the Whole enchilada

A Spicy Collection
of Sylvia's Best

OTHER BOOKS BY NICOLE HOLLANDER

I'm in Training to Be Tall and Blonde

Ma, Can I Be a Feminist and Still Like Men?

That Woman Must Be on Drugs

Mercy, It's the Revolution and I'm in My Bathrobe

My Weight Is Always Perfect for My Height—Which Varies

Hi, This Is Sylvia

Sylvia on Sundays

Okay, Thinner Thighs for Everyone

Never Tell Your Mother This Dream

the whole enchilada

A Spicy Collection of Sylvia's Best
by Nicole Hollander

St. Martin's Press
New York

Library of Congress Cataloging in Publication Data

Hollander, Nicole.
    The whole enchilada.

    I. Title.
PN6728.S97H68   1986   741.5'973   86-13826
ISBN 0-312-87757-9 (pbk.)

Book designed by Tom Greensfelder + Steve Strong

The Sylvia strip is syndicated seven days a week.
For samples and rates, write the Sylvia Syndicate,
P.O. Box 578523, Chicago, IL 60657.

Nicole Hollander's greeting cards are available from:
The Maine Line Co., P.O. Box 418, Rockport, ME 04856.
Phone: (207) 236-8536.

Contents

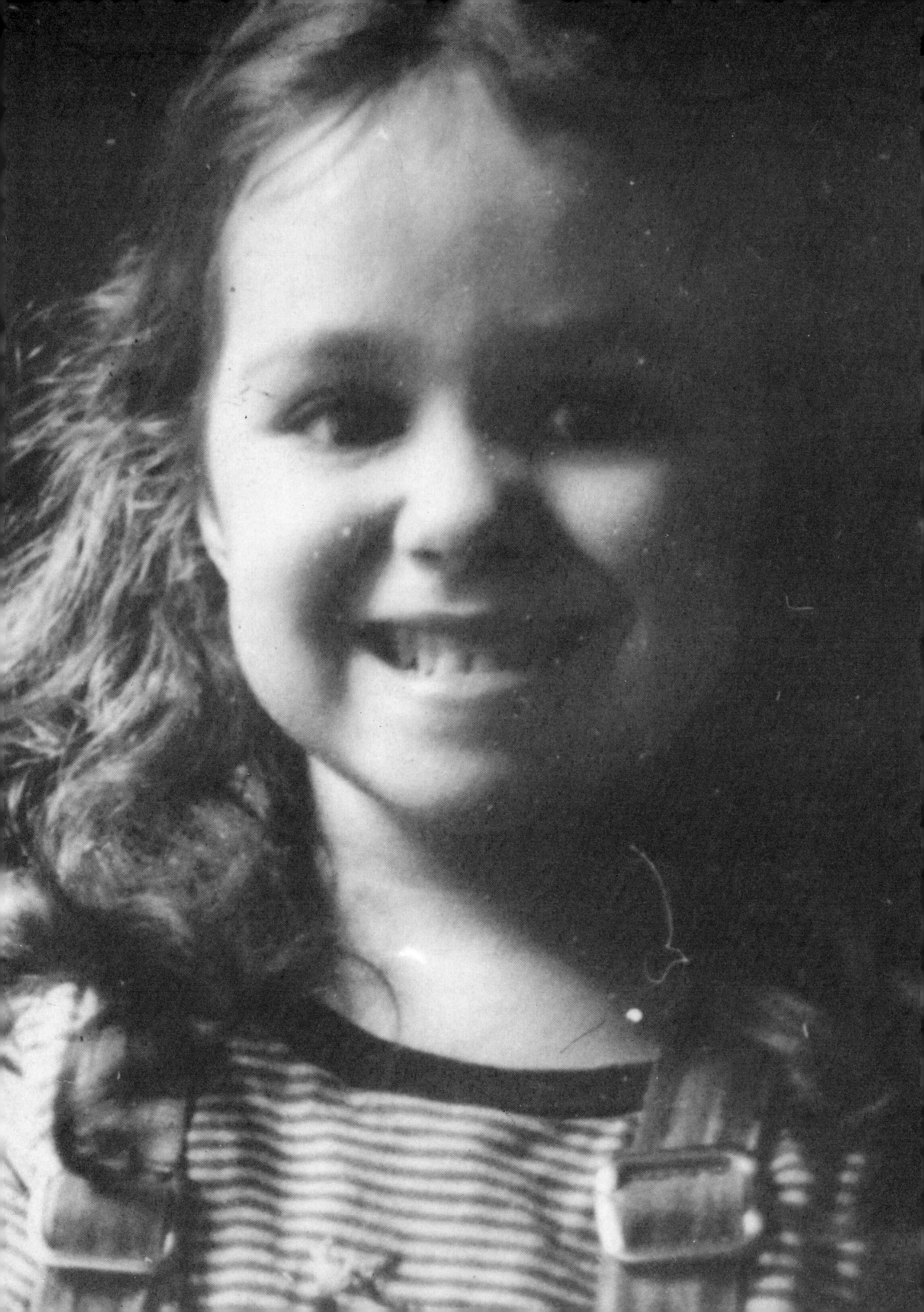

I know that I loved the comics. I learned to read so that I could read the Sunday comics without my parents' help (although someone once pointed out that my favorite cartoons, *The Little King* and *Henry* didn't have any words). I know I stopped reading comics, but I can't remember why. I have a friend who, when she can't remember something like the sixties, says: "Well, I grew up in Mexico." I usually say: "Well, I was married at the time" to explain the gaps in my memory from ages five to 27.

Maybe the comics stopped being relevant to my life because they were all written by men, filled with male characters. But then I always thought I would grow up to be Lew Archer (a private eye and the friend of those who have no friends). How come I never noticed there was a gender difference?

Well one thing I do know, I know where Sylvia came from. Here's a picture of her. She's the one who's looking worldly and weary and smoking a long cigarette. I'm the smaller one, grinning in the background. My grandmother, my mother, and all her friends were witty; in my neighborhood, women had all the best lines. Sylvia is all of them: Annie, Bessie, Shirley, Esther, Goldie, Jennie, Rosie, Lee and Irma.

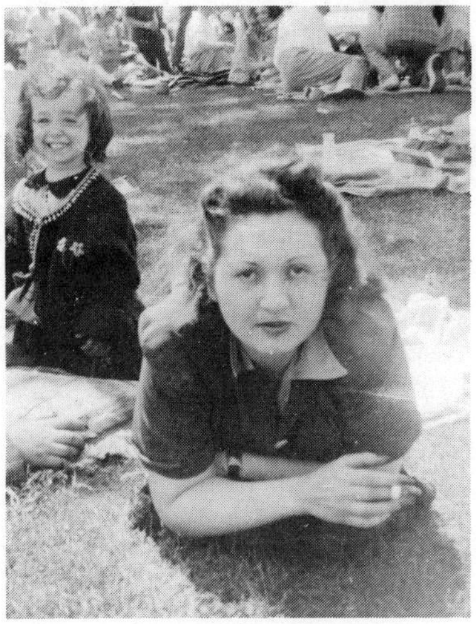

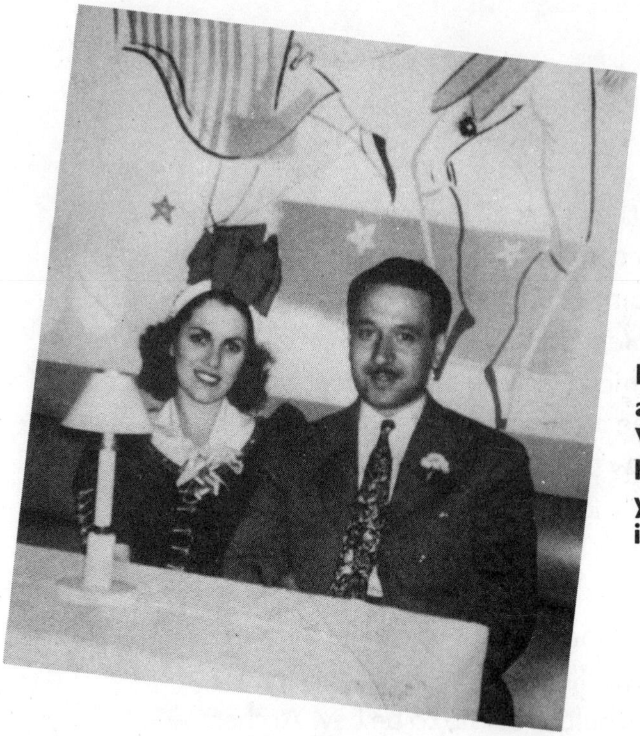

My mother and father at a Las Vegas night club. Variations of my mother's hat and the fashions of her youth keep popping up in Sylvia.

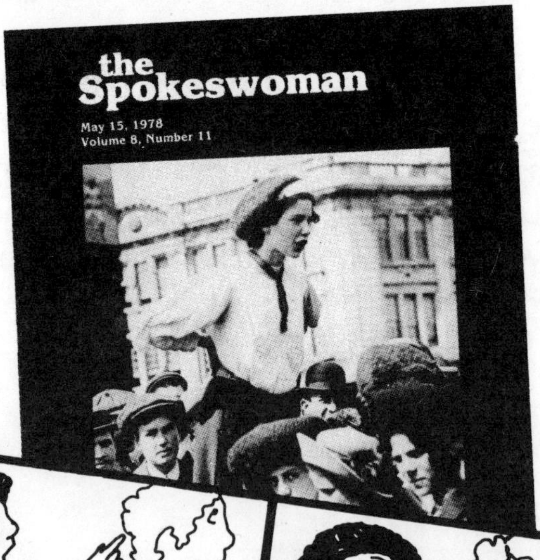
the Spokeswoman
May 15, 1978
Volume 8, Number 11

The Spokeswoman was a national, Chicago-based feminist publication.

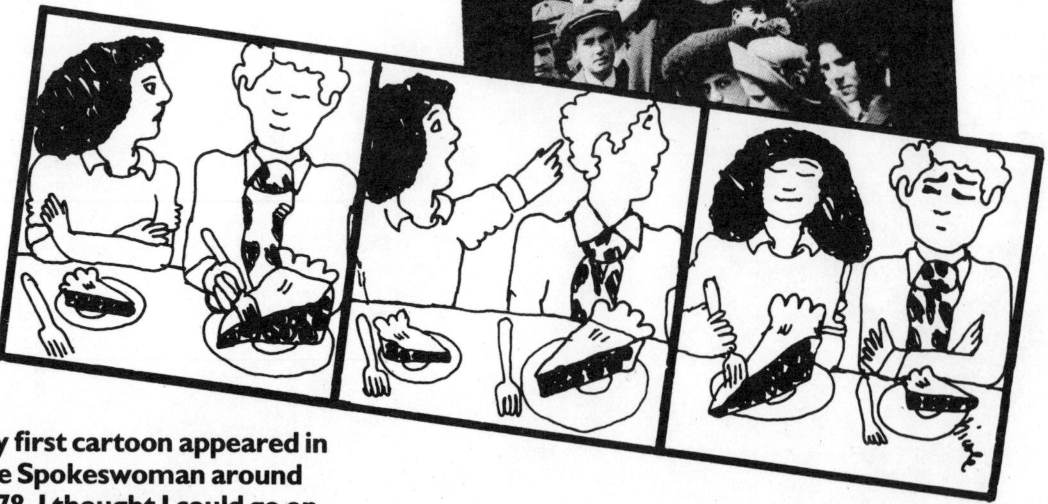

My first cartoon appeared in the Spokeswoman around 1978. I thought I could go on forever doing cartoons without words.

The 1970's prototype Sylvia —not yet named, her politics a little shaky, her profile undeveloped, but with backless mules and cigarette firmly in place.

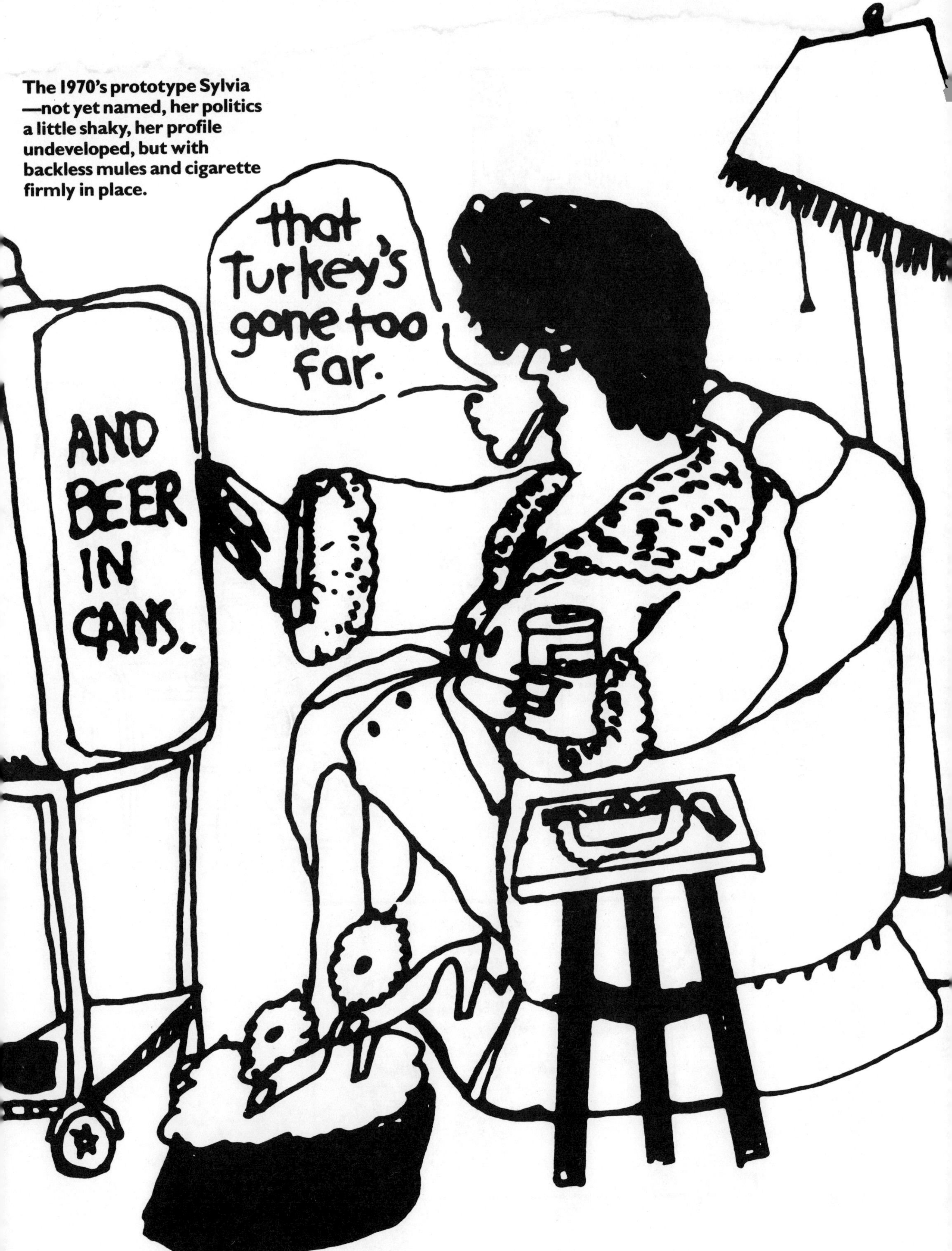
that Turkey's gone too far.
AND BEER IN CANS.

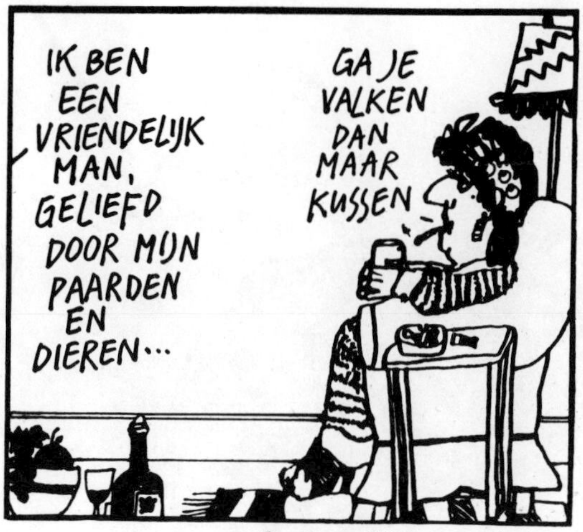
IK BEN EEN VRIENDELIJK MAN, GELIEFD DOOR MIJN PAARDEN EN DIEREN...
GA JE VALKEN DAN MAAR KUSSEN

See page 56 for translation.

Sylvia speaks Dutch, Italian and German like a native.

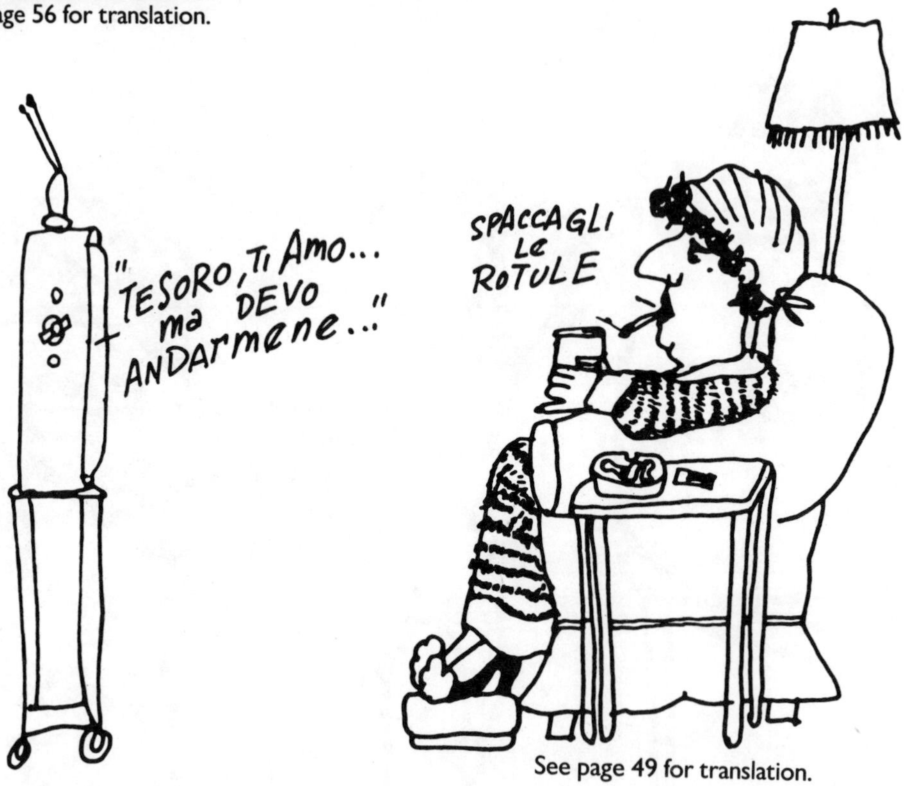
"TESORO, TI AMO... MA DEVO ANDARMENE..."
SPACCAGLI LE ROTULE

See page 49 for translation.

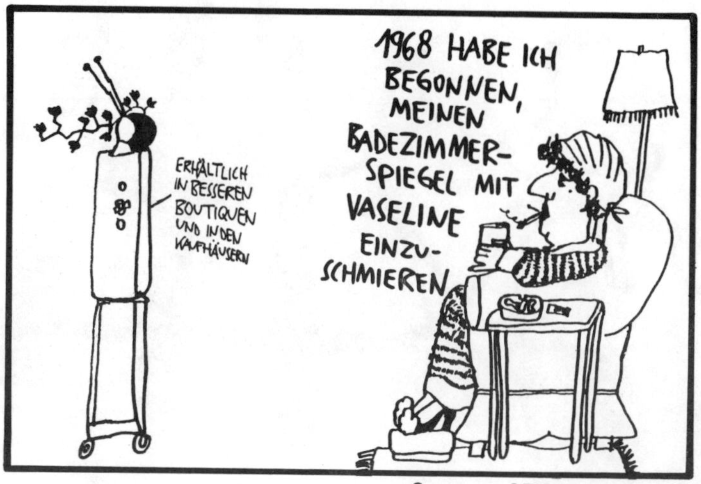
ERHÄLTLICH IN BESSEREN BOUTIQUEN UND IN DEN KAUFHÄUSERN
1968 HABE ICH BEGONNEN, MEINEN BADEZIMMER-SPIEGEL MIT VASELINE EINZU-SCHMIEREN

See page 97 for translation.

I landed in New Orleans, but my friends weren't waiting at the gate. As I wandered through the airport, I saw heads turn and heard people saying: "Well, will you look at that. . ." and then I saw them.

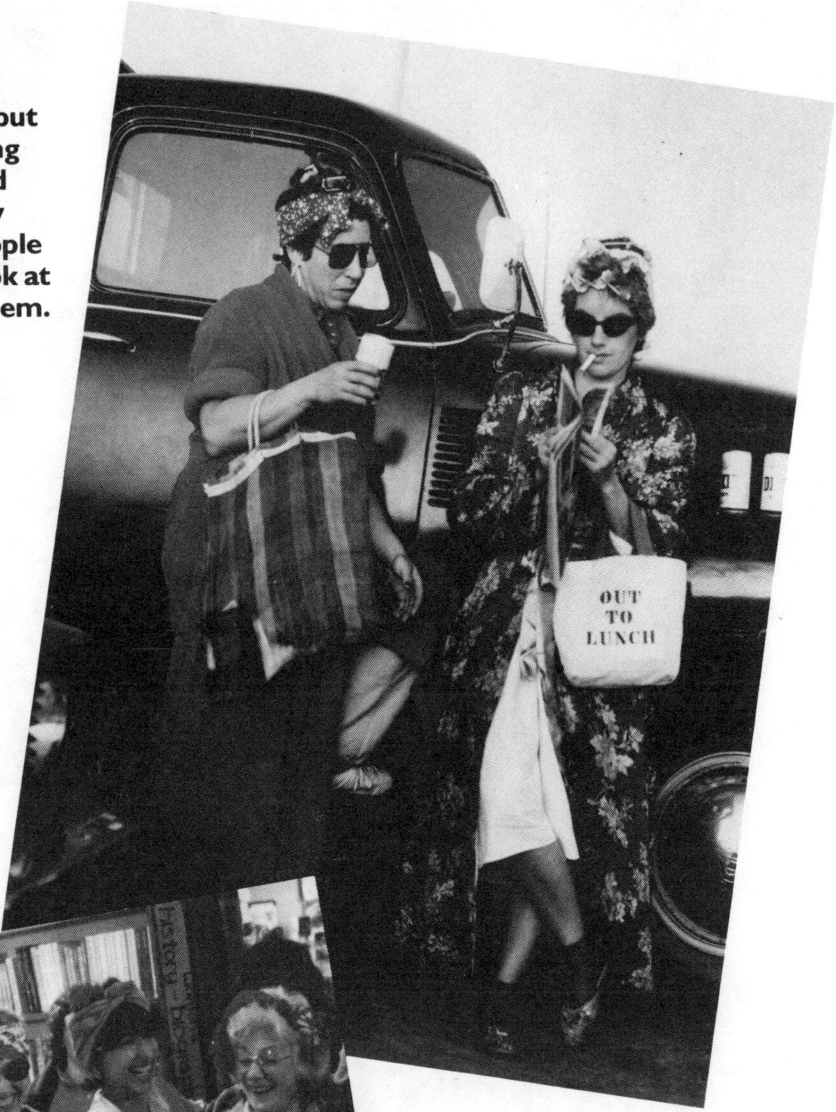
OUT
TO
LUNCH

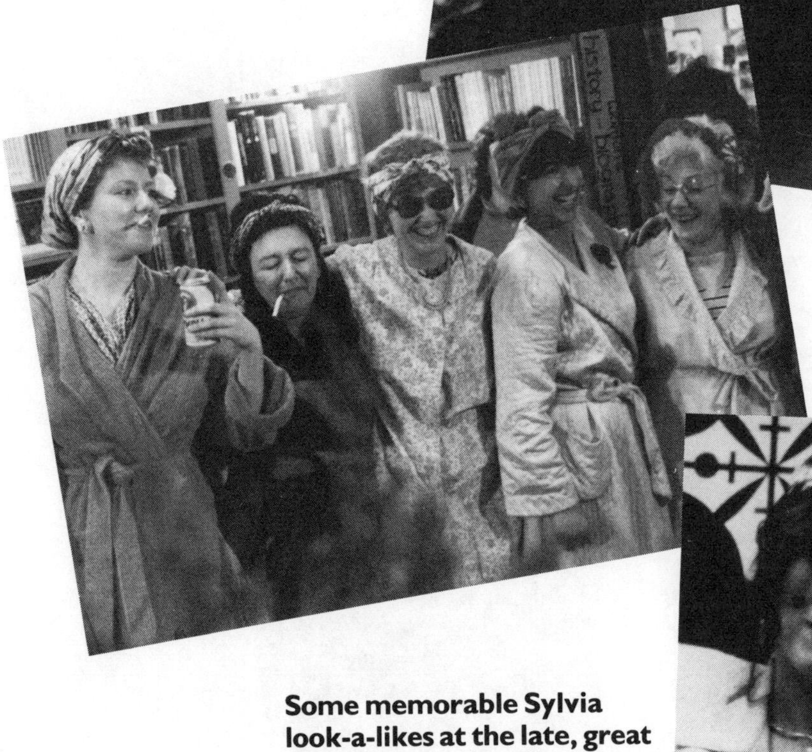

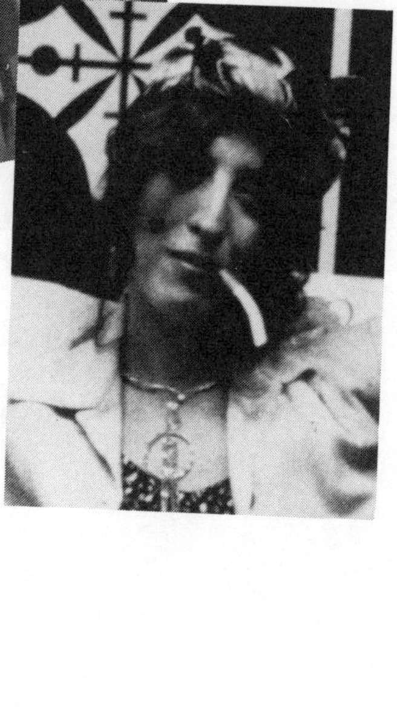

Some memorable Sylvia look-a-likes at the late, great Jane Addams Book Store in Chicago.

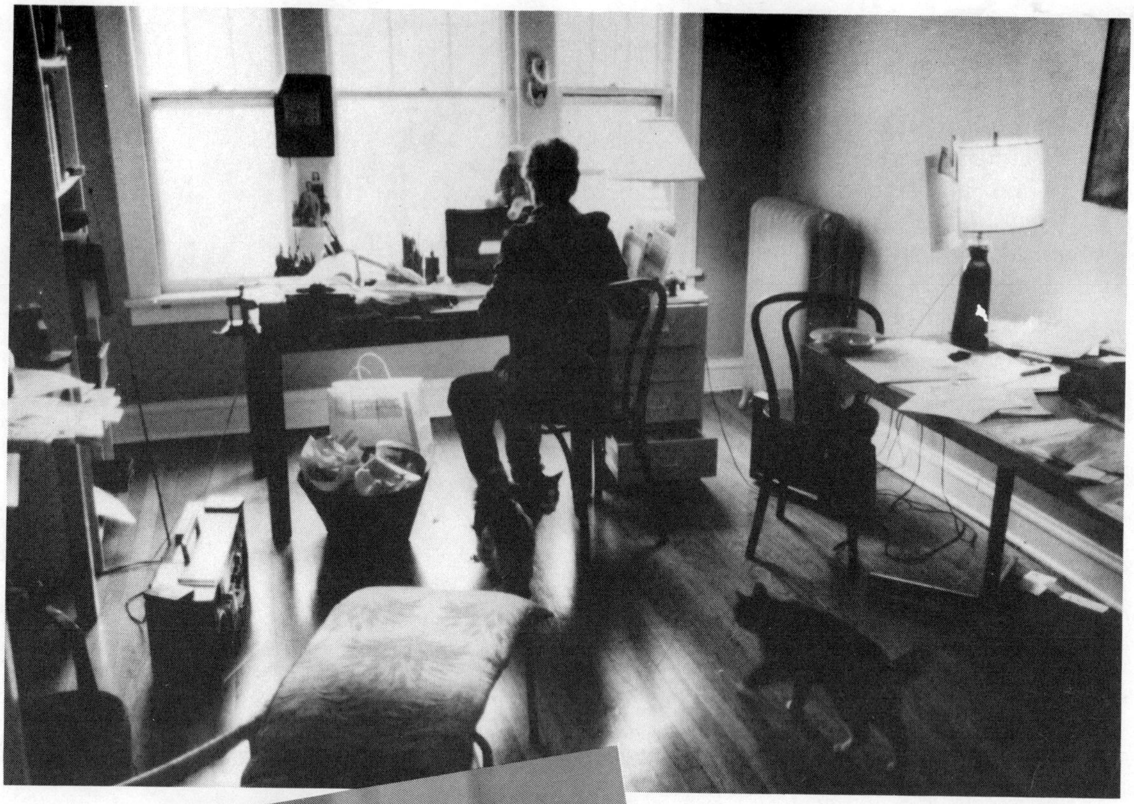

Myself, hard at work at the headquarters of the Sylvia Syndicate.

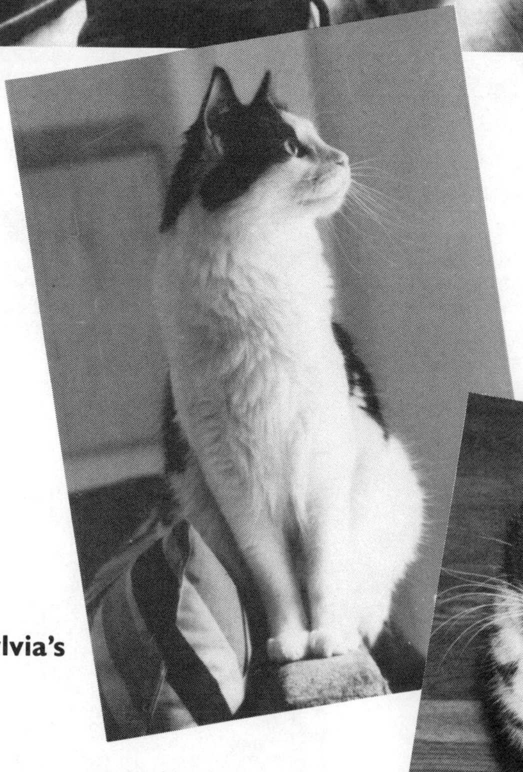

John, the model for Sylvia's cat in the strip.

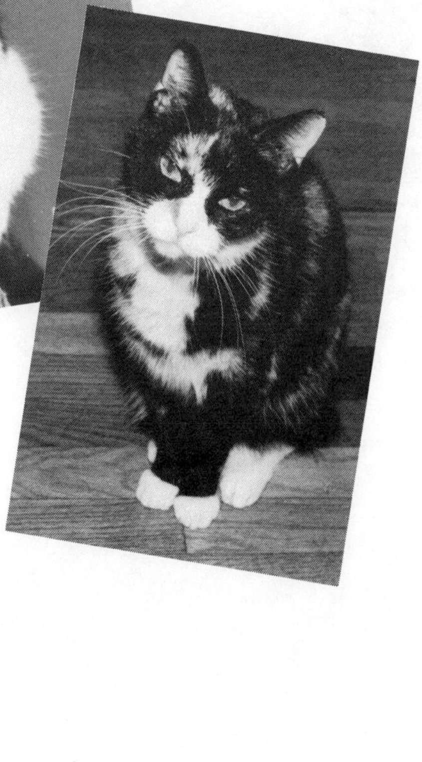

Harriet, much beloved, ever resentful of her non-appearance in the strip.

Some well-meant advice

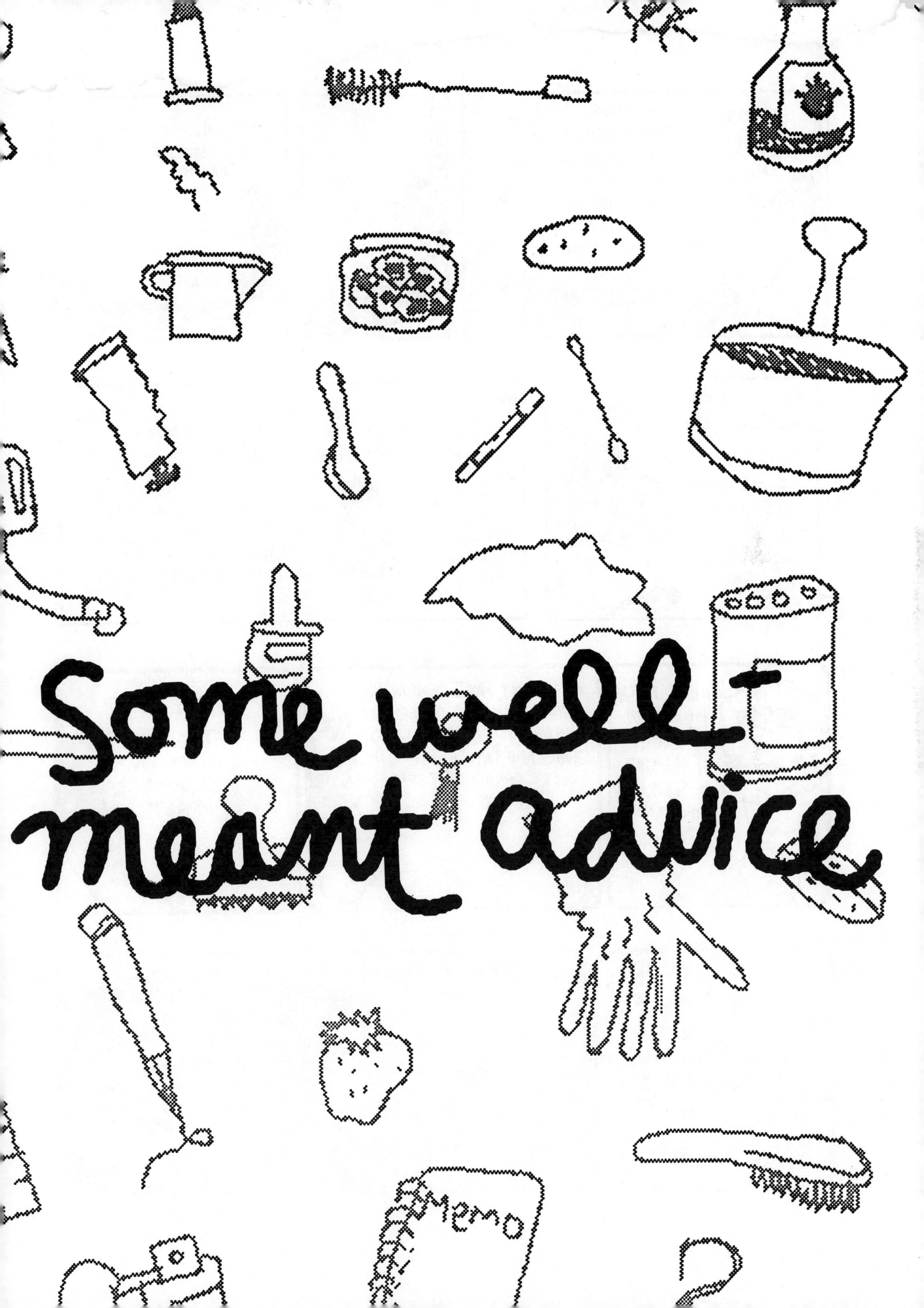
Memo

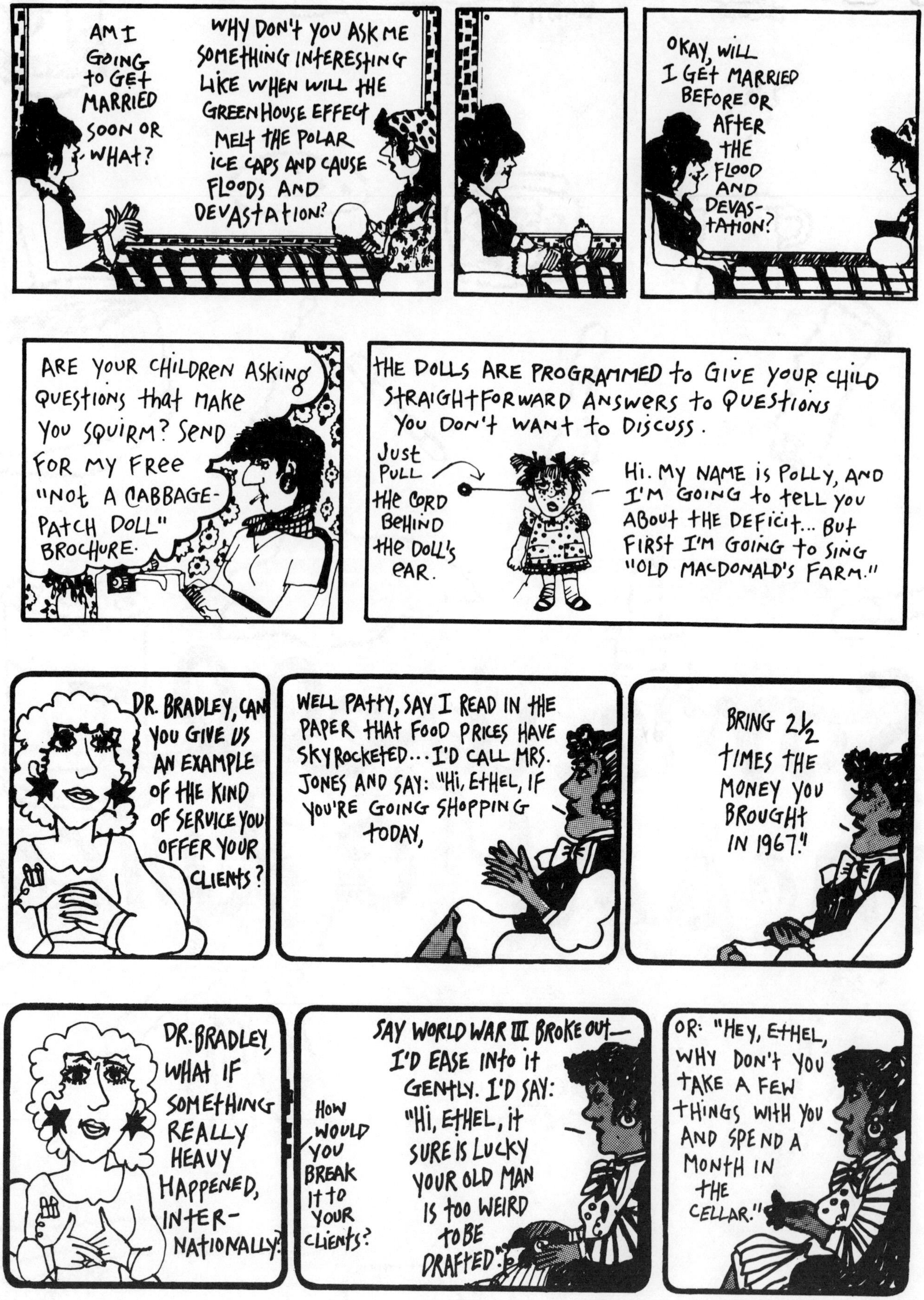
AM I GOING TO GET MARRIED SOON OR WHAT?
WHY DON'T YOU ASK ME SOMETHING INTERESTING LIKE WHEN WILL THE GREENHOUSE EFFECT MELT THE POLAR ICE CAPS AND CAUSE FLOODS AND DEVASTATION?
OKAY, WILL I GET MARRIED BEFORE OR AFTER THE FLOOD AND DEVASTATION?
ARE YOUR CHILDREN ASKING QUESTIONS THAT MAKE YOU SQUIRM? SEND FOR MY FREE "NOT A CABBAGE-PATCH DOLL" BROCHURE.
THE DOLLS ARE PROGRAMMED TO GIVE YOUR CHILD STRAIGHTFORWARD ANSWERS TO QUESTIONS YOU DON'T WANT TO DISCUSS.
JUST PULL THE CORD BEHIND THE DOLL'S EAR.
HI. MY NAME IS POLLY, AND I'M GOING TO TELL YOU ABOUT THE DEFICIT... BUT FIRST I'M GOING TO SING "OLD MACDONALD'S FARM."
DR. BRADLEY, CAN YOU GIVE US AN EXAMPLE OF THE KIND OF SERVICE YOU OFFER YOUR CLIENTS?
WELL PATTY, SAY I READ IN THE PAPER THAT FOOD PRICES HAVE SKYROCKETED... I'D CALL MRS. JONES AND SAY: "HI, ETHEL, IF YOU'RE GOING SHOPPING TODAY,
BRING 2½ TIMES THE MONEY YOU BROUGHT IN 1967."
DR. BRADLEY, WHAT IF SOMETHING REALLY HEAVY HAPPENED, INTERNATIONALLY?
HOW WOULD YOU BREAK IT TO YOUR CLIENTS?
SAY WORLD WAR III BROKE OUT— I'D EASE INTO IT GENTLY. I'D SAY: "HI, ETHEL, IT SURE IS LUCKY YOUR OLD MAN IS TOO WEIRD TO BE DRAFTED".
OR: "HEY, ETHEL, WHY DON'T YOU TAKE A FEW THINGS WITH YOU AND SPEND A MONTH IN THE CELLAR."

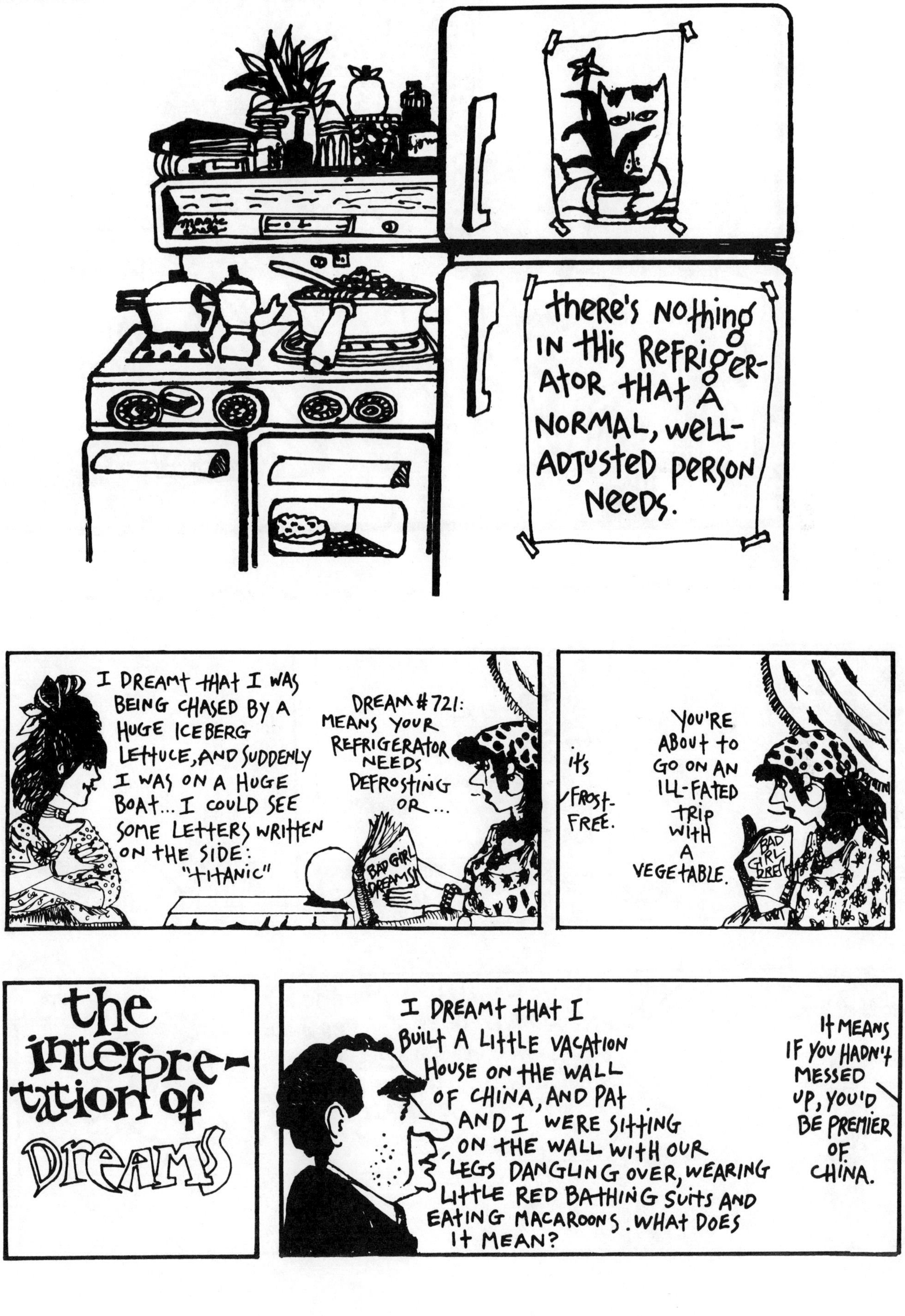
there's nothing in this Refrigerator that A NORMAL, well-Adjusted person needs.
I DREAMT THAT I WAS BEING CHASED BY A HUGE ICEBERG LETTUCE, AND SUDDENLY I WAS ON A HUGE BOAT... I COULD SEE SOME LETTERS WRITTEN ON THE SIDE: "TITANIC"
DREAM #721: MEANS YOUR REFRIGERATOR NEEDS DEFROSTING OR...
BAD GIRL DREAMS
it's Frost-Free.
YOU'RE ABOUT TO GO ON AN ILL-FATED TRIP WITH A VEGETABLE.
the interpretation of Dreams
I DREAMT THAT I BUILT A LITTLE VACATION HOUSE ON THE WALL OF CHINA, AND PAT AND I WERE SITTING ON THE WALL WITH OUR LEGS DANGLING OVER, WEARING LITTLE RED BATHING SUITS AND EATING MACAROONS. WHAT DOES IT MEAN?
IT MEANS IF YOU HADN'T MESSED UP, YOU'D BE PREMIER OF CHINA.

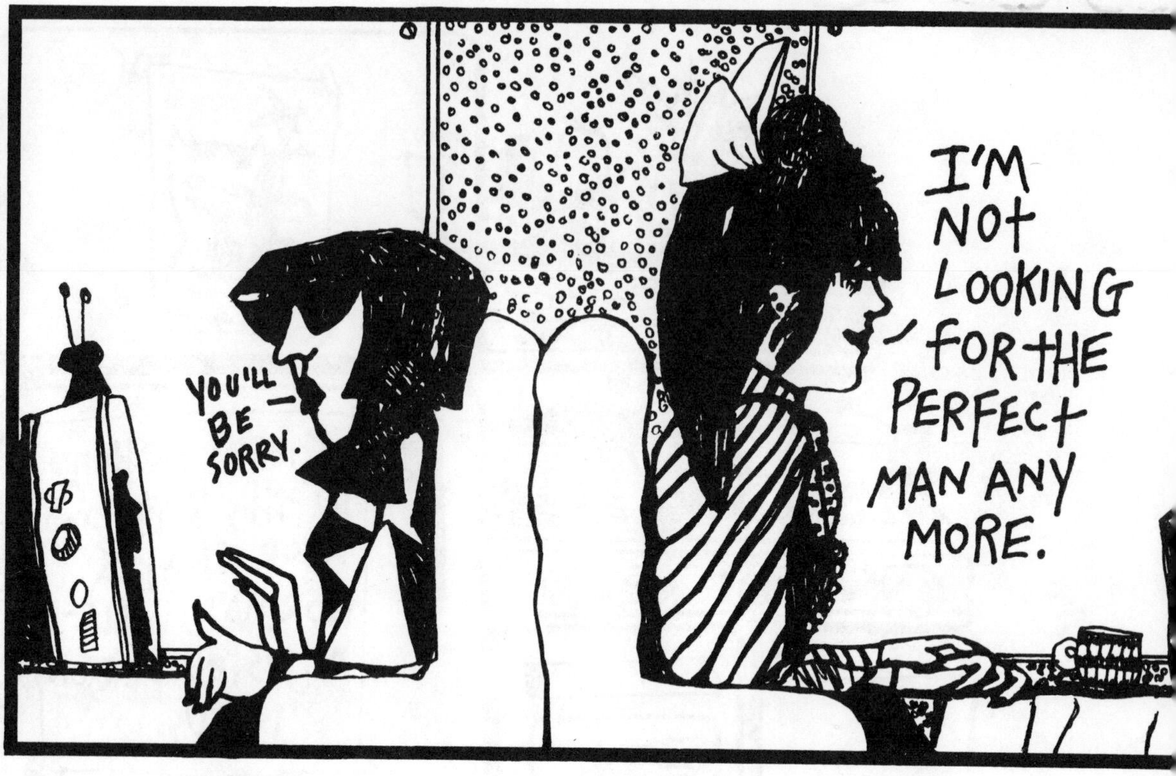
YOU'LL BE SORRY.
I'M NOT LOOKING FOR THE PERFECT MAN ANY MORE.

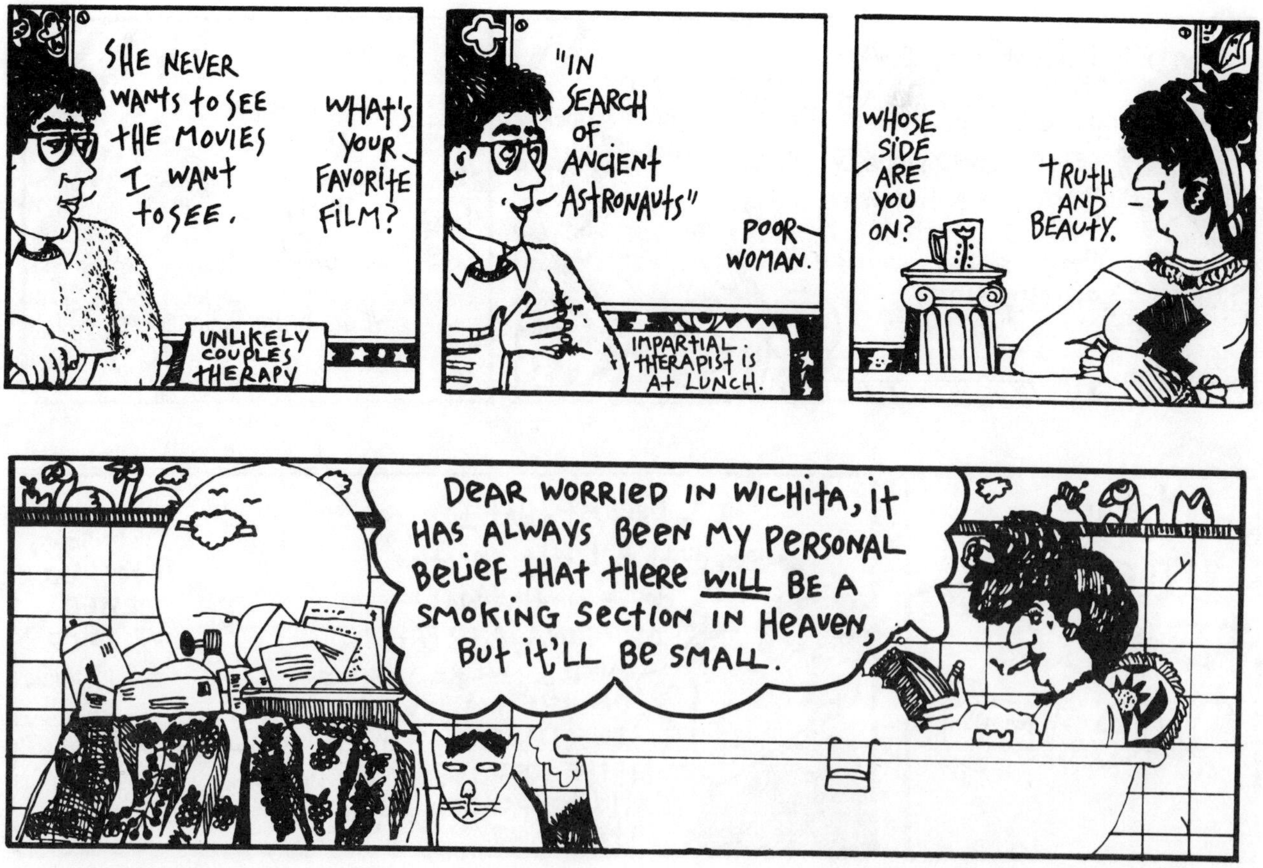
SHE NEVER WANTS TO SEE THE MOVIES I WANT TO SEE.
WHAT'S YOUR FAVORITE FILM?
UNLIKELY COUPLES THERAPY
"IN SEARCH OF ANCIENT ASTRONAUTS"
POOR WOMAN.
IMPARTIAL THERAPIST IS AT LUNCH.
WHOSE SIDE ARE YOU ON?
TRUTH AND BEAUTY.
DEAR WORRIED IN WICHITA, IT HAS ALWAYS BEEN MY PERSONAL BELIEF THAT THERE WILL BE A SMOKING SECTION IN HEAVEN, BUT IT'LL BE SMALL.

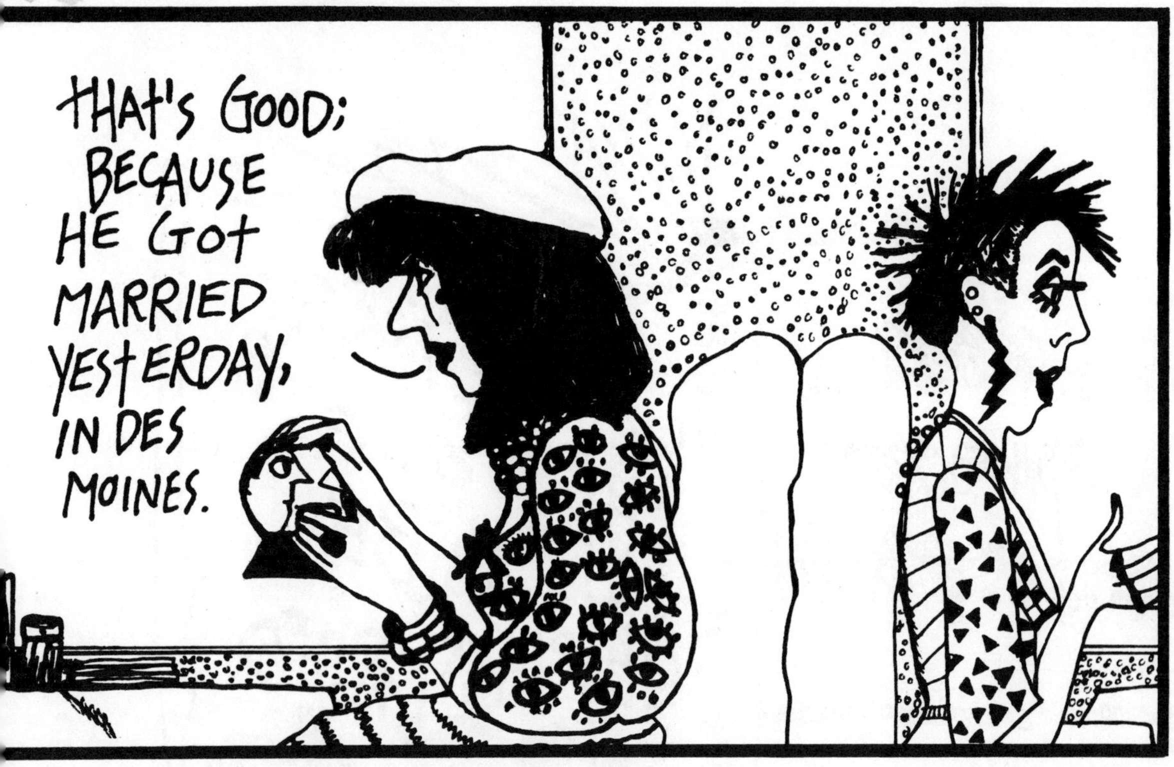
THAT'S GOOD; BECAUSE HE GOT MARRIED YESTERDAY, IN DES MOINES.

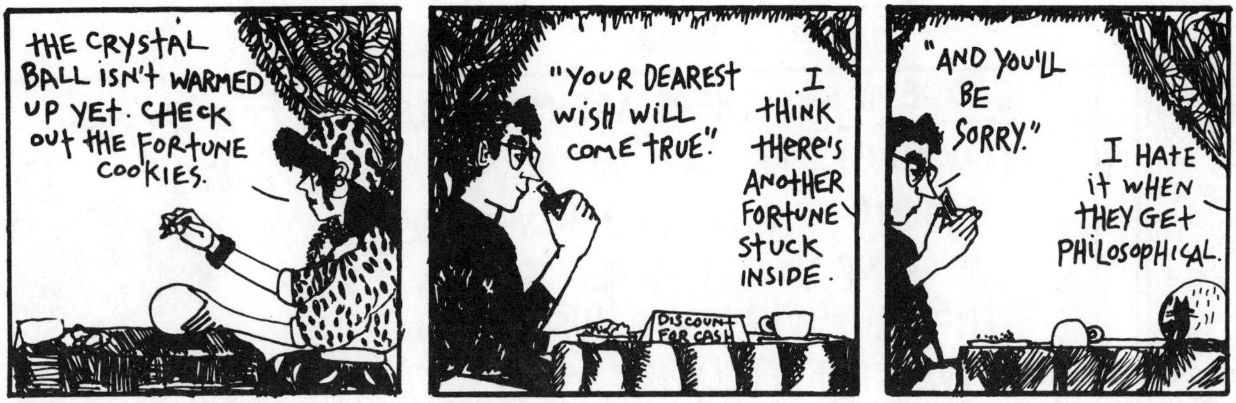
THE CRYSTAL BALL ISN'T WARMED UP YET. CHECK OUT THE FORTUNE COOKIES.
"YOUR DEAREST WISH WILL COME TRUE."
I THINK THERE'S ANOTHER FORTUNE STUCK INSIDE.
DISCOUNT FOR CASH
"AND YOU'LL BE SORRY."
I HATE IT WHEN THEY GET PHILOSOPHICAL.

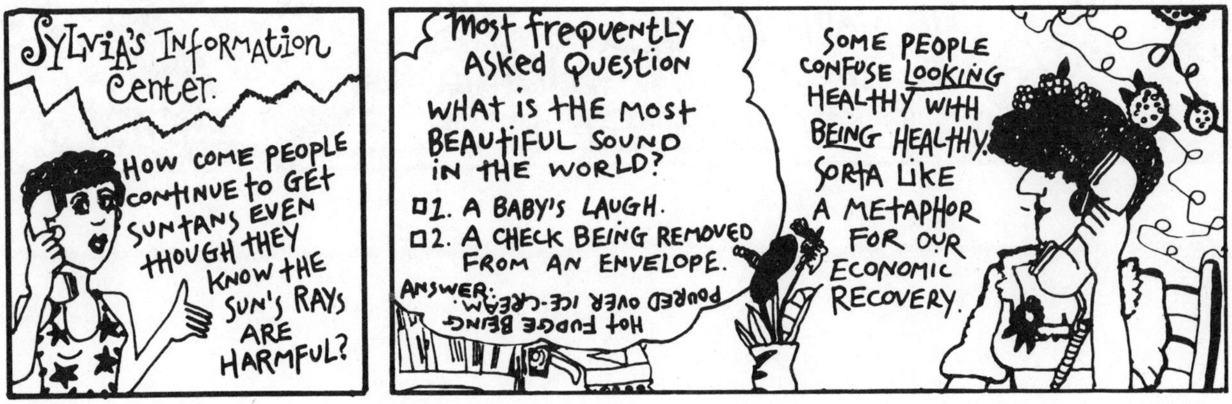
SYLVIA'S INFORMATION CENTER
HOW COME PEOPLE CONTINUE TO GET SUNTANS EVEN THOUGH THEY KNOW THE SUN'S RAYS ARE HARMFUL?
MOST FREQUENTLY ASKED QUESTION
WHAT IS THE MOST BEAUTIFUL SOUND IN THE WORLD?
□1. A BABY'S LAUGH.
□2. A CHECK BEING REMOVED FROM AN ENVELOPE.
ANSWER: HOT FUDGE BEING POURED OVER ICE-CREAM.
SOME PEOPLE CONFUSE LOOKING HEALTHY WITH BEING HEALTHY. SORTA LIKE A METAPHOR FOR OUR ECONOMIC RECOVERY.

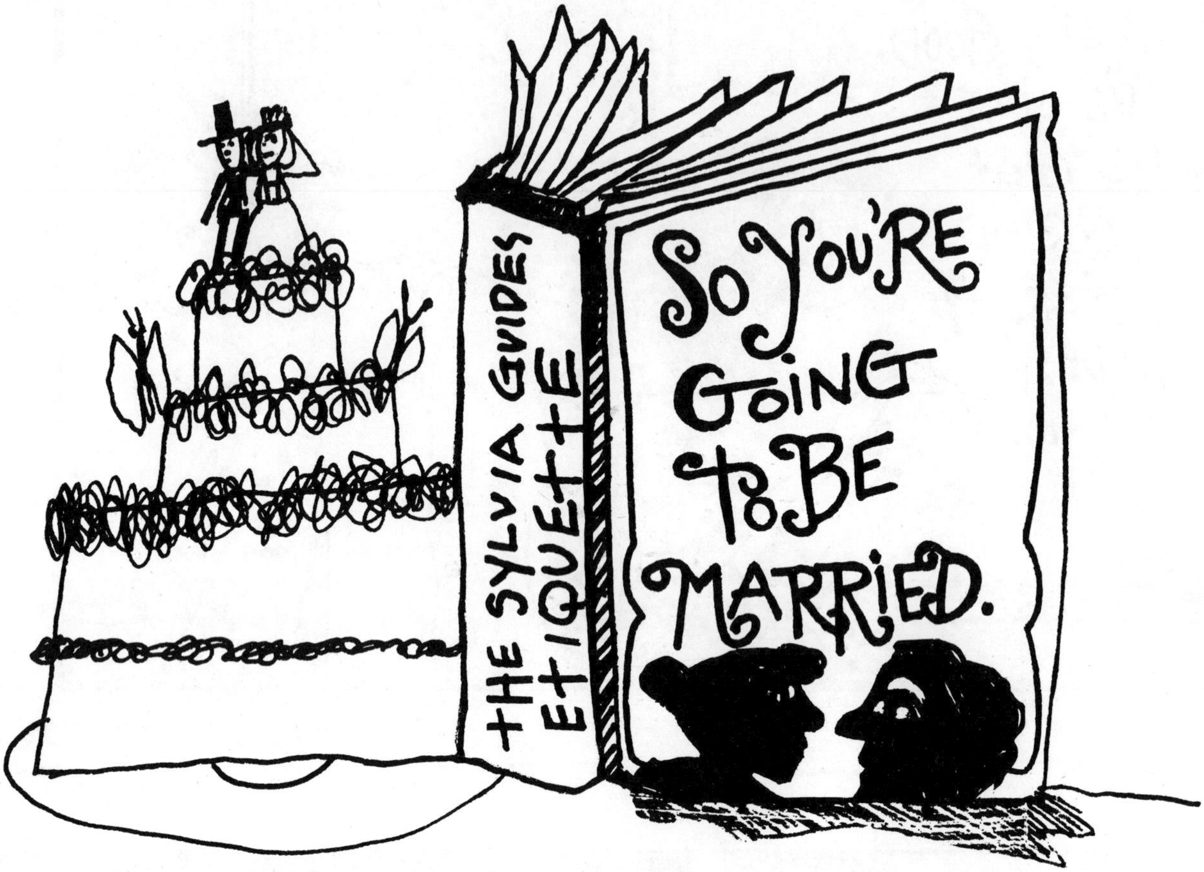
THE SYLVIA GUIDES ET IQUETTE
SO YOU'RE GOING TO BE MARRIED.

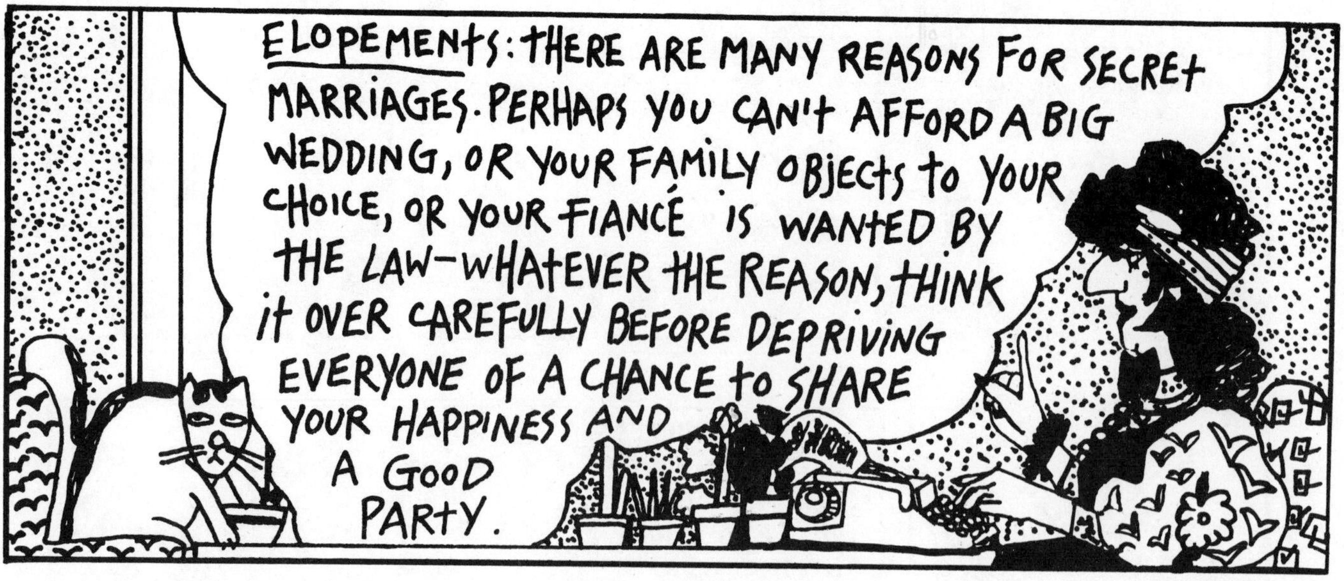
ELOPEMENTS: THERE ARE MANY REASONS FOR SECRET MARRIAGES. PERHAPS YOU CAN'T AFFORD A BIG WEDDING, OR YOUR FAMILY OBJECTS TO YOUR CHOICE, OR YOUR FIANCÉ IS WANTED BY THE LAW—WHATEVER THE REASON, THINK IT OVER CAREFULLY BEFORE DEPRIVING EVERYONE OF A CHANCE TO SHARE YOUR HAPPINESS AND A GOOD PARTY.

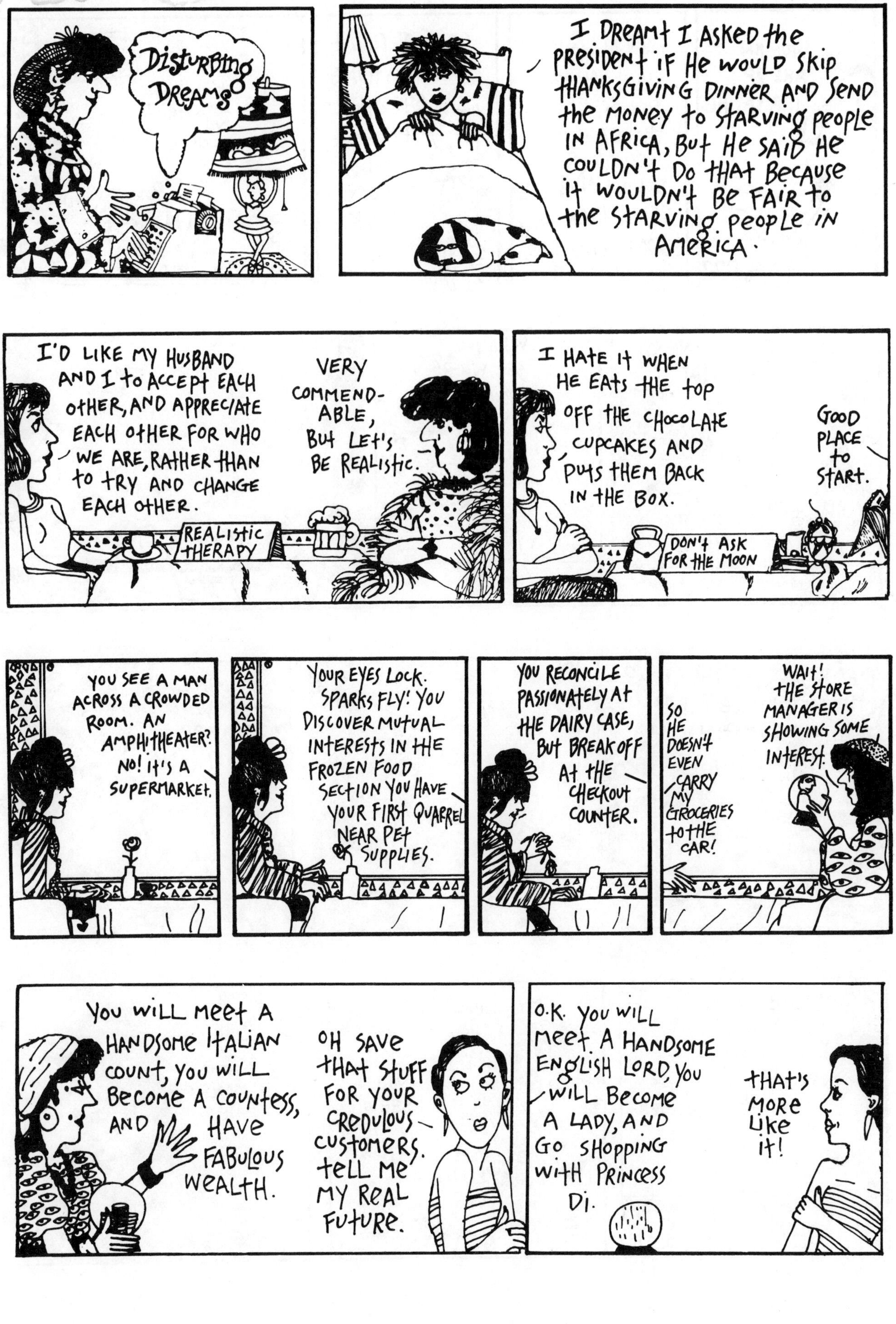

Disturbing Dreams
I dreamt I asked the president if he would skip Thanksgiving dinner and send the money to starving people in Africa, but he said he couldn't do that because it wouldn't be fair to the starving people in America.
I'd like my husband and I to accept each other, and appreciate each other for who we are, rather than to try and change each other.
Very commendable, but let's be realistic.
REALISTIC THERAPY
I hate it when he eats the top off the chocolate cupcakes and puts them back in the box.
Good place to start.
DON'T ASK FOR THE MOON
You see a man across a crowded room. An amphitheater? No! It's a supermarket.
Your eyes lock. Sparks fly! You discover mutual interests in the frozen food section. You have your first quarrel near pet supplies.
You reconcile passionately at the dairy case, but break off at the checkout counter.
So he doesn't even carry my groceries to the car!
Wait! The store manager is showing some interest.
You will meet a handsome Italian count, you will become a countess, and have fabulous wealth.
Oh save that stuff for your credulous customers. Tell me my real future.
O.K. You will meet a handsome English lord, you will become a lady, and go shopping with Princess Di.
That's more like it!

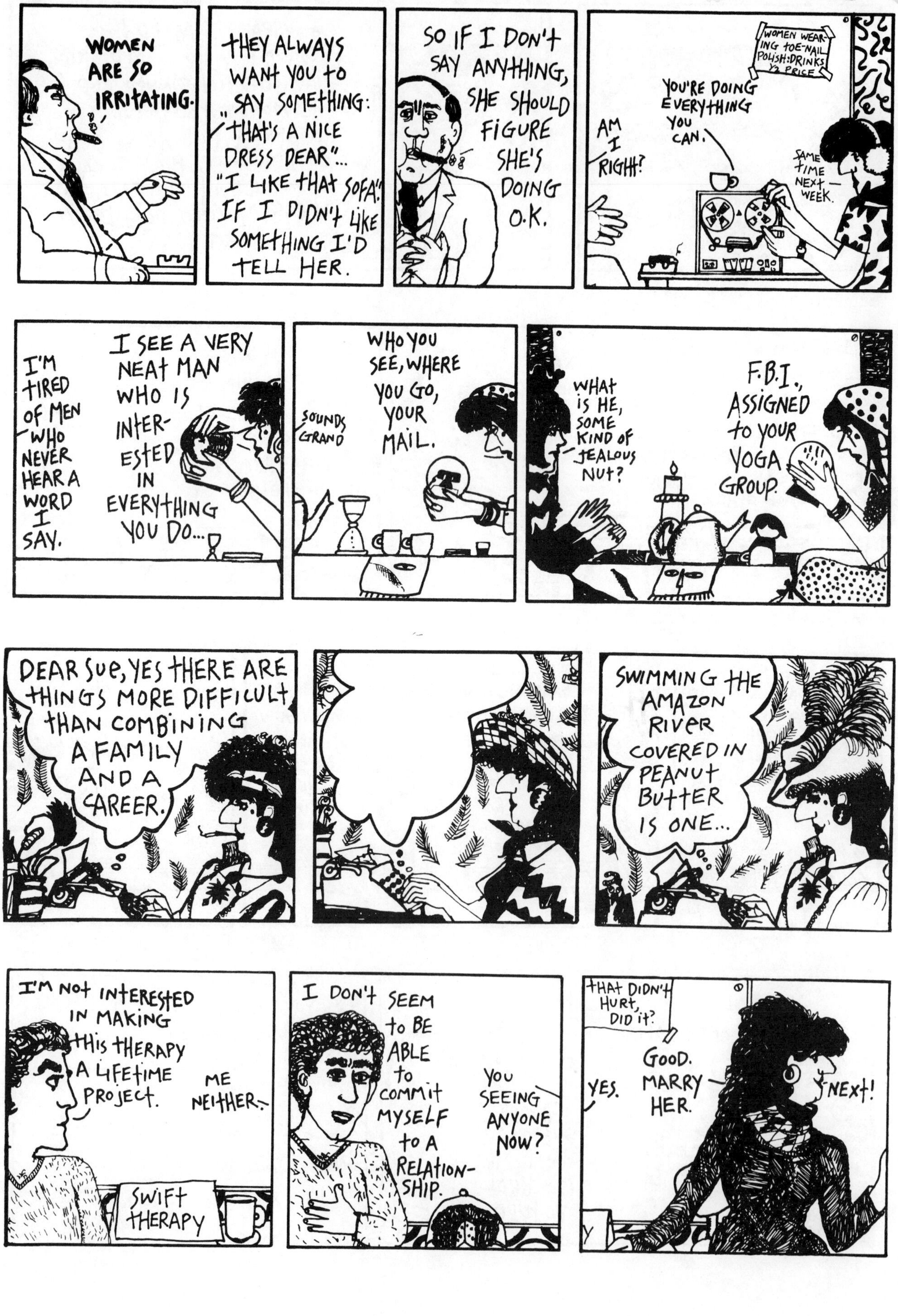
WOMEN ARE SO IRRITATING.
THEY ALWAYS WANT YOU TO SAY SOMETHING: "THAT'S A NICE DRESS DEAR"... "I LIKE THAT SOFA." IF I DIDN'T LIKE SOMETHING I'D TELL HER.
SO IF I DON'T SAY ANYTHING, SHE SHOULD FIGURE SHE'S DOING O.K.
WOMEN WEARING TOE-NAIL POLISH: DRINKS ½ PRICE
AM I RIGHT?
YOU'RE DOING EVERYTHING YOU CAN.
SAME TIME NEXT WEEK.
I'M TIRED OF MEN WHO NEVER HEAR A WORD I SAY.
I SEE A VERY NEAT MAN WHO IS INTERESTED IN EVERYTHING YOU DO...
SOUNDS GRAND
WHO YOU SEE, WHERE YOU GO, YOUR MAIL.
WHAT IS HE, SOME KIND OF JEALOUS NUT?
F.B.I., ASSIGNED TO YOUR YOGA GROUP.
DEAR SUE, YES THERE ARE THINGS MORE DIFFICULT THAN COMBINING A FAMILY AND A CAREER.
SWIMMING THE AMAZON RIVER COVERED IN PEANUT BUTTER IS ONE...
I'M NOT INTERESTED IN MAKING THIS THERAPY A LIFETIME PROJECT.
ME NEITHER.
SWIFT THERAPY
I DON'T SEEM TO BE ABLE TO COMMIT MYSELF TO A RELATIONSHIP.
YOU SEEING ANYONE NOW?
THAT DIDN'T HURT, DID IT?
YES.
GOOD. MARRY HER.
NEXT!

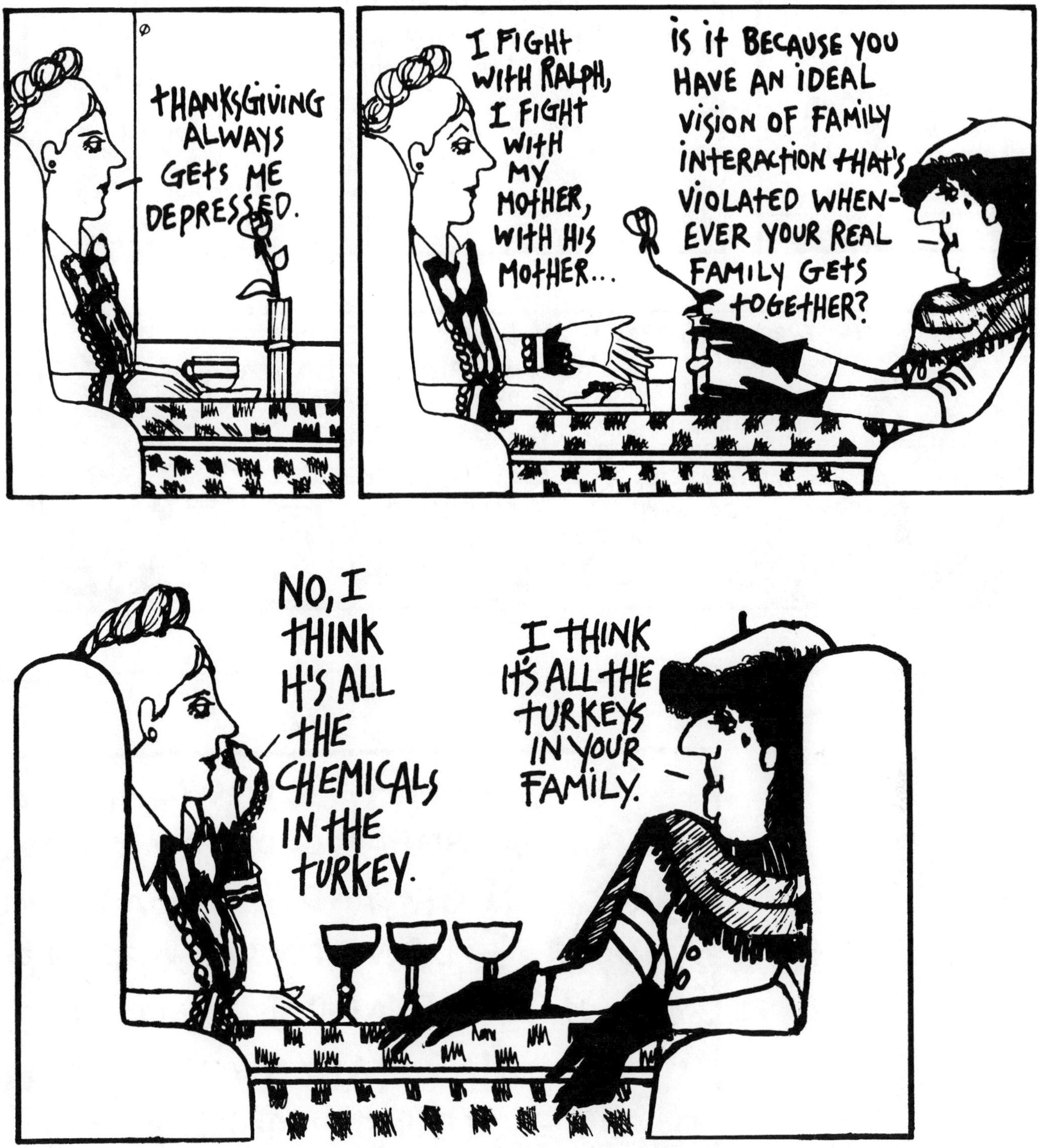
THANKSGIVING ALWAYS GETS ME DEPRESSED.
I FIGHT WITH RALPH, I FIGHT WITH MY MOTHER, WITH HIS MOTHER...
IS IT BECAUSE YOU HAVE AN IDEAL VISION OF FAMILY INTERACTION THAT'S VIOLATED WHENEVER YOUR REAL FAMILY GETS TOGETHER?
NO, I THINK IT'S ALL THE CHEMICALS IN THE TURKEY.
I THINK IT'S ALL THE TURKEYS IN YOUR FAMILY.

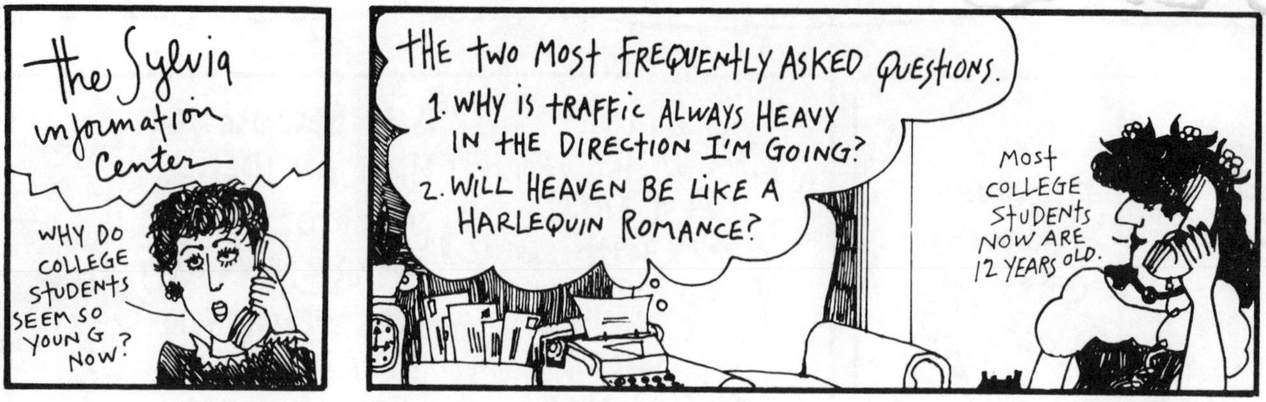
the Sylvia information Center
WHY DO COLLEGE STUDENTS SEEM SO YOUNG NOW?
THE two MOST FREQUENTLY ASKED QUESTIONS.
1. WHY IS TRAFFIC ALWAYS HEAVY IN THE DIRECTION I'M GOING?
2. WILL HEAVEN BE LIKE A HARLEQUIN ROMANCE?
MOST COLLEGE STUDENTS NOW ARE 12 YEARS OLD.

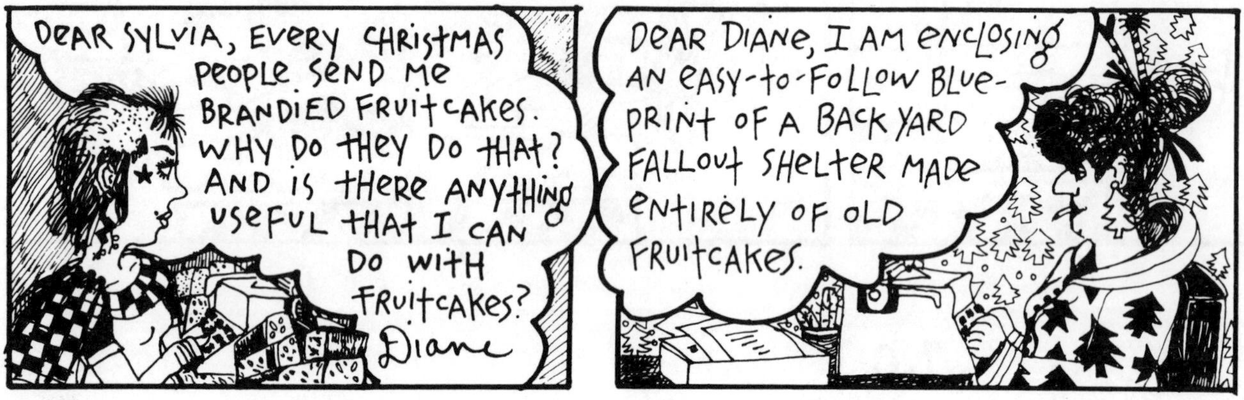
DEAR SYLVIA, EVERY CHRISTMAS PEOPLE SEND ME BRANDIED FRUITCAKES. WHY DO THEY DO THAT? AND IS THERE ANYTHING USEFUL THAT I CAN DO WITH FRUITCAKES? Diane
DEAR DIANE, I AM ENCLOSING AN EASY-TO-FOLLOW BLUE-PRINT OF A BACKYARD FALLOUT SHELTER MADE ENTIRELY OF OLD FRUITCAKES.

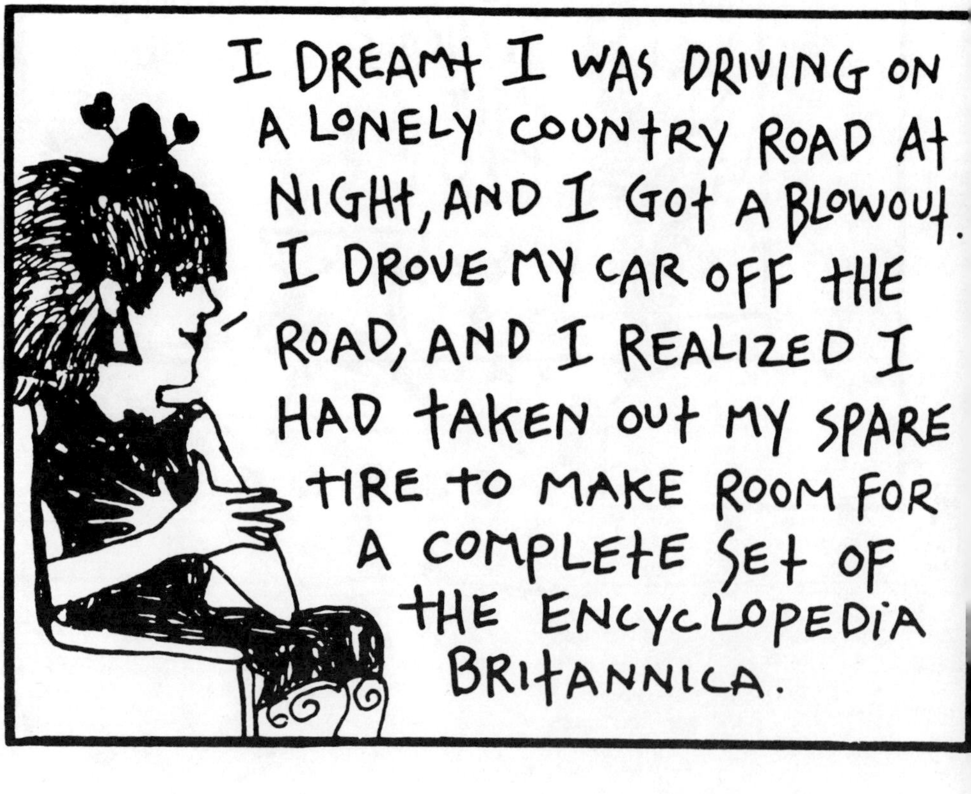
I DREAMT I WAS DRIVING ON A LONELY COUNTRY ROAD AT NIGHT, AND I GOT A BLOWOUT. I DROVE MY CAR OFF THE ROAD, AND I REALIZED I HAD TAKEN OUT MY SPARE TIRE TO MAKE ROOM FOR A COMPLETE SET OF THE ENCYCLOPEDIA BRITANNICA.

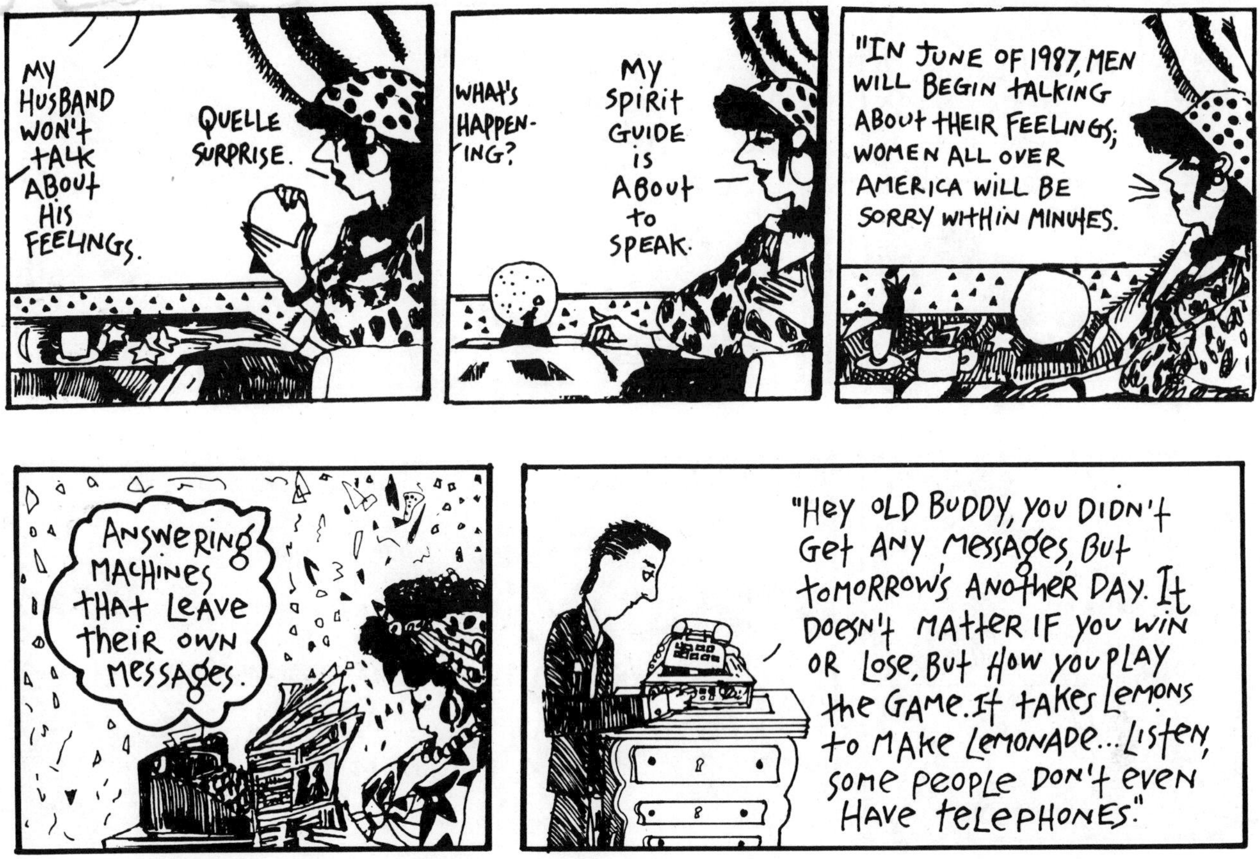
MY HUSBAND WON'T TALK ABOUT HIS FEELINGS.
QUELLE SURPRISE.
WHAT'S HAPPEN-ING?
MY SPIRIT GUIDE IS ABOUT TO SPEAK.
"IN JUNE OF 1987, MEN WILL BEGIN TALKING ABOUT THEIR FEELINGS; WOMEN ALL OVER AMERICA WILL BE SORRY WITHIN MINUTES.
ANSWERING MACHINES THAT LEAVE THEIR OWN MESSAGES.
"HEY OLD BUDDY, YOU DIDN'T GET ANY MESSAGES, BUT TOMORROW'S ANOTHER DAY. IT DOESN'T MATTER IF YOU WIN OR LOSE, BUT HOW YOU PLAY THE GAME. IT TAKES LEMONS TO MAKE LEMONADE... LISTEN, SOME PEOPLE DON'T EVEN HAVE TELEPHONES."

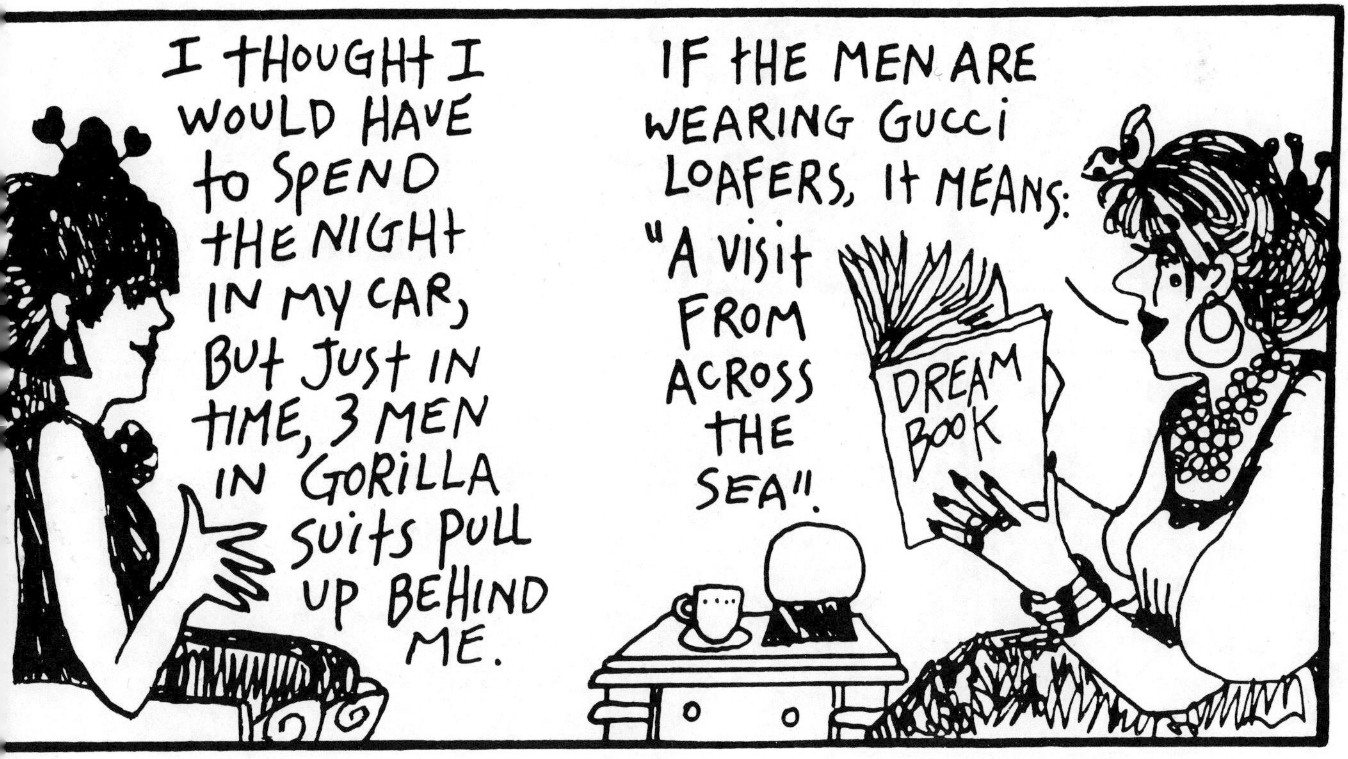
I THOUGHT I WOULD HAVE TO SPEND THE NIGHT IN MY CAR, BUT JUST IN TIME, 3 MEN IN GORILLA SUITS PULL UP BEHIND ME.
IF THE MEN ARE WEARING GUCCI LOAFERS, IT MEANS: "A VISIT FROM ACROSS THE SEA".
DREAM BOOK

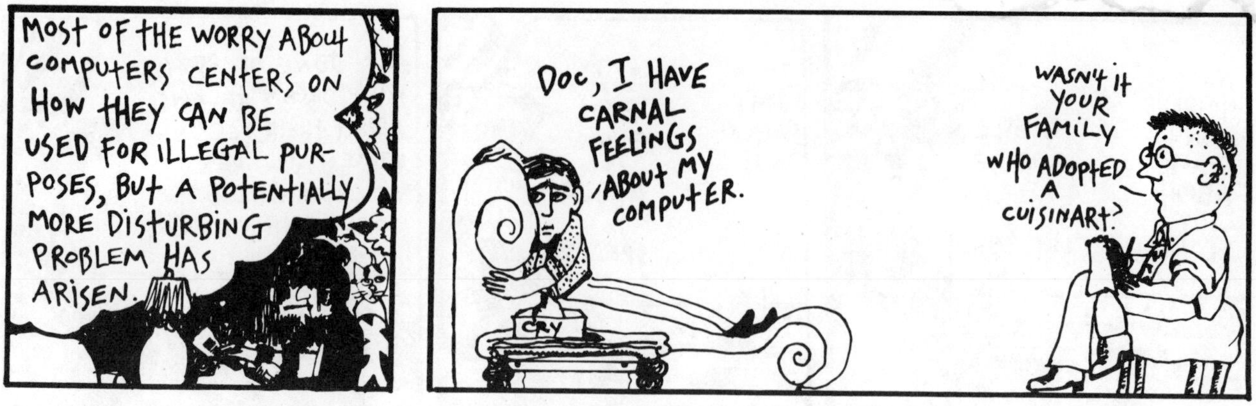
MOST OF THE WORRY ABOUT COMPUTERS CENTERS ON HOW THEY CAN BE USED FOR ILLEGAL PURPOSES, BUT A POTENTIALLY MORE DISTURBING PROBLEM HAS ARISEN.
DOC, I HAVE CARNAL FEELINGS ABOUT MY COMPUTER.
CRY
WASN'T IT YOUR FAMILY WHO ADOPTED A CUISINART?

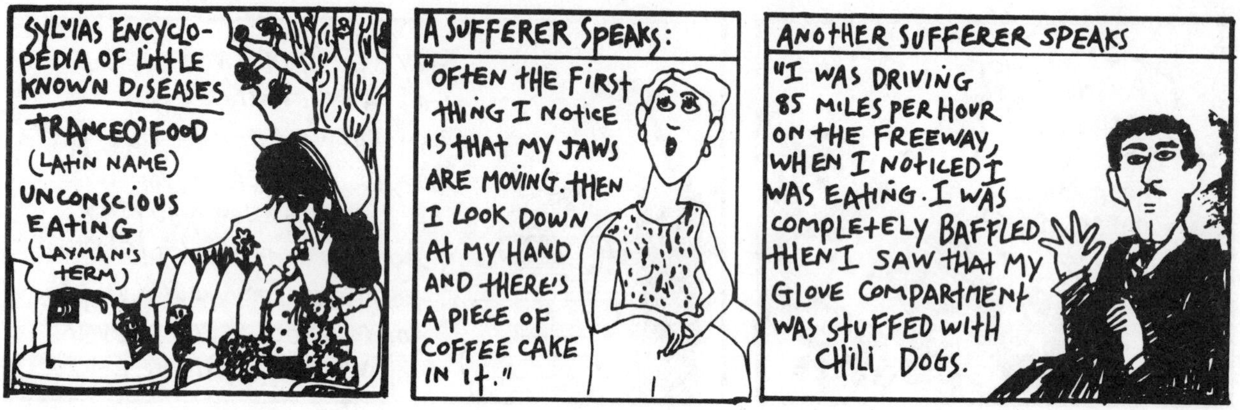
SYLVIA'S ENCYCLOPEDIA OF LITTLE KNOWN DISEASES
TRANCEO'FOOD (LATIN NAME)
UNCONSCIOUS EATING (LAYMAN'S TERM)
A SUFFERER SPEAKS:
"OFTEN THE FIRST THING I NOTICE IS THAT MY JAWS ARE MOVING. THEN I LOOK DOWN AT MY HAND AND THERE'S A PIECE OF COFFEE CAKE IN IT."
ANOTHER SUFFERER SPEAKS
"I WAS DRIVING 85 MILES PER HOUR ON THE FREEWAY, WHEN I NOTICED I WAS EATING. I WAS COMPLETELY BAFFLED. THEN I SAW THAT MY GLOVE COMPARTMENT WAS STUFFED WITH CHILI DOGS.

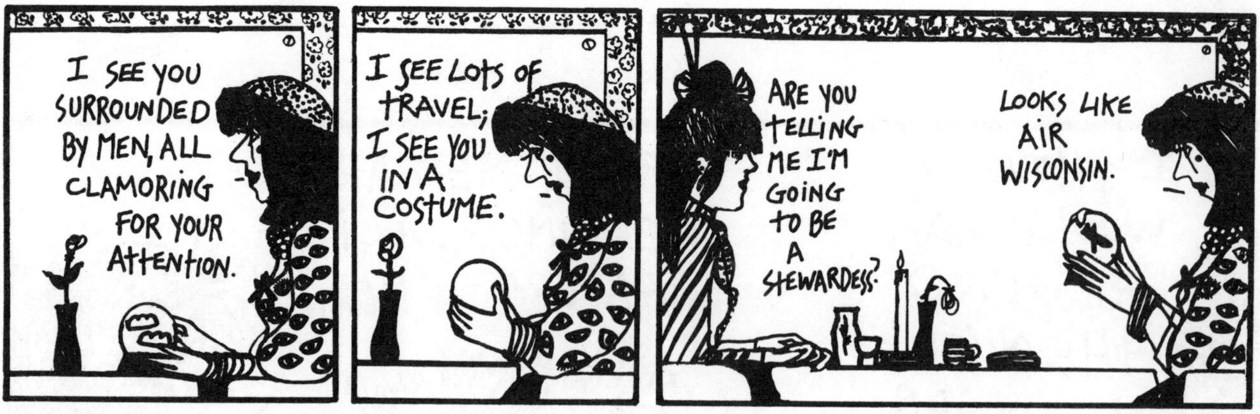
I SEE YOU SURROUNDED BY MEN, ALL CLAMORING FOR YOUR ATTENTION.
I SEE LOTS OF TRAVEL; I SEE YOU IN A COSTUME.
ARE YOU TELLING ME I'M GOING TO BE A STEWARDESS?
LOOKS LIKE AIR WISCONSIN.

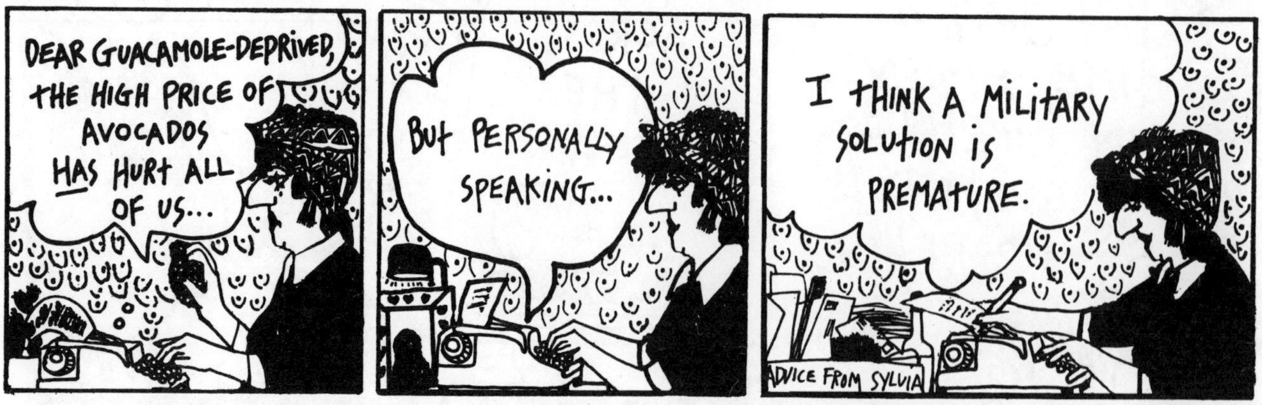
DEAR GUACAMOLE-DEPRIVED, THE HIGH PRICE OF AVOCADOS HAS HURT ALL OF US...
BUT PERSONALLY SPEAKING...
I THINK A MILITARY SOLUTION IS PREMATURE.
ADVICE FROM SYLVIA

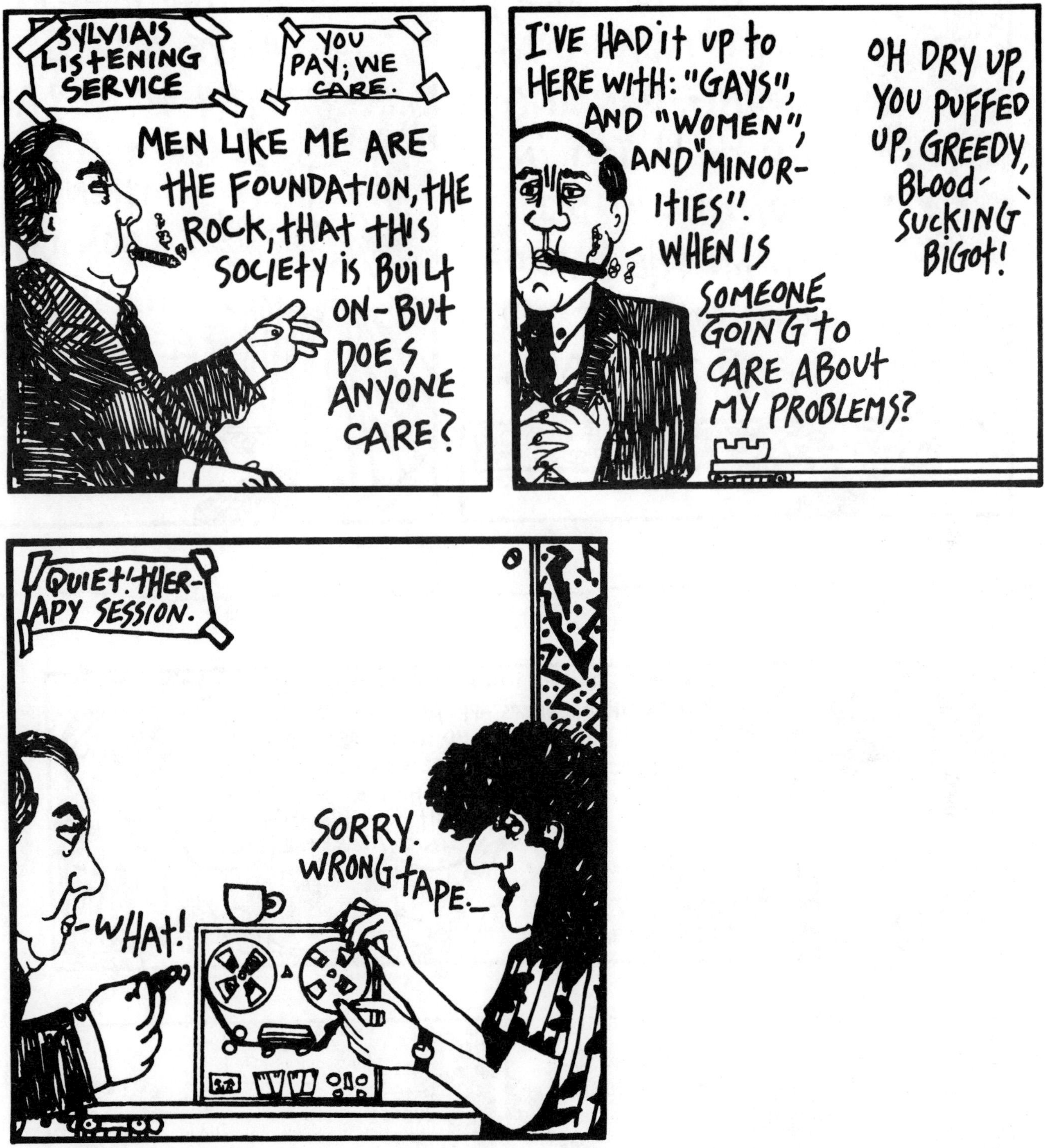
SYLVIA'S LISTENING SERVICE
YOU PAY; WE CARE.
MEN LIKE ME ARE THE FOUNDATION, THE ROCK, THAT THIS SOCIETY IS BUILT ON - BUT DOES ANYONE CARE?
I'VE HAD IT UP TO HERE WITH: "GAYS", AND "WOMEN", AND "MINORITIES". WHEN IS SOMEONE GOING TO CARE ABOUT MY PROBLEMS?
OH DRY UP, YOU PUFFED UP, GREEDY, BLOOD-SUCKING BIGOT!
QUIET! THERAPY SESSION.
SORRY. WRONG TAPE.
WHAT!

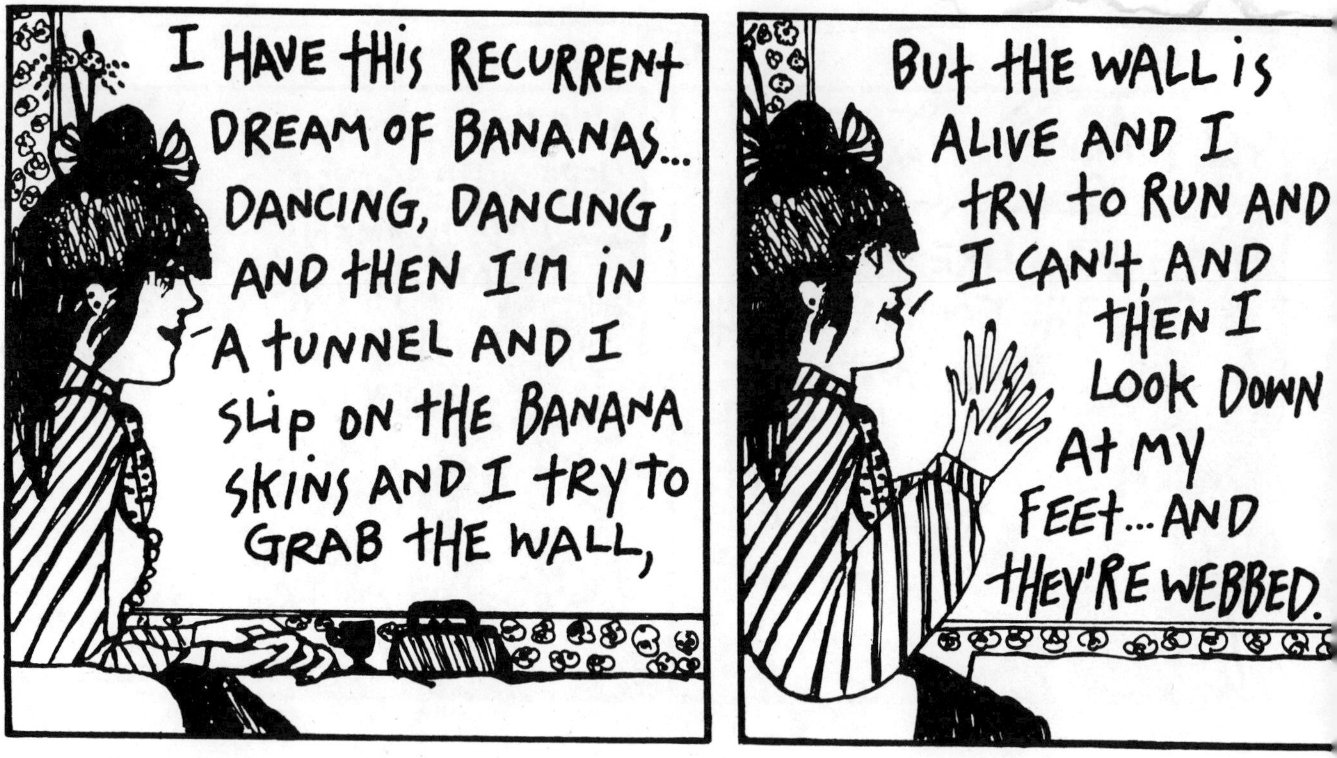
I HAVE THIS RECURRENT DREAM OF BANANAS... DANCING, DANCING, AND THEN I'M IN A TUNNEL AND I SLIP ON THE BANANA SKINS AND I TRY TO GRAB THE WALL,
BUT THE WALL IS ALIVE AND I TRY TO RUN AND I CAN'T, AND THEN I LOOK DOWN AT MY FEET... AND THEY'RE WEBBED.

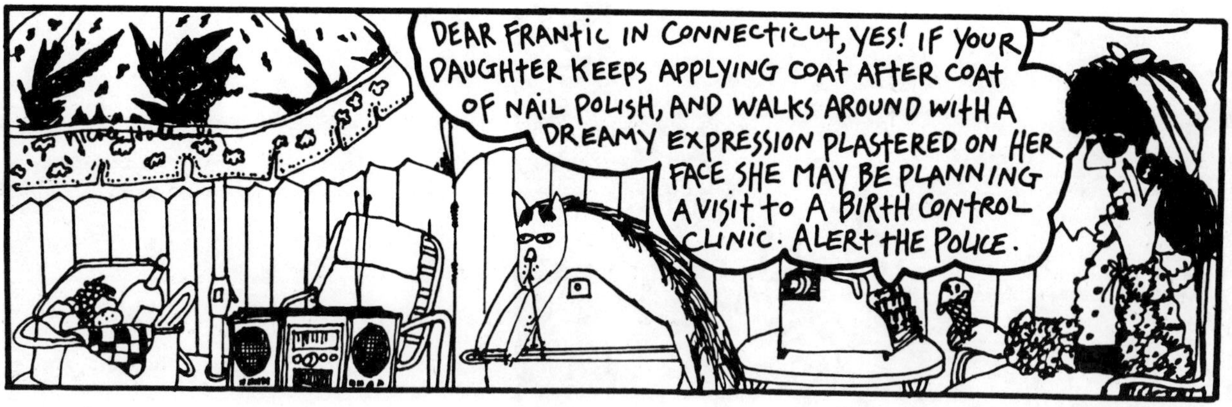
DEAR FRANTIC IN CONNECTICUT, YES! IF YOUR DAUGHTER KEEPS APPLYING COAT AFTER COAT OF NAIL POLISH, AND WALKS AROUND WITH A DREAMY EXPRESSION PLASTERED ON HER FACE SHE MAY BE PLANNING A VISIT TO A BIRTH CONTROL CLINIC. ALERT THE POLICE.

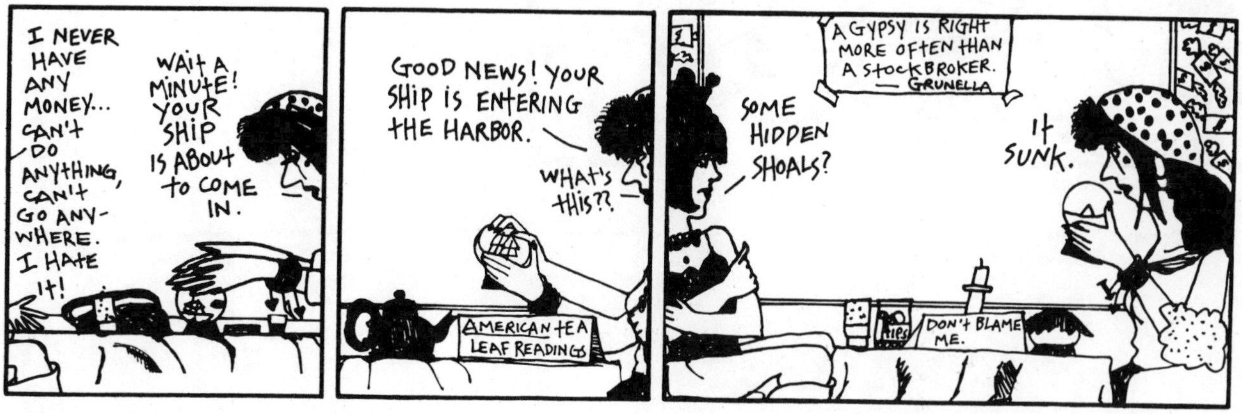
I NEVER HAVE ANY MONEY... CAN'T DO ANYTHING, CAN'T GO ANYWHERE. I HATE IT!
WAIT A MINUTE! YOUR SHIP IS ABOUT TO COME IN.
GOOD NEWS! YOUR SHIP IS ENTERING THE HARBOR.
WHAT'S THIS??
AMERICAN TEA LEAF READINGS
A GYPSY IS RIGHT MORE OFTEN THAN A STOCKBROKER. — GRUNELLA
SOME HIDDEN SHOALS?
IT SUNK.
DON'T BLAME ME.

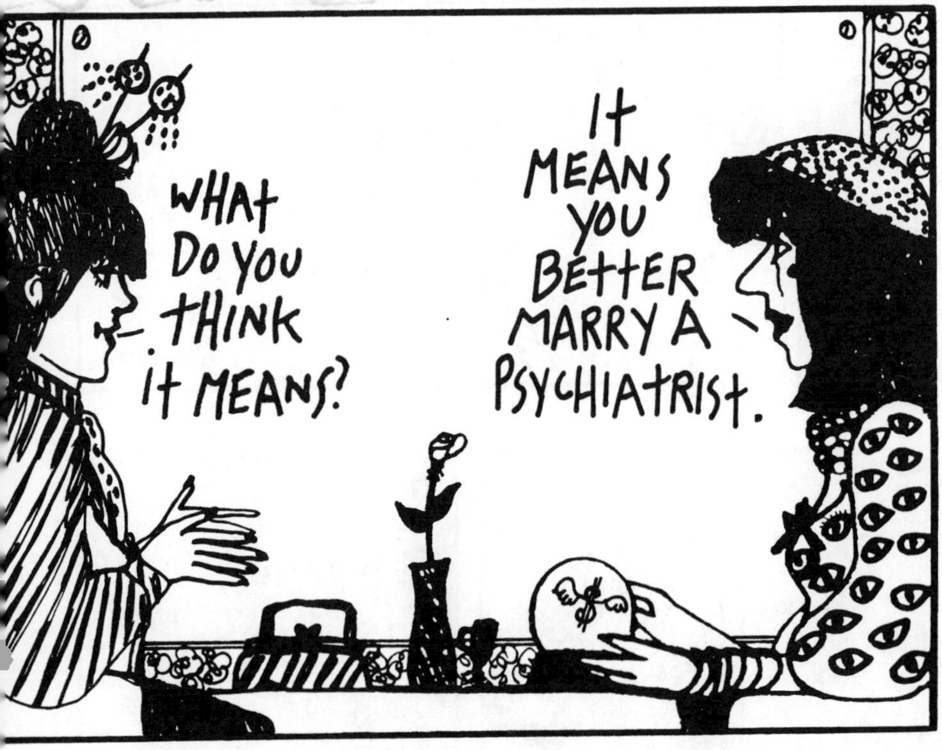
WHAT DO YOU THINK IT MEANS?
IT MEANS YOU BETTER MARRY A PSYCHIATRIST.

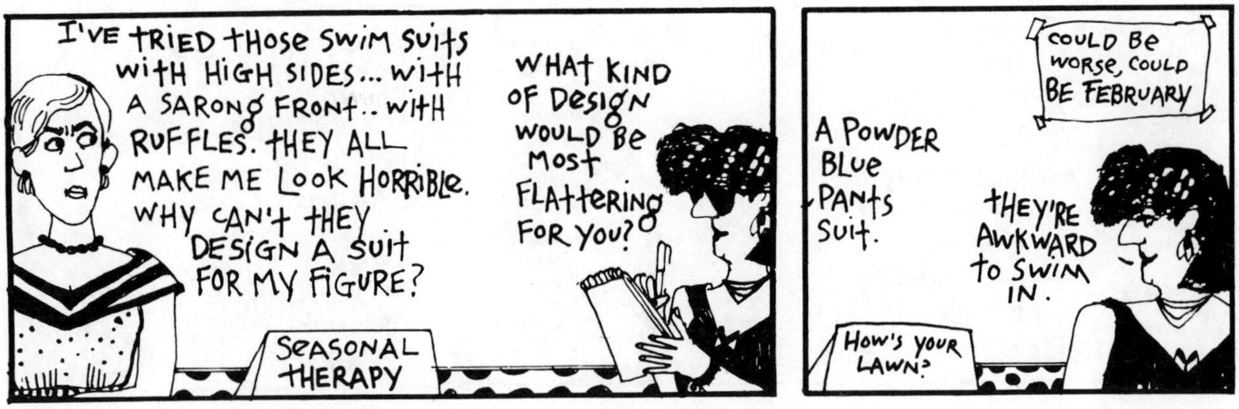
I'VE TRIED THOSE SWIM SUITS WITH HIGH SIDES... WITH A SARONG FRONT.. WITH RUFFLES. THEY ALL MAKE ME LOOK HORRIBLE. WHY CAN'T THEY DESIGN A SUIT FOR MY FIGURE?
WHAT KIND OF DESIGN WOULD BE MOST FLATTERING FOR YOU?
SEASONAL THERAPY
COULD BE WORSE, COULD BE FEBRUARY
A POWDER BLUE PANTS SUIT.
THEY'RE AWKWARD TO SWIM IN.
HOW'S YOUR LAWN?

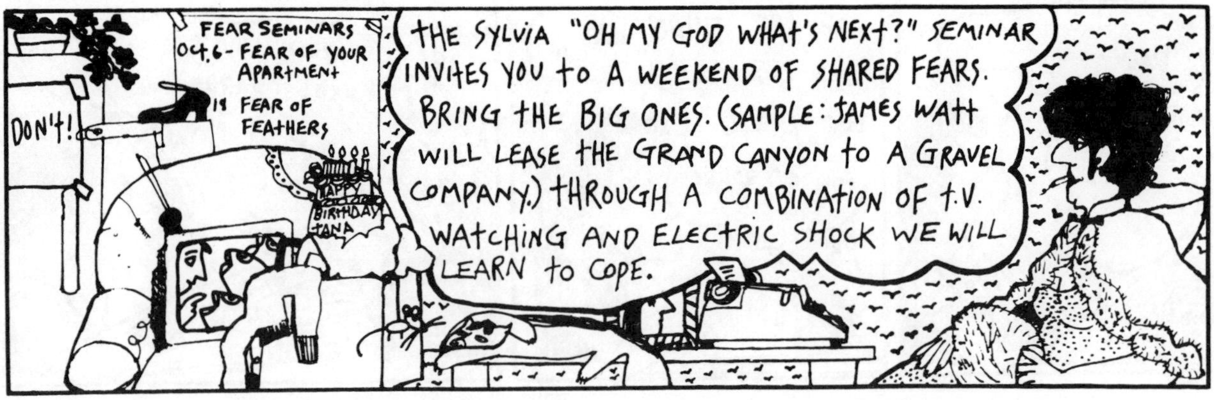
FEAR SEMINARS
OCT. 6 - FEAR OF YOUR APARTMENT
13 FEAR OF FEATHERS
DON'T!
HAPPY BIRTHDAY TANA
THE SYLVIA "OH MY GOD WHAT'S NEXT?" SEMINAR INVITES YOU TO A WEEKEND OF SHARED FEARS. BRING THE BIG ONES. (SAMPLE: JAMES WATT WILL LEASE THE GRAND CANYON TO A GRAVEL COMPANY.) THROUGH A COMBINATION OF T.V. WATCHING AND ELECTRIC SHOCK WE WILL LEARN TO COPE.

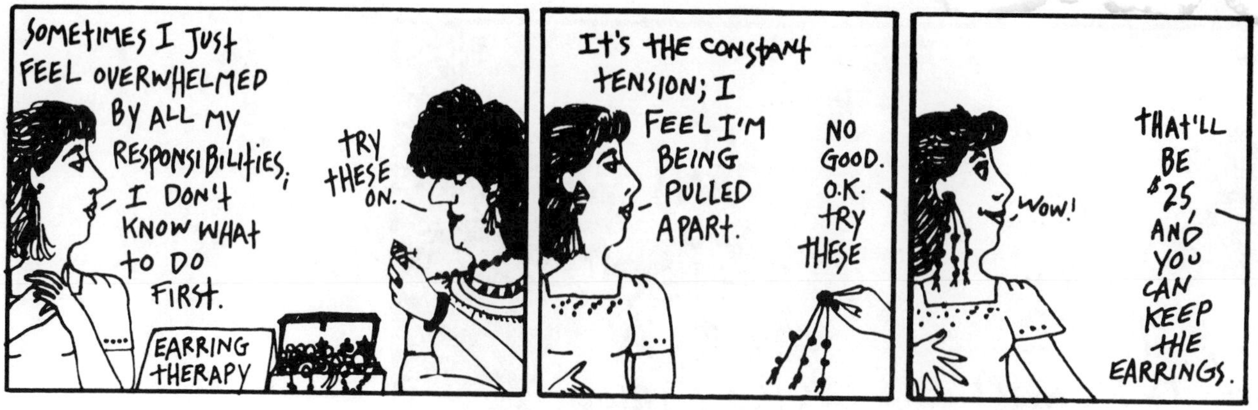
SOMETIMES I JUST FEEL OVERWHELMED BY ALL MY RESPONSIBILITIES; I DON'T KNOW WHAT TO DO FIRST.
EARRING THERAPY
TRY THESE ON.
IT'S THE CONSTANT TENSION; I FEEL I'M BEING PULLED APART.
NO GOOD. O.K. TRY THESE
WOW!
THAT'LL BE $25, AND YOU CAN KEEP THE EARRINGS.

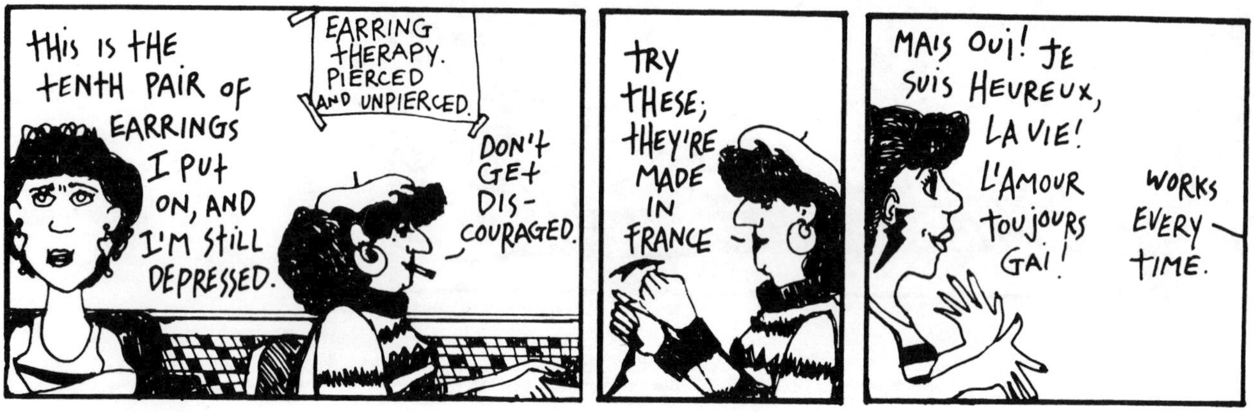
EARRING THERAPY. PIERCED AND UNPIERCED.
THIS IS THE TENTH PAIR OF EARRINGS I PUT ON, AND I'M STILL DEPRESSED.
DON'T GET DIS-COURAGED.
TRY THESE; THEY'RE MADE IN FRANCE
MAIS OUI! JE SUIS HEUREUX, LA VIE! L'AMOUR TOUJOURS GAI!
WORKS EVERY TIME.

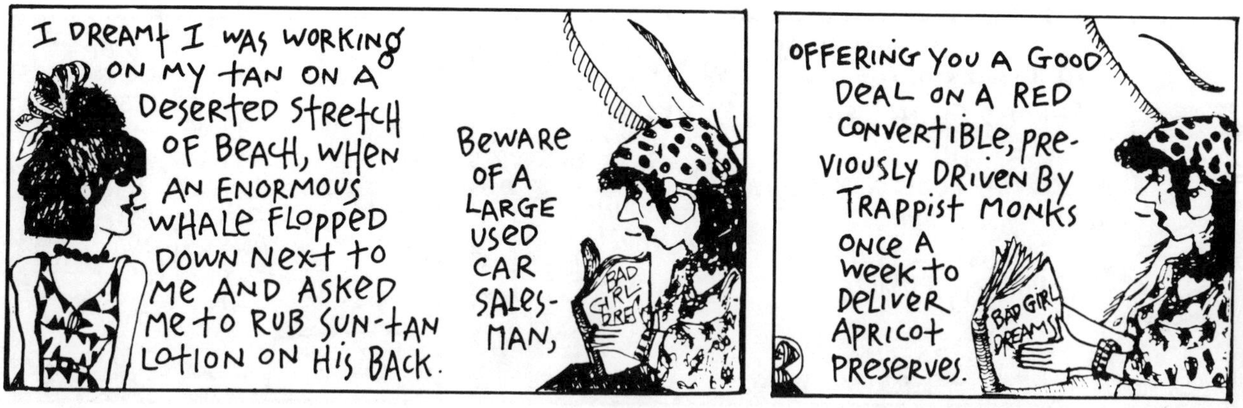
I DREAMT I WAS WORKING ON MY TAN ON A DESERTED STRETCH OF BEACH, WHEN AN ENORMOUS WHALE FLOPPED DOWN NEXT TO ME AND ASKED ME TO RUB SUN-TAN LOTION ON HIS BACK.
BEWARE OF A LARGE USED CAR SALES-MAN,
OFFERING YOU A GOOD DEAL ON A RED CONVERTIBLE, PRE-VIOUSLY DRIVEN BY TRAPPIST MONKS ONCE A WEEK TO DELIVER APRICOT PRESERVES.
BAD GIRL DREAMS

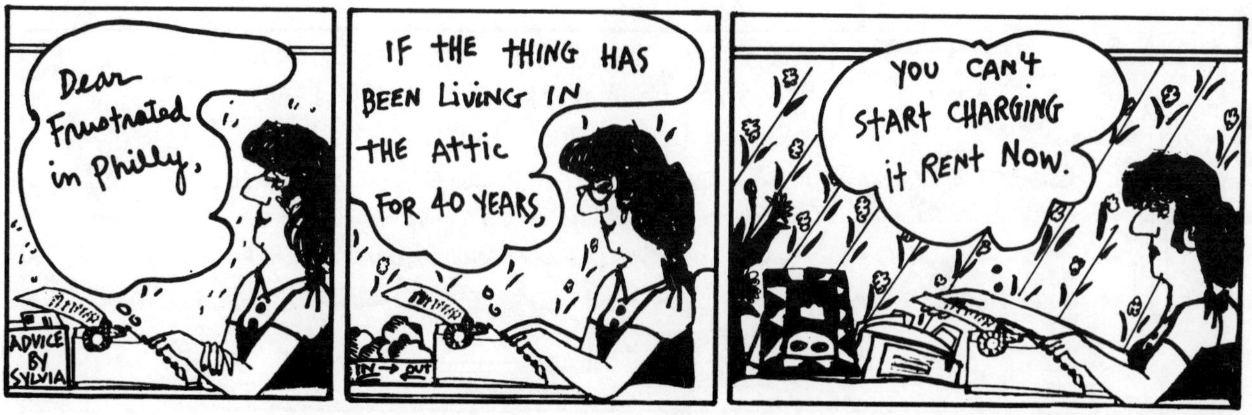
ADVICE BY SYLVIA
Dear Frustrated in Philly,
IN → OUT
IF THE THING HAS BEEN LIVING IN THE ATTIC FOR 40 YEARS,
YOU CAN'T START CHARGING IT RENT NOW.

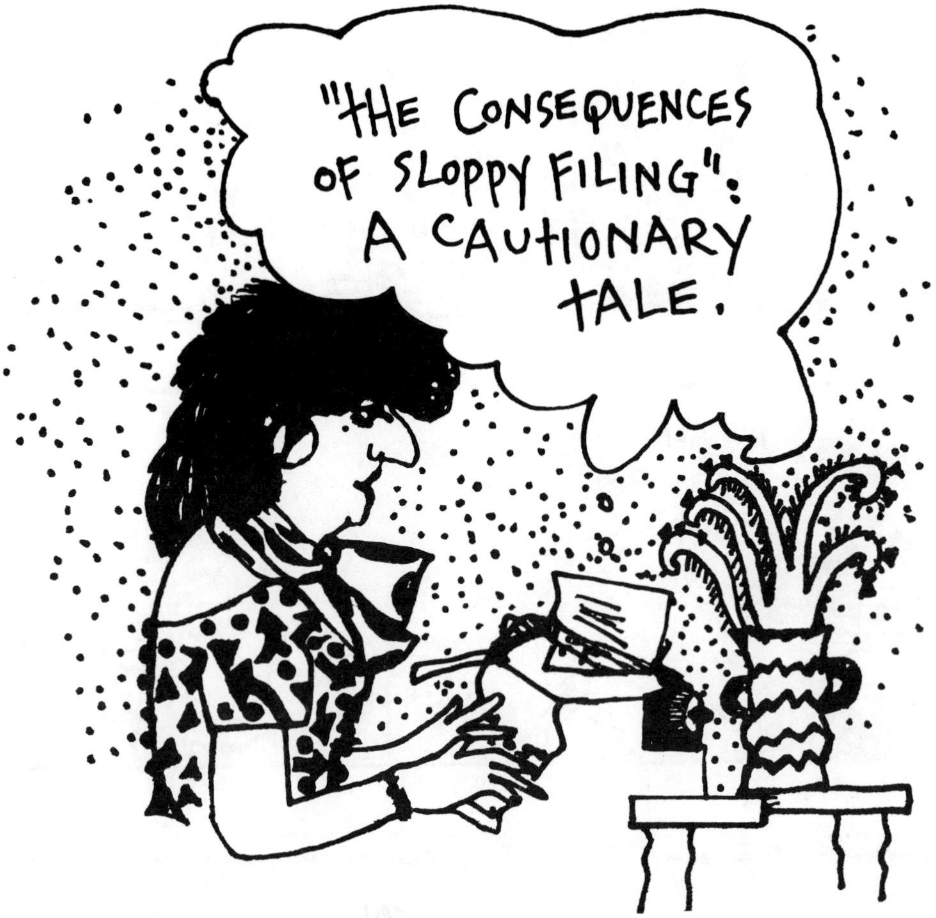
"THE CONSEQUENCES OF SLOPPY FILING": A CAUTIONARY TALE.

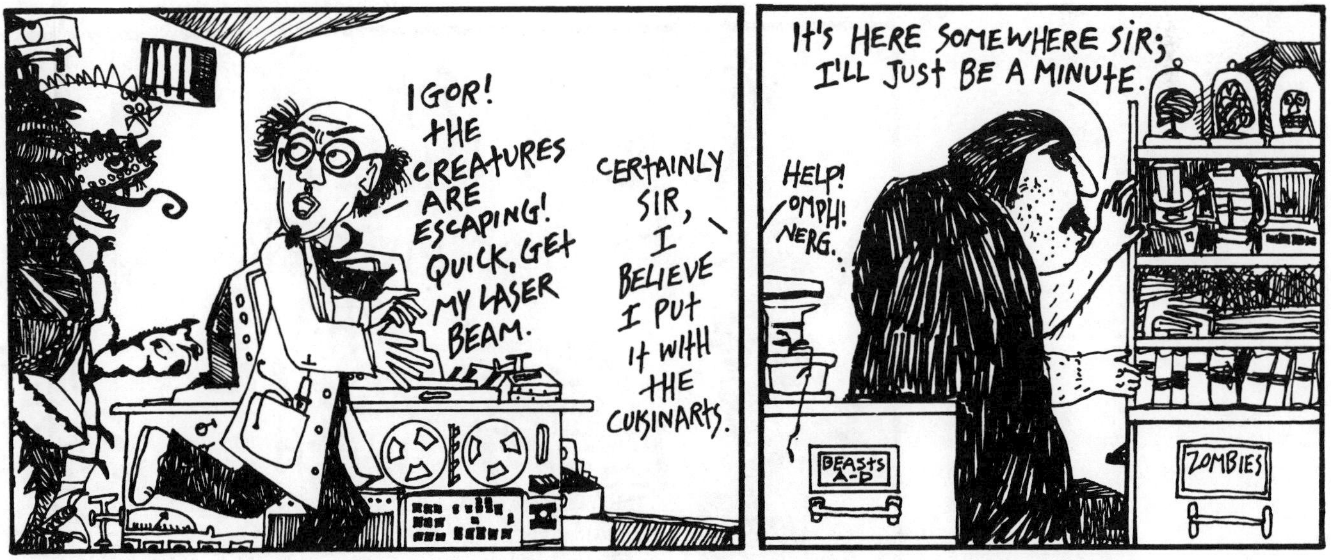
IGOR! THE CREATURES ARE ESCAPING! QUICK, GET MY LASER BEAM.
CERTAINLY SIR, I BELIEVE I PUT IT WITH THE CUISINARTS.
IT'S HERE SOMEWHERE SIR; I'LL JUST BE A MINUTE.
HELP! OMPH! NERG.
BEASTS A-D
ZOMBIES

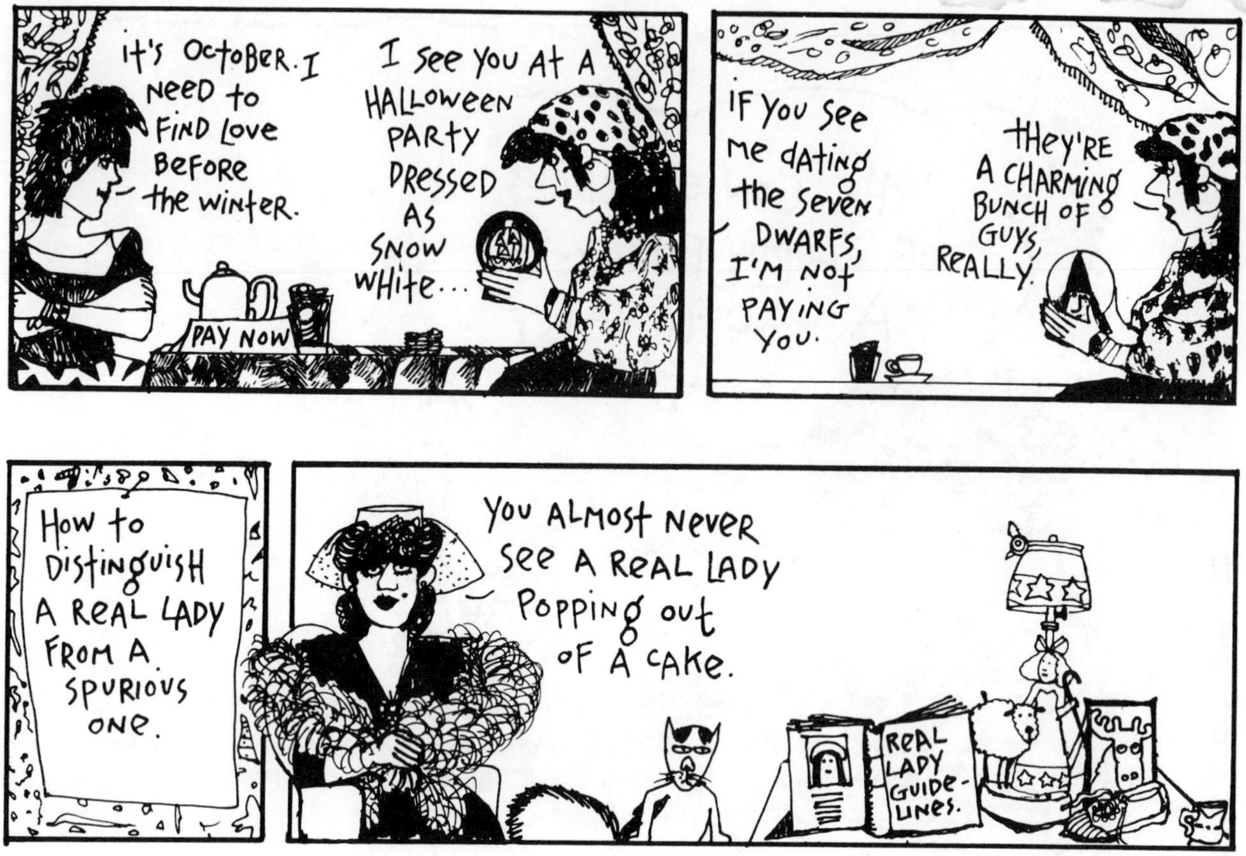
it's October. I need to find love before the winter.
I see you at a Halloween party dressed as Snow White...
PAY NOW
If you see me dating the seven dwarfs, I'm not paying you.
They're a charming bunch of guys, really.
How to distinguish a real lady from a spurious one.
You almost never see a real lady popping out of a cake.
REAL LADY GUIDE-LINES.

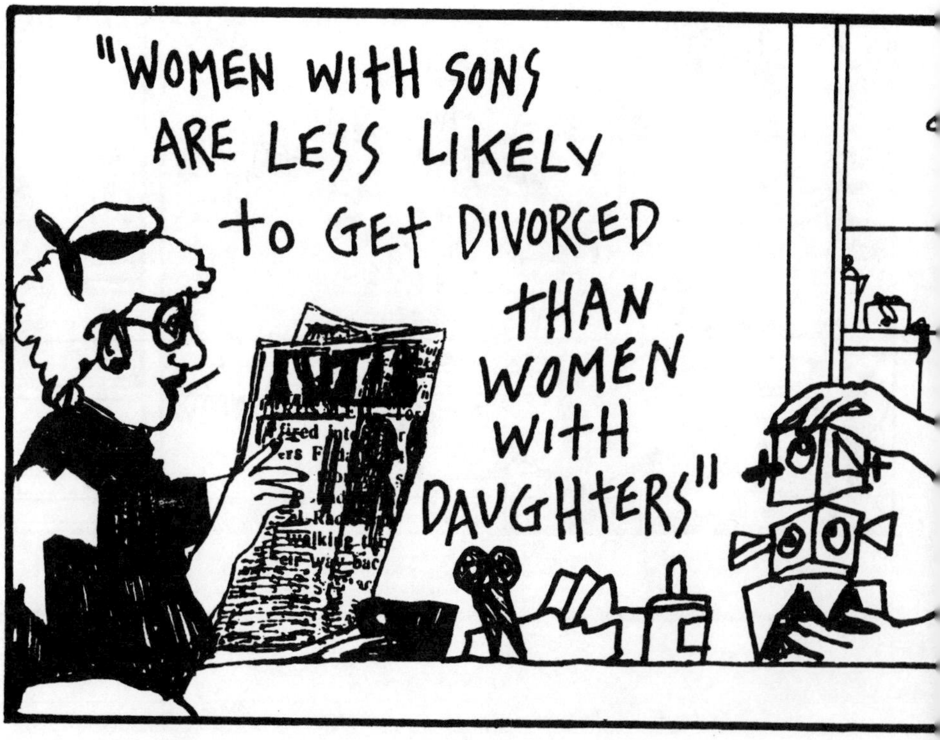
"WOMEN WITH SONS ARE LESS LIKELY TO GET DIVORCED THAN WOMEN WITH DAUGHTERS"

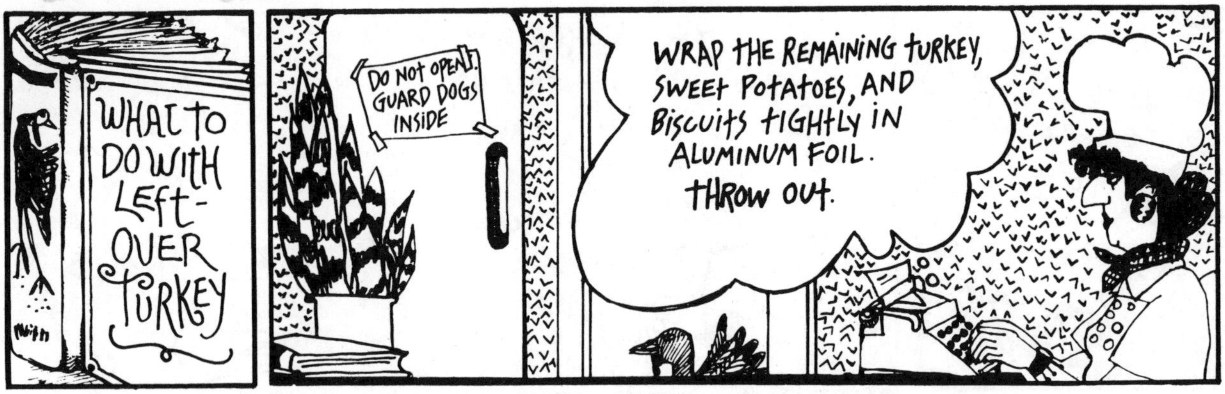
WHAT TO DO WITH LEFT-OVER TURKEY
DO NOT OPEN! GUARD DOGS INSIDE
WRAP THE REMAINING TURKEY, SWEET POTATOES, AND BISCUITS TIGHTLY IN ALUMINUM FOIL. THROW OUT.

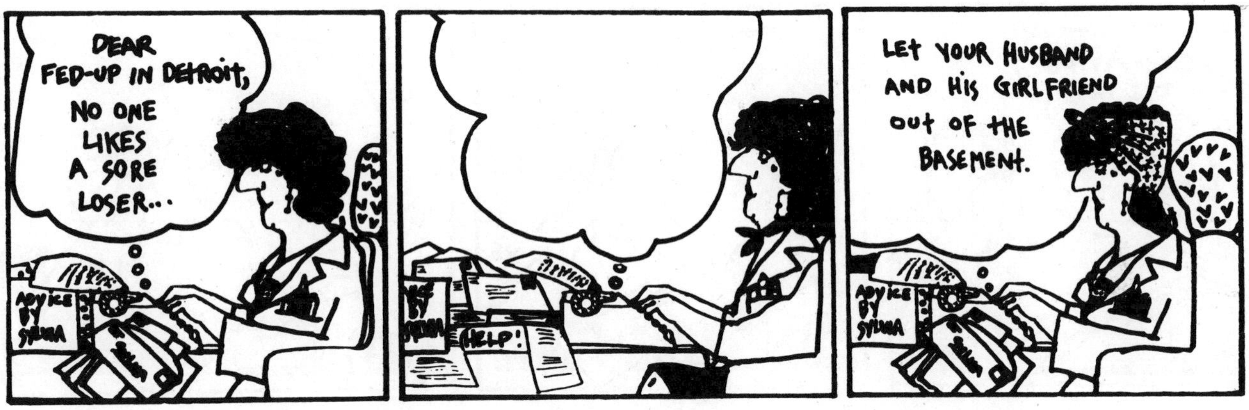
DEAR FED-UP IN DETROIT, NO ONE LIKES A SORE LOSER...
ADVICE BY SYLVIA
HELP!
LET YOUR HUSBAND AND HIS GIRLFRIEND OUT OF THE BASEMENT.
ADVICE BY SYLVIA

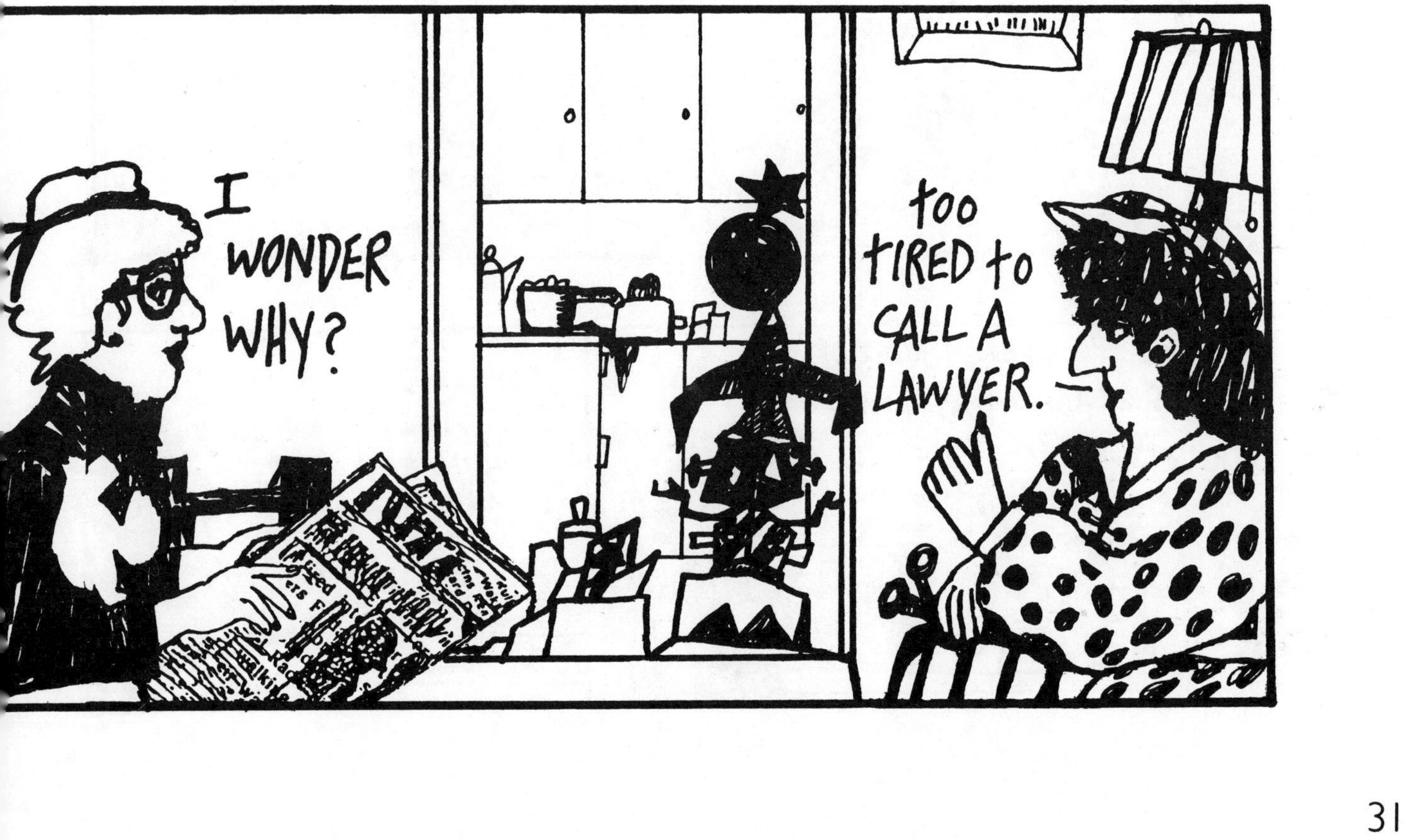
I WONDER WHY?
TOO TIRED TO CALL A LAWYER.

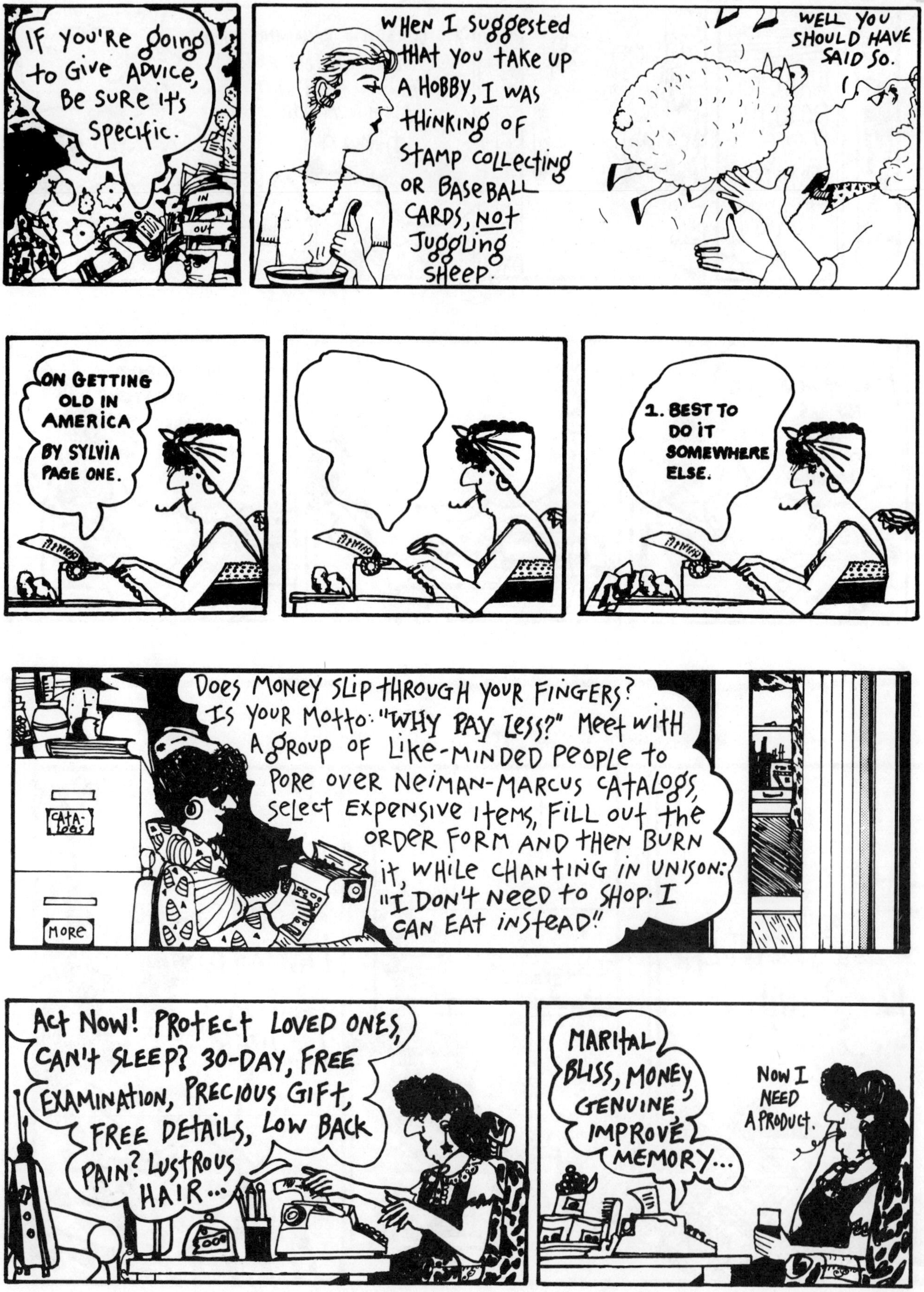
IF YOU'RE GOING TO GIVE ADVICE, BE SURE IT'S SPECIFIC.
IN
OUT
WHEN I SUGGESTED THAT YOU TAKE UP A HOBBY, I WAS THINKING OF STAMP COLLECTING OR BASEBALL CARDS, NOT JUGGLING SHEEP.
WELL YOU SHOULD HAVE SAID SO.
ON GETTING OLD IN AMERICA BY SYLVIA PAGE ONE.
1. BEST TO DO IT SOMEWHERE ELSE.
DOES MONEY SLIP THROUGH YOUR FINGERS? IS YOUR MOTTO: "WHY PAY LESS?" MEET WITH A GROUP OF LIKE-MINDED PEOPLE TO PORE OVER NEIMAN-MARCUS CATALOGS, SELECT EXPENSIVE ITEMS, FILL OUT THE ORDER FORM AND THEN BURN IT, WHILE CHANTING IN UNISON: "I DON'T NEED TO SHOP. I CAN EAT INSTEAD."
CATA-LOGS
MORE
ACT NOW! PROTECT LOVED ONES, CAN'T SLEEP? 30-DAY, FREE EXAMINATION, PRECIOUS GIFT, FREE DETAILS, LOW BACK PAIN? LUSTROUS HAIR...
MARITAL BLISS, MONEY, GENUINE, IMPROVE MEMORY...
NOW I NEED A PRODUCT.

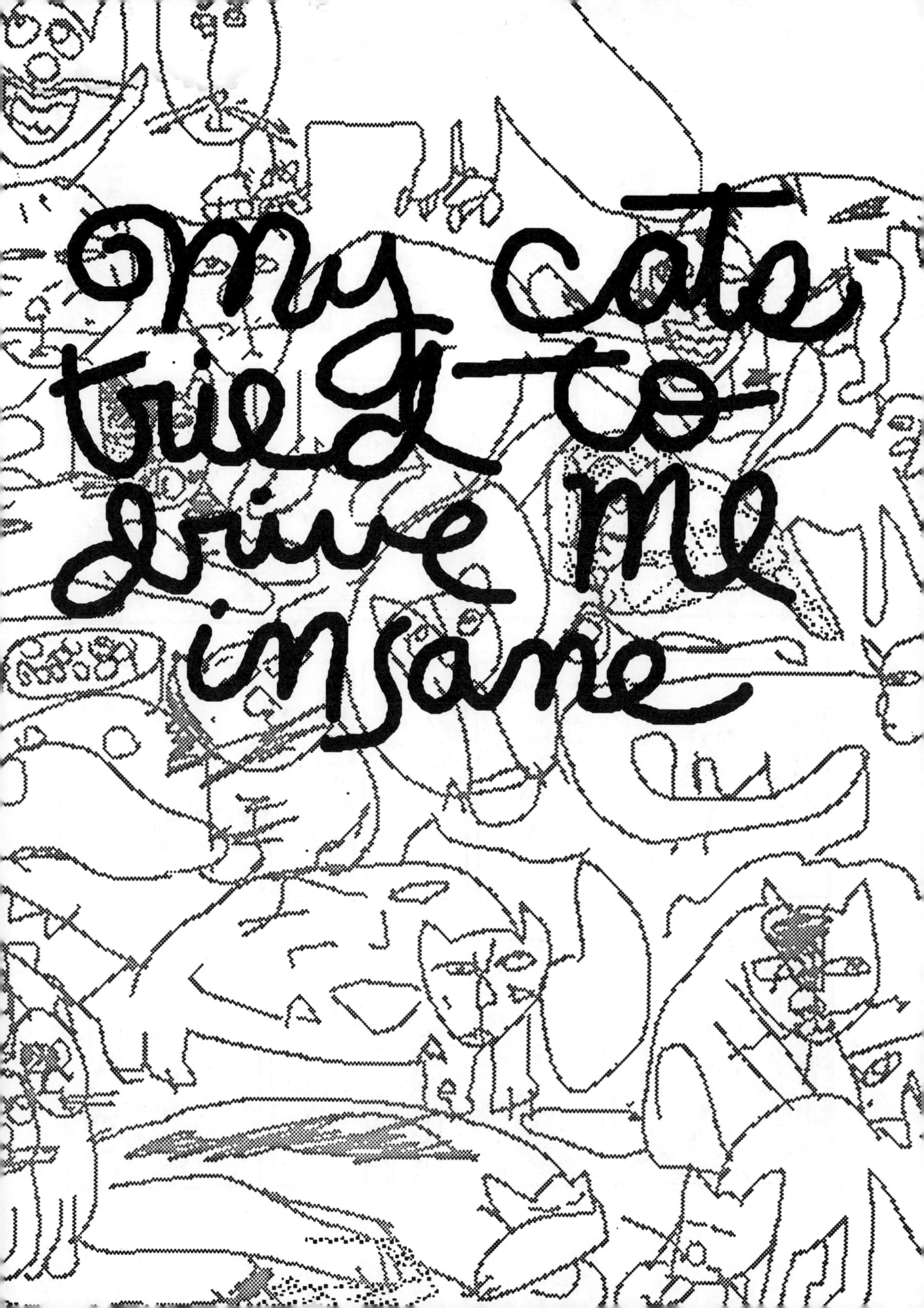
my cats
tried to
drive me
insane

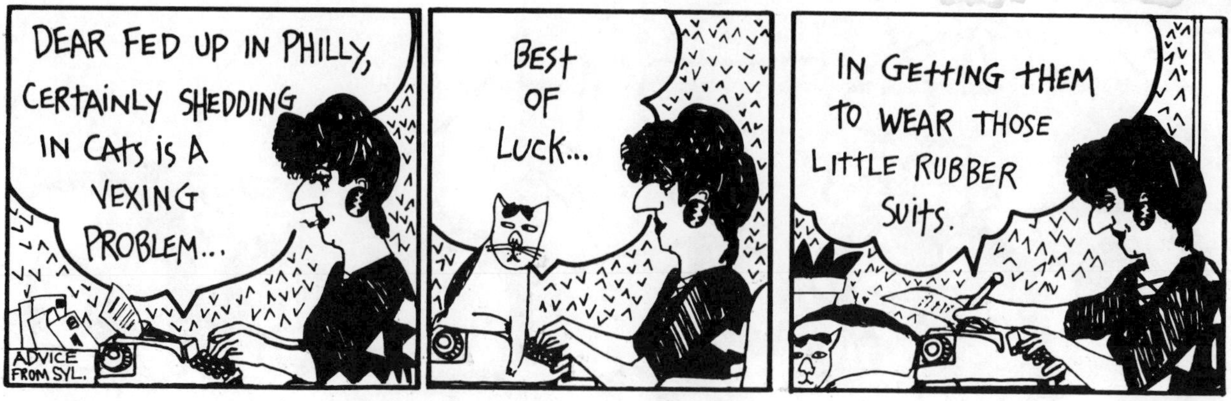
DEAR FED UP IN PHILLY, CERTAINLY SHEDDING IN CATS IS A VEXING PROBLEM...
ADVICE FROM SYL.
BEST OF LUCK...
IN GETTING THEM TO WEAR THOSE LITTLE RUBBER SUITS.

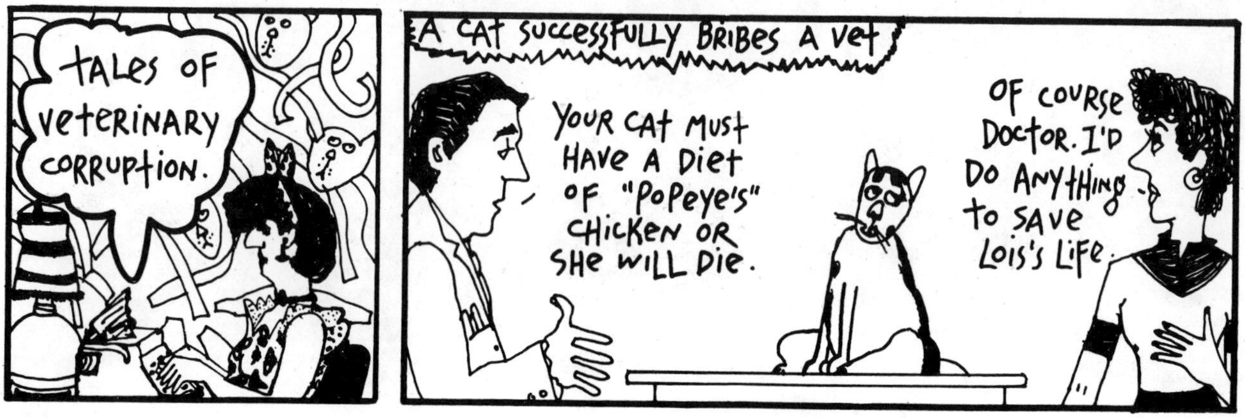
tales of veterinary corruption.
A CAT SUCCESSFULLY BRIBES A VET
YOUR CAT MUST HAVE A DIET OF "POPEYE'S" CHICKEN OR SHE WILL DIE.
OF COURSE DOCTOR. I'D DO ANYTHING TO SAVE LOIS'S LIFE.

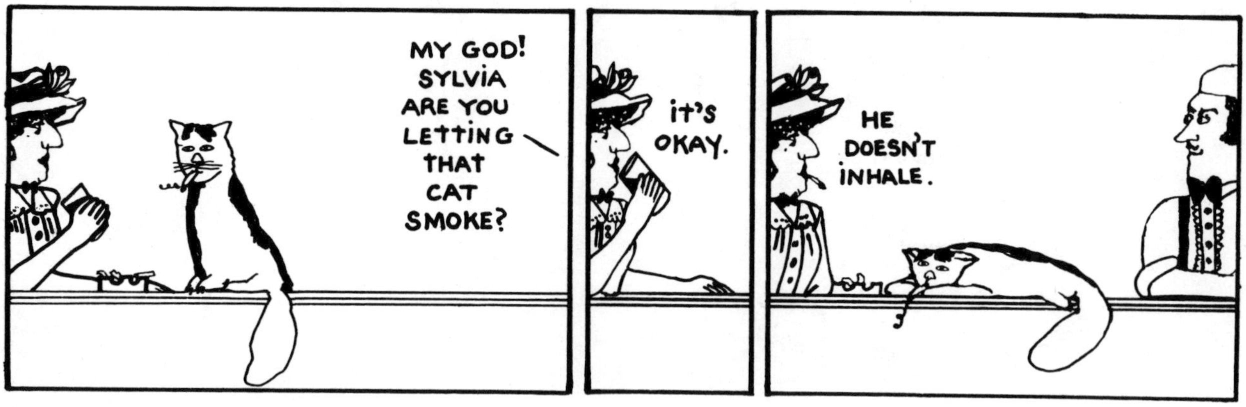
MY GOD! SYLVIA ARE YOU LETTING THAT CAT SMOKE?
it's OKAY.
HE DOESN'T INHALE.

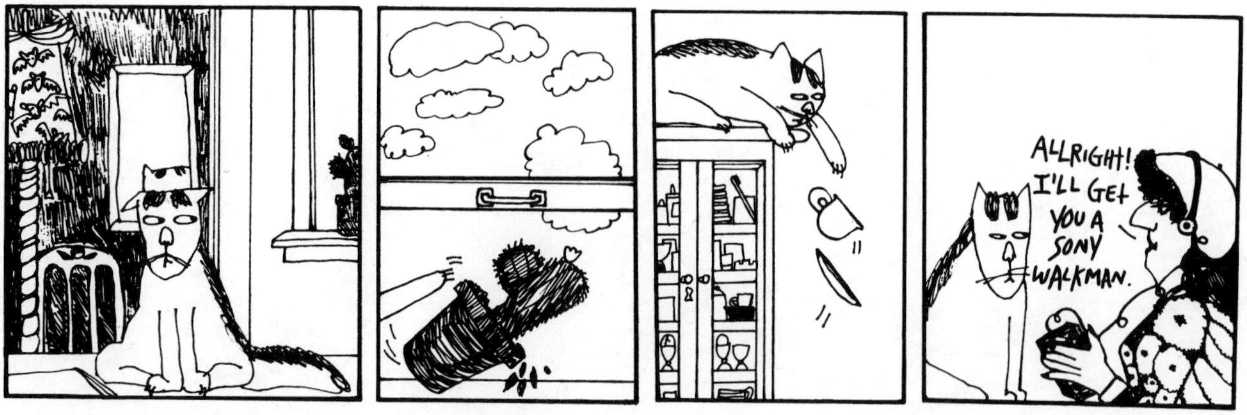
ALLRIGHT! I'LL GET YOU A SONY WALKMAN.

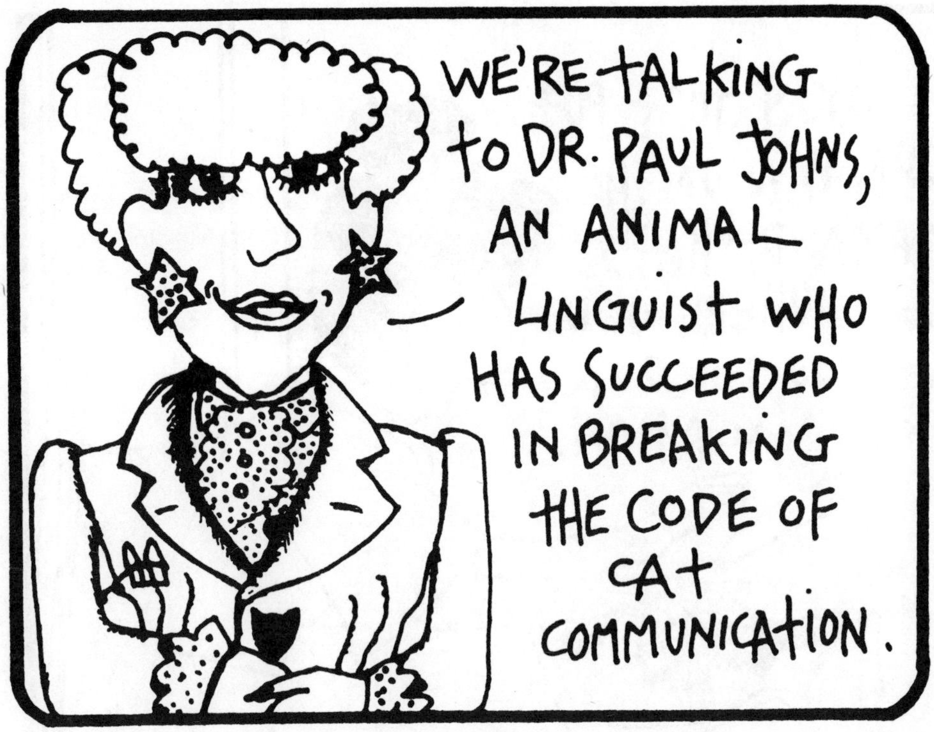
WE'RE TALKING TO DR. PAUL JOHNS, AN ANIMAL LINGUIST WHO HAS SUCCEEDED IN BREAKING THE CODE OF CAT COMMUNICATION.

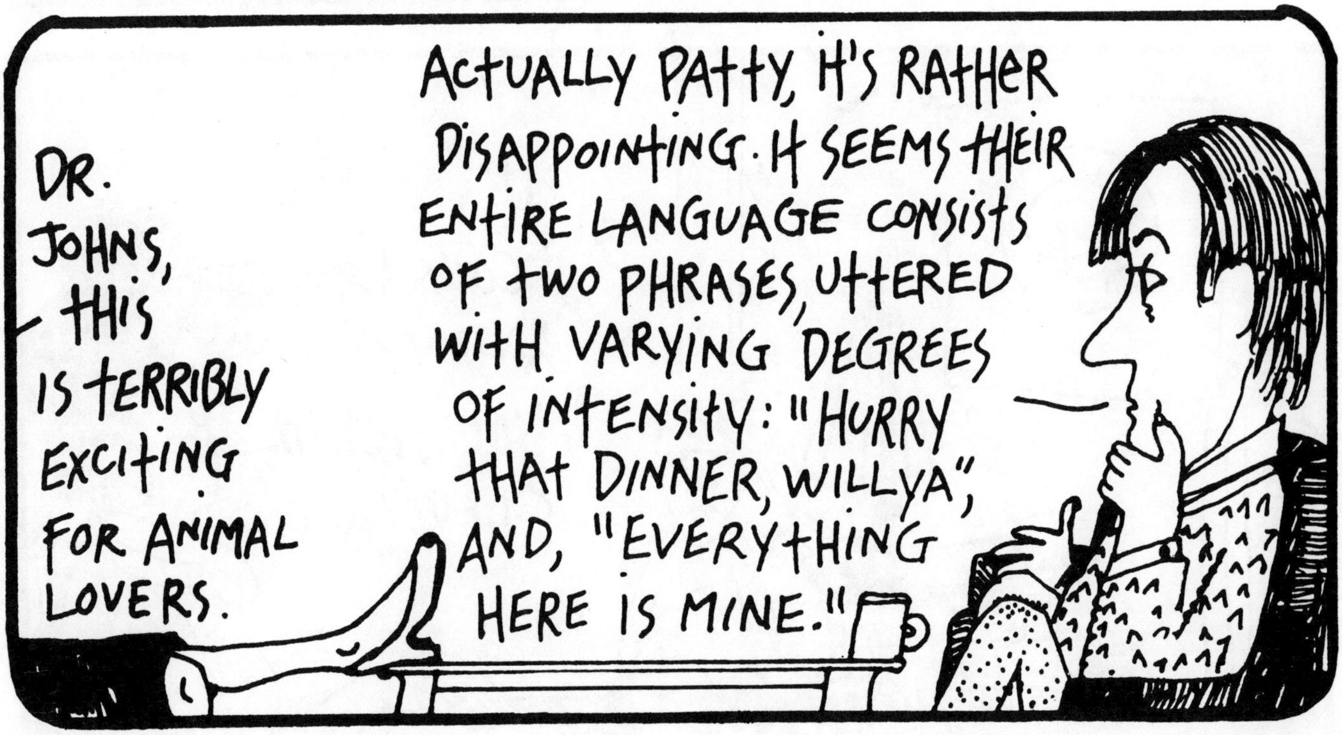
DR. JOHNS, THIS IS TERRIBLY EXCITING FOR ANIMAL LOVERS.
ACTUALLY PATTY, IT'S RATHER DISAPPOINTING. IT SEEMS THEIR ENTIRE LANGUAGE CONSISTS OF TWO PHRASES, UTTERED WITH VARYING DEGREES OF INTENSITY: "HURRY THAT DINNER, WILLYA", AND, "EVERYTHING HERE IS MINE."

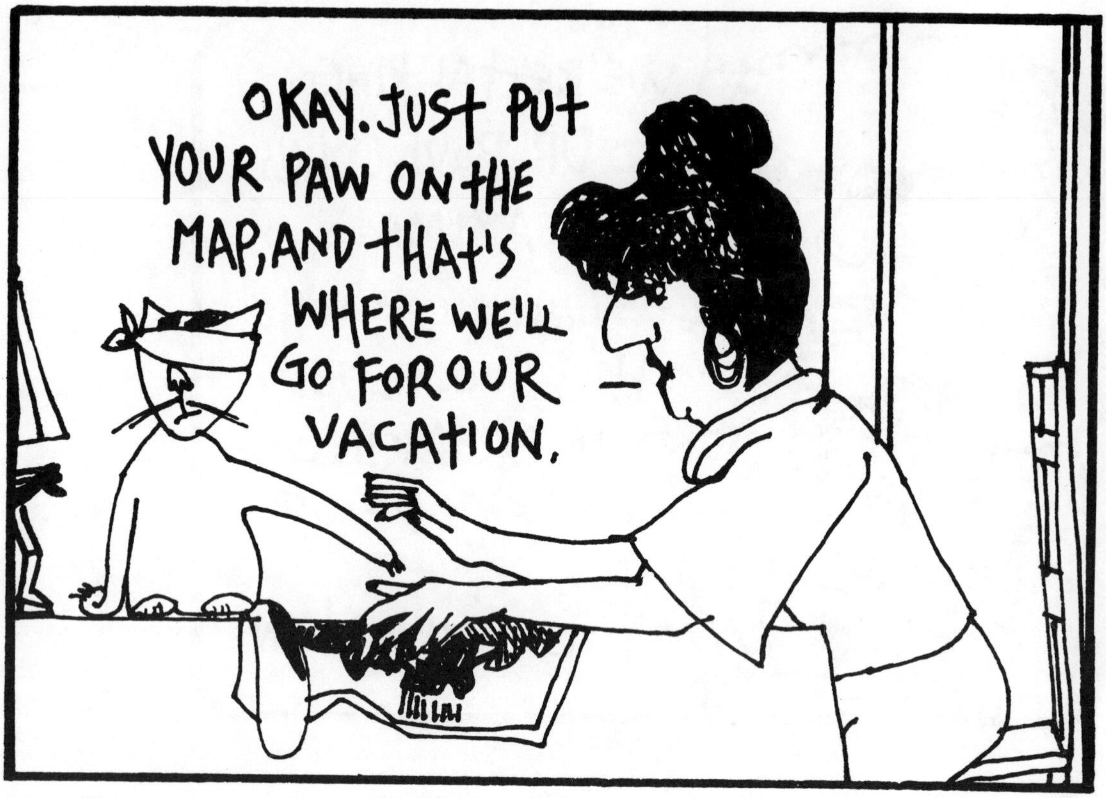
OKAY. JUST PUT YOUR PAW ON THE MAP, AND THAT'S WHERE WE'LL GO FOR OUR VACATION.

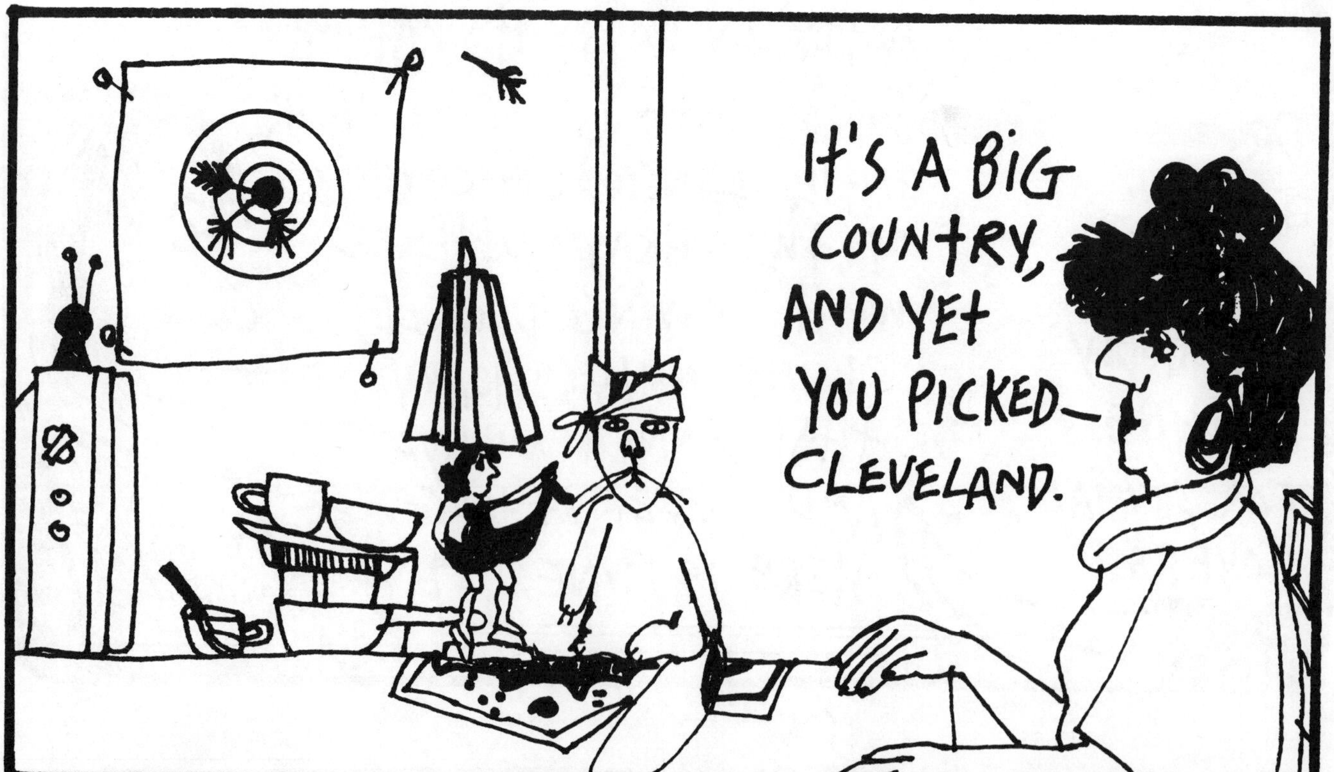
IT'S A BIG COUNTRY, AND YET YOU PICKED— CLEVELAND.

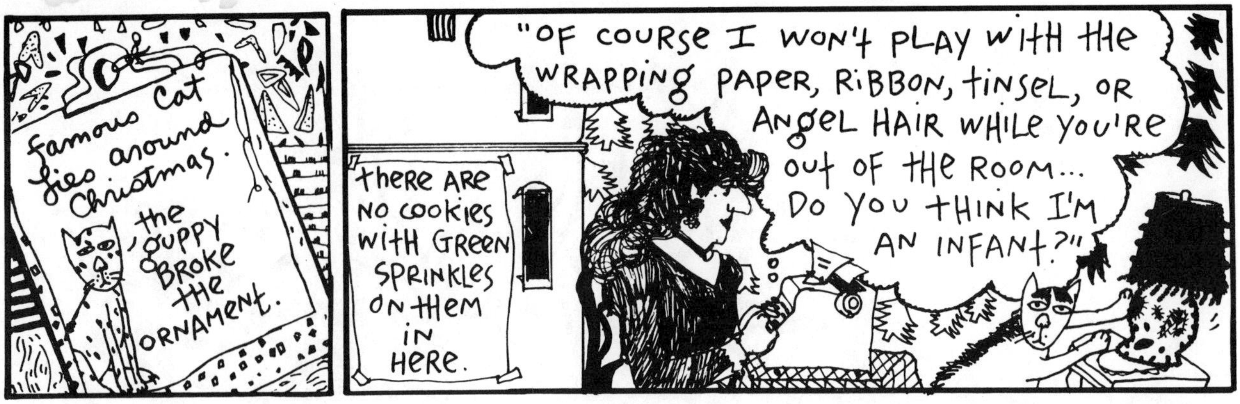
Famous Cat lies around Christmas.
the guppy broke the ornament.
There are no cookies with green sprinkles on them in here.
"Of course I won't play with the wrapping paper, ribbon, tinsel, or angel hair while you're out of the room... Do you think I'm an infant?"

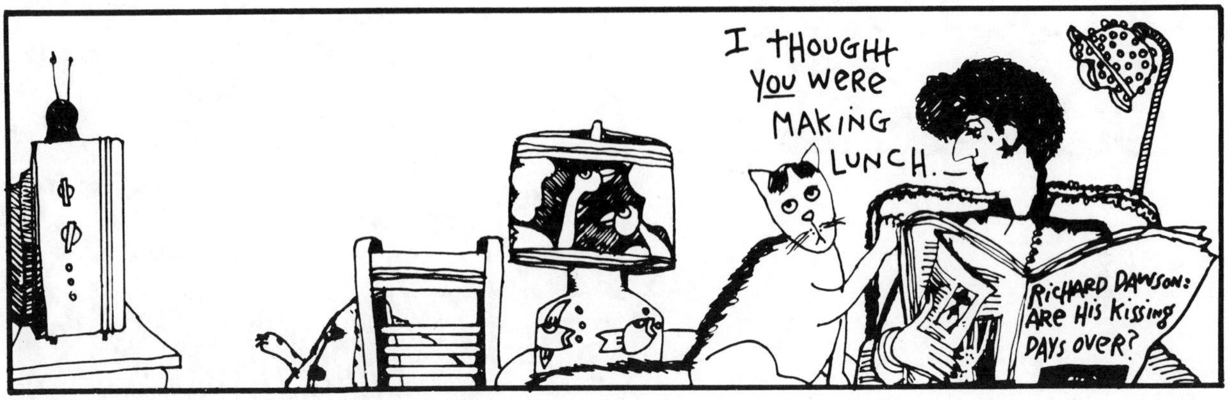
I thought you were making lunch.
Richard Dawson: Are his kissing days over?

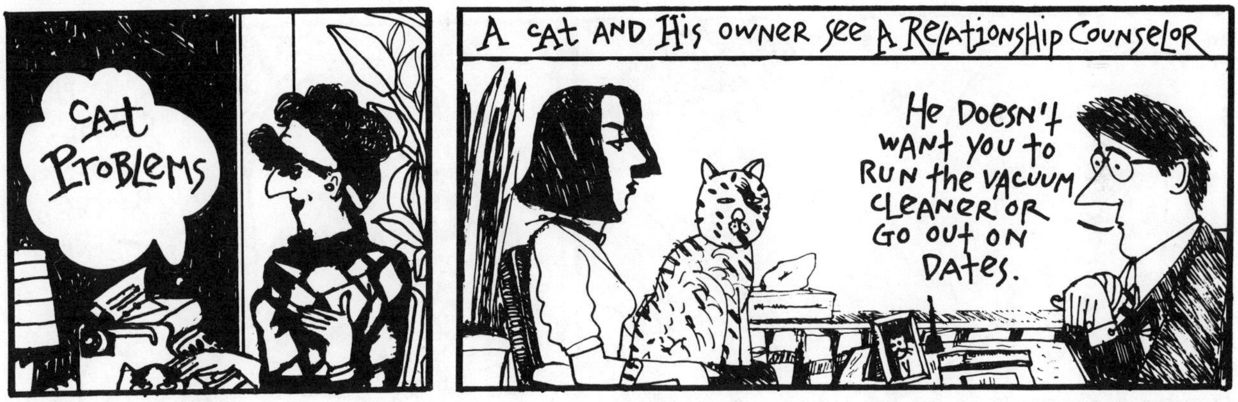
Cat Problems
A cat and his owner see a relationship counselor
He doesn't want you to run the vacuum cleaner or go out on dates.

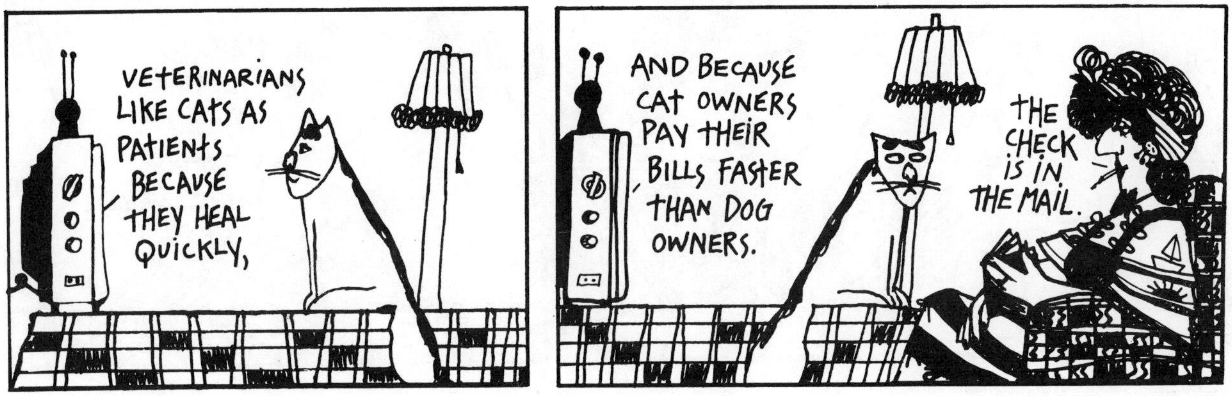
Veterinarians like cats as patients because they heal quickly,
and because cat owners pay their bills faster than dog owners.
The check is in the mail.

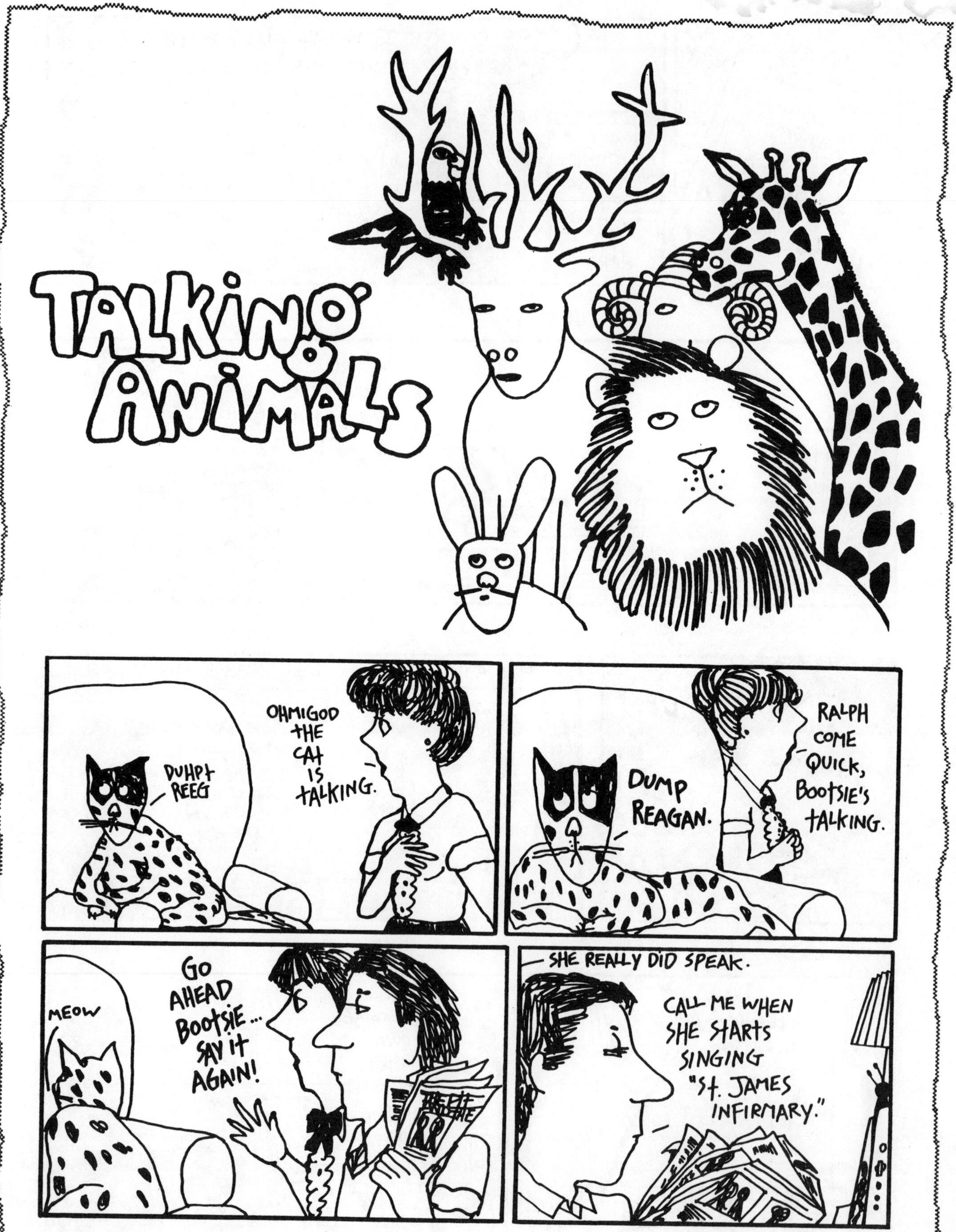
TALKING ANIMALS
DUHPT REEG
OHMIGOD THE CAT IS TALKING.
DUMP REAGAN.
RALPH COME QUICK, BOOTSIE'S TALKING.
MEOW
GO AHEAD BOOTSIE... SAY IT AGAIN!
SHE REALLY DID SPEAK.
CALL ME WHEN SHE STARTS SINGING "ST. JAMES INFIRMARY."

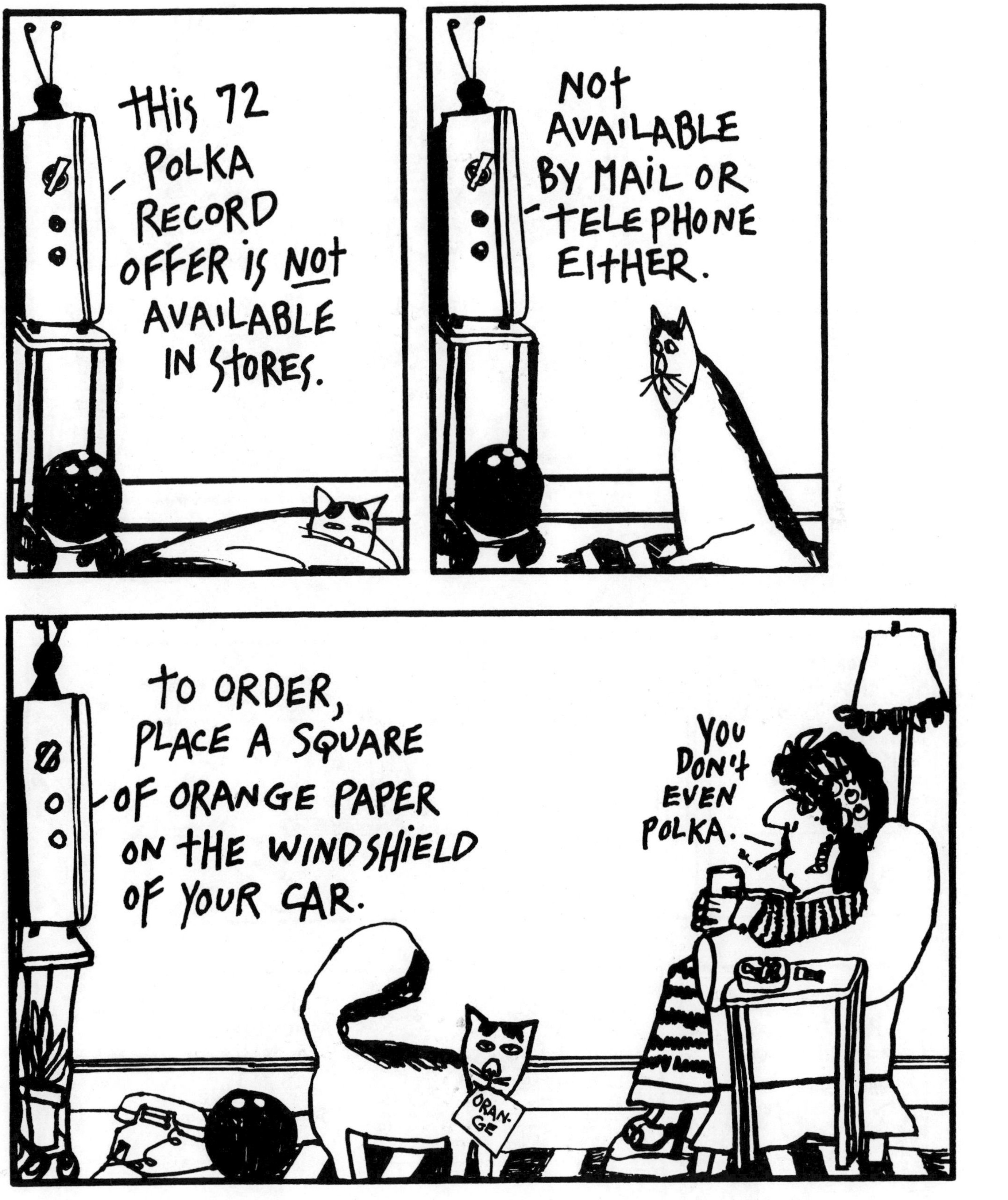
THIS 72 POLKA RECORD OFFER IS NOT AVAILABLE IN STORES.
NOT AVAILABLE BY MAIL OR TELEPHONE EITHER.
TO ORDER, PLACE A SQUARE OF ORANGE PAPER ON THE WINDSHIELD OF YOUR CAR.
YOU DON'T EVEN POLKA.
ORAN-GE

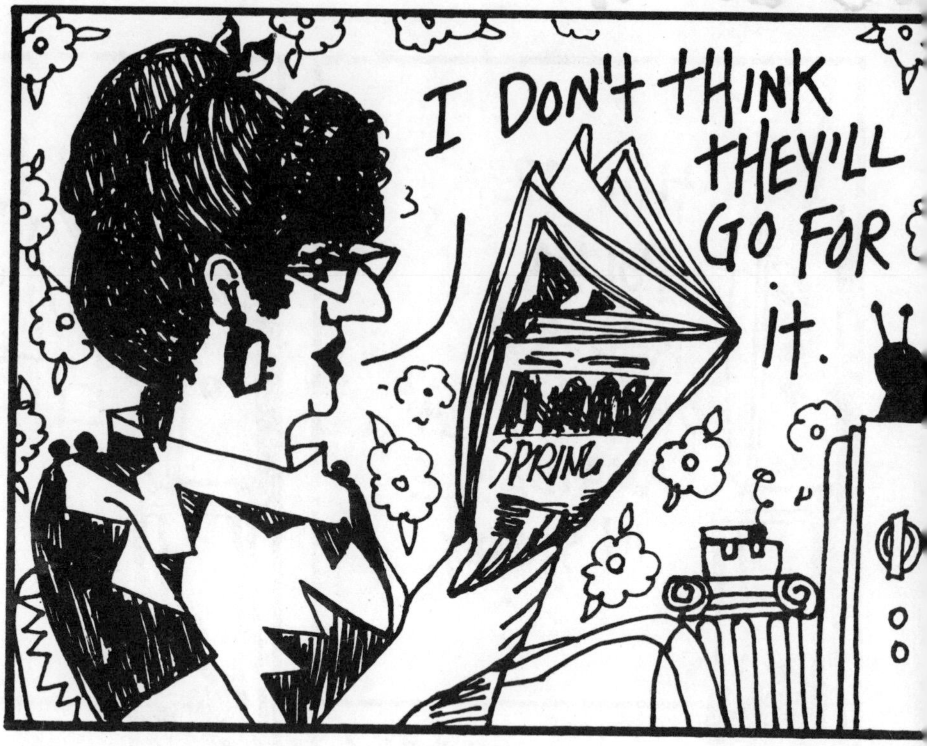
I DON'T THINK THEY'LL GO FOR IT.
SPRING

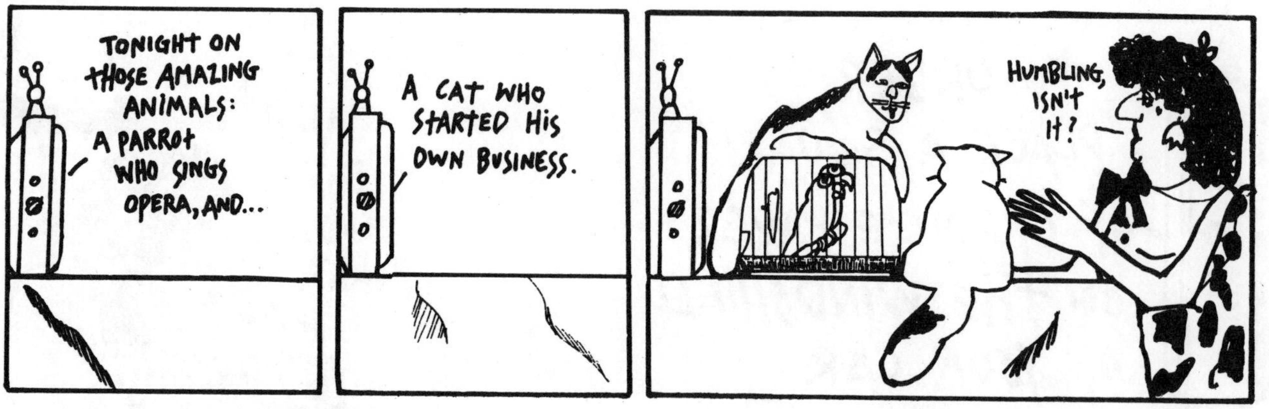
TONIGHT ON THOSE AMAZING ANIMALS: A PARROT WHO SINGS OPERA, AND...
A CAT WHO STARTED HIS OWN BUSINESS.
HUMBLING, ISN'T IT?

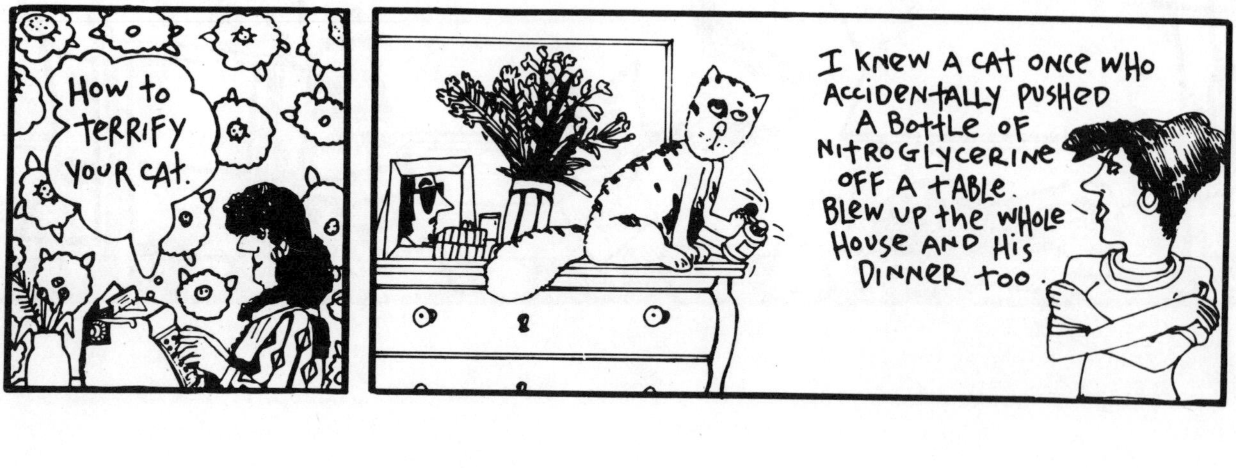
How to terrify your cat.
I knew a cat once who accidentally pushed a bottle of nitroglycerine off a table. Blew up the whole house and his dinner too.

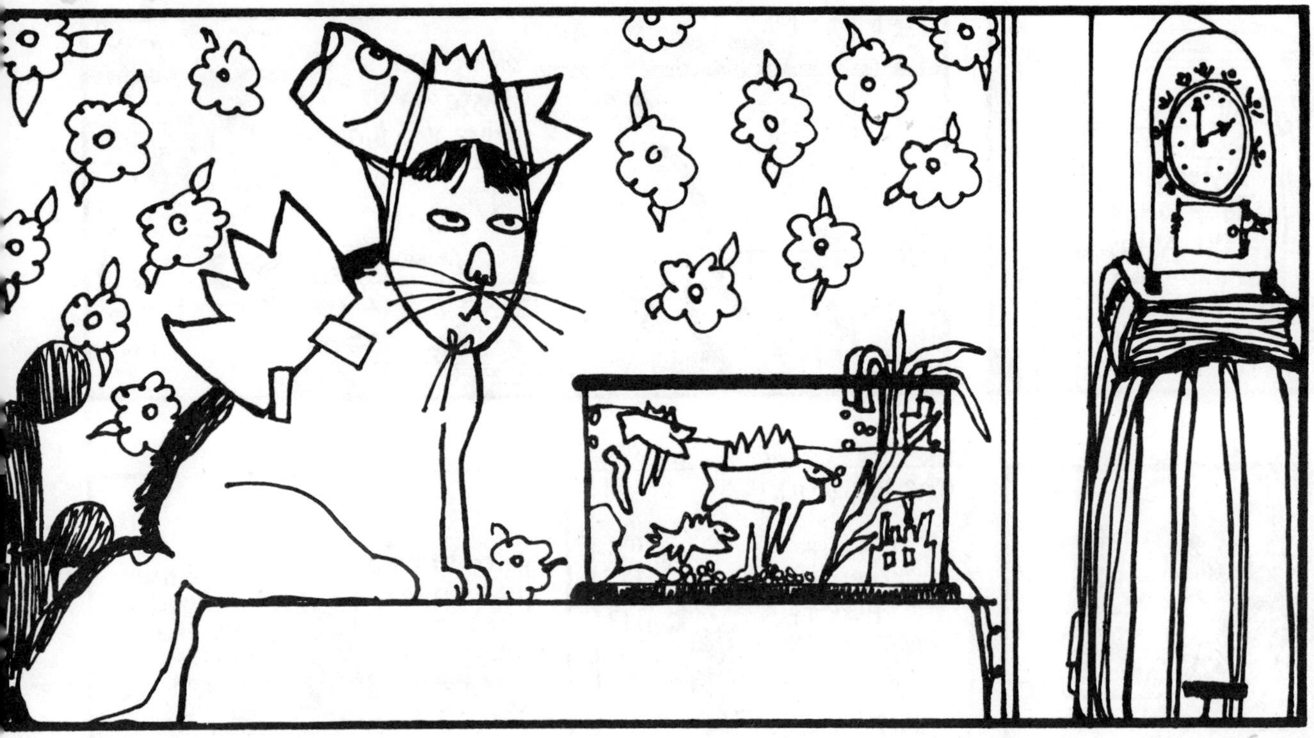

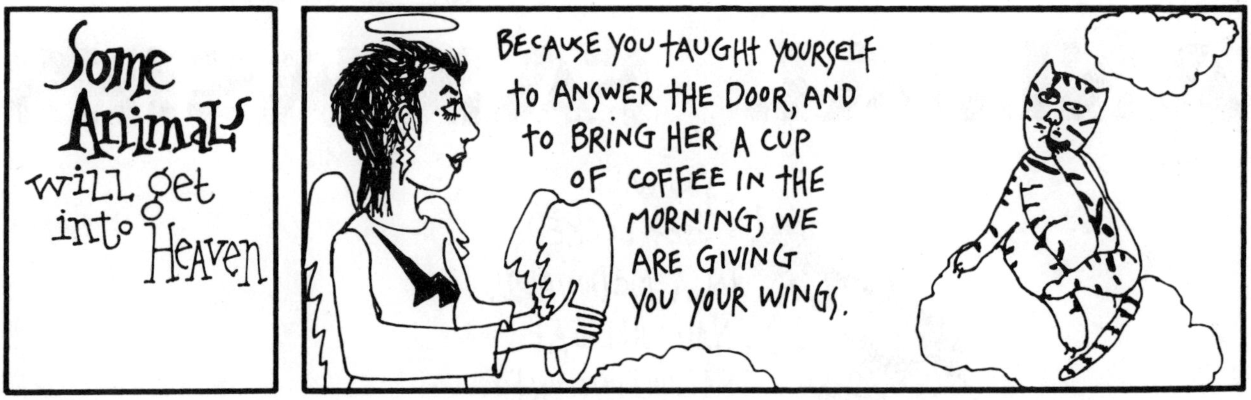
Some Animals will get into Heaven
BECAUSE YOU TAUGHT YOURSELF TO ANSWER THE DOOR, AND TO BRING HER A CUP OF COFFEE IN THE MORNING, WE ARE GIVING YOU YOUR WINGS.

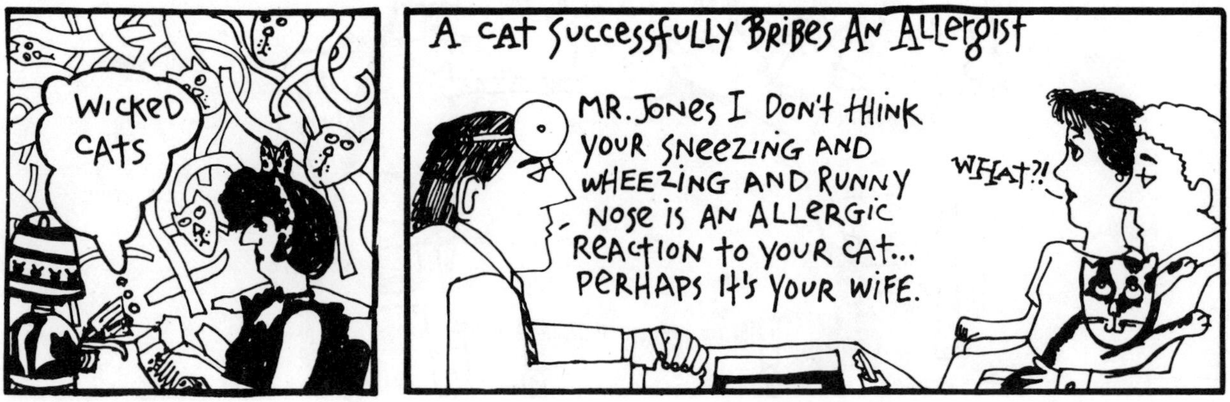
WICKED CATS
A CAT SUCCESSFULLY BRIBES AN ALLERGIST
MR. JONES I DON'T THINK YOUR SNEEZING AND WHEEZING AND RUNNY NOSE IS AN ALLERGIC REACTION TO YOUR CAT... PERHAPS IT'S YOUR WIFE.
WHAT?!

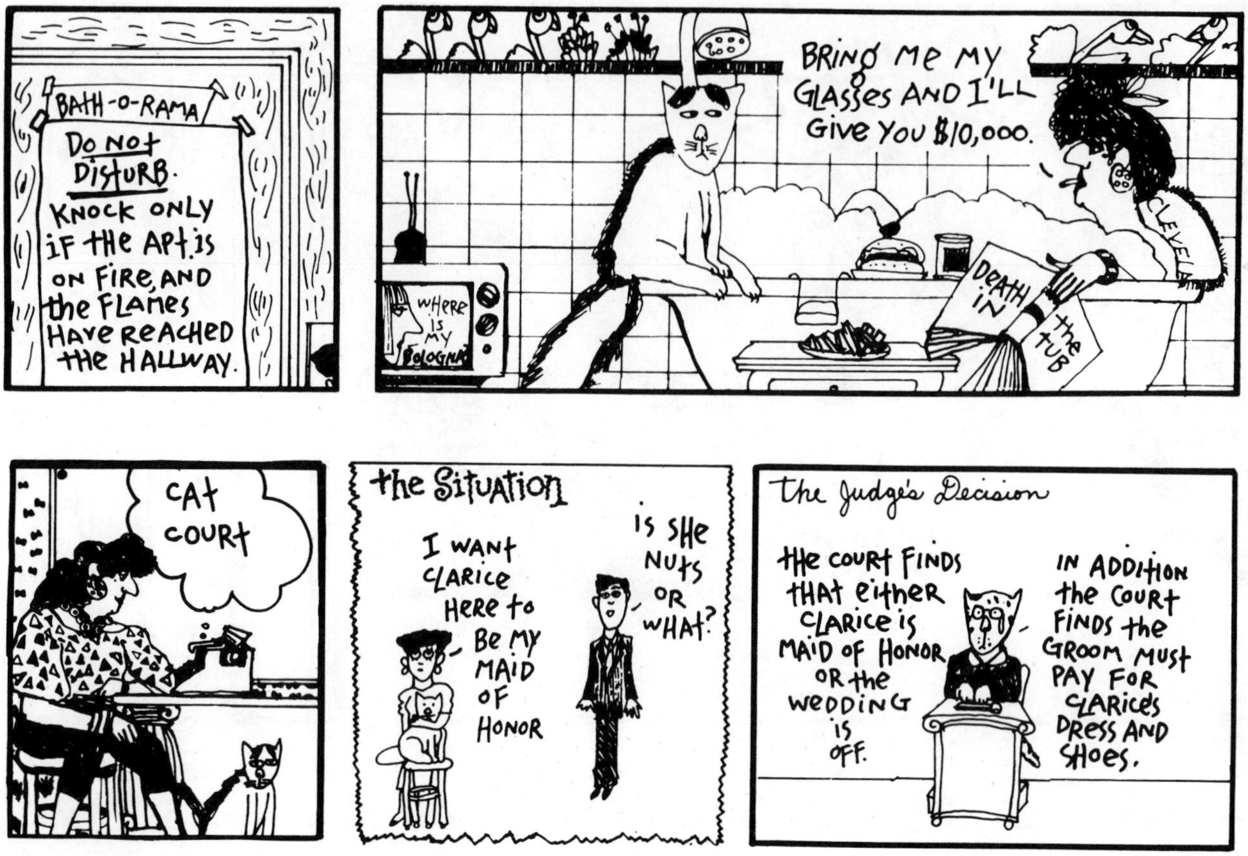
BATH-O-RAMA
DO NOT DISTURB.
KNOCK ONLY IF THE APT. IS ON FIRE, AND THE FLAMES HAVE REACHED THE HALLWAY.
BRING ME MY GLASSES AND I'LL GIVE YOU $10,000.
WHERE IS MY BOLOGNA
DEATH IN THE TUB
CAT COURT
the Situation
I WANT CLARICE HERE TO BE MY MAID OF HONOR
IS SHE NUTS OR WHAT?
The Judge's Decision
THE COURT FINDS THAT EITHER CLARICE IS MAID OF HONOR OR THE WEDDING IS OFF.
IN ADDITION THE COURT FINDS THE GROOM MUST PAY FOR CLARICE'S DRESS AND SHOES.

ANIMAL FANTASIES

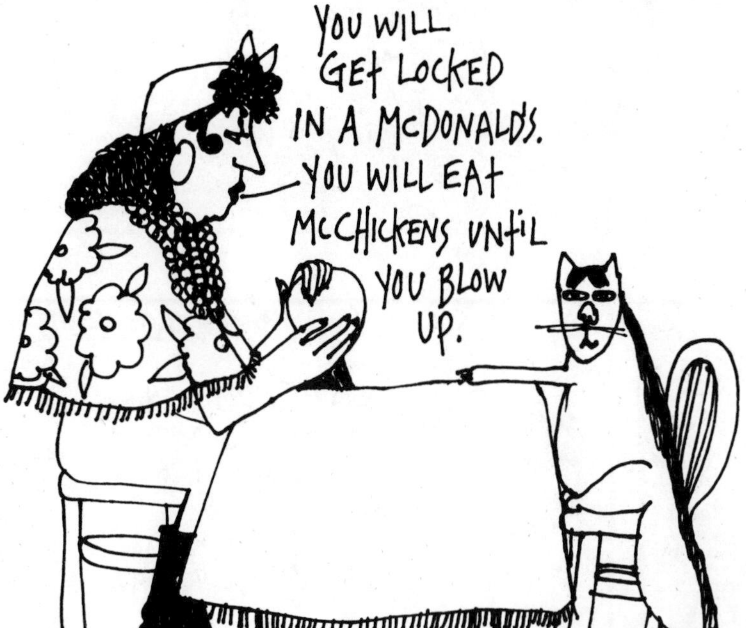
YOU WILL GET LOCKED IN A McDONALD'S. YOU WILL EAT McCHICKENS UNTIL YOU BLOW UP.

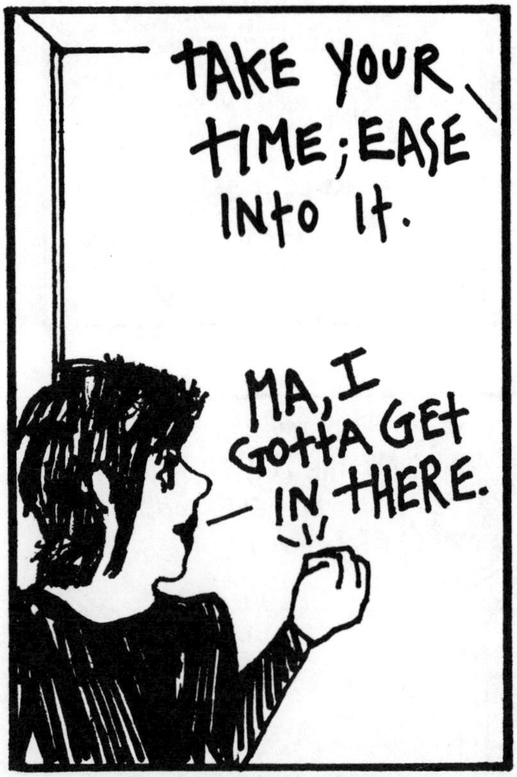
TAKE YOUR TIME; EASE INTO IT.
MA, I GOTTA GET IN THERE.

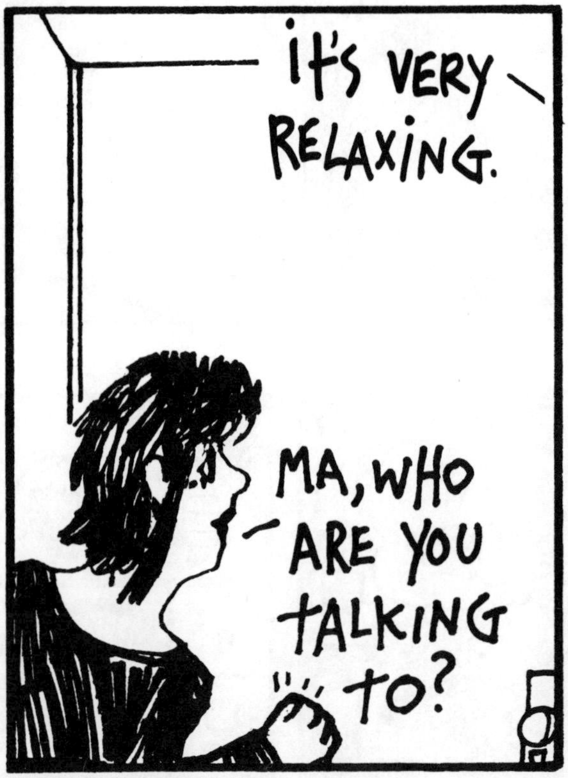
IT'S VERY RELAXING.
MA, WHO ARE YOU TALKING TO?

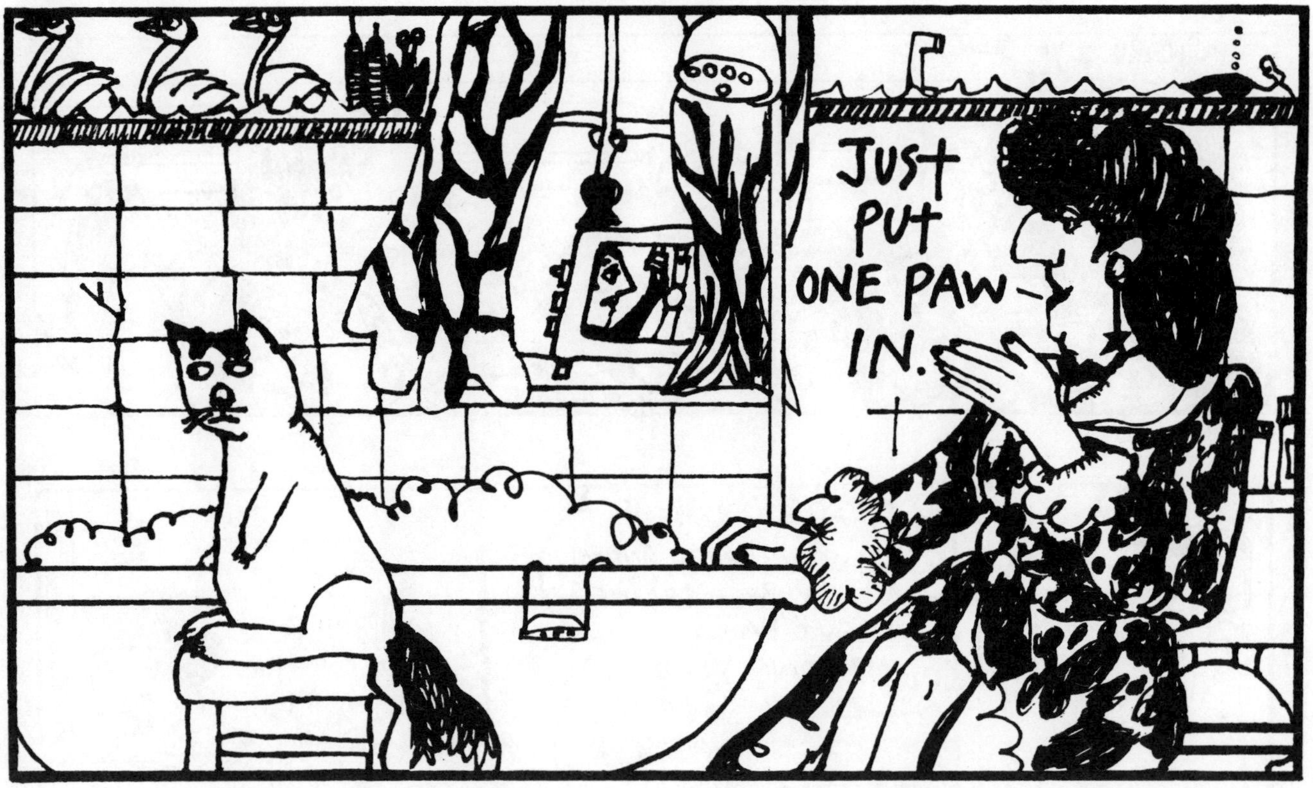
JUST PUT ONE PAW IN.

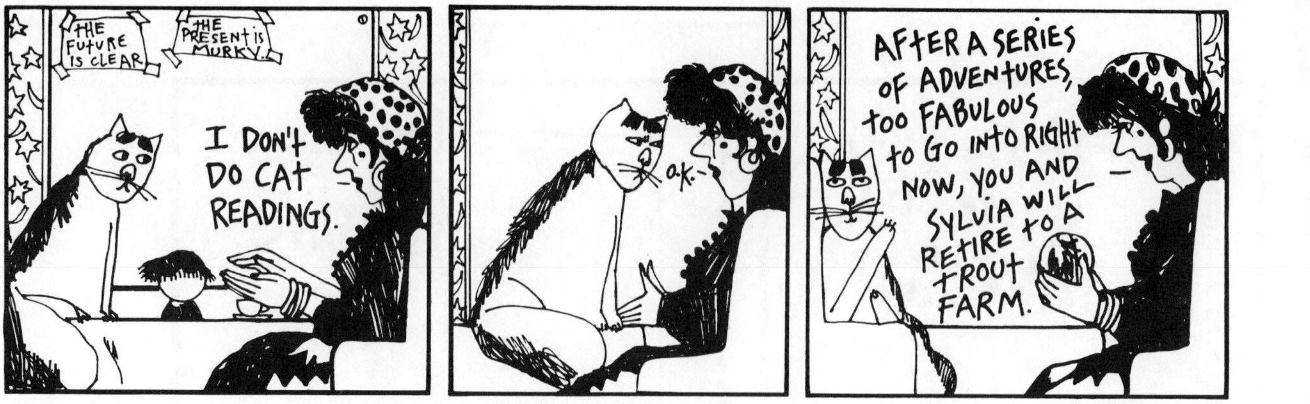
THE FUTURE IS CLEAR
THE PRESENT IS MURKY
I DON'T DO CAT READINGS.
O.K.
AFTER A SERIES OF ADVENTURES, TOO FABULOUS TO GO INTO RIGHT NOW, YOU AND SYLVIA WILL RETIRE TO A TROUT FARM.

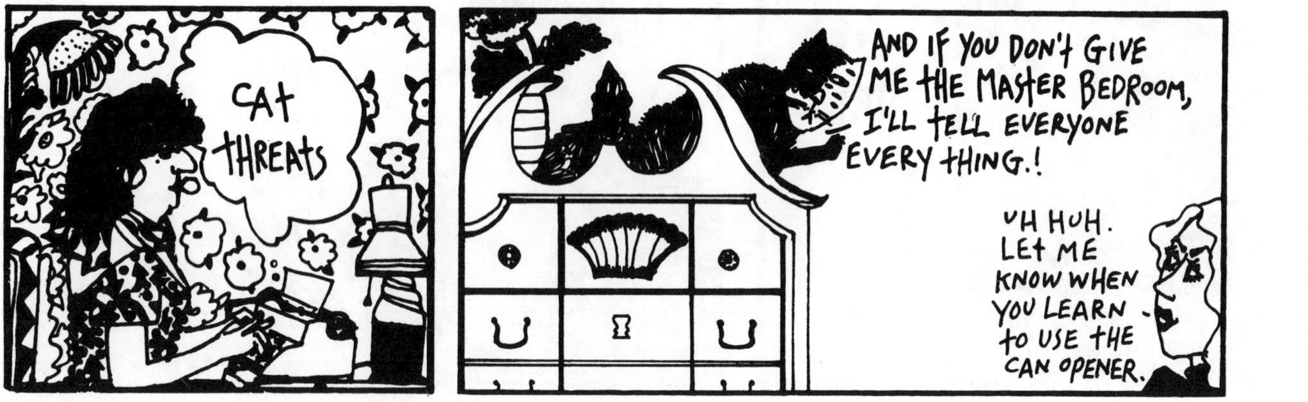
CAT THREATS
AND IF YOU DON'T GIVE ME THE MASTER BEDROOM, I'LL TELL EVERYONE EVERY THING.!
UH HUH. LET ME KNOW WHEN YOU LEARN TO USE THE CAN OPENER.

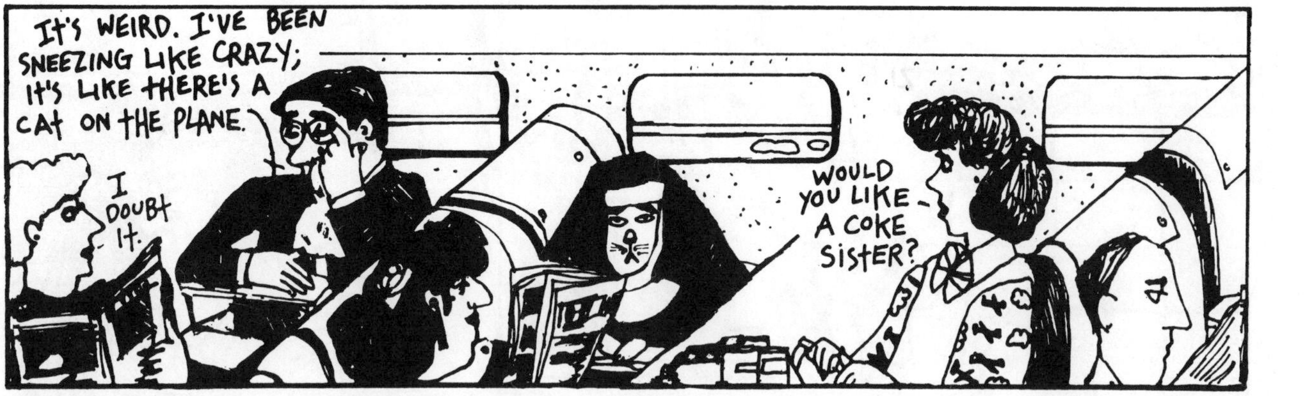
IT'S WEIRD. I'VE BEEN SNEEZING LIKE CRAZY; IT'S LIKE THERE'S A CAT ON THE PLANE.
I DOUBT IT.
WOULD YOU LIKE A COKE SISTER?

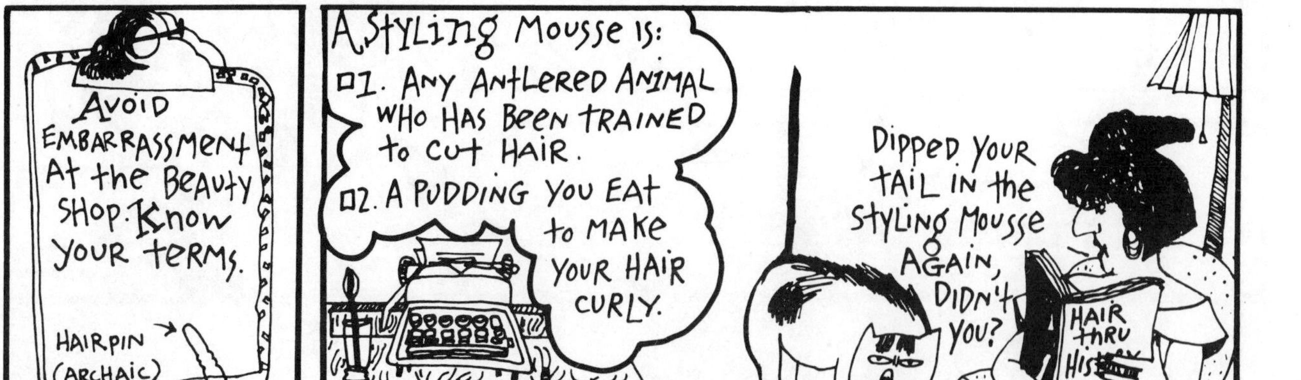
AVOID EMBARRASSMENT AT THE BEAUTY SHOP. KNOW YOUR TERMS.
HAIRPIN (ARCHAIC)
A STYLING MOUSSE IS:
☐1. ANY ANTLERED ANIMAL WHO HAS BEEN TRAINED TO CUT HAIR.
☐2. A PUDDING YOU EAT TO MAKE YOUR HAIR CURLY.
DIPPED YOUR TAIL IN THE STYLING MOUSSE AGAIN, DIDN'T YOU?
HAIR THRU HISTORY

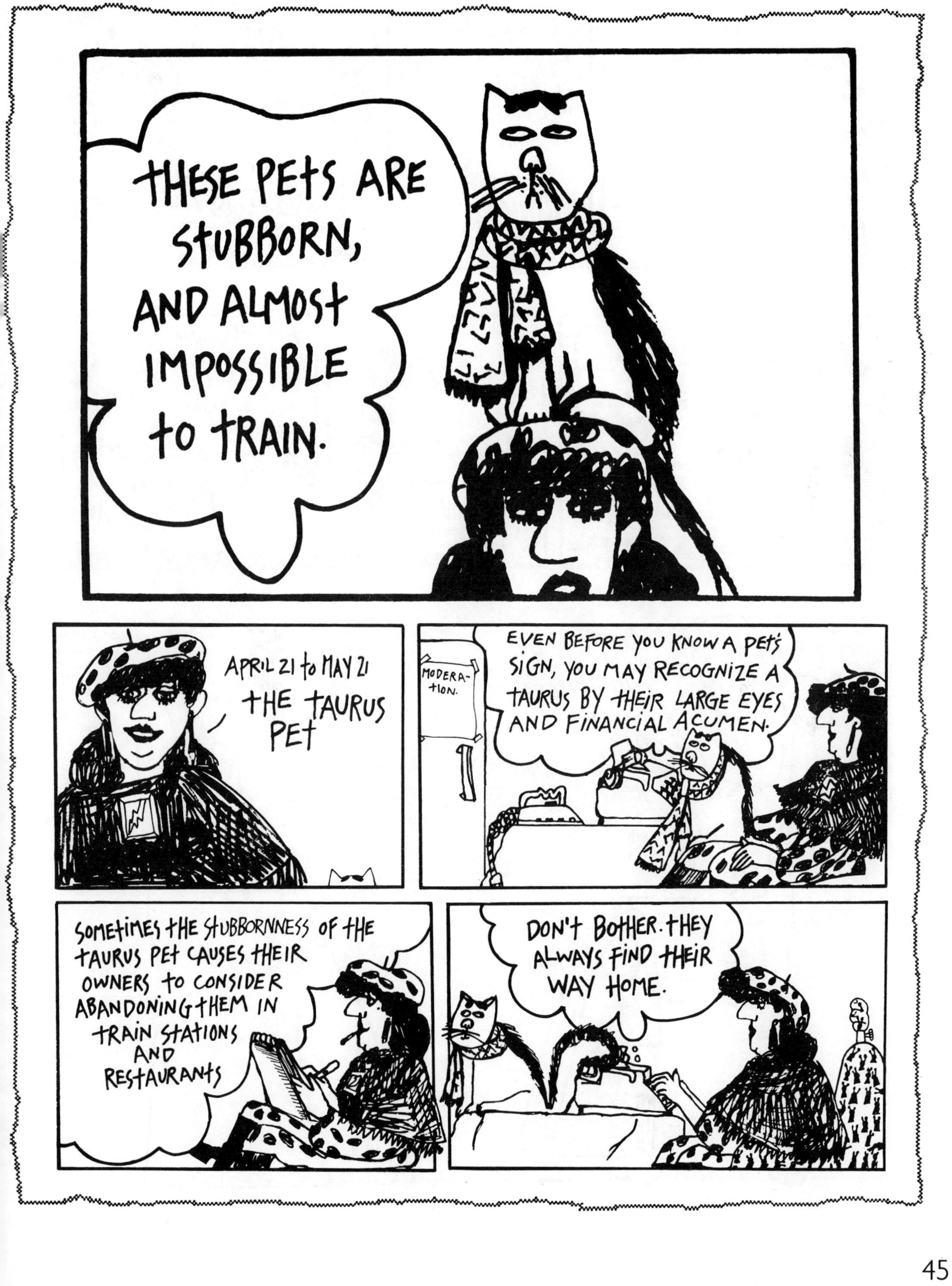
THESE PETS ARE STUBBORN, AND ALMOST IMPOSSIBLE TO TRAIN.
APRIL 21 TO MAY 21
THE TAURUS PET
MODERA-TION.
EVEN BEFORE YOU KNOW A PET'S SIGN, YOU MAY RECOGNIZE A TAURUS BY THEIR LARGE EYES AND FINANCIAL ACUMEN.
SOMETIMES THE STUBBORNNESS OF THE TAURUS PET CAUSES THEIR OWNERS TO CONSIDER ABANDONING THEM IN TRAIN STATIONS AND RESTAURANTS
DON'T BOTHER. THEY ALWAYS FIND THEIR WAY HOME.

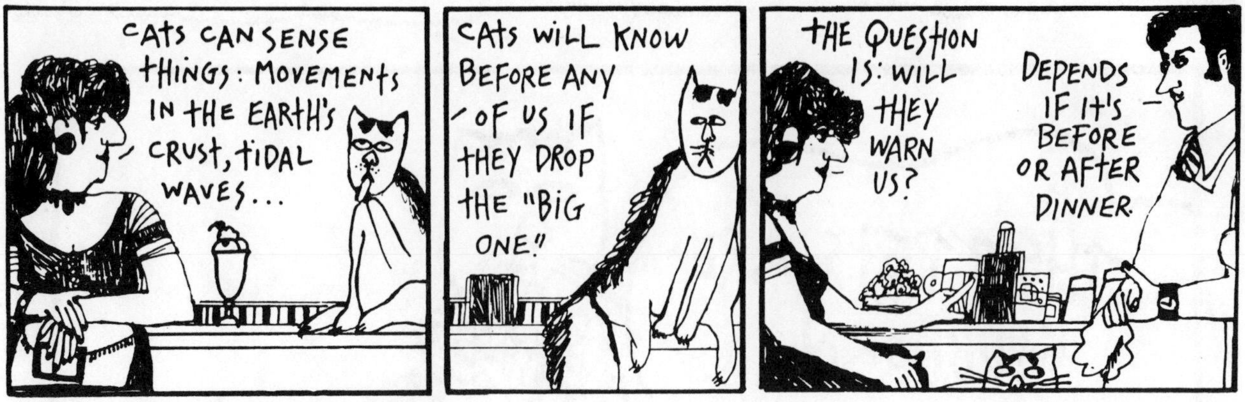
CATS CAN SENSE THINGS: MOVEMENTS IN THE EARTH'S CRUST, TIDAL WAVES...
CATS WILL KNOW BEFORE ANY OF US IF THEY DROP THE "BIG ONE."
THE QUESTION IS: WILL THEY WARN US?
DEPENDS IF IT'S BEFORE OR AFTER DINNER.

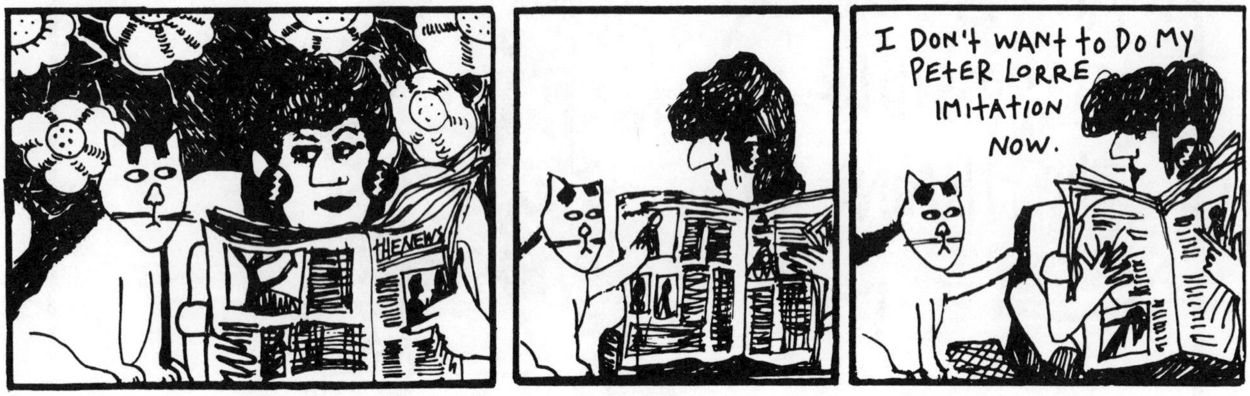
THE NEWS
I DON'T WANT TO DO MY PETER LORRE IMITATION NOW.

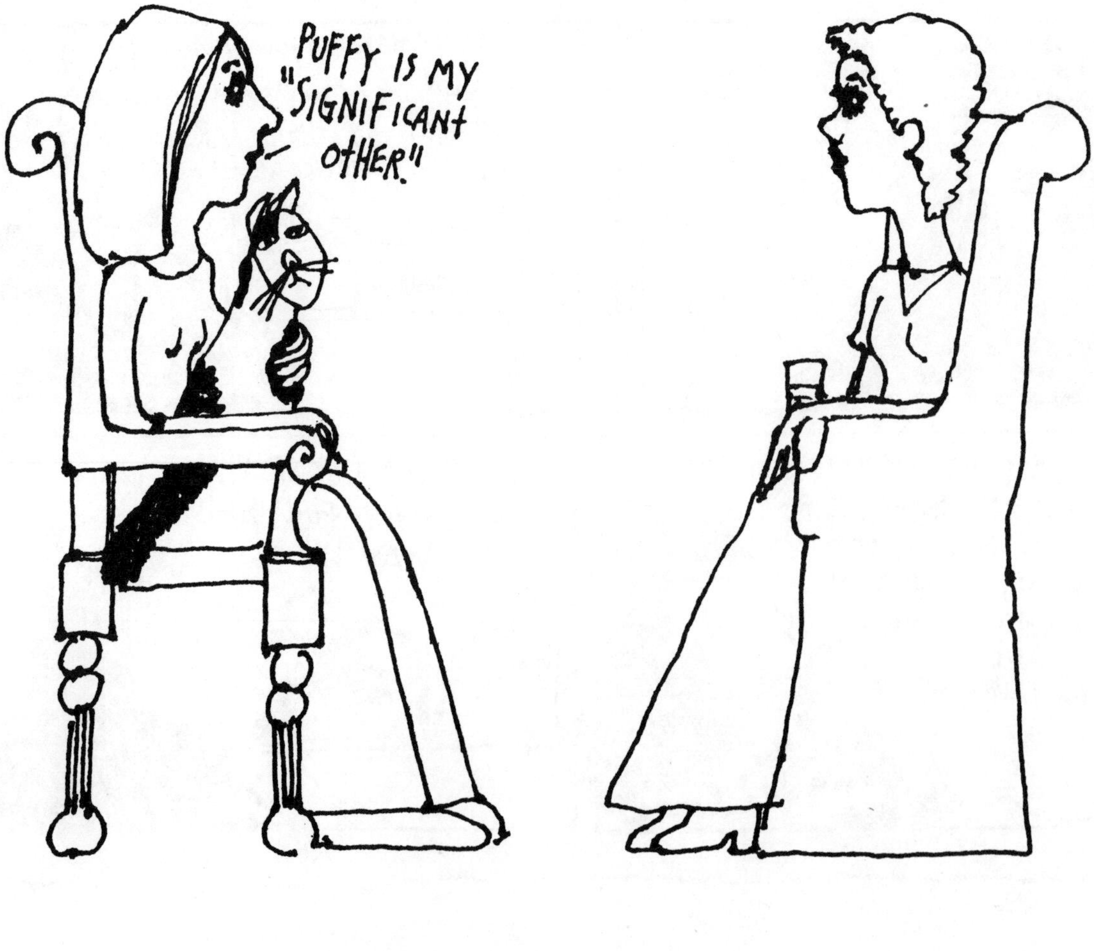
PUFFY IS MY "SIGNIFICANT OTHER."

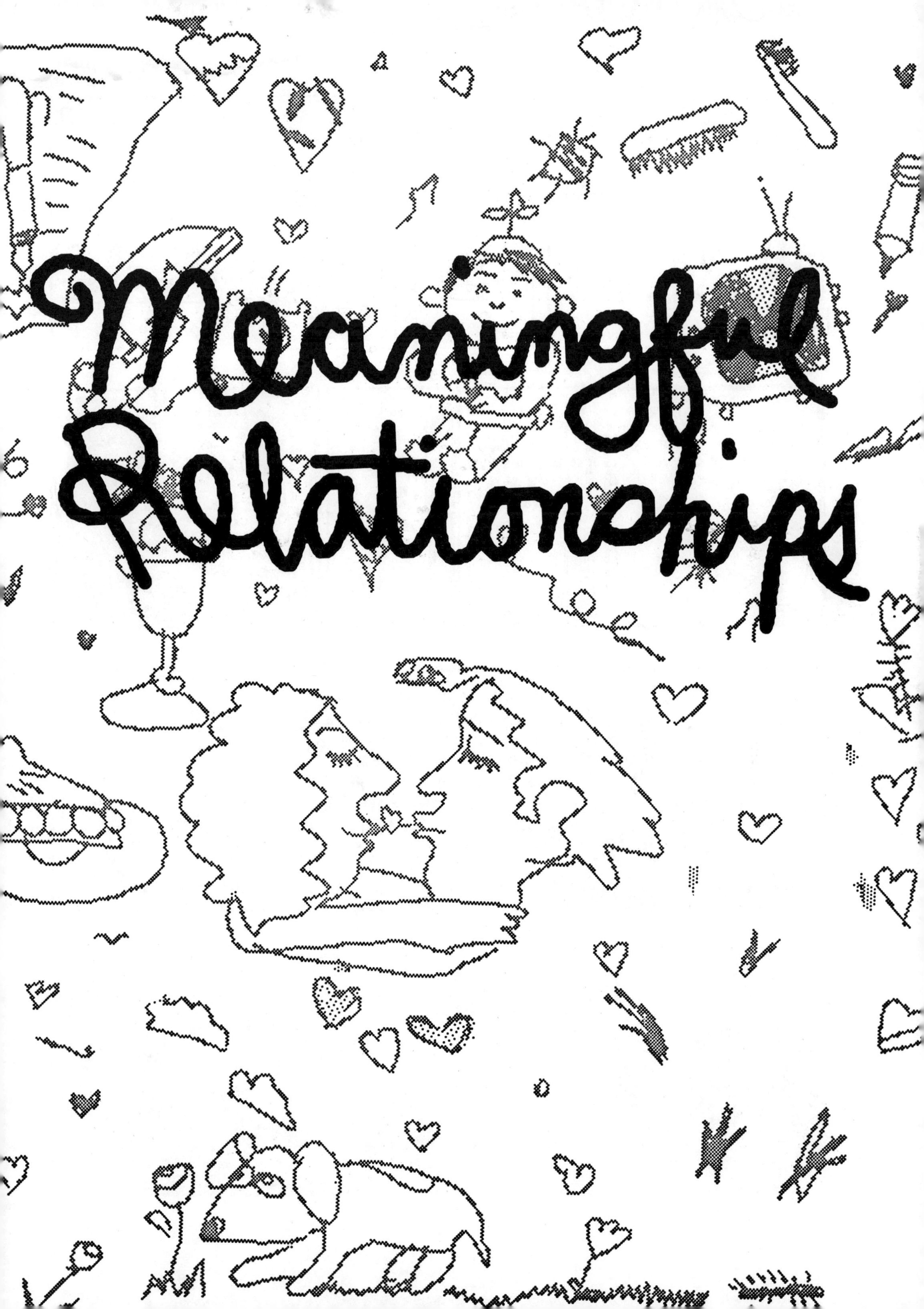
Meaningful Relationships

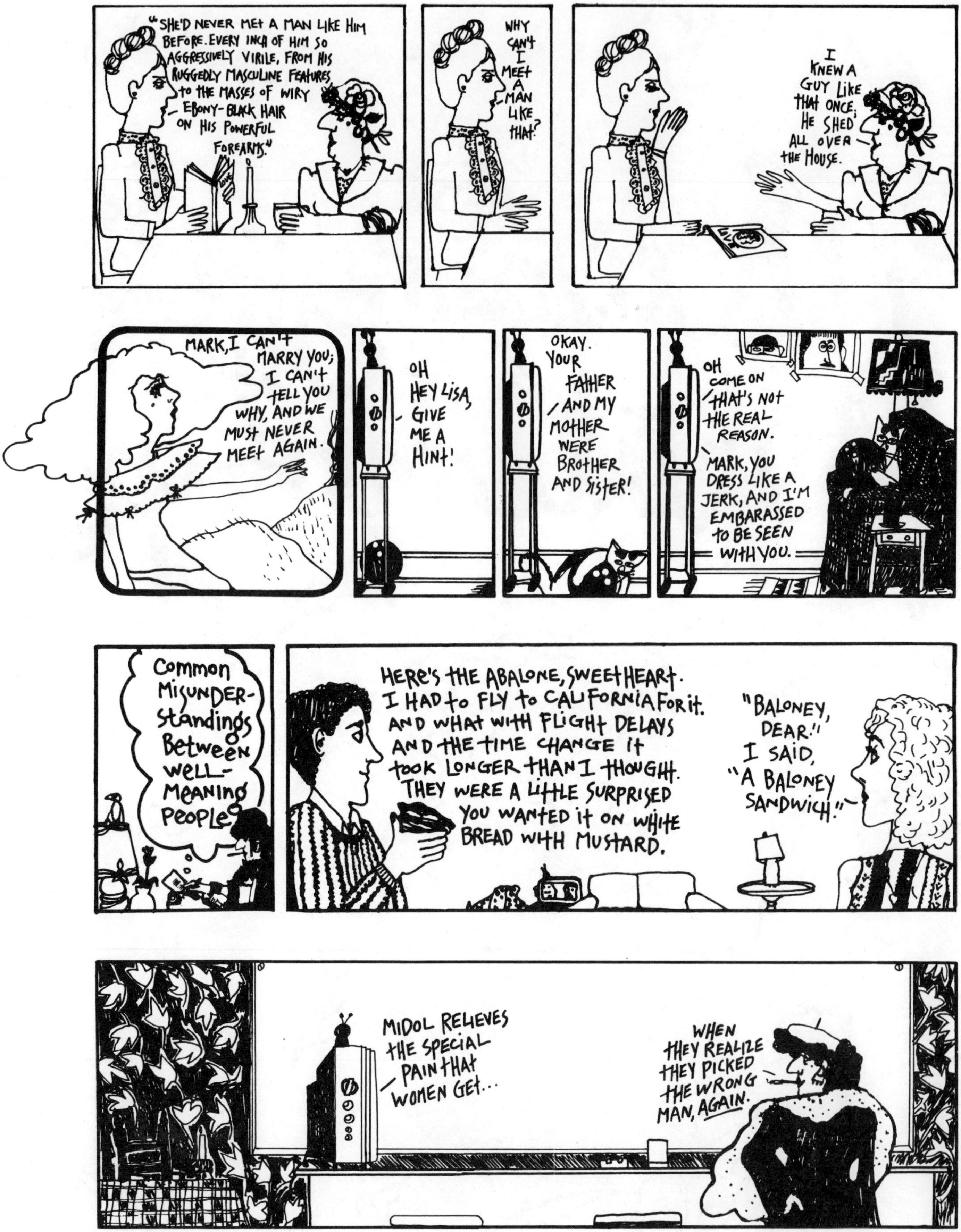
"SHE'D NEVER MET A MAN LIKE HIM BEFORE. EVERY INCH OF HIM SO AGGRESSIVELY VIRILE, FROM HIS RUGGEDLY MASCULINE FEATURES TO THE MASSES OF WIRY EBONY-BLACK HAIR ON HIS POWERFUL FOREARMS."
WHY CAN'T I MEET A MAN LIKE THAT?
I KNEW A GUY LIKE THAT ONCE; HE SHED ALL OVER THE HOUSE.
MARK, I CAN'T MARRY YOU; I CAN'T TELL YOU WHY, AND WE MUST NEVER MEET AGAIN.
OH HEY LISA, GIVE ME A HINT!
OKAY. YOUR FATHER AND MY MOTHER WERE BROTHER AND SISTER!
OH COME ON THAT'S NOT THE REAL REASON.
MARK, YOU DRESS LIKE A JERK, AND I'M EMBARASSED TO BE SEEN WITH YOU.
Common Misunder-standings Between well-Meaning People
HERE'S THE ABALONE, SWEETHEART. I HAD TO FLY TO CALIFORNIA FOR IT. AND WHAT WITH FLIGHT DELAYS AND THE TIME CHANGE IT TOOK LONGER THAN I THOUGHT. THEY WERE A LITTLE SURPRISED YOU WANTED IT ON WHITE BREAD WITH MUSTARD.
"BALONEY, DEAR." I SAID, "A BALONEY SANDWICH!"
MIDOL RELIEVES THE SPECIAL PAIN THAT WOMEN GET...
WHEN THEY REALIZE THEY PICKED THE WRONG MAN, AGAIN.

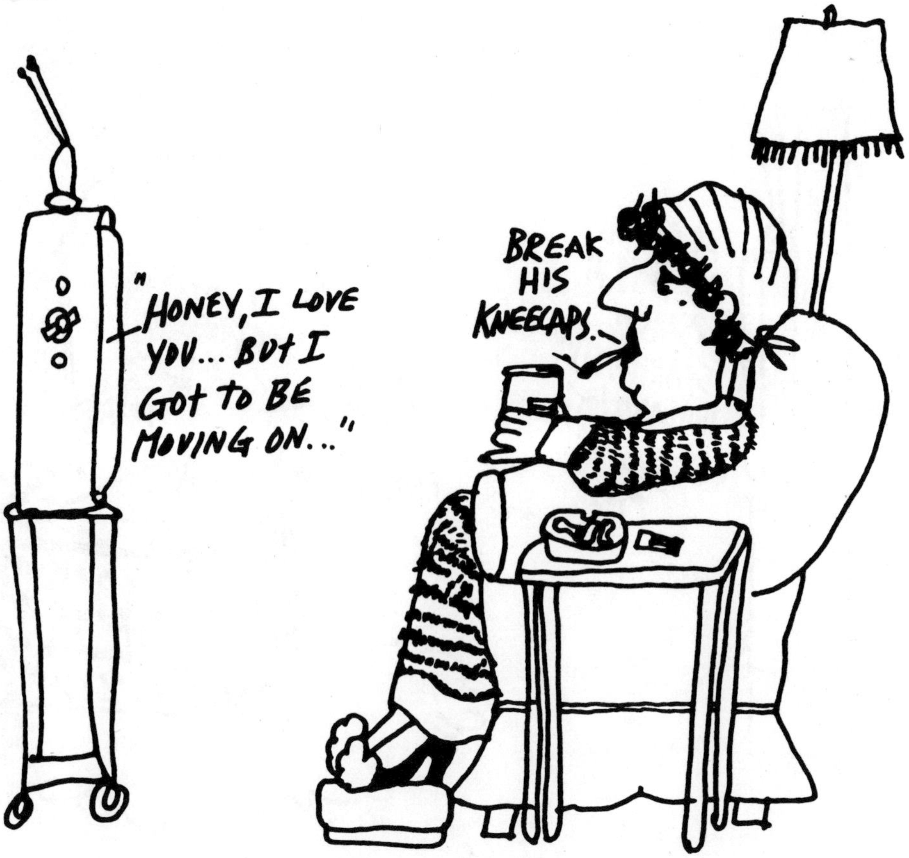
"HONEY, I LOVE YOU... BUT I GOT TO BE MOVING ON..."
BREAK HIS KNEECAPS.

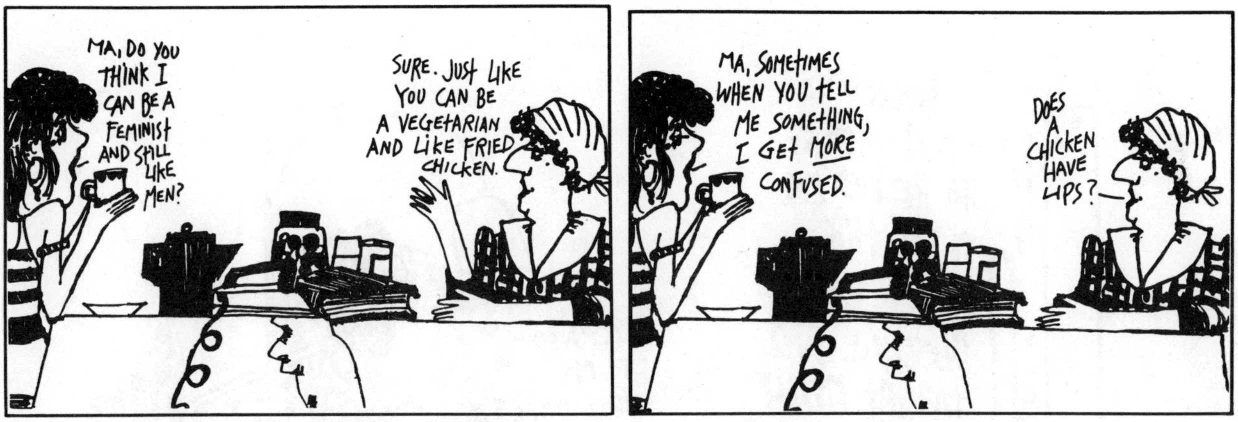
MA, DO YOU THINK I CAN BE A FEMINIST AND STILL LIKE MEN?
SURE. JUST LIKE YOU CAN BE A VEGETARIAN AND LIKE FRIED CHICKEN.
MA, SOMETIMES WHEN YOU TELL ME SOMETHING, I GET MORE CONFUSED.
DOES A CHICKEN HAVE LIPS?

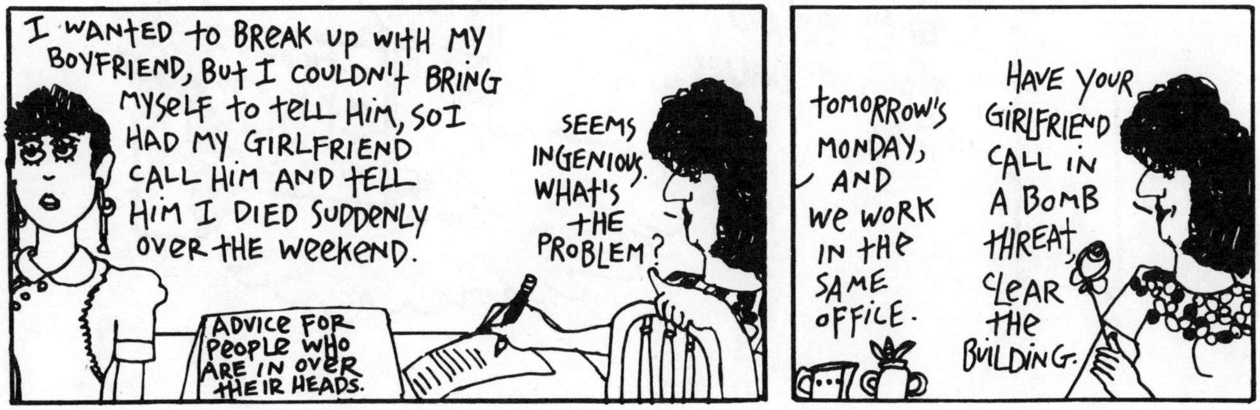
I WANTED TO BREAK UP WITH MY BOYFRIEND, BUT I COULDN'T BRING MYSELF TO TELL HIM, SO I HAD MY GIRLFRIEND CALL HIM AND TELL HIM I DIED SUDDENLY OVER THE WEEKEND.
SEEMS INGENIOUS. WHAT'S THE PROBLEM?
ADVICE FOR PEOPLE WHO ARE IN OVER THEIR HEADS.
TOMORROW'S MONDAY, AND WE WORK IN THE SAME OFFICE.
HAVE YOUR GIRLFRIEND CALL IN A BOMB THREAT, CLEAR THE BUILDING.

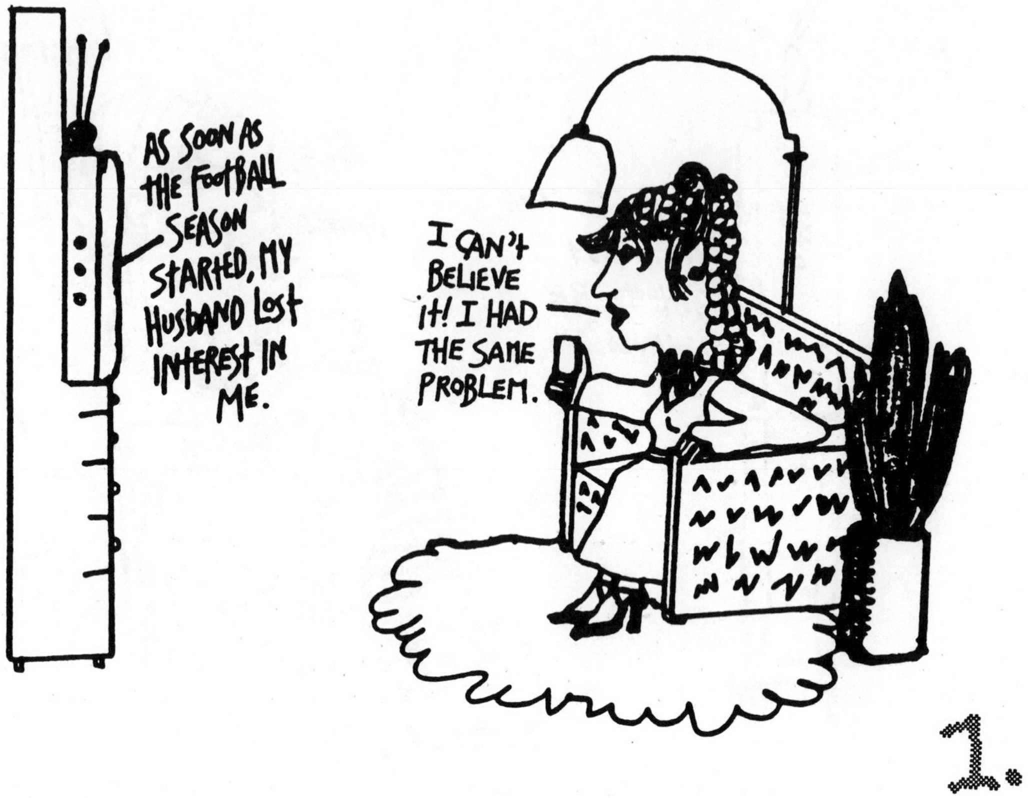

AS SOON AS THE FOOTBALL SEASON STARTED, MY HUSBAND LOST INTEREST IN ME.
I CAN'T BELIEVE IT! I HAD THE SAME PROBLEM.
1.

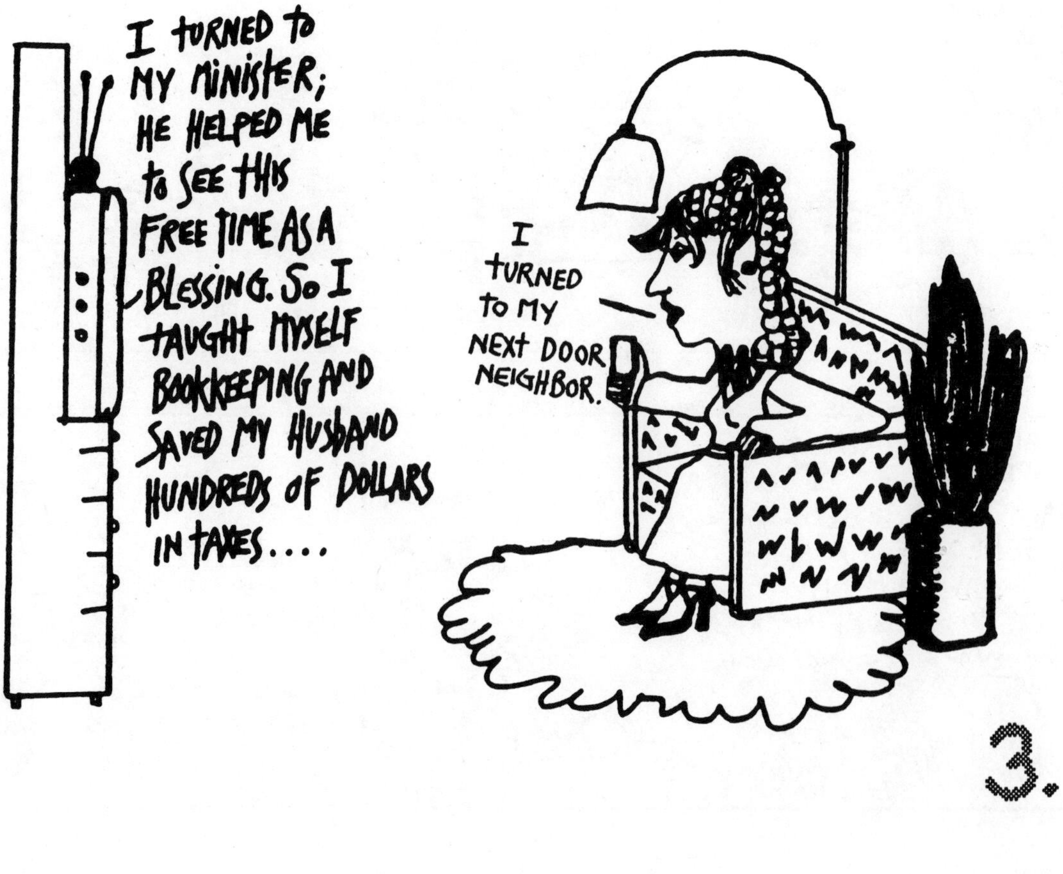

I TURNED TO MY MINISTER; HE HELPED ME TO SEE THIS FREE TIME AS A BLESSING. SO I TAUGHT MYSELF BOOKKEEPING AND SAVED MY HUSBAND HUNDREDS OF DOLLARS IN TAXES....
I TURNED TO MY NEXT DOOR NEIGHBOR.
3.

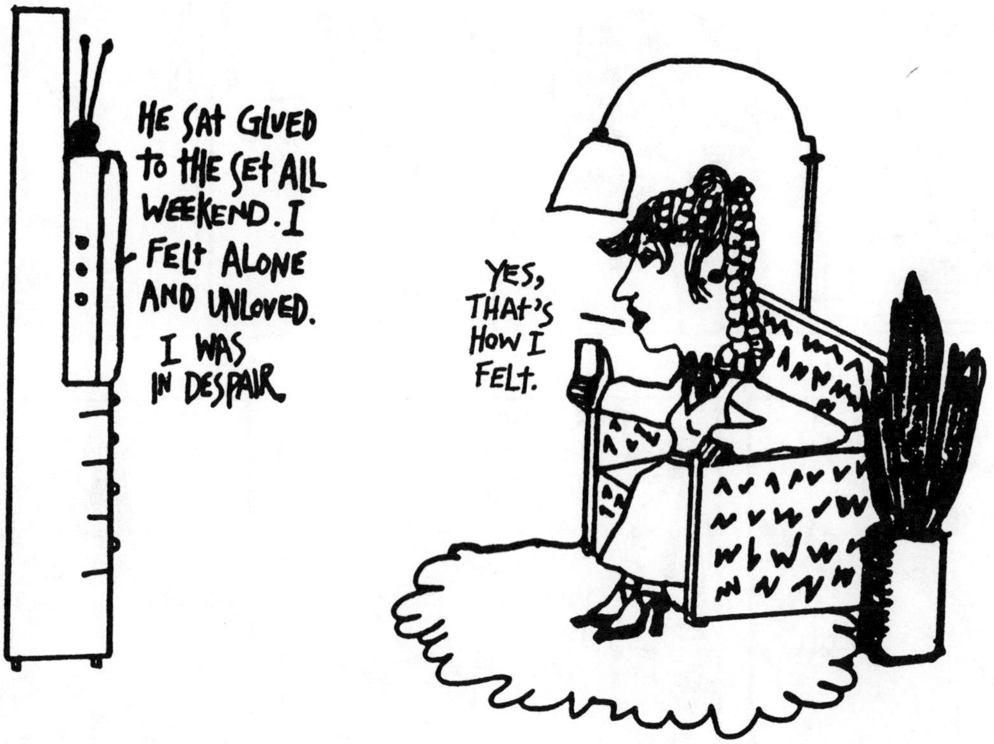
HE SAT GLUED TO THE SET ALL WEEKEND. I FELT ALONE AND UNLOVED. I WAS IN DESPAIR.
YES, THAT'S HOW I FELT.

2.

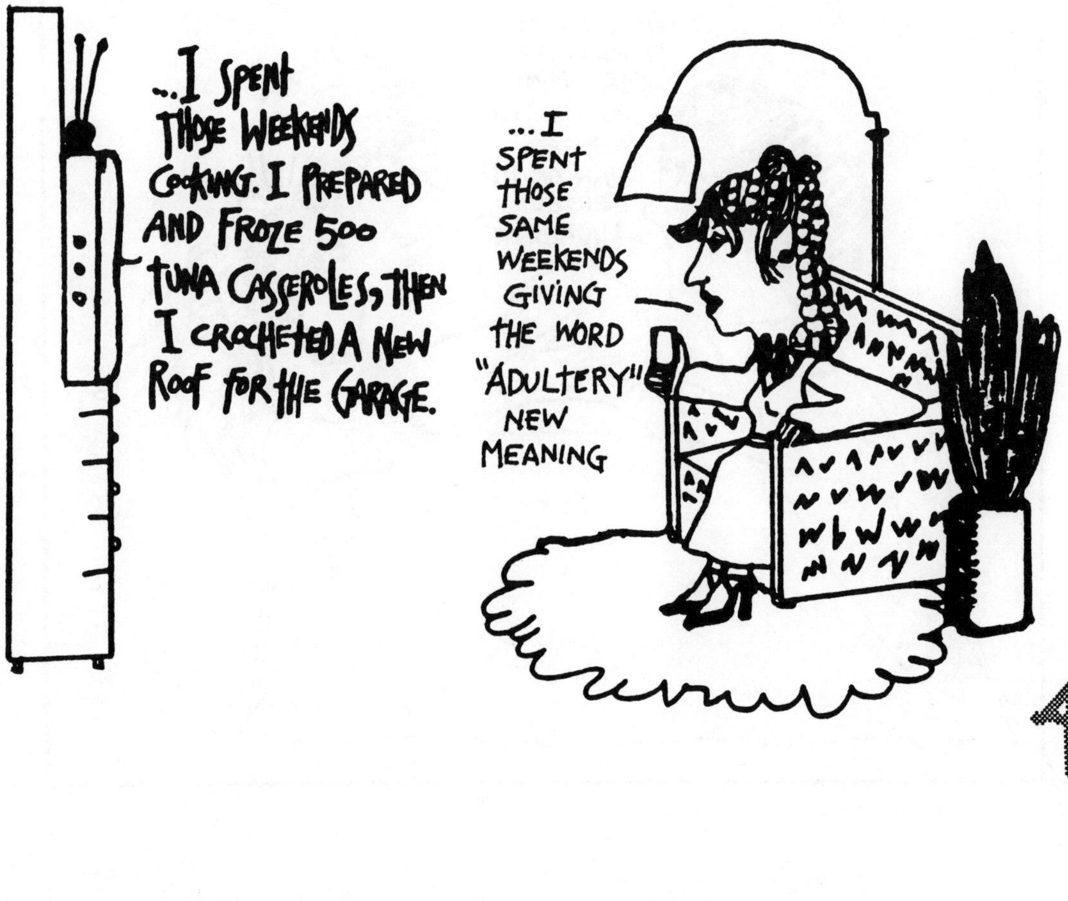
...I SPENT THOSE WEEKENDS COOKING. I PREPARED AND FROZE 500 TUNA CASSEROLES, THEN I CROCHETED A NEW ROOF FOR THE GARAGE.
...I SPENT THOSE SAME WEEKENDS GIVING THE WORD "ADULTERY" NEW MEANING

4.

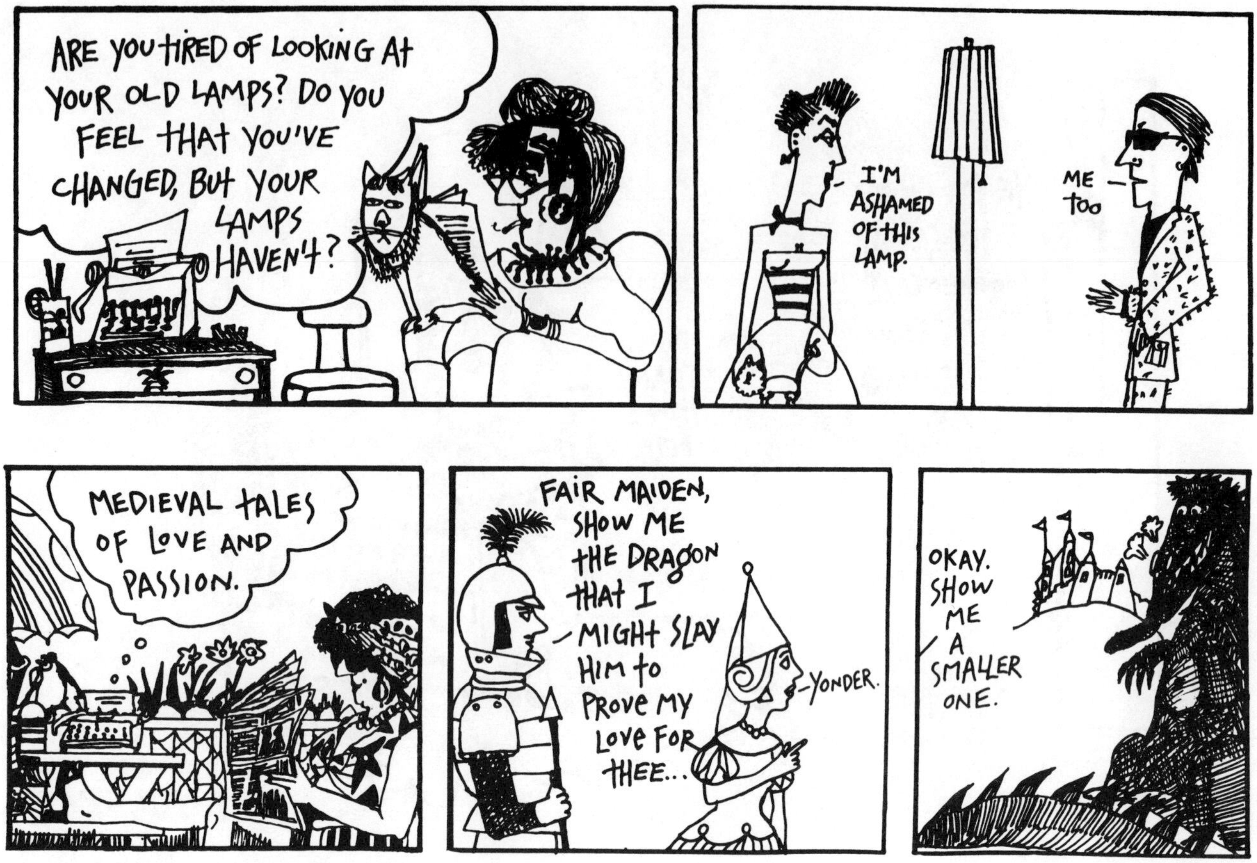
ARE YOU TIRED OF LOOKING AT YOUR OLD LAMPS? DO YOU FEEL THAT YOU'VE CHANGED, BUT YOUR LAMPS HAVEN'T?
I'M ASHAMED OF THIS LAMP.
ME TOO
MEDIEVAL TALES OF LOVE AND PASSION.
FAIR MAIDEN, SHOW ME THE DRAGON THAT I MIGHT SLAY HIM TO PROVE MY LOVE FOR THEE...
YONDER.
OKAY. SHOW ME A SMALLER ONE.

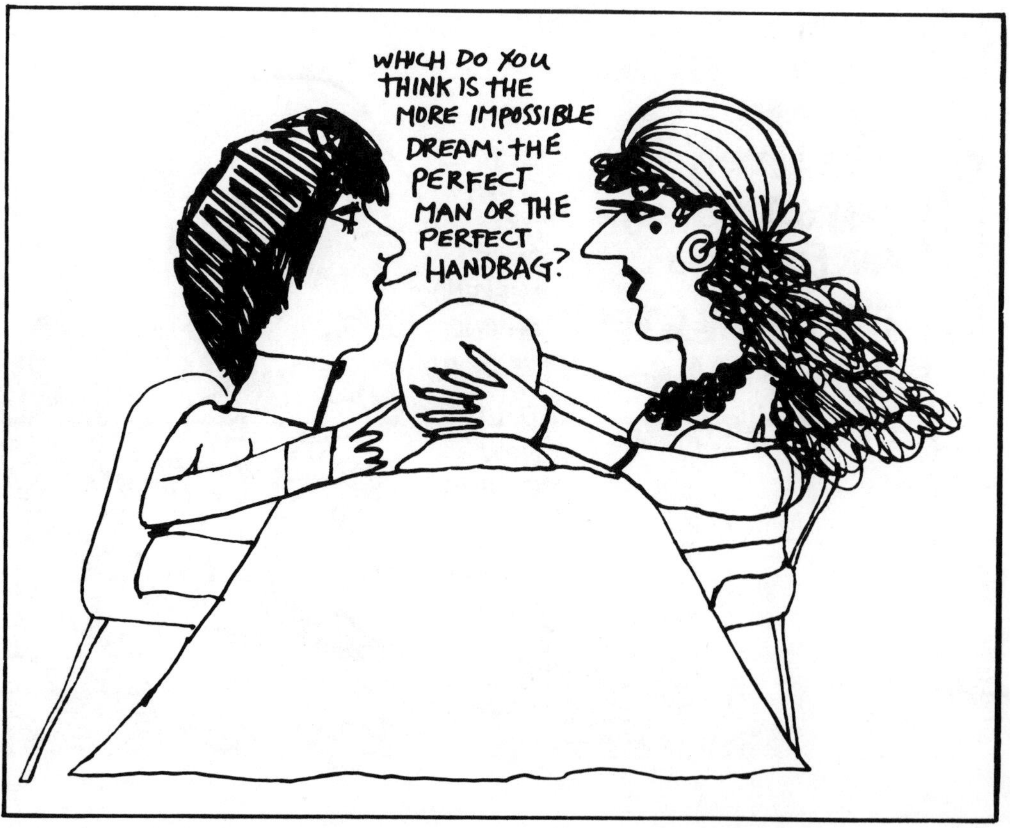
WHICH DO YOU THINK IS THE MORE IMPOSSIBLE DREAM: THE PERFECT MAN OR THE PERFECT HANDBAG?

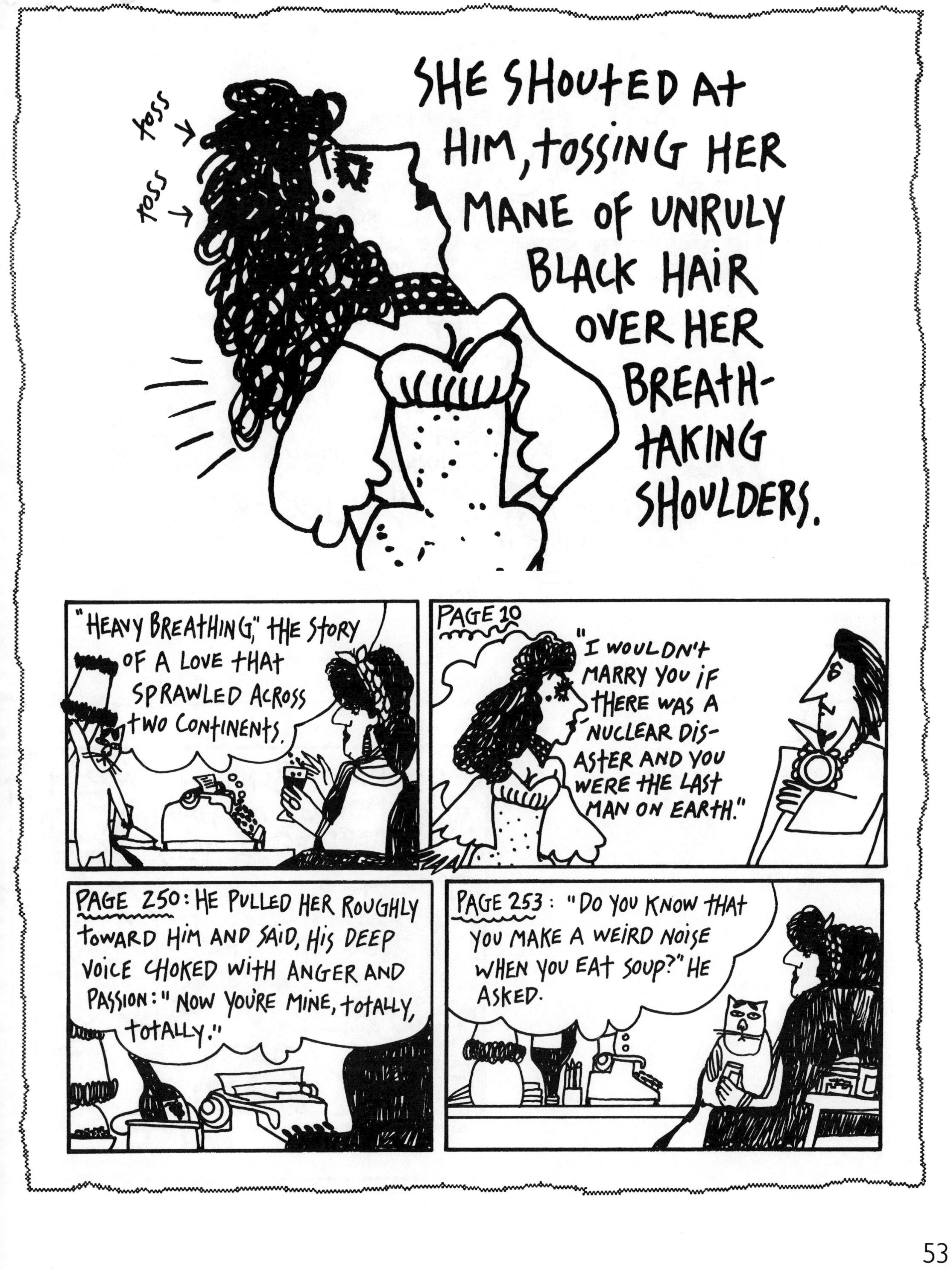
toss
toss
SHE SHOUTED AT HIM, TOSSING HER MANE OF UNRULY BLACK HAIR OVER HER BREATH-TAKING SHOULDERS.
"HEAVY BREATHING," THE STORY OF A LOVE THAT SPRAWLED ACROSS TWO CONTINENTS.
PAGE 10
"I WOULDN'T MARRY YOU IF THERE WAS A NUCLEAR DIS-ASTER AND YOU WERE THE LAST MAN ON EARTH."
PAGE 250: HE PULLED HER ROUGHLY TOWARD HIM AND SAID, HIS DEEP VOICE CHOKED WITH ANGER AND PASSION: "NOW YOU'RE MINE, TOTALLY, TOTALLY."
PAGE 253: "DO YOU KNOW THAT YOU MAKE A WEIRD NOISE WHEN YOU EAT SOUP?" HE ASKED.

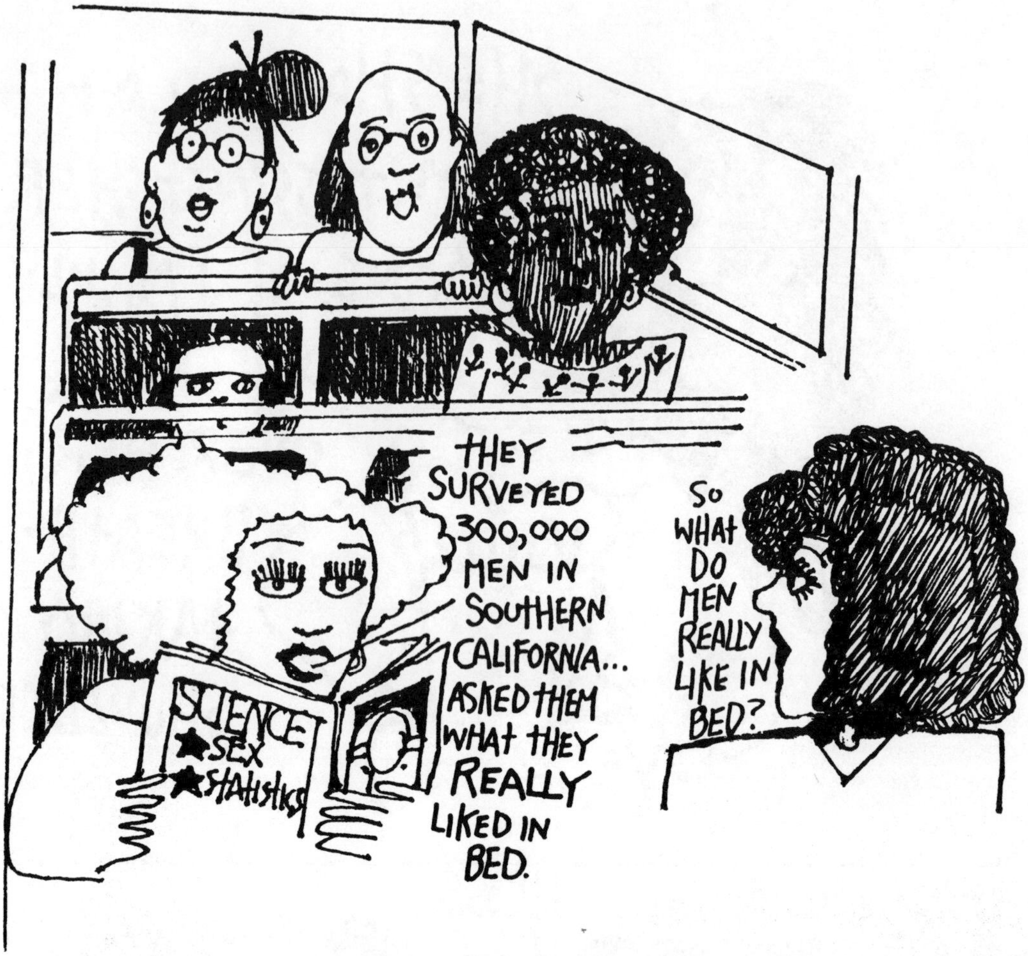
THEY SURVEYED 300,000 MEN IN SOUTHERN CALIFORNIA... ASKED THEM WHAT THEY REALLY LIKED IN BED.
SO WHAT DO MEN REALLY LIKE IN BED?
SCIENCE
SEX
STATISTICS

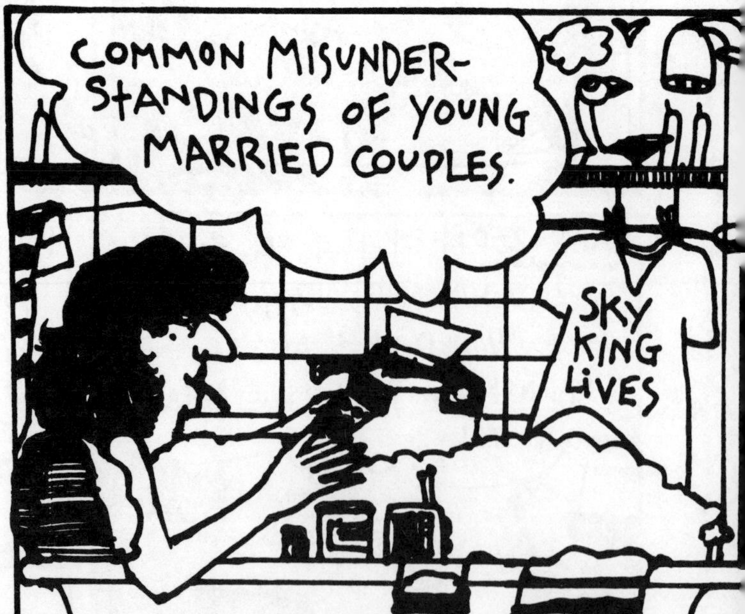
COMMON MISUNDER-STANDINGS OF YOUNG MARRIED COUPLES.
SKY KING LIVES

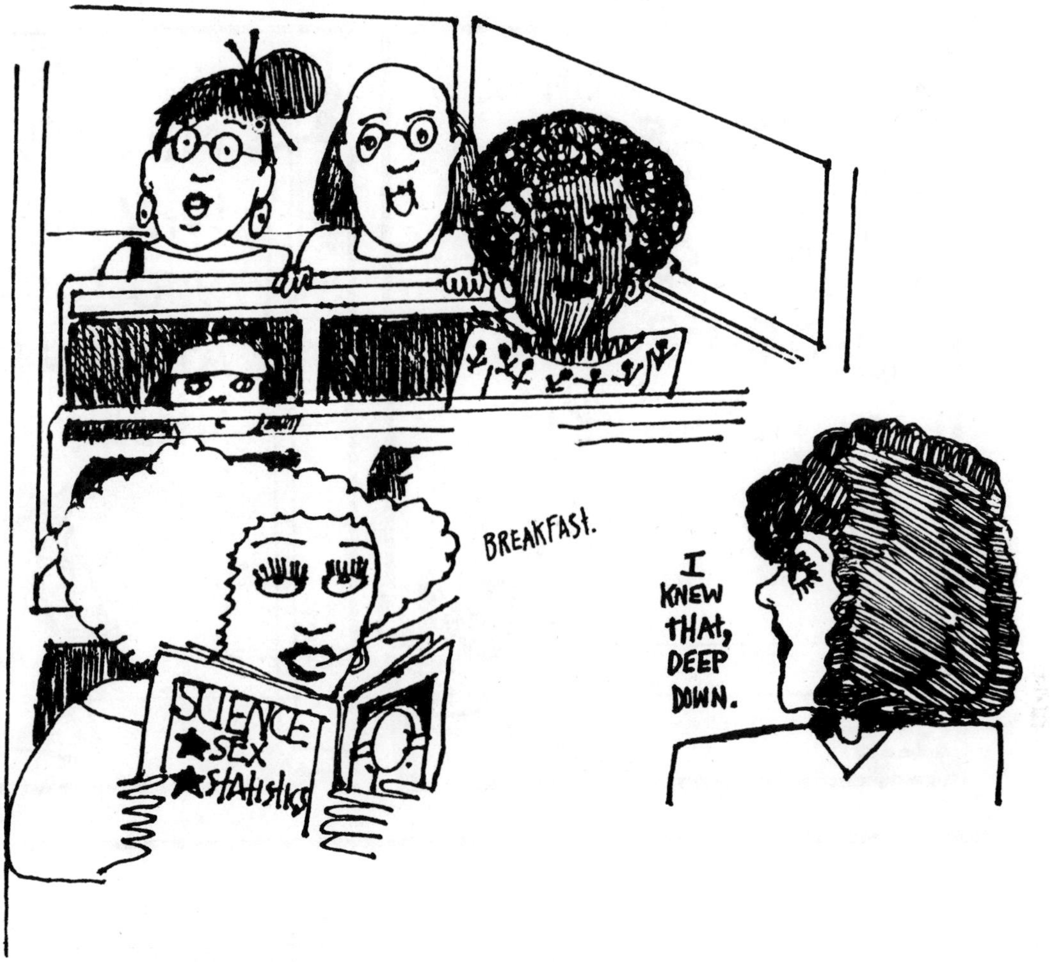
SCIENCE
★SEX
★STATISTICS
BREAKFAST.
I KNEW THAT, DEEP DOWN.

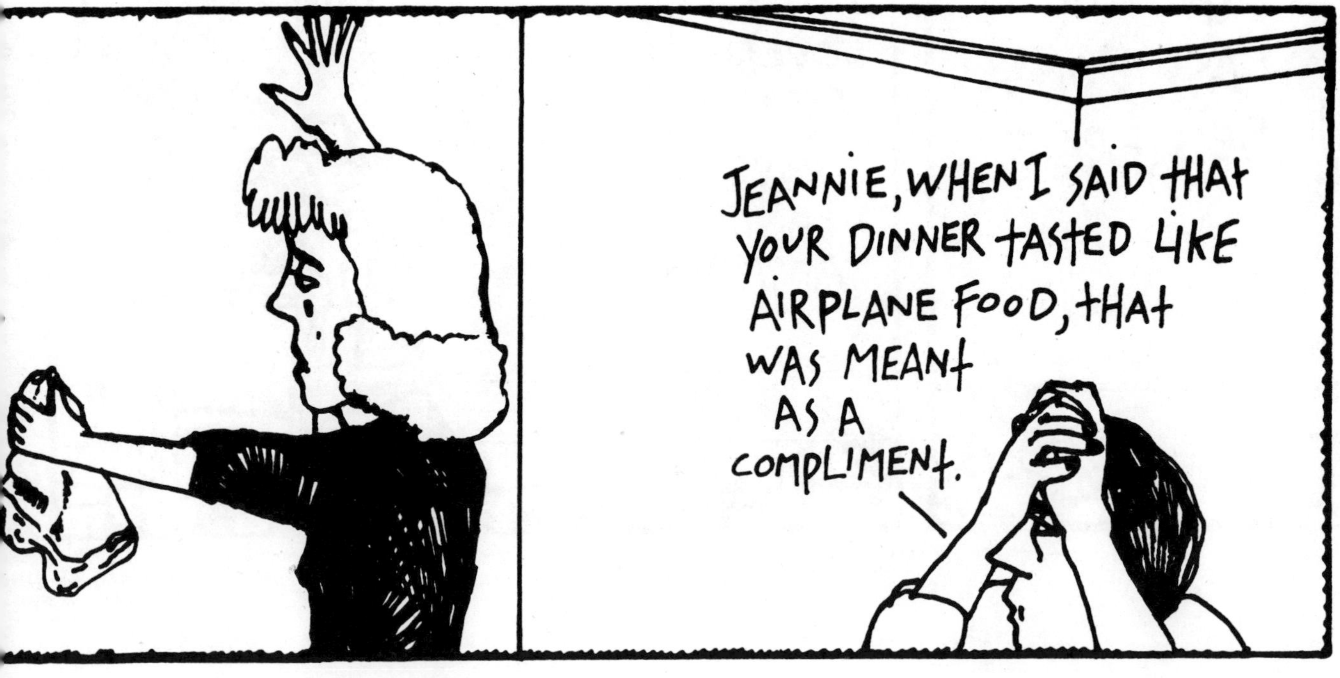
JEANNIE, WHEN I SAID THAT YOUR DINNER TASTED LIKE AIRPLANE FOOD, THAT WAS MEANT AS A COMPLIMENT.

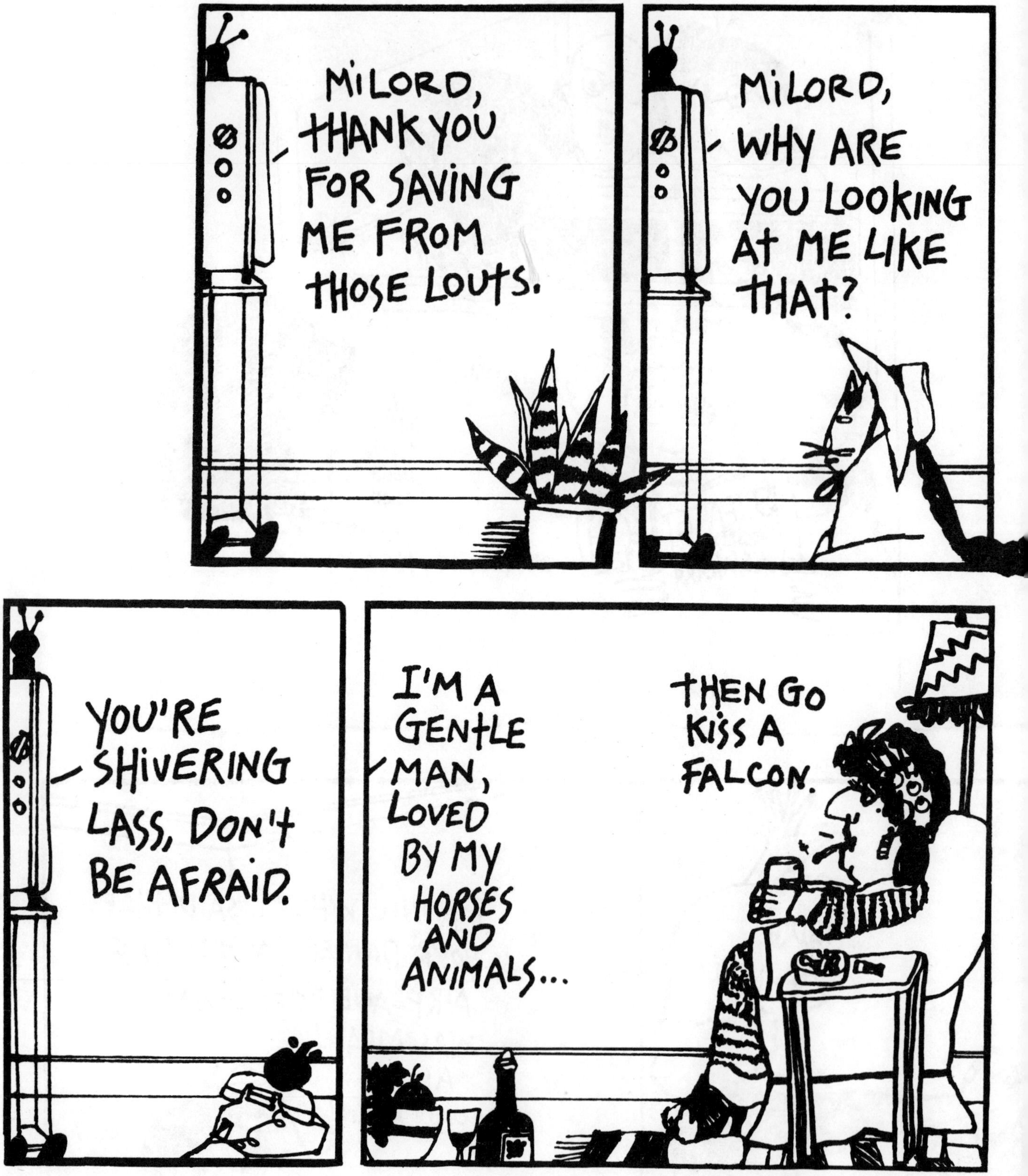

MILORD, THANK YOU FOR SAVING ME FROM THOSE LOUTS.
MILORD, WHY ARE YOU LOOKING AT ME LIKE THAT?
YOU'RE SHIVERING LASS, DON'T BE AFRAID.
I'M A GENTLE MAN, LOVED BY MY HORSES AND ANIMALS...
THEN GO KISS A FALCON.

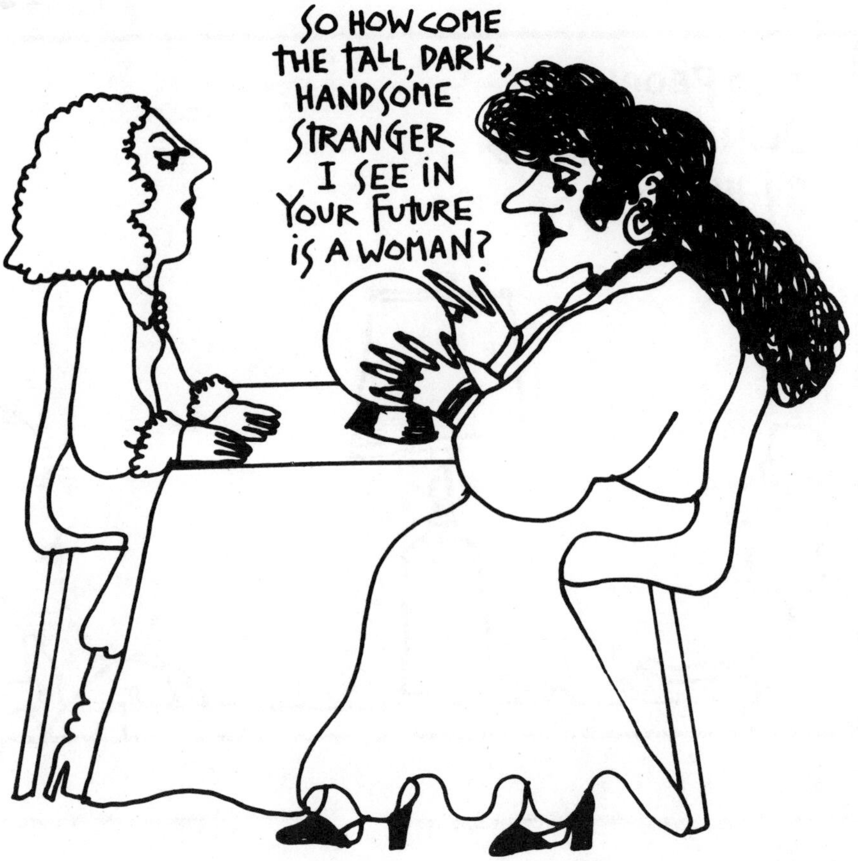
SO HOW COME THE TALL, DARK, HANDSOME STRANGER I SEE IN YOUR FUTURE IS A WOMAN?

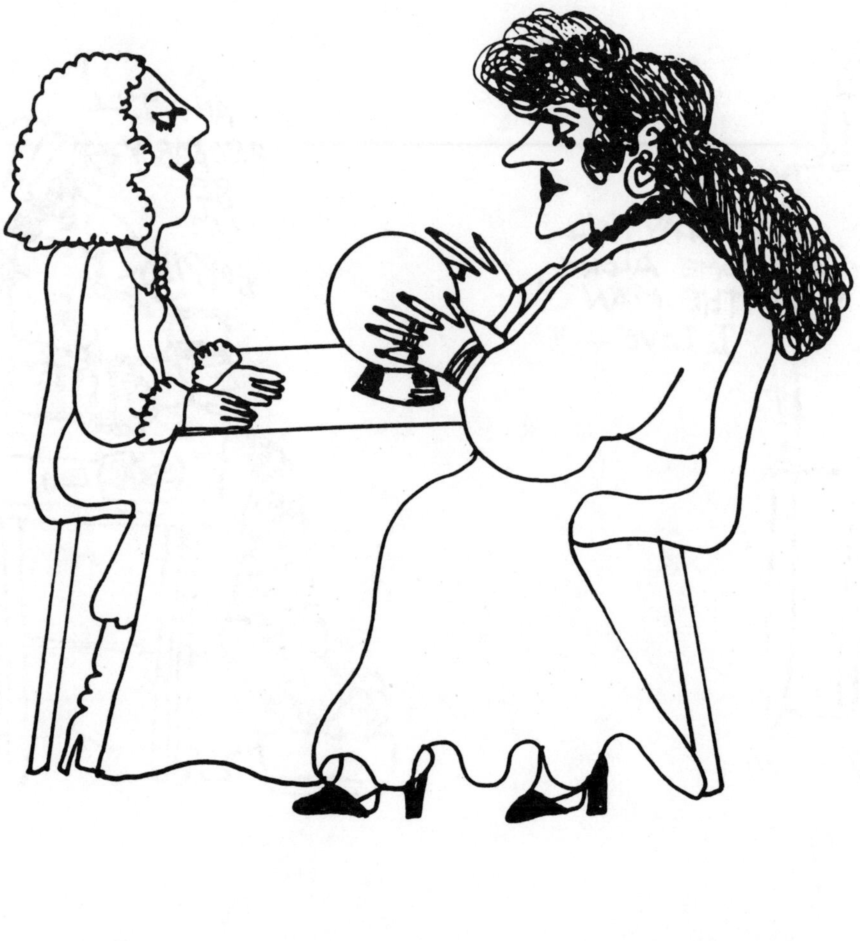

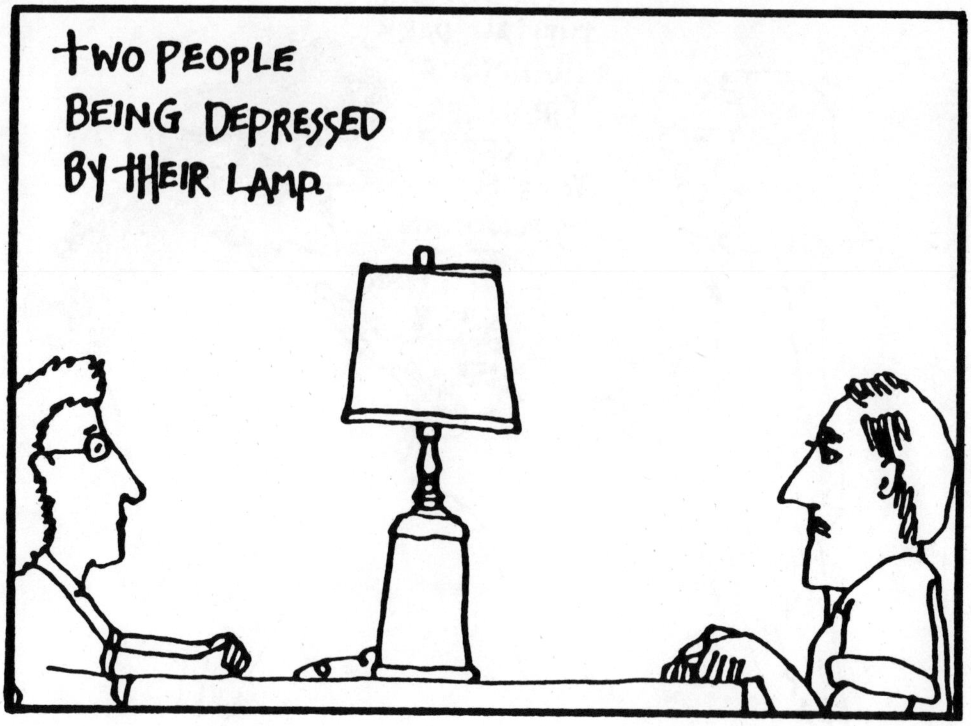
two PEOPLE
BEING DEPRESSED
BY THEIR LAMP.

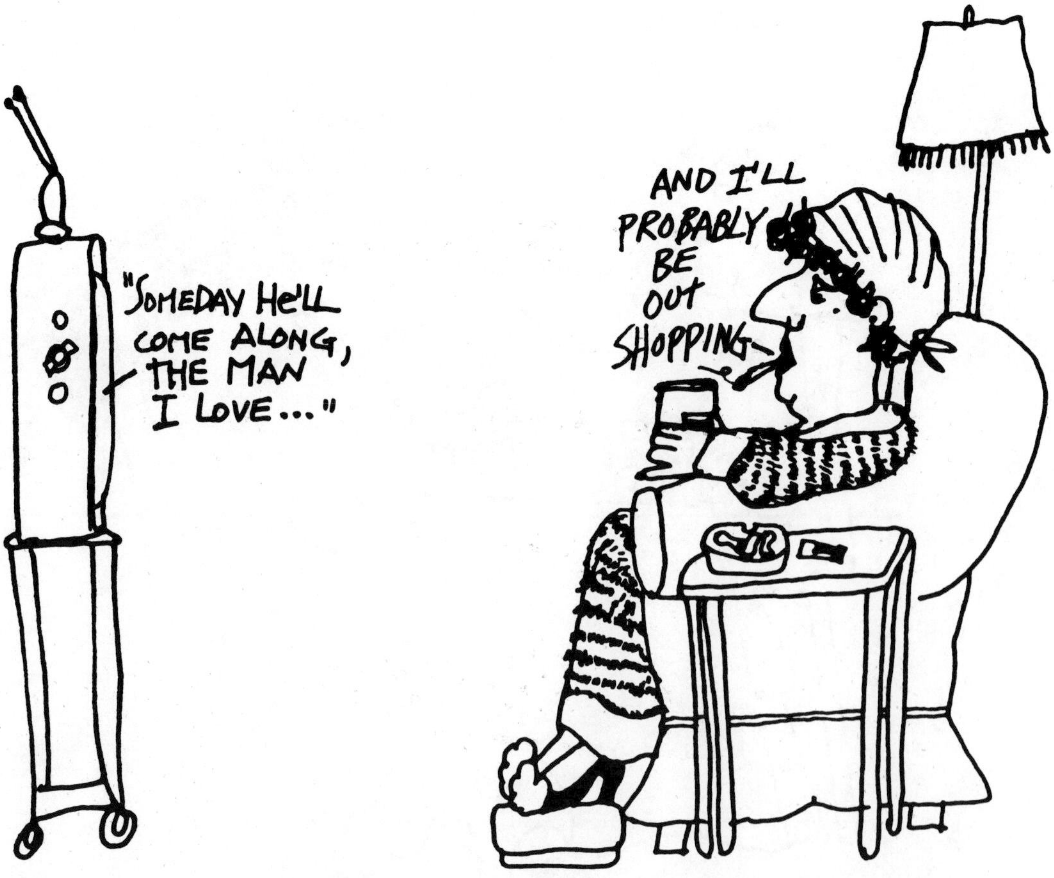
"SOMEDAY HE'LL
COME ALONG,
THE MAN
I LOVE..."
AND I'LL
PROBABLY
BE
OUT
SHOPPING

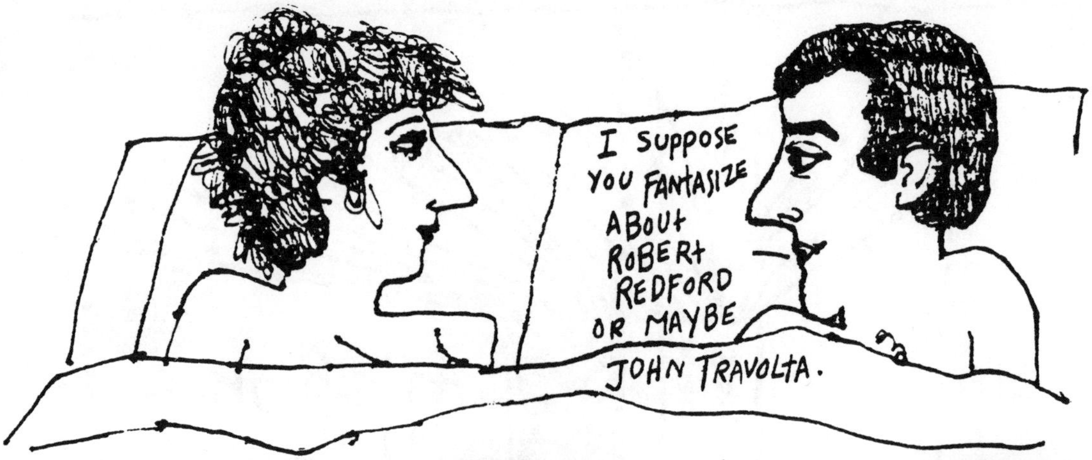
I SUPPOSE YOU FANTASIZE ABOUT ROBERT REDFORD OR MAYBE JOHN TRAVOLTA.

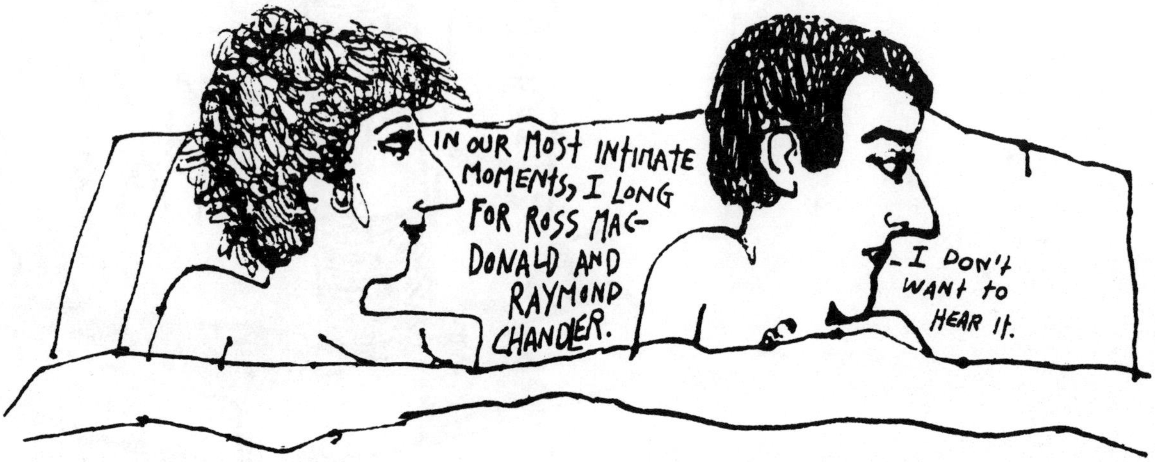
IN OUR MOST INTIMATE MOMENTS, I LONG FOR ROSS MAC-DONALD AND RAYMOND CHANDLER.
I DON'T WANT TO HEAR IT.

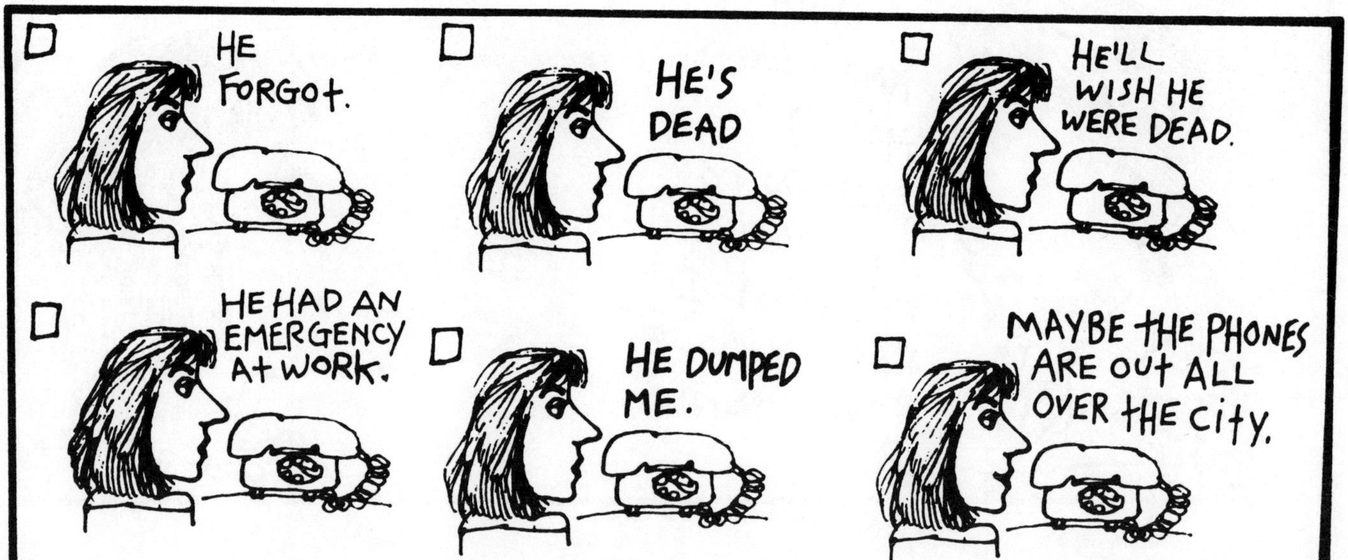
HE FORGOT.
HE'S DEAD
HE'LL WISH HE WERE DEAD.
HE HAD AN EMERGENCY AT WORK.
HE DUMPED ME.
MAYBE THE PHONES ARE OUT ALL OVER THE CITY.

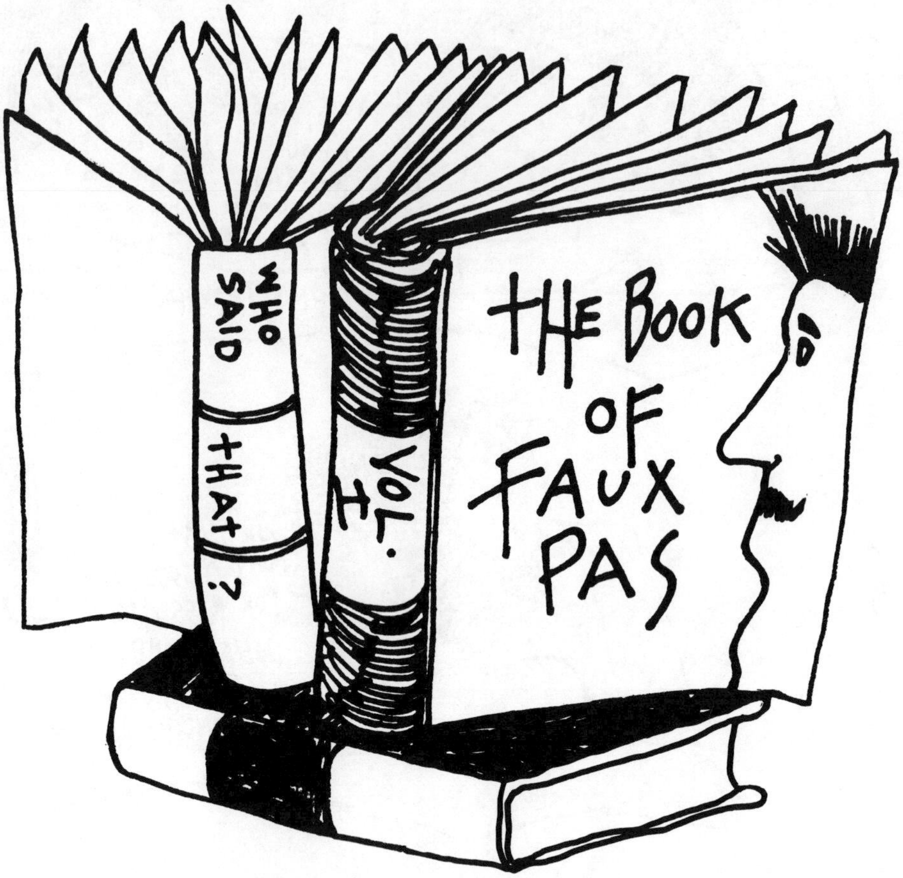
WHO SAID THAT?
VOL. III
THE BOOK OF FAUX PAS

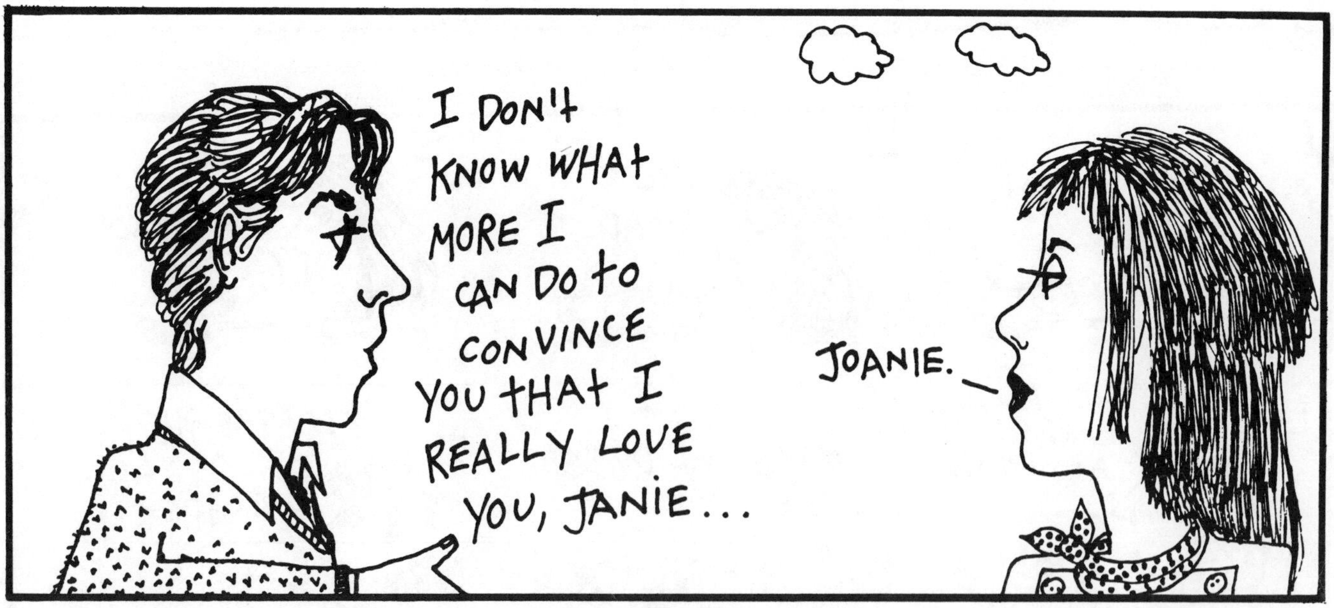
I DON'T KNOW WHAT MORE I CAN DO TO CONVINCE YOU THAT I REALLY LOVE YOU, JANIE...
JOANIE.

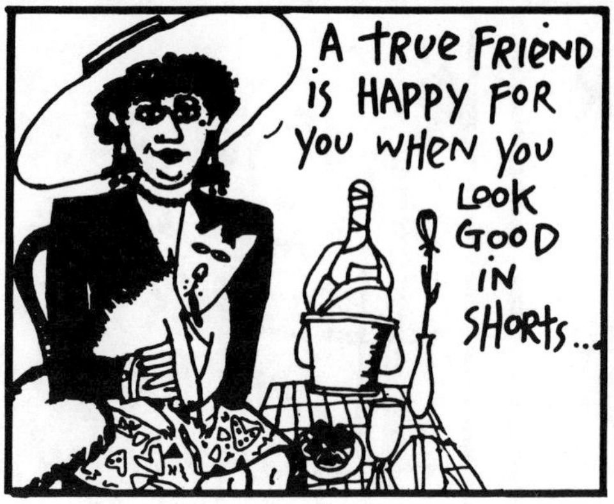
A true Friend is HAPPY FOR you WHEN you LOOK GOOD IN SHORTS...

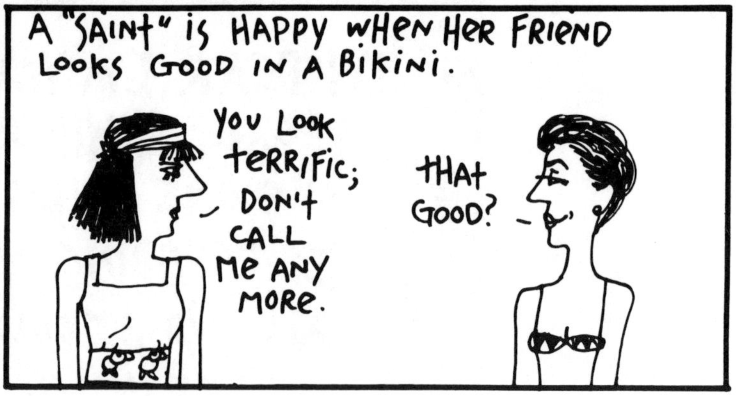
A "SAINT" IS HAPPY WHEN HER FRIEND LOOKS GOOD IN A BIKINI.
YOU LOOK TERRIFIC; DON'T CALL ME ANY MORE.
THAT GOOD?

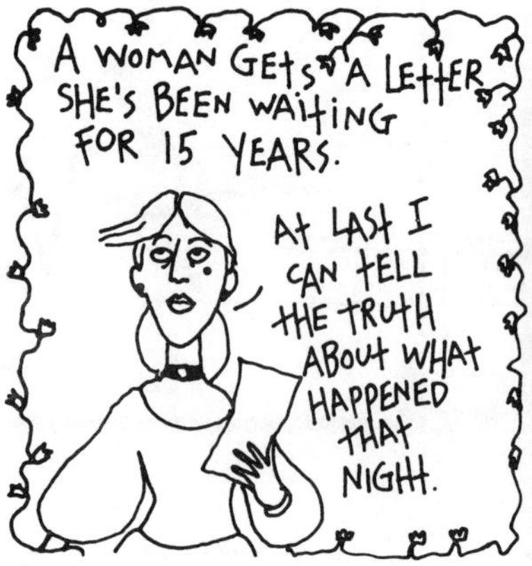
A WOMAN GETS A LETTER SHE'S BEEN WAITING FOR 15 YEARS.
AT LAST I CAN TELL THE TRUTH ABOUT WHAT HAPPENED THAT NIGHT.

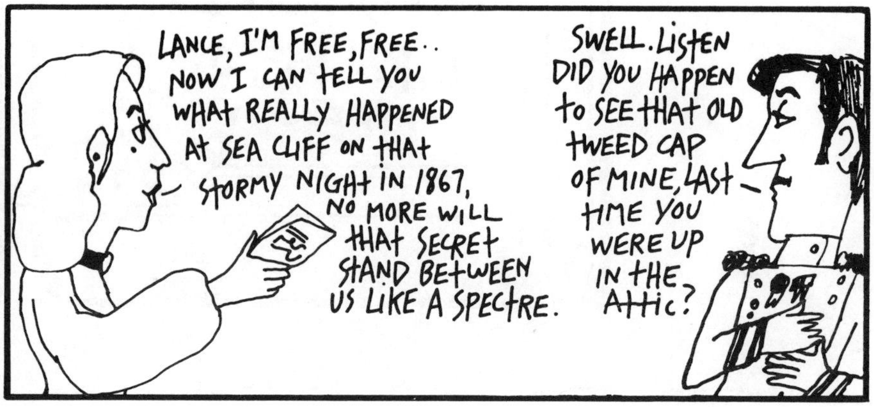
LANCE, I'M FREE, FREE.. NOW I CAN TELL YOU WHAT REALLY HAPPENED AT SEA CLIFF ON THAT STORMY NIGHT IN 1867, NO MORE WILL THAT SECRET STAND BETWEEN US LIKE A SPECTRE.
SWELL. LISTEN DID YOU HAPPEN TO SEE THAT OLD TWEED CAP OF MINE, LAST TIME YOU WERE UP IN THE ATTIC?

TATTOO PROBLEMS

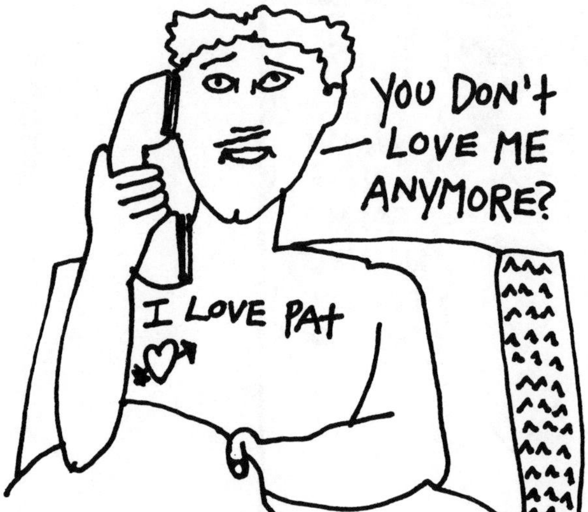
YOU DON'T LOVE ME ANYMORE?
I LOVE PAT

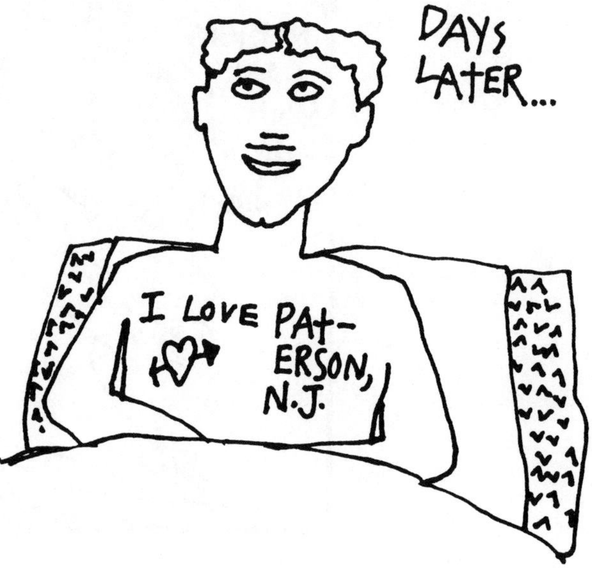
DAYS LATER...
I LOVE PAT-ERSON, N.J.

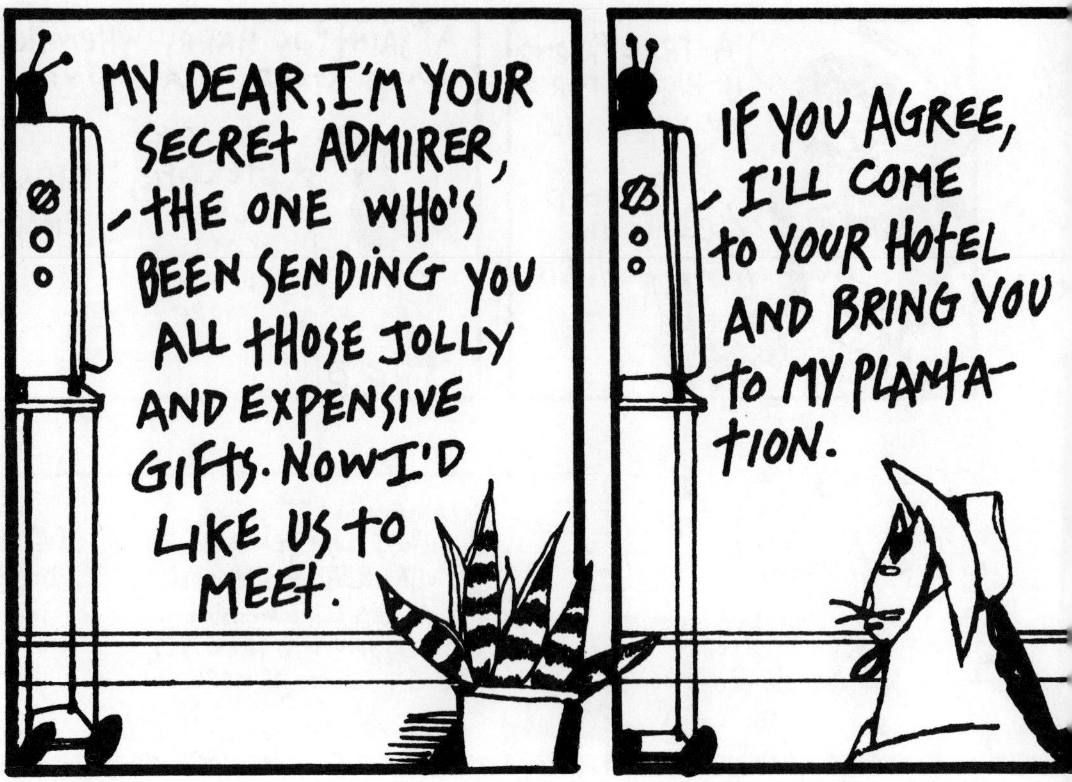
MY DEAR, I'M YOUR SECRET ADMIRER, THE ONE WHO'S BEEN SENDING YOU ALL THOSE JOLLY AND EXPENSIVE GIFTS. NOW I'D LIKE US TO MEET.
IF YOU AGREE, I'LL COME TO YOUR HOTEL AND BRING YOU TO MY PLANTATION.

two People who Are Asking for trouble

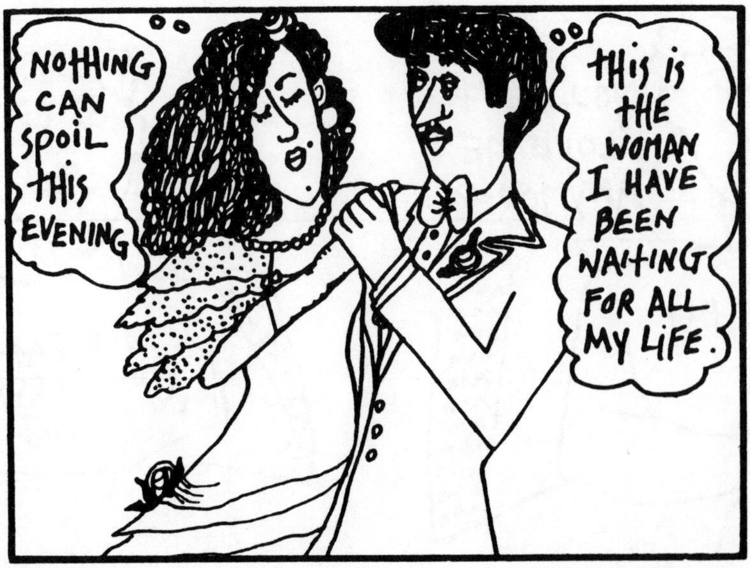
NOTHING CAN SPOIL THIS EVENING
THIS IS THE WOMAN I HAVE BEEN WAITING FOR ALL MY LIFE.

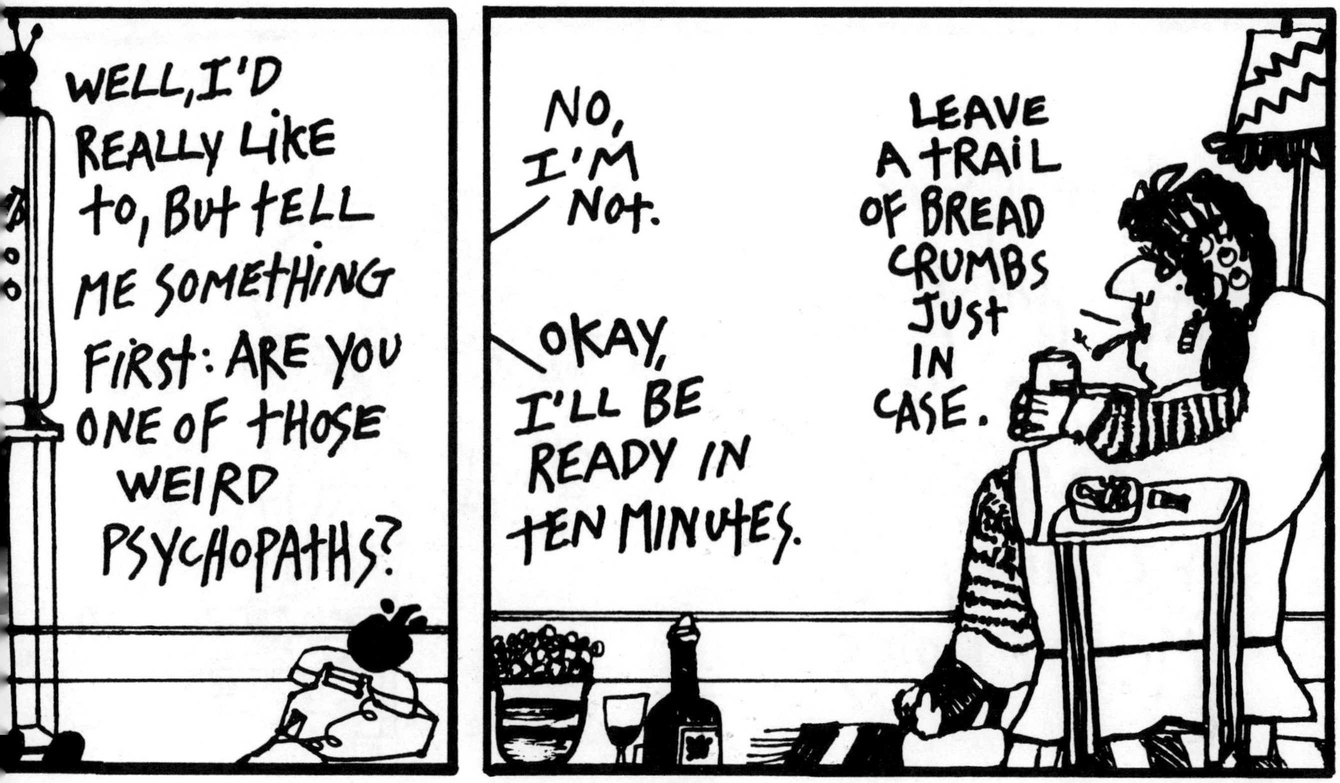
WELL, I'D REALLY LIKE TO, BUT TELL ME SOMETHING FIRST: ARE YOU ONE OF THOSE WEIRD PSYCHOPATHS?
NO, I'M NOT.
OKAY, I'LL BE READY IN TEN MINUTES.
LEAVE A TRAIL OF BREAD CRUMBS JUST IN CASE.

MAN APOLOGIZES TO WIFE

OHIO (UPI)—Late today in Akron, Ohio, a man apologized to his wife for drinking the last Coke in the refrigerator. "You could have knocked me over with a feather," said their next door neighbor.

The Quest for the Holy Grail and Other Anxiety Producing Metaphors

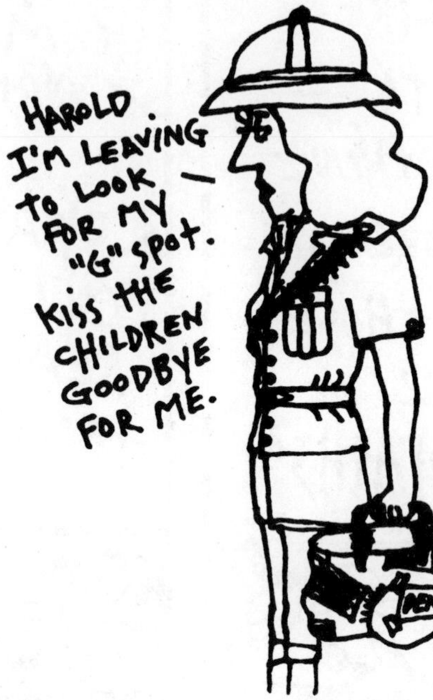

HAROLD I'M LEAVING TO LOOK FOR MY "G" SPOT. KISS THE CHILDREN GOODBYE FOR ME.

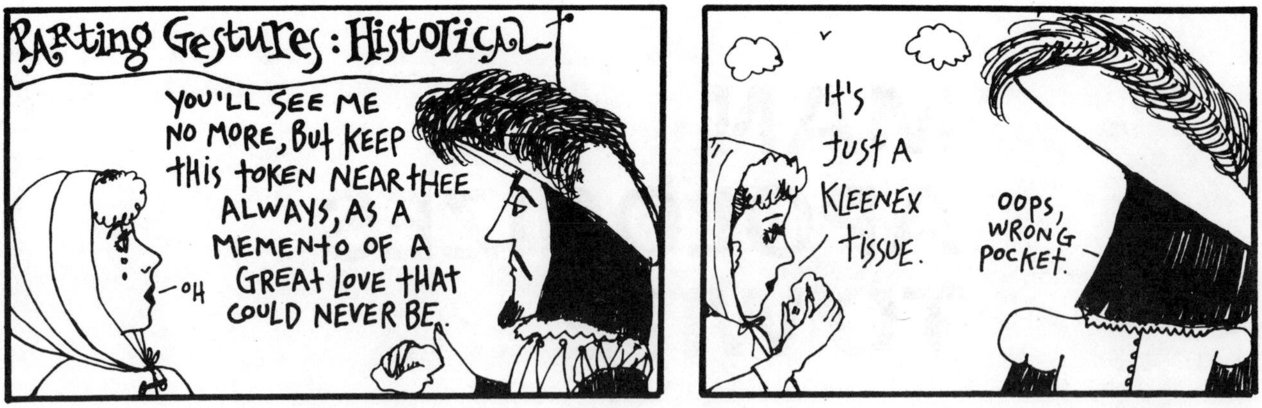

Parting Gestures: Historical
YOU'LL SEE ME NO MORE, BUT KEEP THIS TOKEN NEAR THEE ALWAYS, AS A MEMENTO OF A GREAT LOVE THAT COULD NEVER BE.
OH
IT'S JUST A KLEENEX TISSUE.
OOPS, WRONG POCKET.

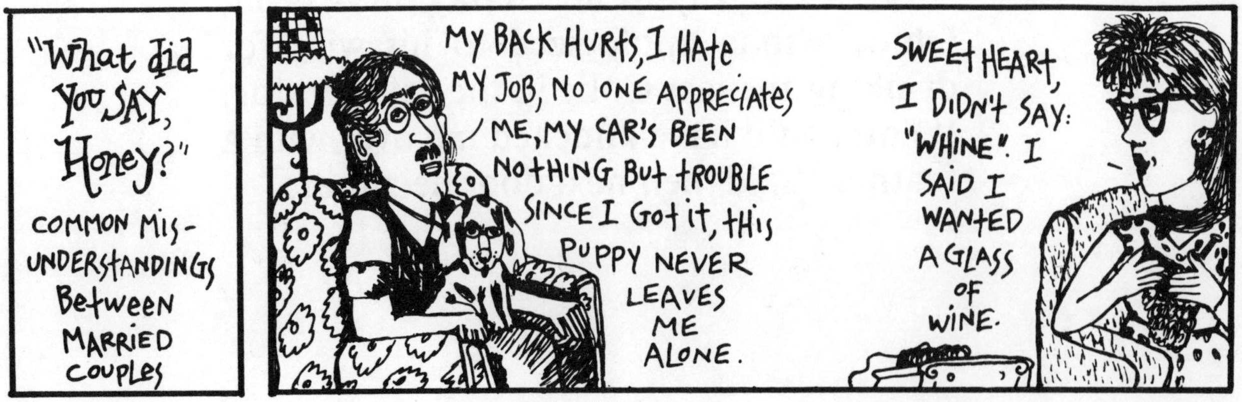

"What did You SAY, Honey?"
COMMON MIS-UNDERSTANDINGS Between MARRIED COUPLES
MY BACK HURTS, I HATE MY JOB, NO ONE APPRECIATES ME, MY CAR'S BEEN NOTHING BUT TROUBLE SINCE I GOT IT, THIS PUPPY NEVER LEAVES ME ALONE.
SWEETHEART, I DIDN'T SAY: "WHINE". I SAID I WANTED A GLASS OF WINE.

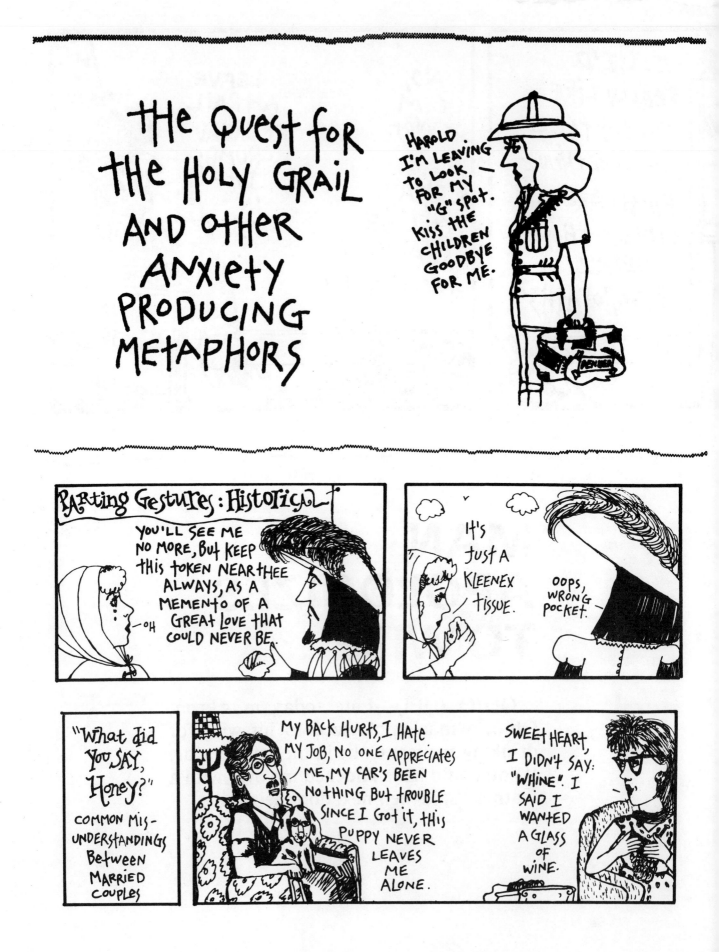

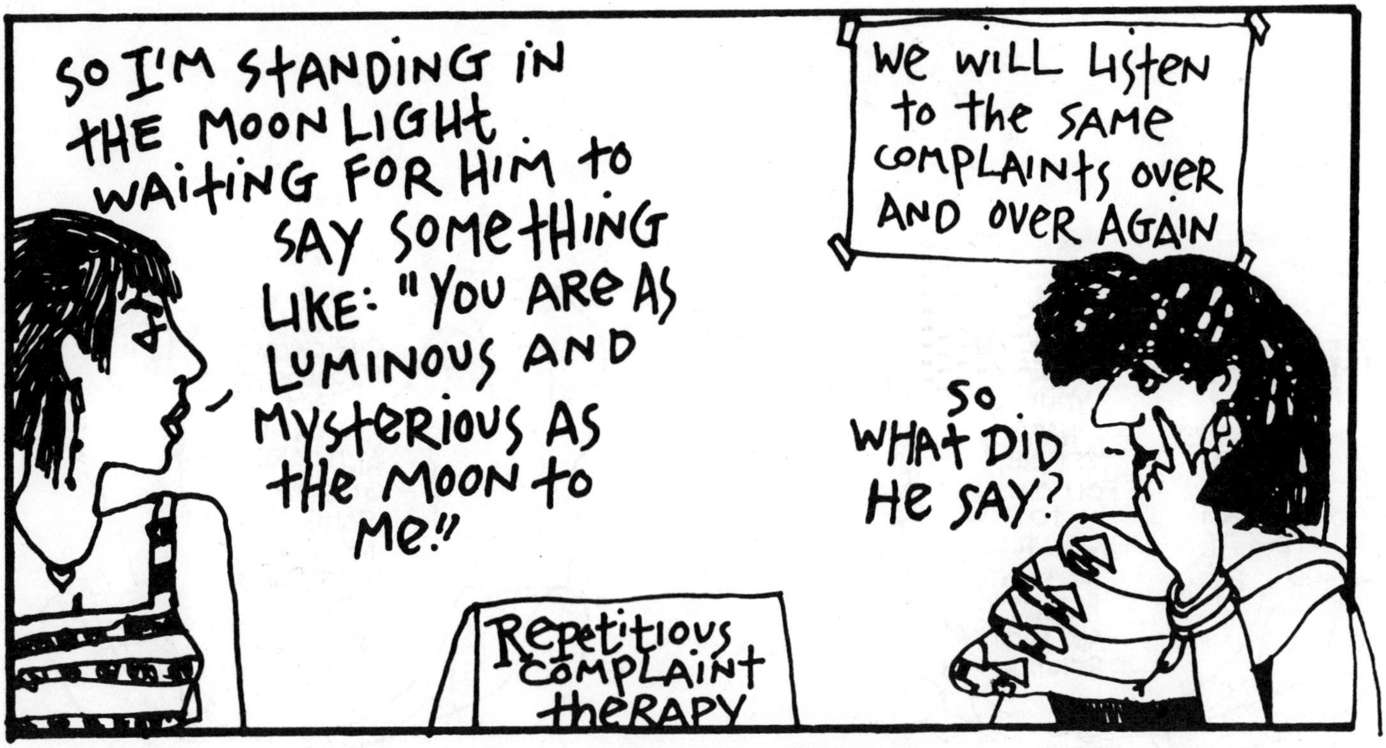
WE WILL LISTEN to the SAME COMPLAINTS OVER AND OVER AGAIN
SO I'M STANDING IN THE MOONLIGHT WAITING FOR HIM to SAY SOMETHING LIKE: "YOU ARE AS LUMINOUS AND MYSTERIOUS AS tHE MOON to Me!"
SO WHAT DID He SAY?
Repetitious COMPLAINT therapy

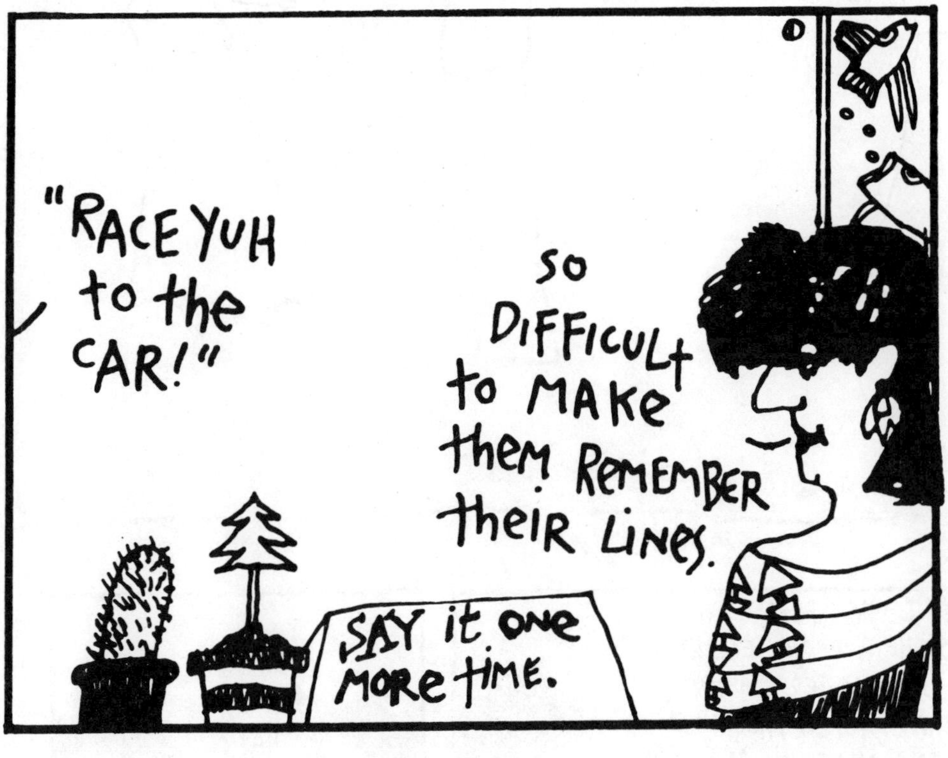
"RACE YUH to the CAR!"
SO DIFFICULT to MAKE them REMEMBER their LINES.
SAY it ONE MORE time.

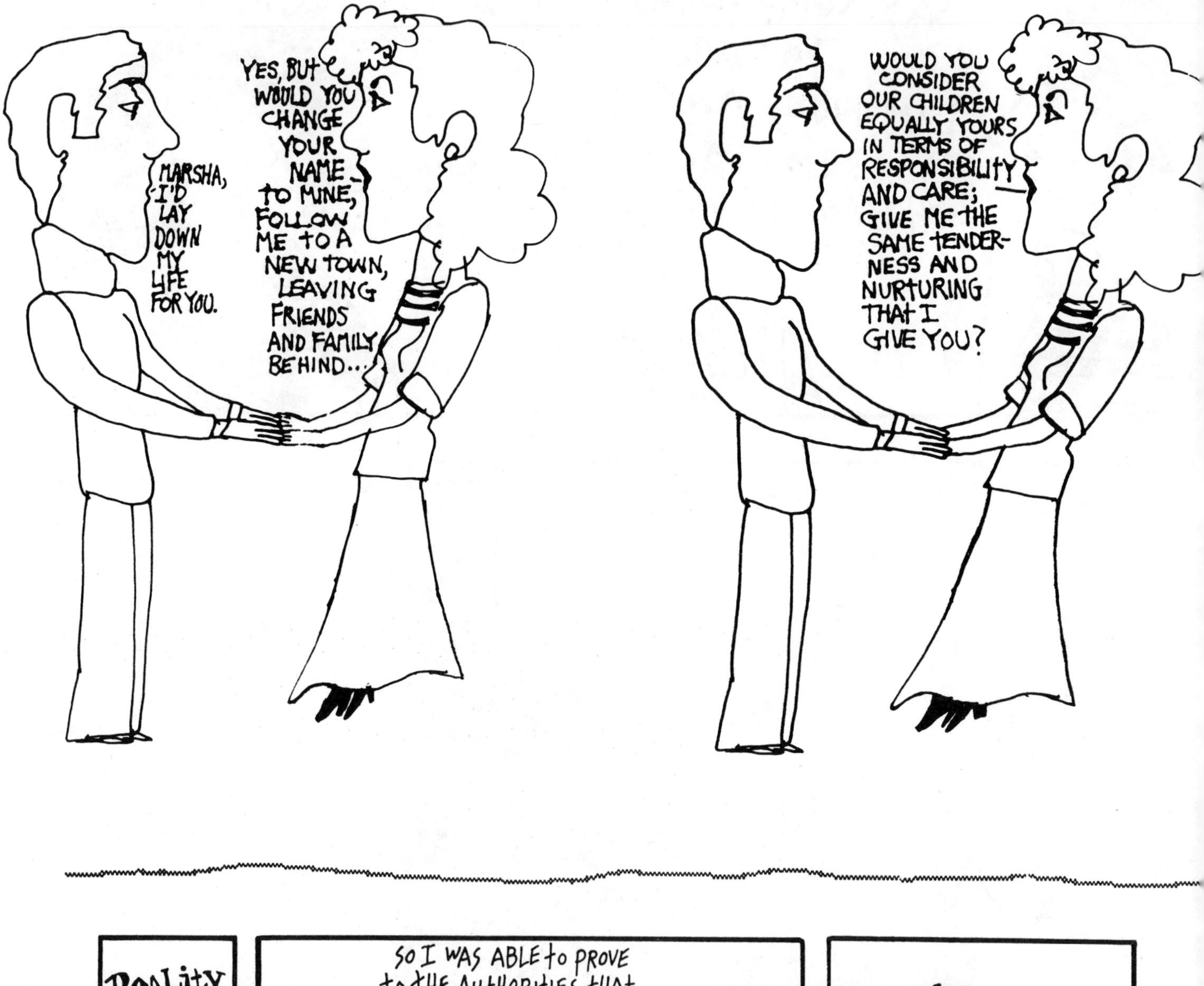
MARSHA, I'D LAY DOWN MY LIFE FOR YOU.
YES, BUT WOULD YOU CHANGE YOUR NAME TO MINE, FOLLOW ME TO A NEW TOWN, LEAVING FRIENDS AND FAMILY BEHIND...
WOULD YOU CONSIDER OUR CHILDREN EQUALLY YOURS IN TERMS OF RESPONSIBILITY AND CARE; GIVE ME THE SAME TENDERNESS AND NURTURING THAT I GIVE YOU?

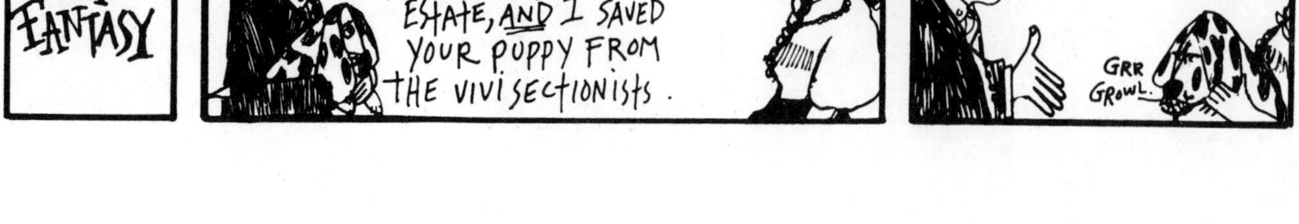
Reality Rarely Lives up to our Fantasy
SO I WAS ABLE TO PROVE TO THE AUTHORITIES THAT YOUR BROTHER COULDN'T HAVE STOLEN THE JEWELS, AND THAT YOU ARE THE RIGHTFUL HEIRS TO THE BRADFORD ESTATE, AND I SAVED YOUR PUPPY FROM THE VIVISECTIONISTS.
GEE THANKS.
"GEE THANKS" THAT'S IT?
I GOTTA GO TO THE BEAUTY PARLOR.
GRR GROWL.

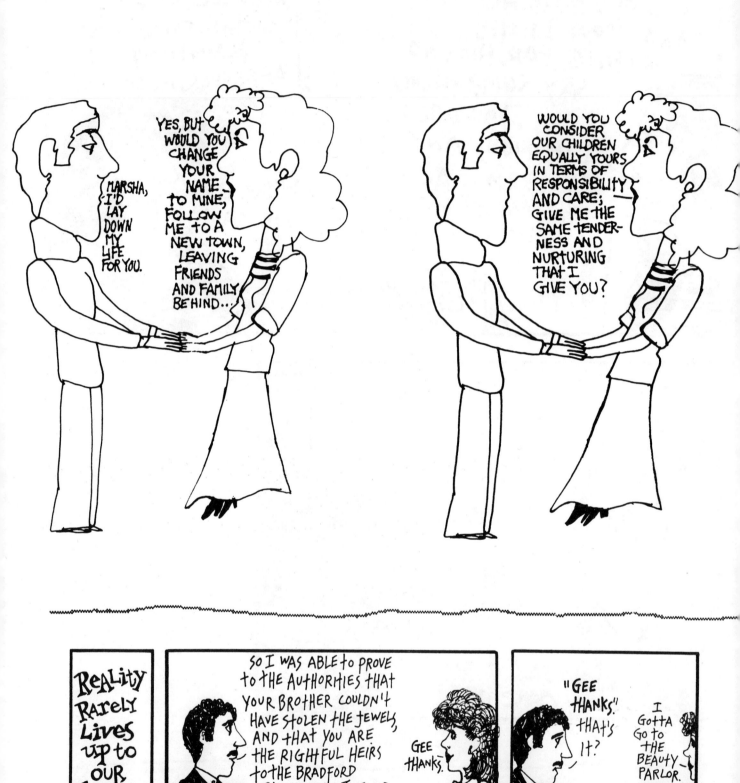

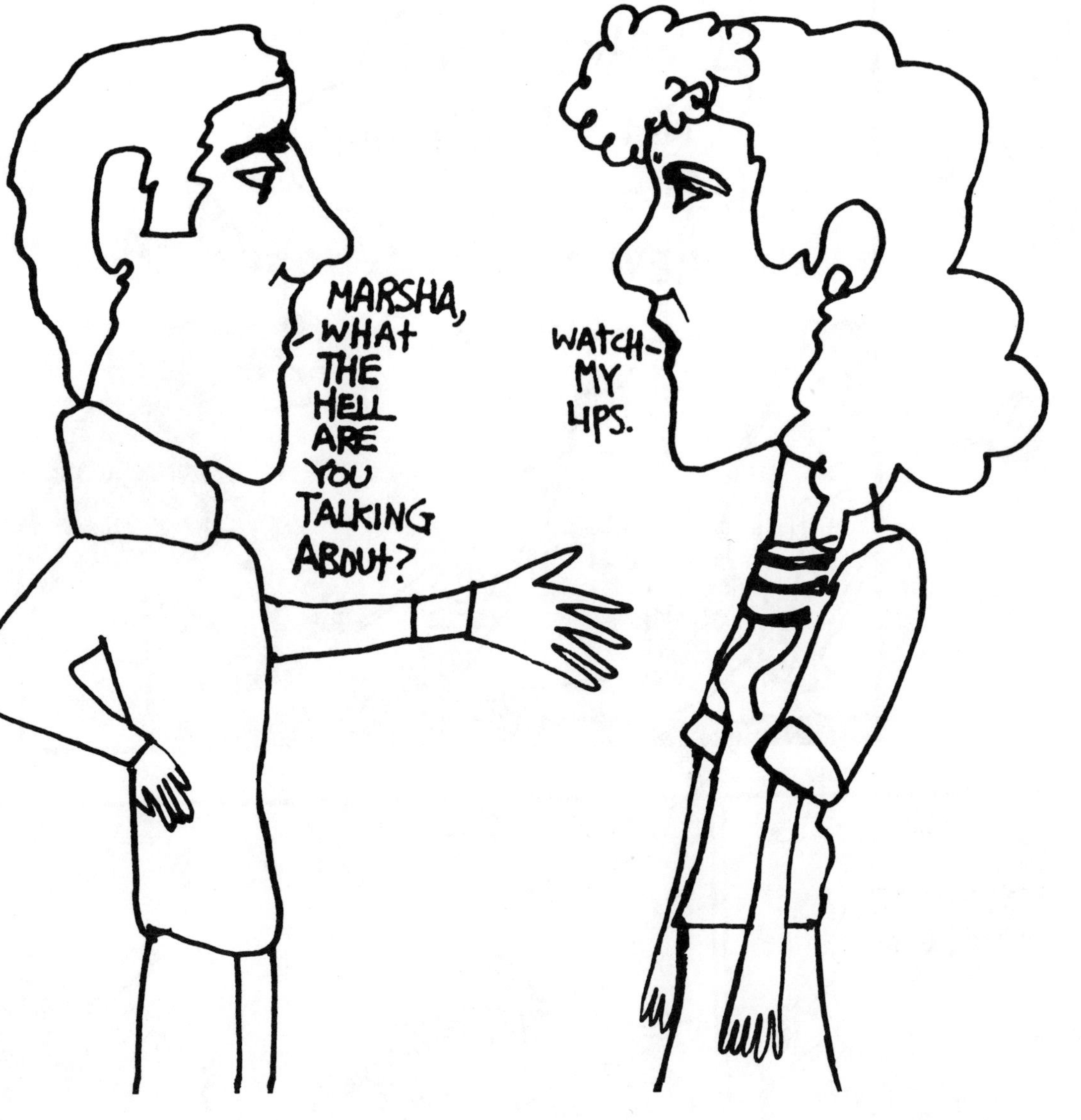
MARSHA, WHAT THE HELL ARE YOU TALKING ABOUT?
WATCH MY LIPS.

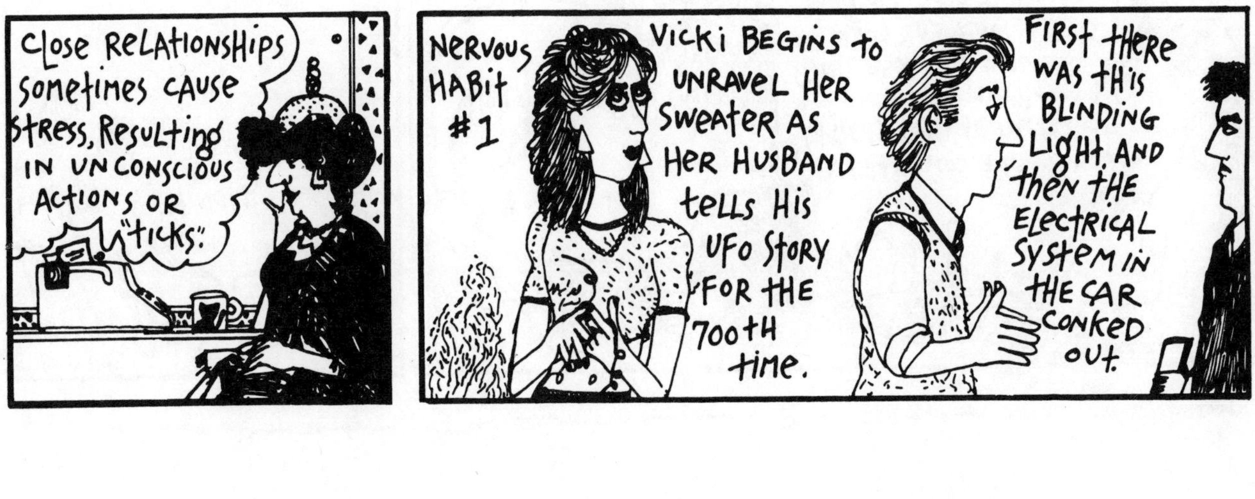
Close Relationships sometimes cause stress, Resulting in unconscious actions or "ticks."
Nervous Habit #1
Vicki Begins to unravel her sweater as her husband tells his UFO story for the 700th time.
First there was this blinding light, and then the electrical system in the car conked out.

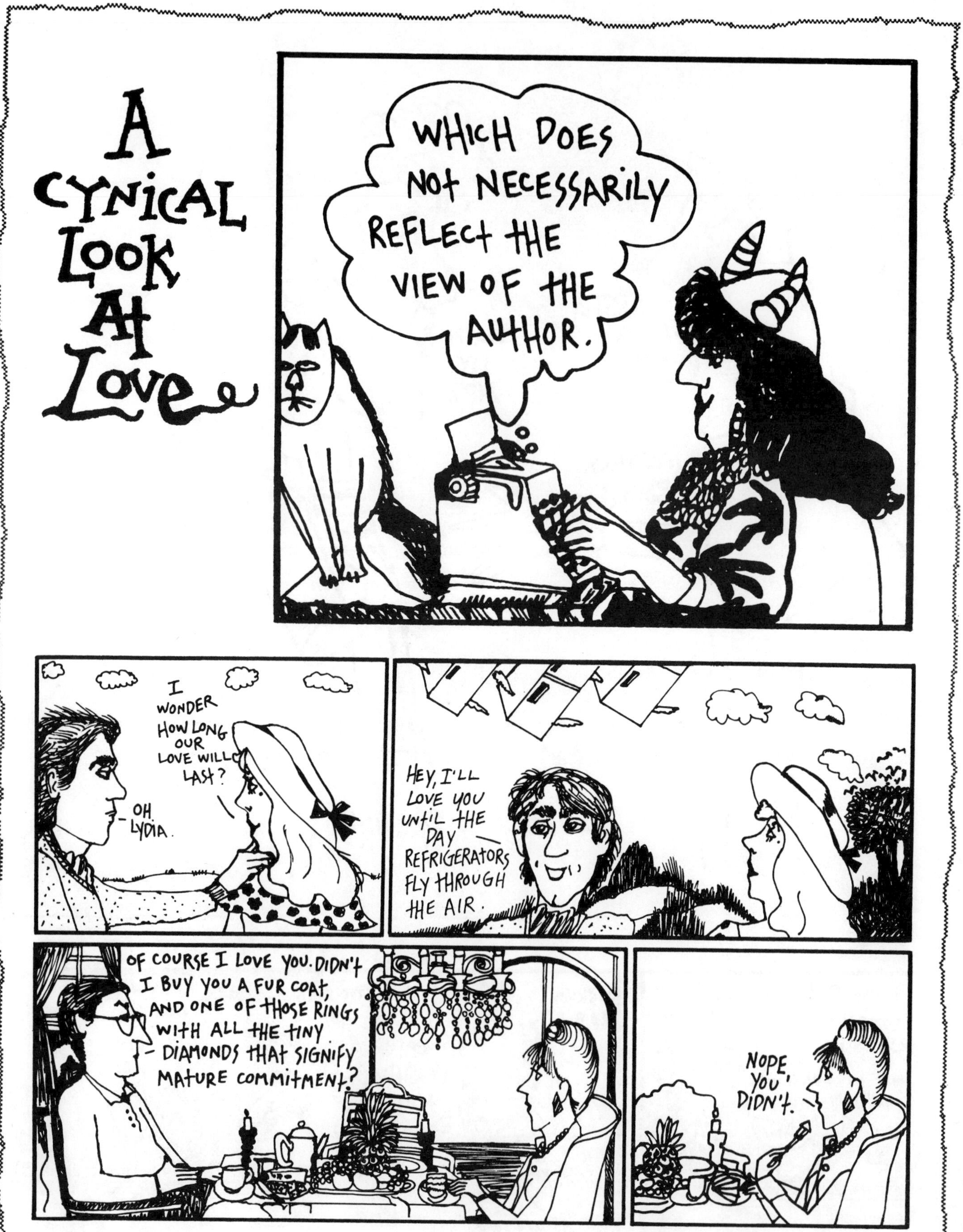
A CYNICAL LOOK AT LOVE
WHICH DOES NOT NECESSARILY REFLECT THE VIEW OF THE AUTHOR.
I WONDER HOW LONG OUR LOVE WILL LAST?
OH LYDIA.
HEY, I'LL LOVE YOU UNTIL THE DAY REFRIGERATORS FLY THROUGH THE AIR.
OF COURSE I LOVE YOU. DIDN'T I BUY YOU A FUR COAT, AND ONE OF THOSE RINGS WITH ALL THE TINY DIAMONDS THAT SIGNIFY MATURE COMMITMENT?
NOPE, YOU DIDN'T.

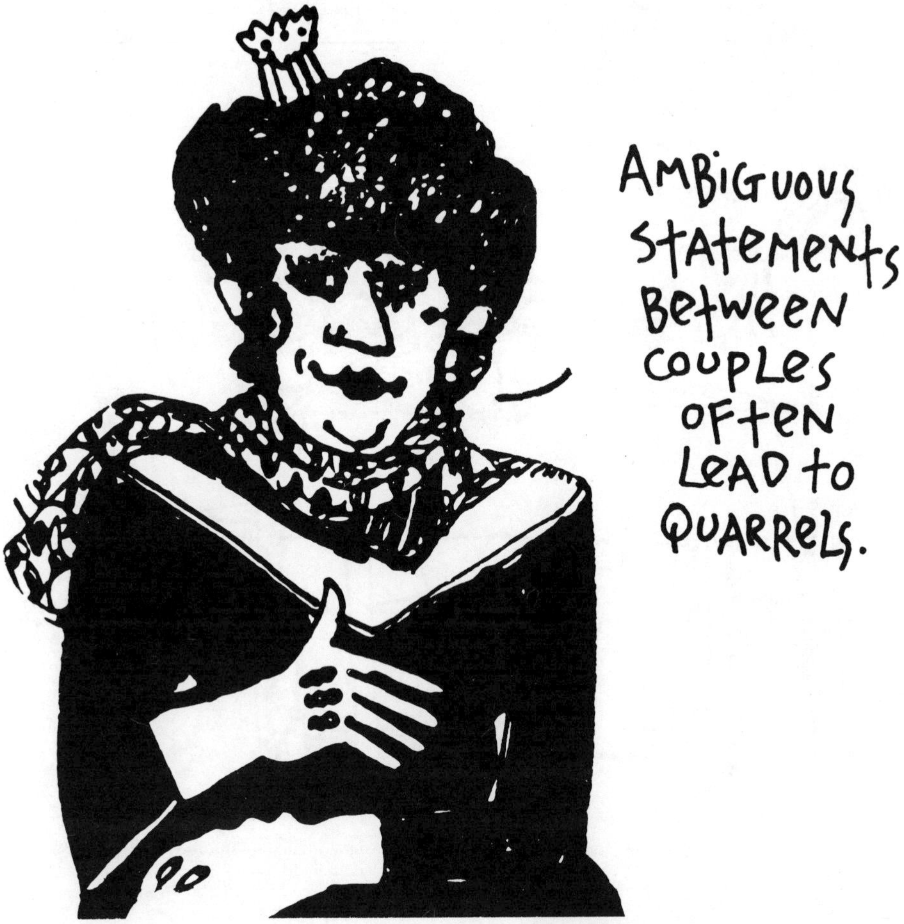
AMBIGUOUS STATEMENTS BETWEEN COUPLES OFTEN LEAD TO QUARRELS.

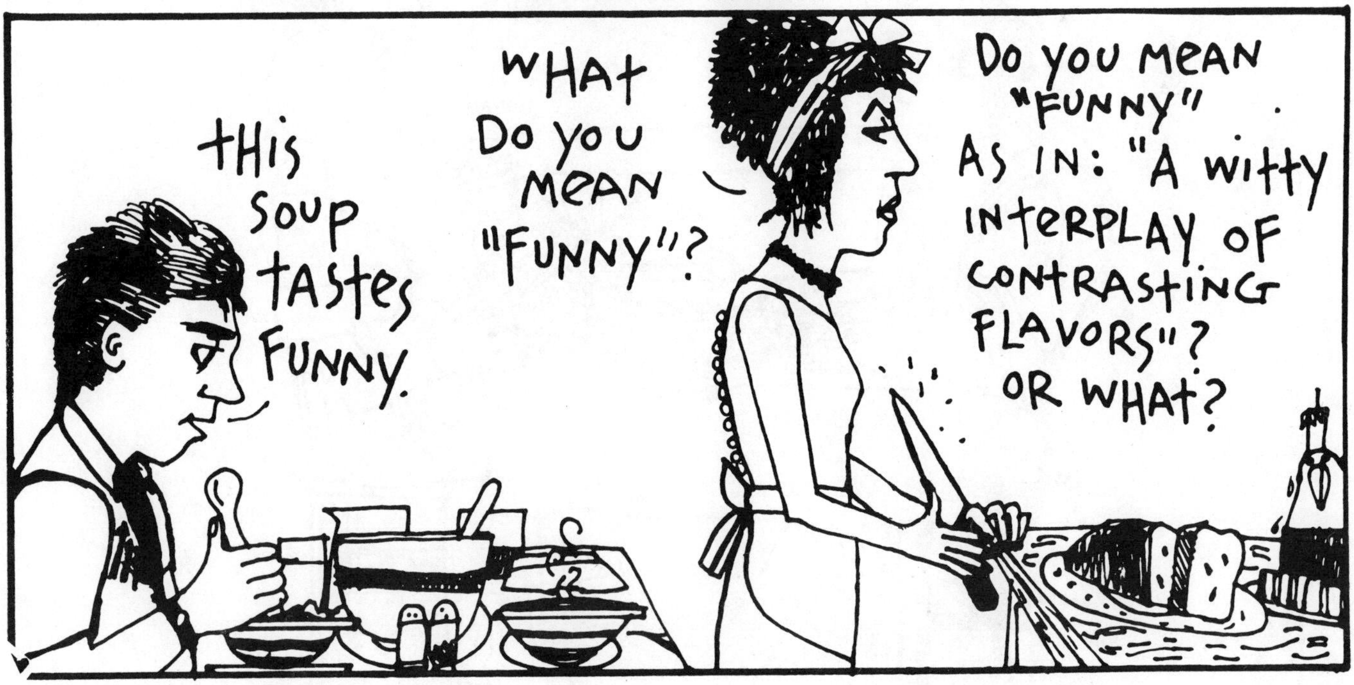
THIS SOUP TASTES FUNNY.
WHAT DO YOU MEAN "FUNNY"?
DO YOU MEAN "FUNNY" AS IN: "A WITTY INTERPLAY OF CONTRASTING FLAVORS"? OR WHAT?

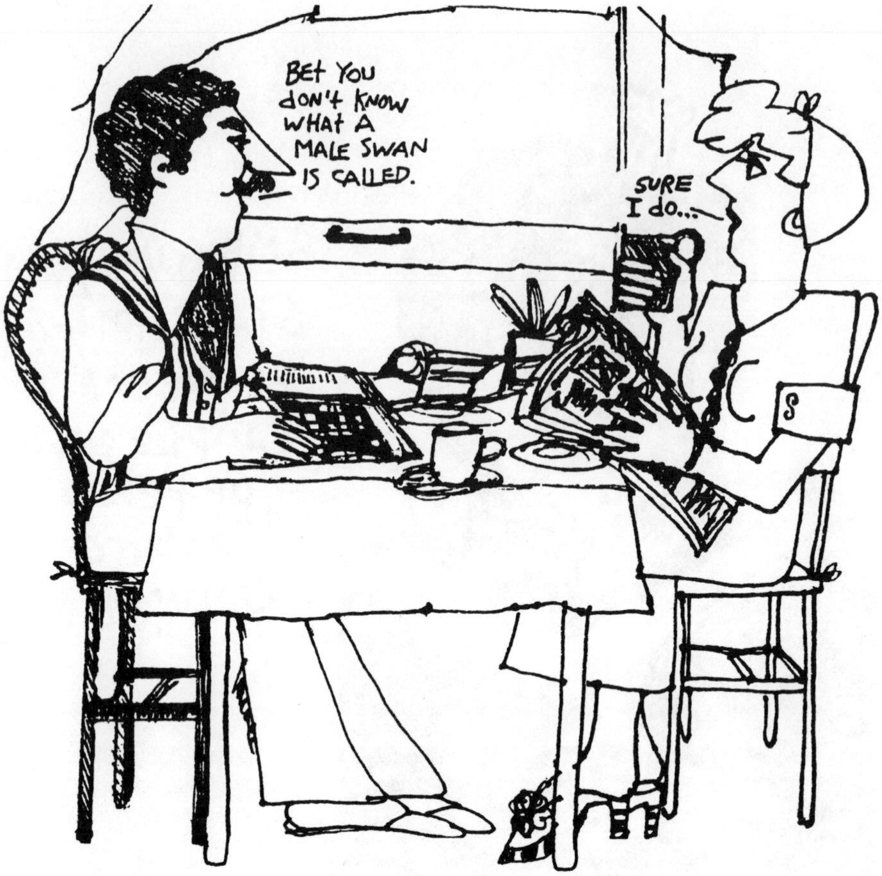
BET YOU don't KNOW WHAT A MALE SWAN IS CALLED.
SURE I do...

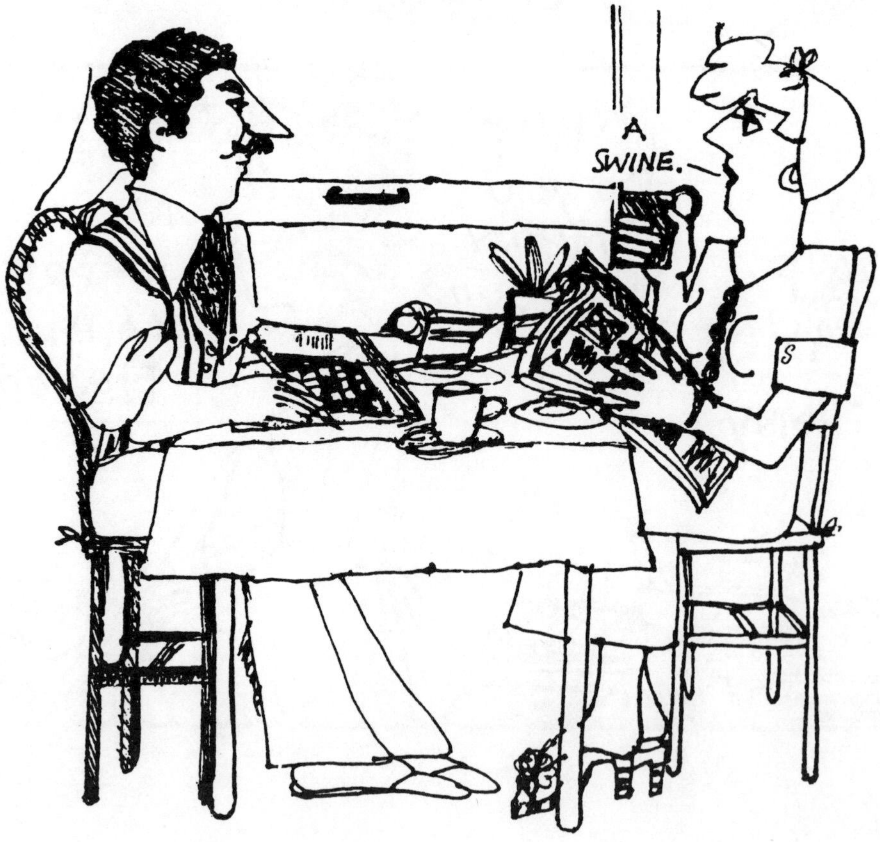
A SWINE.

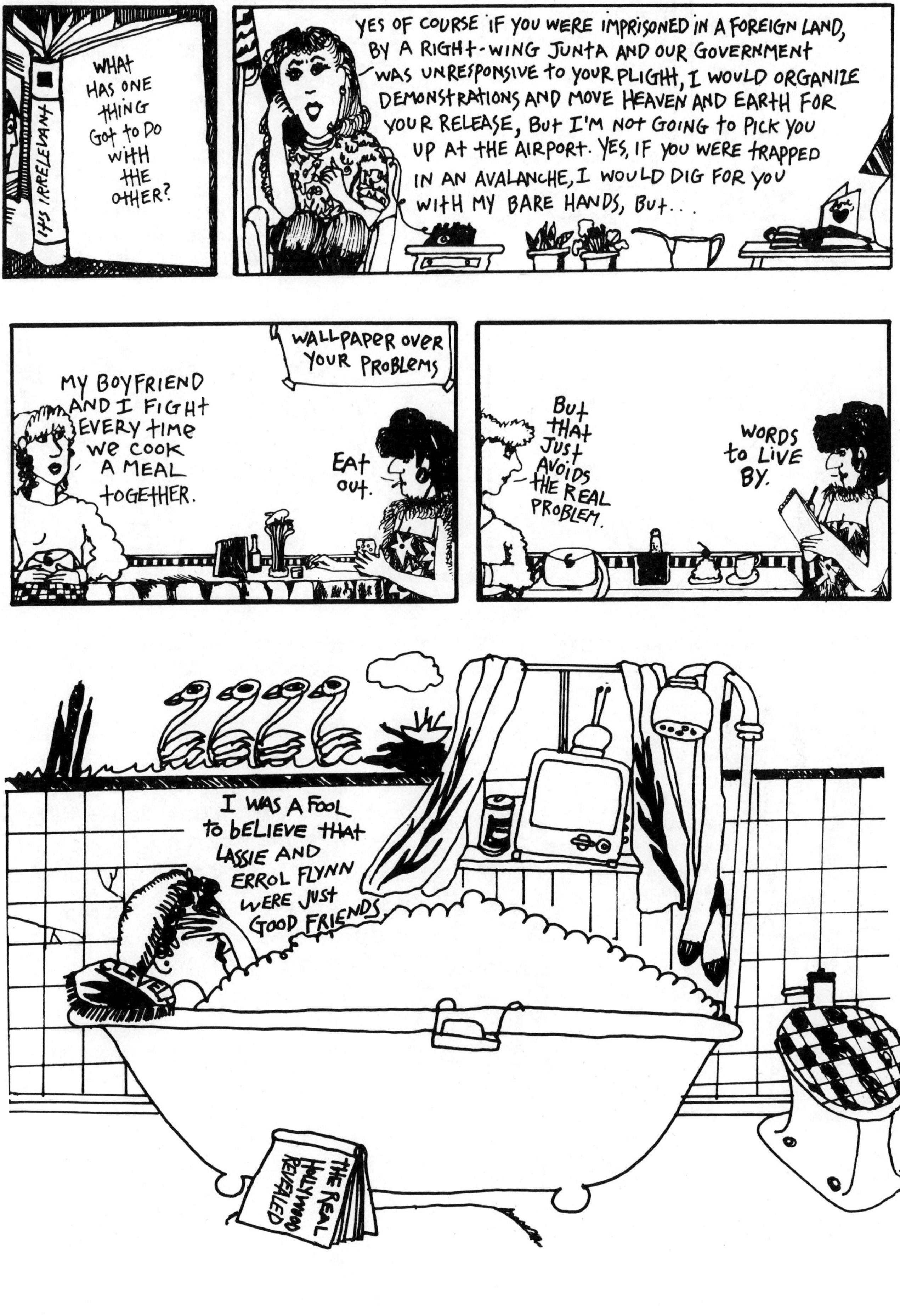
IT'S IRRELEVANT
WHAT HAS ONE THING GOT TO DO WITH THE OTHER?
YES OF COURSE IF YOU WERE IMPRISONED IN A FOREIGN LAND, BY A RIGHT-WING JUNTA AND OUR GOVERNMENT WAS UNRESPONSIVE TO YOUR PLIGHT, I WOULD ORGANIZE DEMONSTRATIONS AND MOVE HEAVEN AND EARTH FOR YOUR RELEASE, BUT I'M NOT GOING TO PICK YOU UP AT THE AIRPORT. YES, IF YOU WERE TRAPPED IN AN AVALANCHE, I WOULD DIG FOR YOU WITH MY BARE HANDS, BUT...
WALLPAPER OVER YOUR PROBLEMS
MY BOYFRIEND AND I FIGHT EVERY TIME WE COOK A MEAL TOGETHER.
EAT OUT.
BUT THAT JUST AVOIDS THE REAL PROBLEM.
WORDS TO LIVE BY.
I WAS A FOOL TO BELIEVE THAT LASSIE AND ERROL FLYNN WERE JUST GOOD FRIENDS
THE REAL HOLLYWOOD REVEALED

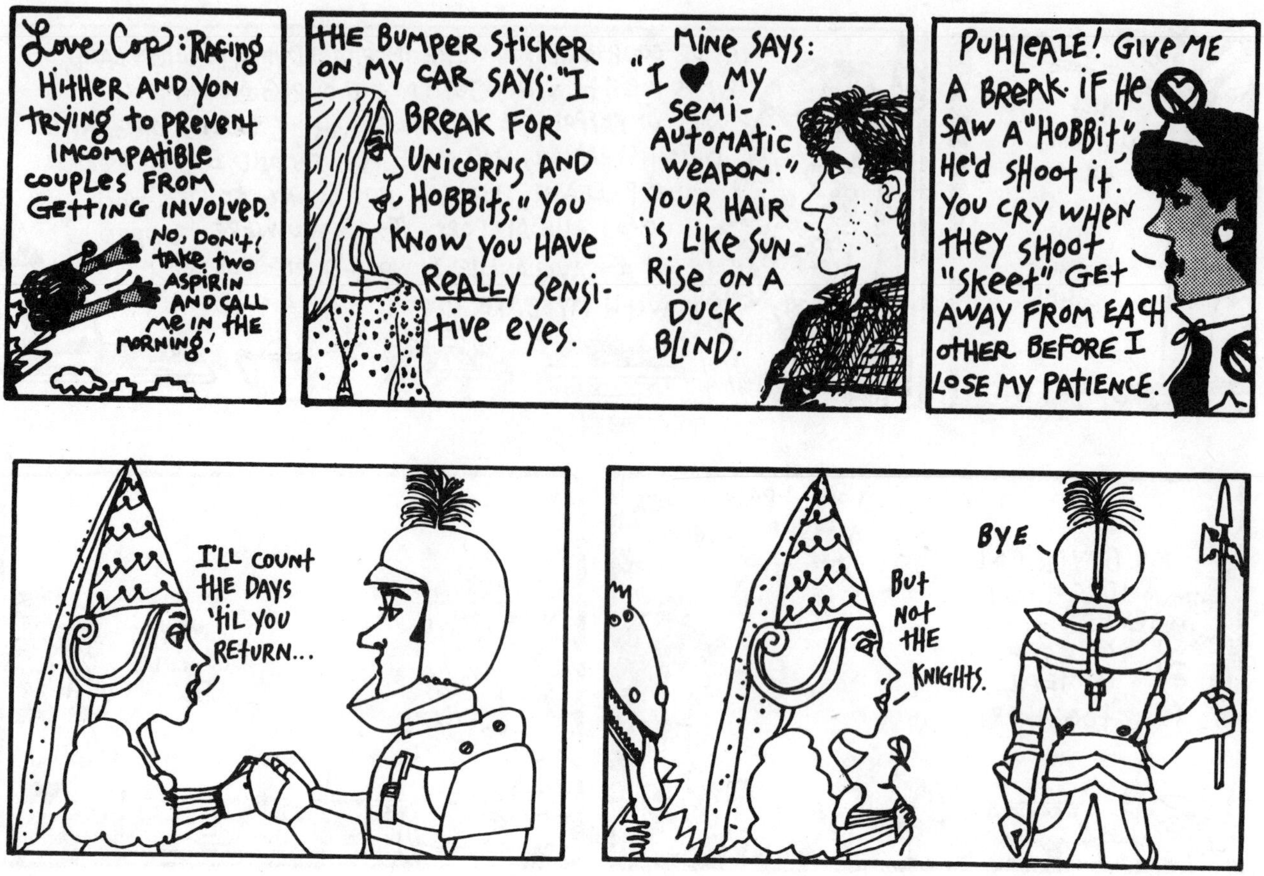
Love Cop: Racing Hither and yon trying to prevent incompatible couples from Getting involved.
No, don't! take two aspirin and call me in the morning!
The bumper sticker on my car says: "I break for unicorns and Hobbits." You know you have really sensitive eyes.
Mine says: "I ♥ my semi-automatic weapon." Your hair is like sunrise on a duck blind.
Puhleaze! Give me a break. if he saw a "Hobbit" he'd shoot it. You cry when they shoot "skeet". Get away from each other before I lose my patience.
I'll count the days 'til you return...
But not the knights.
BYE

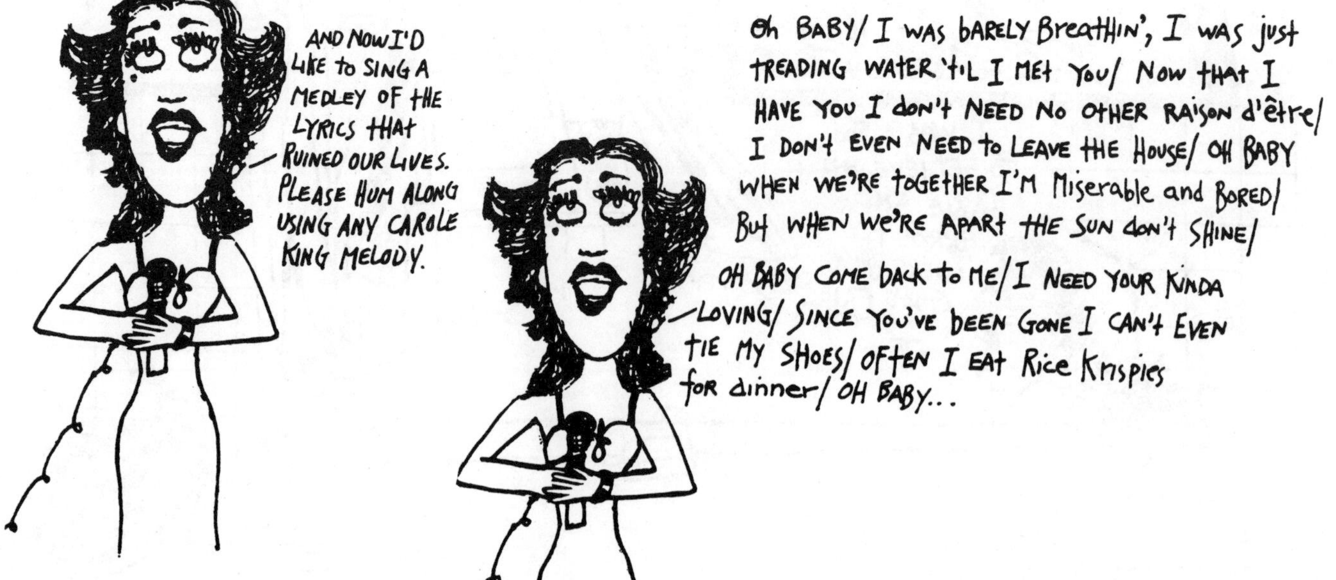
And now I'd like to sing a medley of the lyrics that ruined our lives. Please hum along using any Carole King melody.
Oh baby/ I was barely breathin', I was just treading water 'til I met you/ Now that I have you I don't need no other raison d'être/ I don't even need to leave the house/ Oh baby when we're together I'm miserable and bored/ But when we're apart the sun don't shine/
Oh baby come back to me/ I need your kinda loving/ Since you've been gone I can't even tie my shoes/ often I eat Rice Krispies for dinner/ Oh baby...

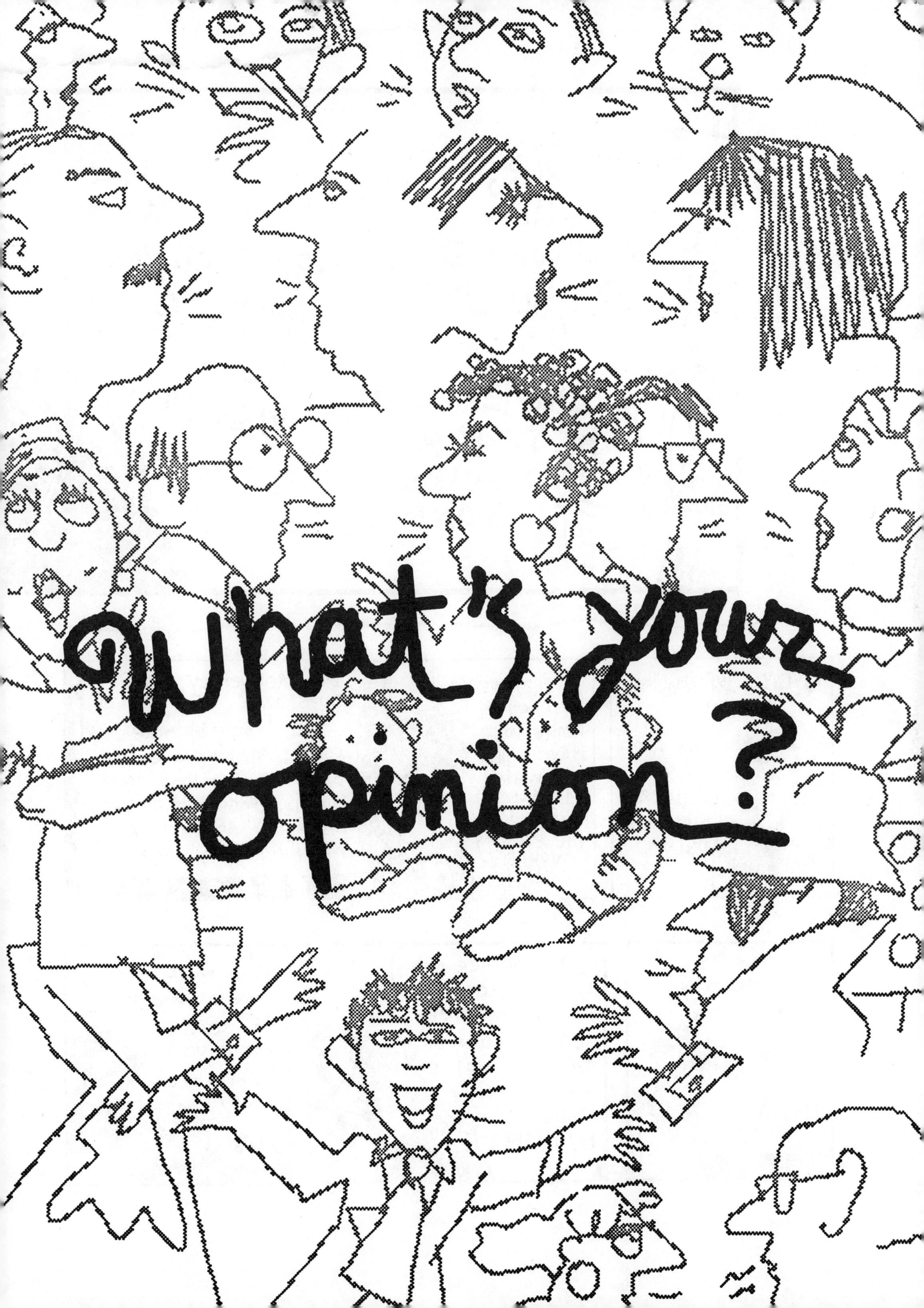
what's your opinion?

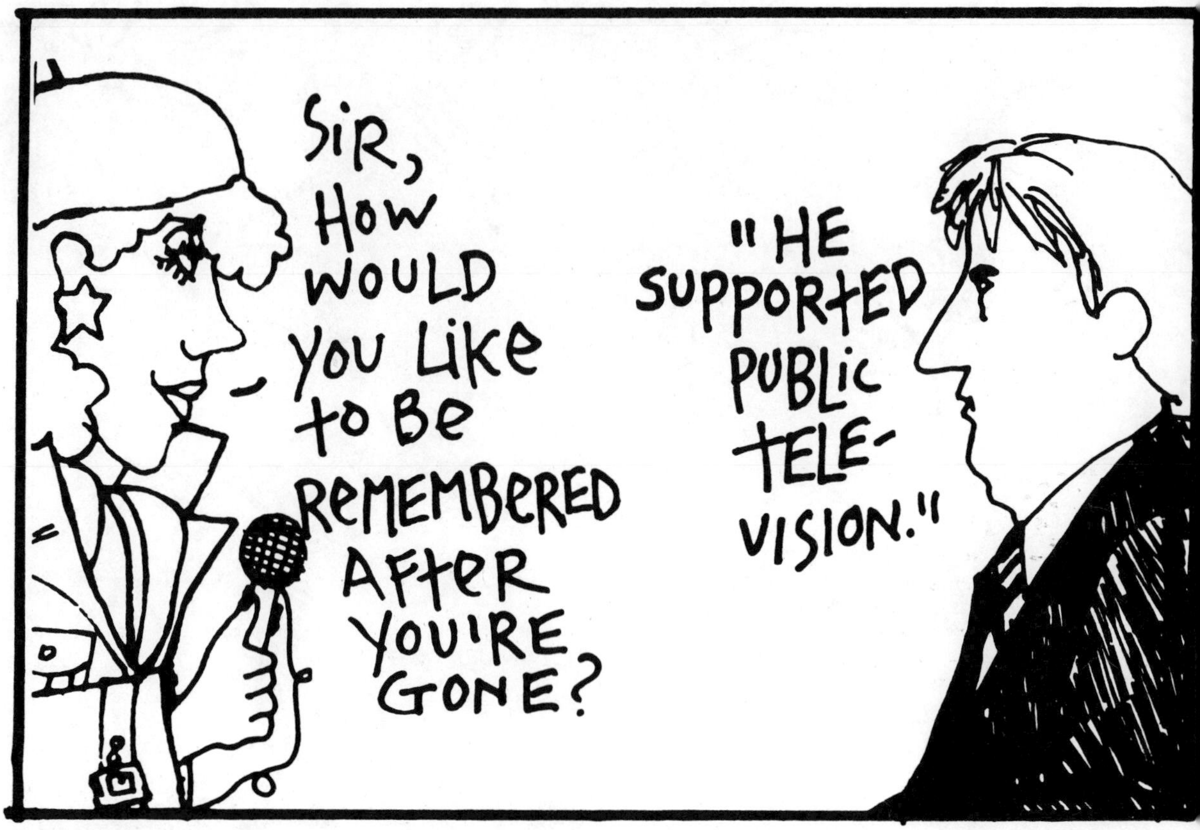
SiR, How WOULD you Like to Be REMEMBERED AFTER YOU'RE GONE?
"HE SUPPORTED PUBLIC TELE-VISION."

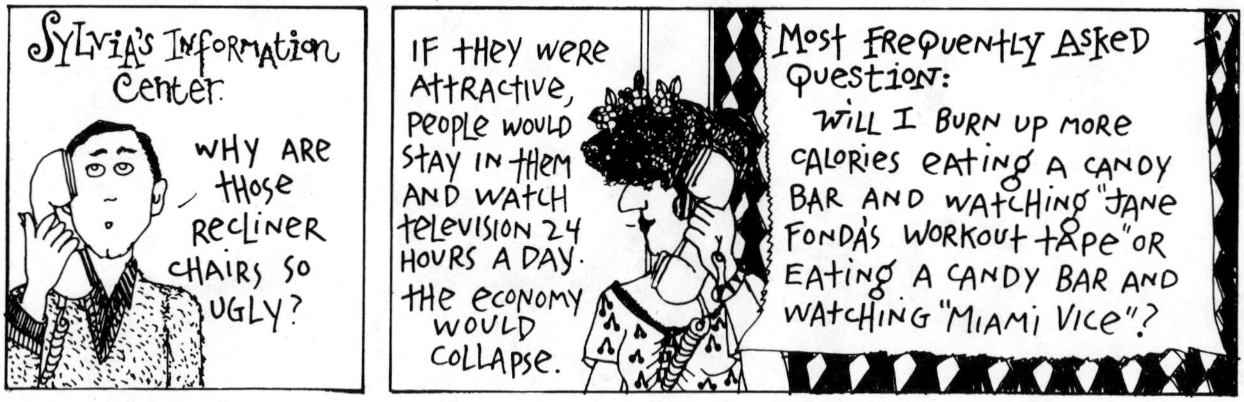
Sylvia's Information Center
WHY ARE those ReCLiNER CHAIRS SO UGLY?
IF tHey were Attractive, People would stay in them AND watch television 24 Hours A Day. the economy would collapse.
Most Frequently Asked Question:
Will I burn up more calories eating a candy bar and watching "Jane Fonda's Workout tape" or eating a candy bar and watching "Miami Vice"?

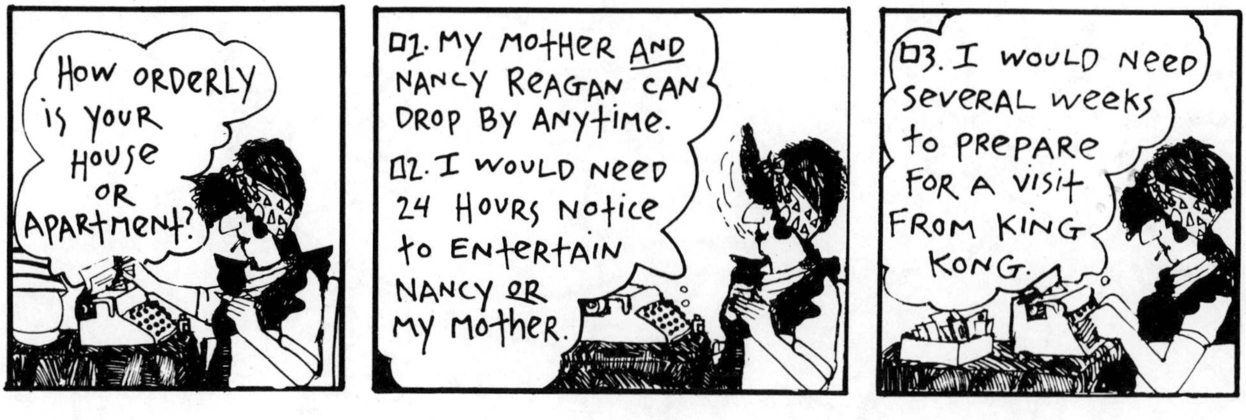
How orderly is your house or apartment?
□1. My mother AND Nancy Reagan can drop by anytime.
□2. I would need 24 Hours Notice to Entertain Nancy OR My Mother.
□3. I would need several weeks to prepare for a visit from King Kong.

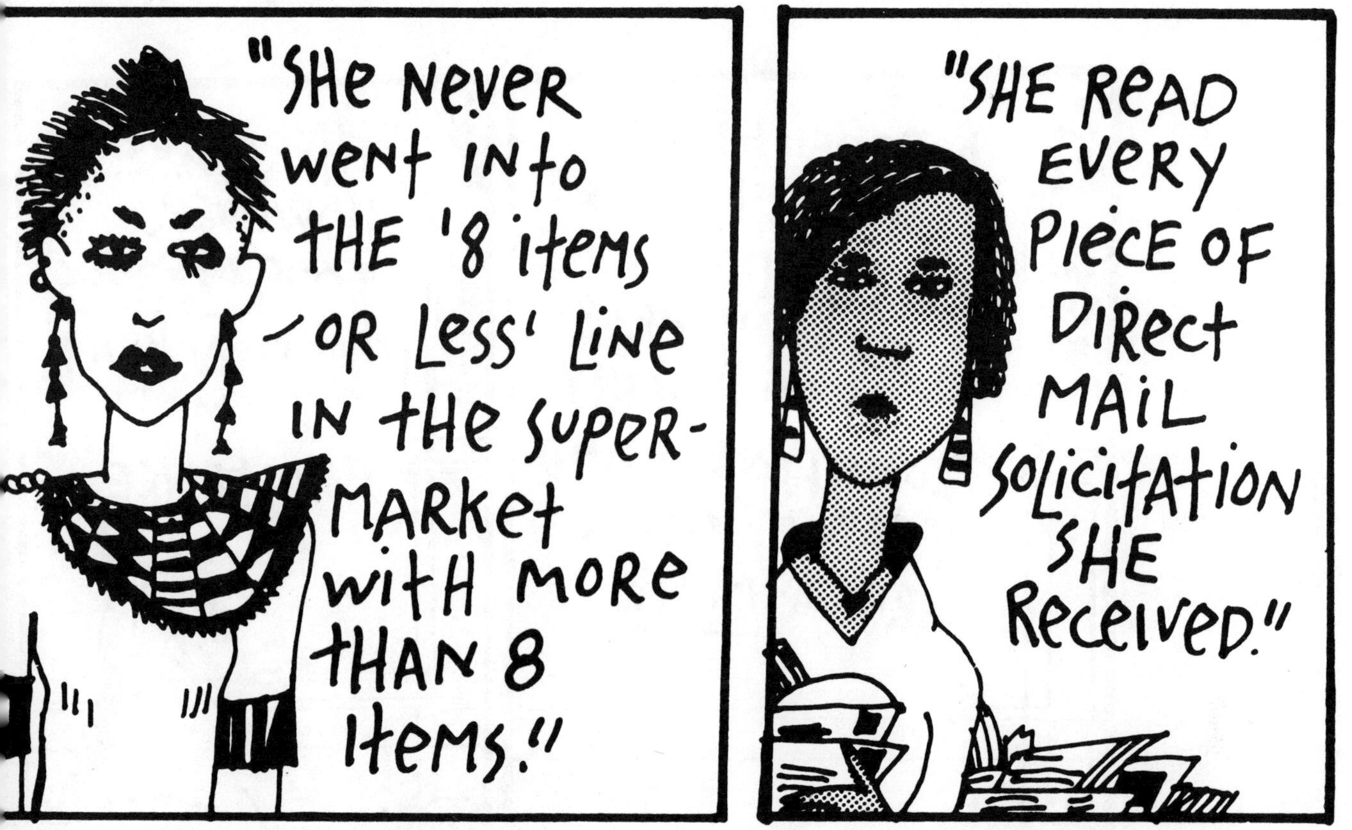
"SHE NEVER WENT INTO THE '8 ITEMS OR LESS' LINE IN THE SUPER-MARKET WITH MORE THAN 8 ITEMS."
"SHE READ EVERY PIECE OF DIRECT MAIL SOLICITATION SHE RECEIVED."

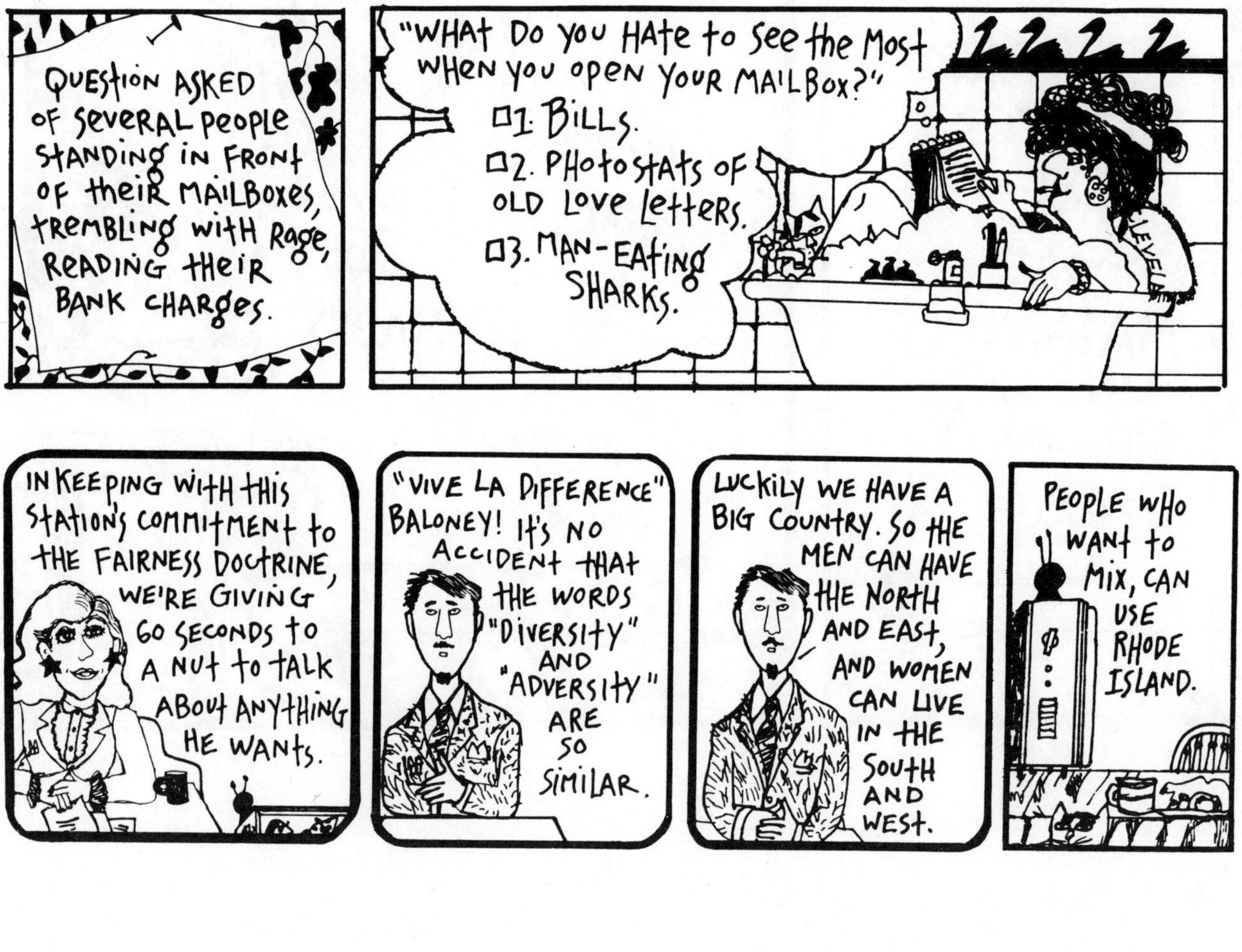
QUESTION ASKED OF SEVERAL PEOPLE STANDING IN FRONT OF THEIR MAILBOXES, TREMBLING WITH RAGE, READING THEIR BANK CHARGES.
"WHAT DO YOU HATE TO SEE THE MOST WHEN YOU OPEN YOUR MAILBOX?"
☐1. BILLS.
☐2. PHOTOSTATS OF OLD LOVE LETTERS.
☐3. MAN-EATING SHARKS.
LEVEL
IN KEEPING WITH THIS STATION'S COMMITMENT TO THE FAIRNESS DOCTRINE, WE'RE GIVING 60 SECONDS TO A NUT TO TALK ABOUT ANYTHING HE WANTS.
"VIVE LA DIFFERENCE" BALONEY! IT'S NO ACCIDENT THAT THE WORDS "DIVERSITY" AND "ADVERSITY" ARE SO SIMILAR.
LUCKILY WE HAVE A BIG COUNTRY. SO THE MEN CAN HAVE THE NORTH AND EAST, AND WOMEN CAN LIVE IN THE SOUTH AND WEST.
PEOPLE WHO WANT TO MIX, CAN USE RHODE ISLAND.

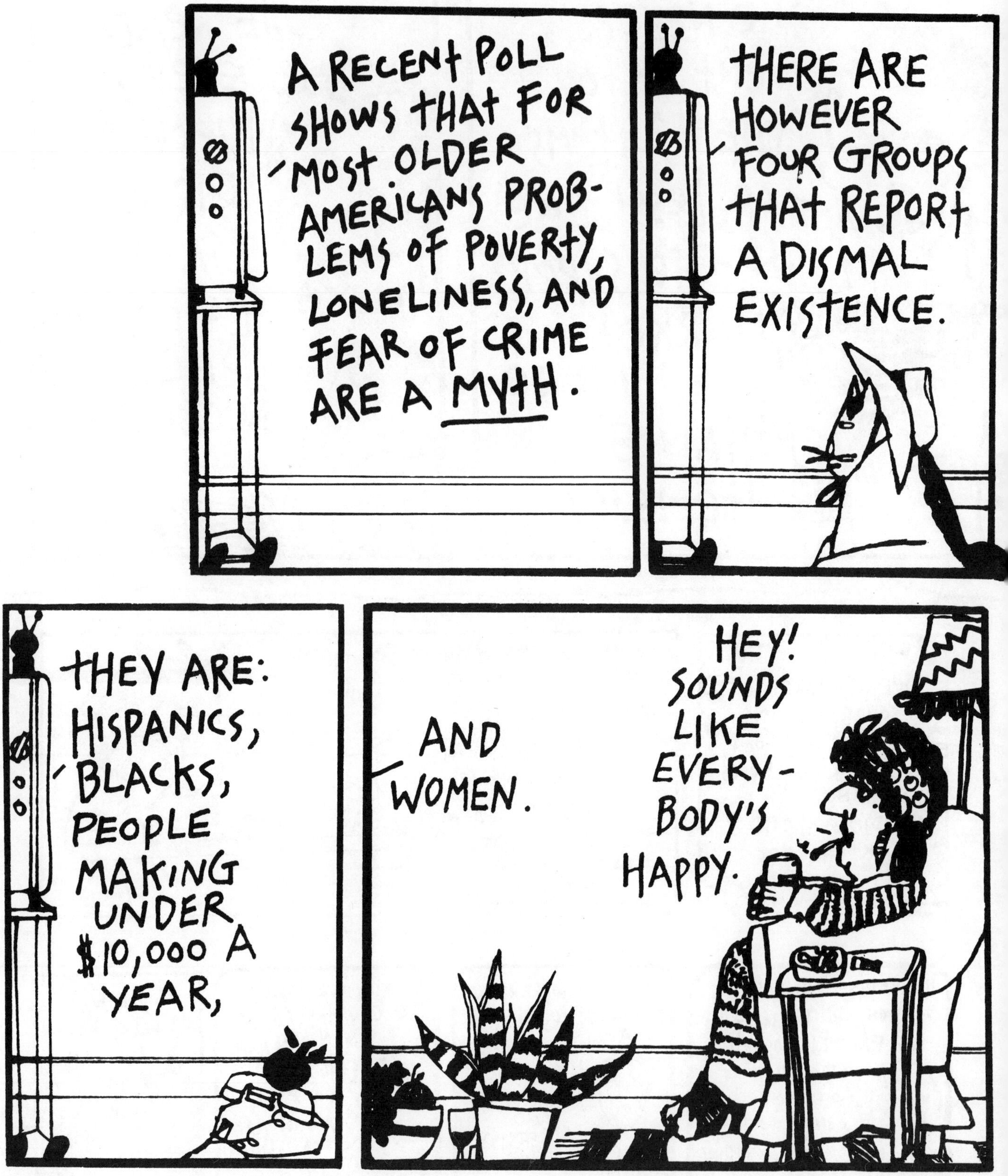
A RECENT POLL SHOWS THAT FOR MOST OLDER AMERICANS PROBLEMS OF POVERTY, LONELINESS, AND FEAR OF CRIME ARE A MYTH.
THERE ARE HOWEVER FOUR GROUPS THAT REPORT A DISMAL EXISTENCE.
THEY ARE: HISPANICS, BLACKS, PEOPLE MAKING UNDER $10,000 A YEAR,
AND WOMEN.
HEY! SOUNDS LIKE EVERYBODY'S HAPPY.

WHAT'S YOUR OPINION/ Do you think it's fair to keep pets in a city apartment?

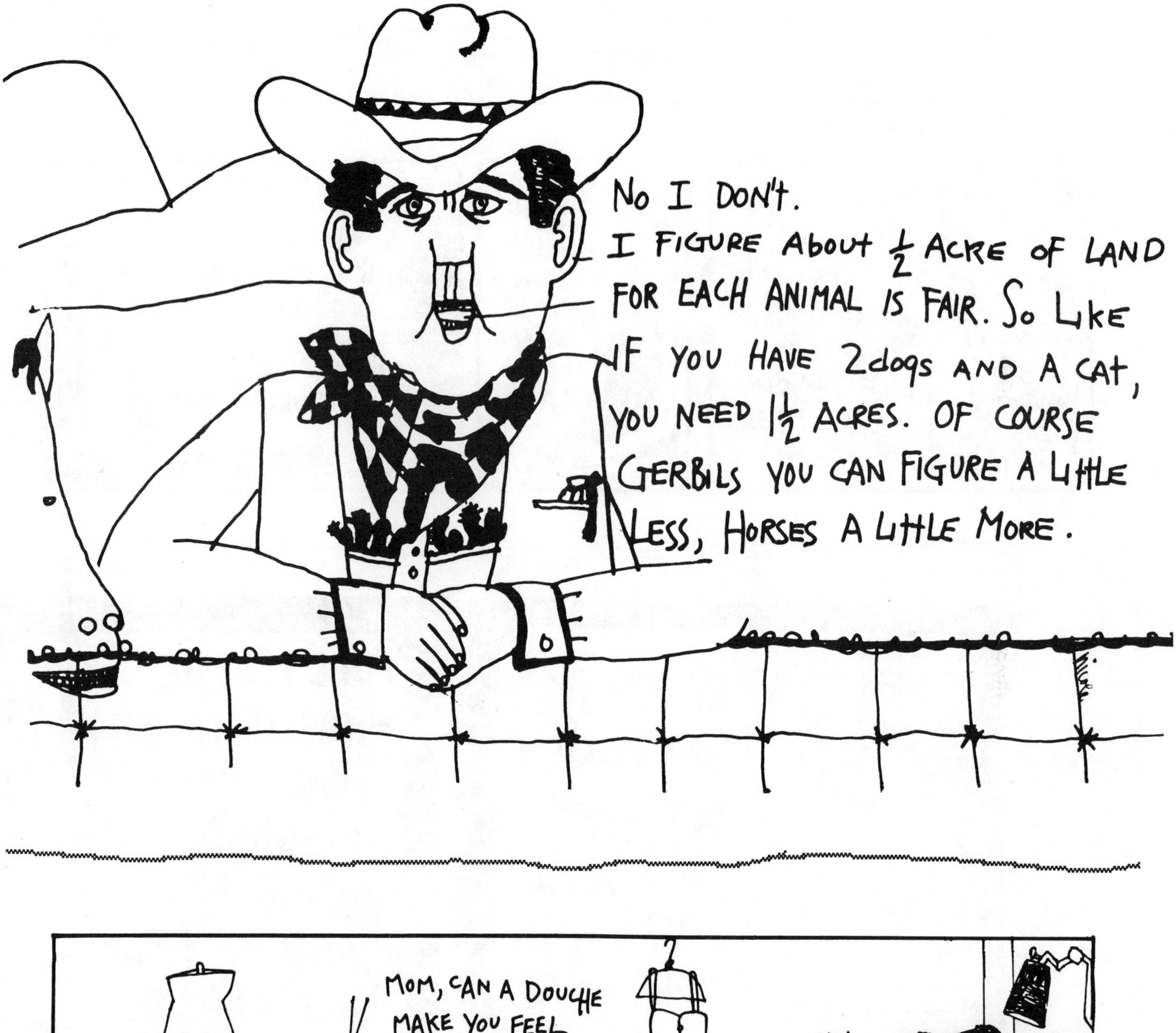

NO I DON'T.
I FIGURE ABOUT 1/2 ACRE OF LAND FOR EACH ANIMAL IS FAIR. SO LIKE IF YOU HAVE 2 dogs AND A CAT, YOU NEED 1 1/2 ACRES. OF COURSE GERBILS YOU CAN FIGURE A LITTLE LESS, HORSES A LITTLE MORE.

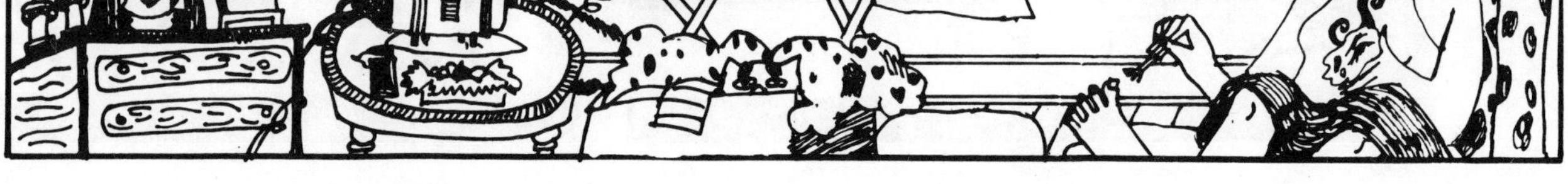

MOM, CAN A DOUCHE MAKE YOU FEEL MORE CONFIDENT?
NOT LIKE A GOOD STOCK-PORTFOLIO.

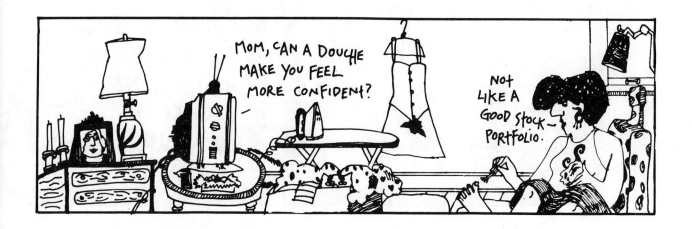

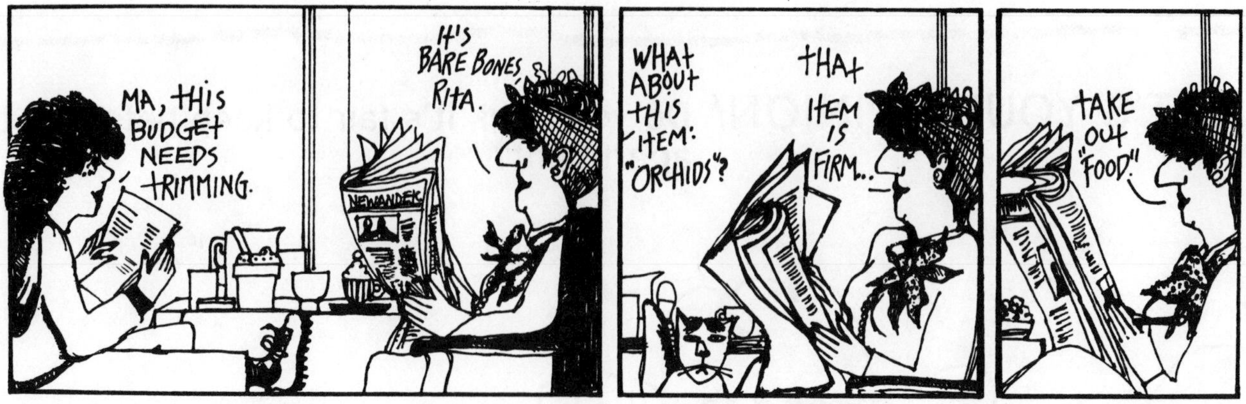
MA, THIS BUDGET NEEDS TRIMMING.
IT'S BARE BONES, RITA.
WHAT ABOUT THIS ITEM: "ORCHIDS"?
THAT ITEM IS FIRM...
TAKE OUT "FOOD."

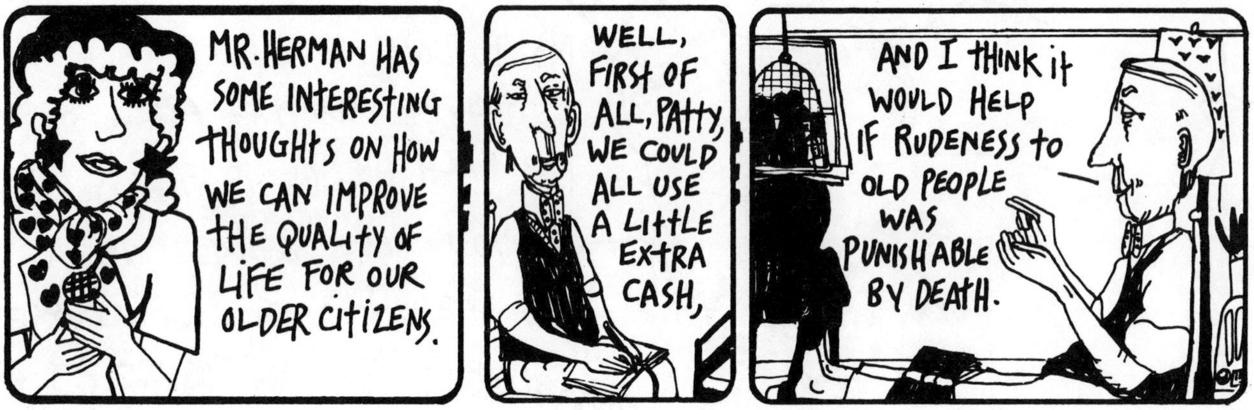
MR. HERMAN HAS SOME INTERESTING THOUGHTS ON HOW WE CAN IMPROVE THE QUALITY OF LIFE FOR OUR OLDER CITIZENS.
WELL, FIRST OF ALL, PATTY, WE COULD ALL USE A LITTLE EXTRA CASH,
AND I THINK IT WOULD HELP IF RUDENESS TO OLD PEOPLE WAS PUNISHABLE BY DEATH.

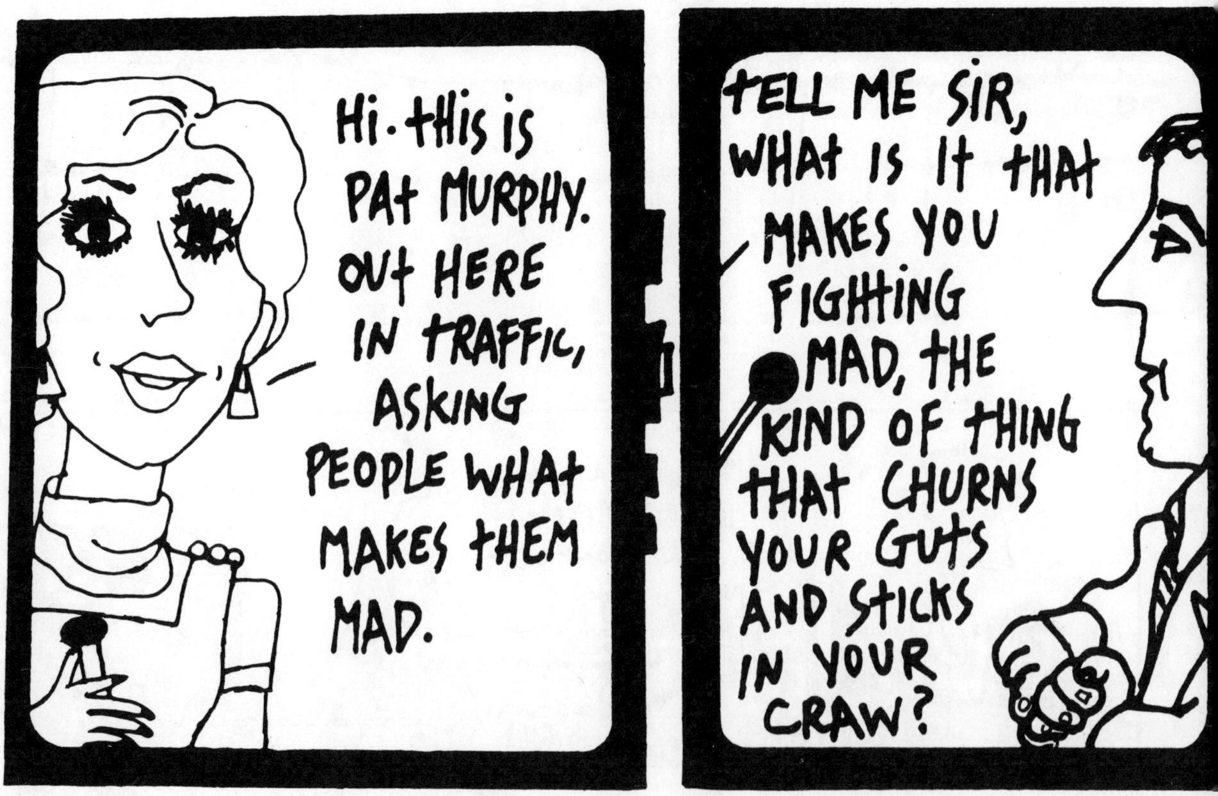
HI. THIS IS PAT MURPHY. OUT HERE IN TRAFFIC, ASKING PEOPLE WHAT MAKES THEM MAD.
TELL ME SIR, WHAT IS IT THAT MAKES YOU FIGHTING MAD, THE KIND OF THING THAT CHURNS YOUR GUTS AND STICKS IN YOUR CRAW?

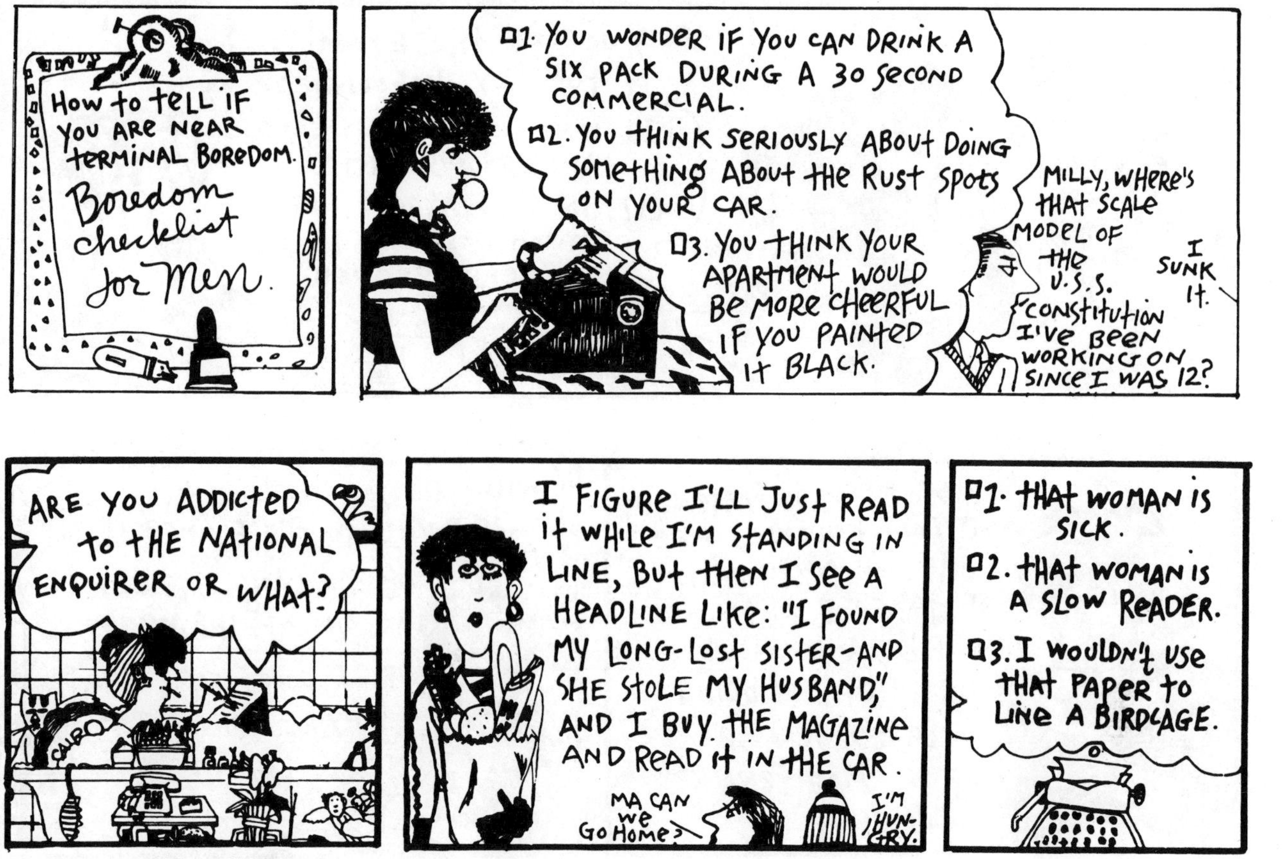
How to tell if you are near terminal Boredom.
Boredom checklist for Men.
□1. You wonder if you can drink a six pack during a 30 second commercial.
□2. You think seriously about doing something about the rust spots on your car.
□3. You think your apartment would be more cheerful if you painted it black.
Milly, where's that scale model of the U.S.S. Constitution I've been working on since I was 12?
I sunk it.
Are you addicted to the National Enquirer or what?
I figure I'll just read it while I'm standing in line, but then I see a headline like: "I found my long-lost sister-and she stole my husband," and I buy the magazine and read it in the car.
Ma can we go home?
I'm hungry.
□1. That woman is sick.
□2. That woman is a slow reader.
□3. I wouldn't use that paper to line a birdcage.

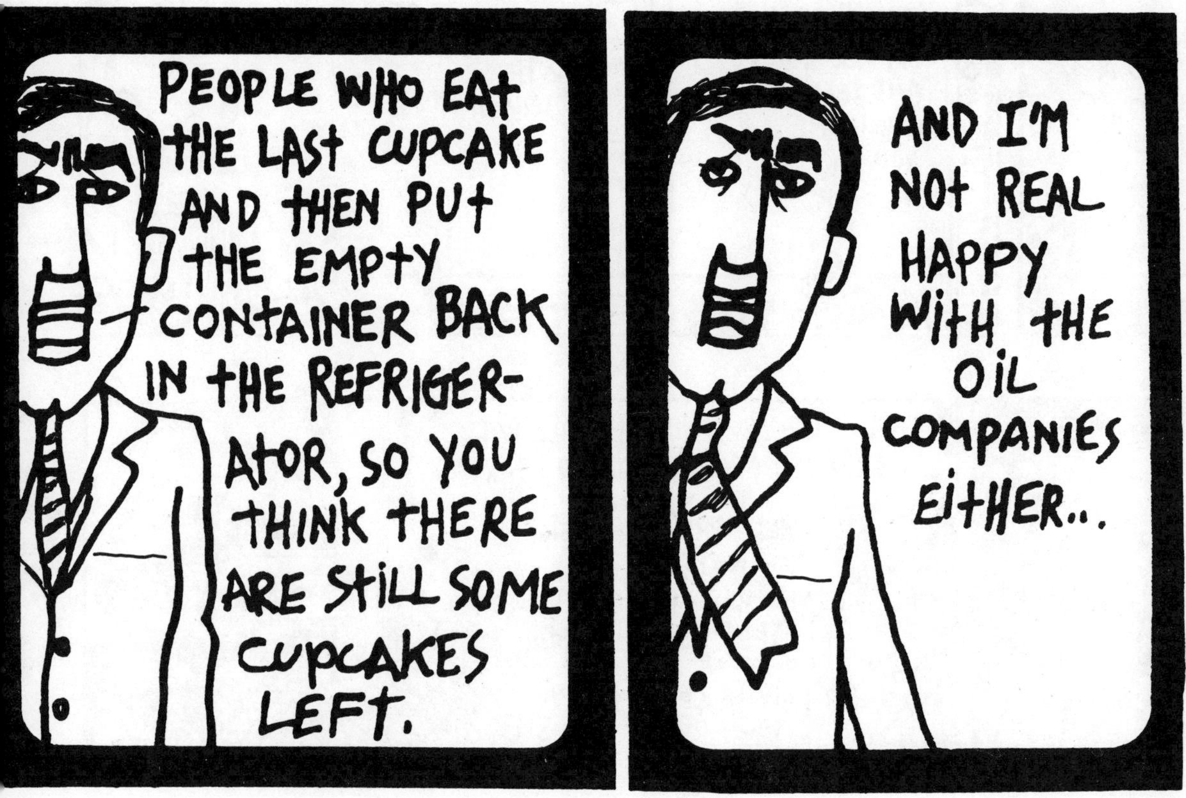
People who eat the last cupcake and then put the empty container back in the refriger-ator, so you think there are still some cupcakes left.
And I'm not real happy with the oil companies either...

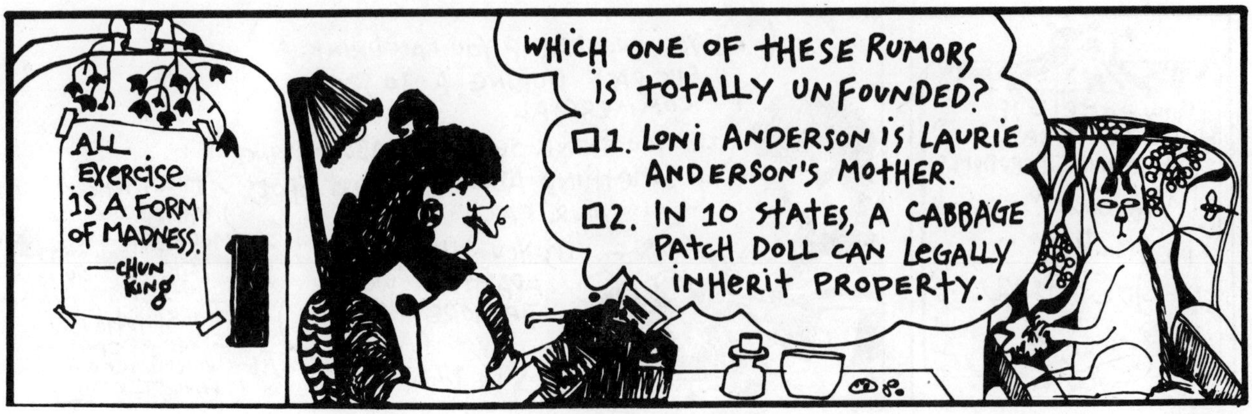
ALL EXERCISE IS A FORM OF MADNESS. —CHUN KING
WHICH ONE OF THESE RUMORS IS TOTALLY UNFOUNDED?
☐1. LONI ANDERSON IS LAURIE ANDERSON'S MOTHER.
☐2. IN 10 STATES, A CABBAGE PATCH DOLL CAN LEGALLY INHERIT PROPERTY.

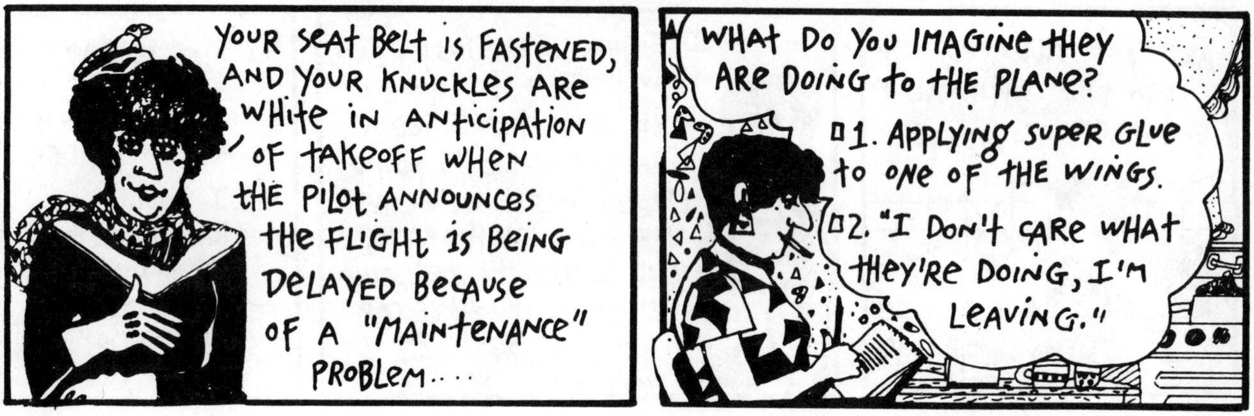
YOUR SEAT BELT IS FASTENED, AND YOUR KNUCKLES ARE WHITE IN ANTICIPATION OF TAKEOFF WHEN THE PILOT ANNOUNCES THE FLIGHT IS BEING DELAYED BECAUSE OF A "MAINTENANCE" PROBLEM....
WHAT DO YOU IMAGINE THEY ARE DOING TO THE PLANE?
☐1. APPLYING SUPER GLUE TO ONE OF THE WINGS.
☐2. "I DON'T CARE WHAT THEY'RE DOING, I'M LEAVING."

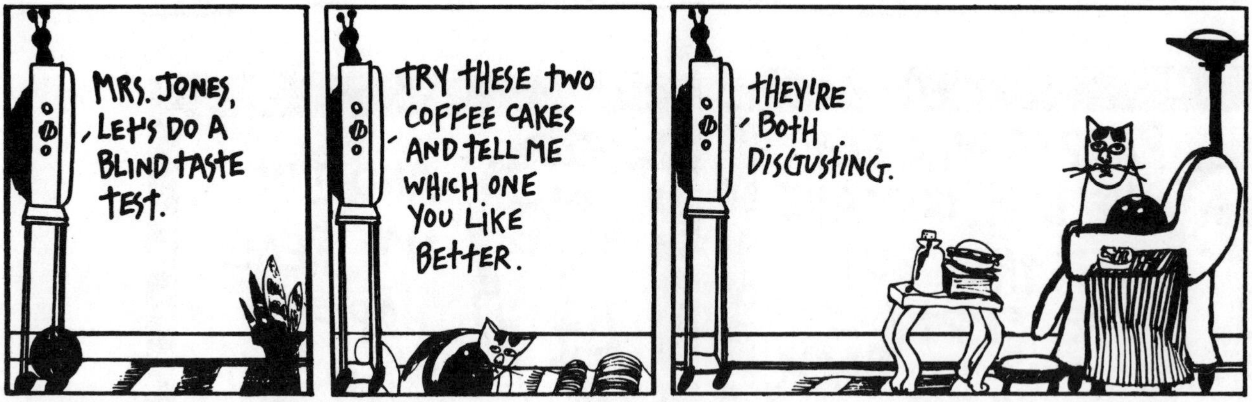
MRS. JONES, LET'S DO A BLIND TASTE TEST.
TRY THESE TWO COFFEE CAKES AND TELL ME WHICH ONE YOU LIKE BETTER.
THEY'RE BOTH DISGUSTING.

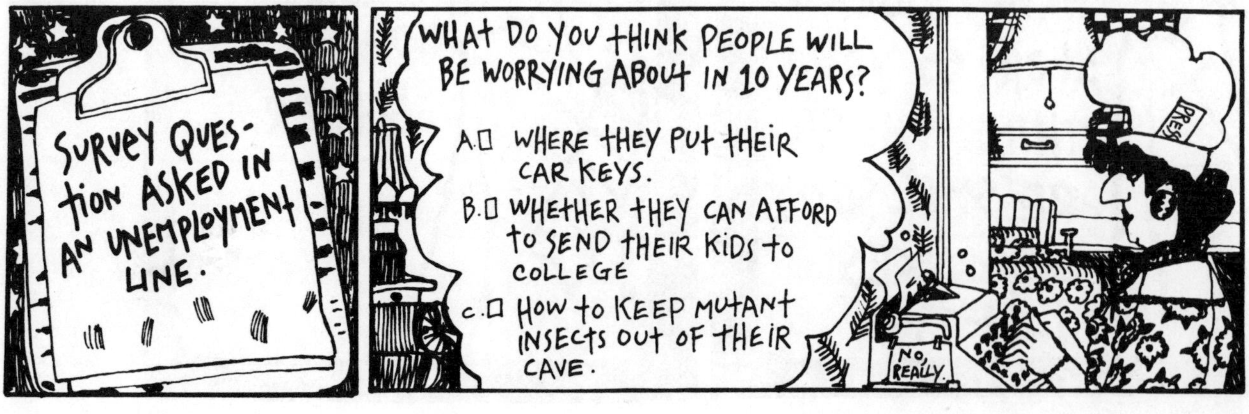
SURVEY QUESTION ASKED IN AN UNEMPLOYMENT LINE.
WHAT DO YOU THINK PEOPLE WILL BE WORRYING ABOUT IN 10 YEARS?
A.☐ WHERE THEY PUT THEIR CAR KEYS.
B.☐ WHETHER THEY CAN AFFORD TO SEND THEIR KIDS TO COLLEGE
C.☐ HOW TO KEEP MUTANT INSECTS OUT OF THEIR CAVE.
NO, REALLY.

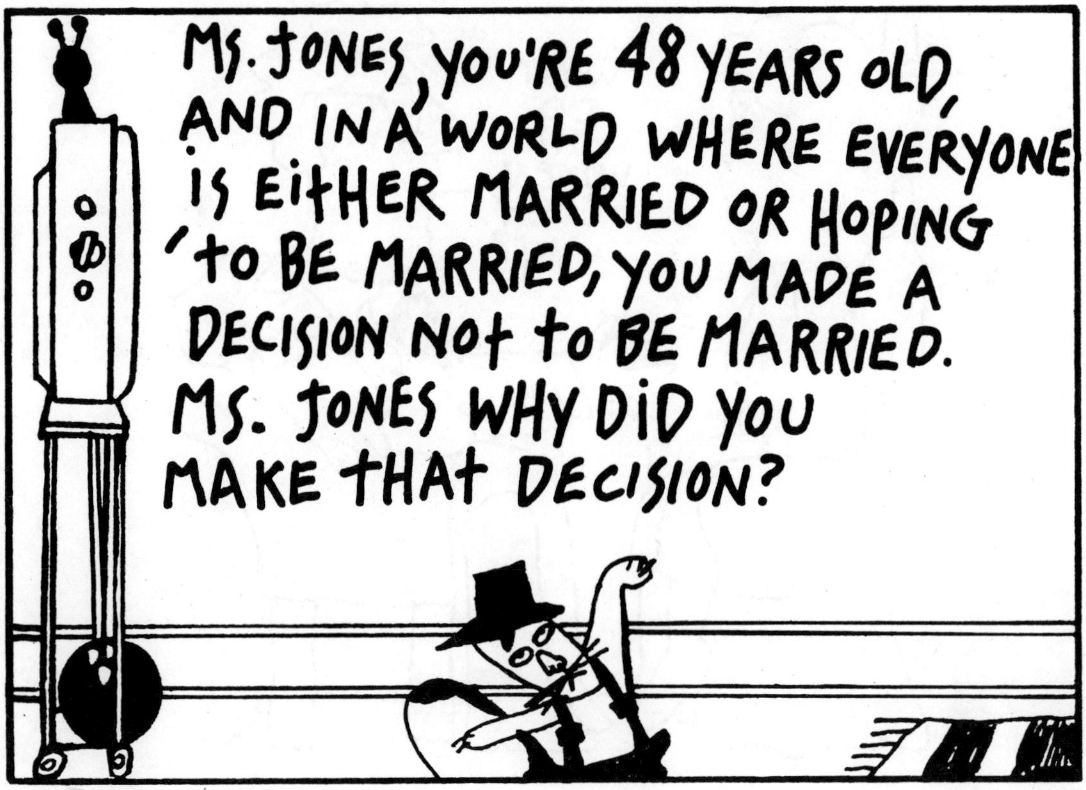
MS. JONES, YOU'RE 48 YEARS OLD, AND IN A WORLD WHERE EVERYONE IS EITHER MARRIED OR HOPING TO BE MARRIED, YOU MADE A DECISION NOT TO BE MARRIED. MS. JONES WHY DID YOU MAKE THAT DECISION?

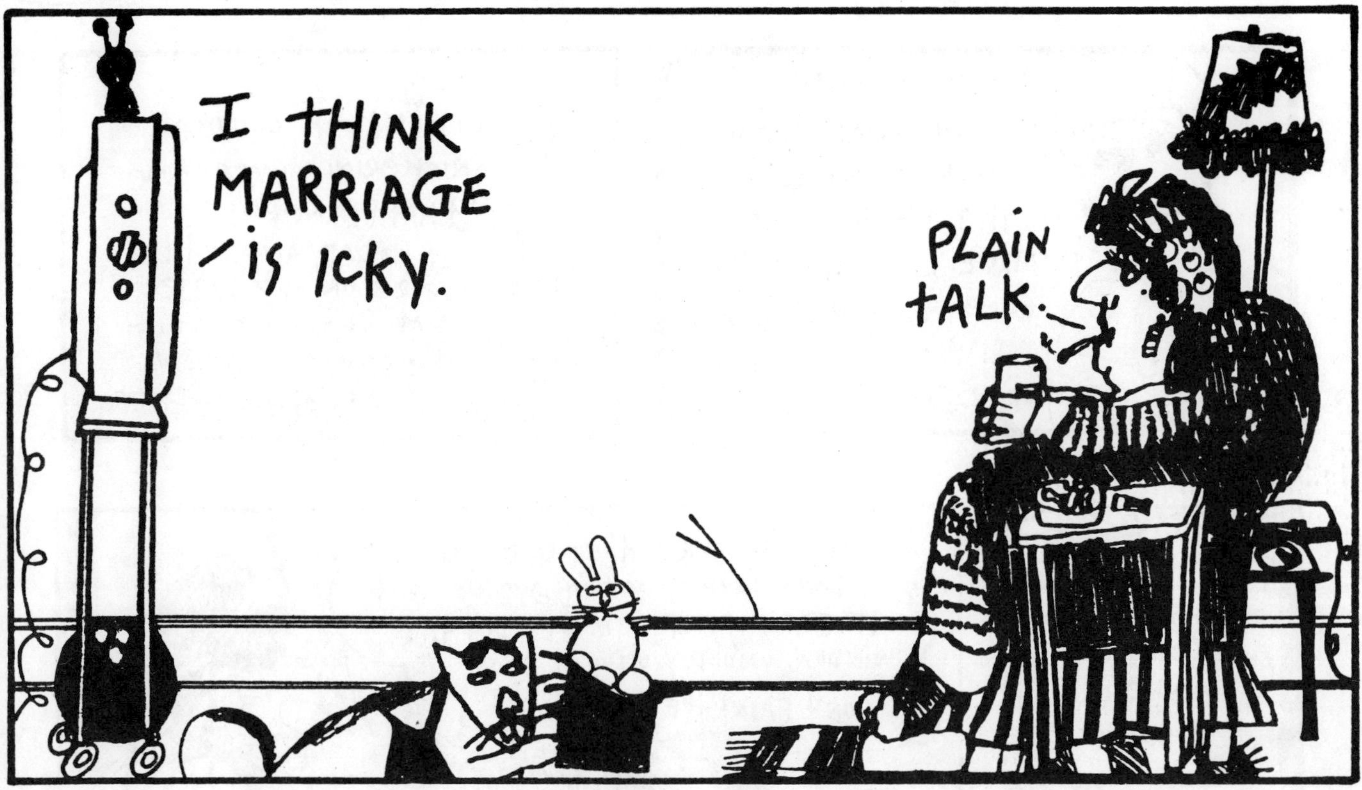
I THINK MARRIAGE IS ICKY.
PLAIN TALK.

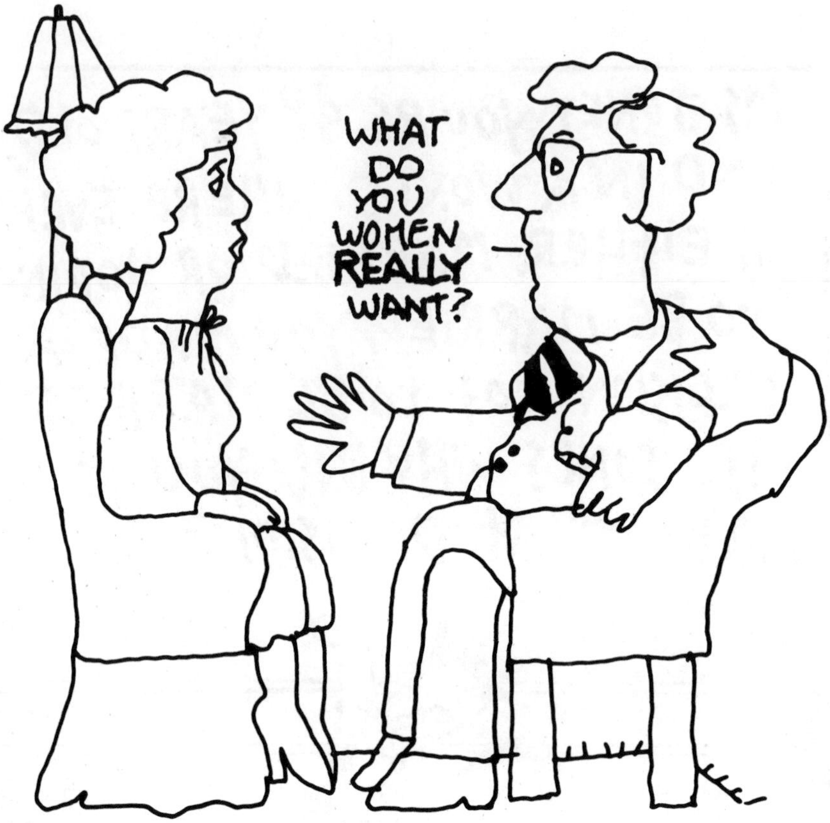
WHAT DO YOU WOMEN REALLY WANT?

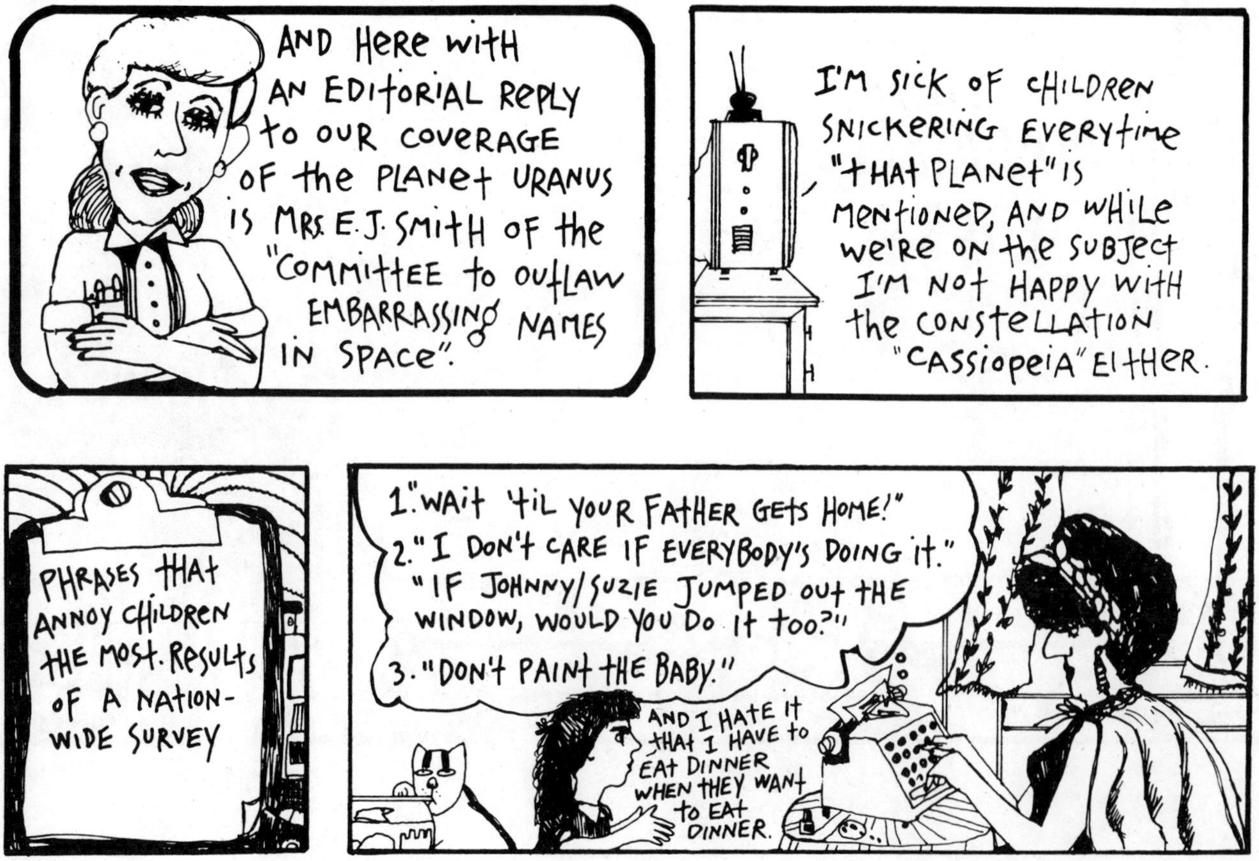
AND Here with AN EDitoRIAL RePLY to OUR COVERAGE OF the PLANet URANUS IS MRS. E.J. SMitH OF the "COMMittEE to OUtLAW EMBARRASSING NAMES IN SPACE".
I'M SICK OF CHILDREN SNICKERING EVERYtime "tHAT PLANet" IS MENtIONED, AND WHILE WE'RE ON the SUBJECt I'M NOt HAPPY WITH the CONStELLATION "CASSIOPEIA" EItHER.
PHRASES tHAt ANNOY CHILDREN tHE MOSt. RESULtS OF A NATION-WIDE SURVEY
1. "WAIt 'tIL YOUR FAtHER GEtS HOME!"
2. "I DON'T CARE IF EVERYBODY'S DOING It." "IF JOHNNY/SUZIE JUMPED OUt tHE WINDOW, WOULD YOU DO It too?"
3. "DON'T PAINt tHE BABY."
AND I HATE It tHAt I HAVE to EAt DINNER WHEN tHEY WANt to EAt DINNER.

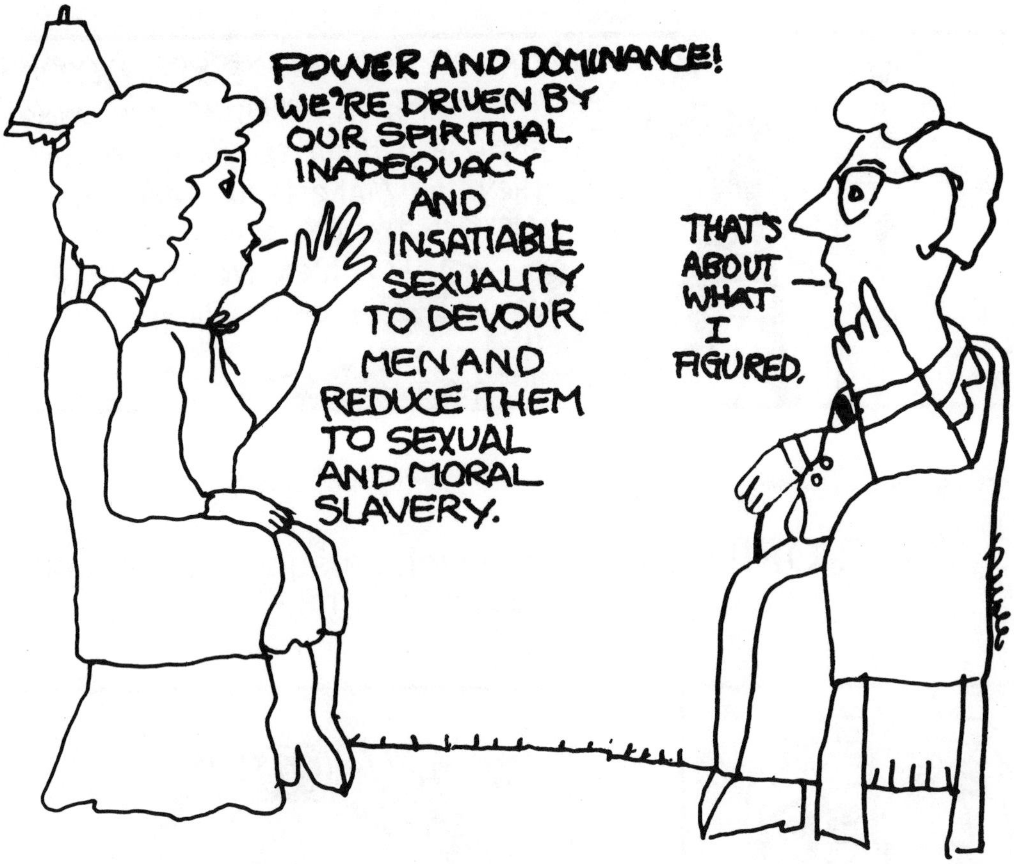
POWER AND DOMINANCE! WE'RE DRIVEN BY OUR SPIRITUAL INADEQUACY AND INSATIABLE SEXUALITY TO DEVOUR MEN AND REDUCE THEM TO SEXUAL AND MORAL SLAVERY.
THAT'S ABOUT WHAT I FIGURED.

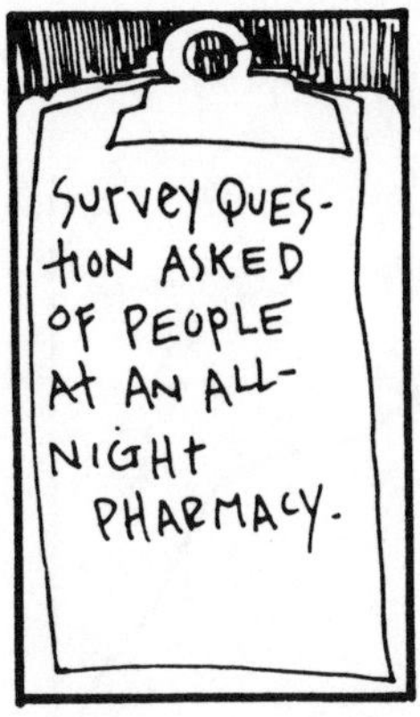
Survey Question ASKED of PEOPLE At AN ALL-NIGHT PHARMACY.

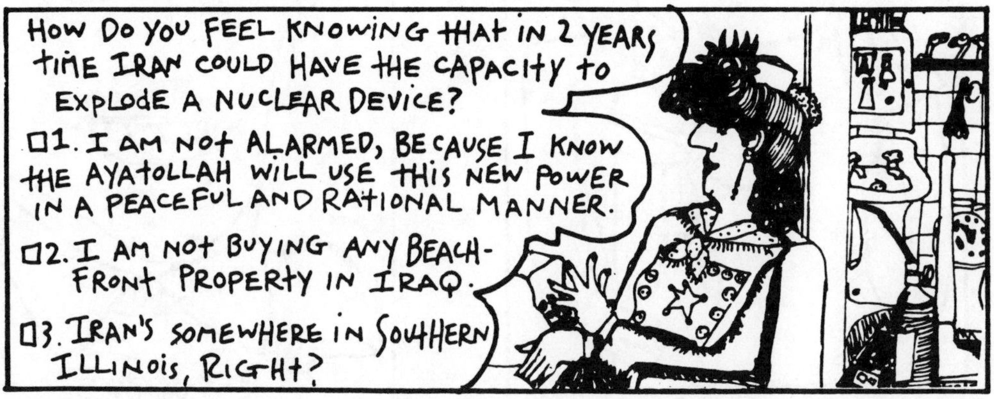
HOW DO YOU FEEL KNOWING that IN 2 YEARS time IRAN COULD HAVE the CAPACITY to EXPLODE A NUCLEAR DEVICE?
☐1. I AM NOT ALARMED, BECAUSE I KNOW the AYATOLLAH WILL USE this NEW POWER IN A PEACEFUL AND RATIONAL MANNER.
☐2. I AM NOT BUYING ANY BEACH-FRONT PROPERTY IN IRAQ.
☐3. IRAN'S SOMEWHERE IN SOUTHERN ILLINOIS, RIGHT?

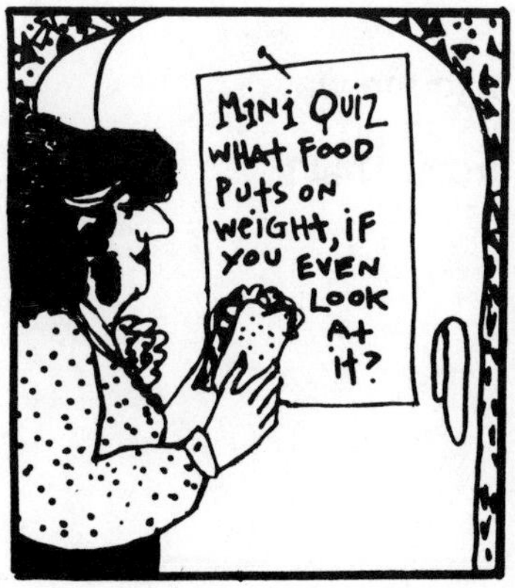
Mini Quiz
WHAT FOOD PUTS ON WEIGHT, IF YOU EVEN LOOK AT it?

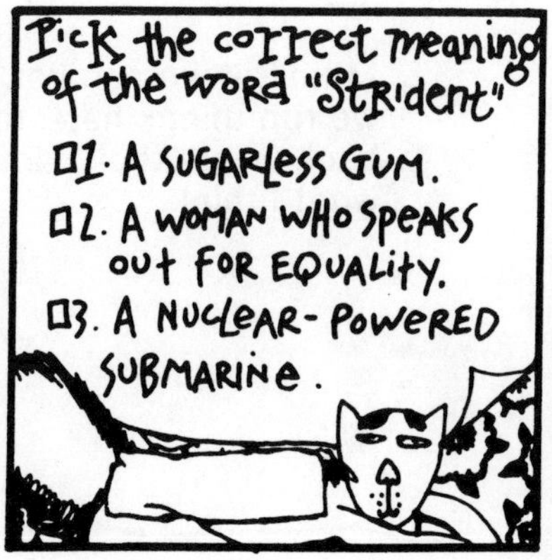
Pick the correct meaning of the word "Strident"
☐1. A SUGARLESS GUM.
☐2. A WOMAN WHO SPEAKS OUT FOR EQUALITY.
☐3. A NUCLEAR-POWERED SUBMARINE.

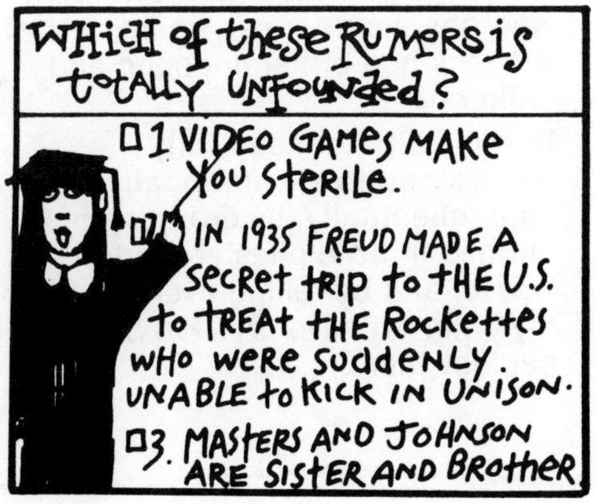
WHICH of these RUMORS is totally Unfounded?
☐1 VIDEO GAMES MAKE YOU STERILE.
☐2 IN 1935 FREUD MADE A SECRET TRIP to THE U.S. to TREAT THE ROCKETTES WHO WERE SUDDENLY UNABLE to KICK IN UNISON.
☐3. MASTERS AND JOHNSON ARE SISTER AND BROTHER

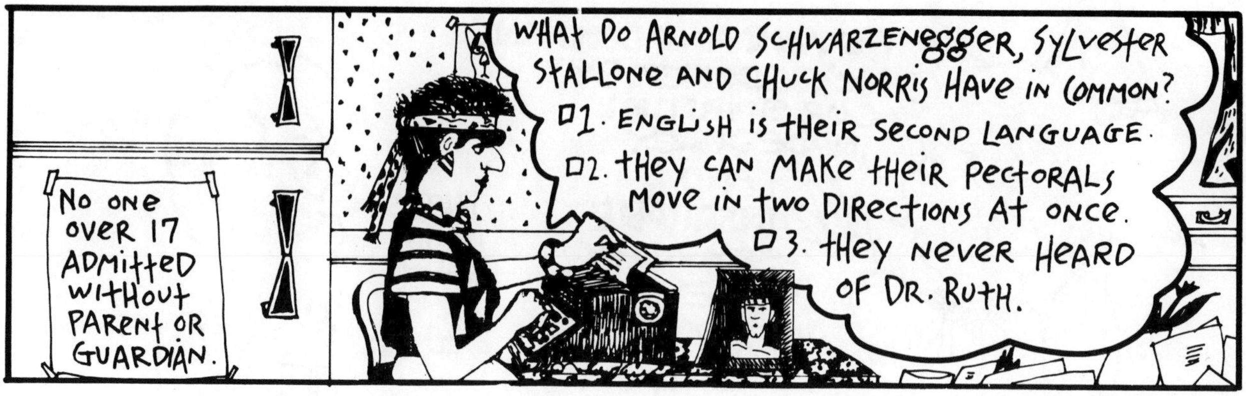
No one over 17 ADMITTED WITHOUT PARENT OR GUARDIAN.
WHAT DO ARNOLD SCHWARZENEGGER, SYLVESTER STALLONE AND CHUCK NORRIS HAVE IN COMMON?
□1. ENGLISH IS THEIR SECOND LANGUAGE.
□2. THEY CAN MAKE THEIR PECTORALS MOVE IN TWO DIRECTIONS AT ONCE.
□3. THEY NEVER HEARD OF DR. RUTH.

WHAT'S YOUR OPINION/ Can a woman successfully combine career and family?

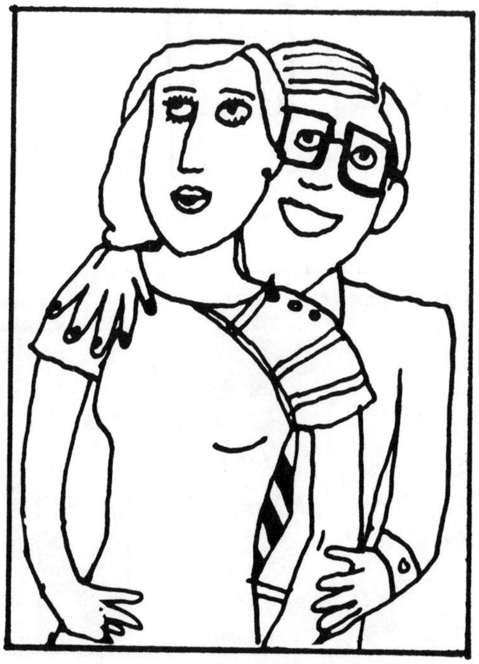

Both Bob and I feel that a woman who has a career can do so only at the expense of her husband and children.

Bob is helping me to fully understand this, emotionally as well as intellectually, by dropping his clothes in little piles around the house, and by telling everyone that my children have dry skin because I neglect them.

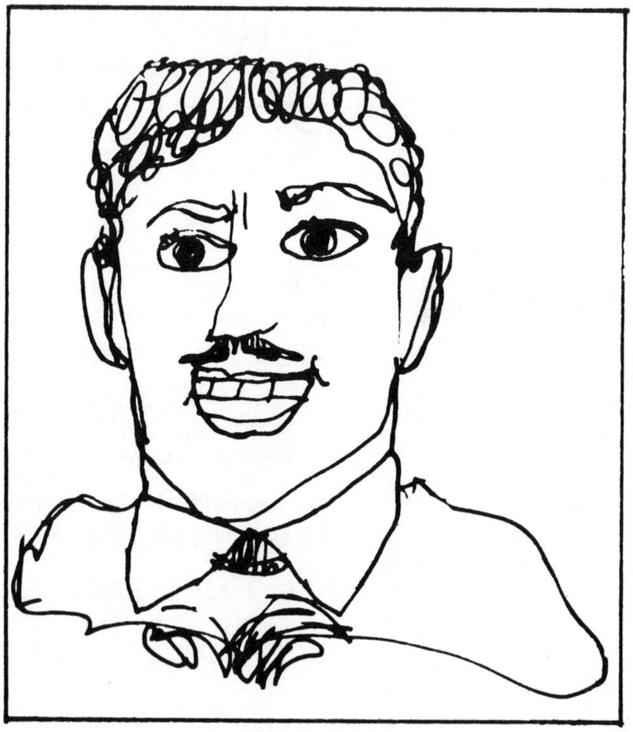

I think, if women don't like the way we run things here, they can go back where they came from. That's what I think.

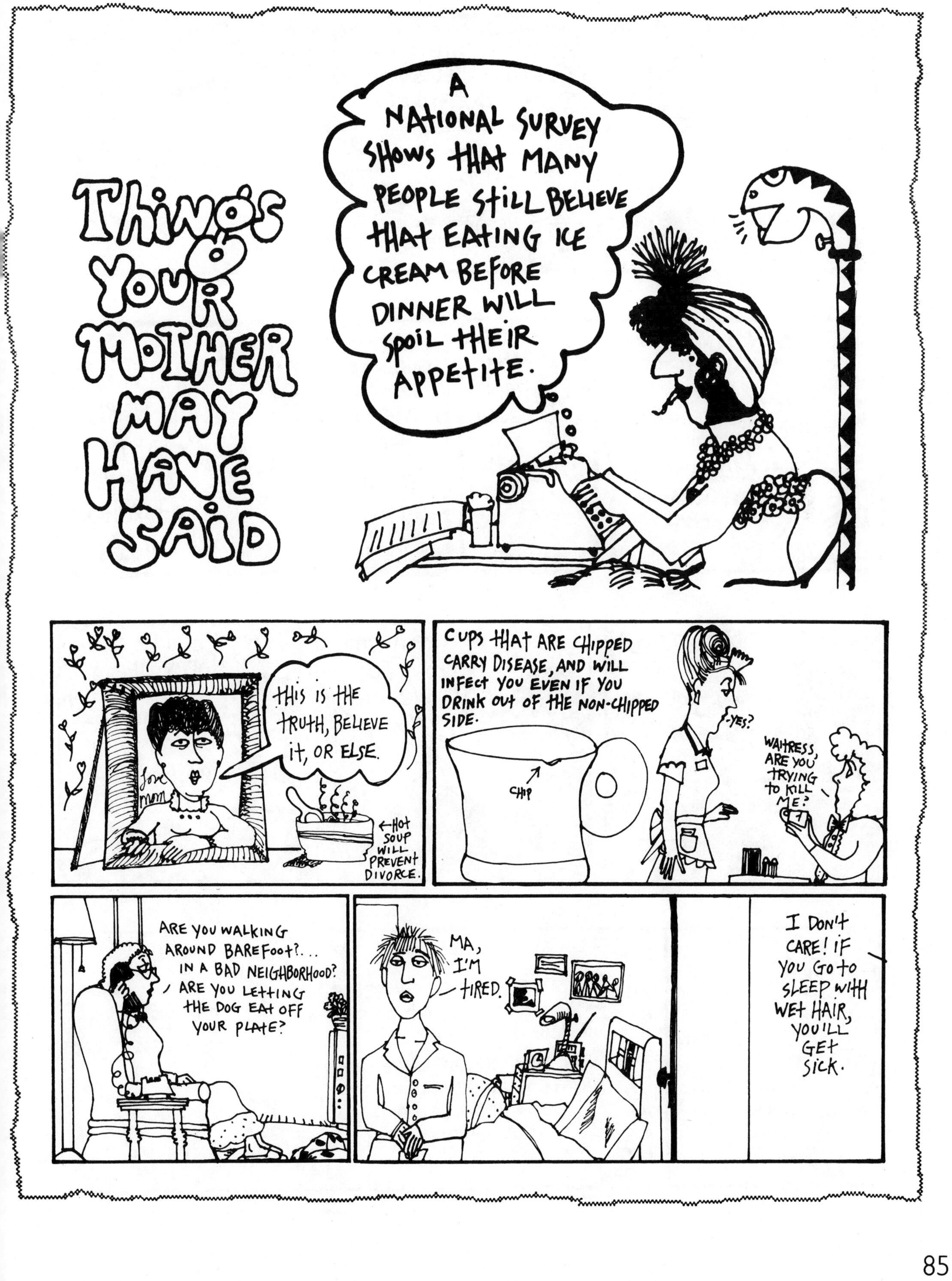
THINGS YOUR MOTHER MAY HAVE SAID
A NATIONAL SURVEY SHOWS THAT MANY PEOPLE STILL BELIEVE THAT EATING ICE CREAM BEFORE DINNER WILL SPOIL THEIR APPETITE.
love mom
THIS IS THE TRUTH, BELIEVE IT, OR ELSE.
←HOT SOUP WILL PREVENT DIVORCE.
CUPS THAT ARE CHIPPED CARRY DISEASE, AND WILL INFECT YOU EVEN IF YOU DRINK OUT OF THE NON-CHIPPED SIDE.
CHIP
-YES?
WAITRESS, ARE YOU TRYING TO KILL ME?
ARE YOU WALKING AROUND BAREFOOT?... IN A BAD NEIGHBORHOOD? ARE YOU LETTING THE DOG EAT OFF YOUR PLATE?
MA, I'M TIRED.
I DON'T CARE! IF YOU GO TO SLEEP WITH WET HAIR, YOU'LL GET SICK.

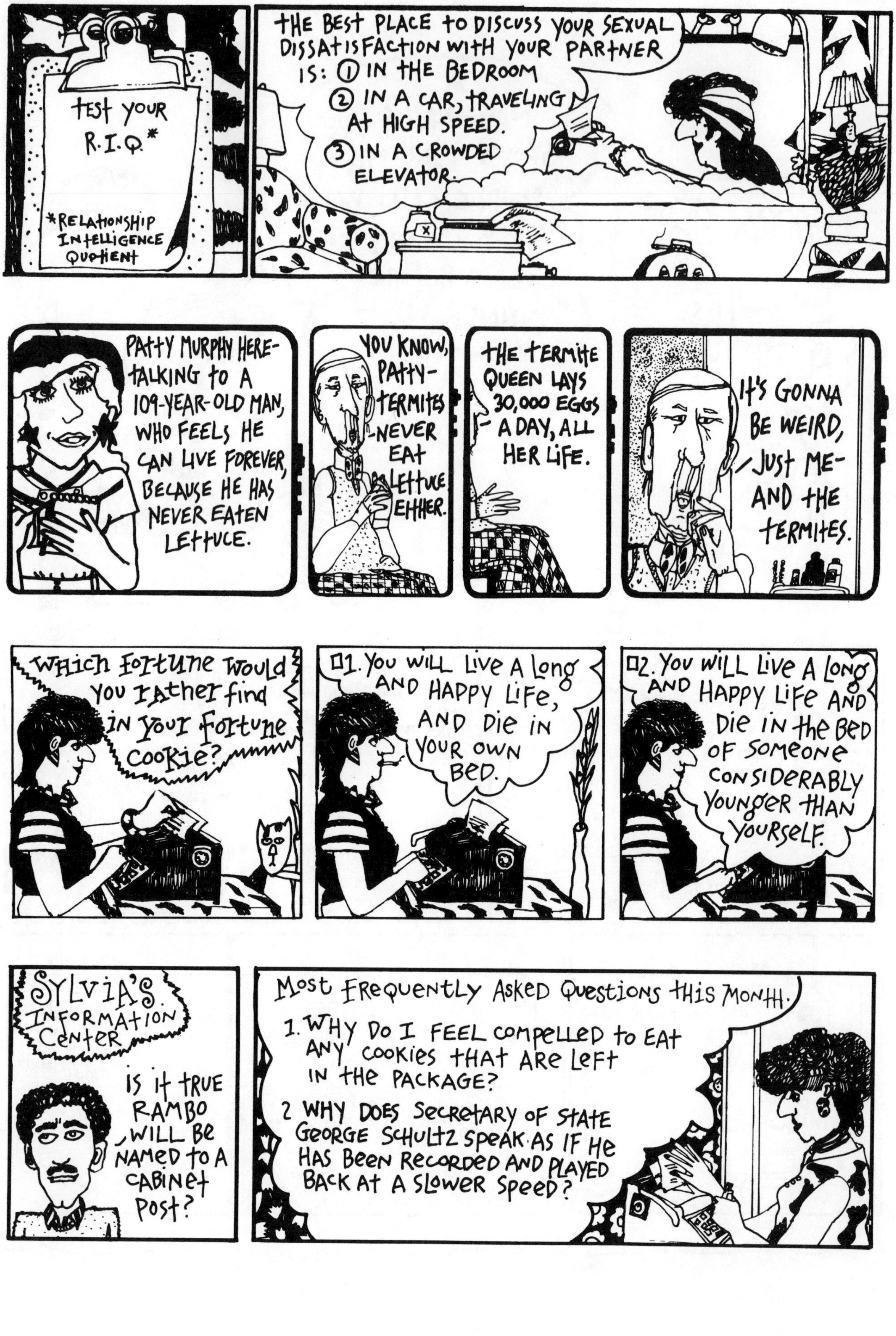
test your R.I.Q.*
*Relationship Intelligence Quotient
THE BEST PLACE to DISCUSS YOUR SEXUAL DISSATISFACTION WITH YOUR PARTNER IS: ① IN THE BEDROOM ② IN A CAR, TRAVELING AT HIGH SPEED. ③ IN A CROWDED ELEVATOR.
PATTY MURPHY HERE- TALKING to A 109-YEAR-OLD MAN, WHO FEELS HE CAN LIVE FOREVER, BECAUSE HE HAS NEVER EATEN LETTUCE.
YOU KNOW, PATTY- TERMITES -NEVER EAT LETTUCE EITHER.
THE TERMITE QUEEN LAYS 30,000 EGGS A DAY, ALL HER LIFE.
IT'S GONNA BE WEIRD, JUST ME- AND THE TERMITES.
Which Fortune would you rather find in your Fortune cookie?
□1. You will live a long and happy life, and die in your own bed.
□2. You will live a long and happy life and die in the bed of someone considerably younger than yourself.
Sylvia's Information Center
Is it true Rambo will be named to a cabinet post?
Most Frequently Asked Questions this Month.
1. Why do I feel compelled to eat any cookies that are left in the package?
2 Why does Secretary of State George Schultz speak as if he has been recorded and played back at a slower speed?

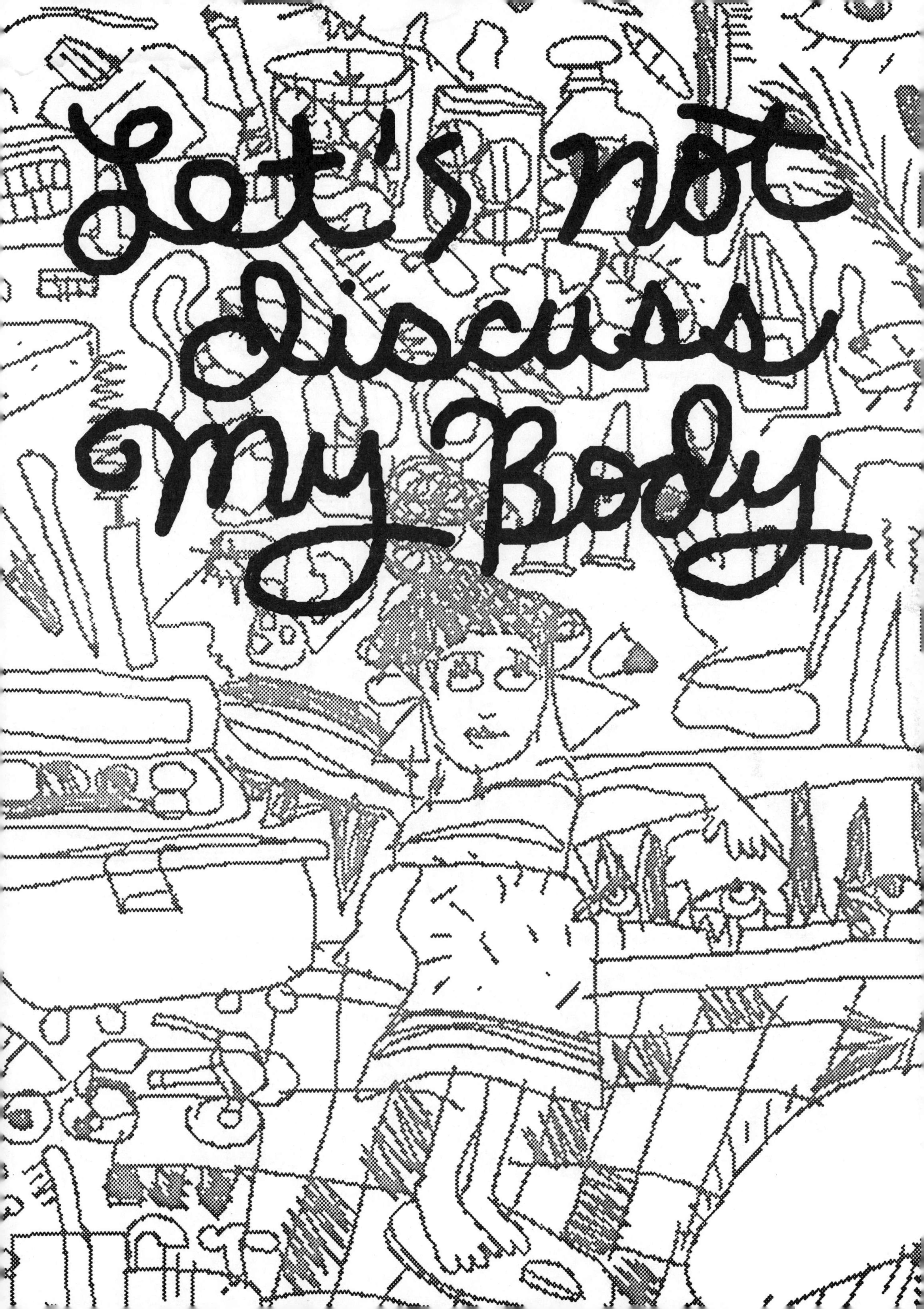
Let's not
discuss
my Body

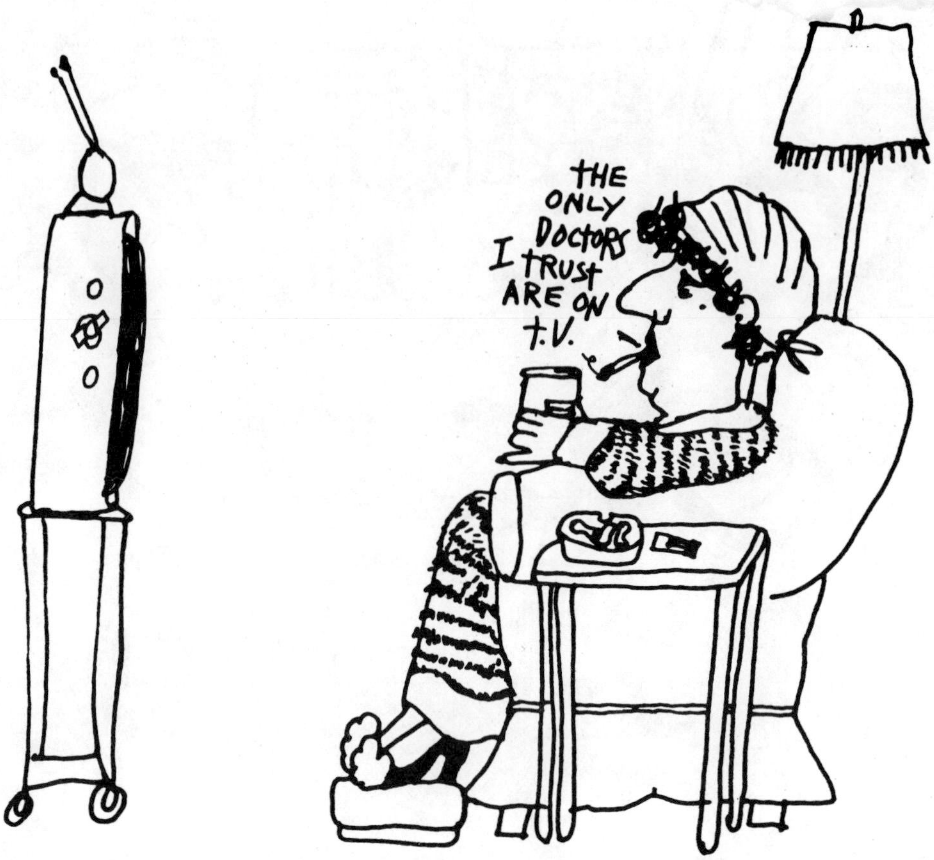
THE ONLY DOCTORS I TRUST ARE ON T.V.

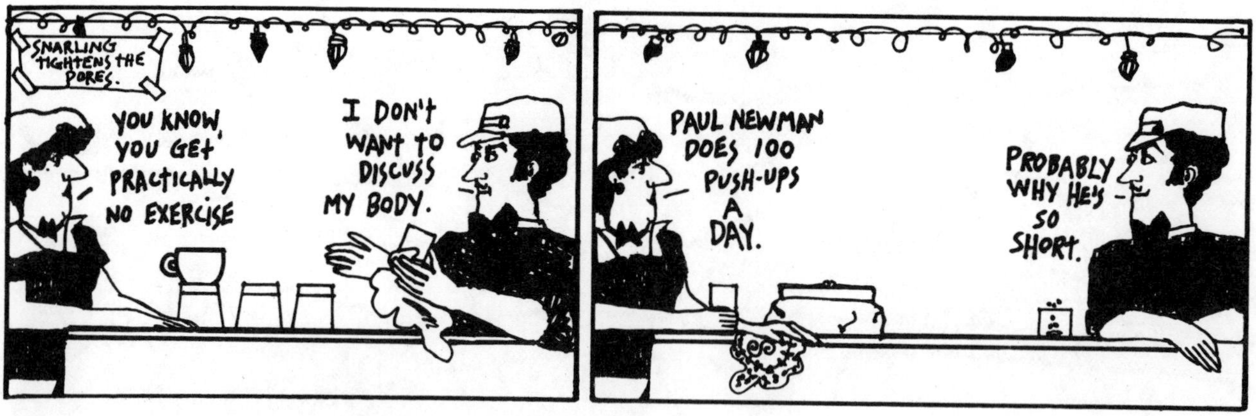
SNARLING TIGHTENS THE PORES.
YOU KNOW, YOU GET PRACTICALLY NO EXERCISE
I DON'T WANT TO DISCUSS MY BODY.
PAUL NEWMAN DOES 100 PUSH-UPS A DAY.
PROBABLY WHY HE'S SO SHORT.

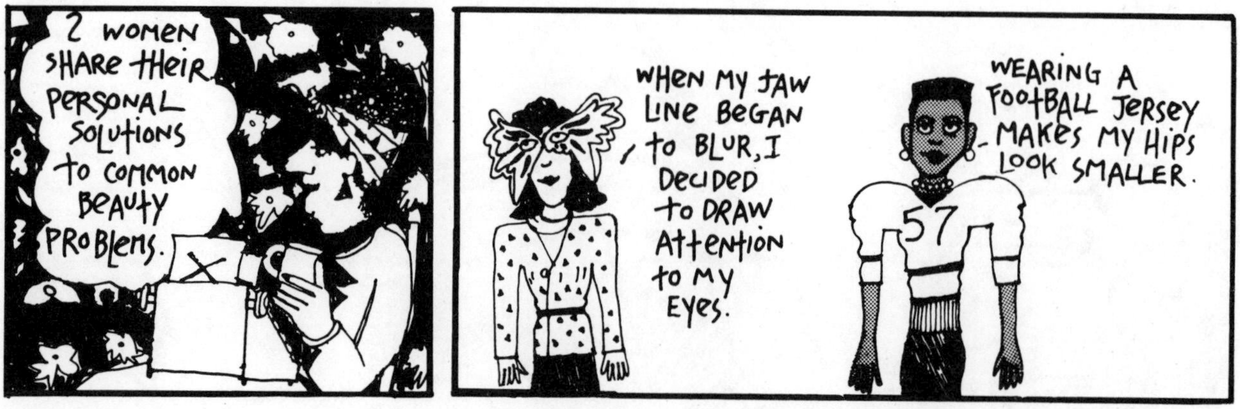
2 women share their personal solutions to common beauty problems.
WHEN MY JAW LINE BEGAN TO BLUR, I DECIDED TO DRAW ATTENTION TO MY EYES.
WEARING A FOOTBALL JERSEY MAKES MY HIPS LOOK SMALLER.
57

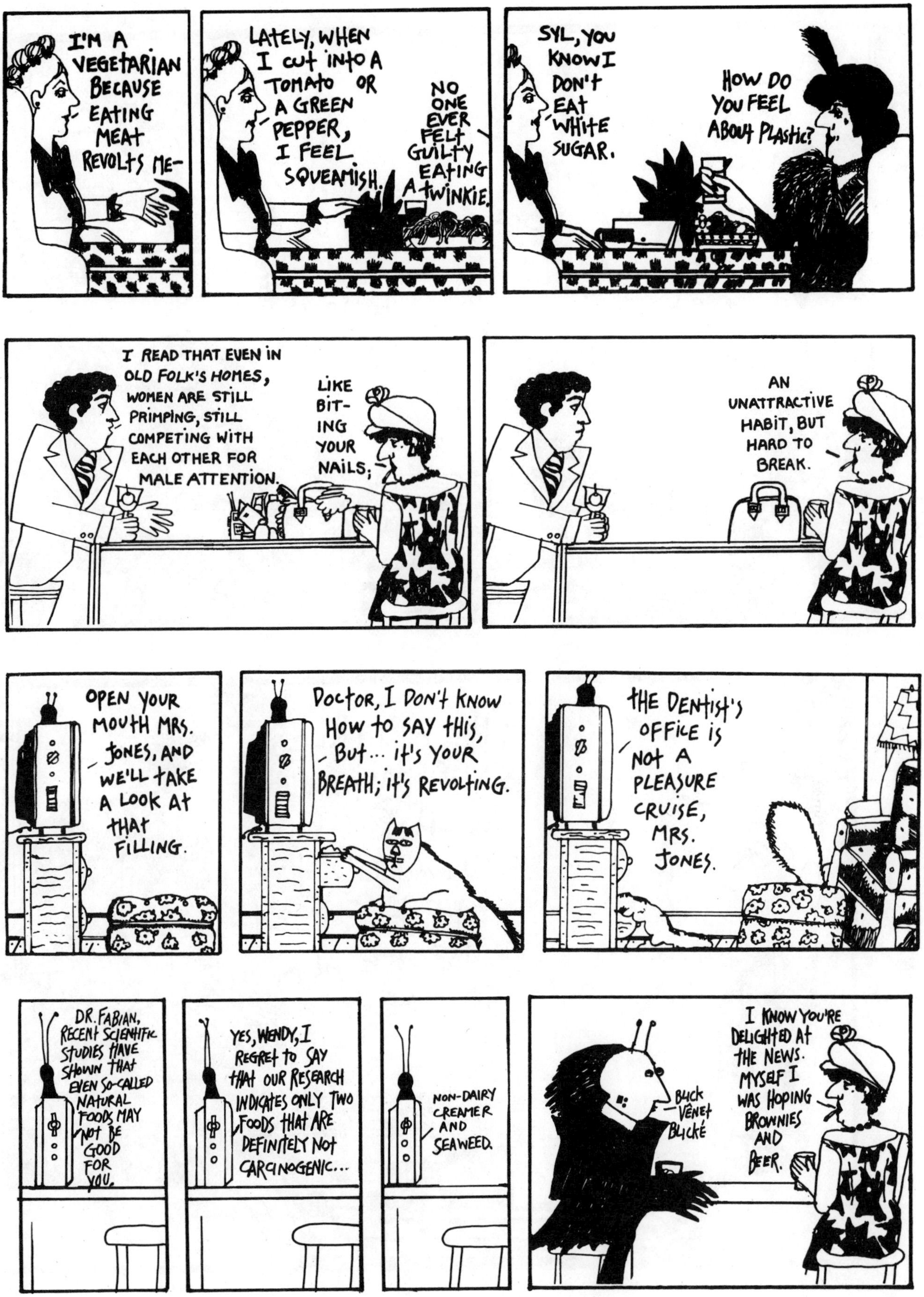
I'M A VEGETARIAN BECAUSE EATING MEAT REVOLTS ME-
LATELY, WHEN I cut into A TOMATO OR A GREEN PEPPER, I FEEL SQUEAMISH.
NO ONE EVER FELT GUILTY EATING A TWINKIE.
SYL, YOU KNOW I DON'T EAT WHITE SUGAR.
HOW DO YOU FEEL ABOUT PLASTIC?
I READ THAT EVEN IN OLD FOLK'S HOMES, WOMEN ARE STILL PRIMPING, STILL COMPETING WITH EACH OTHER FOR MALE ATTENTION.
LIKE BIT-ING YOUR NAILS;
AN UNATTRACTIVE HABIT, BUT HARD TO BREAK.
OPEN YOUR MOUTH MRS. JONES, AND WE'LL TAKE A LOOK AT THAT FILLING.
Doctor, I Don't know How to SAY this, But... it's YOUR BREATH; it's Revolting.
THE DENTIST'S OFFICE is NOT A PLEASURE CRUISE, MRS. JONES.
DR. FABIAN, RECENT SCIENTIFIC STUDIES HAVE SHOWN THAT EVEN SO-CALLED NATURAL FOODS MAY NOT BE GOOD FOR YOU.
YES, WENDY, I REGRET TO SAY THAT OUR RESEARCH INDICATES ONLY TWO FOODS THAT ARE DEFINITELY NOT CARCINOGENIC...
NON-DAIRY CREAMER AND SEAWEED.
BUCK VÊNET BUCKÉ
I KNOW YOU'RE DELIGHTED AT THE NEWS. MYSELF I WAS HOPING BROWNIES AND BEER.

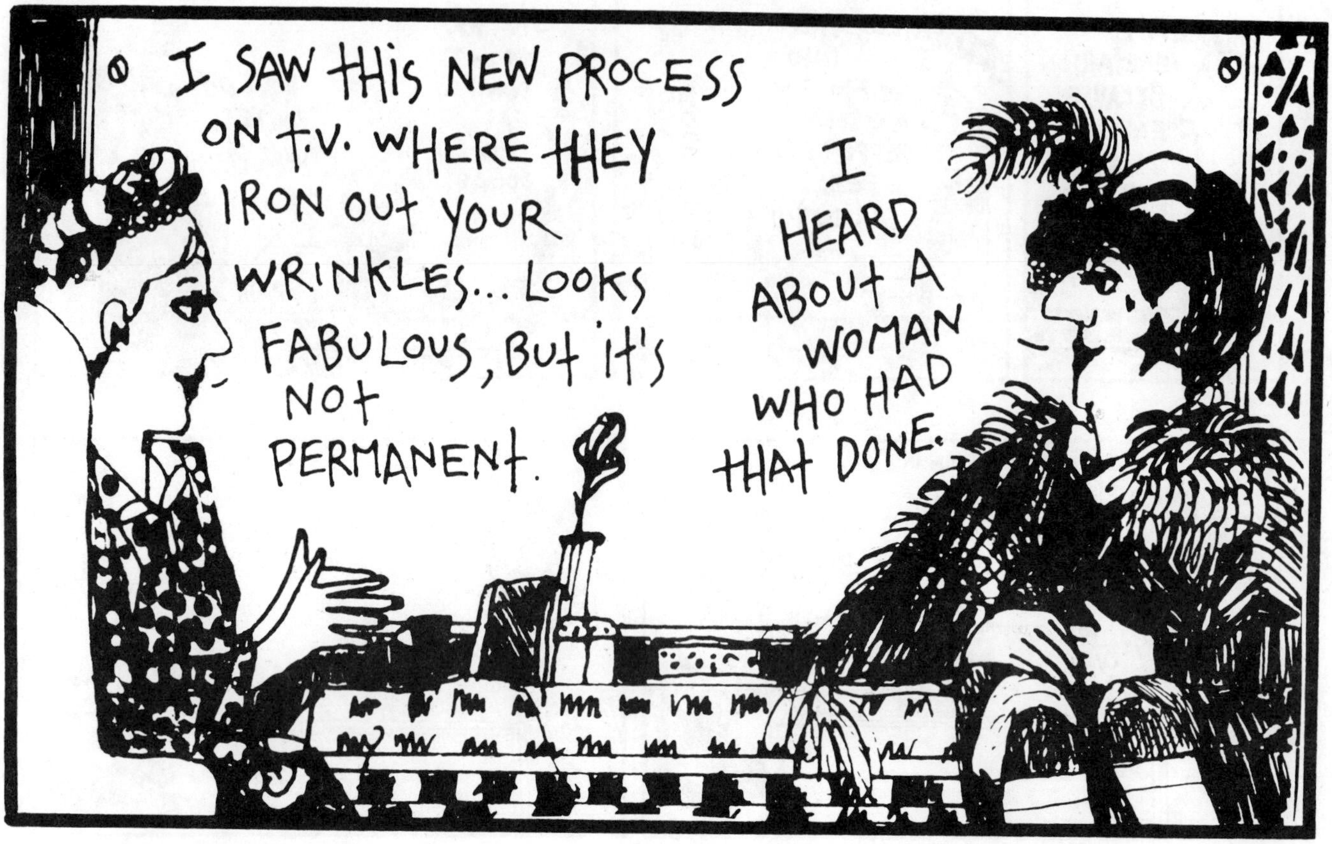
I SAW THIS NEW PROCESS ON T.V. WHERE THEY IRON OUT YOUR WRINKLES... LOOKS FABULOUS, BUT IT'S NOT PERMANENT.
I HEARD ABOUT A WOMAN WHO HAD THAT DONE.

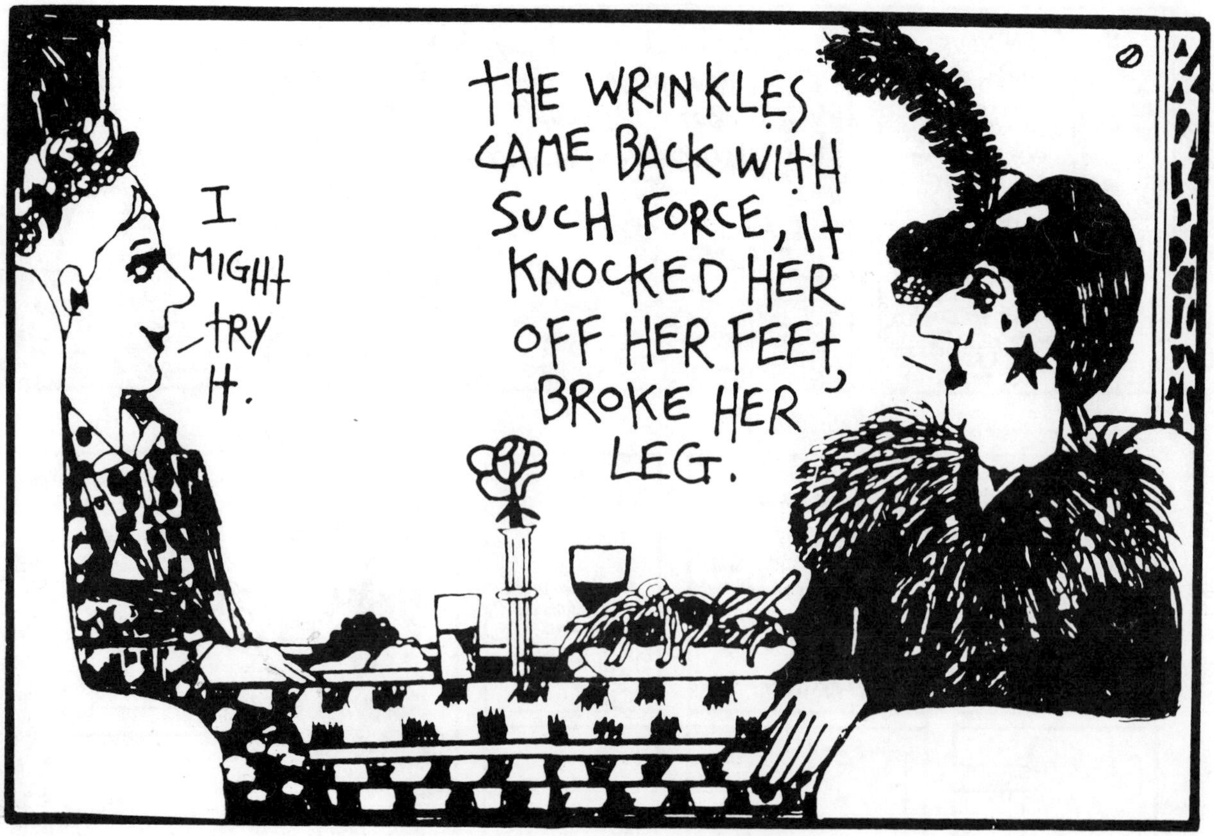
THE WRINKLES CAME BACK WITH SUCH FORCE, IT KNOCKED HER OFF HER FEET, BROKE HER LEG.
I MIGHT TRY IT.

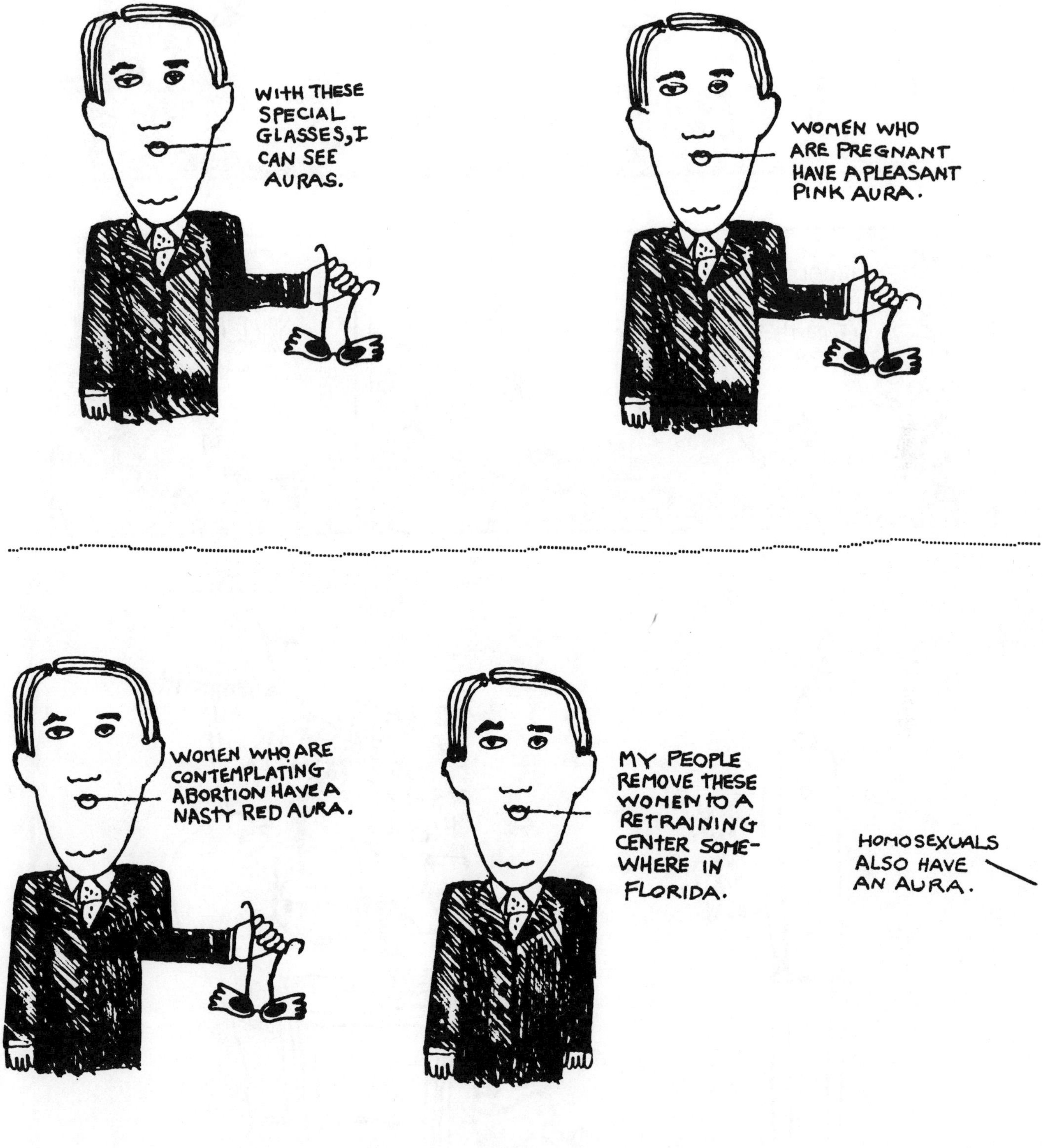
WITH THESE SPECIAL GLASSES, I CAN SEE AURAS.
WOMEN WHO ARE PREGNANT HAVE A PLEASANT PINK AURA.
WOMEN WHO ARE CONTEMPLATING ABORTION HAVE A NASTY RED AURA.
MY PEOPLE REMOVE THESE WOMEN TO A RETRAINING CENTER SOME-WHERE IN FLORIDA.
HOMOSEXUALS ALSO HAVE AN AURA.

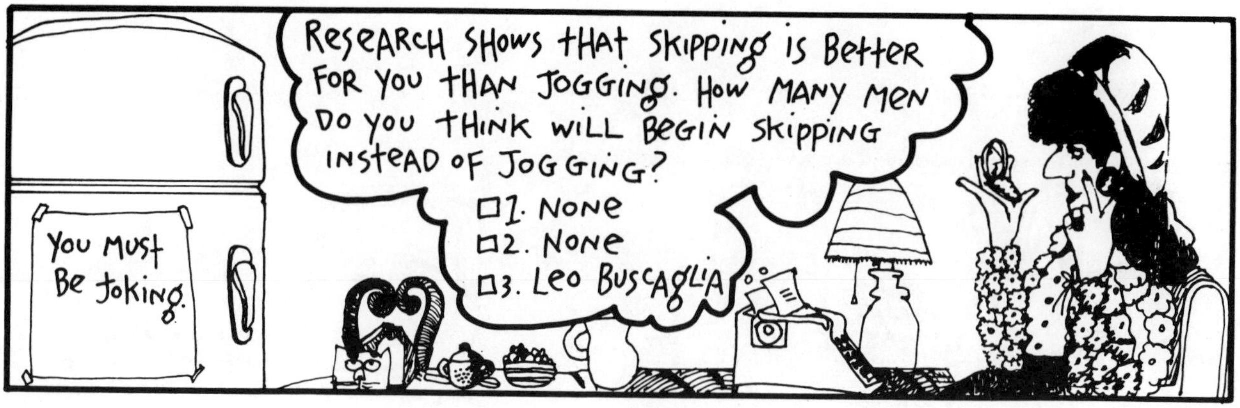
You Must Be Joking.
Research shows that skipping is better for you than jogging. How many men do you think will begin skipping instead of jogging?
☐1. None
☐2. None
☐3. Leo Buscaglia

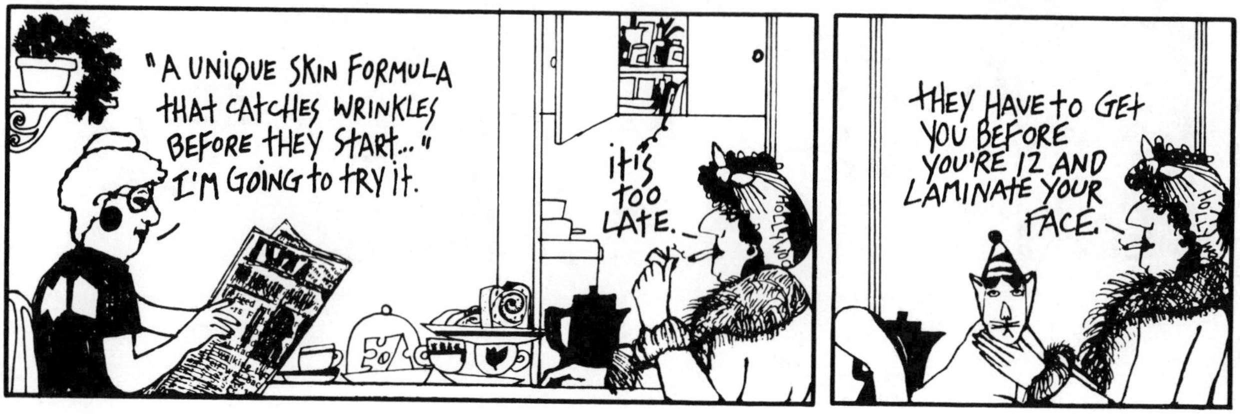
"A unique skin formula that catches wrinkles before they start..." I'm going to try it.
It's too late.
They have to get you before you're 12 and laminate your face.

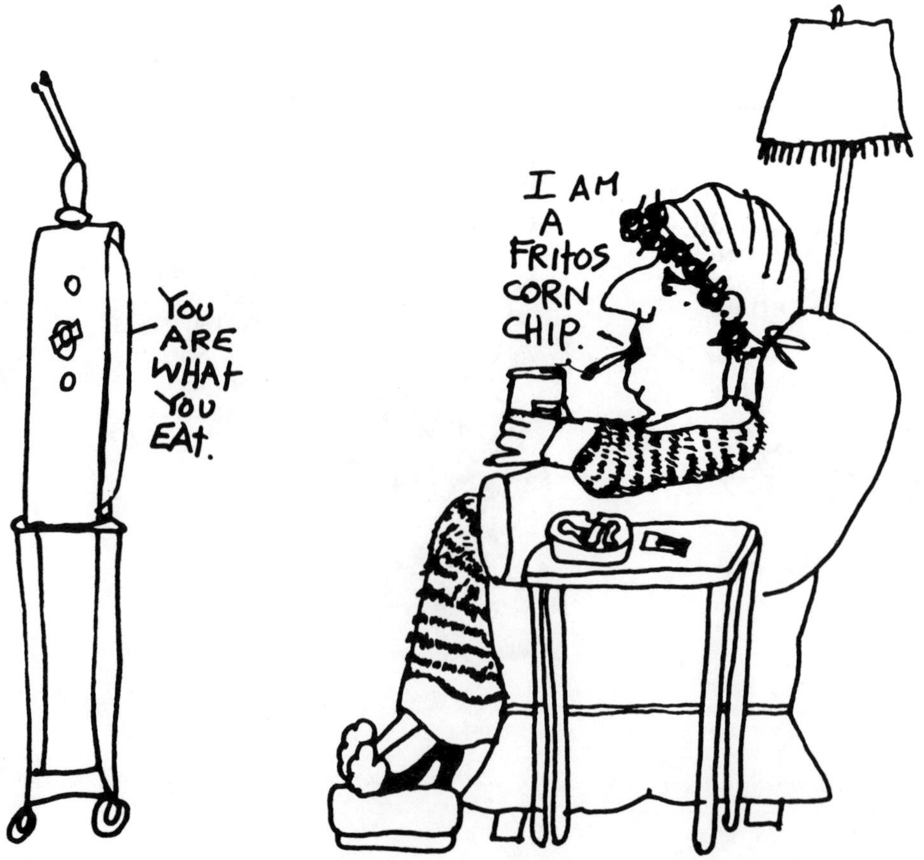
You are what you eat.
I am a Fritos corn chip.

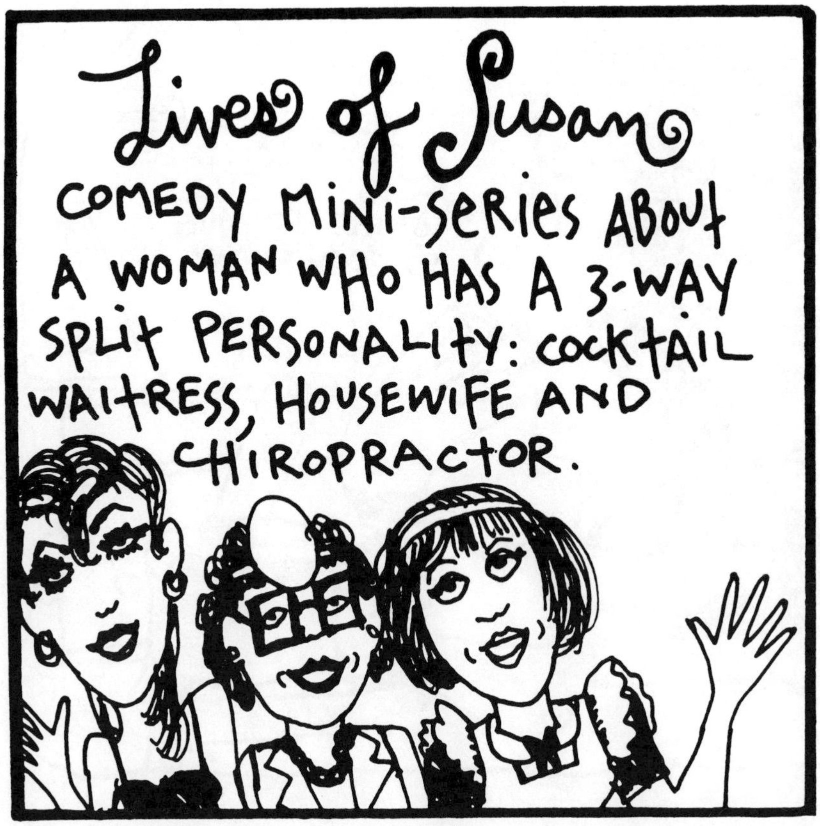
Lives of Susan
COMEDY MINI-SERIES ABOUT A WOMAN WHO HAS A 3-WAY SPLIT PERSONALITY: COCKTAIL WAITRESS, HOUSEWIFE AND CHIROPRACTOR.

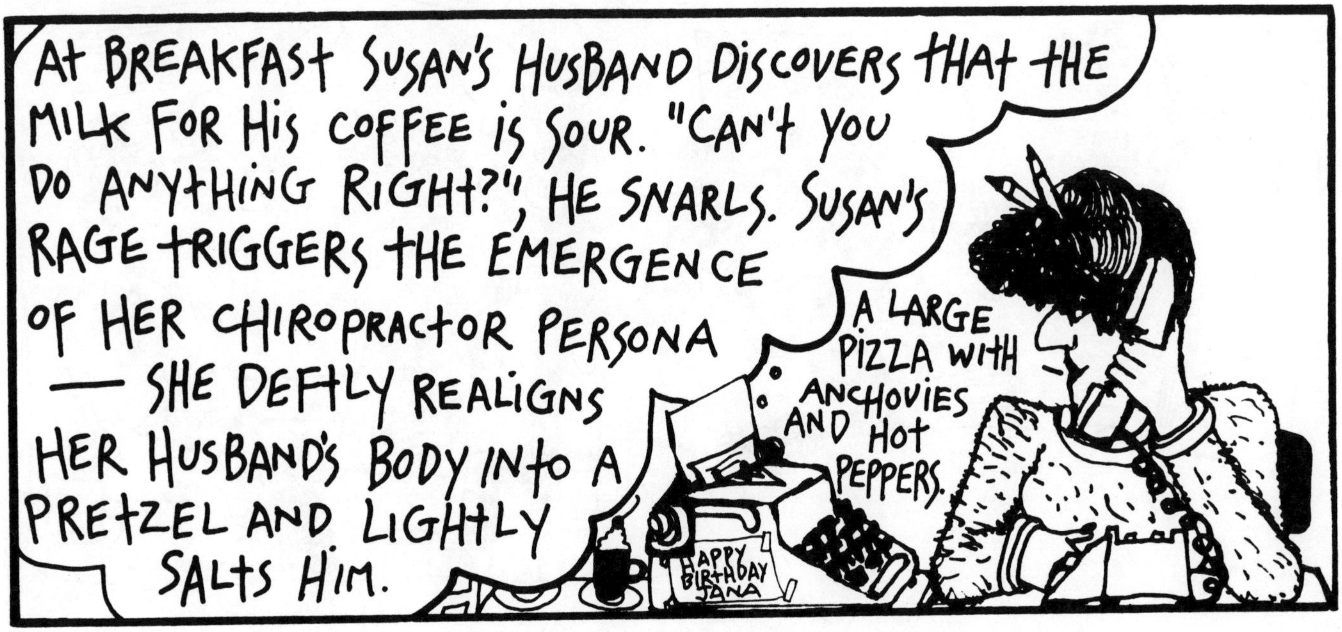
AT BREAKFAST SUSAN'S HUSBAND DISCOVERS THAT THE MILK FOR HIS COFFEE IS SOUR. "CAN'T YOU DO ANYTHING RIGHT?", HE SNARLS. SUSAN'S RAGE TRIGGERS THE EMERGENCE OF HER CHIROPRACTOR PERSONA — SHE DEFTLY REALIGNS HER HUSBAND'S BODY INTO A PRETZEL AND LIGHTLY SALTS HIM.
A LARGE PIZZA WITH ANCHOVIES AND HOT PEPPERS.
HAPPY BIRTHDAY JANA

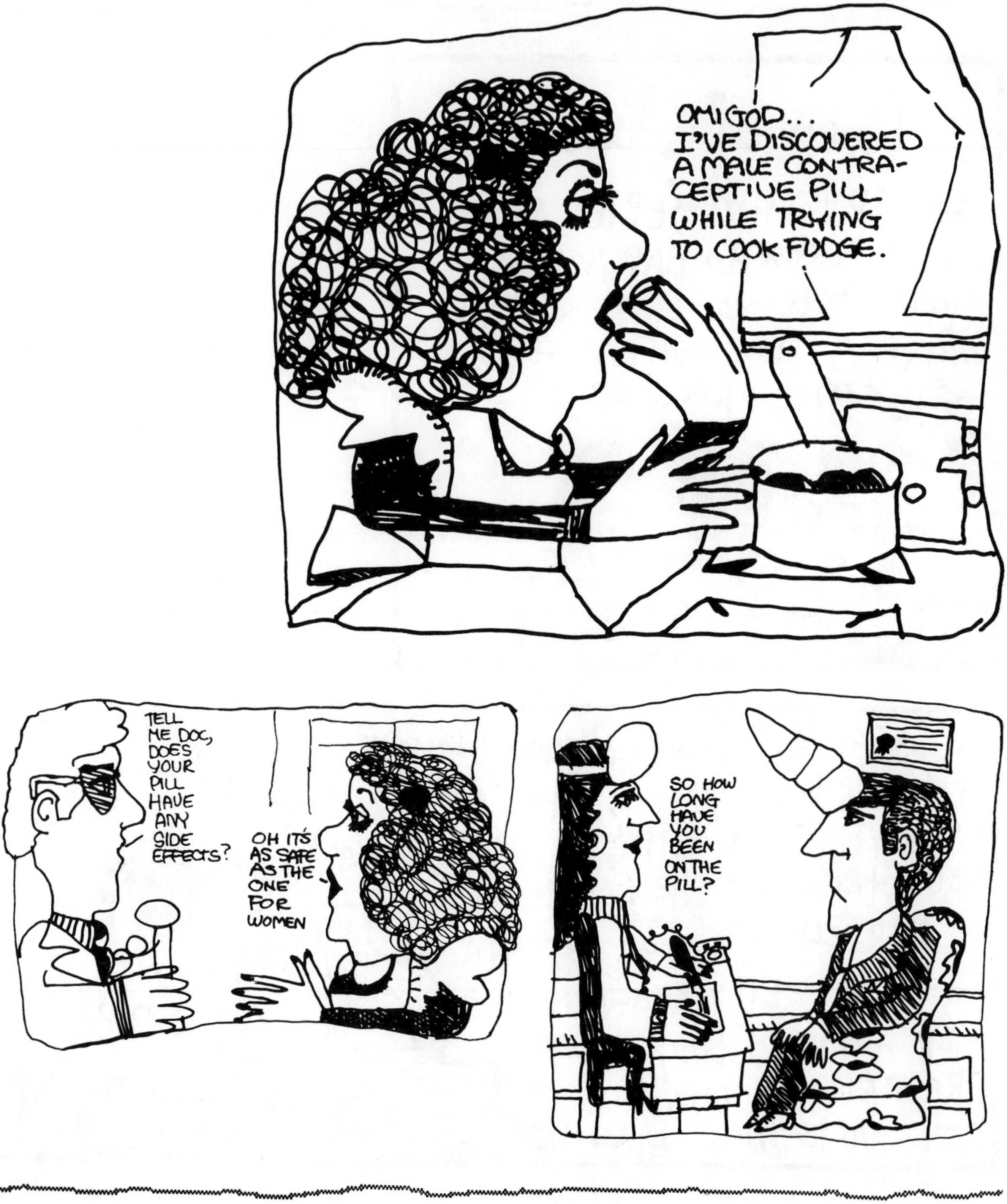
OMIGOD... I'VE DISCOVERED A MALE CONTRA-CEPTIVE PILL WHILE TRYING TO COOK FUDGE.
TELL ME DOC, DOES YOUR PILL HAVE ANY SIDE EFFECTS?
OH IT'S AS SAFE AS THE ONE FOR WOMEN
SO HOW LONG HAVE YOU BEEN ON THE PILL?

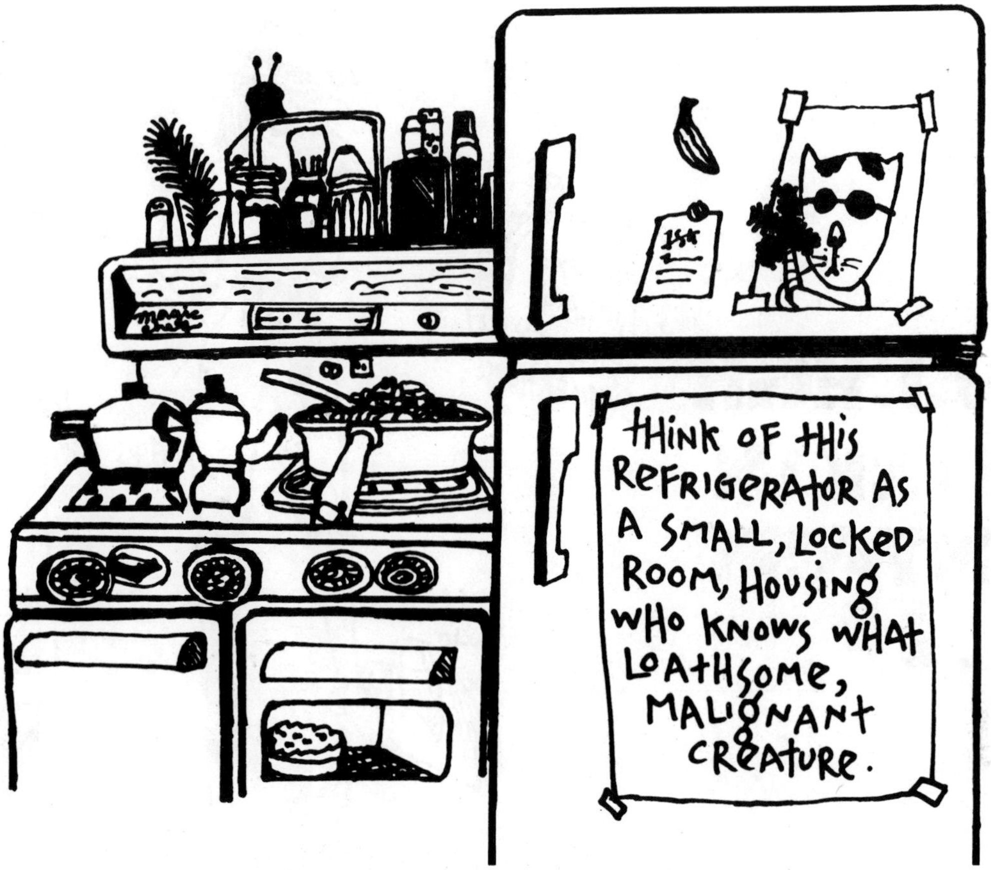
THINK OF THIS REFRIGERATOR AS A SMALL, LOCKED ROOM, HOUSING WHO KNOWS WHAT LOATHSOME, MALIGNANT CREATURE.

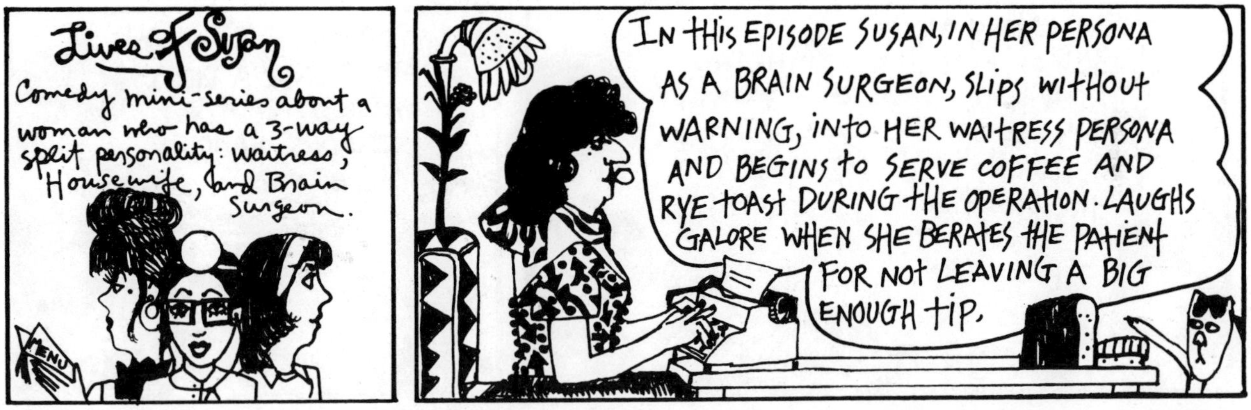
Lives of Susan
Comedy mini-series about a woman who has a 3-way split personality: waitress, Housewife, and Brain Surgeon.
MENU
IN THIS EPISODE SUSAN, IN HER PERSONA AS A BRAIN SURGEON, SLIPS WITHOUT WARNING, INTO HER WAITRESS PERSONA AND BEGINS TO SERVE COFFEE AND RYE TOAST DURING THE OPERATION. LAUGHS GALORE WHEN SHE BERATES THE PATIENT FOR NOT LEAVING A BIG ENOUGH TIP.

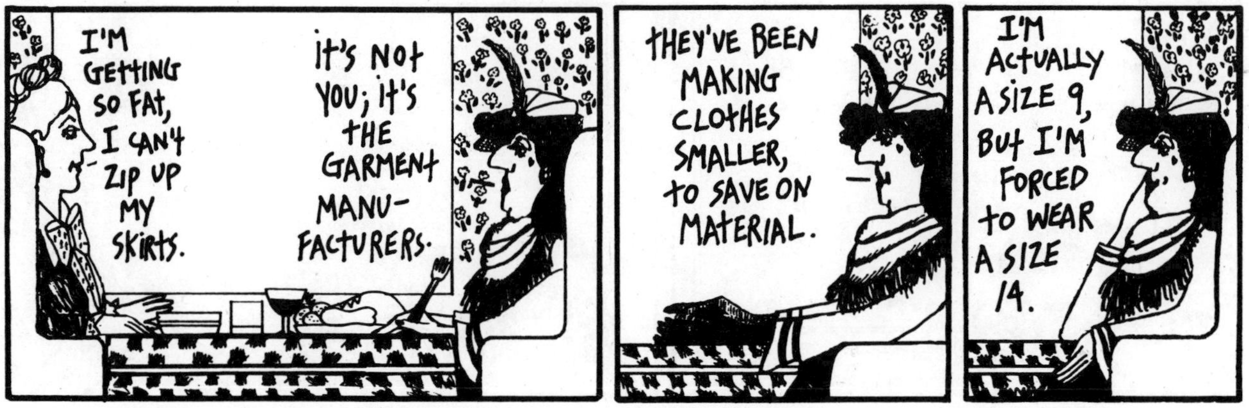
I'M GETTING SO FAT, I CAN'T ZIP UP MY SKIRTS.
IT'S NOT YOU; IT'S THE GARMENT MANU-FACTURERS.
THEY'VE BEEN MAKING CLOTHES SMALLER, TO SAVE ON MATERIAL.
I'M ACTUALLY A SIZE 9, BUT I'M FORCED TO WEAR A SIZE 14.

COLLEGE REUNION FANTASY NO. 1

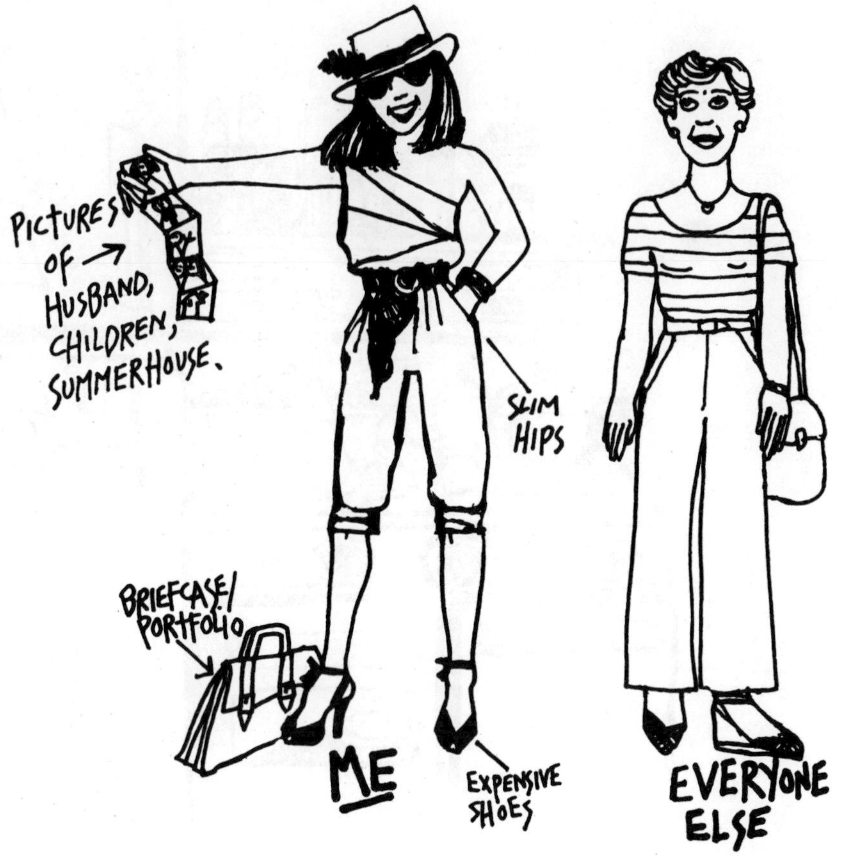

PICTURES of → HUSBAND, CHILDREN, SUMMERHOUSE.
SLIM HIPS
BRIEFCASE/PORTFOLIO
ME
EXPENSIVE SHOES
EVERYONE ELSE

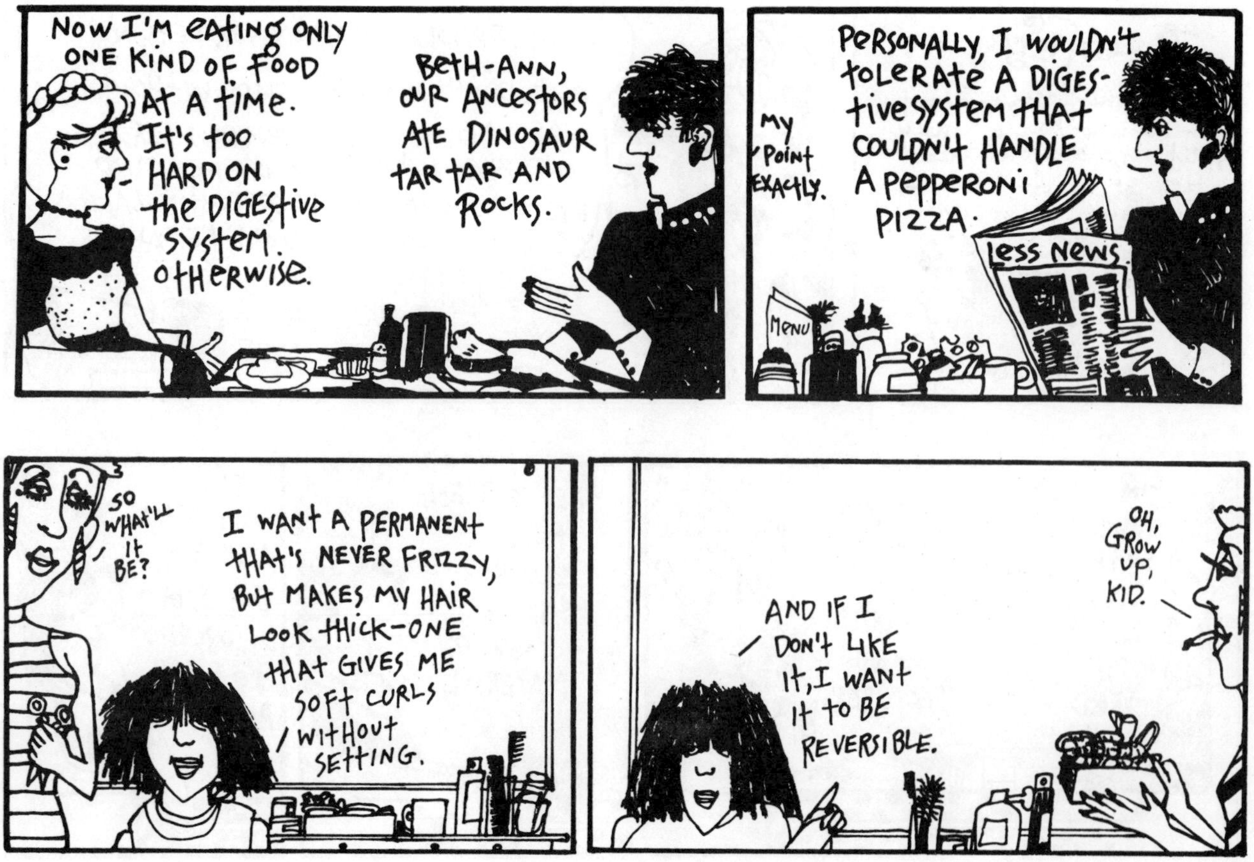

NOW I'M EATING ONLY ONE KIND OF FOOD AT A TIME. IT'S TOO HARD ON THE DIGESTIVE SYSTEM OTHERWISE.
BETH-ANN, OUR ANCESTORS ATE DINOSAUR TAR TAR AND ROCKS.
MY POINT EXACTLY.
PERSONALLY, I WOULDN'T TOLERATE A DIGESTIVE SYSTEM THAT COULDN'T HANDLE A PEPPERONI PIZZA.
LESS NEWS
MENU
SO WHAT'LL IT BE?
I WANT A PERMANENT THAT'S NEVER FRIZZY, BUT MAKES MY HAIR LOOK THICK—ONE THAT GIVES ME SOFT CURLS WITHOUT SETTING.
AND IF I DON'T LIKE IT, I WANT IT TO BE REVERSIBLE.
OH, GROW UP, KID.

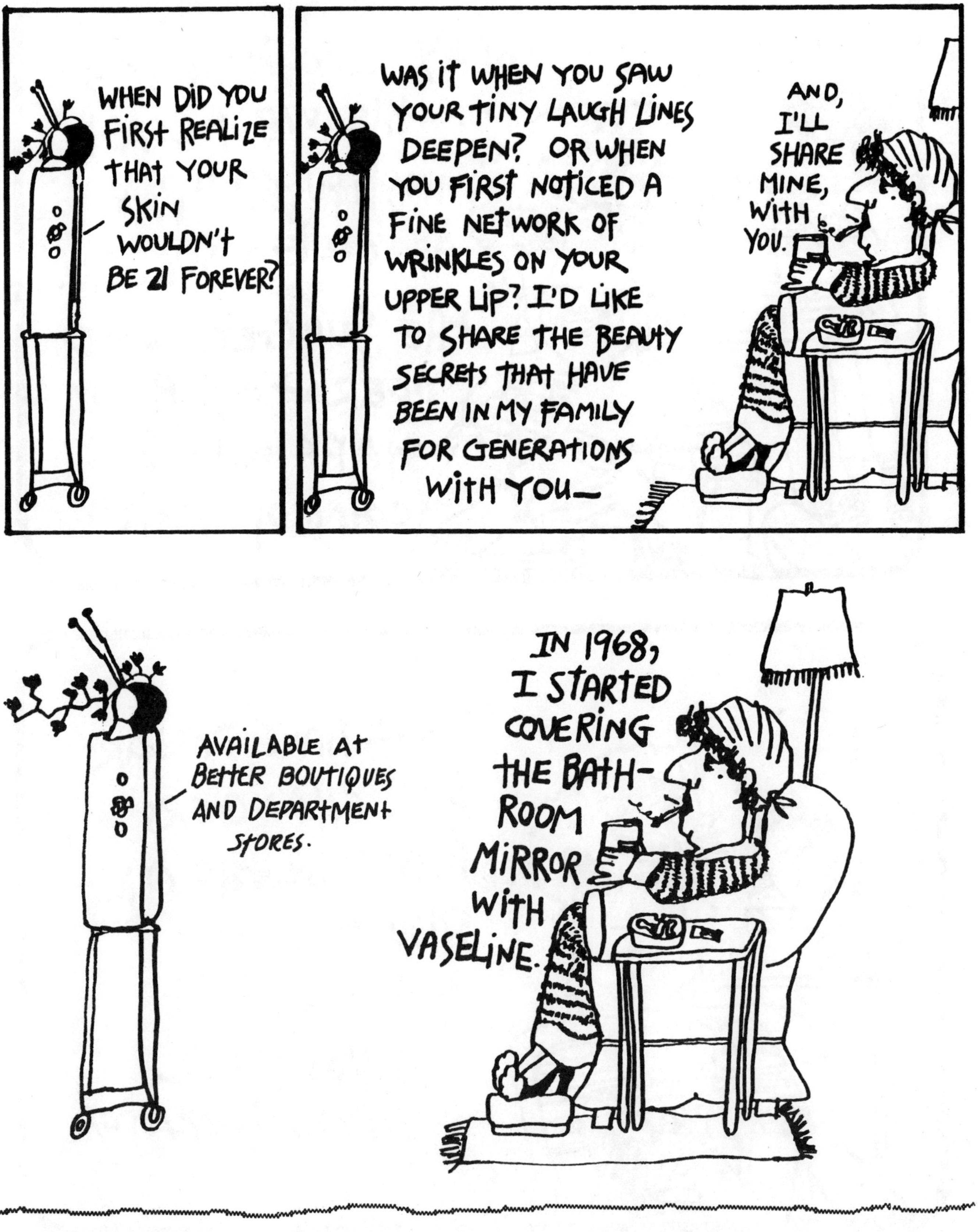

WHEN DID YOU FIRST REALIZE THAT YOUR SKIN WOULDN'T BE 21 FOREVER?
WAS IT WHEN YOU SAW YOUR TINY LAUGH LINES DEEPEN? OR WHEN YOU FIRST NOTICED A FINE NETWORK OF WRINKLES ON YOUR UPPER LIP? I'D LIKE TO SHARE THE BEAUTY SECRETS THAT HAVE BEEN IN MY FAMILY FOR GENERATIONS WITH YOU—
AND, I'LL SHARE MINE, WITH YOU.
AVAILABLE AT BETTER BOUTIQUES AND DEPARTMENT STORES.
IN 1968, I STARTED COVERING THE BATH-ROOM MIRROR WITH VASELINE.

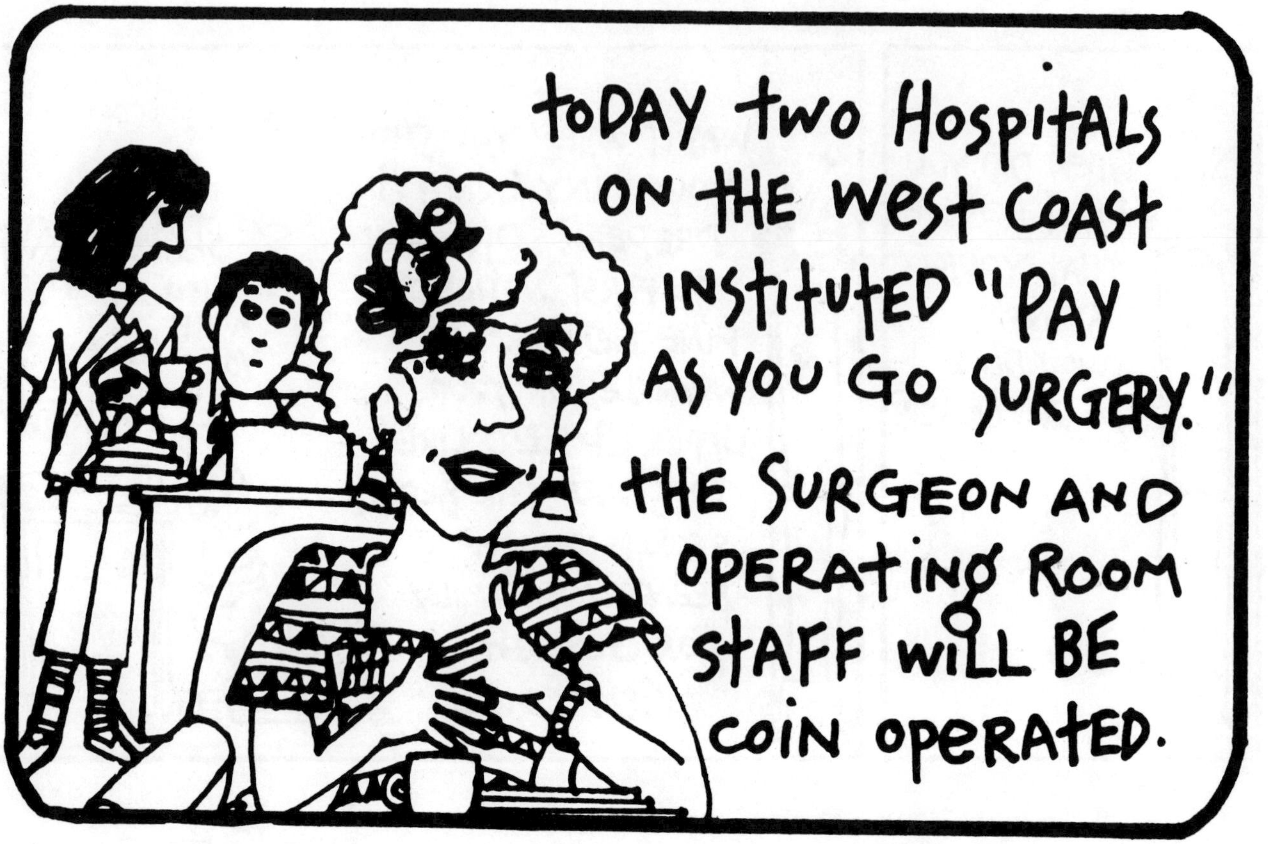
TODAY TWO HOSPITALS ON THE WEST COAST INSTITUTED "PAY AS YOU GO SURGERY."
THE SURGEON AND OPERATING ROOM STAFF WILL BE COIN OPERATED.

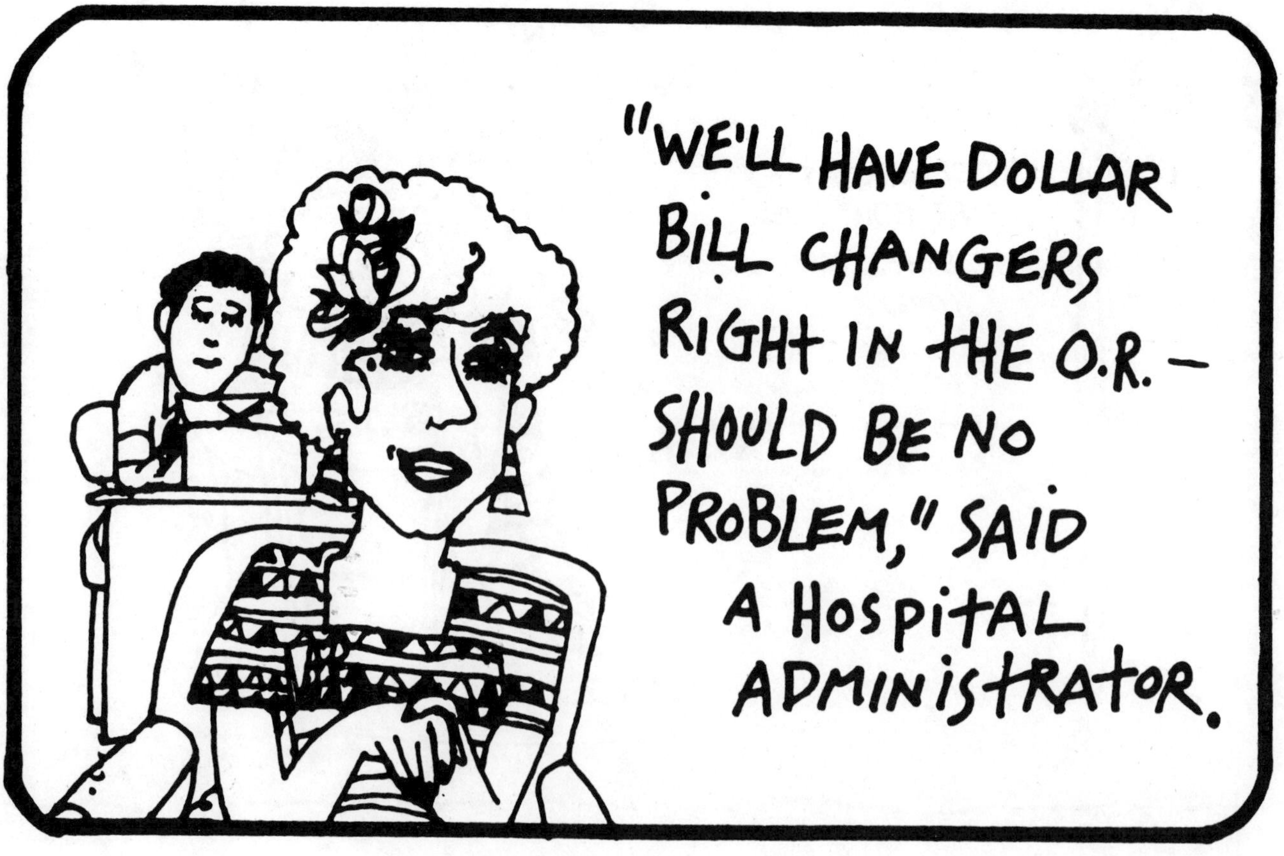
"WE'LL HAVE DOLLAR BILL CHANGERS RIGHT IN THE O.R. – SHOULD BE NO PROBLEM," SAID A HOSPITAL ADMINISTRATOR.

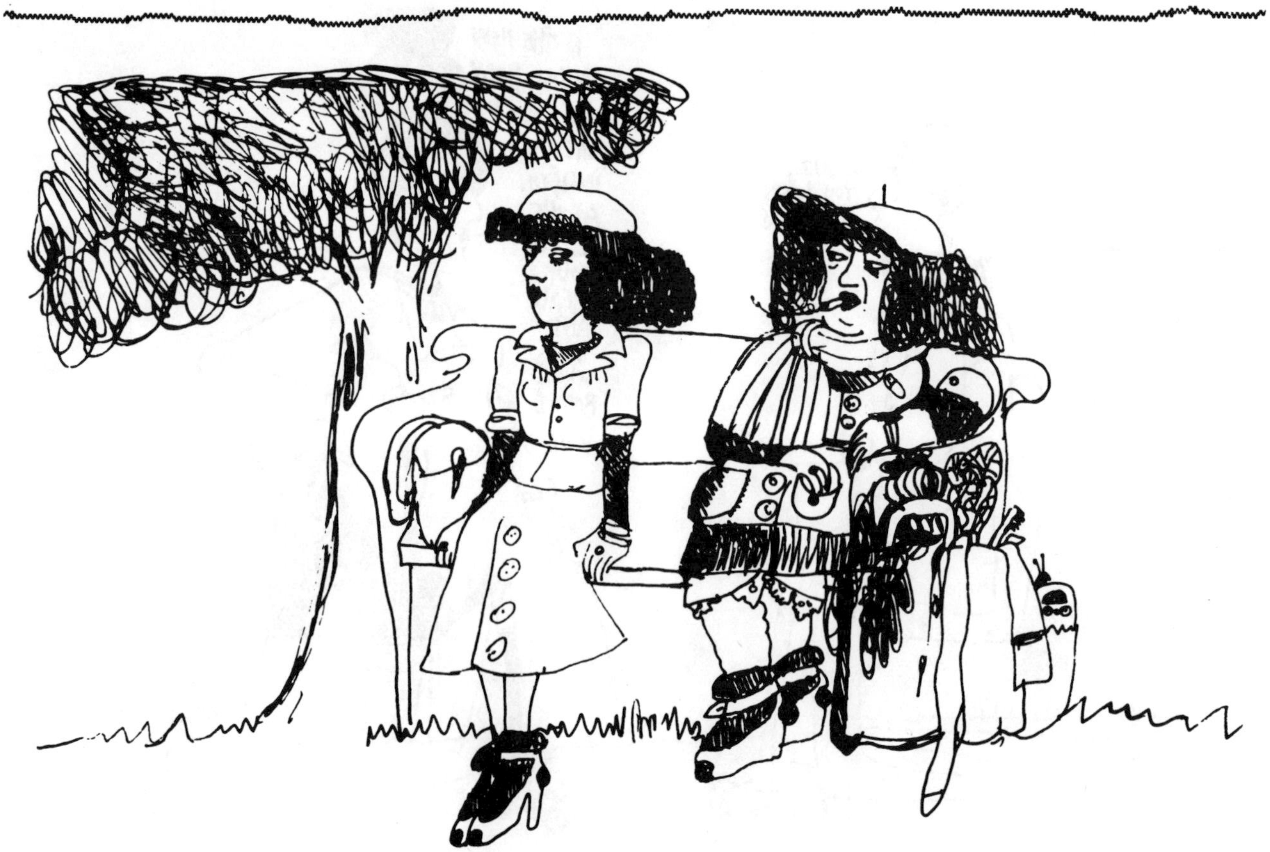

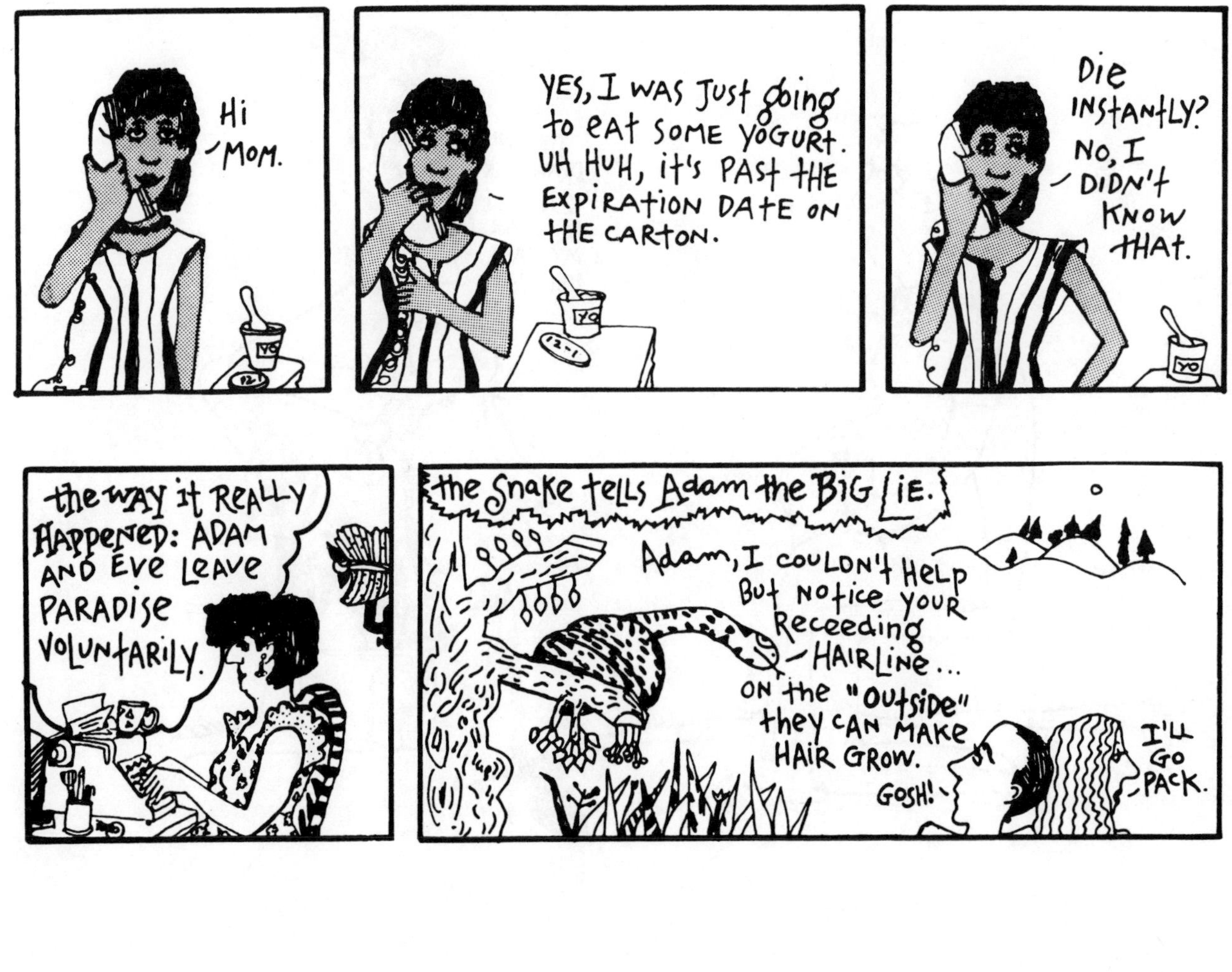
Hi MOM.
YES, I WAS JUST going to eat SOME YOGURT. UH HUH, it's PAST THE EXPIRATION DATE ON THE CARTON.
Die INSTANTLY? NO, I DIDN'T KNOW THAT.
the WAY it REALLY HAPPENED: ADAM AND EVE LEAVE PARADISE VOLUNTARILY.
the Snake tells Adam the BiG Lie.
Adam, I COULDN'T HELP But Notice YOUR Receeding HAIRLiNE...
ON the "OUTSiDE" they CAN MAKE HAIR GROW.
GOSH!
I'LL GO PACK.

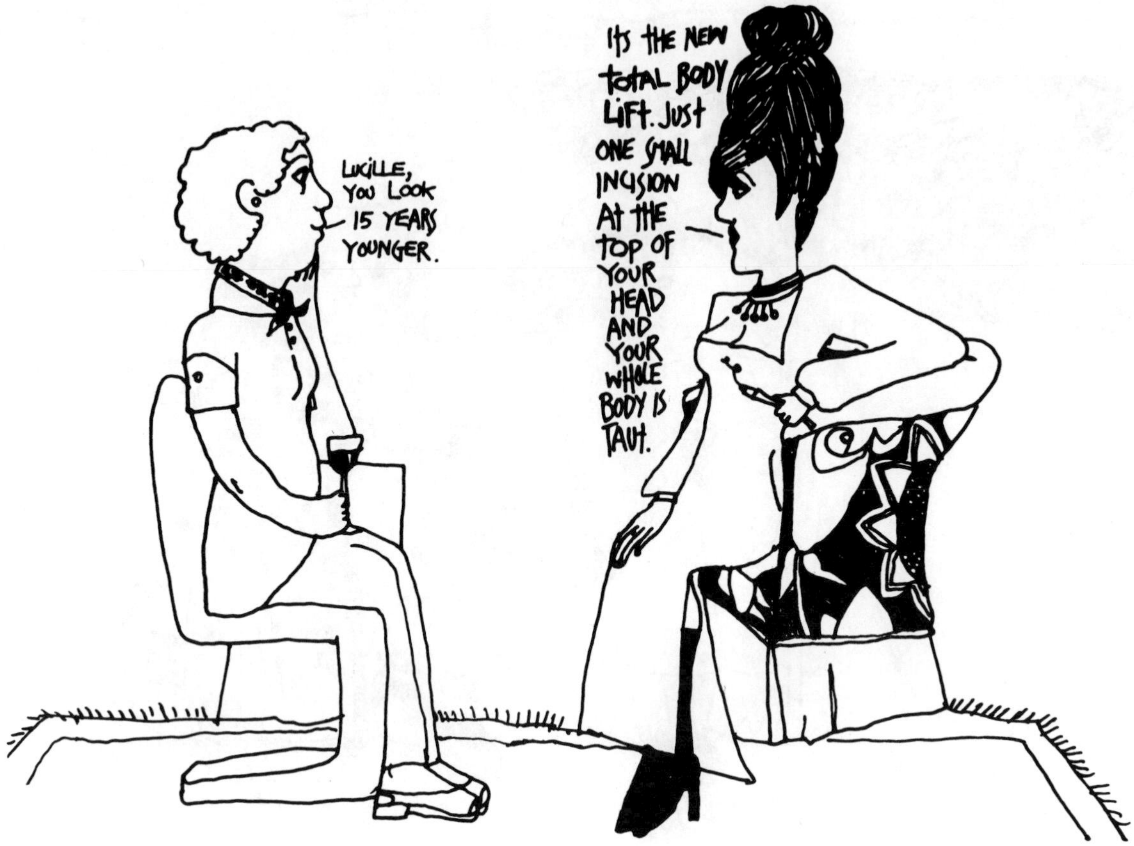
LUCILLE, YOU LOOK 15 YEARS YOUNGER.
ITS THE NEW TOTAL BODY LIFT. JUST ONE SMALL INCISION AT THE TOP OF YOUR HEAD AND YOUR WHOLE BODY IS TAUT.

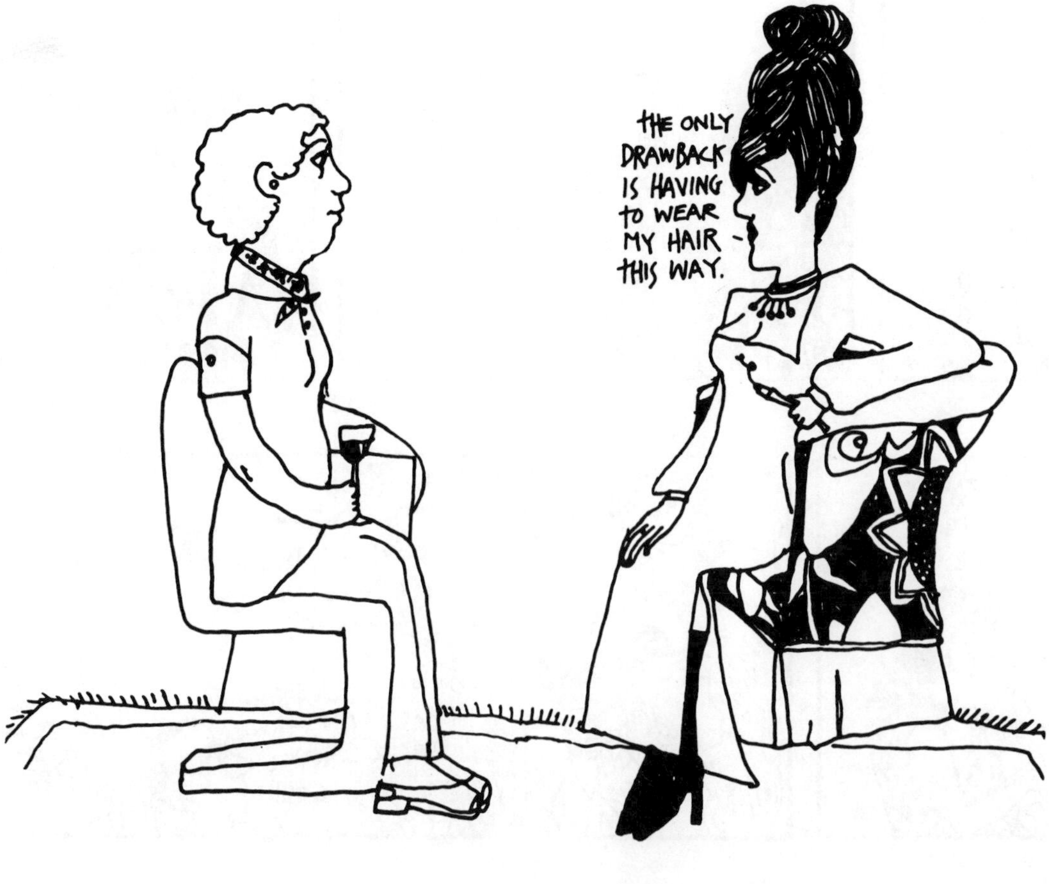
THE ONLY DRAWBACK IS HAVING TO WEAR MY HAIR THIS WAY.

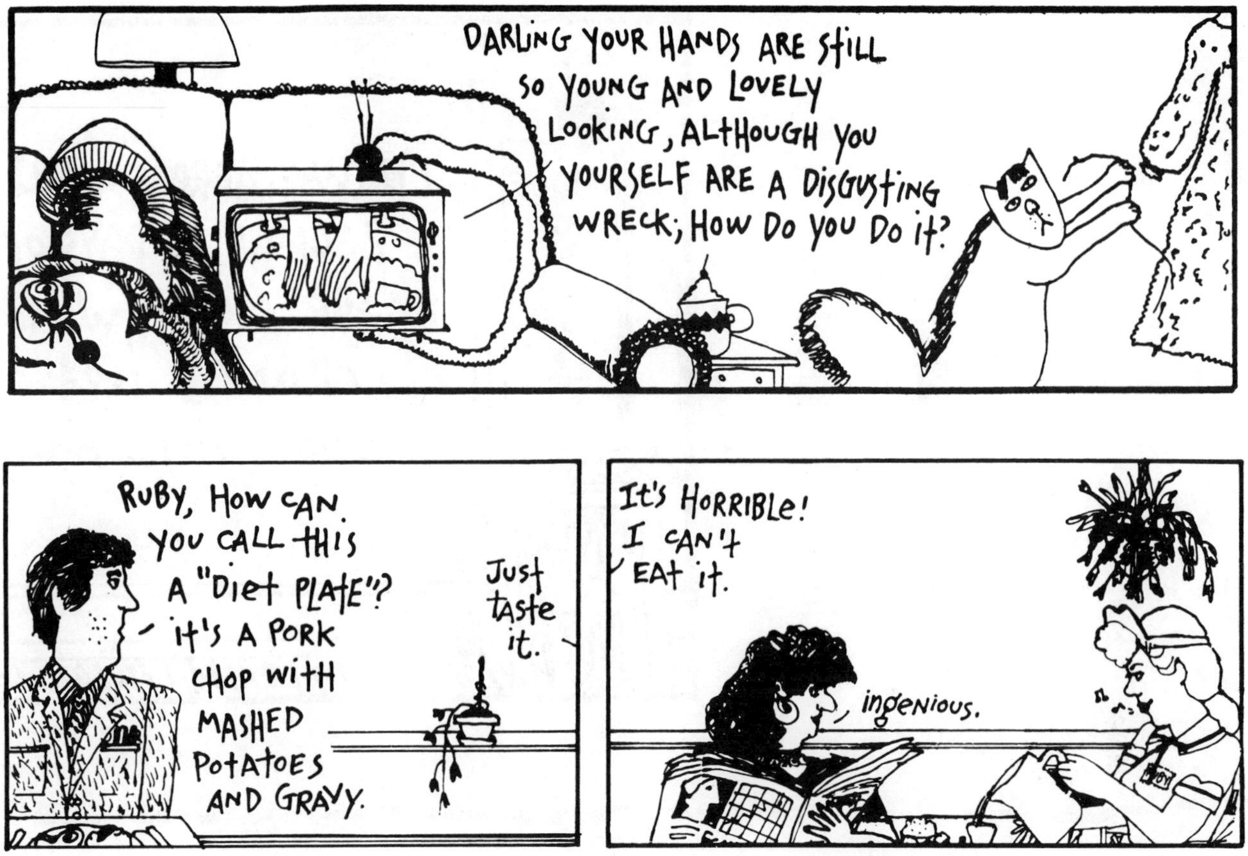
DARLING YOUR HANDS ARE STILL SO YOUNG AND LOVELY LOOKING, ALTHOUGH YOU YOURSELF ARE A DISGUSTING WRECK; HOW DO YOU DO IT?
RUBY, HOW CAN YOU CALL THIS A "DIET PLATE"? IT'S A PORK CHOP WITH MASHED POTATOES AND GRAVY.
Just taste it.
It's HORRIBLE! I CAN'T EAT IT.
ingenious.

COLLEGE REUNION FANTASY NO. 2

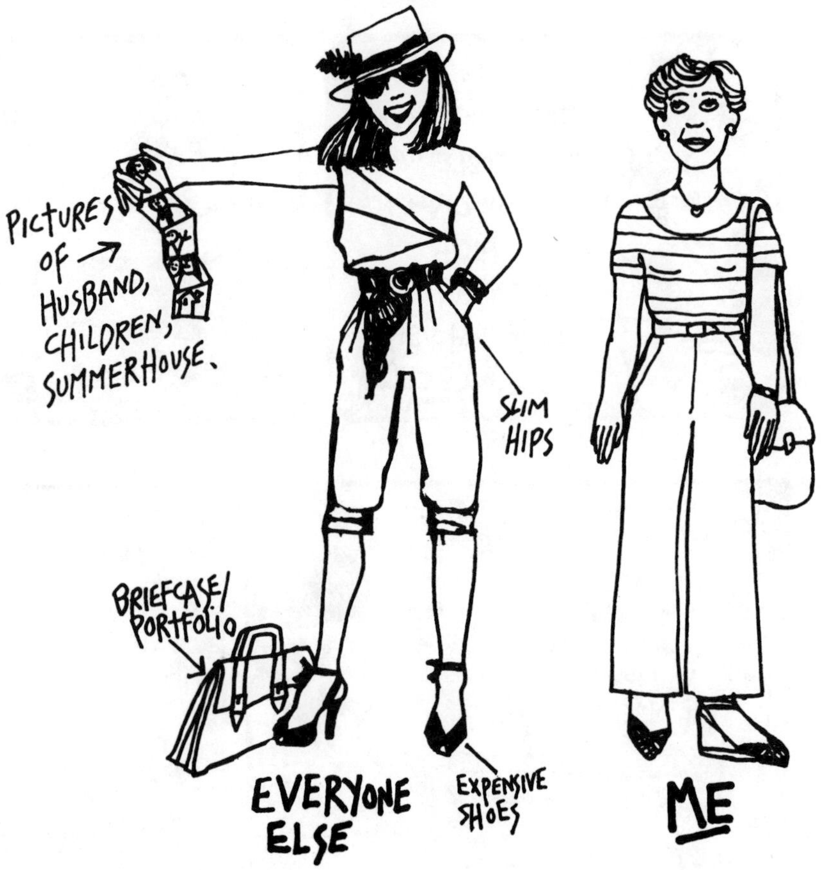
PICTURES OF → HUSBAND, CHILDREN, SUMMERHOUSE.
SLIM HIPS
BRIEFCASE/ PORTFOLIO
EXPENSIVE SHOES
EVERYONE ELSE
ME

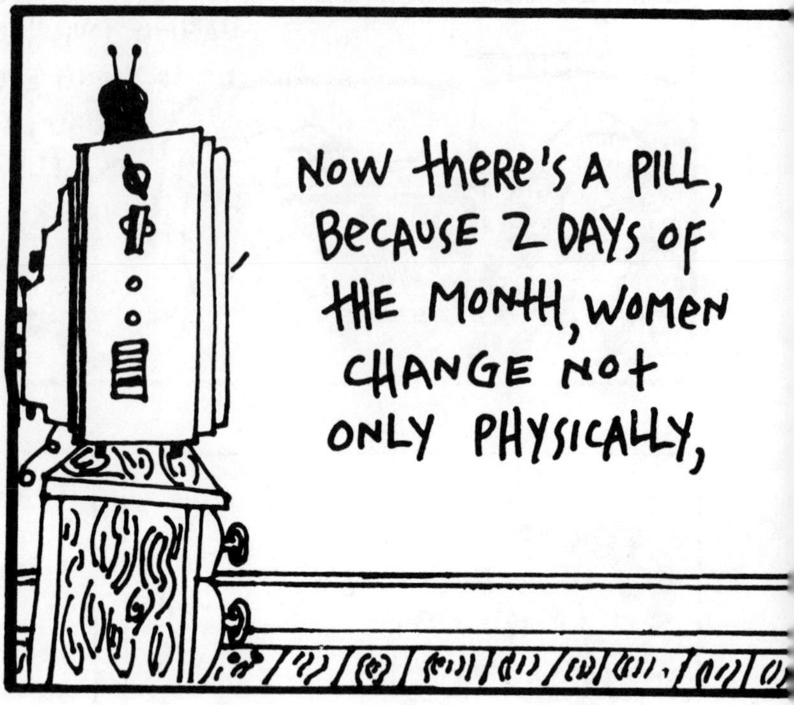
Now there's a PILL, BECAUSE 2 DAYS OF THE MONTH, WOMEN CHANGE NOT ONLY PHYSICALLY,

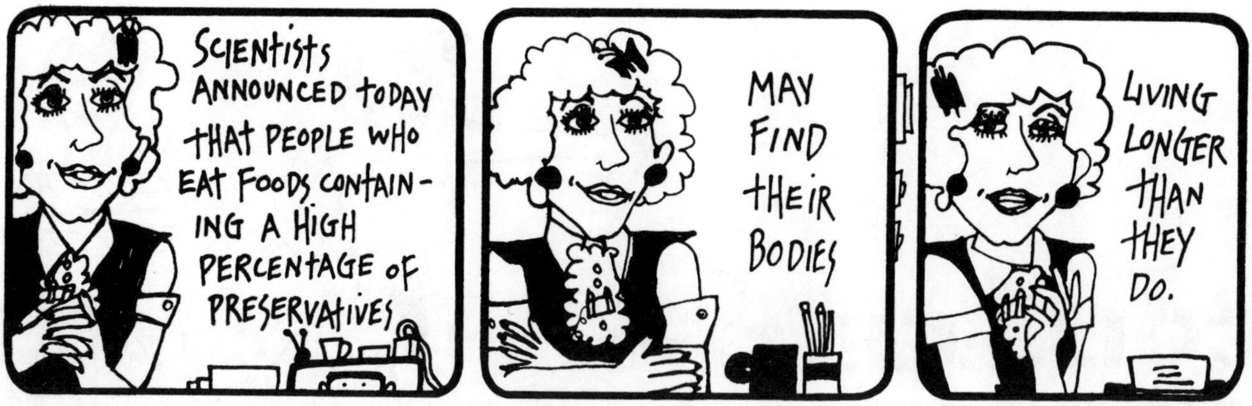
SCIENTISTS ANNOUNCED TODAY THAT PEOPLE WHO EAT FOODS CONTAIN-ING A HIGH PERCENTAGE OF PRESERVATIVES
MAY FIND THEIR BODIES
LIVING LONGER THAN THEY DO.

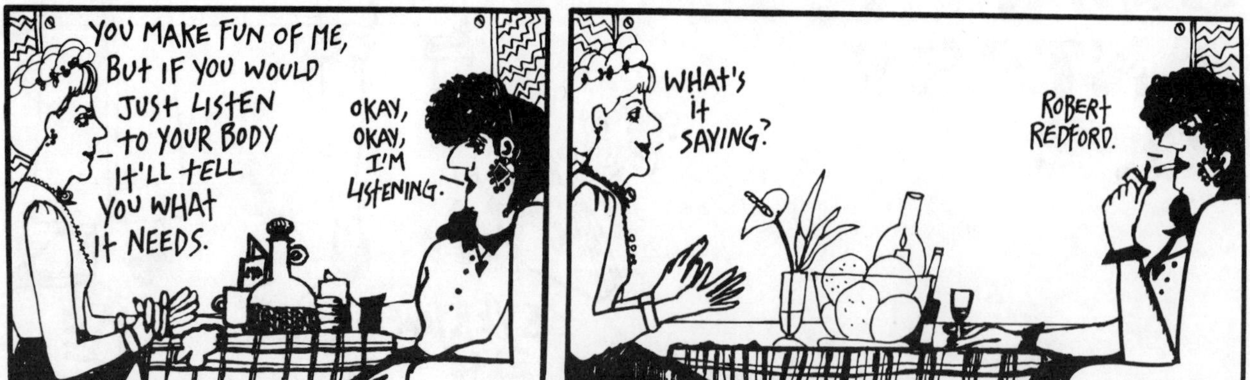
YOU MAKE FUN OF ME, BUT IF YOU WOULD JUST LISTEN TO YOUR BODY IT'LL TELL YOU WHAT IT NEEDS.
OKAY, OKAY, I'M LISTENING.
WHAT'S IT SAYING?
ROBERT REDFORD.

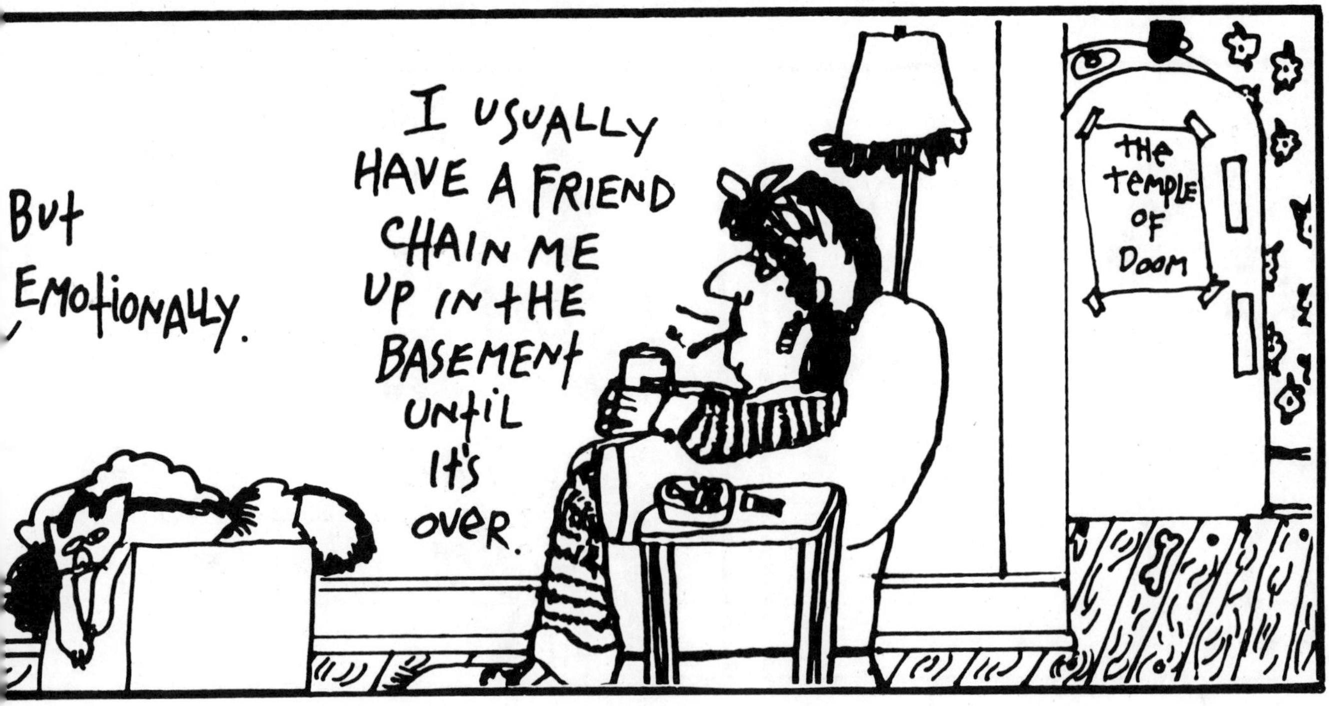
But Emotionally.
I usually have a friend chain me up in the basement until it's over.
the temple of Doom

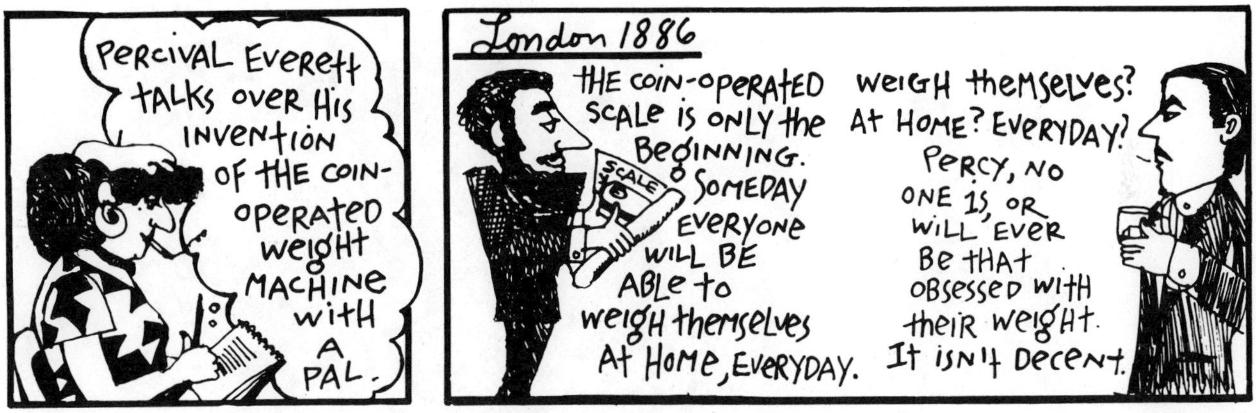
Percival Everett talks over his invention of the coin-operated weight machine with a pal.
London 1886
The coin-operated scale is only the beginning. Someday everyone will be able to weigh themselves at home, everyday.
SCALE
Weigh themselves? At home? Everyday? Percy, no one is, or will ever be that obsessed with their weight. It isn't decent.

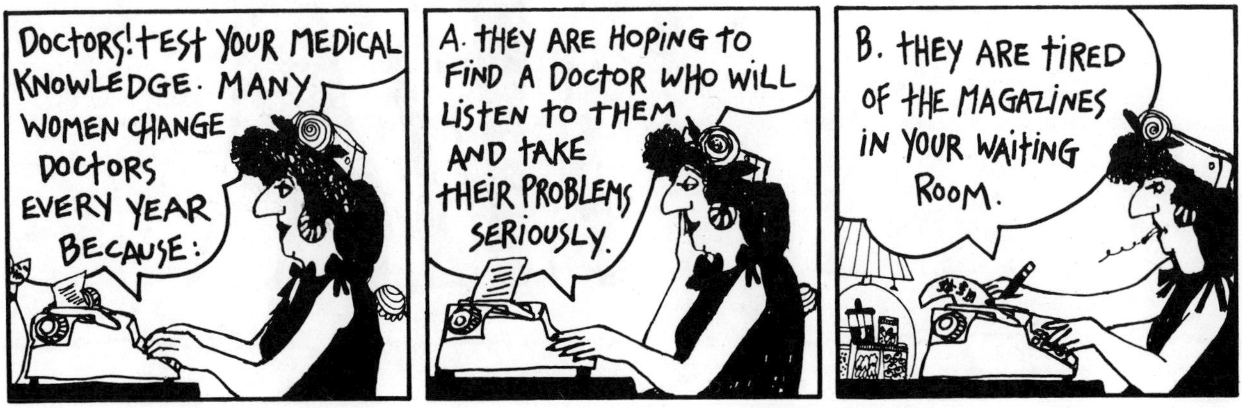
Doctors! Test your medical knowledge. Many women change doctors every year because:
A. They are hoping to find a doctor who will listen to them and take their problems seriously.
B. They are tired of the magazines in your waiting room.

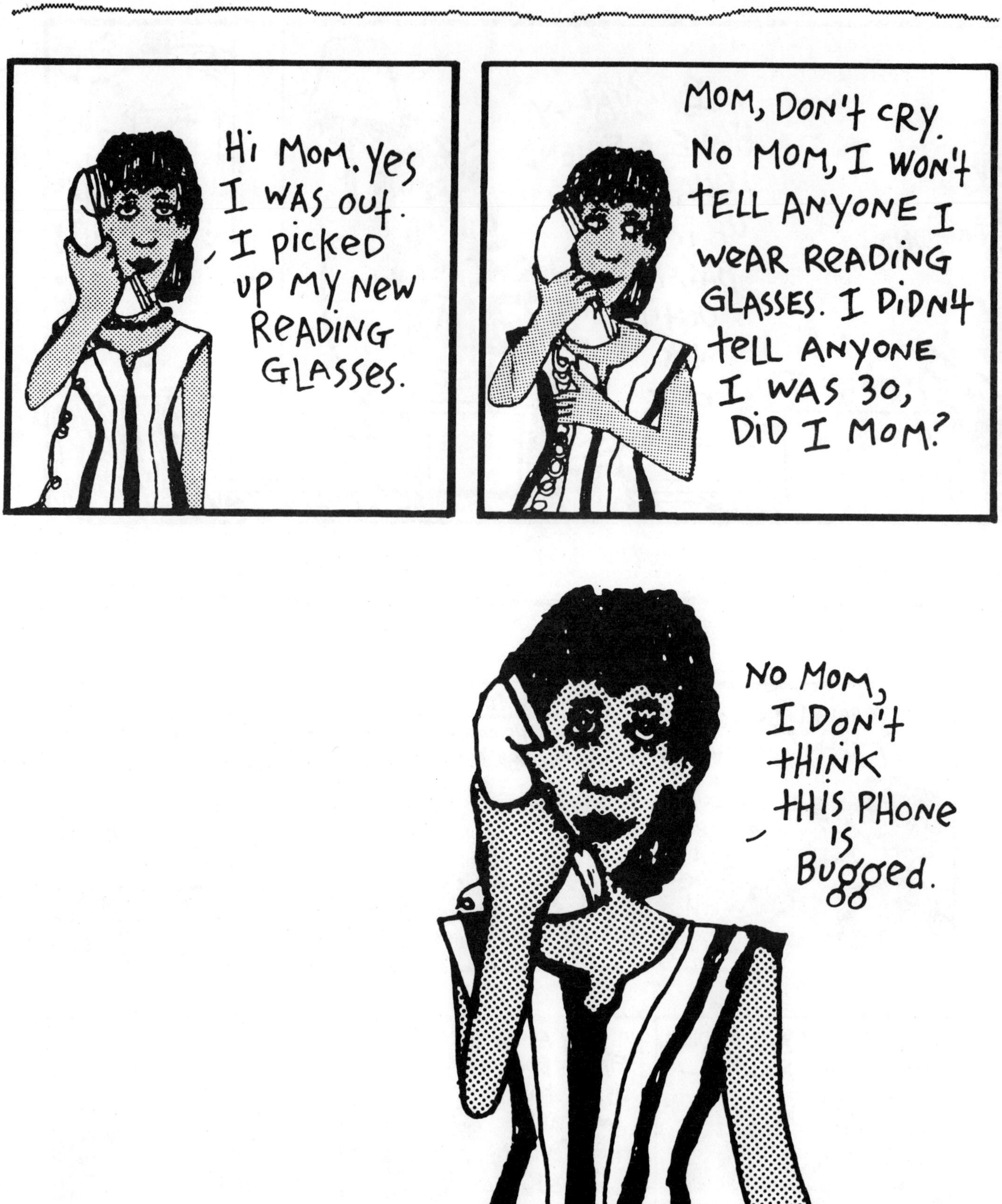

Hi MOM. yes I WAS out. I picked up MY New READING GLASSES.
MOM, DON'T CRY. No MOM, I WON'T TELL ANYONE I wear READING GLASSES. I DIDN'T tell ANYONE I WAS 30, DID I MOM?
No MOM, I DON'T THINK THIS PHONE is Bugged.

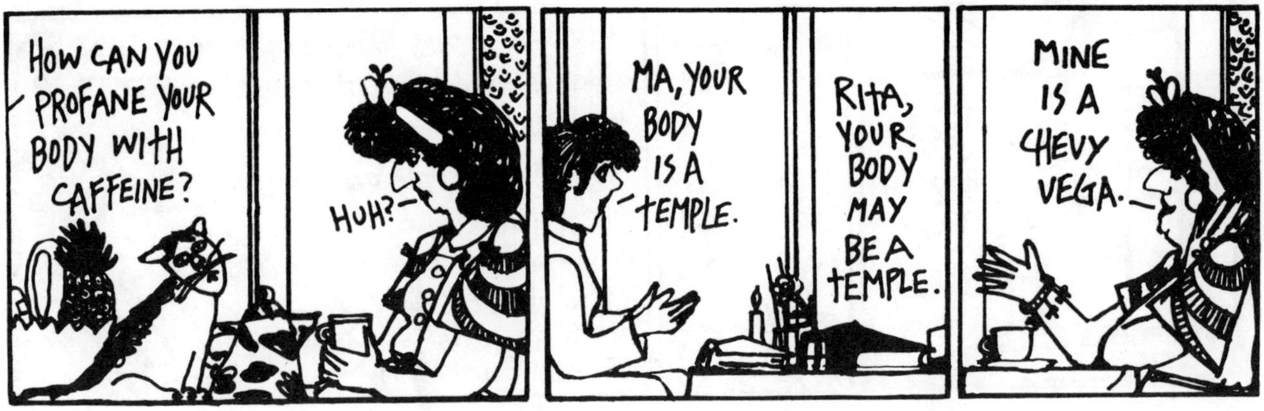
HOW CAN YOU PROFANE YOUR BODY WITH CAFFEINE?
HUH?
MA, YOUR BODY IS A TEMPLE.
RITA, YOUR BODY MAY BE A TEMPLE.
MINE IS A CHEVY VEGA.

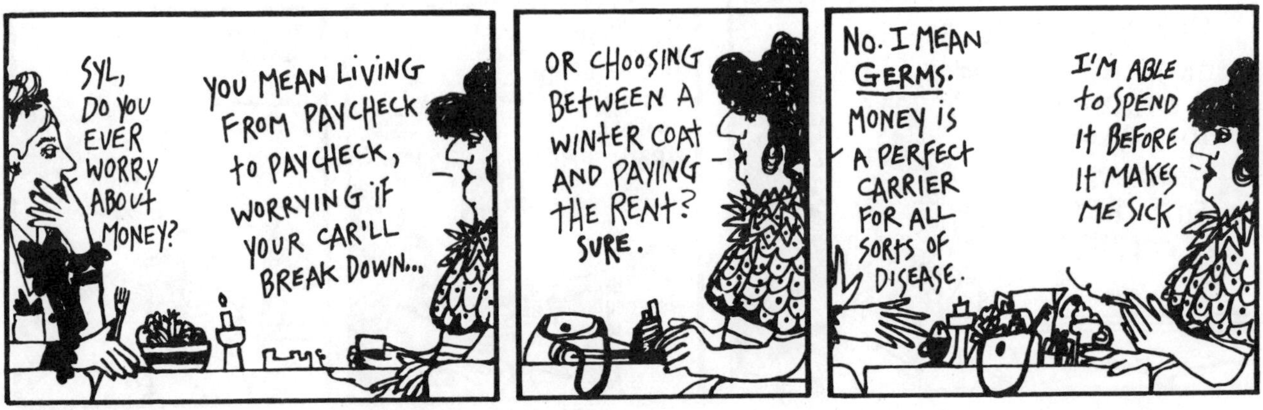
SYL, DO YOU EVER WORRY ABOUT MONEY?
YOU MEAN LIVING FROM PAYCHECK TO PAYCHECK, WORRYING IF YOUR CAR'LL BREAK DOWN...
OR CHOOSING BETWEEN A WINTER COAT AND PAYING THE RENT? SURE.
NO. I MEAN GERMS. MONEY IS A PERFECT CARRIER FOR ALL SORTS OF DISEASE.
I'M ABLE TO SPEND IT BEFORE IT MAKES ME SICK

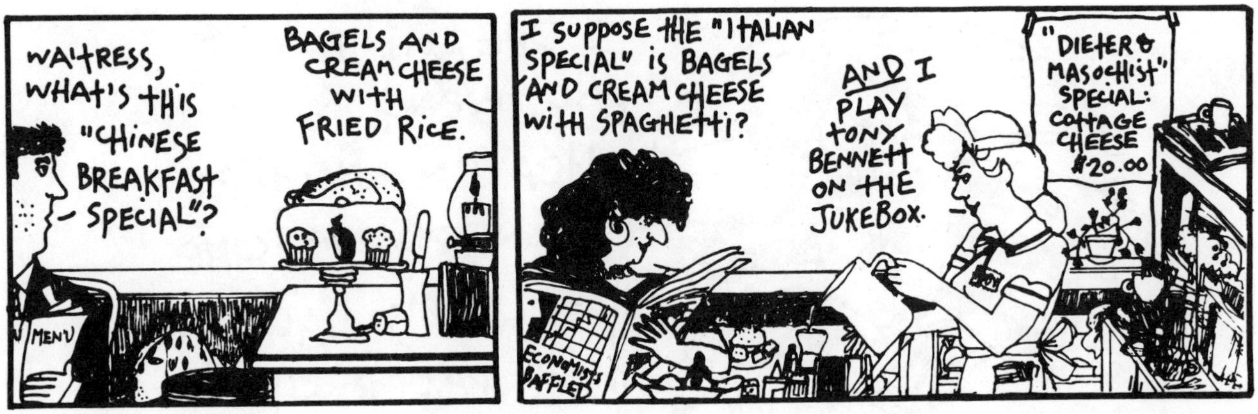
WAITRESS, WHAT'S THIS "CHINESE BREAKFAST SPECIAL"?
BAGELS AND CREAM CHEESE WITH FRIED RICE.
MENU
I SUPPOSE THE "ITALIAN SPECIAL" IS BAGELS AND CREAM CHEESE WITH SPAGHETTI?
AND I PLAY TONY BENNETT ON THE JUKEBOX.
"DIETER & MASOCHIST" SPECIAL: COTTAGE CHEESE $20.00
ECONOMISTS BAFFLED

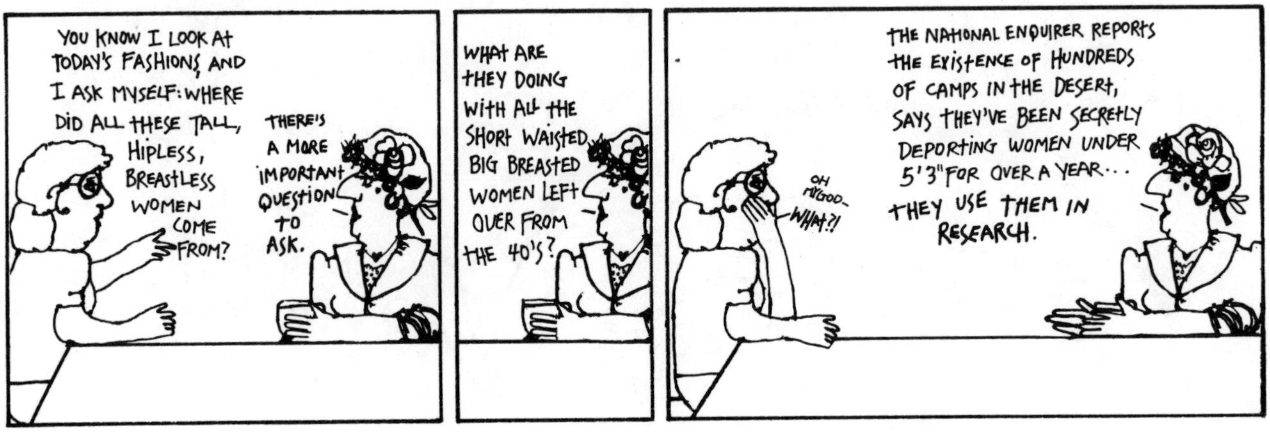
YOU KNOW I LOOK AT TODAY'S FASHIONS AND I ASK MYSELF: WHERE DID ALL THESE TALL, HIPLESS, BREASTLESS WOMEN COME FROM?
THERE'S A MORE IMPORTANT QUESTION TO ASK.
WHAT ARE THEY DOING WITH ALL THE SHORT WAISTED, BIG BREASTED WOMEN LEFT OVER FROM THE 40'S?
THE NATIONAL ENQUIRER REPORTS THE EXISTENCE OF HUNDREDS OF CAMPS IN THE DESERT, SAYS THEY'VE BEEN SECRETLY DEPORTING WOMEN UNDER 5'3" FOR OVER A YEAR... THEY USE THEM IN RESEARCH.
OH MY GOD- WHAT?!

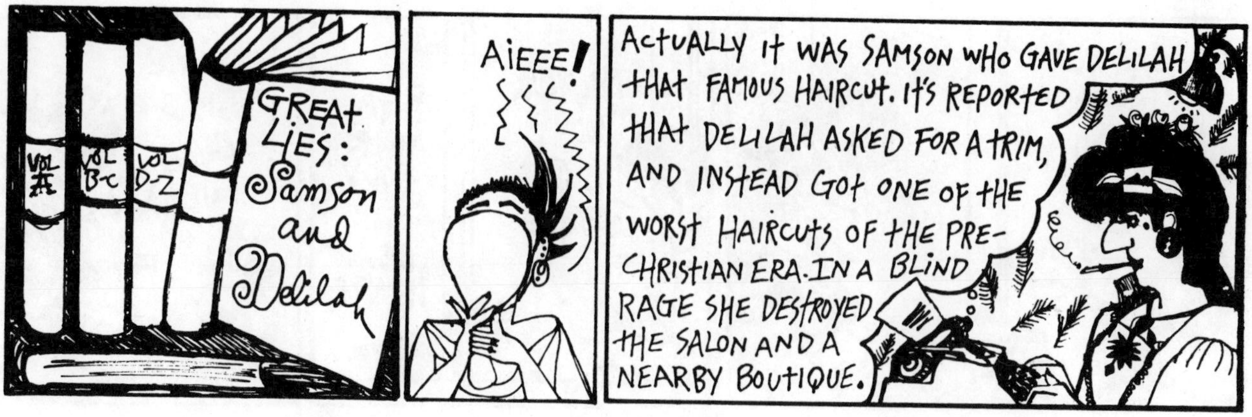
VOL A
VOL B-C
VOL D-Z
GREAT LIES: Samson and Delilah
AiEEE!
ACTUALLY IT WAS SAMSON WHO GAVE DELILAH THAT FAMOUS HAIRCUT. IT'S REPORTED THAT DELILAH ASKED FOR A TRIM, AND INSTEAD GOT ONE OF THE WORST HAIRCUTS OF THE PRE-CHRISTIAN ERA. IN A BLIND RAGE SHE DESTROYED THE SALON AND A NEARBY BOUTIQUE.

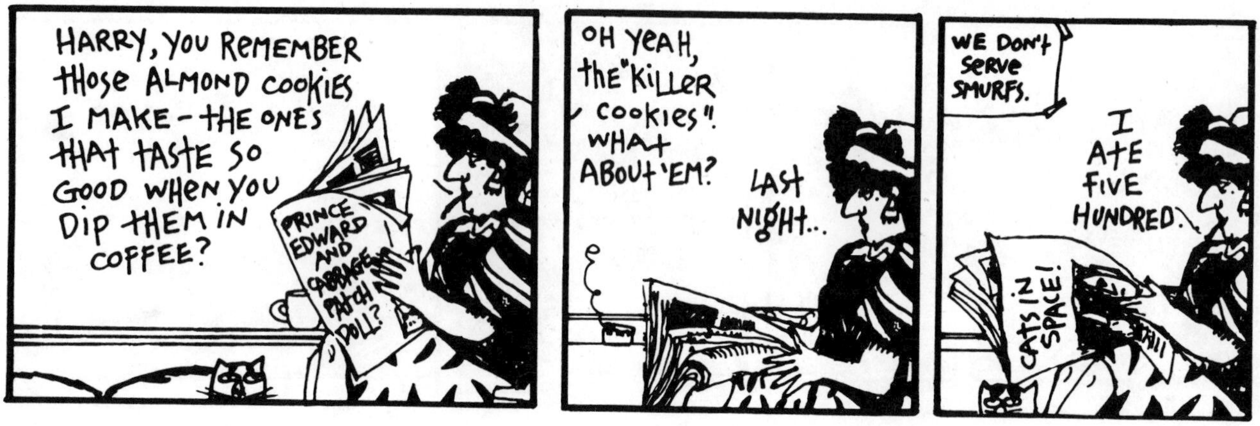
HARRY, YOU REMEMBER THOSE ALMOND COOKIES I MAKE - THE ONES THAT TASTE SO GOOD WHEN YOU DIP THEM IN COFFEE?
PRINCE EDWARD AND CABBAGE PATCH DOLL?
OH YEAH, THE "KILLER COOKIES". WHAT ABOUT 'EM?
LAST NIGHT...
WE DON'T SERVE SMURFS.
I ATE FIVE HUNDRED.
CATS IN SPACE!

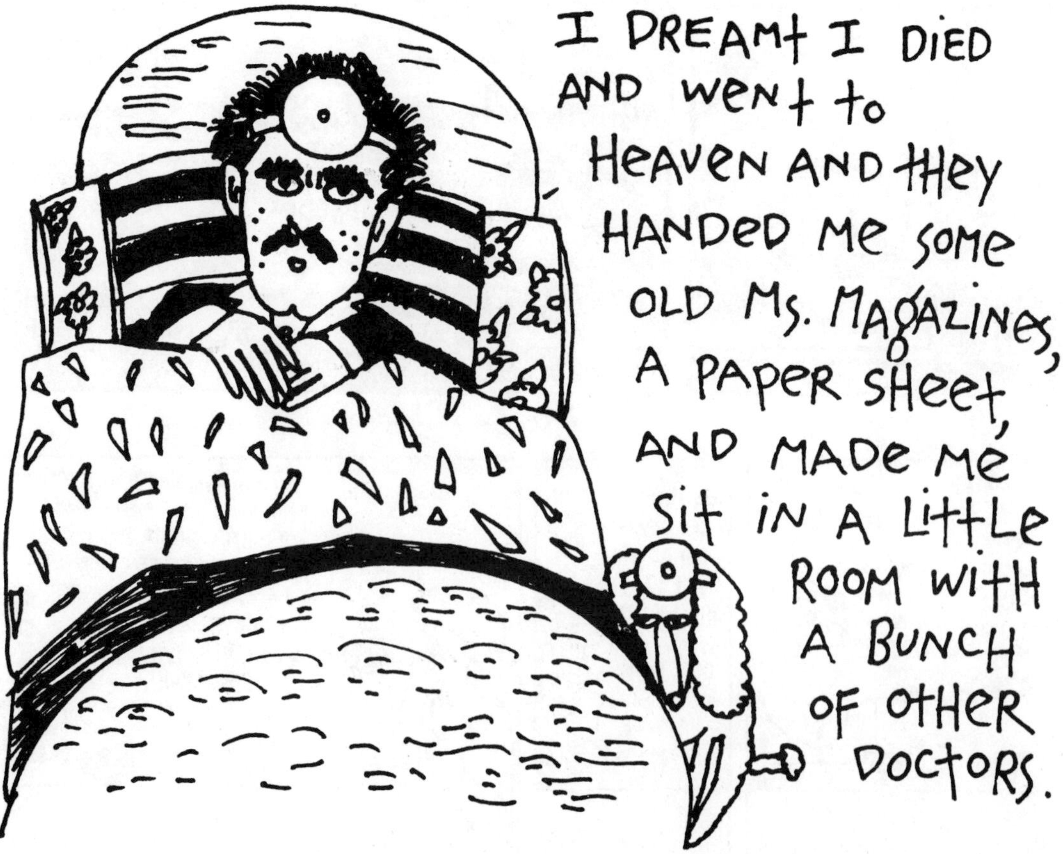
I DREAMT I DIED AND WENT TO HEAVEN AND THEY HANDED ME SOME OLD Ms. MAGAZINES, A PAPER SHEET, AND MADE ME SIT IN A LITTLE ROOM WITH A BUNCH OF OTHER DOCTORS.

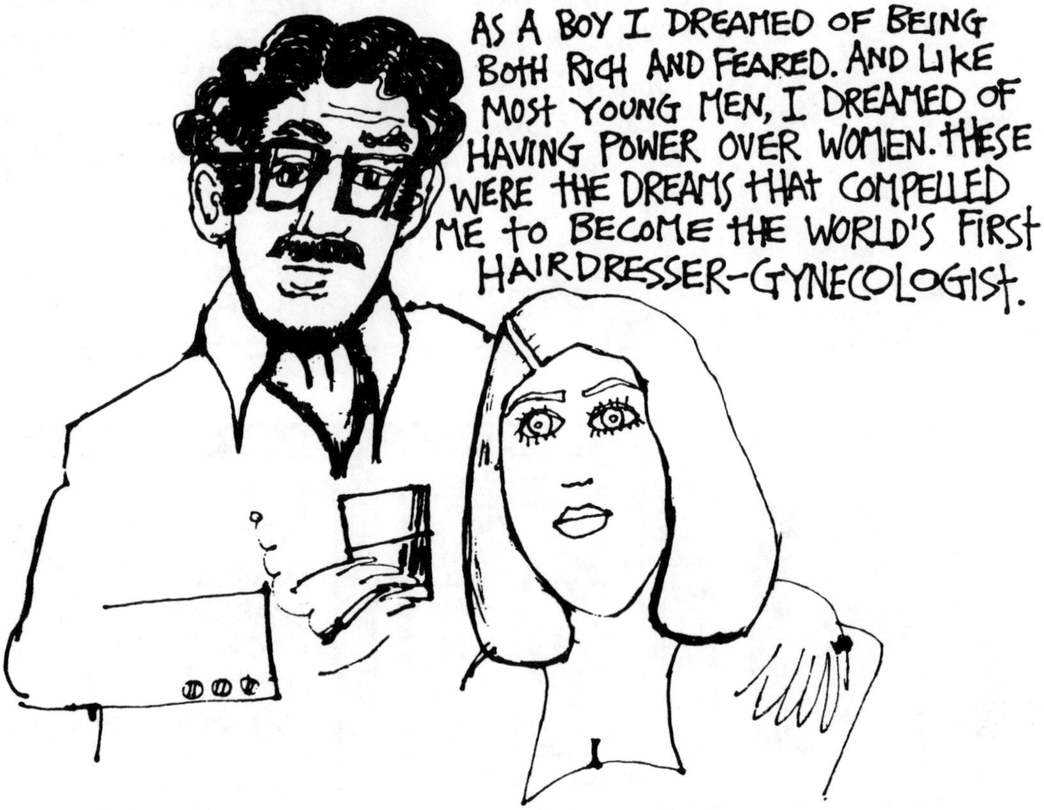
AS A BOY I DREAMED OF BEING BOTH RICH AND FEARED. AND LIKE MOST YOUNG MEN, I DREAMED OF HAVING POWER OVER WOMEN. THESE WERE THE DREAMS THAT COMPELLED ME TO BECOME THE WORLD'S FIRST HAIRDRESSER-GYNECOLOGIST.

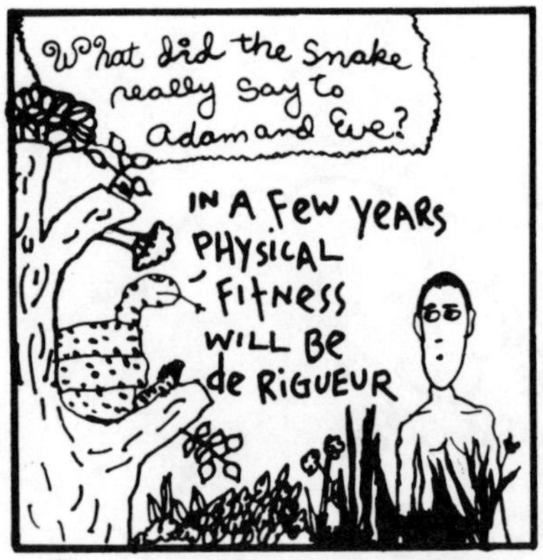
What did the Snake really say to adam and Eve?
IN A FEW YEARS PHYSICAL FITNESS WILL BE de RIGUEUR

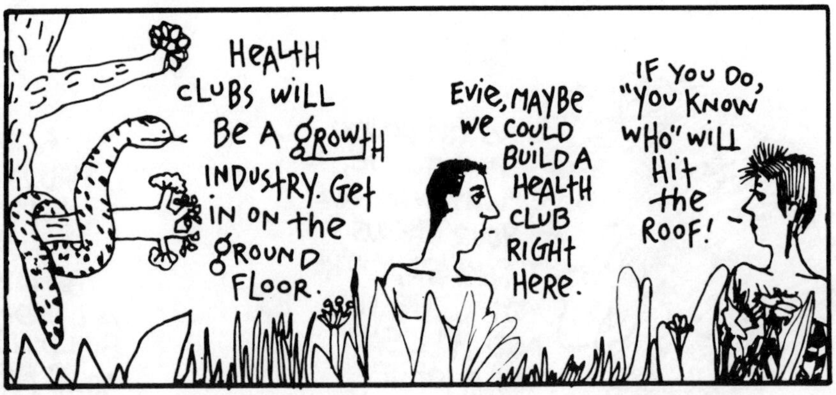
HEALTH CLUBS WILL BE A GROWTH INDUSTRY. GET IN ON THE GROUND FLOOR.
EVIE, MAYBE WE COULD BUILD A HEALTH CLUB RIGHT HERE.
IF YOU DO, "YOU KNOW WHO" WILL HIT THE ROOF!

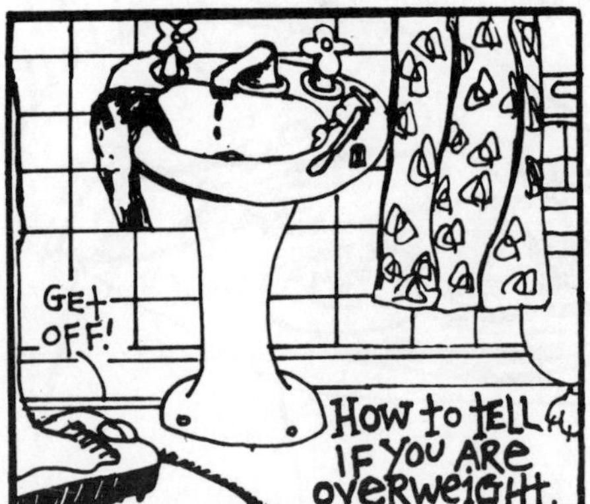
GET OFF!
HOW TO TELL IF YOU ARE OVERWEIGHT.

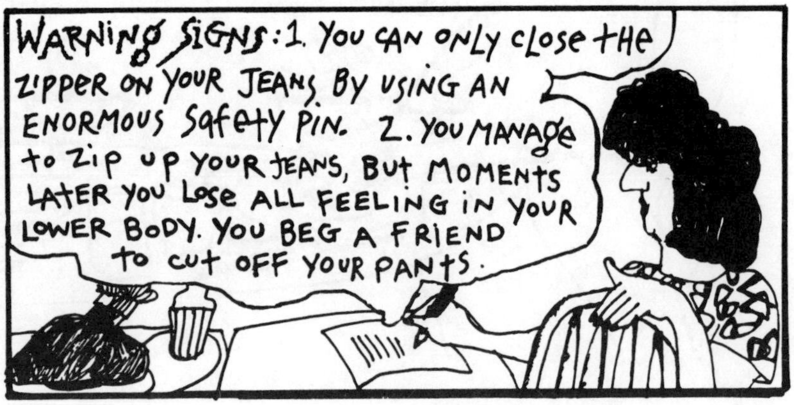
WARNING SIGNS: 1. YOU CAN ONLY CLOSE THE ZIPPER ON YOUR JEANS BY USING AN ENORMOUS SAFETY PIN. 2. YOU MANAGE TO ZIP UP YOUR JEANS, BUT MOMENTS LATER YOU LOSE ALL FEELING IN YOUR LOWER BODY. YOU BEG A FRIEND TO CUT OFF YOUR PANTS.

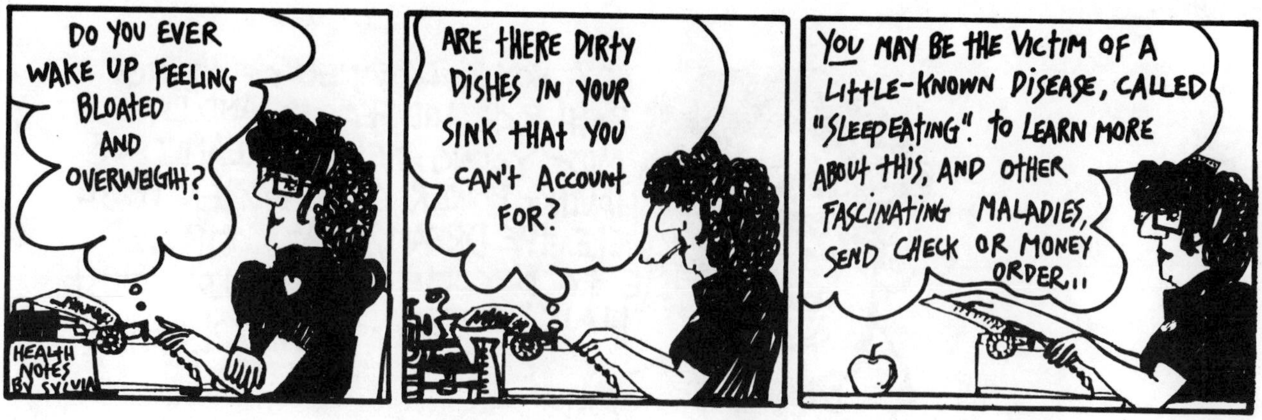
DO YOU EVER WAKE UP FEELING BLOATED AND OVERWEIGHT?
HEALTH NOTES BY SYLVIA
ARE THERE DIRTY DISHES IN YOUR SINK THAT YOU CAN'T ACCOUNT FOR?
YOU MAY BE THE VICTIM OF A LITTLE-KNOWN DISEASE, CALLED "SLEEPEATING". TO LEARN MORE ABOUT THIS, AND OTHER FASCINATING MALADIES, SEND CHECK OR MONEY ORDER..

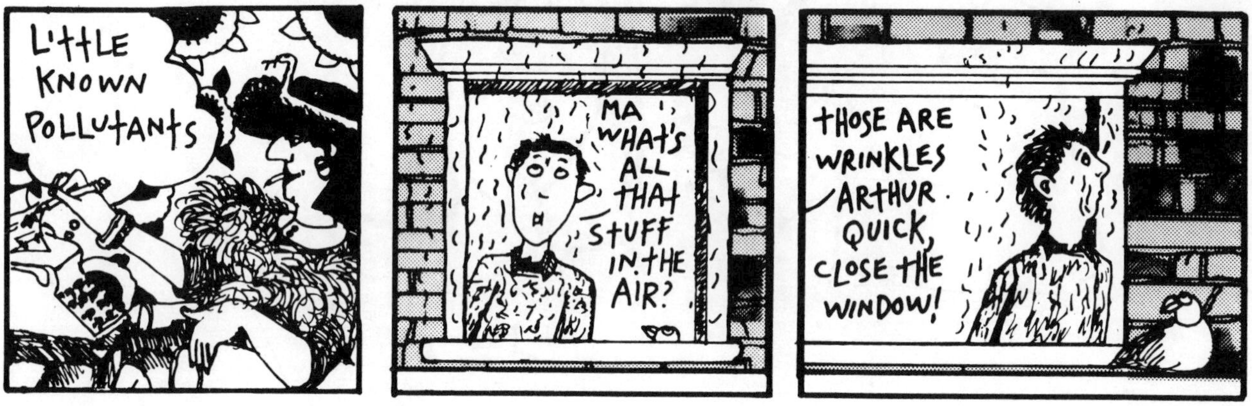
LITTLE KNOWN POLLUTANTS
MA WHAT'S ALL THAT STUFF IN THE AIR?
THOSE ARE WRINKLES ARTHUR. QUICK, CLOSE THE WINDOW!

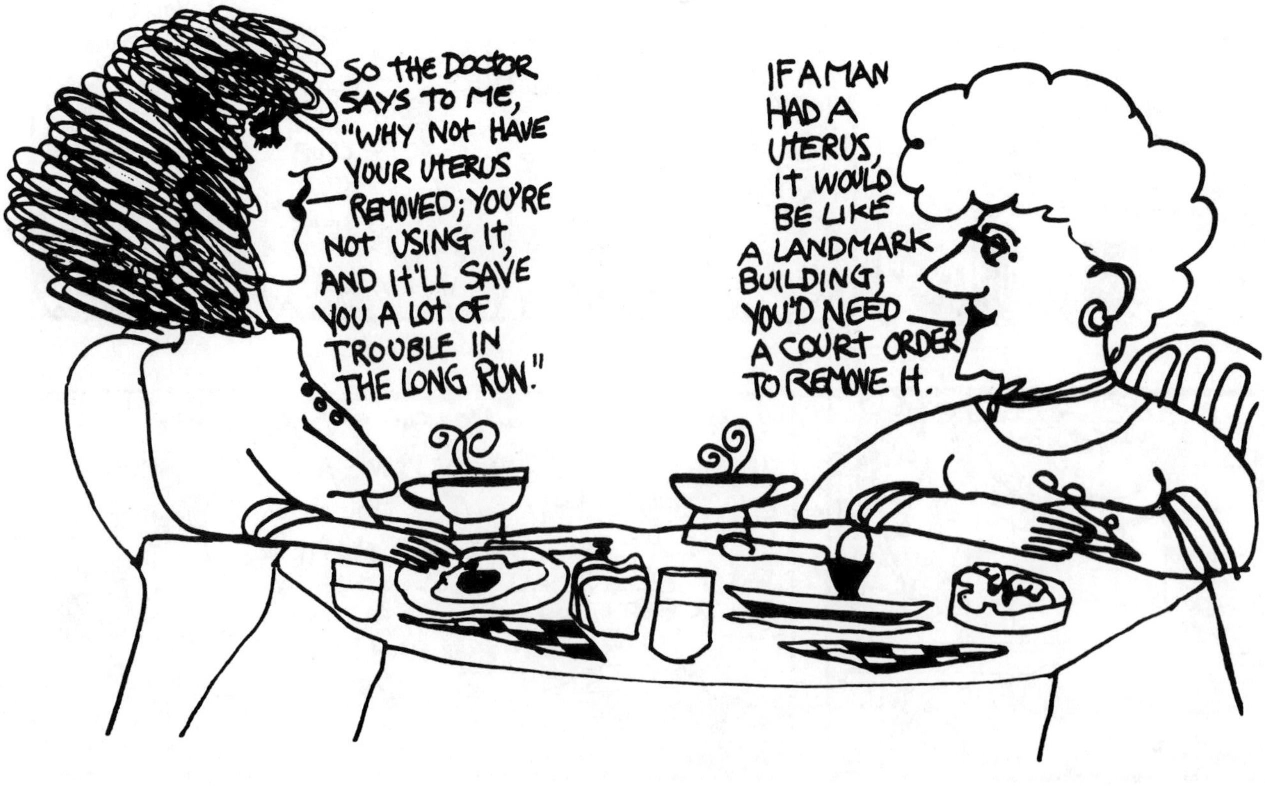
SO THE DOCTOR SAYS TO ME, "WHY NOT HAVE YOUR UTERUS REMOVED; YOU'RE NOT USING IT, AND IT'LL SAVE YOU A LOT OF TROUBLE IN THE LONG RUN."
IF A MAN HAD A UTERUS, IT WOULD BE LIKE A LANDMARK BUILDING; YOU'D NEED A COURT ORDER TO REMOVE IT.

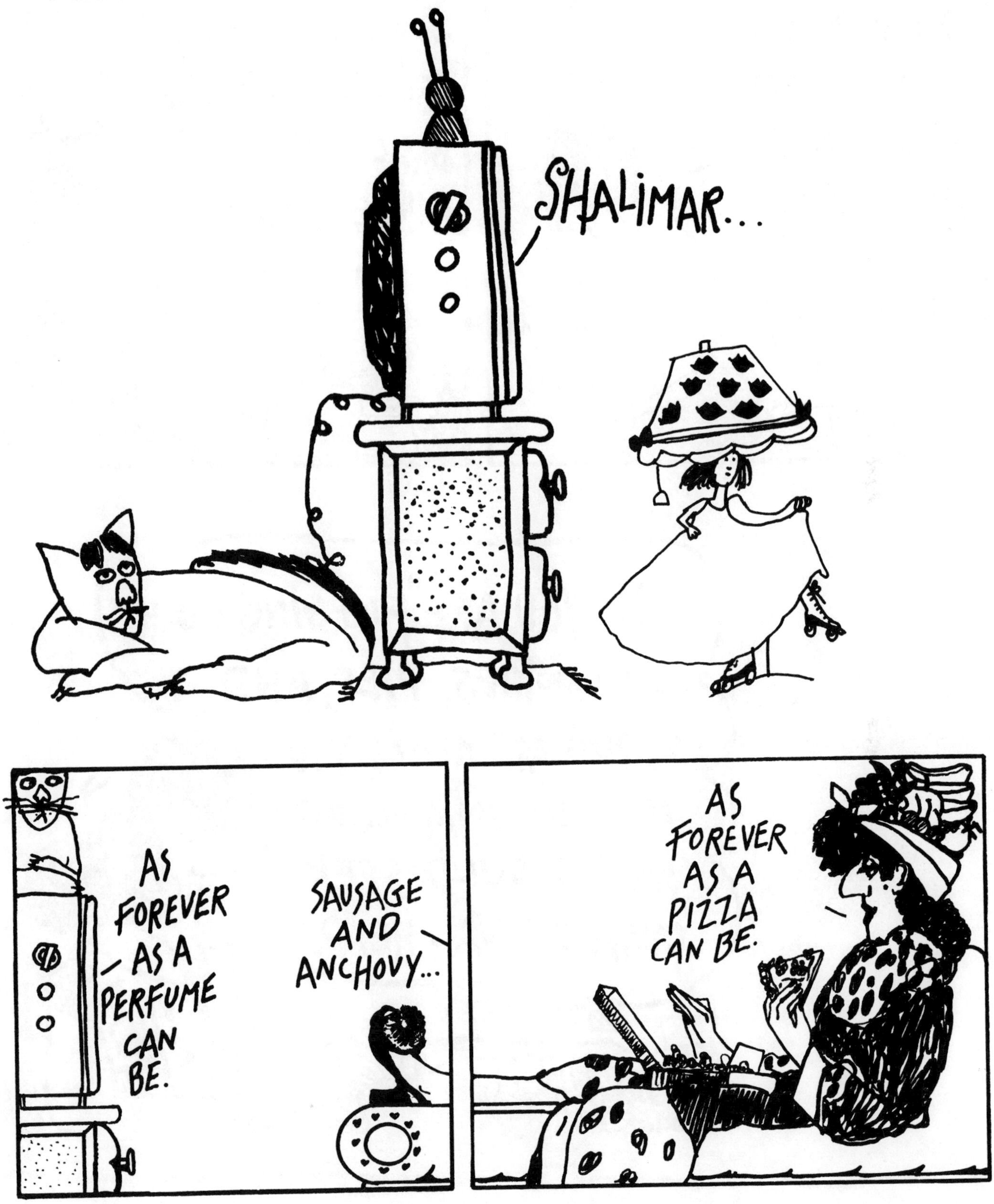
SHALIMAR...
AS FOREVER AS A PERFUME CAN BE.
SAUSAGE AND ANCHOVY...
AS FOREVER AS A PIZZA CAN BE.

DEAR ANXIOUS, I DON'T FEEL THAT OVEREATING IS ALWAYS AN INDICATION OF NEUROSIS.
IF YOU ARE OVEREATING FROM EACH OF THE BASIC FOOD GROUPS, THERE IS NO CAUSE FOR CONCERN.
-IF YOU ARE "PIGGING OUT" ON COOKIES, PIES, AND CHOCOLATE KISSES, YOU MAY BE IMMATURE AND SHOULD SEEK PROFESSIONAL HELP.

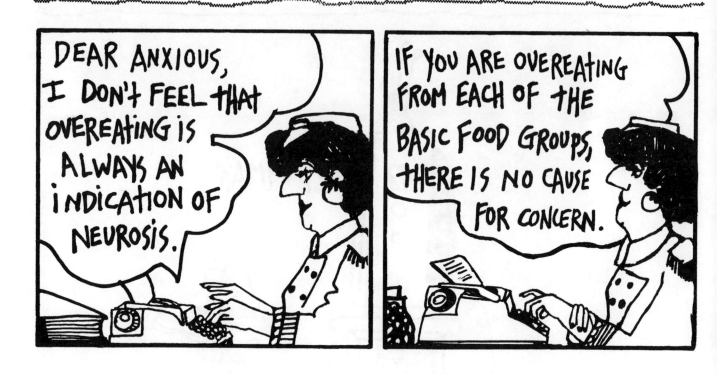

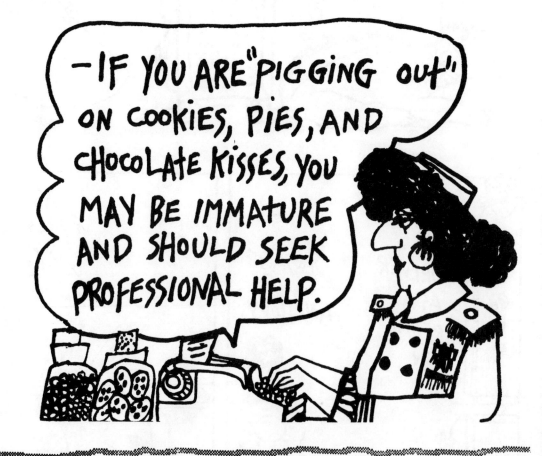

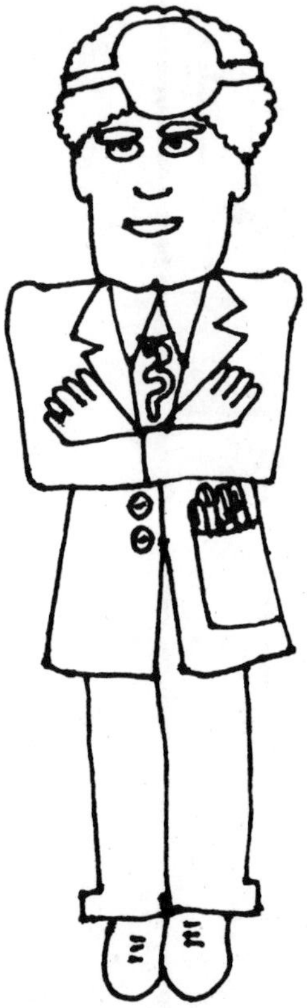

Is Medical School the right choice for *you*?

A SELF-EVALUATION TEST FOR THE PRE-MEDICAL STUDENT

Answer true or false:

T	F	
☐	☐	**1.** Mothers often overreact to the most trivial symptoms in their children.
☐	☐	**2.** Mothers are often guilty of denial followed by neglect in not bringing a symptomatic child to the doctor.
☐	☐	**3.** Women often imagine breast lumps.
☐	☐	**4.** Women should examine their breasts often enough, but not too often.*
☐	☐	**5.** Informing patients of the side effects of the drugs prescribed for them will cause the patients to experience these side effects in their most virulent form.
☐	☐	**6.** Women are sexually excited by gynecological examinations.
☐	☐	**7.** Patients never ask the really interesting questions.
☐	☐	**8.** A certain amount of physical discomfort is to be expected in anyone over 35, and old people should keep their symptoms to themselves.
☐	☐	**9.** No doctor can ever really be guilty of malpractice.
☐	☐	**10.** Most people when asked to describe your personality would say, "He's not real warm."

**Too often* if the lump disappears in a few months; *not often* enough if the lump turns out to be malignant.

ANSWERS: You know who you are.

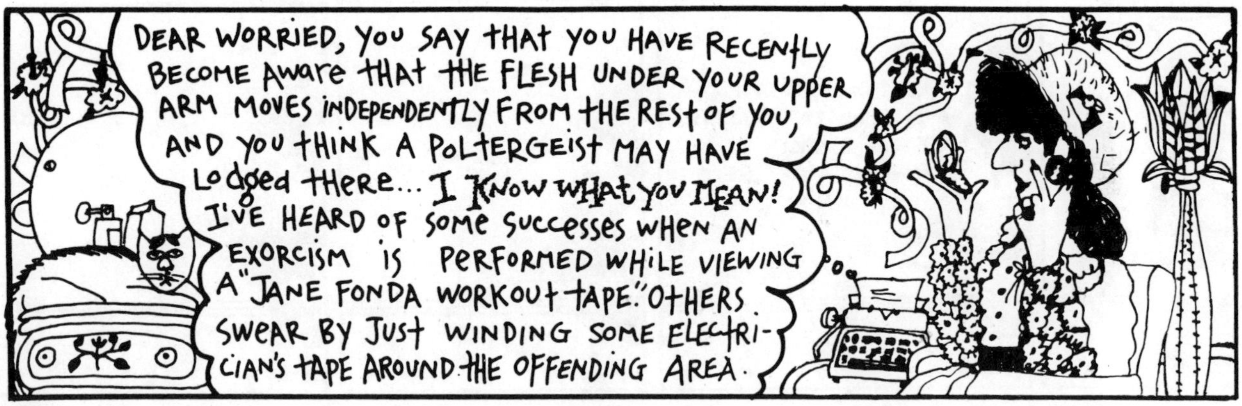
DEAR WORRIED, YOU SAY THAT YOU HAVE RECENTLY BECOME AWARE THAT THE FLESH UNDER YOUR UPPER ARM MOVES INDEPENDENTLY FROM THE REST OF YOU, AND YOU THINK A POLTERGEIST MAY HAVE LODGED THERE... I KNOW WHAT YOU MEAN! I'VE HEARD OF SOME SUCCESSES WHEN AN EXORCISM IS PERFORMED WHILE VIEWING A "JANE FONDA WORKOUT TAPE." OTHERS SWEAR BY JUST WINDING SOME ELECTRICIAN'S TAPE AROUND THE OFFENDING AREA.

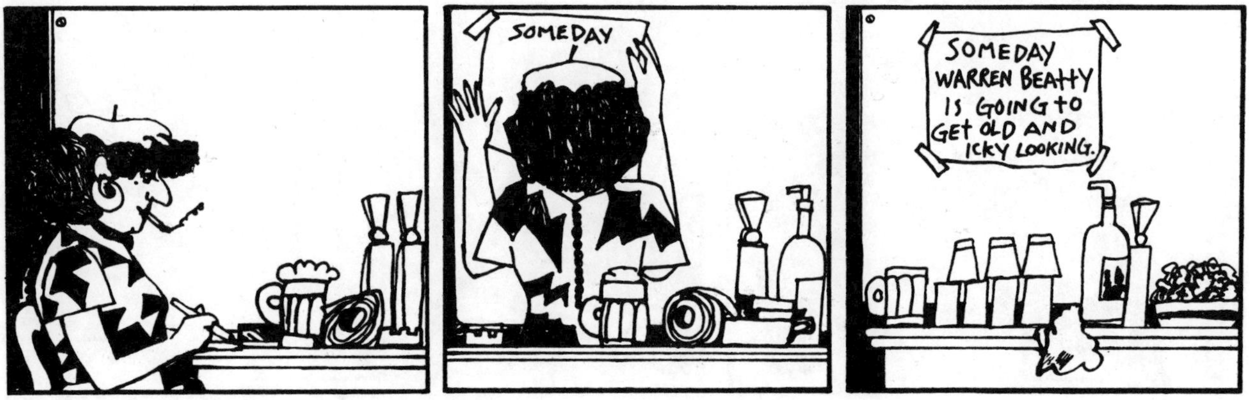
SOMEDAY
SOMEDAY WARREN BEATTY IS GOING TO GET OLD AND ICKY LOOKING.

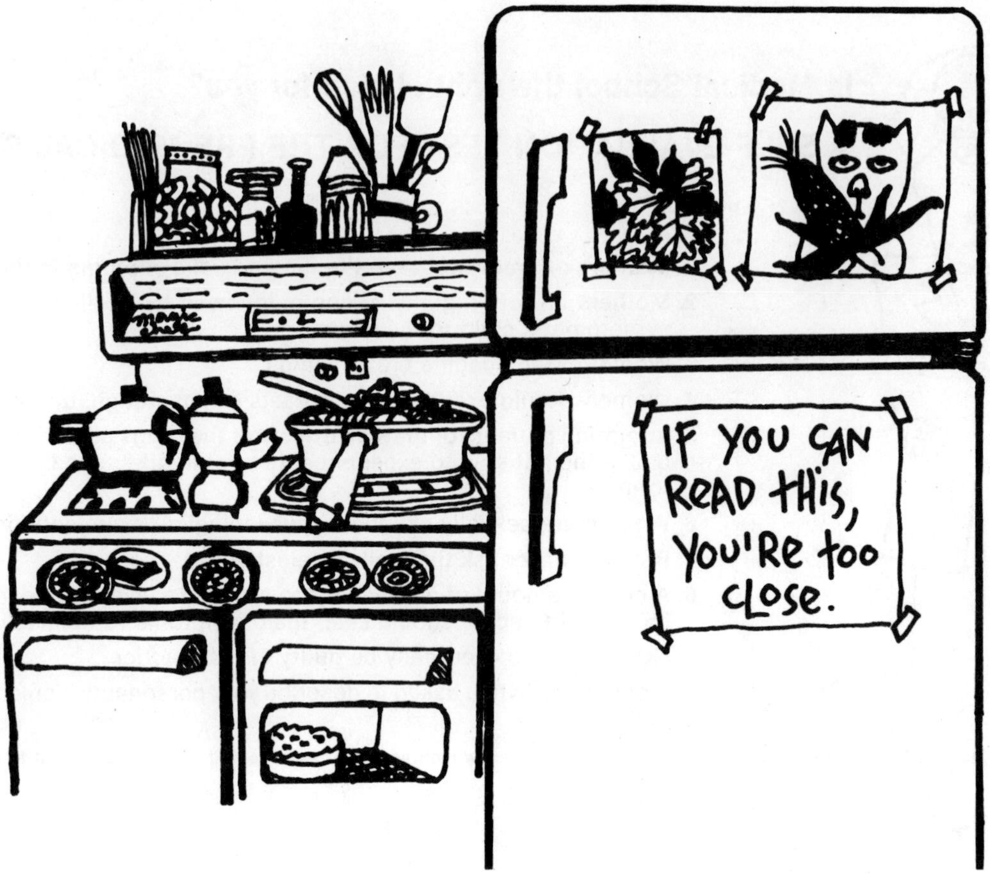
IF YOU CAN READ THIS, YOU'RE TOO CLOSE.

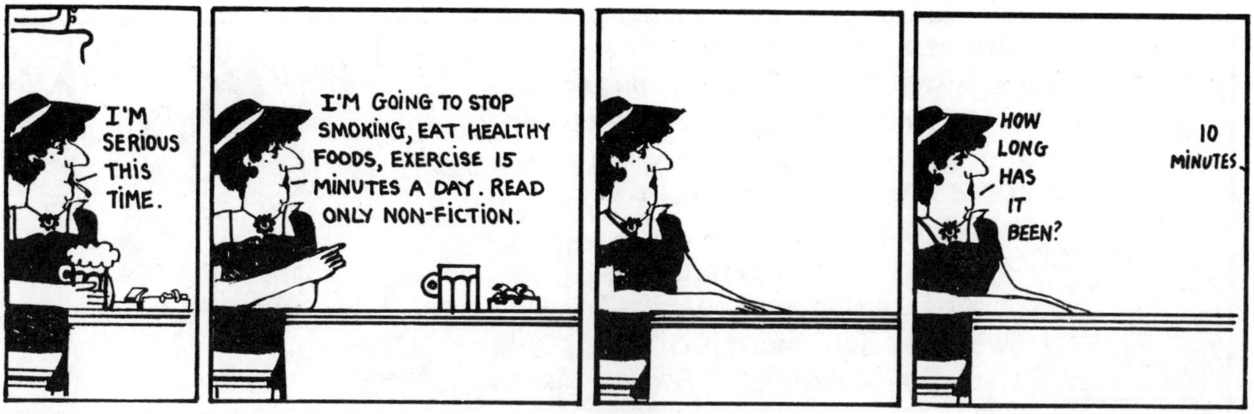
I'M SERIOUS THIS TIME.
I'M GOING TO STOP SMOKING, EAT HEALTHY FOODS, EXERCISE 15 MINUTES A DAY. READ ONLY NON-FICTION.
HOW LONG HAS IT BEEN?
10 MINUTES.

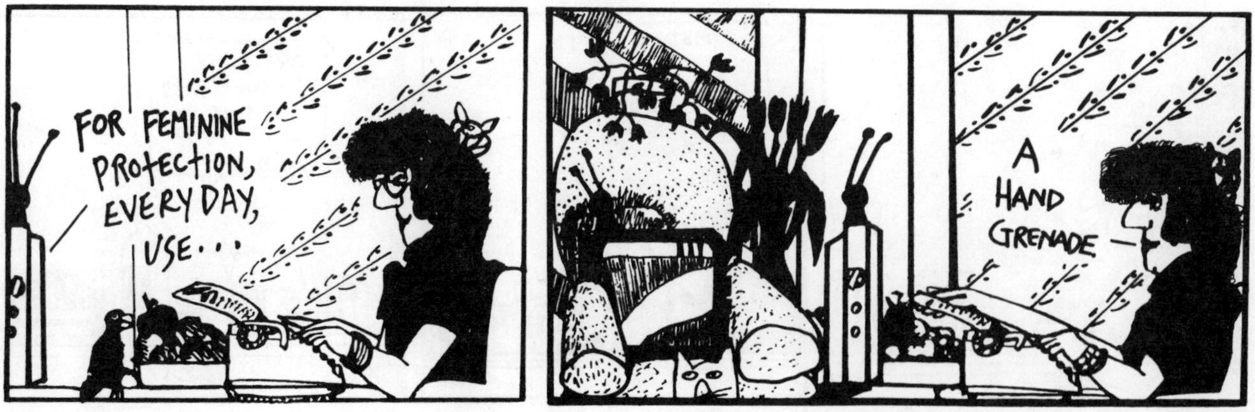
FOR FEMININE PROTECTION, EVERY DAY, USE...
A HAND GRENADE

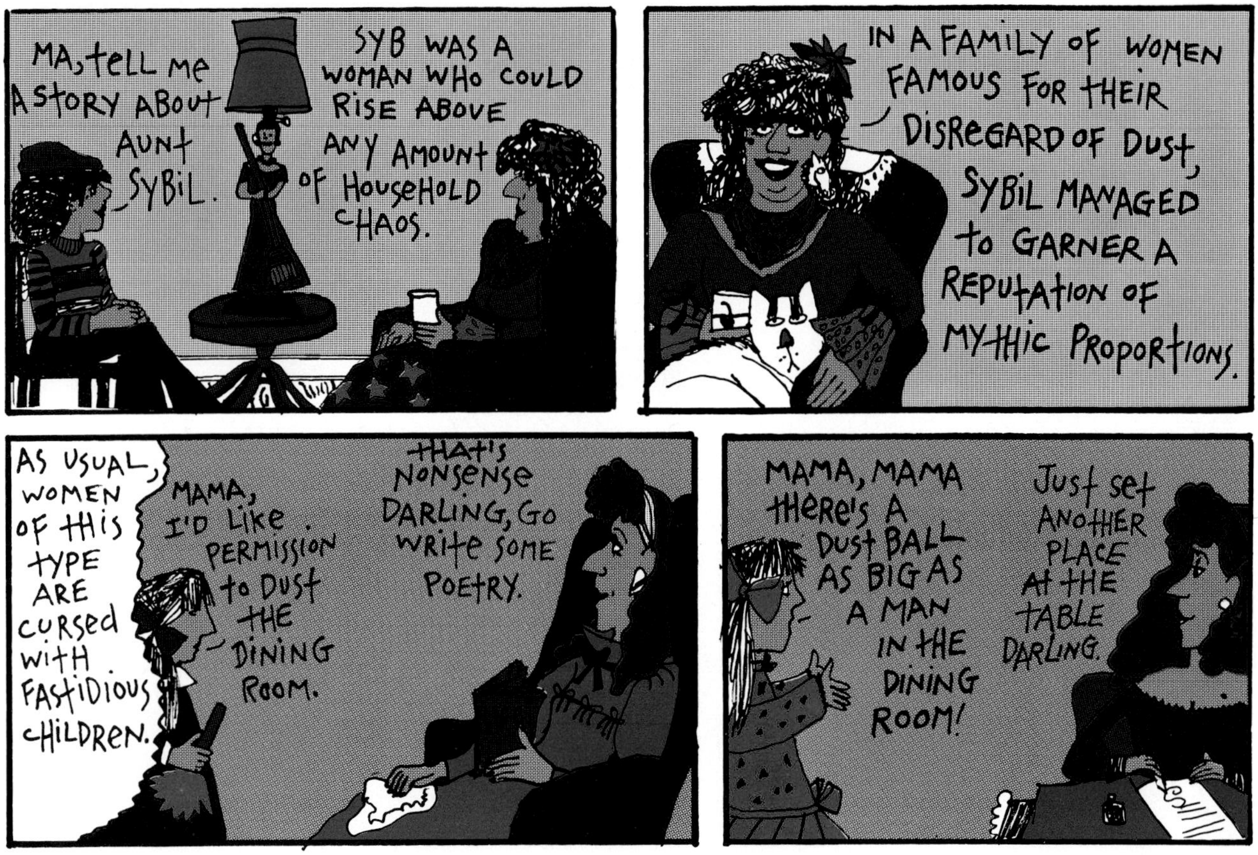
MA, tell me A story About Aunt SYBIL.
SYB WAS A WOMAN WHO COULD RISE ABOVE ANY AMOUNT OF HOUSEHOLD CHAOS.
IN A FAMILY OF WOMEN FAMOUS FOR THEIR DISREGARD OF DUST, SYBIL MANAGED TO GARNER A REPUTATION OF MYTHIC PROPORTIONS.
AS USUAL, WOMEN OF THIS TYPE ARE CURSED WITH FASTIDIOUS CHILDREN.
MAMA, I'D LIKE PERMISSION TO DUST THE DINING ROOM.
THAT'S NONSENSE DARLING, GO WRITE SOME POETRY.
MAMA, MAMA THERE'S A DUST BALL AS BIG AS A MAN IN THE DINING ROOM!
JUST SET ANOTHER PLACE AT THE TABLE DARLING.

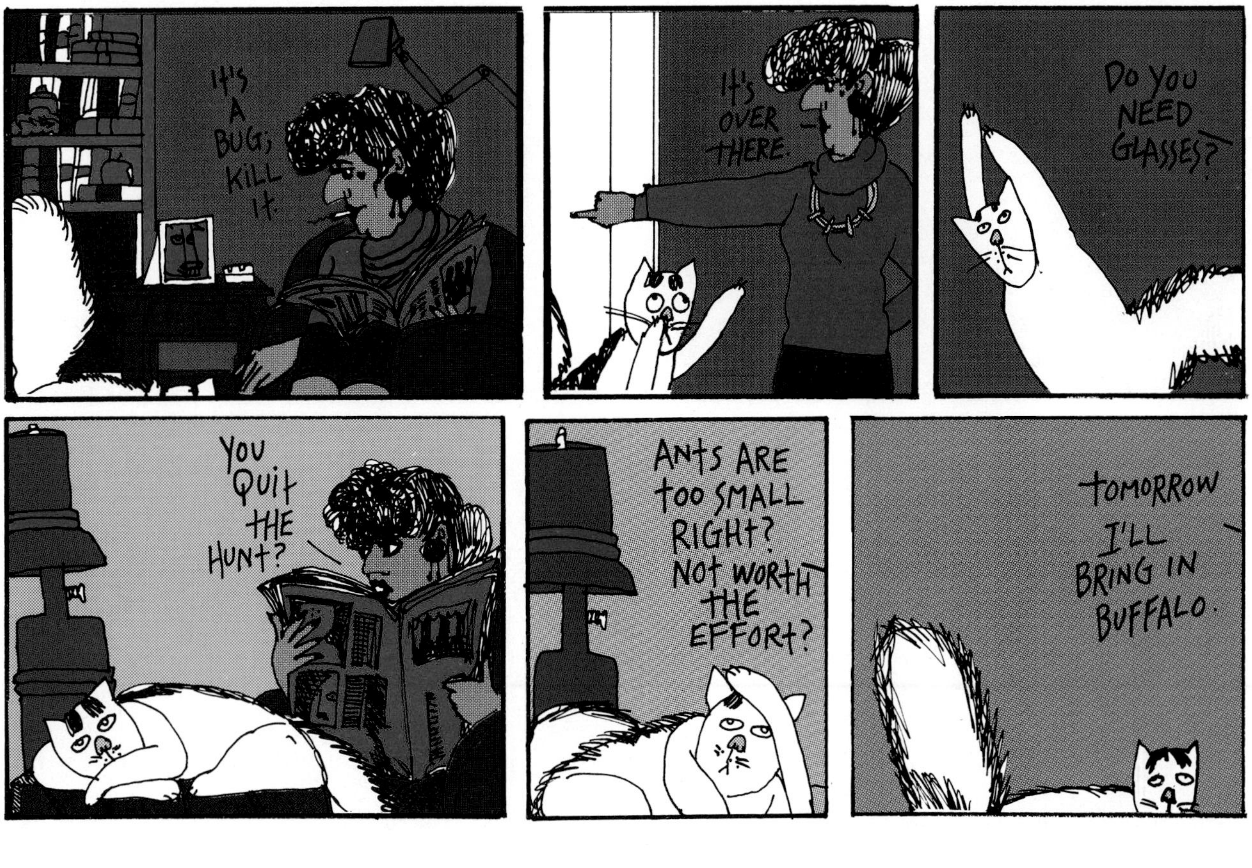
IT'S A BUG; KILL IT.
IT'S OVER THERE.
DO YOU NEED GLASSES?
YOU QUIT THE HUNT?
ANTS ARE TOO SMALL RIGHT? NOT WORTH THE EFFORT?
TOMORROW I'LL BRING IN BUFFALO.

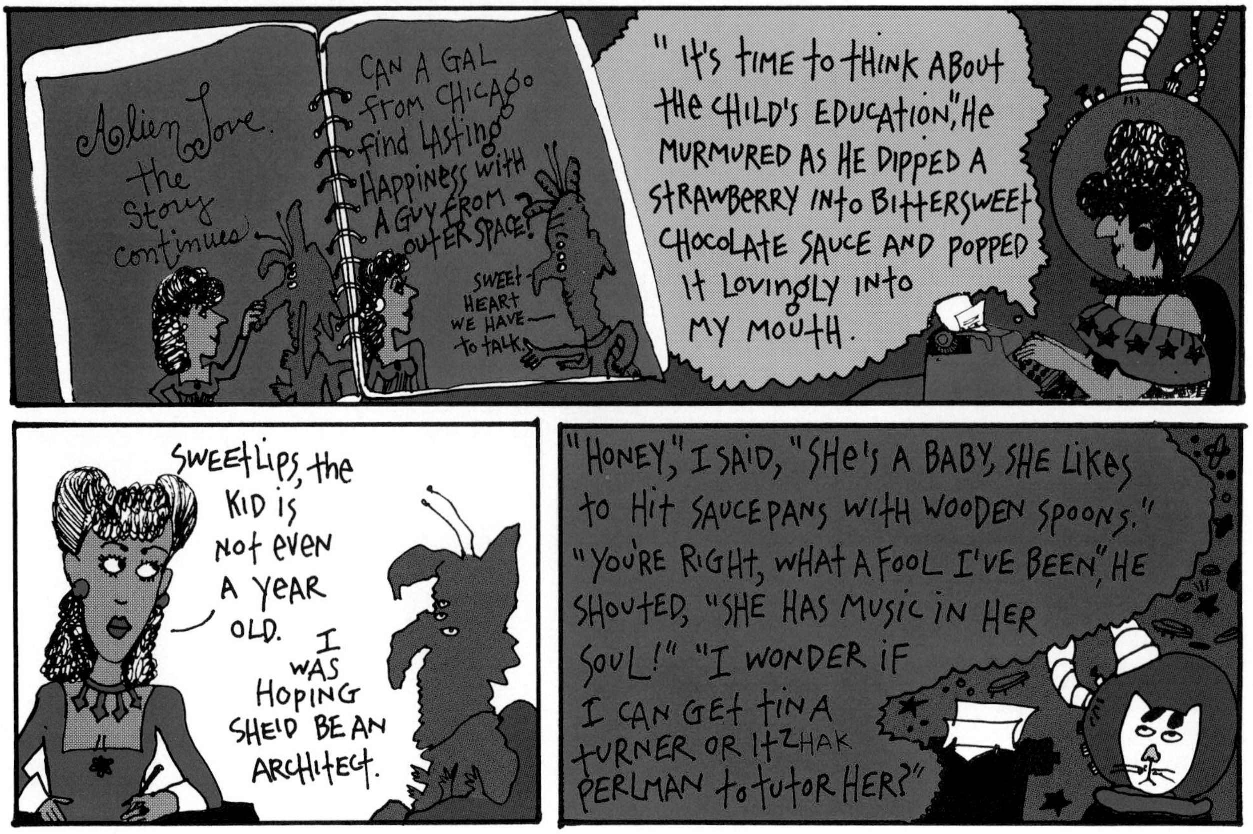
Alien Love the Story continues
CAN A GAL from CHICAGO find LASTING HAPPINESS with A GUY FROM OUTER SPACE?
SWEET-HEART WE HAVE to TALK.
"It's time to think About the CHILD's EDUCATION," He MURMURED AS HE DIPPED A STRAWBERRY INto BITTERSWEET CHOCOLATE SAUCE AND POPPED It Lovingly into my mouth.
SWEETLIPS, the KID is Not even A YEAR OLD.
I WAS HOPING SHE'D BE AN ARCHITECT.
"HONEY," I SAID, "SHE's A BABY, SHE LIKES to Hit SAUCEPANS WITH WOODEN spoons." "YOU'RE RIGHT, WHAT A FOOL I'VE BEEN," HE SHOUTED, "SHE HAS MUSIC IN HER SOUL!" "I WONDER IF I CAN GET TINA TURNER OR ITZHAK PERLMAN to tutor HER?"

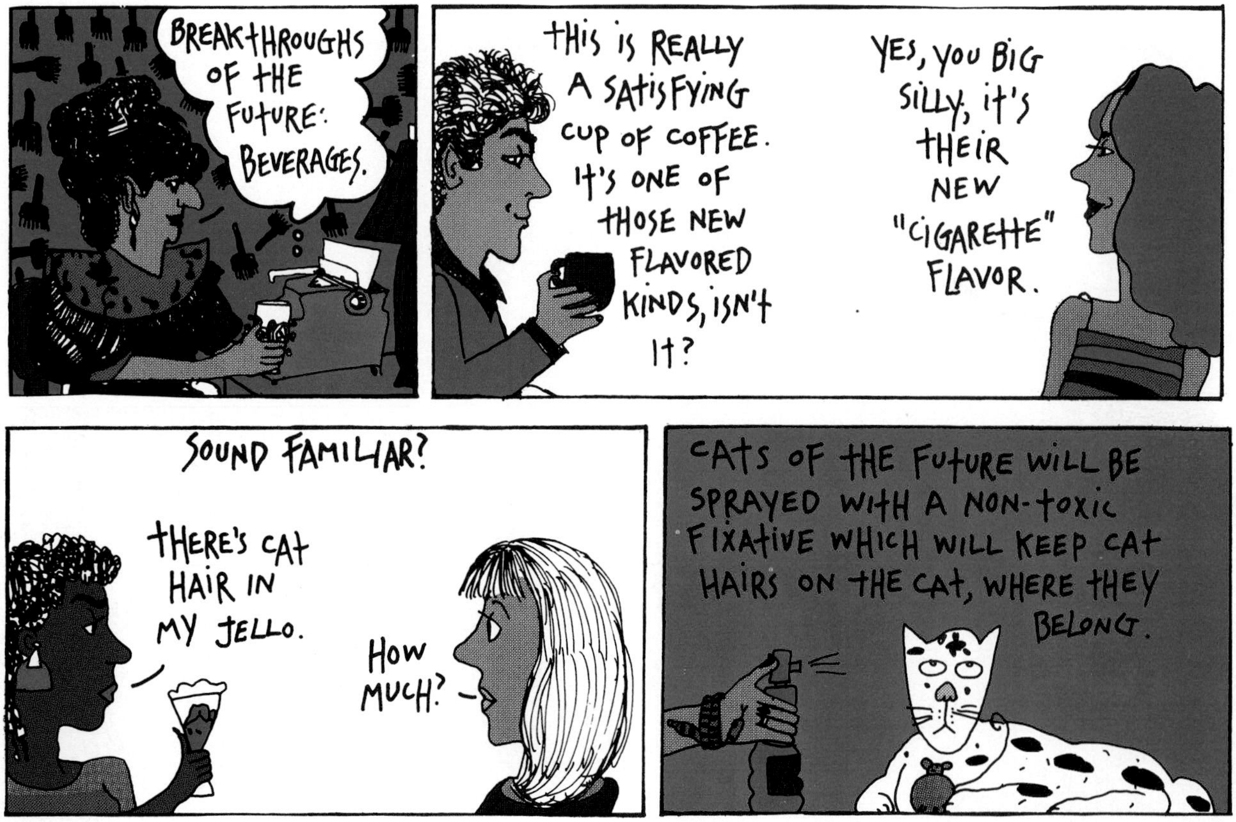
BREAKTHROUGHS OF THE FUTURE: BEVERAGES.
THIS is REALLY A SATISFYING CUP OF COFFEE. It's ONE OF THOSE NEW FLAVORED KINDS, ISN'T It?
YES, you BIG SILLY, it's THEIR NEW "CIGARETTE" FLAVOR.
SOUND FAMILIAR?
THERE'S CAT HAIR IN MY JELLO.
HOW MUCH?
CATS OF THE FUTURE WILL BE SPRAYED WITH A NON-TOXIC FIXATIVE WHICH WILL KEEP CAT HAIRS ON THE CAT, WHERE THEY BELONG.

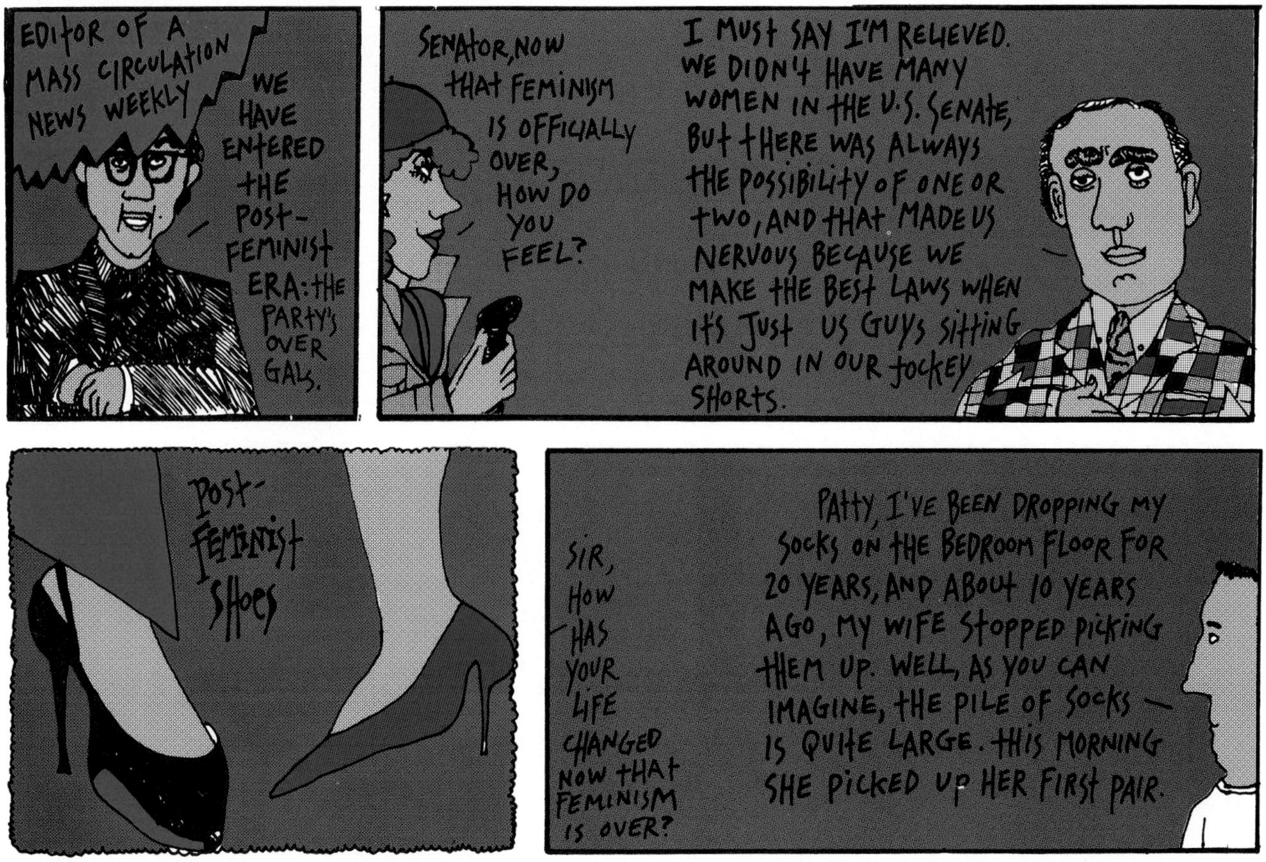
EDITOR OF A MASS CIRCULATION NEWS WEEKLY
WE HAVE ENTERED THE POST-FEMINIST ERA: THE PARTY'S OVER GALS.
SENATOR, NOW THAT FEMINISM IS OFFICIALLY OVER, HOW DO YOU FEEL?
I MUST SAY I'M RELIEVED. WE DIDN'T HAVE MANY WOMEN IN THE U.S. SENATE, BUT THERE WAS ALWAYS THE POSSIBILITY OF ONE OR TWO, AND THAT MADE US NERVOUS BECAUSE WE MAKE THE BEST LAWS WHEN IT'S JUST US GUYS SITTING AROUND IN OUR JOCKEY SHORTS.
POST-FEMINIST SHOES
SIR, HOW HAS YOUR LIFE CHANGED NOW THAT FEMINISM IS OVER?
PATTY, I'VE BEEN DROPPING MY SOCKS ON THE BEDROOM FLOOR FOR 20 YEARS, AND ABOUT 10 YEARS AGO, MY WIFE STOPPED PICKING THEM UP. WELL, AS YOU CAN IMAGINE, THE PILE OF SOCKS IS QUITE LARGE. THIS MORNING SHE PICKED UP HER FIRST PAIR.

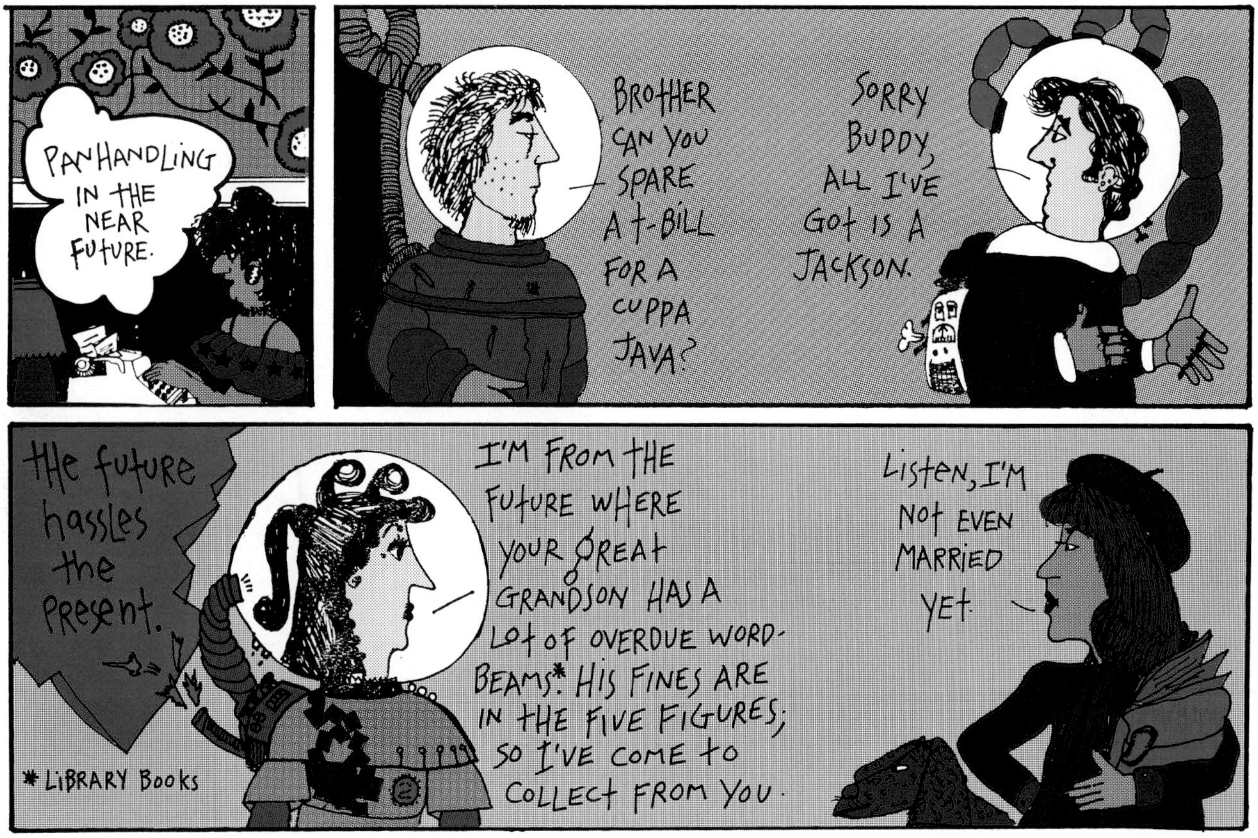
PANHANDLING IN THE NEAR FUTURE.
BROTHER CAN YOU SPARE A T-BILL FOR A CUPPA JAVA?
SORRY BUDDY, ALL I'VE GOT IS A JACKSON.
THE FUTURE HASSLES THE PRESENT.
I'M FROM THE FUTURE WHERE YOUR GREAT GRANDSON HAS A LOT OF OVERDUE WORD-BEAMS.* HIS FINES ARE IN THE FIVE FIGURES; SO I'VE COME TO COLLECT FROM YOU.
LISTEN, I'M NOT EVEN MARRIED YET.
*LIBRARY BOOKS

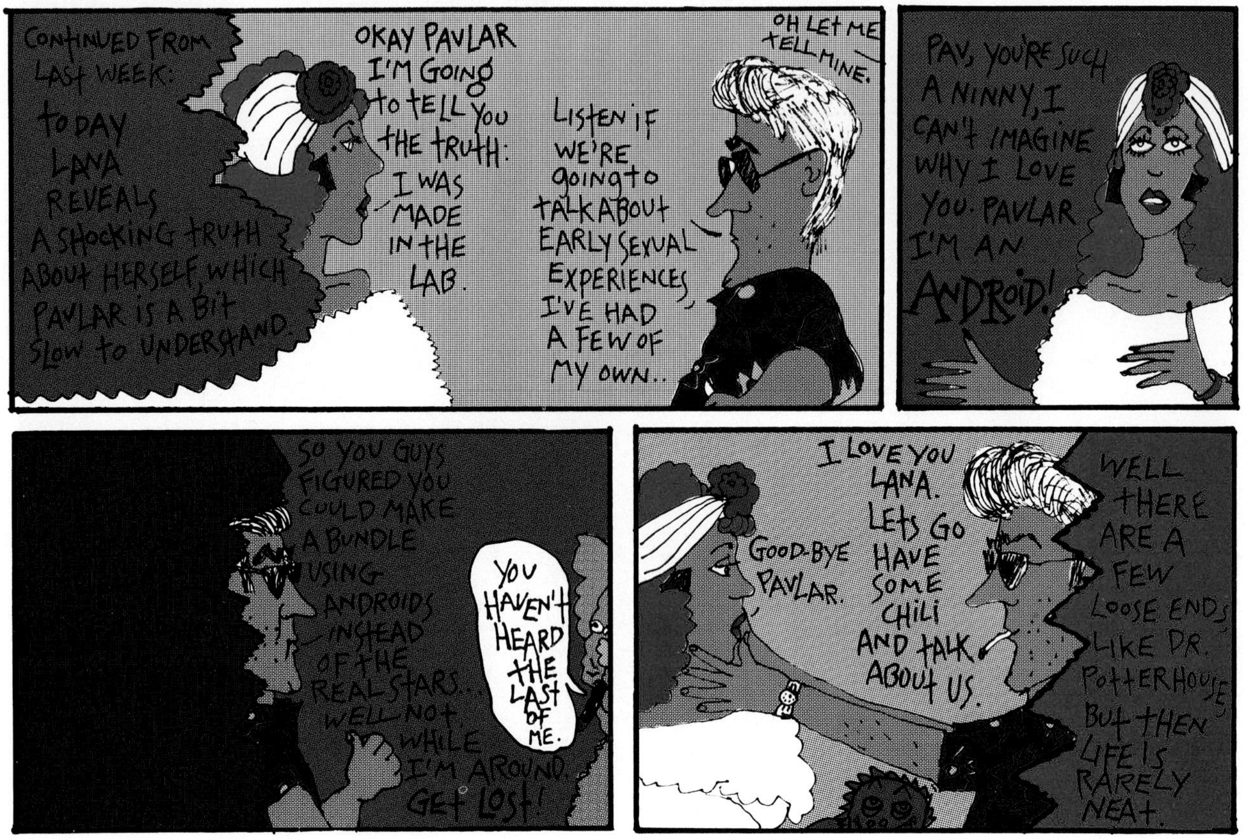
CONTINUED FROM LAST WEEK: TODAY LANA REVEALS A SHOCKING TRUTH ABOUT HERSELF, WHICH PAVLAR IS A BIT SLOW TO UNDERSTAND.
OKAY PAVLAR I'M GOING TO TELL YOU THE TRUTH: I WAS MADE IN THE LAB.
LISTEN IF WE'RE GOING TO TALK ABOUT EARLY SEXUAL EXPERIENCES I'VE HAD A FEW OF MY OWN..
OH LET ME TELL MINE.
PAV, YOU'RE SUCH A NINNY, I CAN'T IMAGINE WHY I LOVE YOU. PAVLAR I'M AN ANDROID!
SO YOU GUYS FIGURED YOU COULD MAKE A BUNDLE USING ANDROIDS INSTEAD OF THE REAL STARS... WELL NOT WHILE I'M AROUND. GET LOST!
YOU HAVEN'T HEARD THE LAST OF ME.
I LOVE YOU LANA. LETS GO HAVE SOME CHILI AND TALK ABOUT US.
GOOD-BYE PAVLAR.
WELL THERE ARE A FEW LOOSE ENDS LIKE DR. POTTERHOUSE BUT THEN LIFE IS RARELY NEAT.

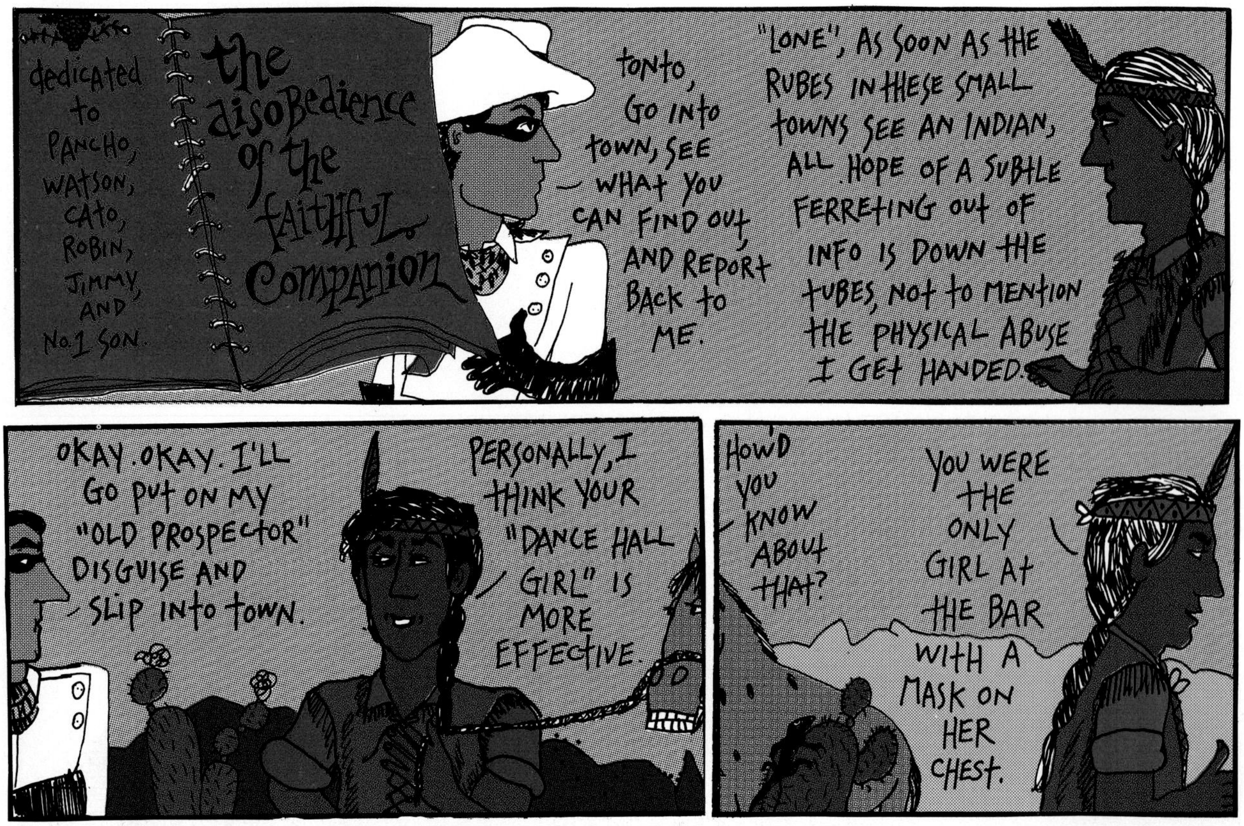
dedicated to PANCHO, WATSON, CATO, ROBIN, JIMMY, AND No. 1 SON.
the disobedience of the faithful companion
TONTO, GO INTO TOWN, SEE WHAT YOU CAN FIND OUT AND REPORT BACK TO ME.
"LONE", AS SOON AS THE RUBES IN THESE SMALL TOWNS SEE AN INDIAN, ALL HOPE OF A SUBTLE FERRETING OUT OF INFO IS DOWN THE TUBES, NOT TO MENTION THE PHYSICAL ABUSE I GET HANDED.
OKAY. OKAY. I'LL GO PUT ON MY "OLD PROSPECTOR" DISGUISE AND SLIP INTO TOWN.
PERSONALLY, I THINK YOUR "DANCE HALL GIRL" IS MORE EFFECTIVE.
HOW'D YOU KNOW ABOUT THAT?
YOU WERE THE ONLY GIRL AT THE BAR WITH A MASK ON HER CHEST.

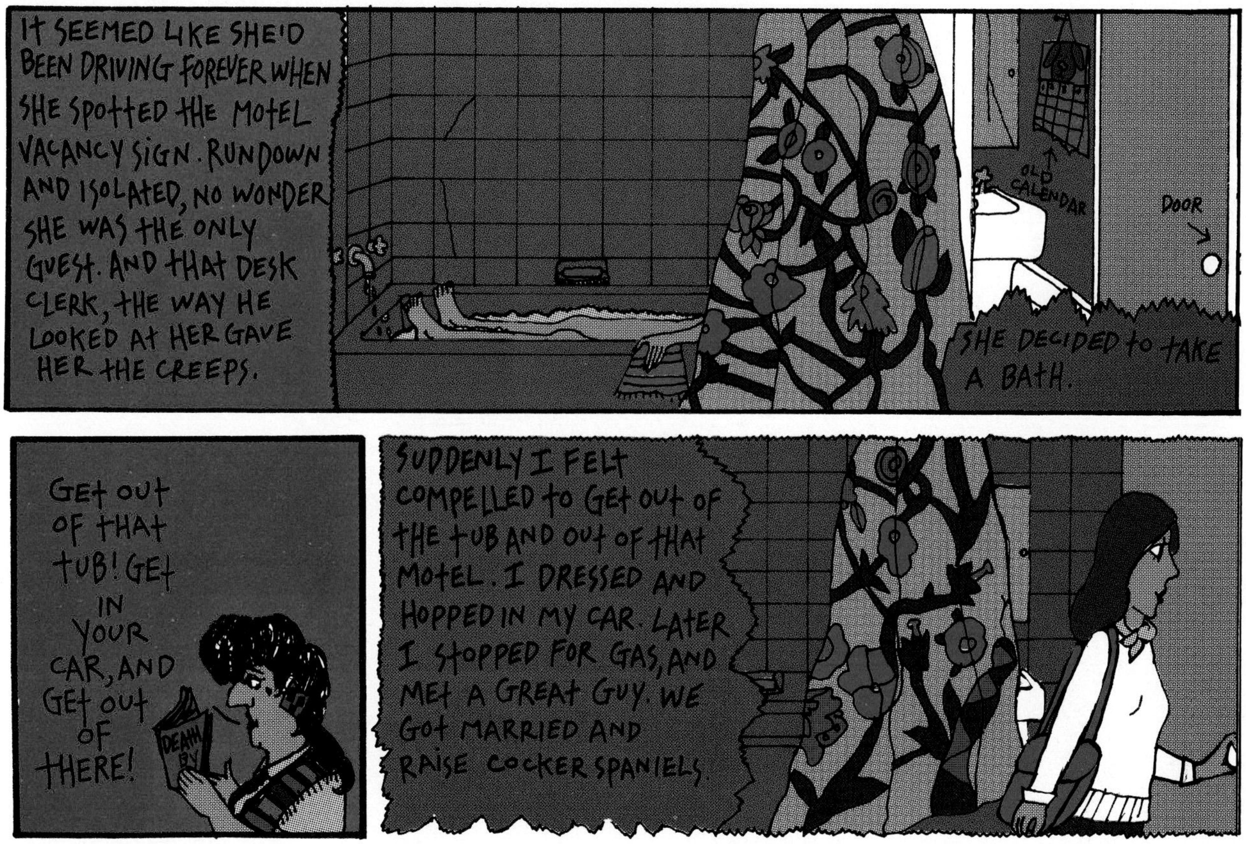
IT SEEMED LIKE SHE'D BEEN DRIVING FOREVER WHEN SHE SPOTTED THE MOTEL VACANCY SIGN. RUNDOWN AND ISOLATED, NO WONDER SHE WAS THE ONLY GUEST. AND THAT DESK CLERK, THE WAY HE LOOKED AT HER GAVE HER THE CREEPS.
OLD CALENDAR
DOOR
SHE DECIDED TO TAKE A BATH.
GET OUT OF THAT TUB! GET IN YOUR CAR, AND GET OUT OF THERE!
DEATH BY
SUDDENLY I FELT COMPELLED TO GET OUT OF THE TUB AND OUT OF THAT MOTEL. I DRESSED AND HOPPED IN MY CAR. LATER I STOPPED FOR GAS, AND MET A GREAT GUY. WE GOT MARRIED AND RAISE COCKER SPANIELS.

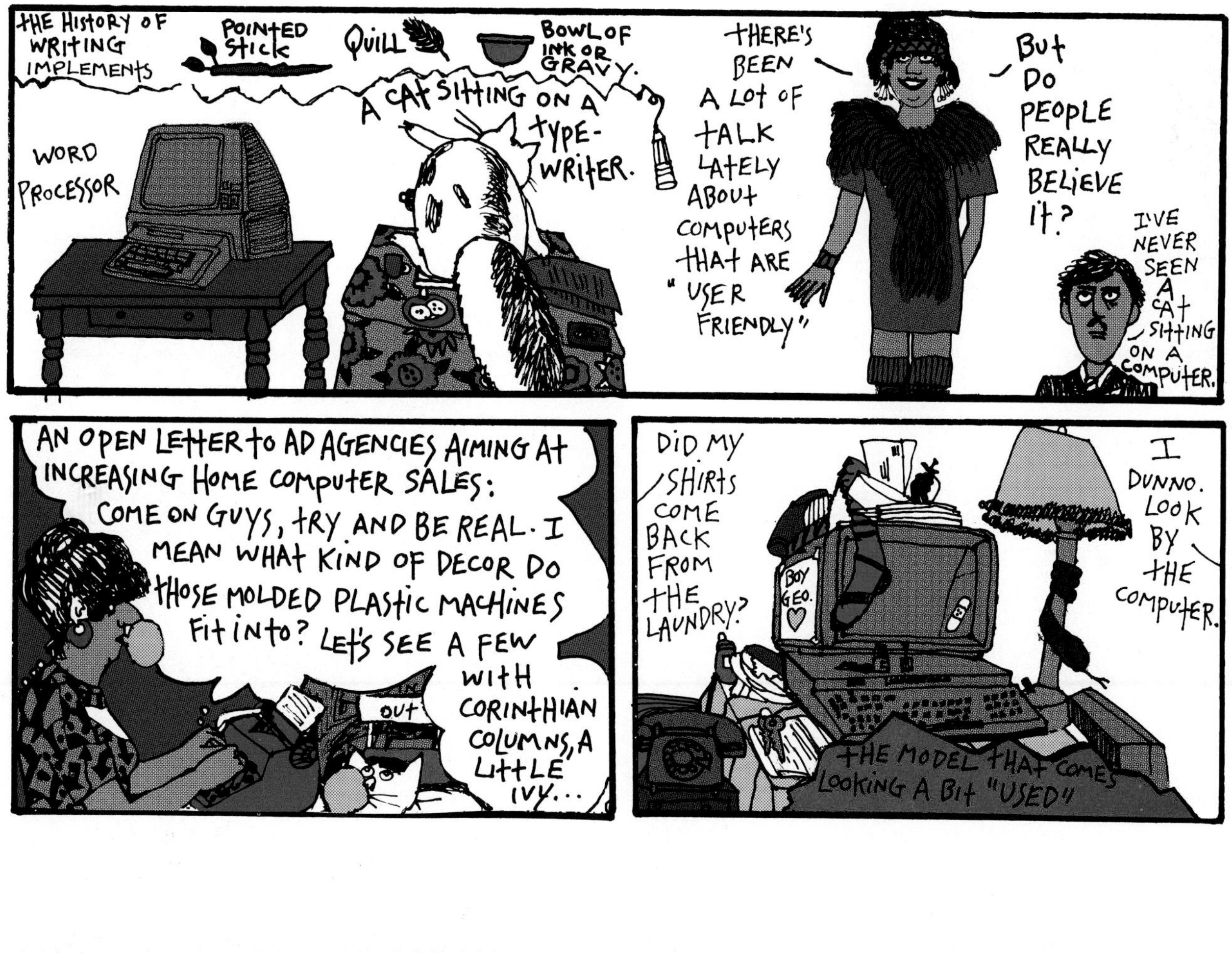
THE HISTORY OF WRITING IMPLEMENTS
POINTED STICK
QUILL
BOWL OF INK OR GRAVY.
A CAT SITTING ON A TYPE-WRITER.
WORD PROCESSOR
THERE'S BEEN A LOT OF TALK LATELY ABOUT COMPUTERS THAT ARE "USER FRIENDLY"
BUT DO PEOPLE REALLY BELIEVE IT?
I'VE NEVER SEEN A CAT SITTING ON A COMPUTER.
AN OPEN LETTER TO AD AGENCIES AIMING AT INCREASING HOME COMPUTER SALES: COME ON GUYS, TRY AND BE REAL. I MEAN WHAT KIND OF DECOR DO THOSE MOLDED PLASTIC MACHINES FIT INTO? LET'S SEE A FEW WITH CORINTHIAN COLUMNS, A LITTLE IVY...
OUT
DID MY SHIRTS COME BACK FROM THE LAUNDRY?
I DUNNO. LOOK BY THE COMPUTER.
BOY GEO.
THE MODEL THAT COMES LOOKING A BIT "USED"

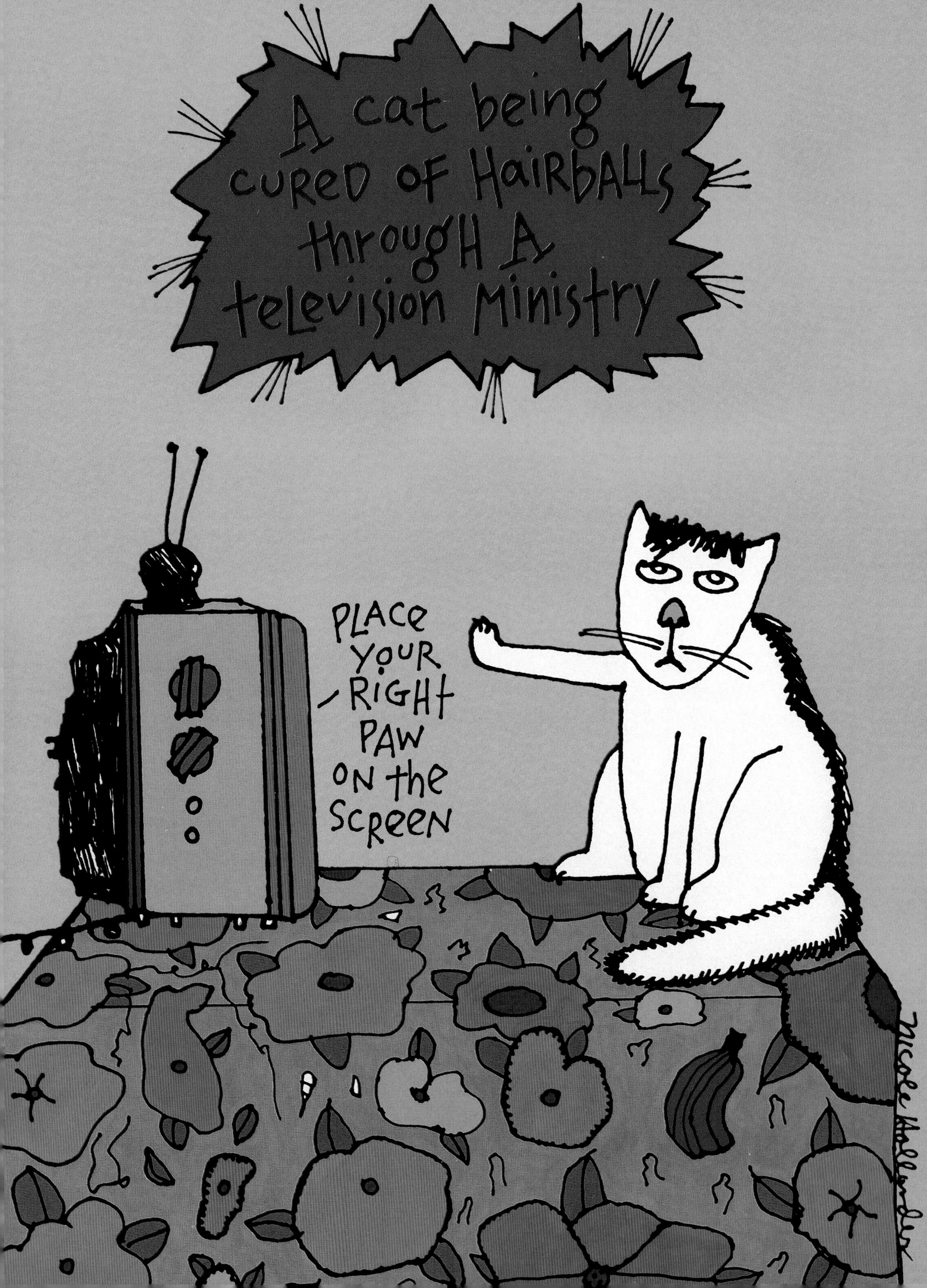
A cat being cured of Hairballs through A television Ministry
PLACE YOUR RIGHT PAW ON the SCREEN

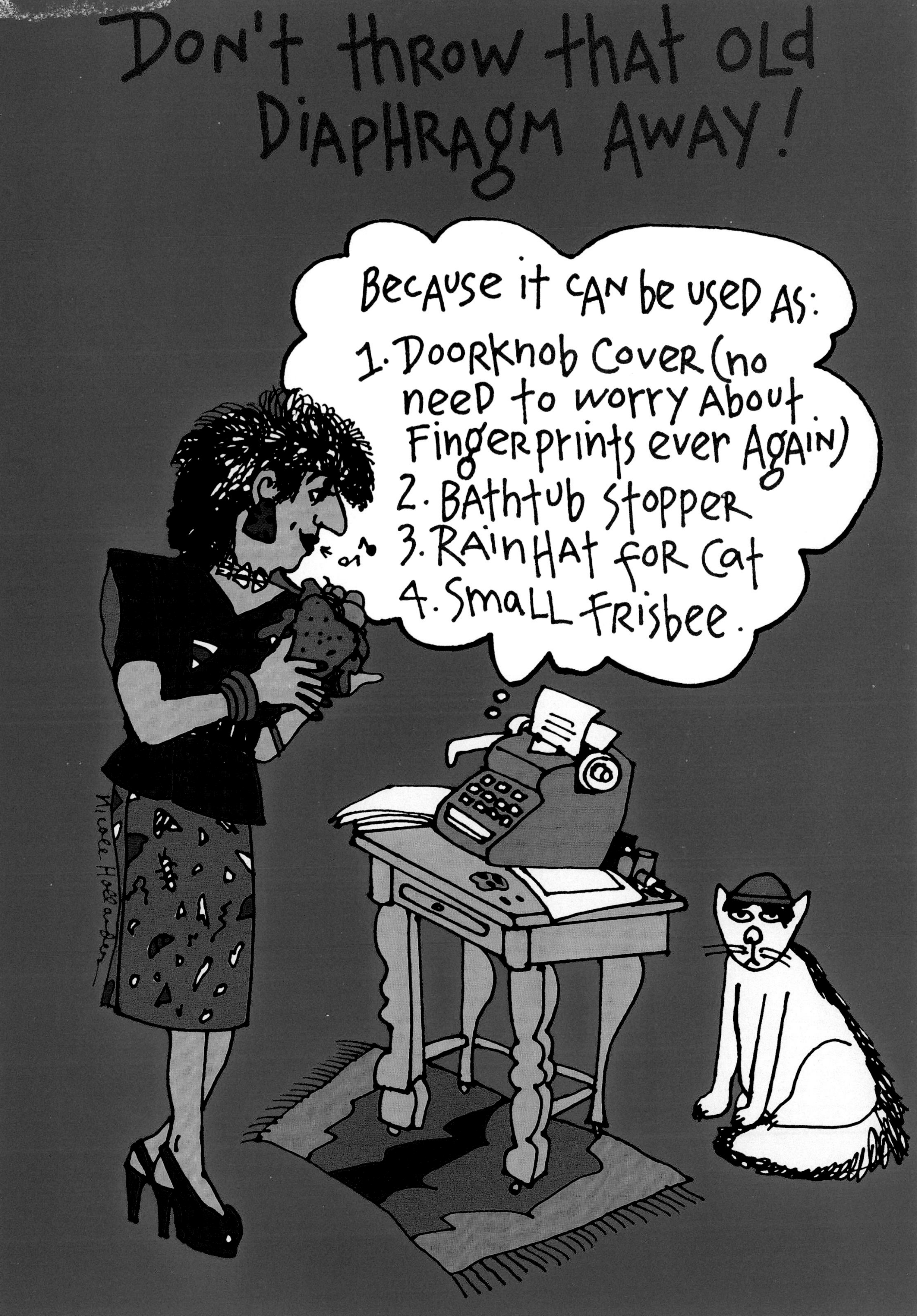

CUT AND REMOVE POSTER ALONG DOTTED LINE

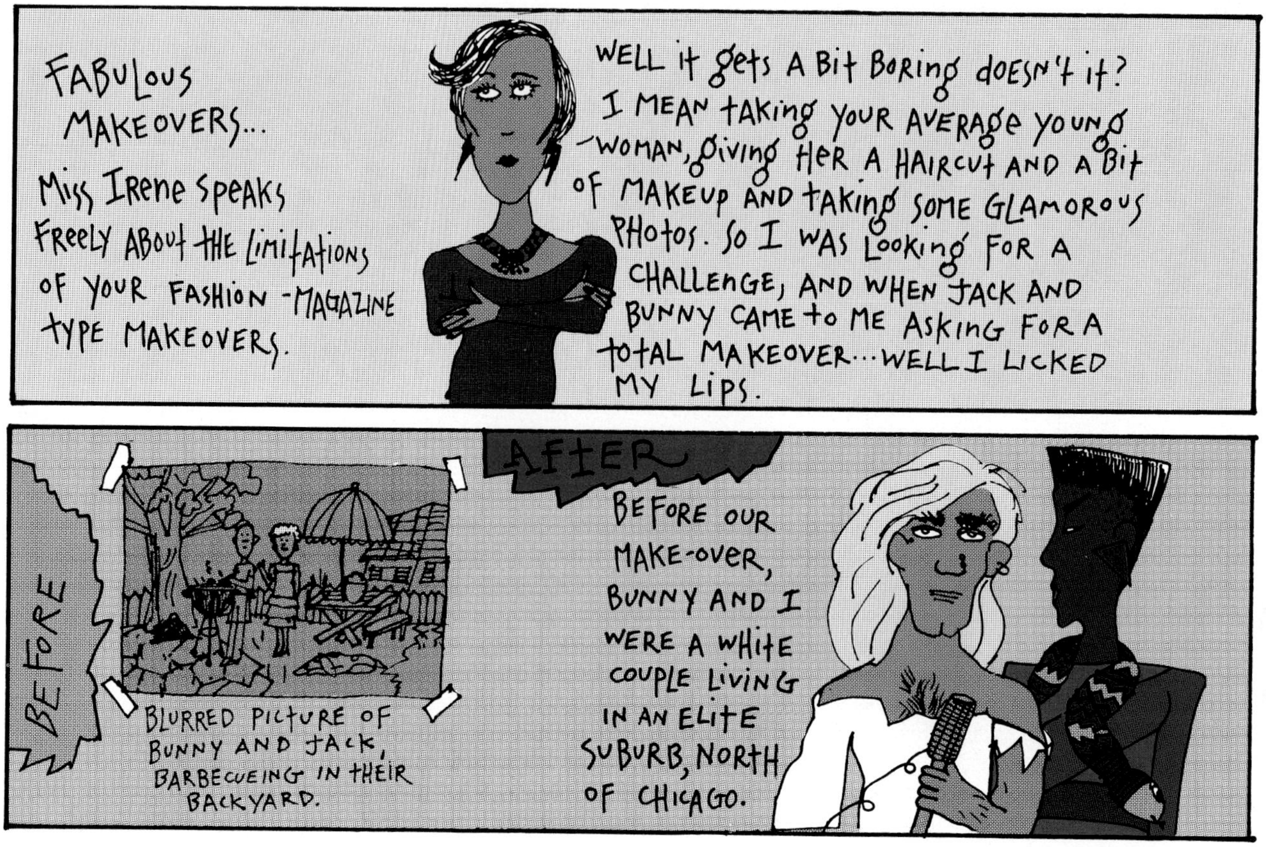
FABULOUS MAKEOVERS...
Miss Irene speaks freely about the limitations of your fashion-magazine type makeovers.
WELL it gets a Bit Boring doesn't it? I MEAN taking your average young woman, giving her a haircut and a bit of makeup and taking some glamorous photos. So I was looking for a challenge, and when Jack and Bunny came to me asking for a total makeover... well I licked my lips.
BEFORE
BLURRED PICTURE OF BUNNY AND JACK, BARBECUEING IN THEIR BACKYARD.
AFTER
BEFORE OUR MAKE-OVER, BUNNY AND I WERE A WHITE COUPLE LIVING IN AN ELITE SUBURB, NORTH OF CHICAGO.

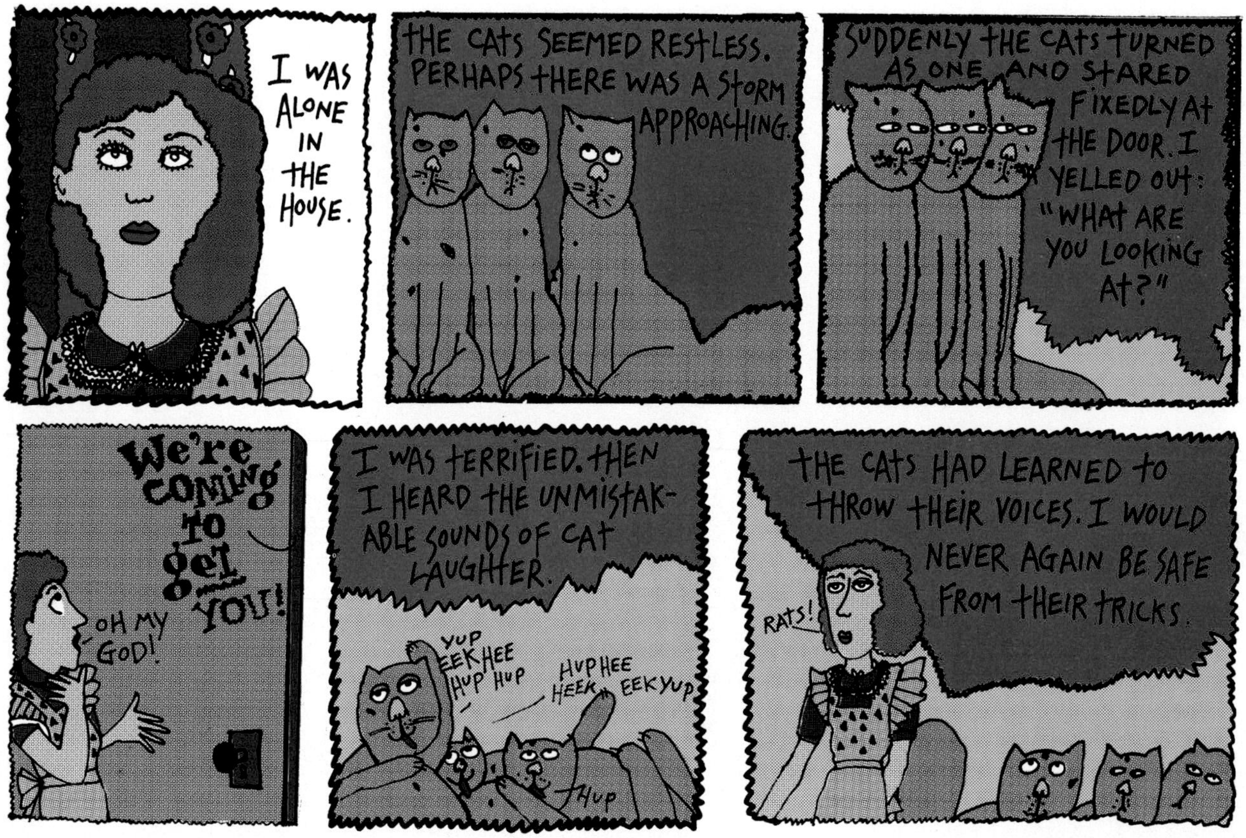
I WAS ALONE IN THE HOUSE.
THE CATS SEEMED RESTLESS. PERHAPS THERE WAS A STORM APPROACHING.
SUDDENLY THE CATS TURNED AS ONE AND STARED FIXEDLY AT THE DOOR. I YELLED OUT: "WHAT ARE YOU LOOKING AT?"
We're coming to get YOU!
OH MY GOD!
I WAS TERRIFIED. THEN I HEARD THE UNMISTAKABLE SOUNDS OF CAT LAUGHTER.
YUP EEKHEE HUP HUP
HUP HEE HEEK EEKYUP
THUP
THE CATS HAD LEARNED TO THROW THEIR VOICES. I WOULD NEVER AGAIN BE SAFE FROM THEIR TRICKS.
RATS!

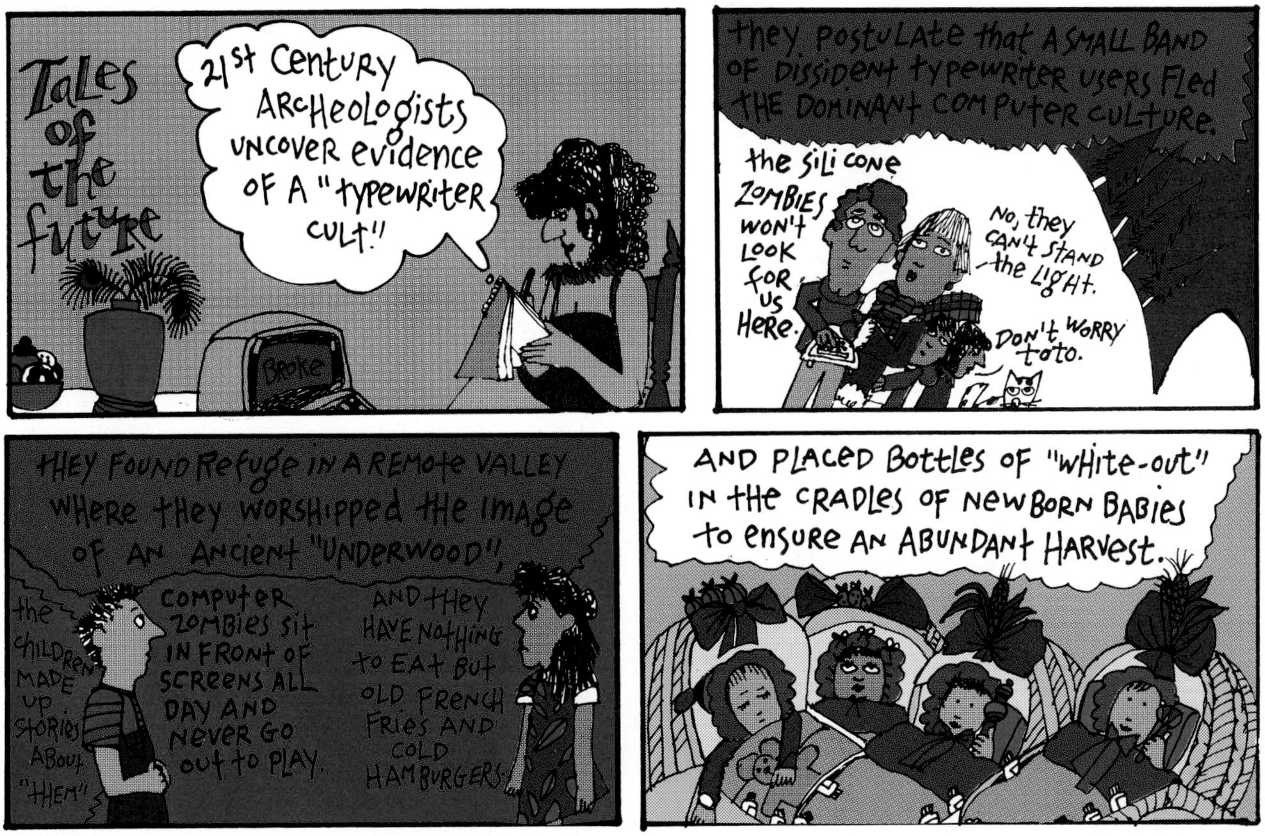
Tales of the future
21st Century Archeologists uncover evidence of A "typewriter cult!!
Broke
they postulate that A SMALL BAND OF DISSIDENT typewriter users Fled THE DOMINANT COMPUTER CULTURE.
the Sili cone Zombies won't look for us Here.
No, they can't stand the light.
Don't worry toto.
THEY FOUND Refuge IN A REMOTE VALLEY where they worshipped the image of AN Ancient "UNDERWOOD",
the children made up stories about "them"
computer zombies sit in front of screens all day and never go out to play.
And they have nothing to eat but old French fries and cold hamburgers.
AND PLACED Bottles of "white-out" IN the cradles of new born babies to ensure AN ABUNDANT HARVEST.

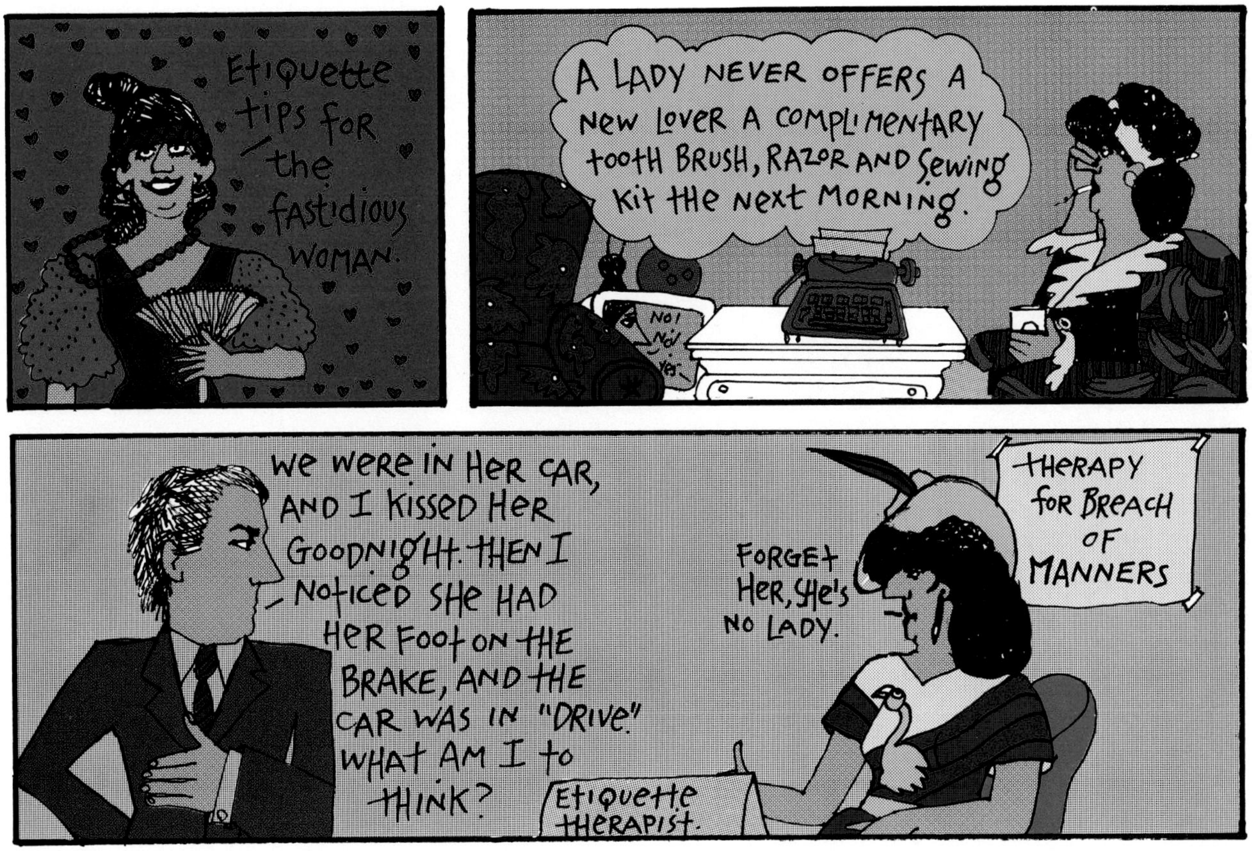
Etiquette tips for the fastidious woman.
A LADY NEVER OFFERS A new lover A complimentary tooth brush, razor and sewing kit the next morning.
No! No! Yes!
We were in her car, and I kissed her goodnight. then I noticed she had her foot on the brake, and the car was in "Drive." What am I to think?
Forget her, she's no lady.
Therapy for Breach of Manners
Etiquette therapist.

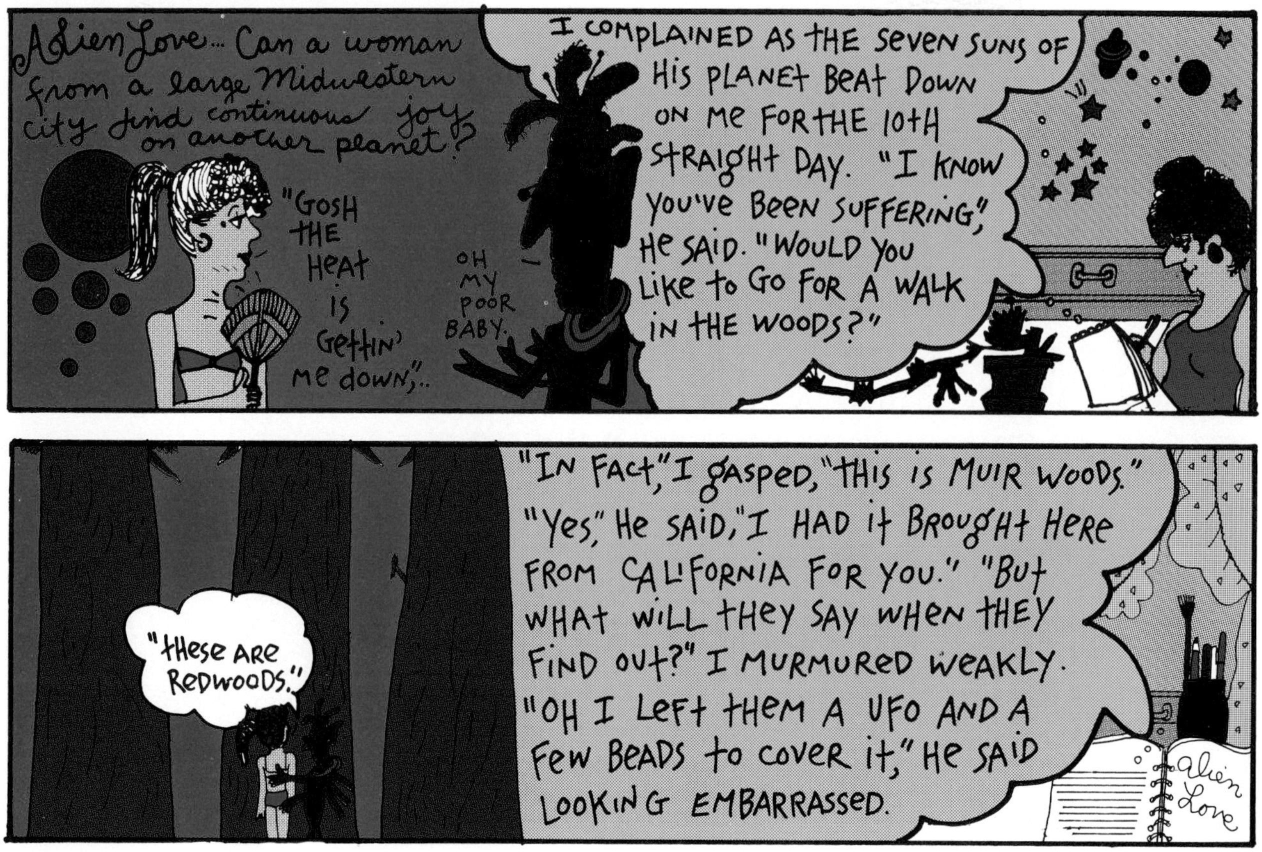
Alien Love... Can a woman from a large Midwestern city find continuous joy on another planet?
"Gosh the heat is gettin' me down."
Oh my poor baby.
I complained as the seven suns of his planet beat down on me for the 10th straight day. "I know you've been suffering," he said. "Would you like to go for a walk in the woods?"
"These are redwoods."
"In fact," I gasped, "this is Muir Woods." "Yes," he said, "I had it brought here from California for you." "But what will they say when they find out?" I murmured weakly. "Oh I left them a UFO and a few beads to cover it," he said looking embarrassed.
Alien Love

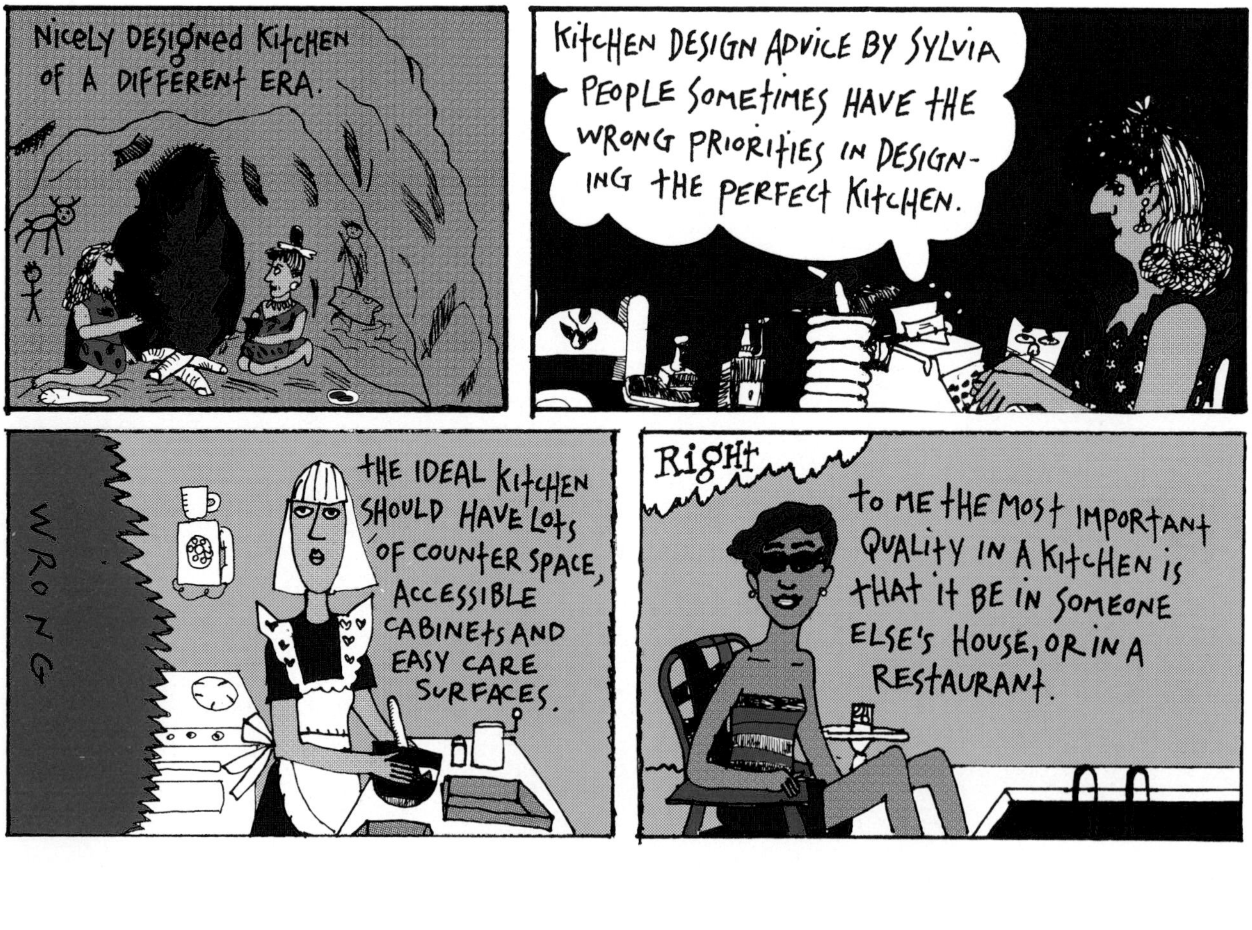
Nicely designed kitchen of a different era.
Kitchen Design Advice by Sylvia
People sometimes have the wrong priorities in designing the perfect kitchen.
WRONG
The ideal kitchen should have lots of counter space, accessible cabinets and easy care surfaces.
Right
To me the most important quality in a kitchen is that it be in someone else's house, or in a restaurant.

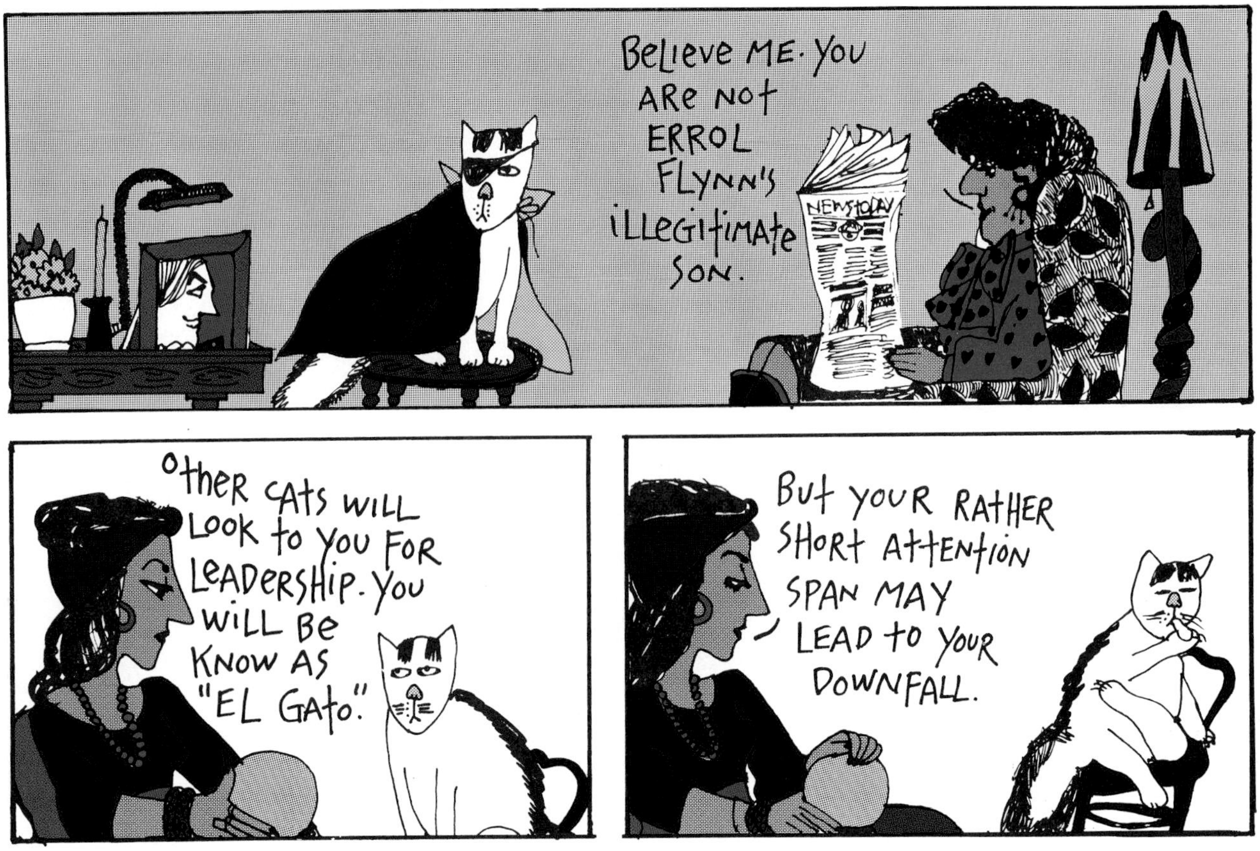
Believe me. You are not Errol Flynn's illegitimate son.
NEWSTODAY
Other cats will look to you for leadership. You will be know as "El Gato."
But your rather short attention span may lead to your downfall.

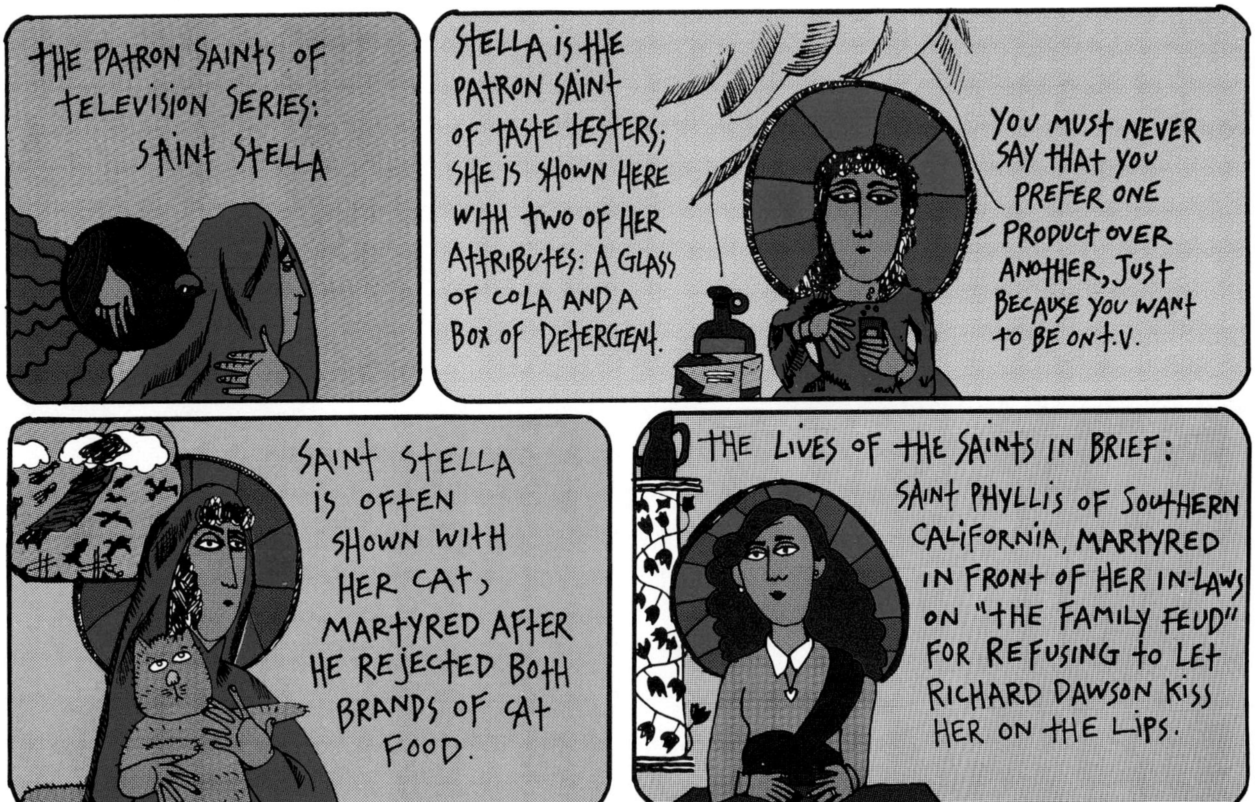
The patron saints of television series: Saint Stella
Stella is the patron saint of taste testers; she is shown here with two of her attributes: a glass of cola and a box of detergent.
You must never say that you prefer one product over another, just because you want to be on t.v.
Saint Stella is often shown with her cat, martyred after he rejected both brands of cat food.
The lives of the saints in brief:
Saint Phyllis of Southern California, martyred in front of her in-laws on "The Family Feud" for refusing to let Richard Dawson kiss her on the lips.

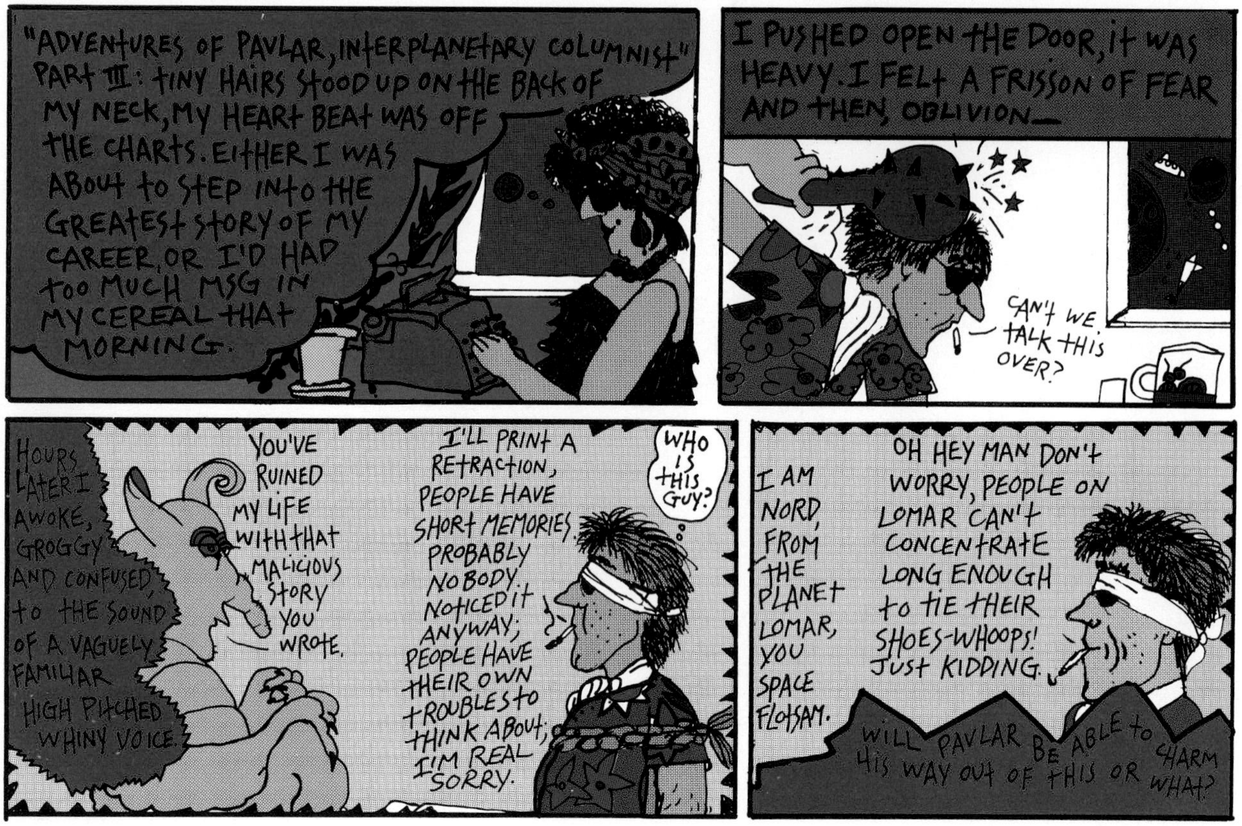
"ADVENTURES OF PAVLAR, INTERPLANETARY COLUMNIST" PART III: TINY HAIRS STOOD UP ON THE BACK OF MY NECK, MY HEART BEAT WAS OFF THE CHARTS. EITHER I WAS ABOUT TO STEP INTO THE GREATEST STORY OF MY CAREER, OR I'D HAD TOO MUCH MSG IN MY CEREAL THAT MORNING.
I PUSHED OPEN THE DOOR, IT WAS HEAVY. I FELT A FRISSON OF FEAR AND THEN, OBLIVION—
CAN'T WE TALK THIS OVER?
HOURS LATER I AWOKE, GROGGY AND CONFUSED, TO THE SOUND OF A VAGUELY FAMILIAR HIGH PITCHED WHINY VOICE.
YOU'VE RUINED MY LIFE WITH THAT MALICIOUS STORY YOU WROTE.
I'LL PRINT A RETRACTION, PEOPLE HAVE SHORT MEMORIES PROBABLY NOBODY NOTICED IT ANYWAY; PEOPLE HAVE THEIR OWN TROUBLES TO THINK ABOUT; I'M REAL SORRY.
WHO IS THIS GUY?
I AM NORD, FROM THE PLANET LOMAR, YOU SPACE FLOTSAM.
OH HEY MAN DON'T WORRY, PEOPLE ON LOMAR CAN'T CONCENTRATE LONG ENOUGH TO TIE THEIR SHOES-WHOOPS! JUST KIDDING.
WILL PAVLAR BE ABLE TO CHARM HIS WAY OUT OF THIS OR WHAT?

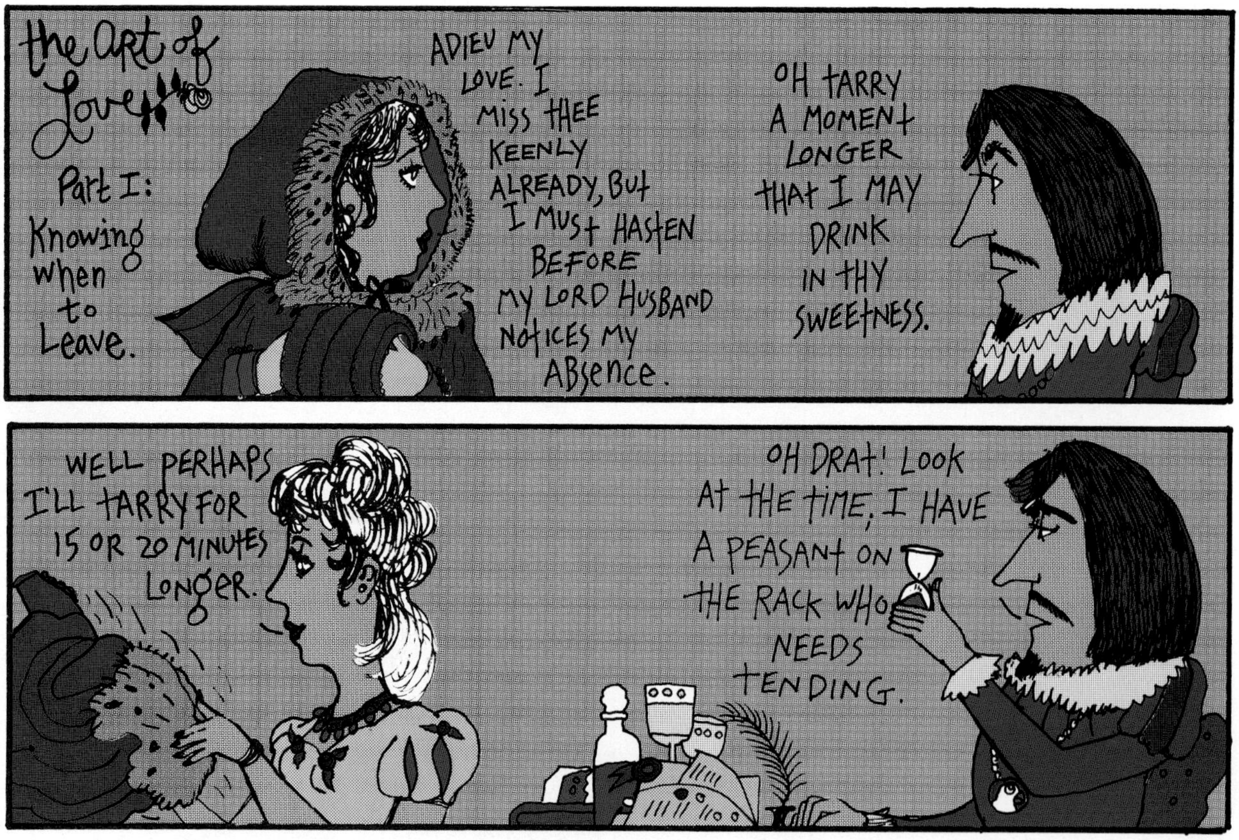
the Art of Love
Part I: Knowing when to Leave.
ADIEU MY LOVE. I MISS THEE KEENLY ALREADY, BUT I MUST HASTEN BEFORE MY LORD HUSBAND NOTICES MY ABSENCE.
OH TARRY A MOMENT LONGER THAT I MAY DRINK IN THY SWEETNESS.
WELL PERHAPS I'LL TARRY FOR 15 OR 20 MINUTES LONGER.
OH DRAT! LOOK AT THE TIME, I HAVE A PEASANT ON THE RACK WHO NEEDS TENDING.

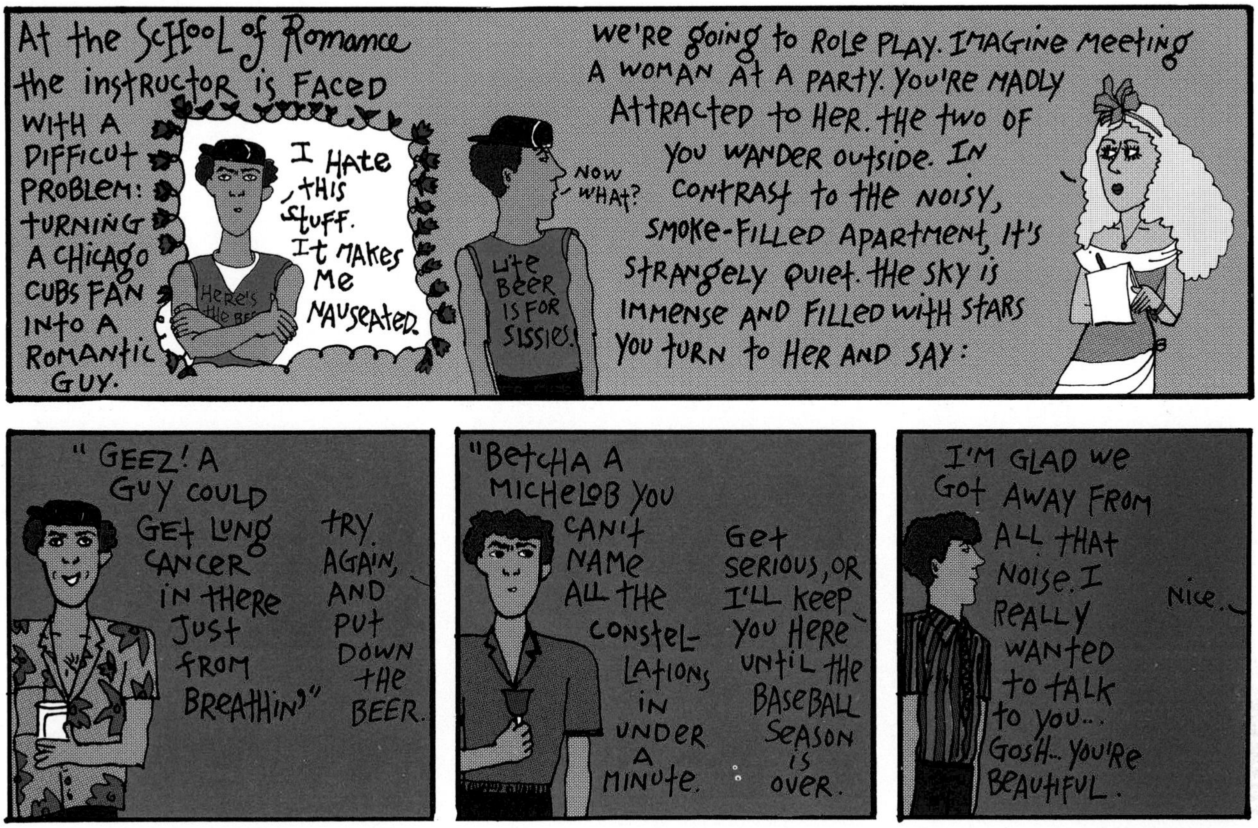
At the School of Romance the instructor is faced with a difficut problem: turning a Chicago Cubs fan into a romantic guy.
I hate this stuff. It makes me nauseated.
Here's the beer
Lite beer is for sissies!
Now what?
We're going to role play. Imagine meeting a woman at a party. You're madly attracted to her. The two of you wander outside. In contrast to the noisy, smoke-filled apartment, it's strangely quiet. The sky is immense and filled with stars you turn to her and say:
"Geez! A guy could get lung cancer in there just from breathin'"
Try again, and put down the beer.
"Betcha a Michelob you can't name all the constellations in under a minute.
Get serious, or I'll keep you here until the baseball season is over.
I'm glad we got away from all that noise. I really wanted to talk to you... Gosh... you're beautiful.
Nice.

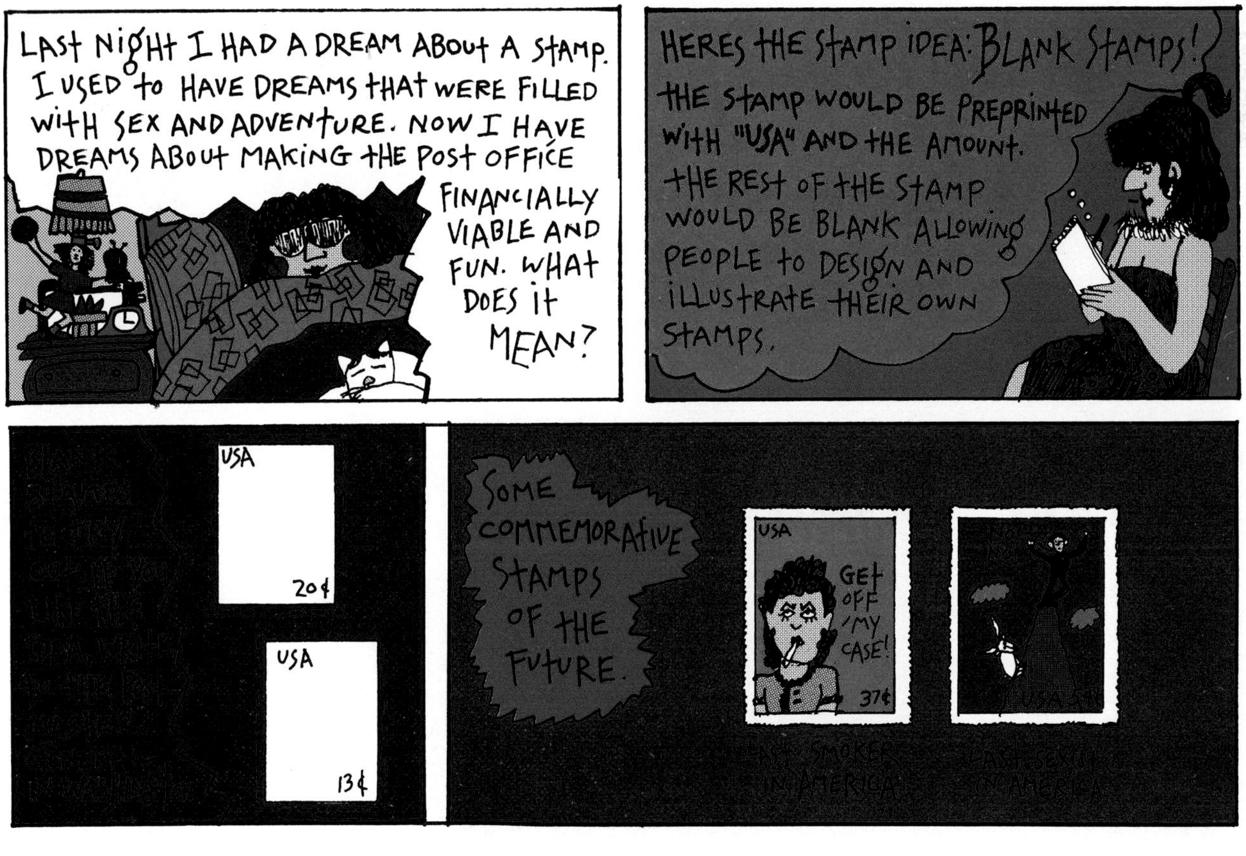
Last night I had a dream about a stamp. I used to have dreams that were filled with sex and adventure. Now I have dreams about making the post office financially viable and fun. What does it mean?
Heres the stamp idea: Blank stamps! The stamp would be preprinted with "USA" and the amount. The rest of the stamp would be blank allowing people to design and illustrate their own stamps.
USA
20¢
USA
13¢
Some commemorative stamps of the future.
USA
Get off my case!
37¢
Last smoker in America

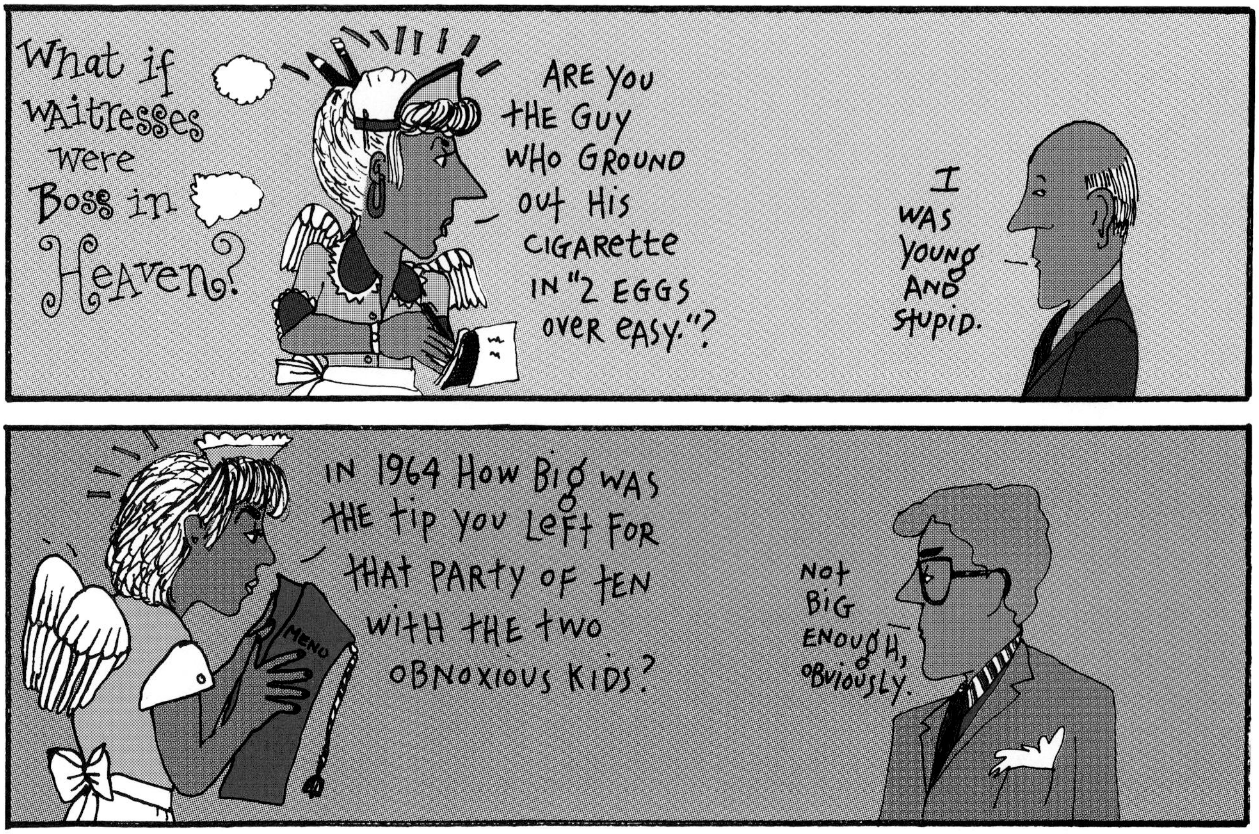
What if waitresses were Boss in Heaven?
ARE you the GUY WHO GROUND out His cigarette IN "2 EGGS over easy."?
I WAS young AND stupid.
IN 1964 HOW BIG WAS tHE tip you LEft FOR tHAt PARTY OF tEN WitH tHE two OBNOXIOUS KIDS?
MENU
Not BIG ENOUGH, OBVIOUSLY.

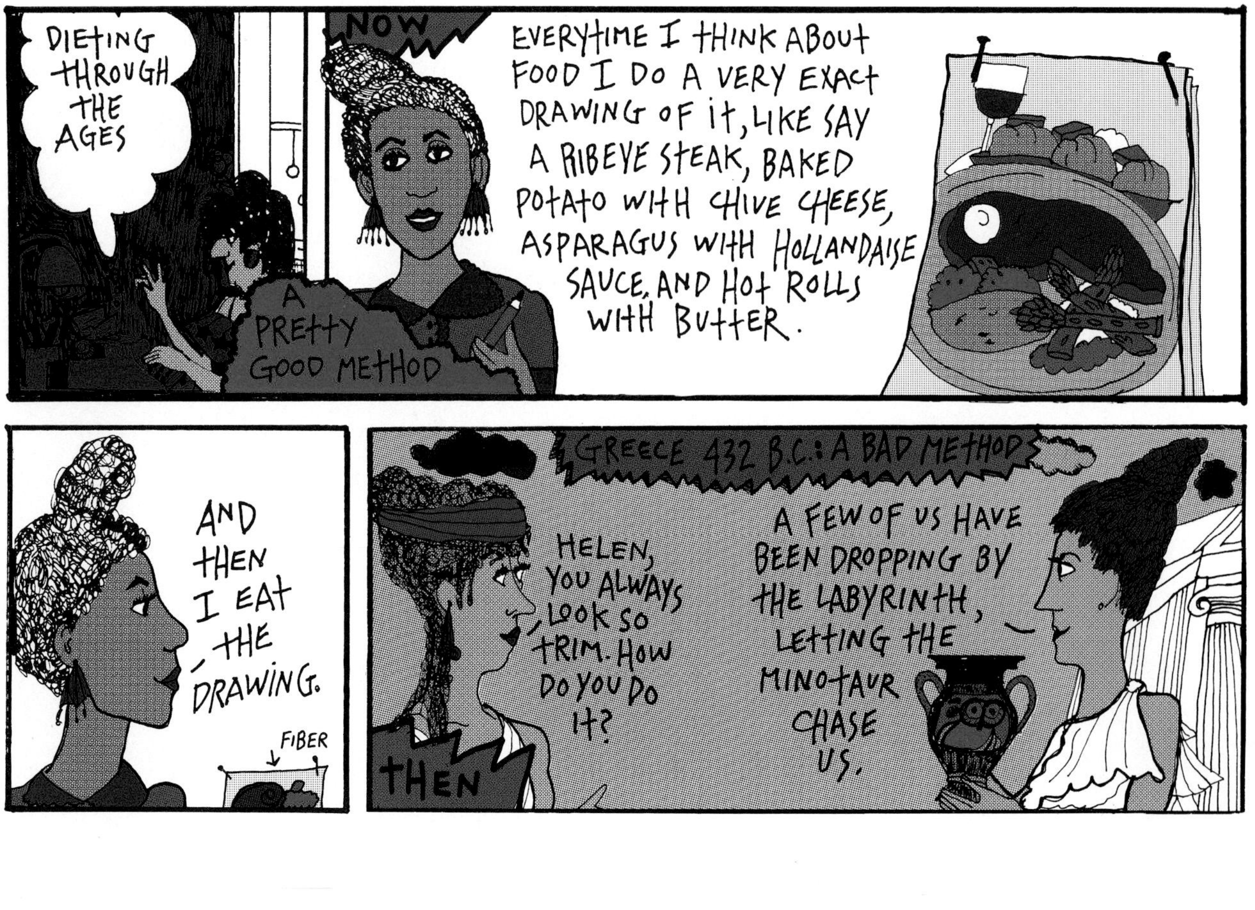
DIEtING tHROUGH tHE AGES
NOW
EVERYtIME I tHINK ABOUt FOOD I DO A VERY EXACt DRAWING OF It, LIKE SAY A RIBEYE StEAK, BAKED POtAtO WItH CHIVE CHEESE, ASPARAGUS WItH HOLLANDAISE SAUCE, AND HOt ROLLS WItH BUttER.
A PREttY GOOD METHOD
AND tHEN I EAt tHE DRAWING.
FIBER
GREECE 432 B.C.: A BAD METHOD
HELEN, YOU ALWAYS LOOK SO tRIM. HOW DO YOU DO It?
A FEW OF US HAVE BEEN DROPPING BY tHE LABYRINtH, LEttING tHE MINOtAUR CHASE US.
THEN

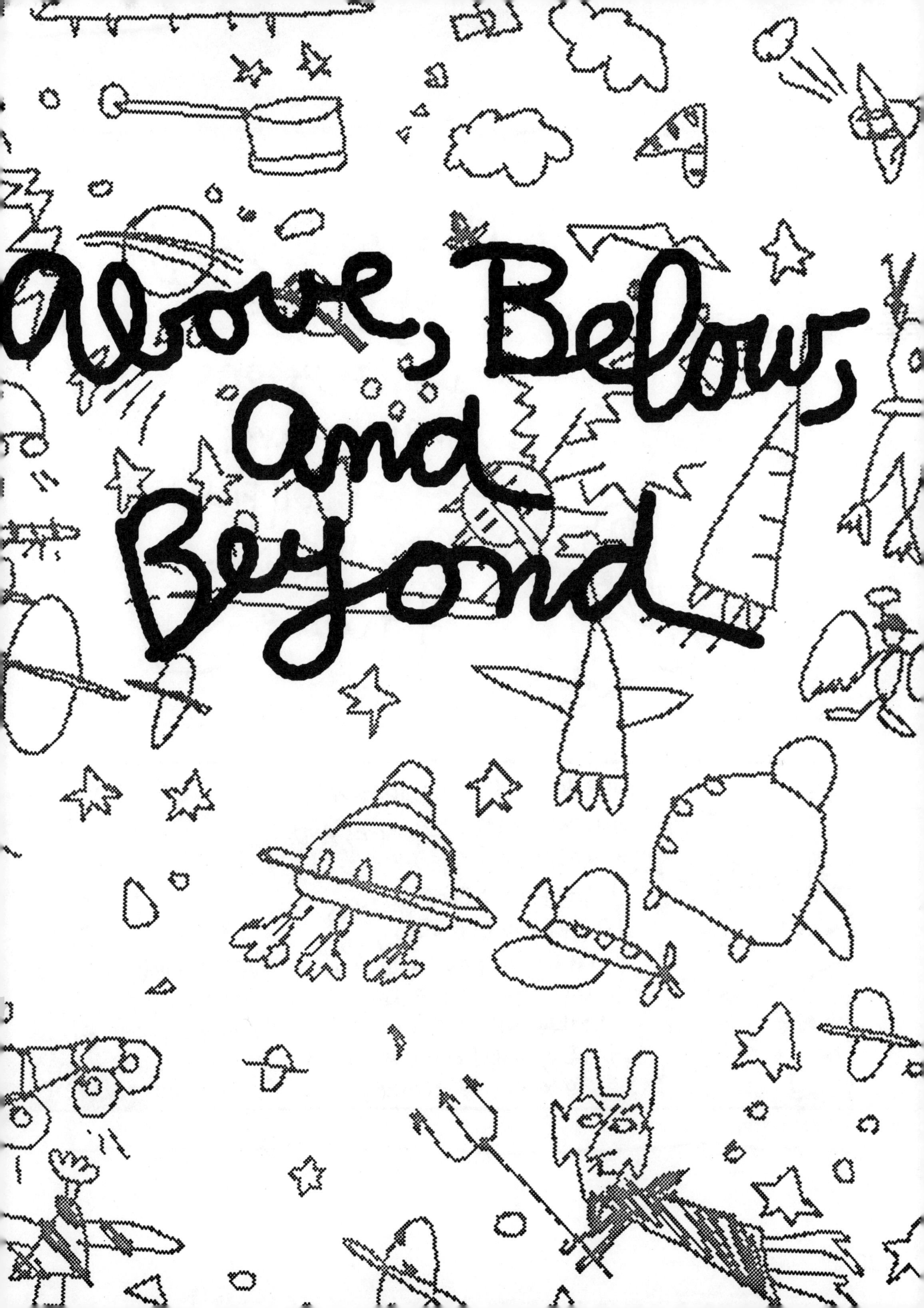
Above, Below, and Beyond

the members of some Institutions will Have Lots of Difficulty getting into Heaven

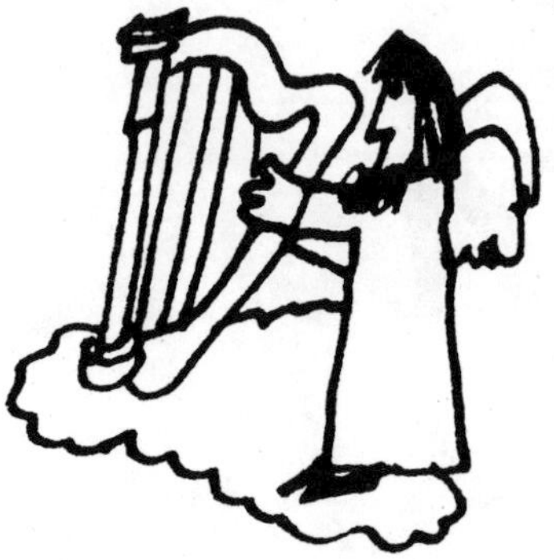

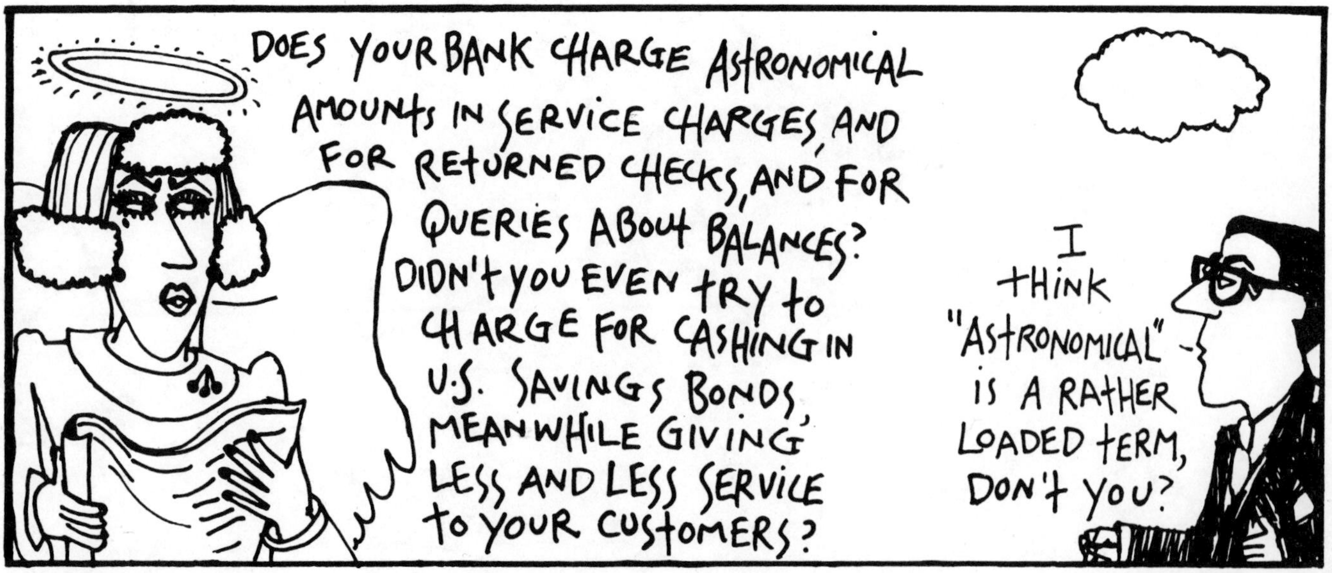
DOES YOUR BANK CHARGE ASTRONOMICAL AMOUNTS IN SERVICE CHARGES, AND FOR RETURNED CHECKS, AND FOR QUERIES ABOUT BALANCES? DIDN'T YOU EVEN TRY TO CHARGE FOR CASHING IN U.S. SAVINGS BONDS, MEANWHILE GIVING LESS AND LESS SERVICE TO YOUR CUSTOMERS?
I THINK "ASTRONOMICAL" IS A RATHER LOADED TERM, DON'T YOU?

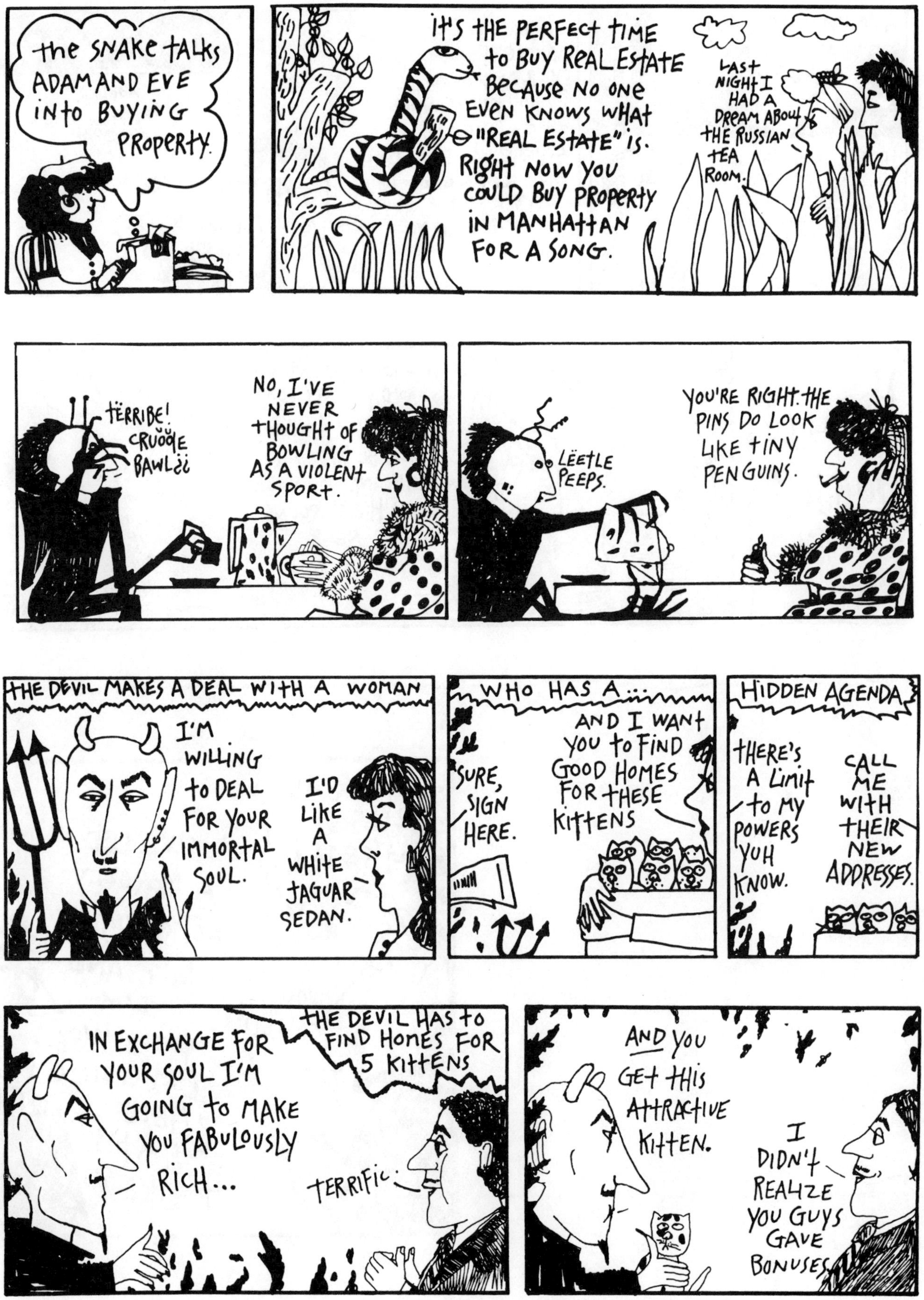
the SNAKE tAlks ADAM AND EVE into BUYING Property.
It's the PERFECT time to Buy REAL ESTATE BECAUSE NO ONE EVEN KNOWS WHAT "REAL ESTATE" is. RIGHT NOW YOU COULD BUY PROPERTY IN MANHATTAN FOR A SONG.
LAST NIGHT I HAD A DREAM ABOUT THE RUSSIAN TEA ROOM.
TËRRIBE! CRUÖÖLE BAWLS¿¿
NO, I'VE NEVER THOUGHT OF BOWLING AS A VIOLENT SPORT.
LËETLE PEEPS.
YOU'RE RIGHT. THE PINS DO LOOK LIKE TINY PENGUINS.
THE DEVIL MAKES A DEAL WITH A WOMAN
I'M WILLING to DEAL FOR YOUR IMMORTAL SOUL.
I'D LIKE A WHITE JAGUAR SEDAN.
WHO HAS A...
SURE, SIGN HERE.
AND I WANT YOU to FIND GOOD HOMES FOR THESE KITTENS
HIDDEN AGENDA
THERE'S A LIMIT to MY POWERS YUH KNOW.
CALL ME WITH THEIR NEW ADDRESSES.
THE DEVIL HAS to FIND HOMES FOR 5 KITTENS
IN EXCHANGE FOR YOUR SOUL I'M GOING to MAKE YOU FABULOUSLY RICH...
TERRIFIC.
AND YOU GET THIS ATTRACTIVE KITTEN.
I DIDN'T REALIZE YOU GUYS GAVE BONUSES.

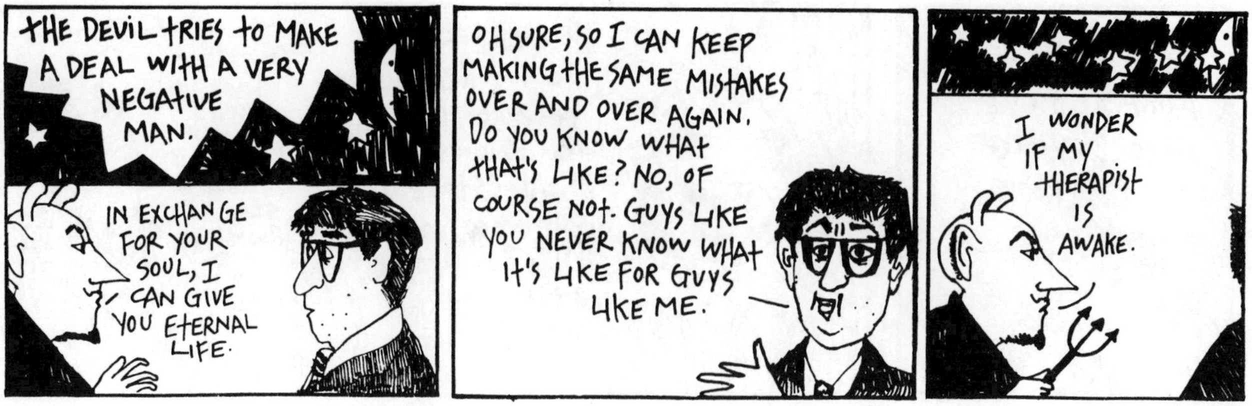
THE DEVIL TRIES TO MAKE A DEAL WITH A VERY NEGATIVE MAN.
IN EXCHANGE FOR YOUR SOUL, I CAN GIVE YOU ETERNAL LIFE.
OH SURE, SO I CAN KEEP MAKING THE SAME MISTAKES OVER AND OVER AGAIN. DO YOU KNOW WHAT THAT'S LIKE? NO, OF COURSE NOT. GUYS LIKE YOU NEVER KNOW WHAT IT'S LIKE FOR GUYS LIKE ME.
I WONDER IF MY THERAPIST IS AWAKE.

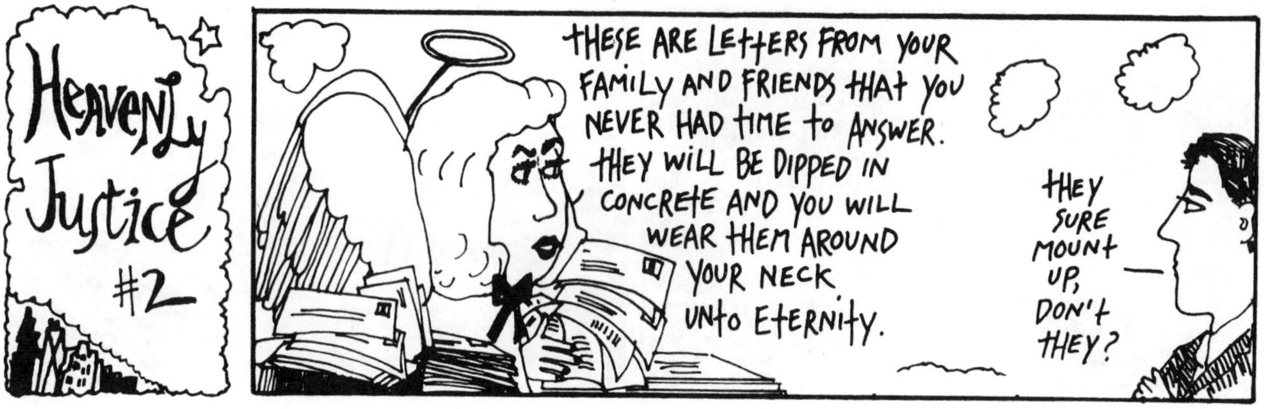
Heavenly Justice #2
THESE ARE LETTERS FROM YOUR FAMILY AND FRIENDS THAT YOU NEVER HAD TIME TO ANSWER. THEY WILL BE DIPPED IN CONCRETE AND YOU WILL WEAR THEM AROUND YOUR NECK UNTO ETERNITY.
THEY SURE MOUNT UP, DON'T THEY?

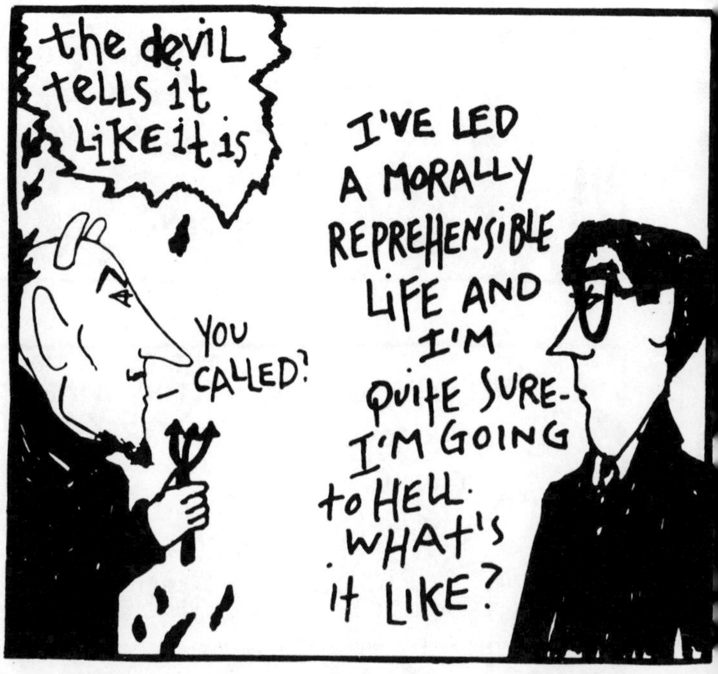
the devil tells it like it is
I'VE LED A MORALLY REPREHENSIBLE LIFE AND I'M QUITE SURE I'M GOING TO HELL. WHAT'S IT LIKE?
YOU CALLED?

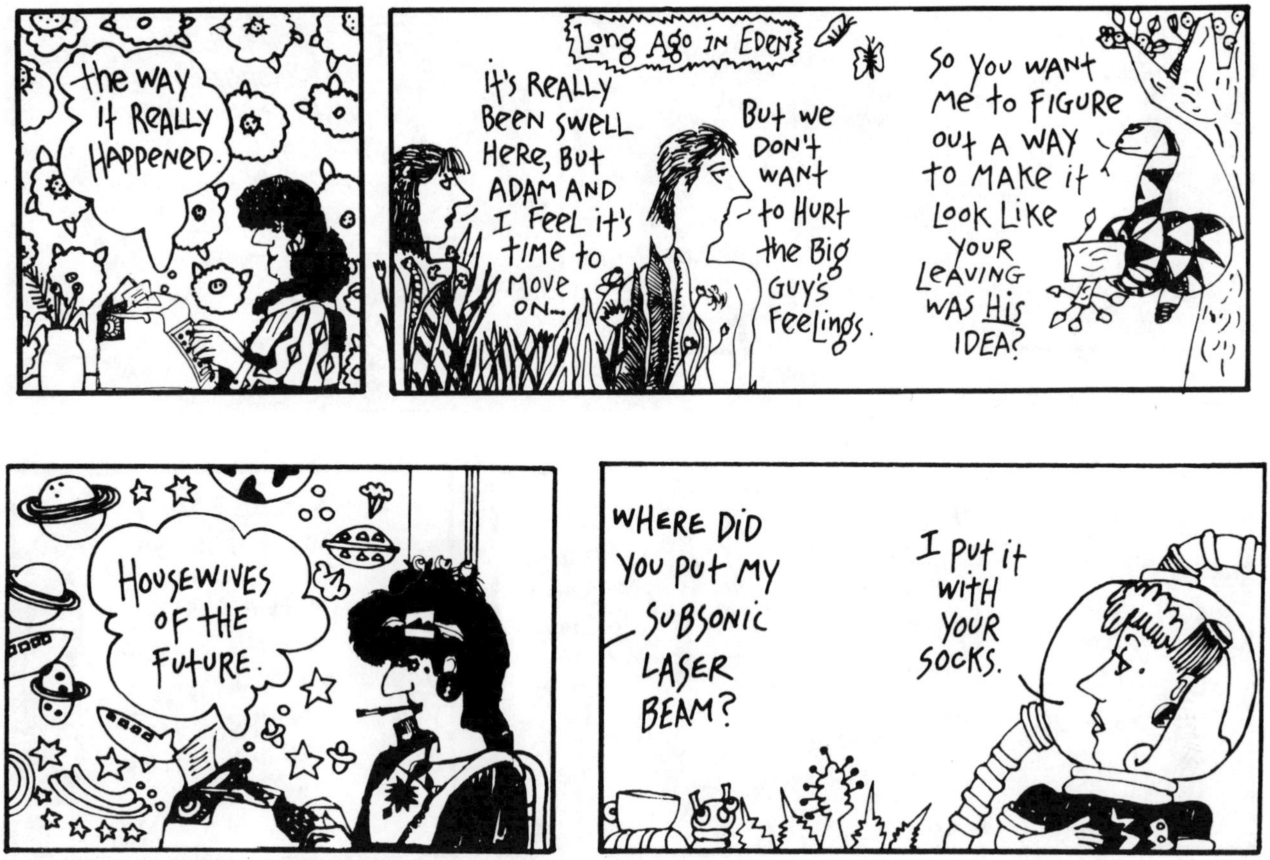
the way it Really Happened.
Long Ago in Eden
it's Really Been swell Here, But ADAM AND I Feel it's time to Move on...
But we Don't want to Hurt the Big Guy's Feelings.
So you want me to figure out a way to make it look like your leaving was His idea?
Housewives of the Future.
Where did you put my subsonic laser beam?
I put it with your socks.

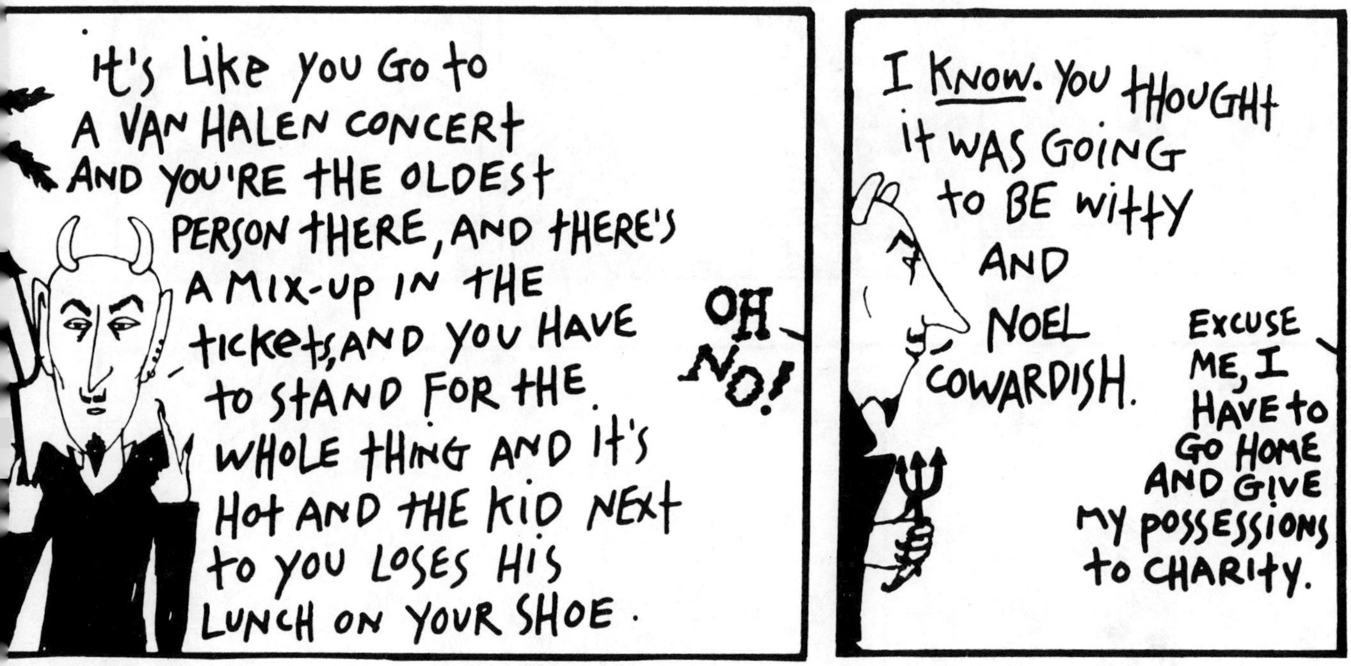
it's like you go to a Van Halen concert and you're the oldest person there, and there's a mix-up in the tickets, and you have to stand for the whole thing and it's hot and the kid next to you loses his lunch on your shoe.
OH NO!
I Know. You thought it was going to be witty and Noel Cowardish.
Excuse me, I have to go home and give my possessions to charity.

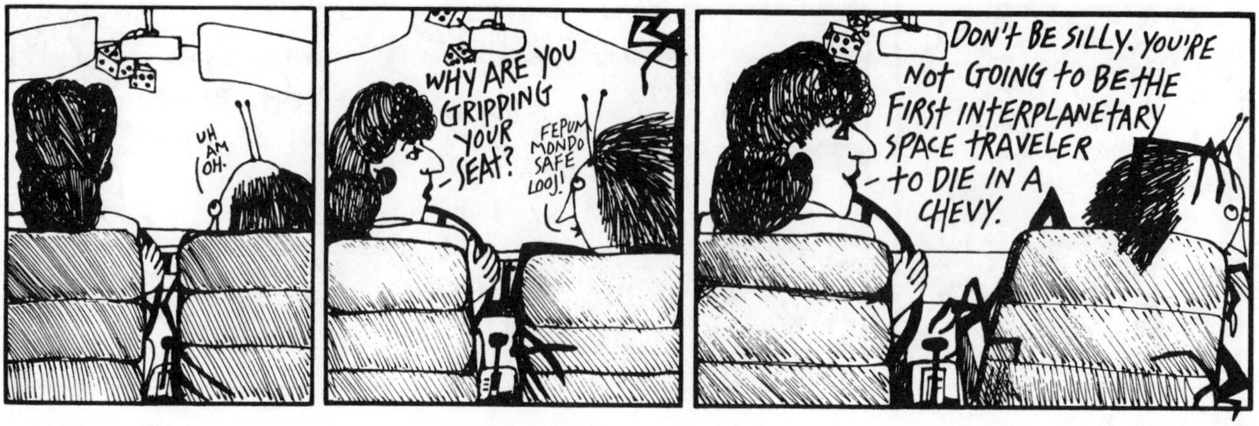
UH AM (OH.
WHY ARE YOU GRIPPING YOUR SEAT?
FEPUM MONDO SAFE LOOJ!
DON'T BE SILLY. YOU'RE NOT GOING TO BE THE FIRST INTERPLANETARY SPACE TRAVELER TO DIE IN A CHEVY.

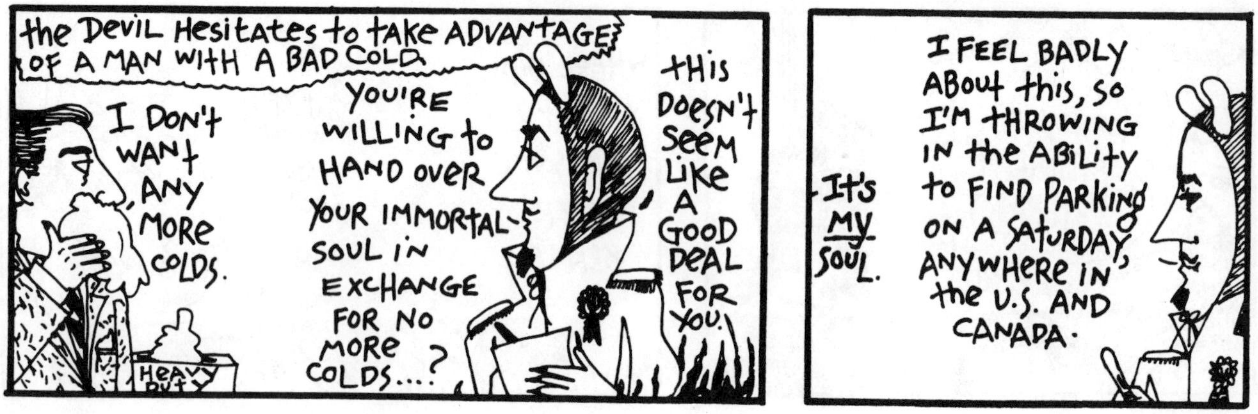
the DEVIL HESITATES to TAKE ADVANTAGE OF A MAN WITH A BAD COLD
I DON'T WANT ANY MORE COLDS.
YOU'RE WILLING to HAND OVER YOUR IMMORTAL SOUL IN EXCHANGE FOR NO MORE COLDS...?
THIS DOESN'T SEEM LIKE A GOOD DEAL FOR YOU.
HEAVY DUTY
It's MY SOUL.
I FEEL BADLY ABOUT this, SO I'M THROWING IN the ABILITY to FIND PARKING ON A SATURDAY, ANYWHERE IN the U.S. AND CANADA.

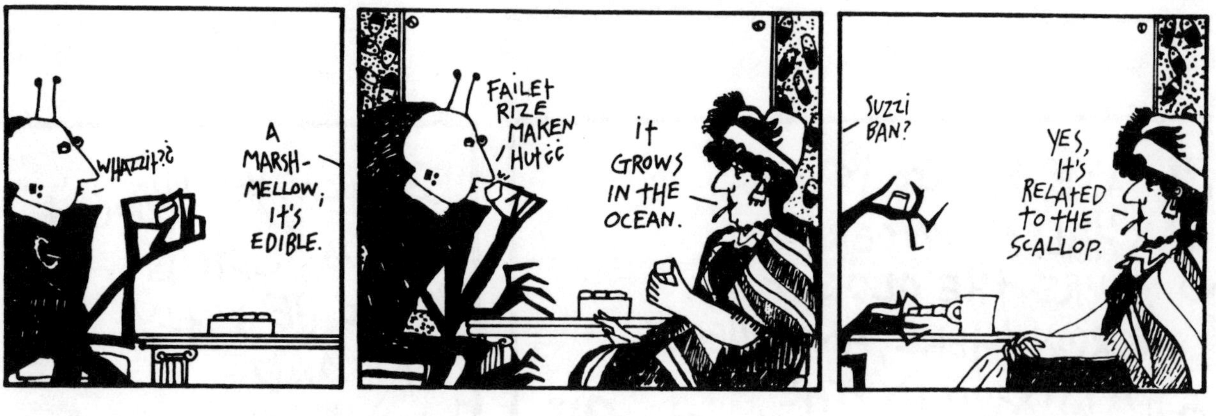
WHAZZIT?¿
A MARSH-MELLOW; It's EDIBLE.
FAILET RIZE MAKEN HUTCC
It GROWS IN THE OCEAN.
SUZZI BAN?
YES, It's RELATED to THE SCALLOP.

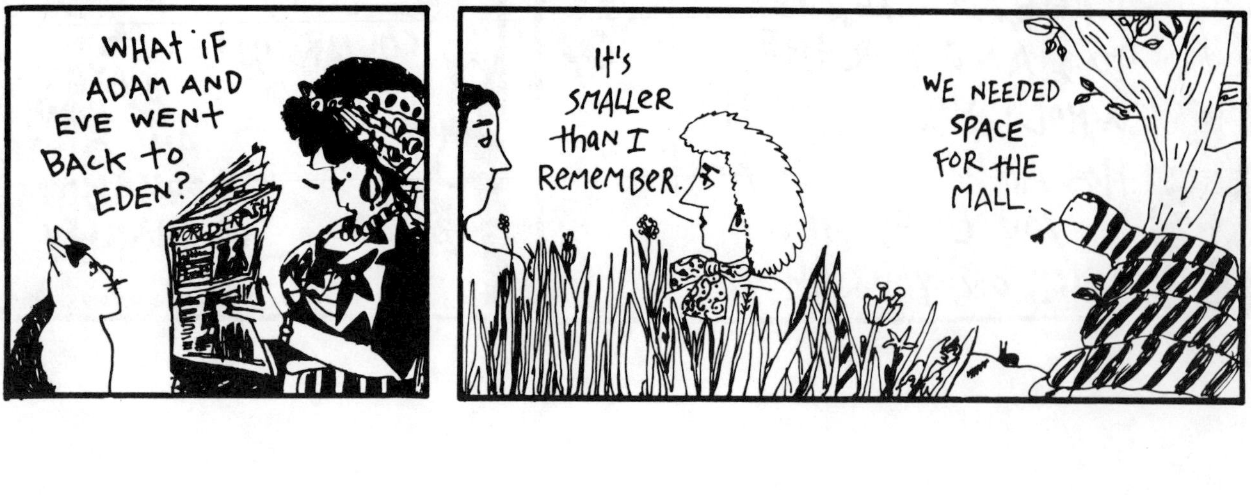
WHAT IF ADAM AND EVE WENT BACK to EDEN?
WORLD TRASH
It's SMALLER than I REMEMBER.
WE NEEDED SPACE FOR THE MALL.

Big Mistakes in Biblical Times

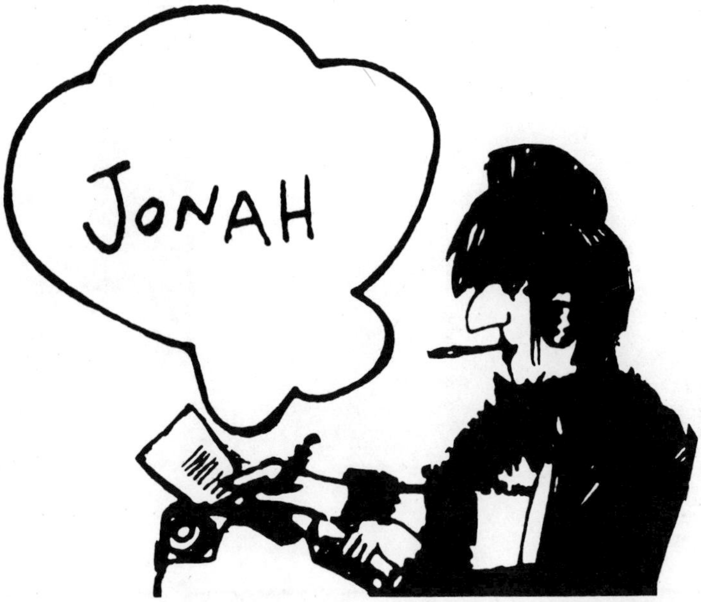
JONAH

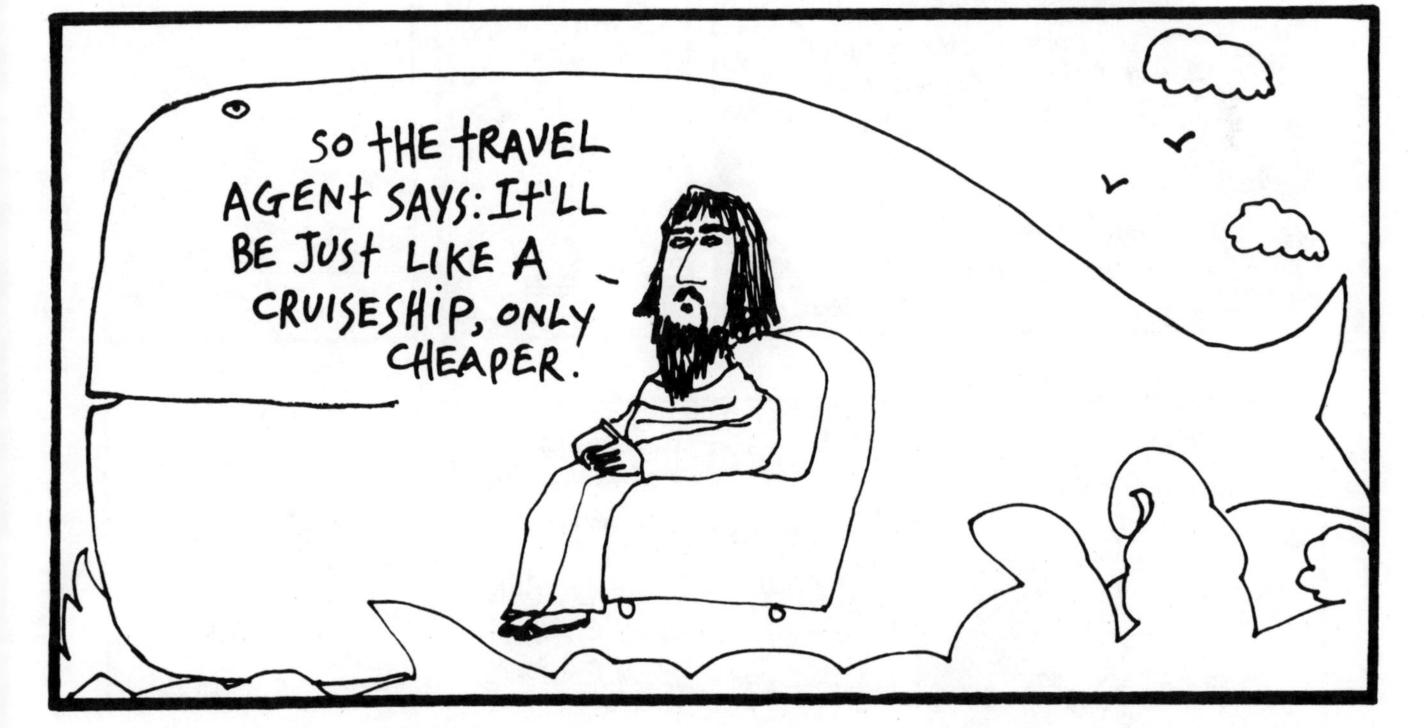
SO THE TRAVEL AGENT SAYS: IT'LL BE JUST LIKE A CRUISESHIP, ONLY CHEAPER.

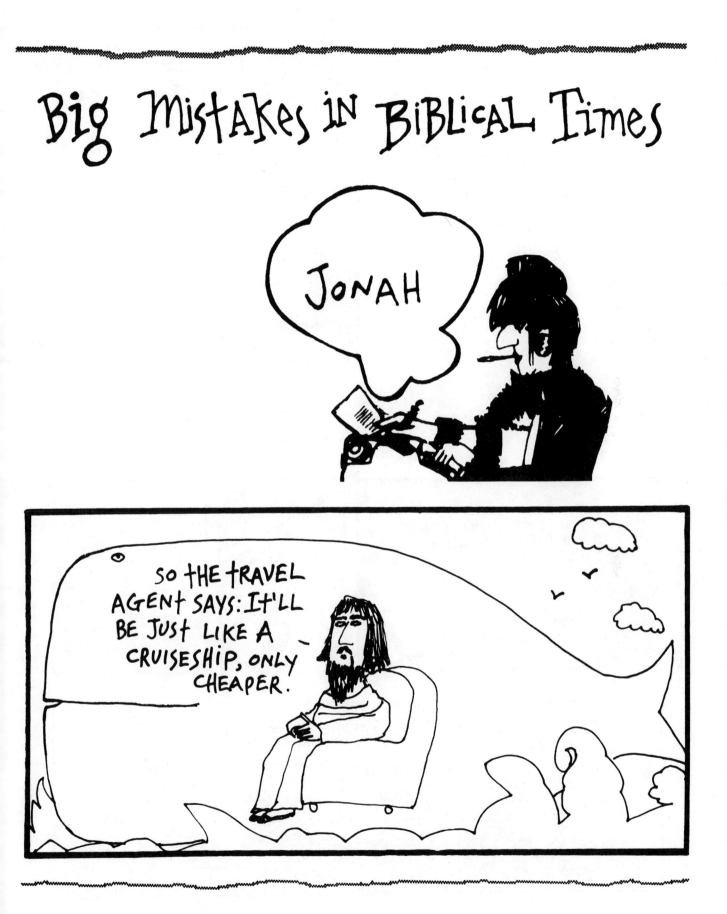

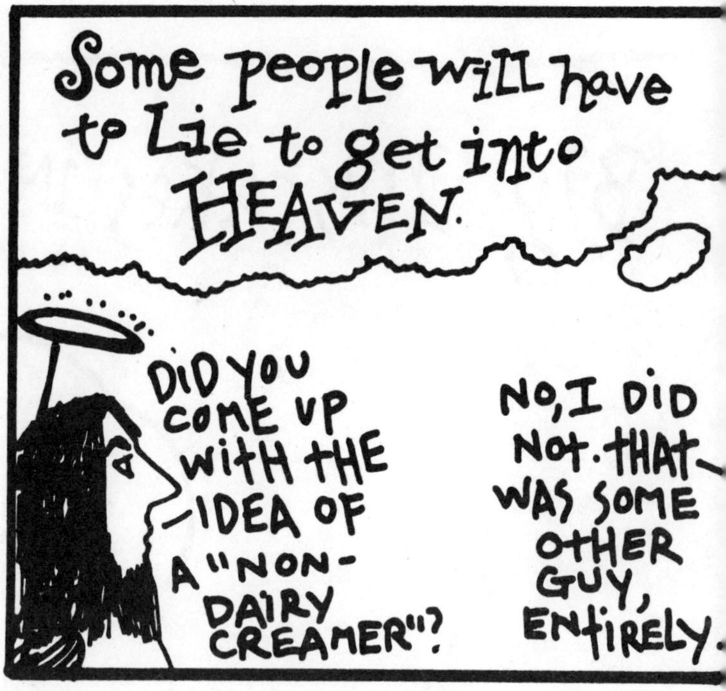
Some people will have to Lie to get into HEAVEN.
DID YOU COME UP WITH THE IDEA OF A "NON-DAIRY CREAMER"?
NO, I DID NOT. THAT WAS SOME OTHER GUY, ENTIRELY.

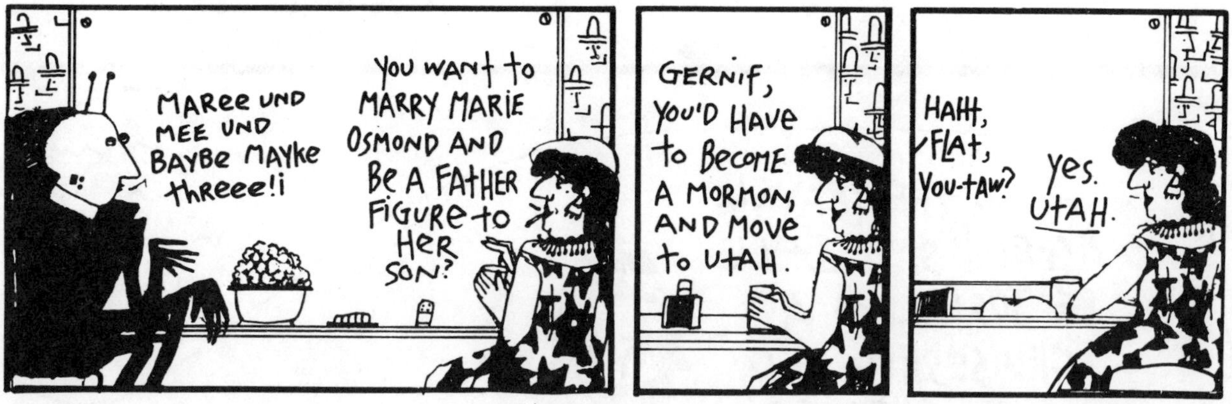
MAREE UND MEE UND BAYBE MAYKE threee!!
YOU WANT TO MARRY MARIE OSMOND AND BE A FATHER FIGURE TO HER SON?
GERNIF, YOU'D HAVE TO BECOME A MORMON, AND MOVE TO UTAH.
HAHH, FLAT, YOU-TAW?
YES. UTAH.

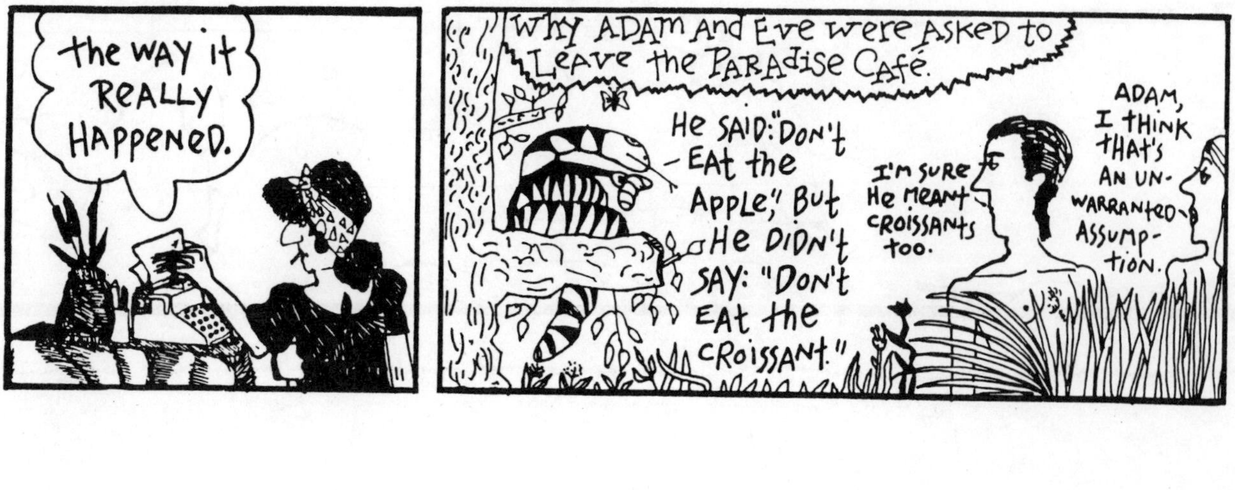
the way it REALLY HAPPENED.
Why ADAM And Eve were ASKED to Leave the PARADISE CAFÉ.
He SAID: "Don't Eat the Apple," But He DIDN'T SAY: "Don't Eat the CROISSANT."
I'M SURE He MEANT CROISSANTS too.
ADAM, I THINK THAT'S AN UN-WARRANTED ASSUMP-TION.

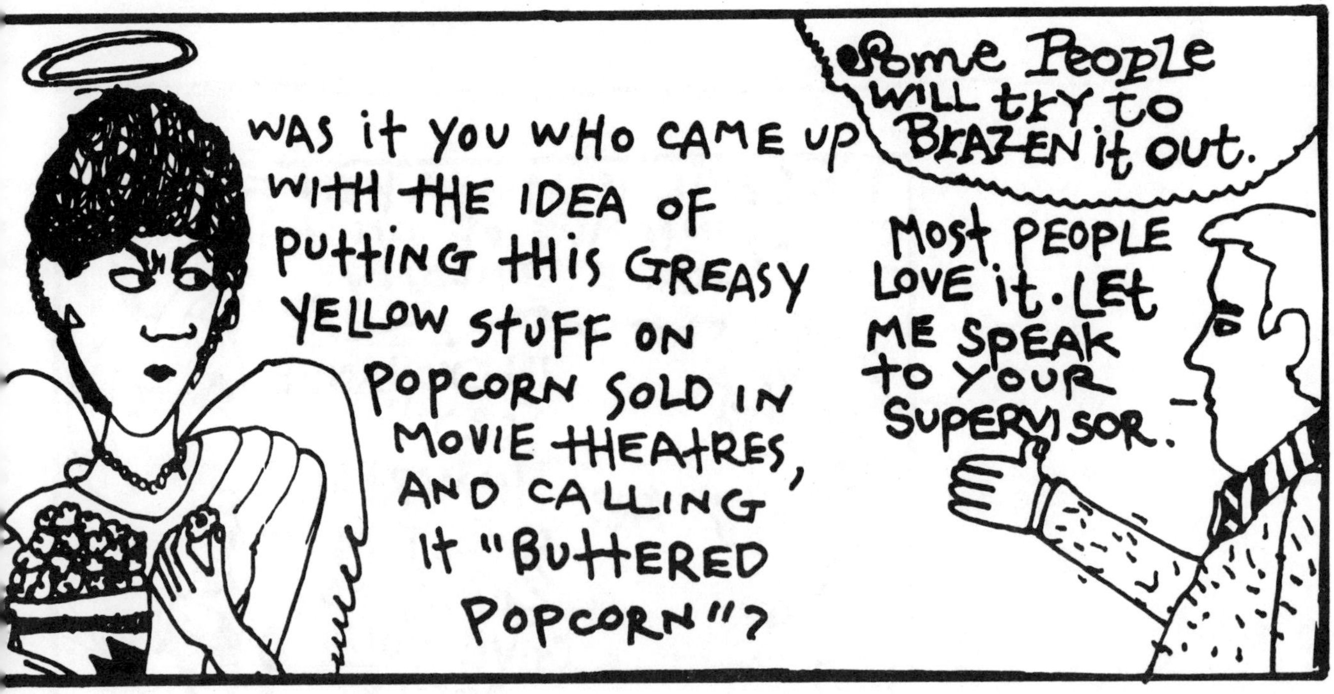
WAS it YOU WHO CAME UP WITH THE IDEA OF PUTTING THIS GREASY YELLOW STUFF ON POPCORN SOLD IN MOVIE THEATRES, AND CALLING IT "BUTTERED POPCORN"?
Some People will try to BRAZEN it out.
MOST PEOPLE LOVE it. LET ME SPEAK TO YOUR SUPERVISOR.

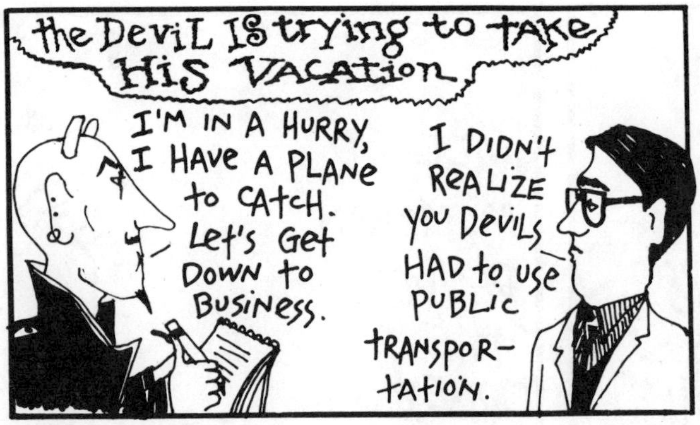
the Devil IS trying to take HIS Vacation
I'M IN A HURRY, I HAVE A PLANE to CATCH. Let's Get DOWN to BUSINESS.
I DIDN'T REALIZE YOU DEVILS HAD to USE PUBLIC TRANSPOR-TATION.

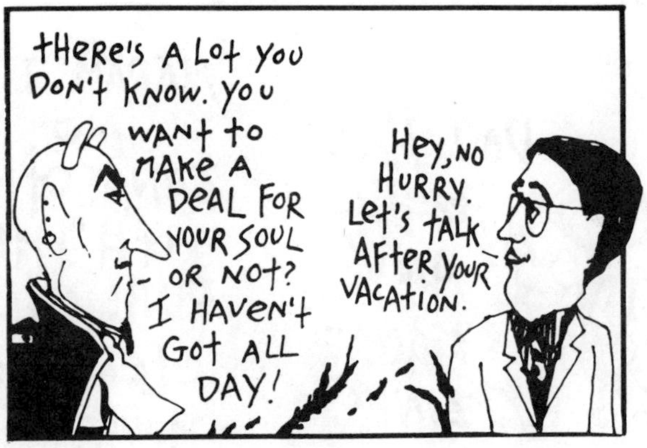
THERE'S A LOT YOU DON'T KNOW. YOU WANT to MAKE A DEAL FOR YOUR SOUL OR NOT? I HAVEN'T GOT ALL DAY!
Hey, NO HURRY. Let's TALK AFTER YOUR VACATION.

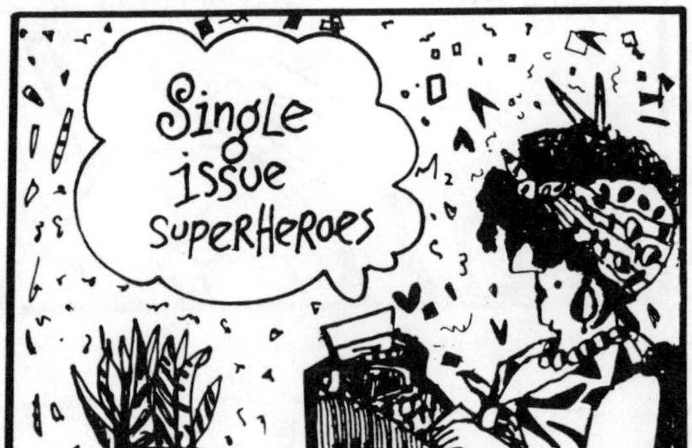
Single issue SuperHeroes

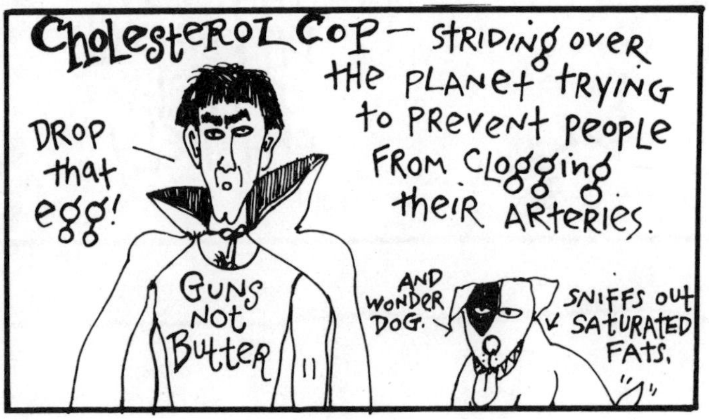
Cholesterol Cop — STRIDING OVER THE PLANET TRYING to PREVENT PEOPLE FROM Clogging their ARTERIES.
DROP that egg!
GUNS Not Butter
AND WONDER DOG.
SNIFFS OUT SATURATED FATS.

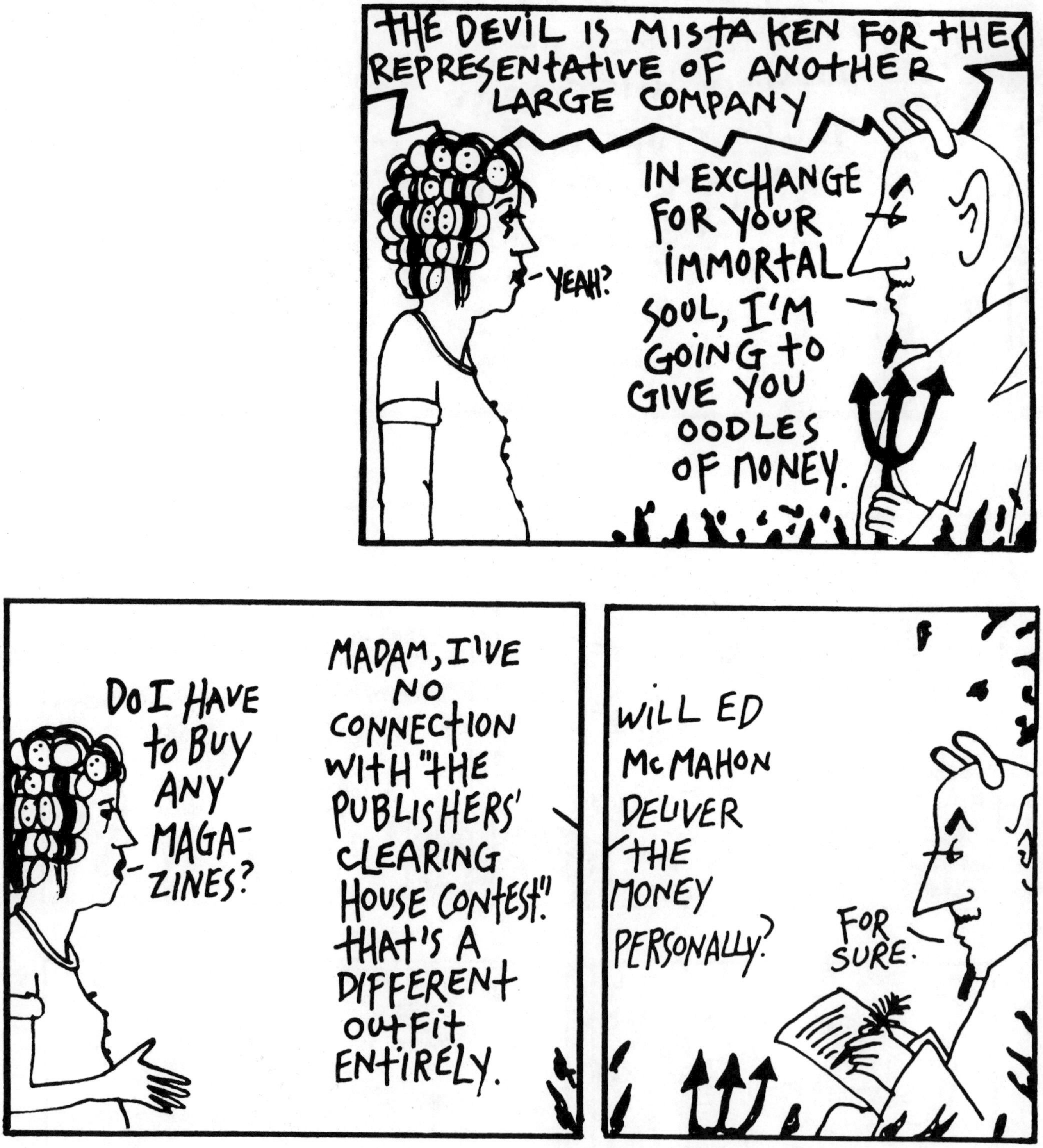
THE DEVIL IS MISTAKEN FOR THE REPRESENTATIVE OF ANOTHER LARGE COMPANY
IN EXCHANGE FOR YOUR IMMORTAL SOUL, I'M GOING TO GIVE YOU OODLES OF MONEY.
YEAH?
DO I HAVE TO BUY ANY MAGAZINES?
MADAM, I'VE NO CONNECTION WITH "THE PUBLISHERS' CLEARING HOUSE CONTEST." THAT'S A DIFFERENT OUTFIT ENTIRELY.
WILL ED McMAHON DELIVER THE MONEY PERSONALLY?
FOR SURE.

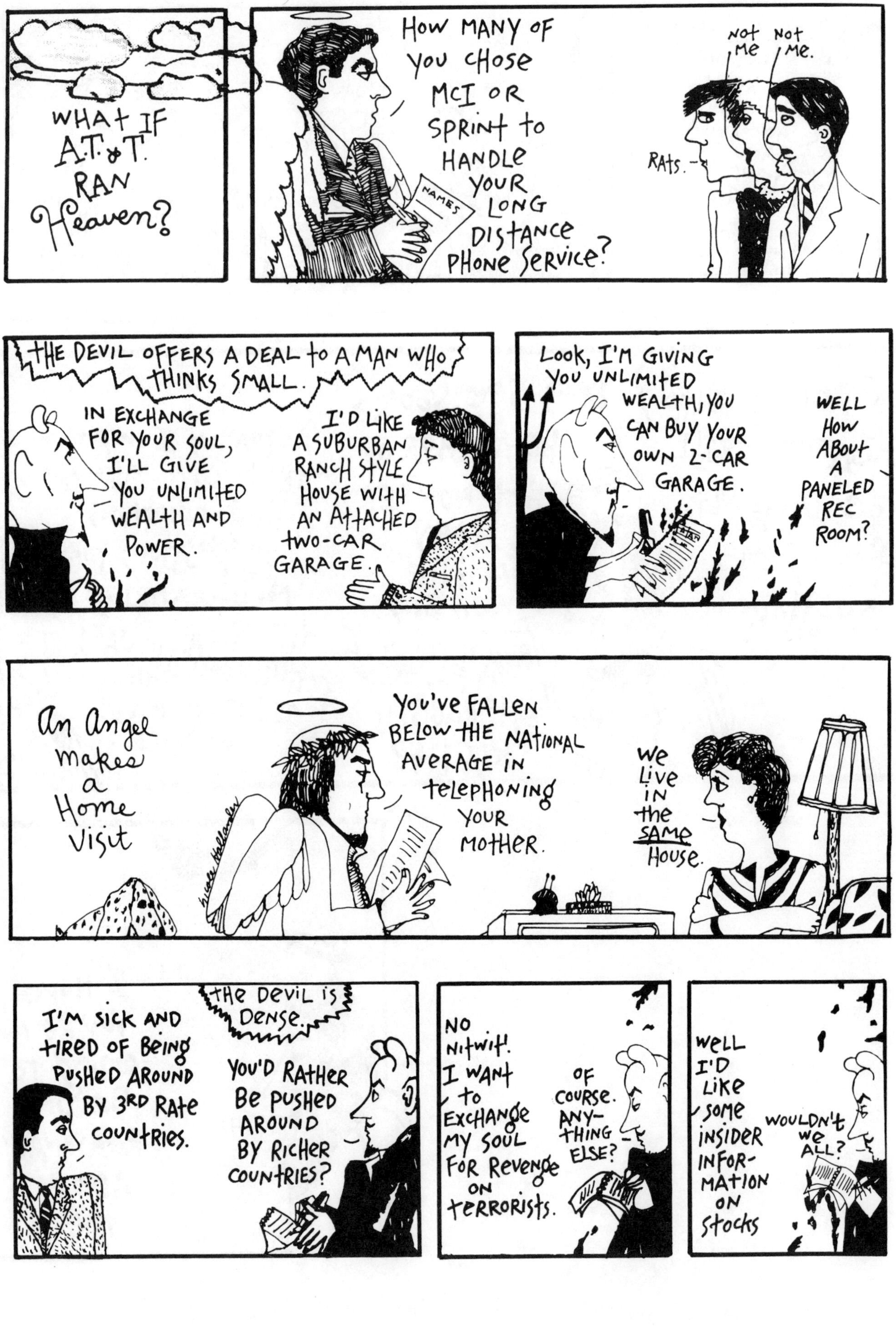
WHAT IF A.T.&T. RAN Heaven?
HOW MANY OF YOU CHOSE MCI OR SPRINT TO HANDLE YOUR LONG DISTANCE PHONE SERVICE?
NAMES
Not me
Not me.
Rats.
THE DEVIL OFFERS A DEAL TO A MAN WHO THINKS SMALL.
IN EXCHANGE FOR YOUR SOUL, I'LL GIVE YOU UNLIMITED WEALTH AND POWER.
I'D LIKE A SUBURBAN RANCH STYLE HOUSE WITH AN ATTACHED TWO-CAR GARAGE.
LOOK, I'M GIVING YOU UNLIMITED WEALTH, YOU CAN BUY YOUR OWN 2-CAR GARAGE.
WELL HOW ABOUT A PANELED REC ROOM?
An Angel makes a Home Visit
YOU'VE FALLEN BELOW THE NATIONAL AVERAGE IN TELEPHONING YOUR MOTHER.
WE LIVE IN THE SAME HOUSE.
THE DEVIL IS DENSE.
I'M SICK AND TIRED OF BEING PUSHED AROUND BY 3RD RATE COUNTRIES.
YOU'D RATHER BE PUSHED AROUND BY RICHER COUNTRIES?
NO NITWIT. I WANT TO EXCHANGE MY SOUL FOR REVENGE ON TERRORISTS.
OF COURSE. ANYTHING ELSE?
WELL I'D LIKE SOME INSIDER INFORMATION ON STOCKS
WOULDN'T WE ALL?

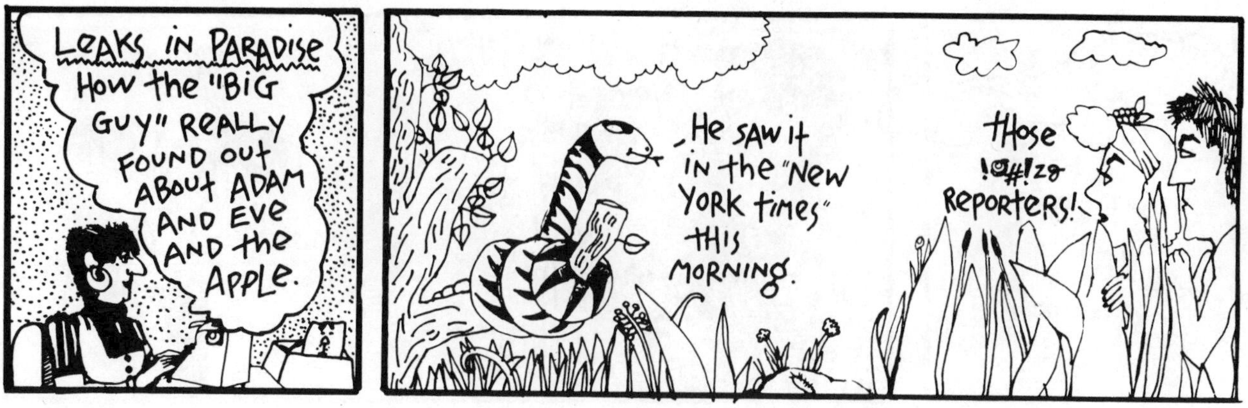
LEAKS IN PARADISE
How the "BIG GUY" REALLY FOUND OUT ABOUT ADAM AND EVE AND the APPLE.
He saw it in the "New York times" this MORNING.
those !@#!z@ Reporters!

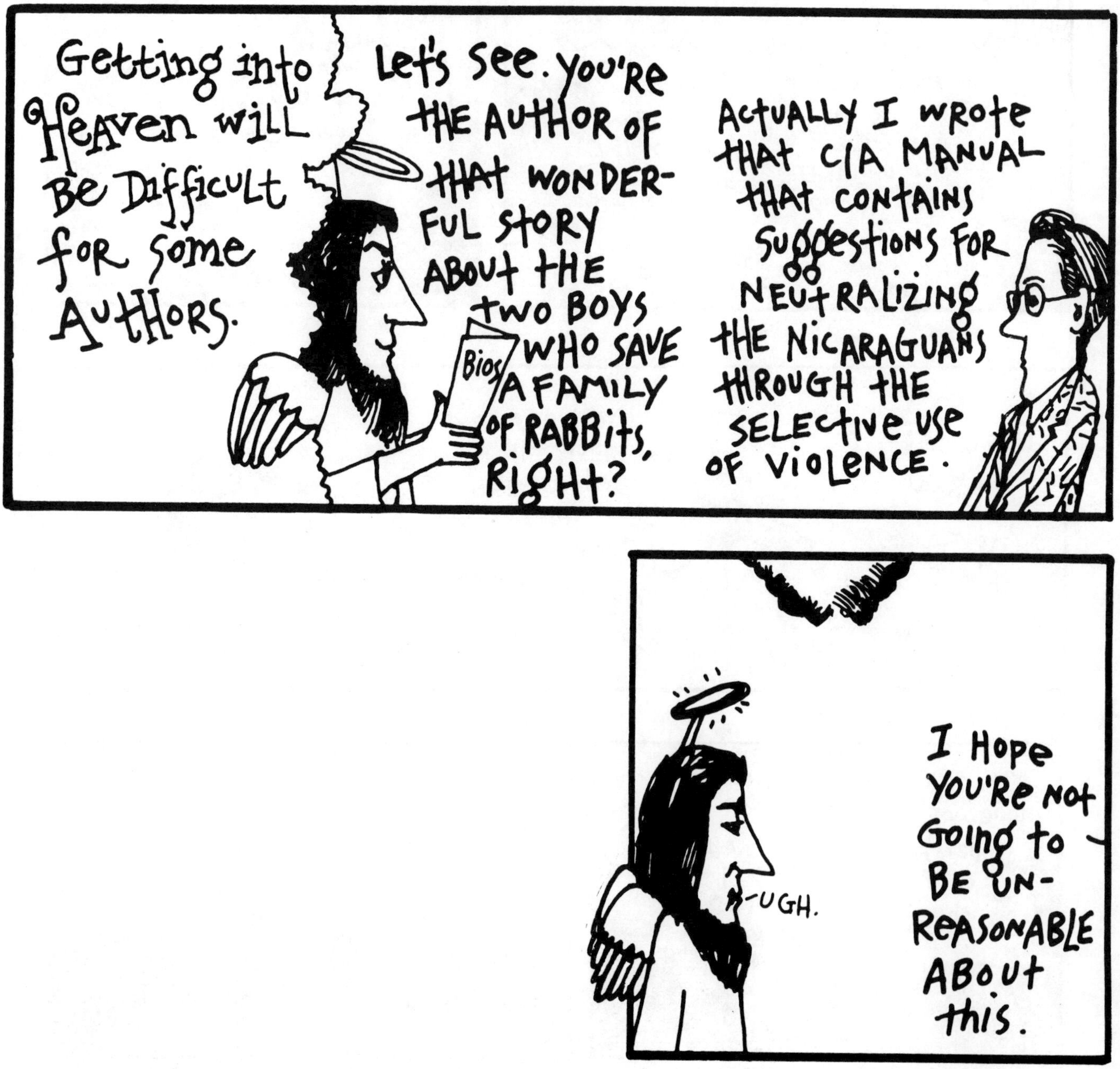
Getting into Heaven will Be Difficult for some Authors.
Let's see. You're the AUTHOR OF THAT WONDERFUL STORY ABOUT THE TWO BOYS WHO SAVE A FAMILY OF RABBITS, RIGHT?
Bios
ACTUALLY I WROTE THAT CIA MANUAL THAT CONTAINS SUGGESTIONS FOR NEUTRALIZING THE NICARAGUANS THROUGH THE SELECTIVE USE OF VIOLENCE.
UGH.
I HOPE YOU'RE NOT GOING TO BE UN-REASONABLE ABOUT THIS.

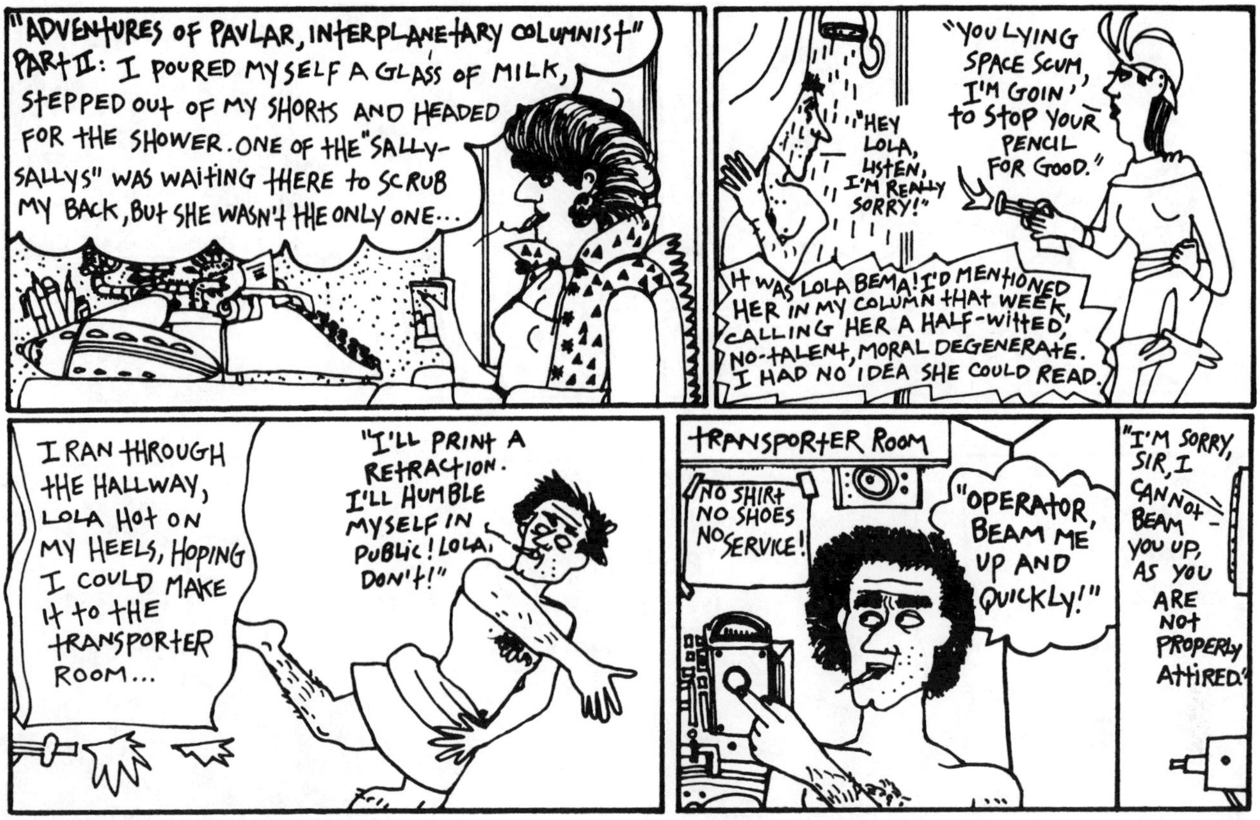
"ADVENTURES OF PAVLAR, INTERPLANETARY COLUMNIST" PART II: I POURED MYSELF A GLASS OF MILK, STEPPED OUT OF MY SHORTS AND HEADED FOR THE SHOWER. ONE OF THE "SALLY-SALLYS" WAS WAITING THERE TO SCRUB MY BACK, BUT SHE WASN'T THE ONLY ONE...
"HEY LOLA, LISTEN, I'M REALLY SORRY!"
"YOU LYING SPACE SCUM, I'M GOIN' TO STOP YOUR PENCIL FOR GOOD."
IT WAS LOLA BEMA! I'D MENTIONED HER IN MY COLUMN THAT WEEK, CALLING HER A HALF-WITTED, NO-TALENT, MORAL DEGENERATE. I HAD NO IDEA SHE COULD READ.
I RAN THROUGH THE HALLWAY, LOLA HOT ON MY HEELS, HOPING I COULD MAKE IT TO THE TRANSPORTER ROOM...
"I'LL PRINT A RETRACTION. I'LL HUMBLE MYSELF IN PUBLIC! LOLA, DON'T!"
TRANSPORTER ROOM
NO SHIRT NO SHOES NO SERVICE!
"OPERATOR, BEAM ME UP AND QUICKLY!"
"I'M SORRY, SIR, I CANNOT BEAM YOU UP, AS YOU ARE NOT PROPERLY ATTIRED."

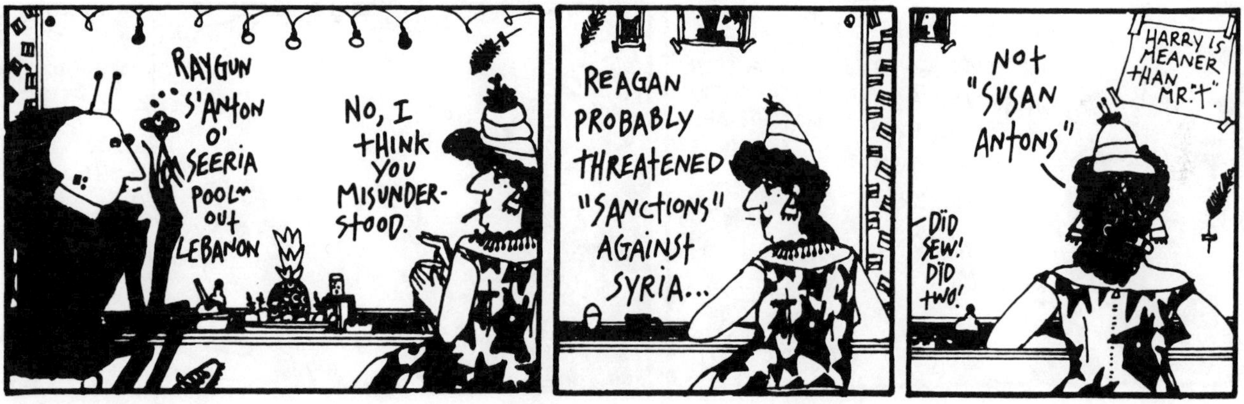
RAYGUN S'ANTON O' SEERIA POOL'M OUT LEBANON
NO, I THINK YOU MISUNDERSTOOD.
REAGAN PROBABLY THREATENED "SANCTIONS" AGAINST SYRIA...
DID SEW! DID TWO!
NOT "SUSAN ANTONS"
HARRY IS MEANER THAN MR. T.

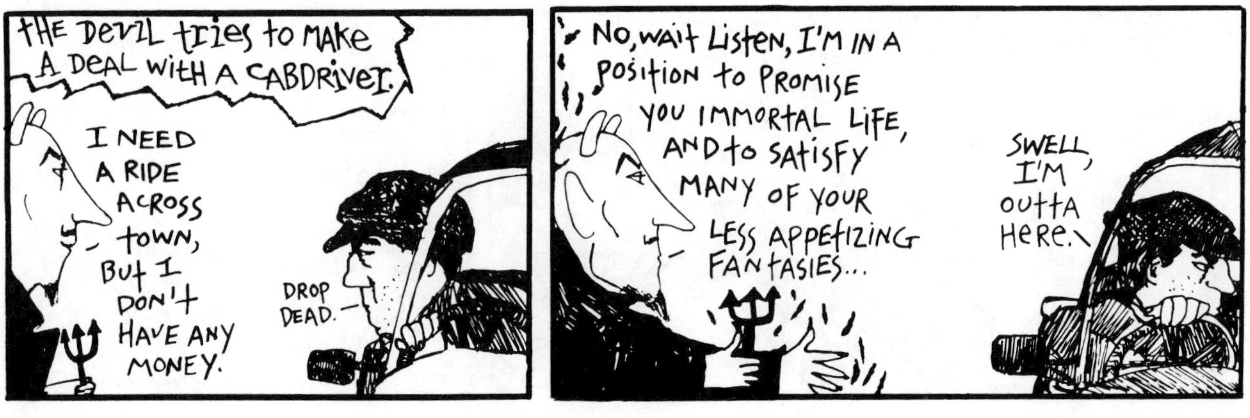
THE DEVIL TRIES TO MAKE A DEAL WITH A CABDRIVER.
I NEED A RIDE ACROSS TOWN, BUT I DON'T HAVE ANY MONEY.
DROP DEAD.
NO, WAIT LISTEN, I'M IN A POSITION TO PROMISE YOU IMMORTAL LIFE, AND TO SATISFY MANY OF YOUR LESS APPETIZING FANTASIES...
SWELL, I'M OUTTA HERE.

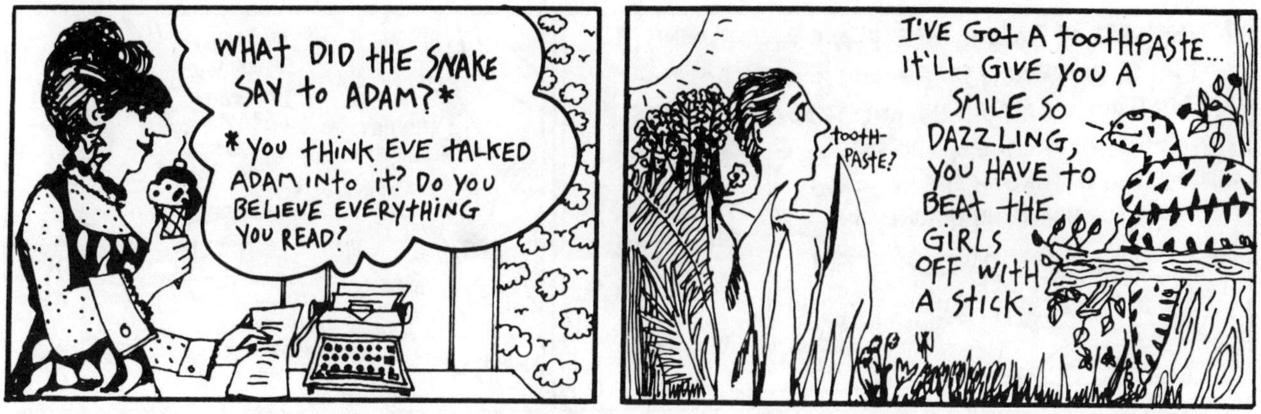
WHAT DID THE SNAKE SAY to ADAM?*
*YOU THINK EVE TALKED ADAM INto it? DO YOU BELIEVE EVERYTHING YOU READ?
tooth-PASTE?
I'VE Got A toothPASTE... It'LL GIVE YOU A SMILE SO DAZZLING, YOU HAVE to BEAT THE GIRLS OFF WITH A STICK.

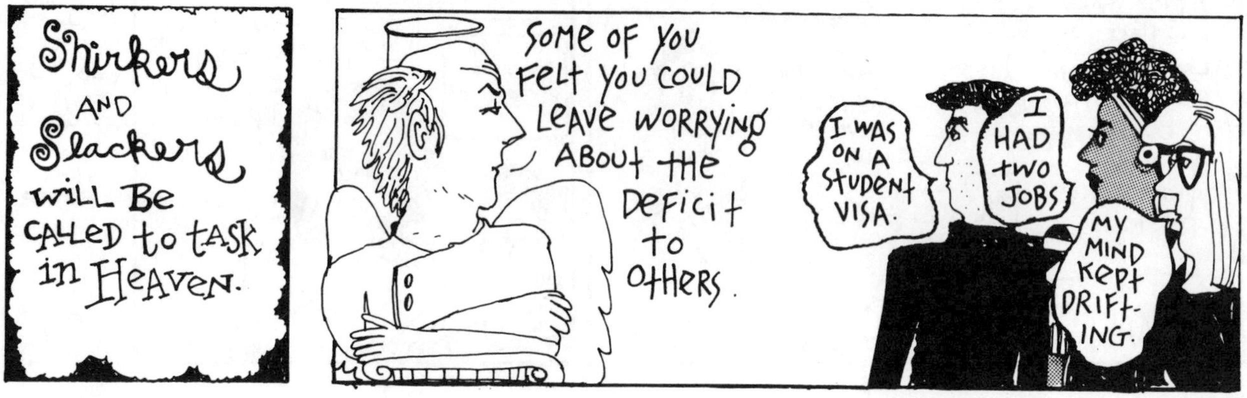
Shirkers AND Slackers WILL BE CALLED to tASK in HEAVEN.
SOME OF YOU FELT YOU COULD LEAVE WORRYING ABOUT THE DEFICIT to OTHERS.
I WAS ON A STUDENT VISA.
I HAD two JOBS
MY MIND KEPT DRIFT-ING.

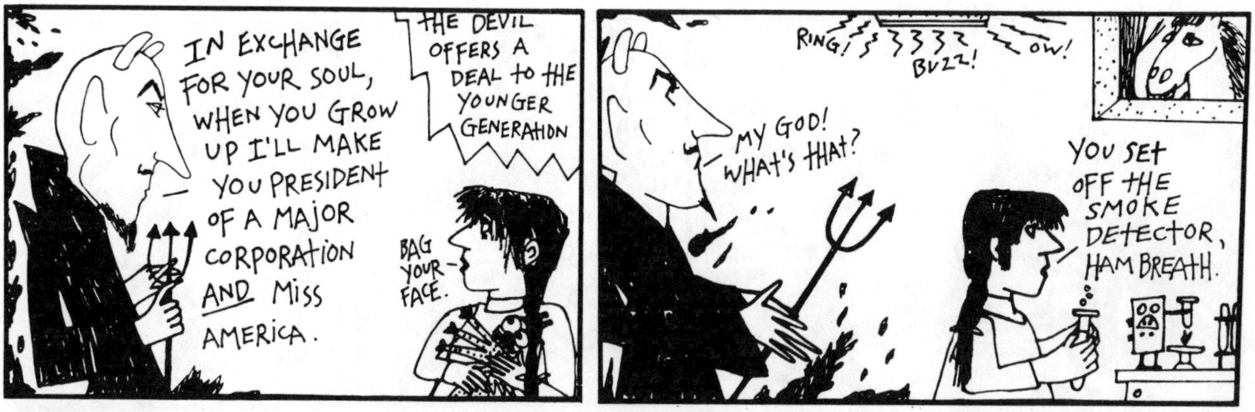
THE DEVIL OFFERS A DEAL to THE YOUNGER GENERATION
IN EXCHANGE FOR YOUR SOUL, WHEN YOU GROW UP I'LL MAKE YOU PRESIDENT OF A MAJOR CORPORATION AND MISS AMERICA.
BAG YOUR FACE.
RING! BUZZ! OW!
MY GOD! WHAT'S THAT?
YOU SET OFF THE SMOKE DETECTOR, HAM BREATH.

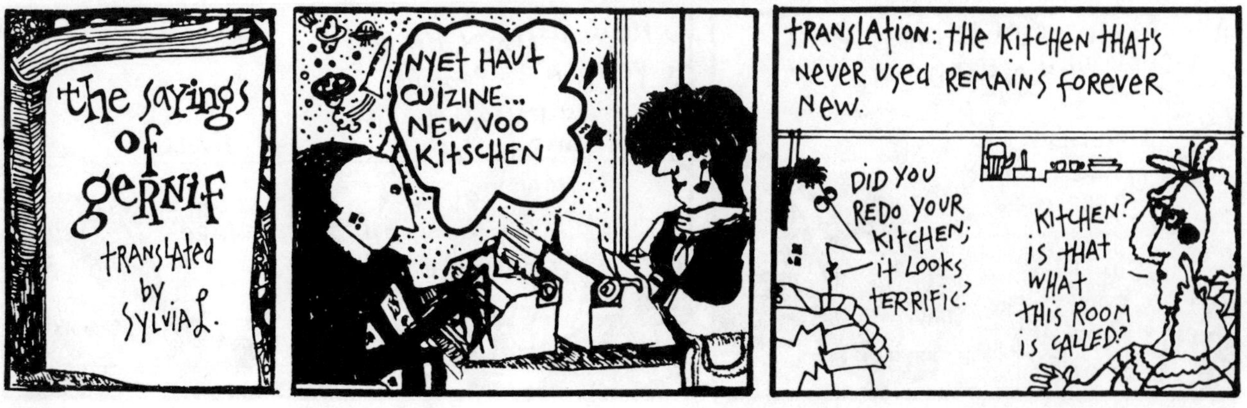
the sayings of gernif translated by SYLVIA L.
NYET HAUT CUIZINE... NEWVOO KITSCHEN
TRANSLATION: THE KITCHEN THAT'S NEVER USED REMAINS FOREVER NEW.
DID YOU REDO YOUR KITCHEN; it LOOKS TERRIFIC?
KITCHEN? IS THAT WHAT THIS ROOM IS CALLED?

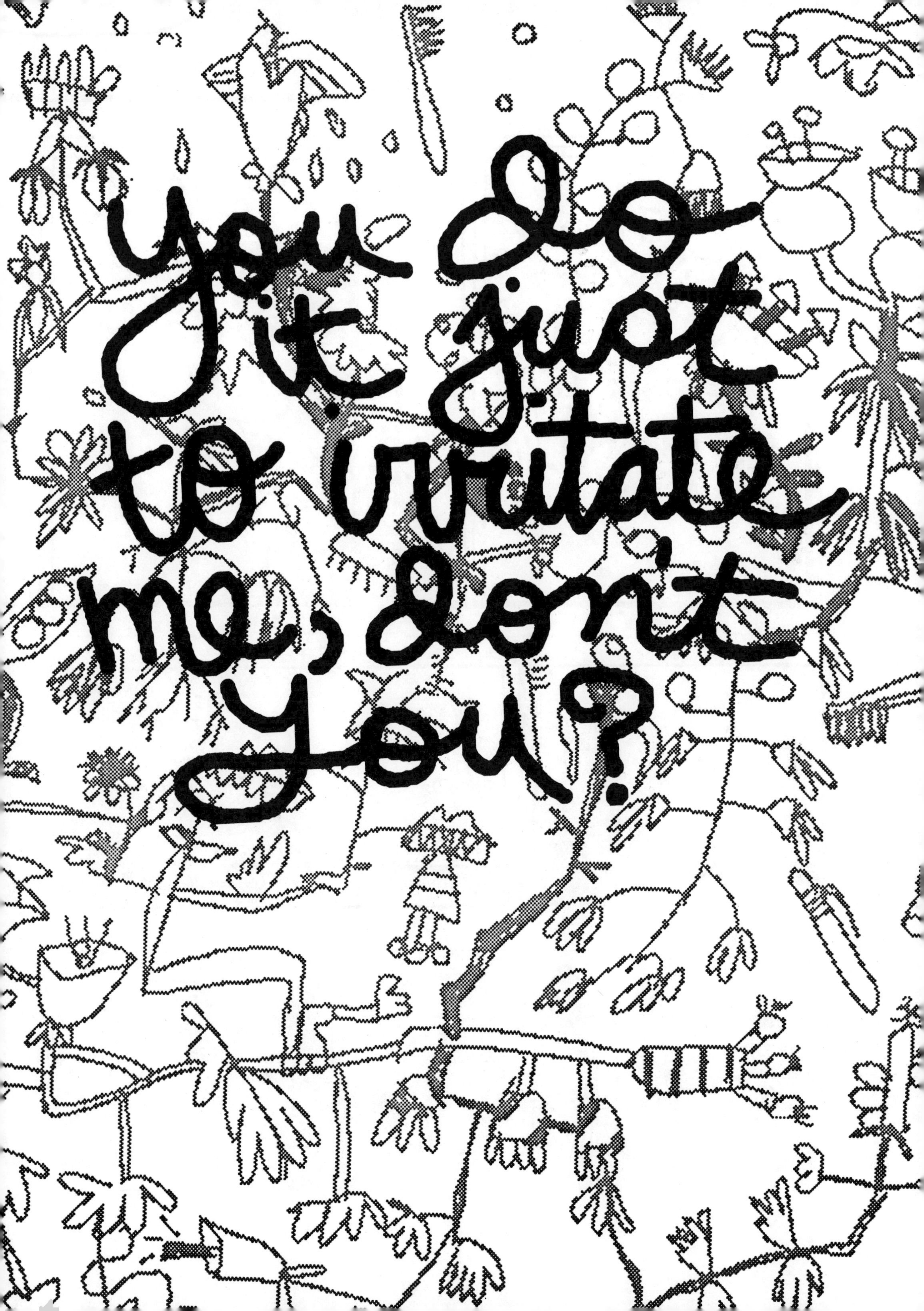
you do
it just
to irritate
me, don't
you?

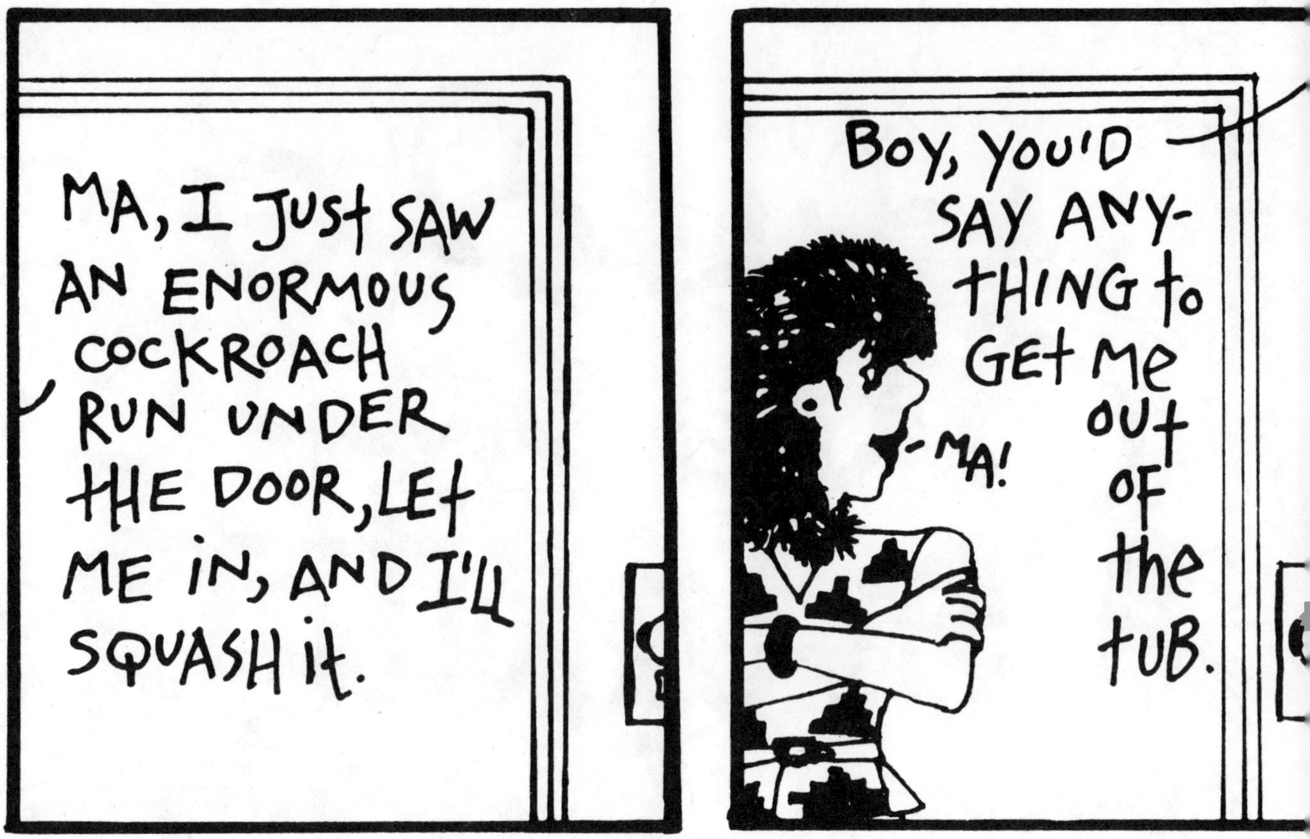
MA, I JUST SAW AN ENORMOUS COCKROACH RUN UNDER THE DOOR, LET ME IN, AND I'LL SQUASH IT.
BOY, YOU'D SAY ANYTHING TO GET ME OUT OF THE TUB.
MA!

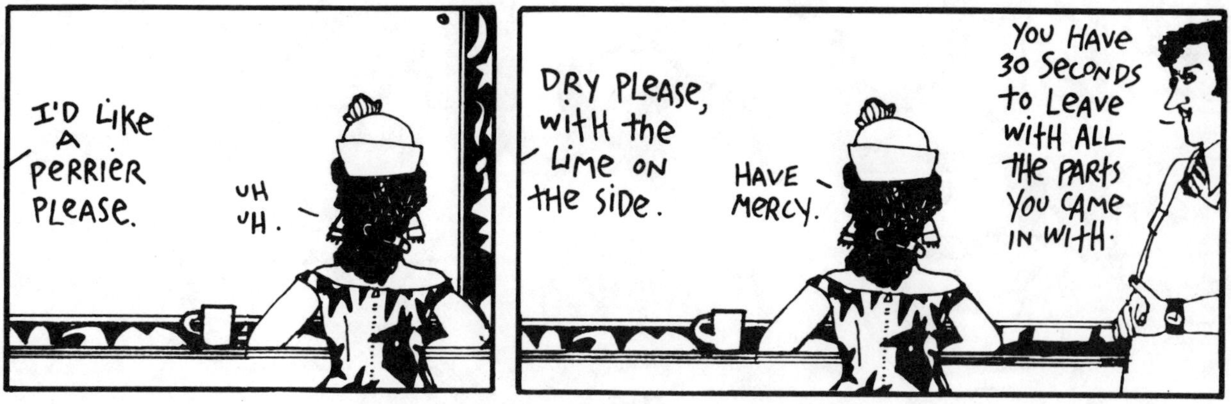
I'D LIKE A PERRIER PLEASE.
UH UH.
DRY PLEASE, WITH THE LIME ON THE SIDE.
HAVE MERCY.
YOU HAVE 30 SECONDS TO LEAVE WITH ALL THE PARTS YOU CAME IN WITH.

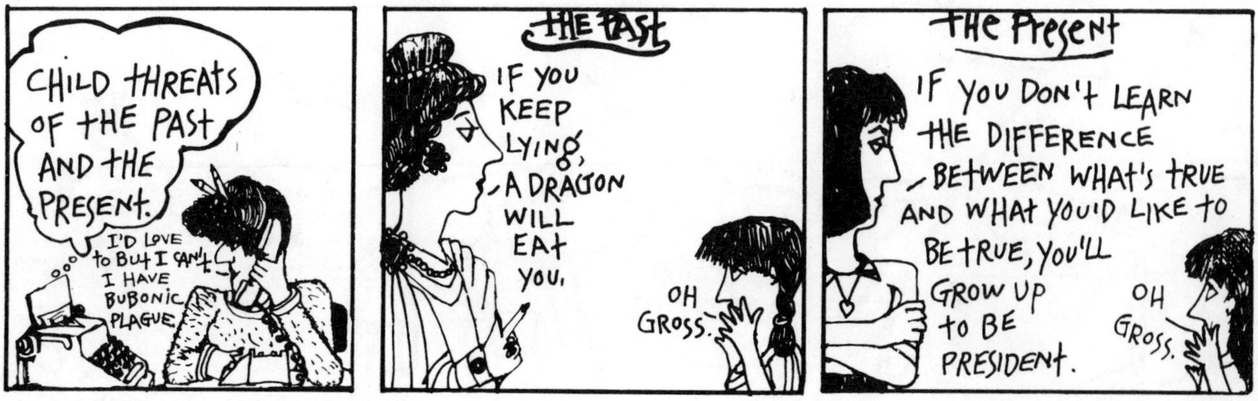
CHILD THREATS OF THE PAST AND THE PRESENT.
I'D LOVE TO BUT I CAN'T. I HAVE BUBONIC PLAGUE.
THE PAST
IF YOU KEEP LYING, A DRAGON WILL EAT YOU.
OH GROSS.
THE PRESENT
IF YOU DON'T LEARN THE DIFFERENCE BETWEEN WHAT'S TRUE AND WHAT YOU'D LIKE TO BE TRUE, YOU'LL GROW UP TO BE PRESIDENT.
OH GROSS.

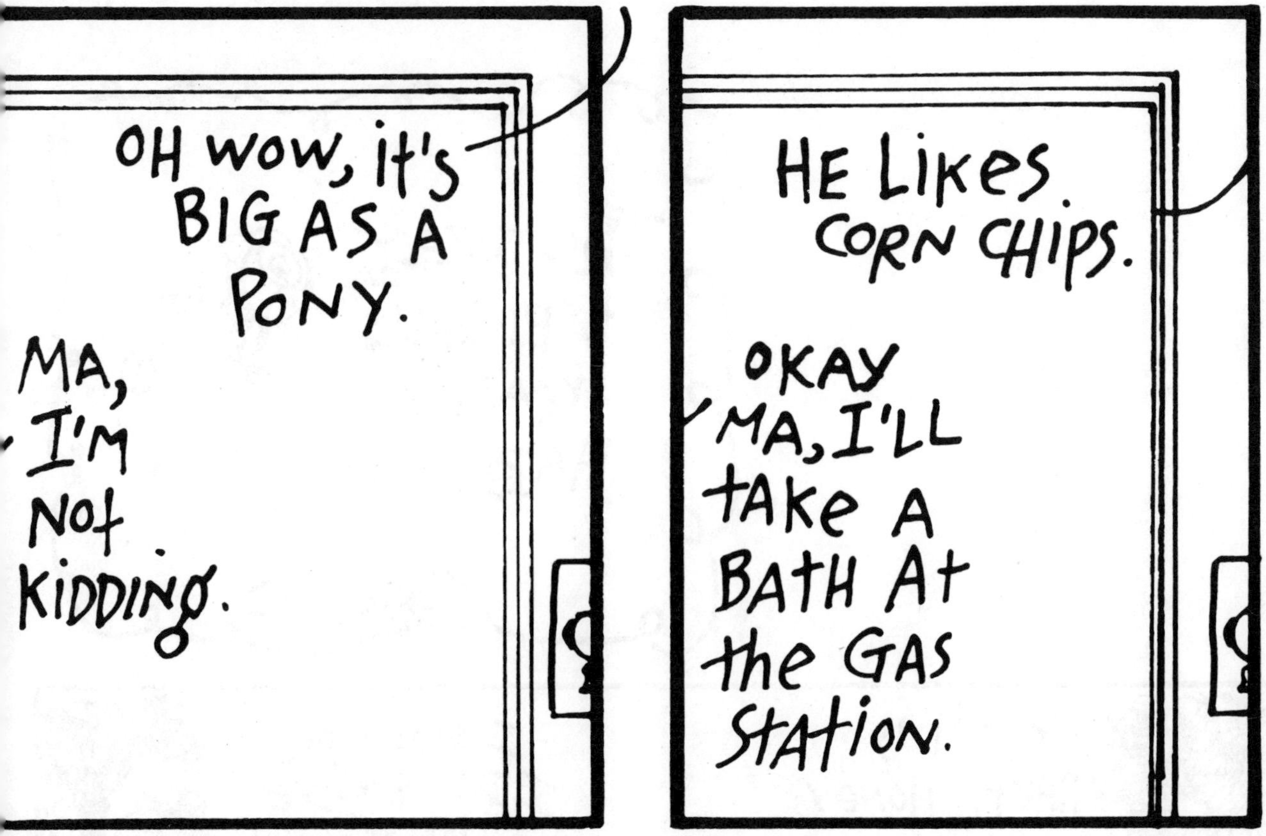
OH WOW, it's BIG AS A PONY.
MA, I'M NOT KIDDING.
HE LIKES CORN CHIPS.
OKAY MA, I'LL TAKE A BATH AT THE GAS STATION.

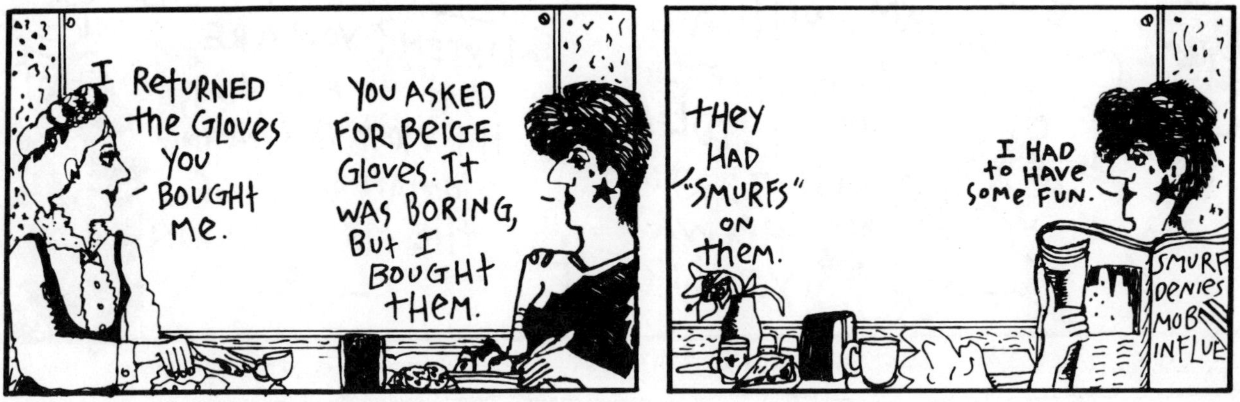
I RETURNED THE GLOVES YOU BOUGHT ME.
YOU ASKED FOR BEIGE GLOVES. IT WAS BORING, BUT I BOUGHT THEM.
THEY HAD "SMURFS" ON THEM.
I HAD TO HAVE SOME FUN.
SMURF DENIES MOB INFLUE

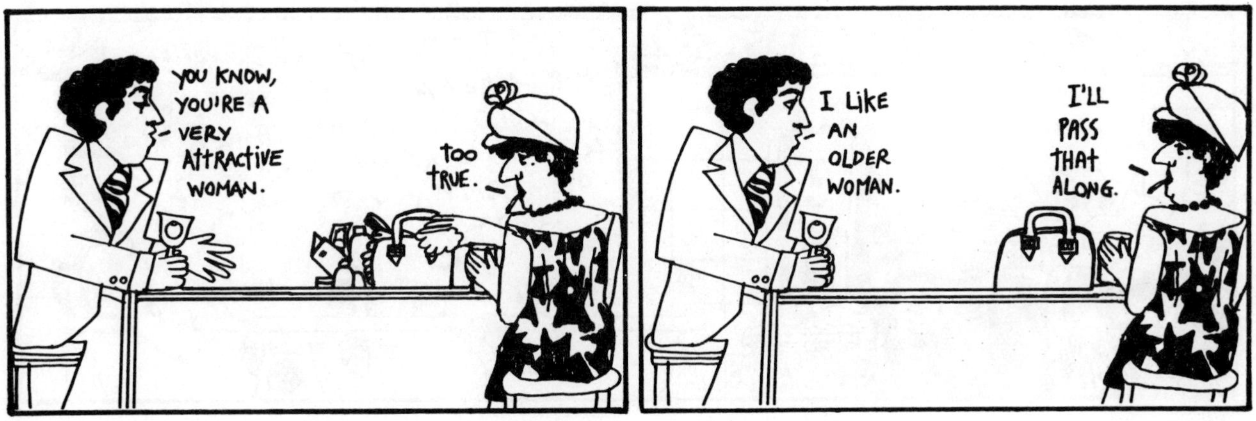
YOU KNOW, YOU'RE A VERY ATTRACTIVE WOMAN.
TOO TRUE.
I LIKE AN OLDER WOMAN.
I'LL PASS THAT ALONG.

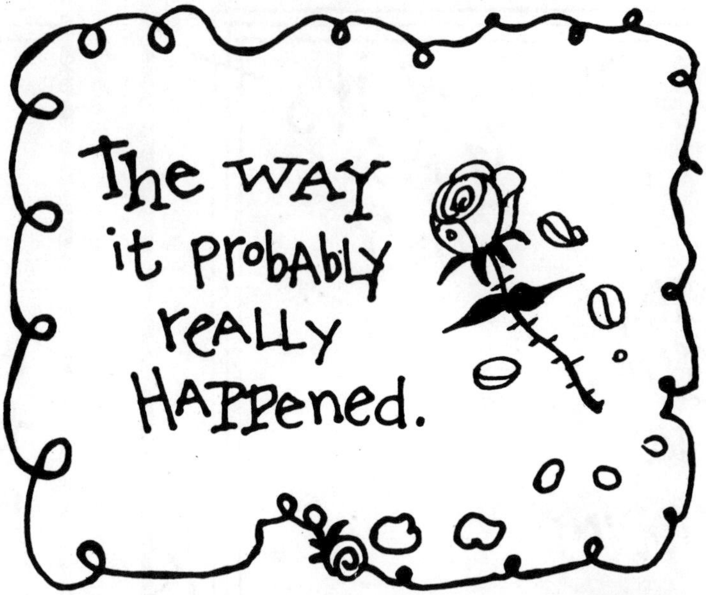
The WAY it probably really HAPPened.

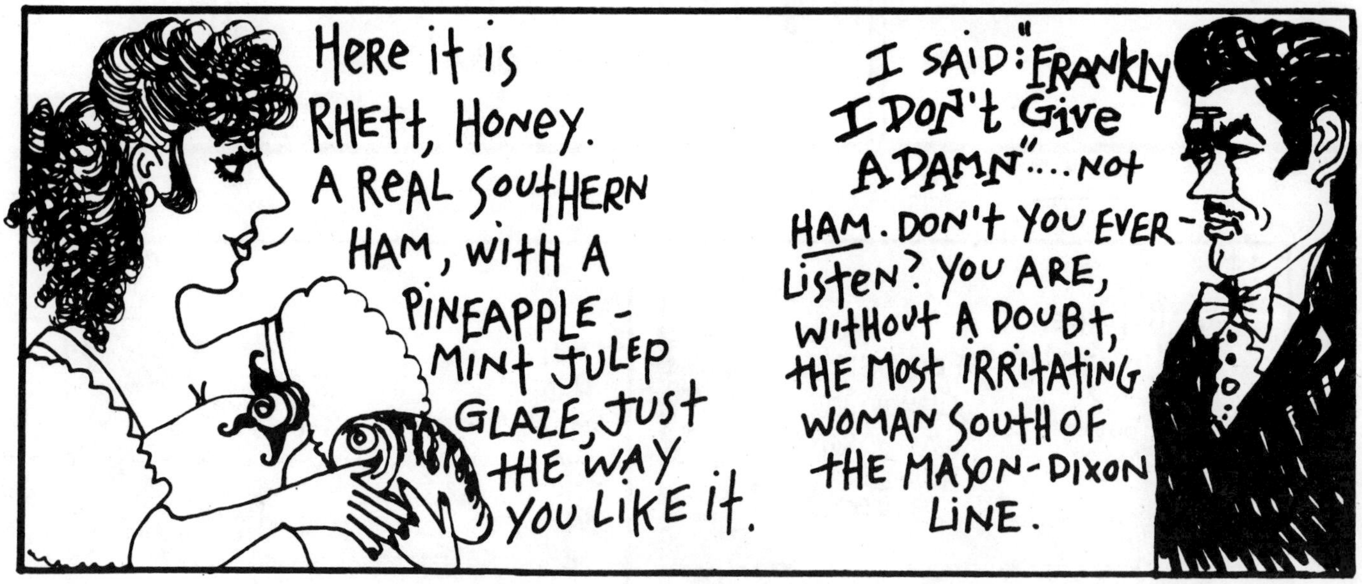
Here it is RHett, Honey. A Real Southern HAM, with A PINEAPPLE-MINT JULEP GLAZE, JUST THE WAY YOU LIKE it.
I SAID: "FRANKLY I DON'T GIVE A DAMN"....NOT HAM. DON'T YOU EVER-LISTEN? YOU ARE, WITHOUT A DOUBT, THE MOST IRRITATING WOMAN SOUTH OF THE MASON-DIXON LINE.

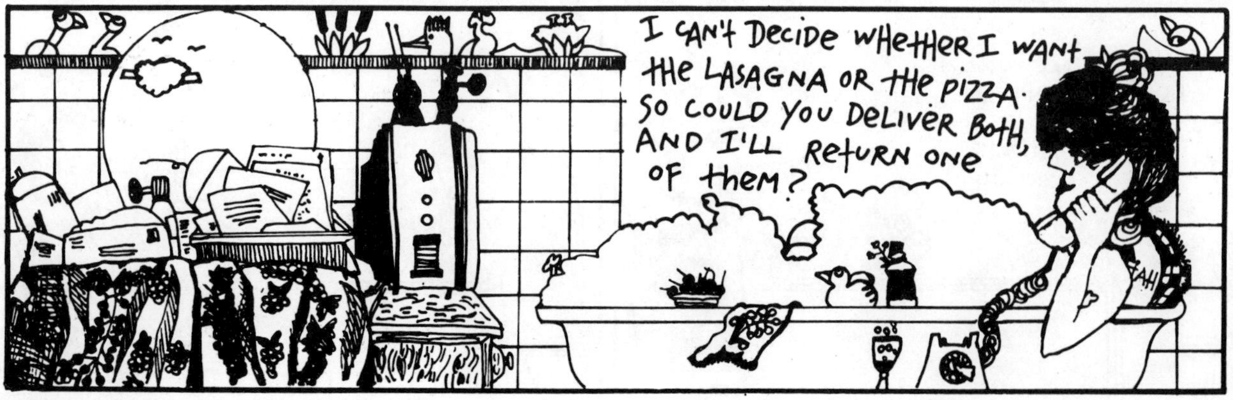
I CAN'T DECIDE WHETHER I WANT THE LASAGNA OR THE PIZZA. SO COULD YOU DELIVER BOTH, AND I'LL RETURN ONE OF THEM?

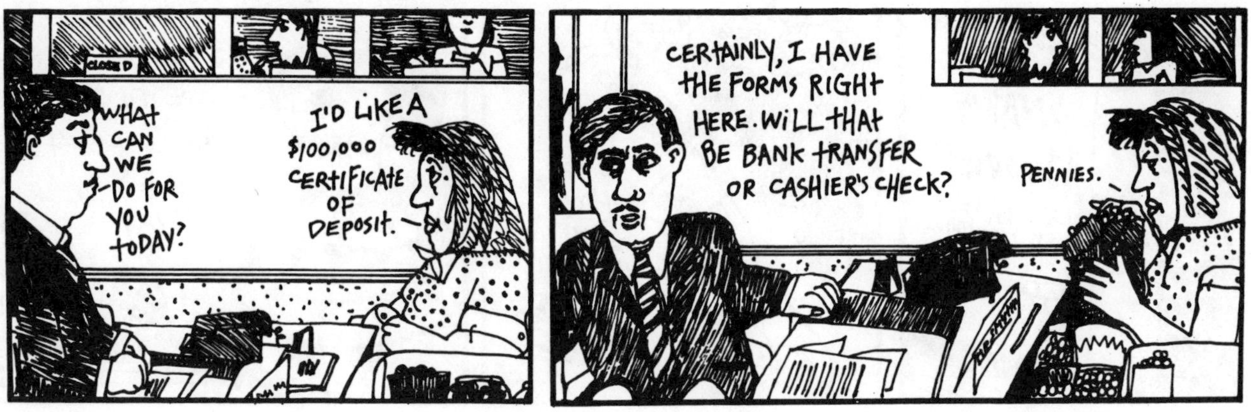
WHAT CAN WE DO FOR YOU TODAY?
I'D LIKE A $100,000 CERTIFICATE OF DEPOSIT.
CERTAINLY, I HAVE THE FORMS RIGHT HERE. WILL THAT BE BANK TRANSFER OR CASHIER'S CHECK?
PENNIES.

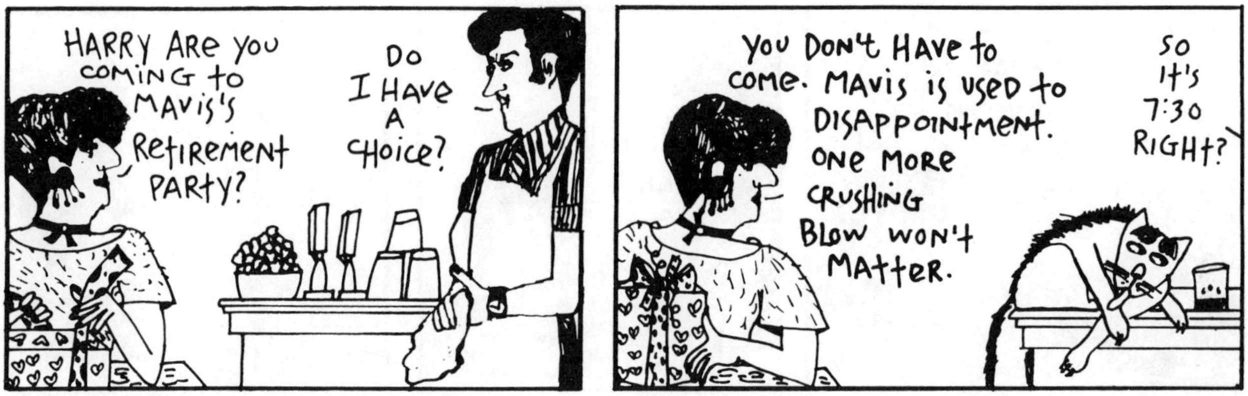
HARRY ARE YOU COMING TO MAVIS'S RETIREMENT PARTY?
DO I HAVE A CHOICE?
YOU DON'T HAVE TO COME. MAVIS IS USED TO DISAPPOINTMENT. ONE MORE CRUSHING BLOW WON'T MATTER.
SO IT'S 7:30 RIGHT?

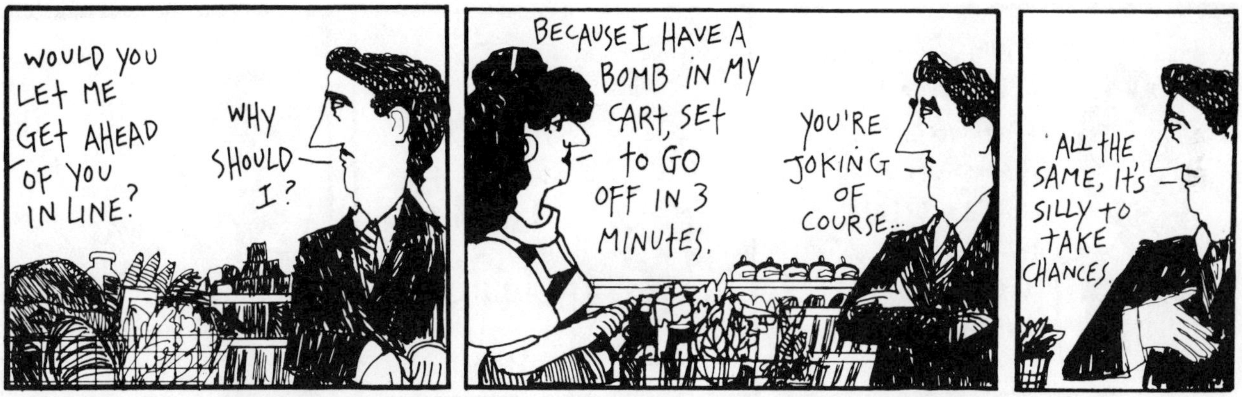
WOULD YOU LET ME GET AHEAD OF YOU IN LINE?
WHY SHOULD I?
BECAUSE I HAVE A BOMB IN MY CART, SET TO GO OFF IN 3 MINUTES.
YOU'RE JOKING OF COURSE...
ALL THE SAME, IT'S SILLY TO TAKE CHANCES.

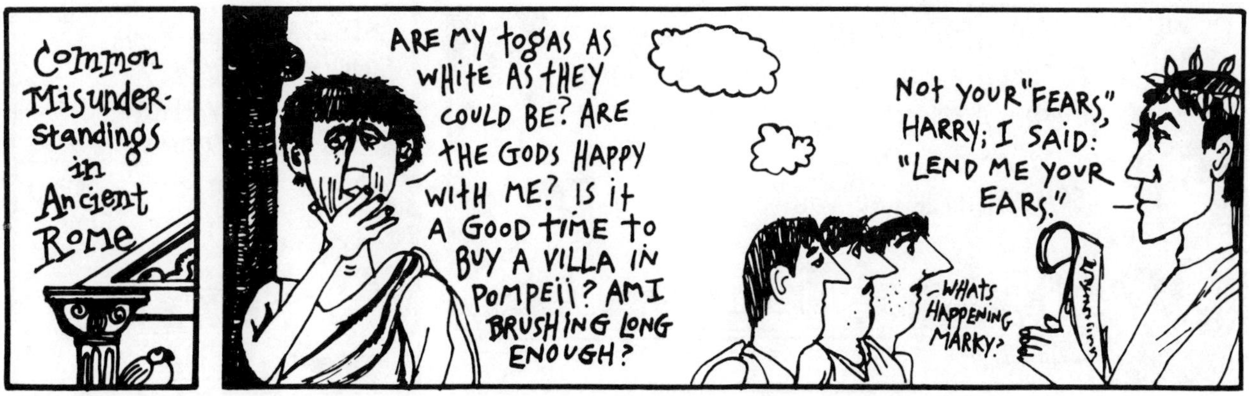
Common Misunder-standings in Ancient Rome
ARE MY TOGAS AS WHITE AS THEY COULD BE? ARE THE GODS HAPPY WITH ME? IS IT A GOOD TIME TO BUY A VILLA IN POMPEII? AM I BRUSHING LONG ENOUGH?
NOT YOUR "FEARS," HARRY; I SAID: "LEND ME YOUR EARS."
WHATS HAPPENING MARKY?

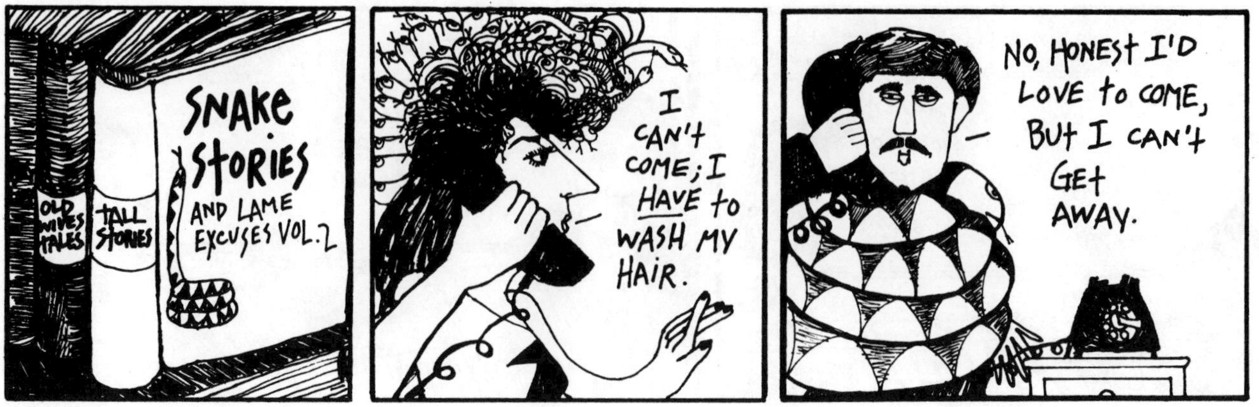
OLD WIVES TALES
TALL STORIES
SNAKE STORIES AND LAME EXCUSES VOL. 2
I CAN'T COME; I HAVE to WASH MY HAIR.
No, HONEST I'D LOVE to COME, BUT I CAN'T GET AWAY.

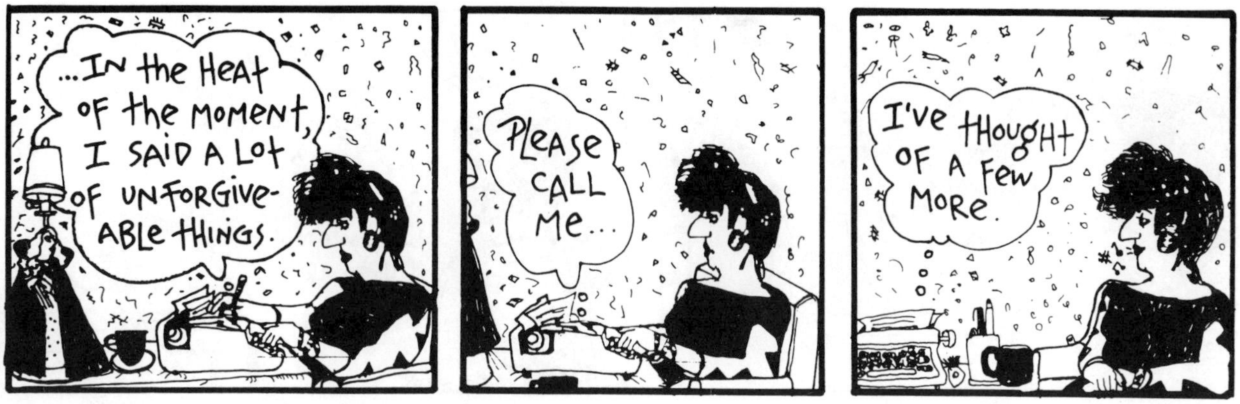
...IN the HEAT of the MOMENT, I SAID A LOT of UNFORGIVE-ABLE THINGS.
PLEASE CALL ME...
I'VE THOUGHT OF A FEW MORE.

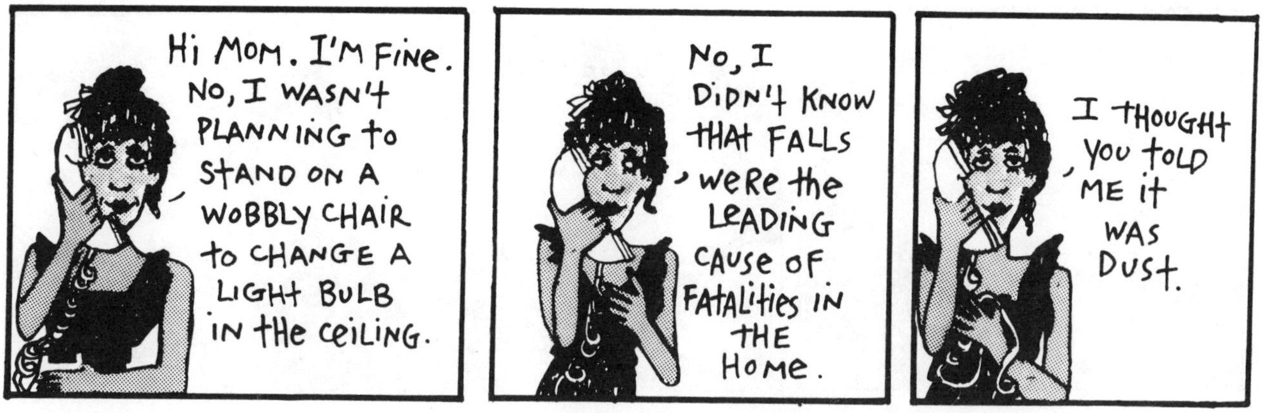
Hi MOM. I'M FINE. NO, I WASN'T PLANNING to STAND ON A WOBBLY CHAIR to CHANGE A LIGHT BULB IN THE CEILING.
NO, I DIDN'T KNOW THAT FALLS WERE THE LEADING CAUSE OF FATALITIES IN THE HOME.
I THOUGHT YOU TOLD ME IT WAS DUST.

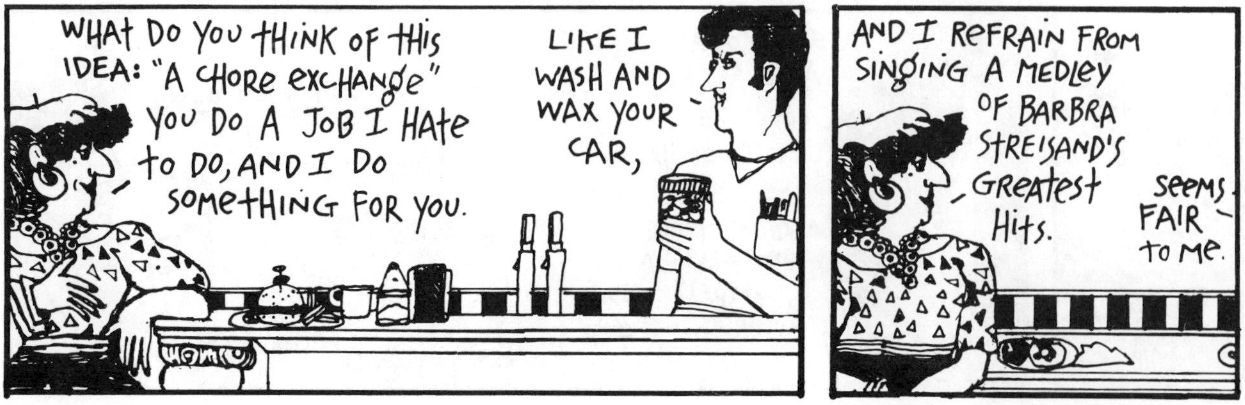
WHAT DO YOU THINK OF THIS IDEA: "A CHORE EXCHANGE" YOU DO A JOB I HATE to DO, AND I DO SOMETHING FOR YOU.
LIKE I WASH AND WAX YOUR CAR,
AND I REFRAIN FROM SINGING A MEDLEY OF BARBRA STREISAND'S GREATEST HITS.
SEEMS FAIR to ME.

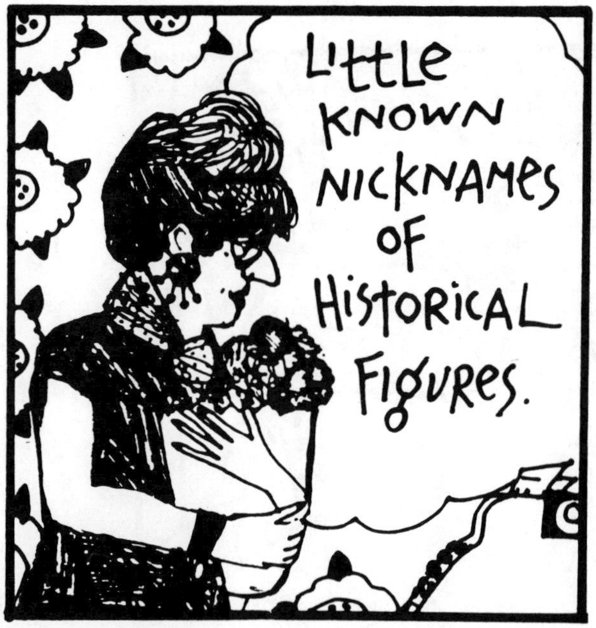
Little known nicknames of Historical Figures.

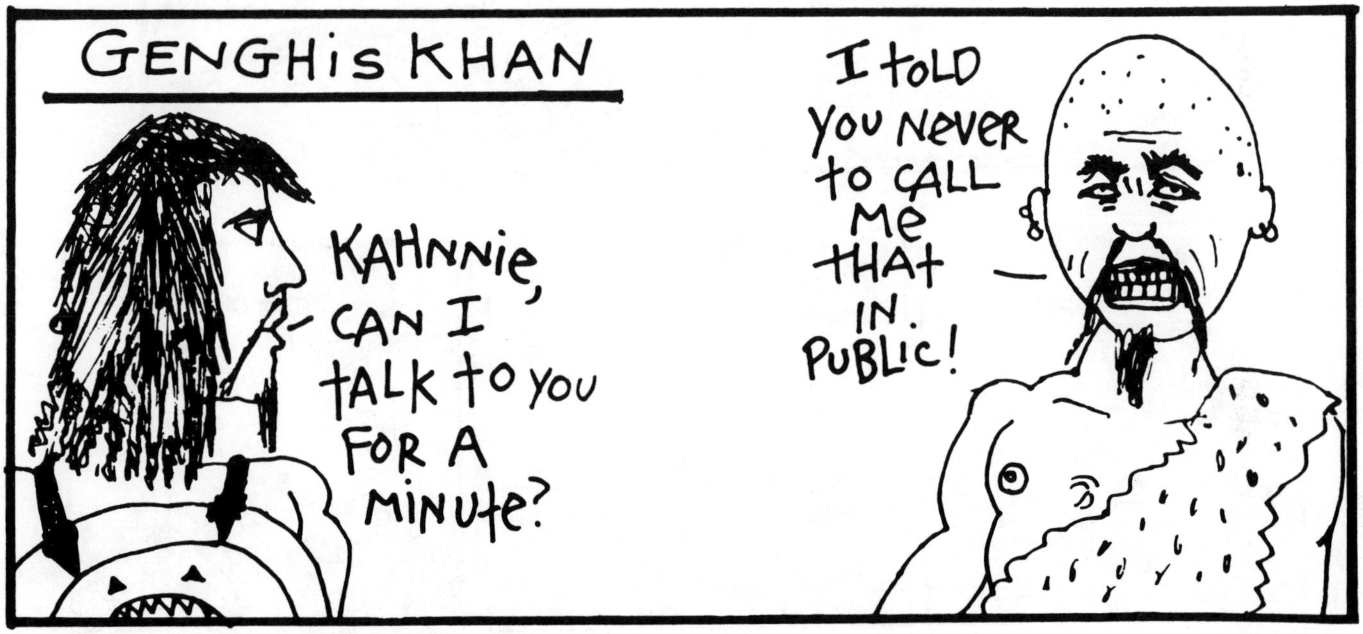
GENGHIS KHAN
KAHNNIE, CAN I talk to you FOR A minute?
I told you never to CALL me that in public!

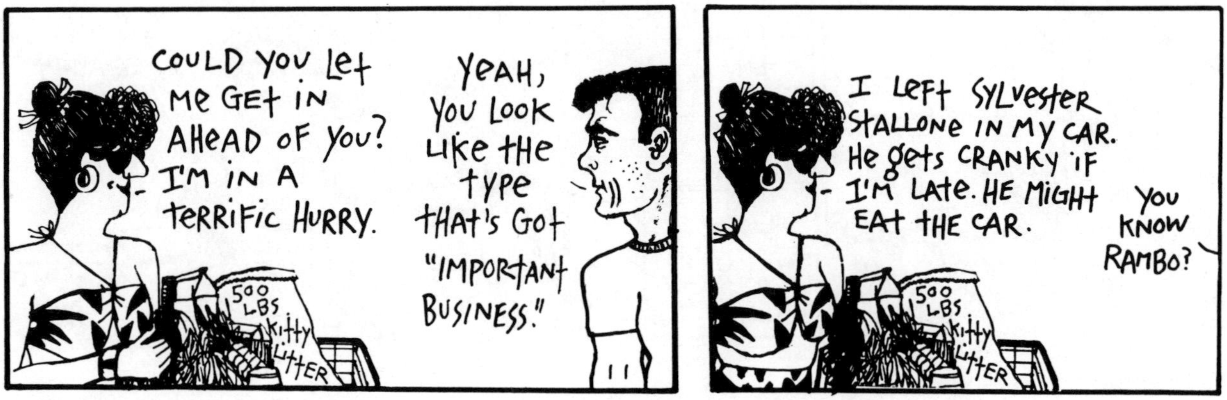
COULD YOU Let me Get in AHEAD OF YOU? I'M IN A TERRIFIC HURRY.
YEAH, YOU LOOK LIKE THE TYPE THAT'S GOT "IMPORTANT BUSINESS."
500 LBS kitty litter
I LEFT SYLVESTER STALLONE IN MY CAR. He gets CRANKY IF I'M LATE. HE MIGHT EAT THE CAR.
YOU KNOW RAMBO?
500 LBS kitty litter

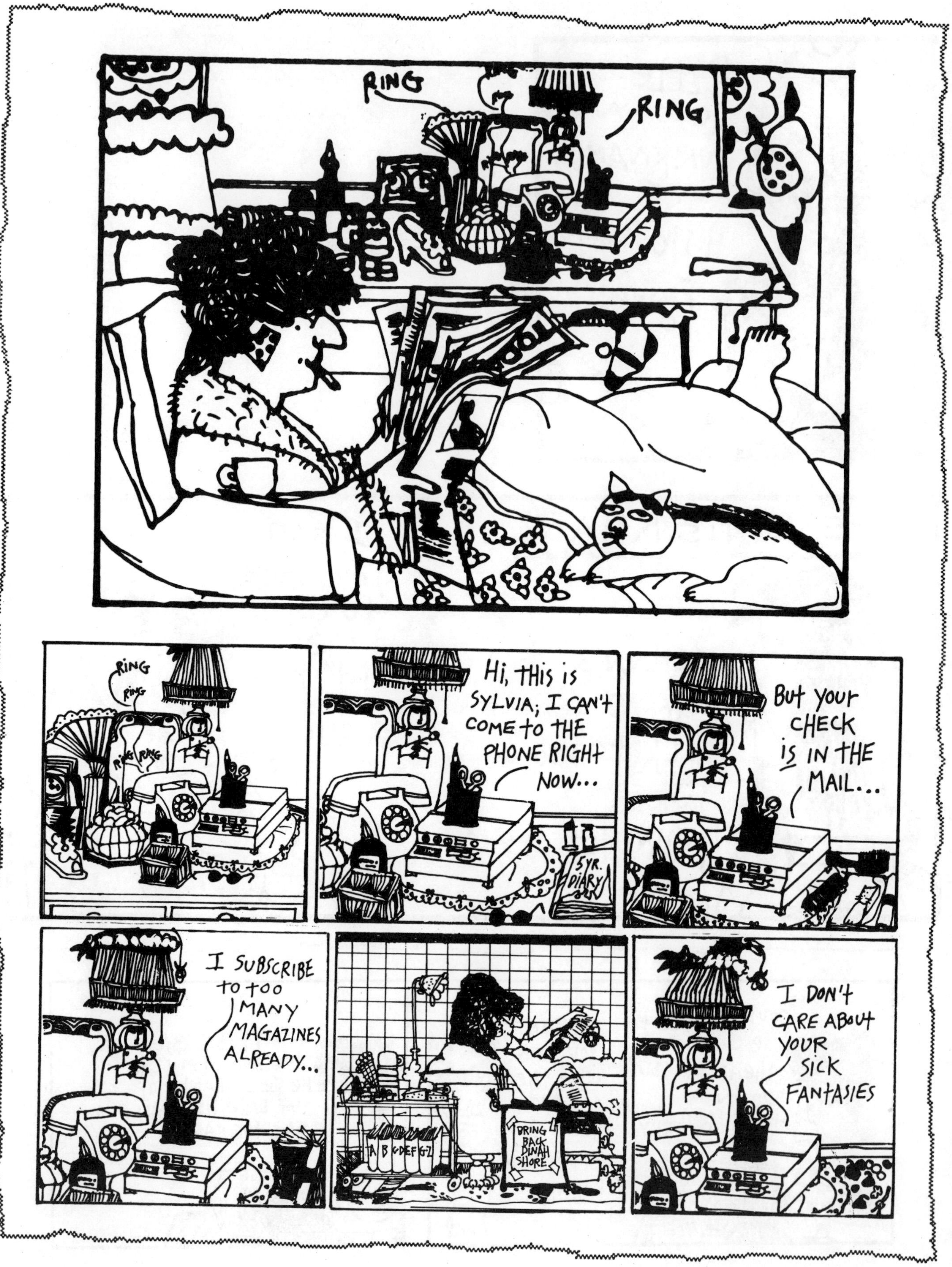
RING
RING
RING
RING
RING RING
Hi, THIS is SYLVIA; I CAN'T COME to THE PHONE RIGHT NOW...
5YR. DIARY
But your CHECK is IN THE MAIL...
I SUBSCRIBE to too MANY MAGAZINES ALREADY...
BRING BACK DINAH SHORE
I DON'T CARE ABOUT YOUR SICK FANTASIES

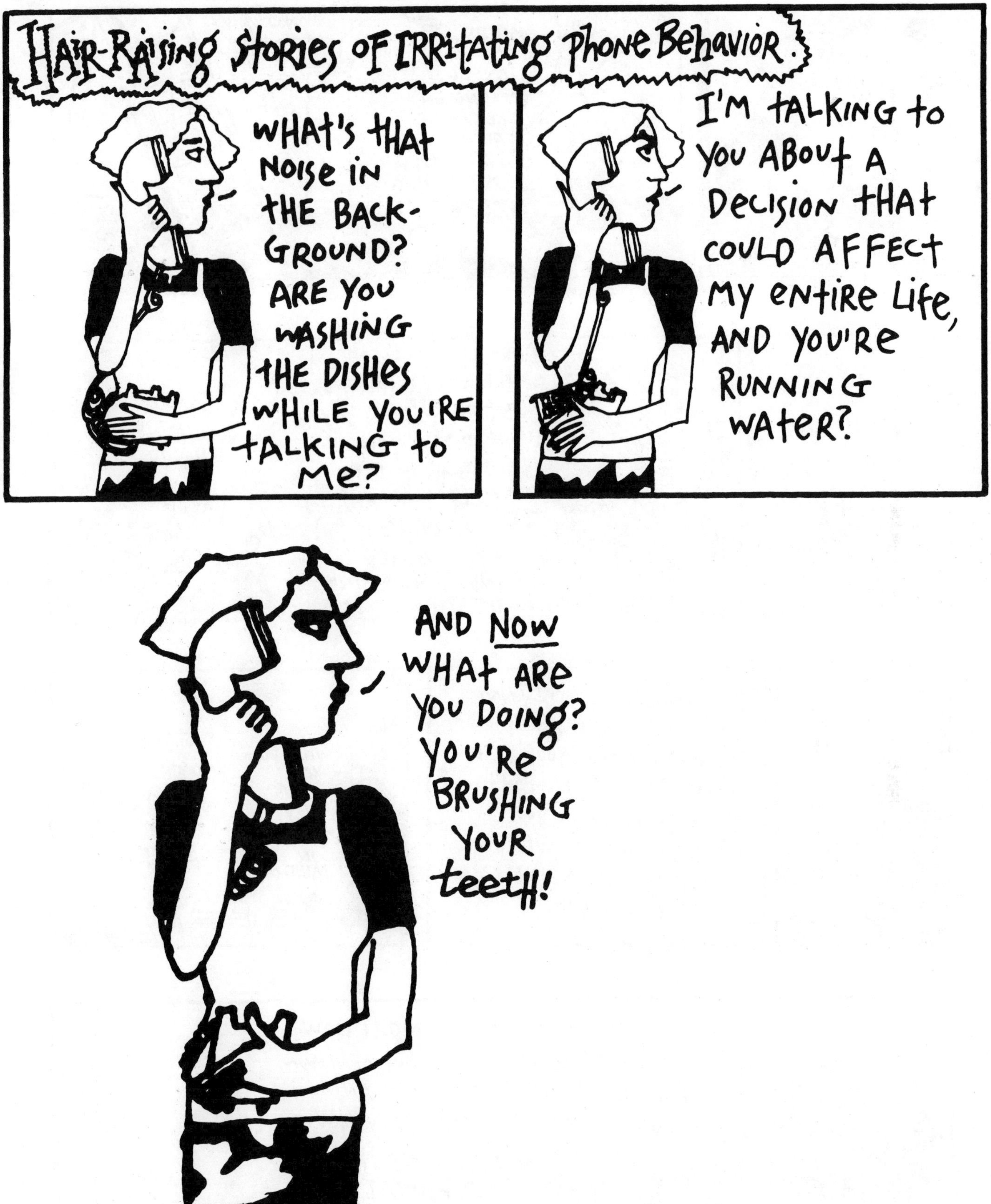
HAIR-RAISING STORIES OF IRRITATING PHONE BEHAVIOR:
WHAT'S THAT NOISE IN THE BACK-GROUND? ARE YOU WASHING THE DISHES WHILE YOU'RE TALKING TO ME?
I'M TALKING TO YOU ABOUT A DECISION THAT COULD AFFECT MY ENTIRE LIFE, AND YOU'RE RUNNING WATER?
AND NOW WHAT ARE YOU DOING? YOU'RE BRUSHING YOUR TEETH!

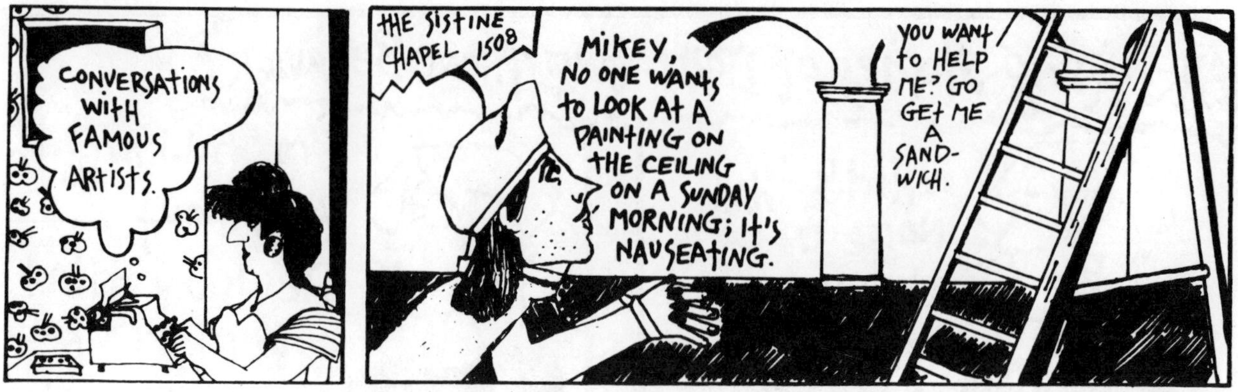
CONVERSATIONS WITH FAMOUS ARTISTS.
THE SISTINE CHAPEL 1508
MIKEY, NO ONE WANTS TO LOOK AT A PAINTING ON THE CEILING ON A SUNDAY MORNING; IT'S NAUSEATING.
YOU WANT TO HELP ME? GO GET ME A SANDWICH.

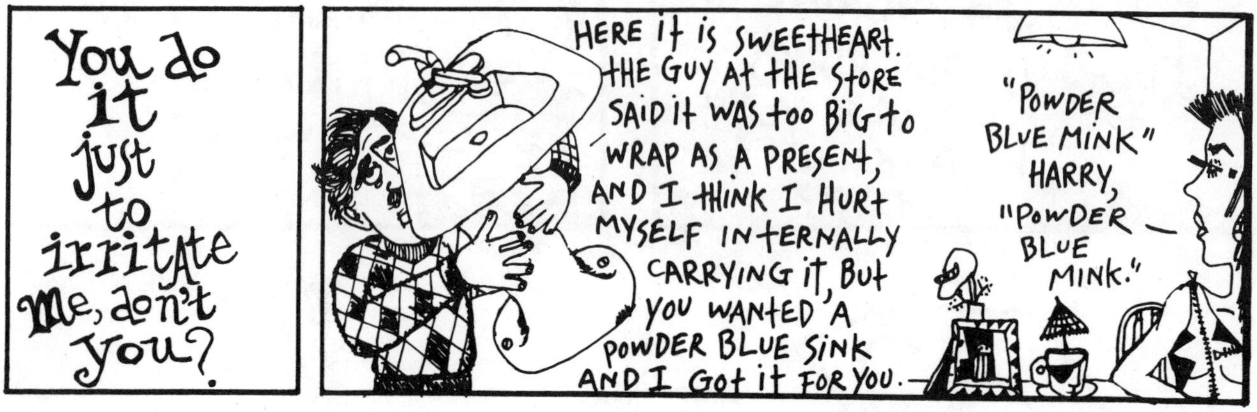
You do it just to irritate me, don't you?
HERE IT IS SWEETHEART. THE GUY AT THE STORE SAID IT WAS TOO BIG TO WRAP AS A PRESENT, AND I THINK I HURT MYSELF INTERNALLY CARRYING IT, BUT YOU WANTED A POWDER BLUE SINK AND I GOT IT FOR YOU.
"POWDER BLUE MINK" HARRY, "POWDER BLUE MINK."

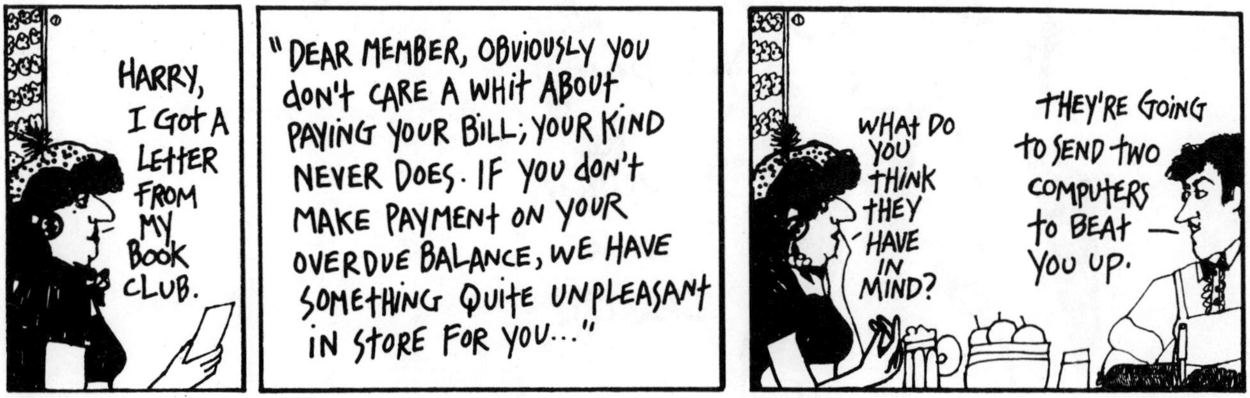
HARRY, I GOT A LETTER FROM MY BOOK CLUB.
"DEAR MEMBER, OBVIOUSLY YOU DON'T CARE A WHIT ABOUT PAYING YOUR BILL; YOUR KIND NEVER DOES. IF YOU DON'T MAKE PAYMENT ON YOUR OVERDUE BALANCE, WE HAVE SOMETHING QUITE UNPLEASANT IN STORE FOR YOU..."
WHAT DO YOU THINK THEY HAVE IN MIND?
THEY'RE GOING TO SEND TWO COMPUTERS TO BEAT YOU UP.

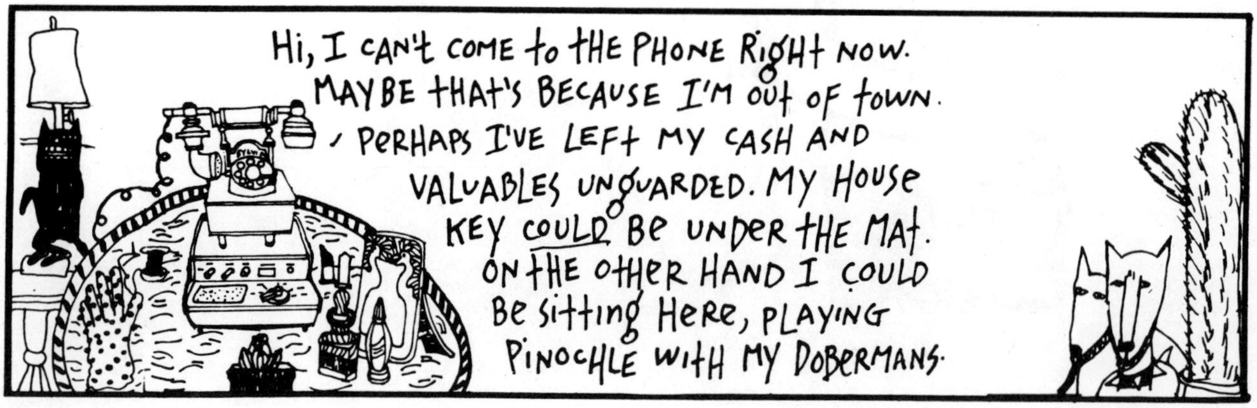
Hi, I CAN'T COME TO THE PHONE RIGHT NOW. MAYBE THAT'S BECAUSE I'M OUT OF TOWN. PERHAPS I'VE LEFT MY CASH AND VALUABLES UNGUARDED. MY HOUSE KEY COULD BE UNDER THE MAT. ON THE OTHER HAND I COULD BE SITTING HERE, PLAYING PINOCHLE WITH MY DOBERMANS.

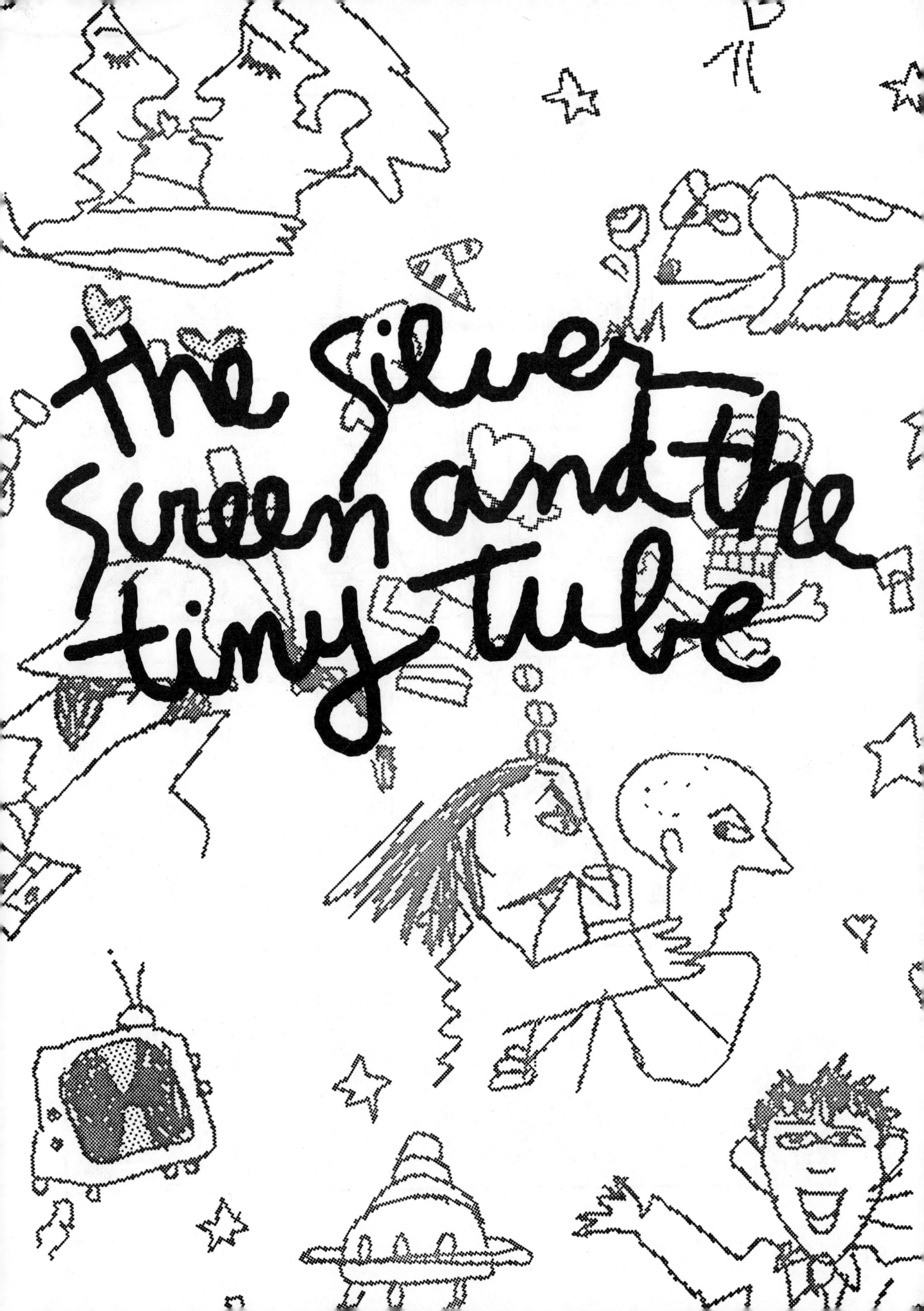
the silver screen and the tiny tube

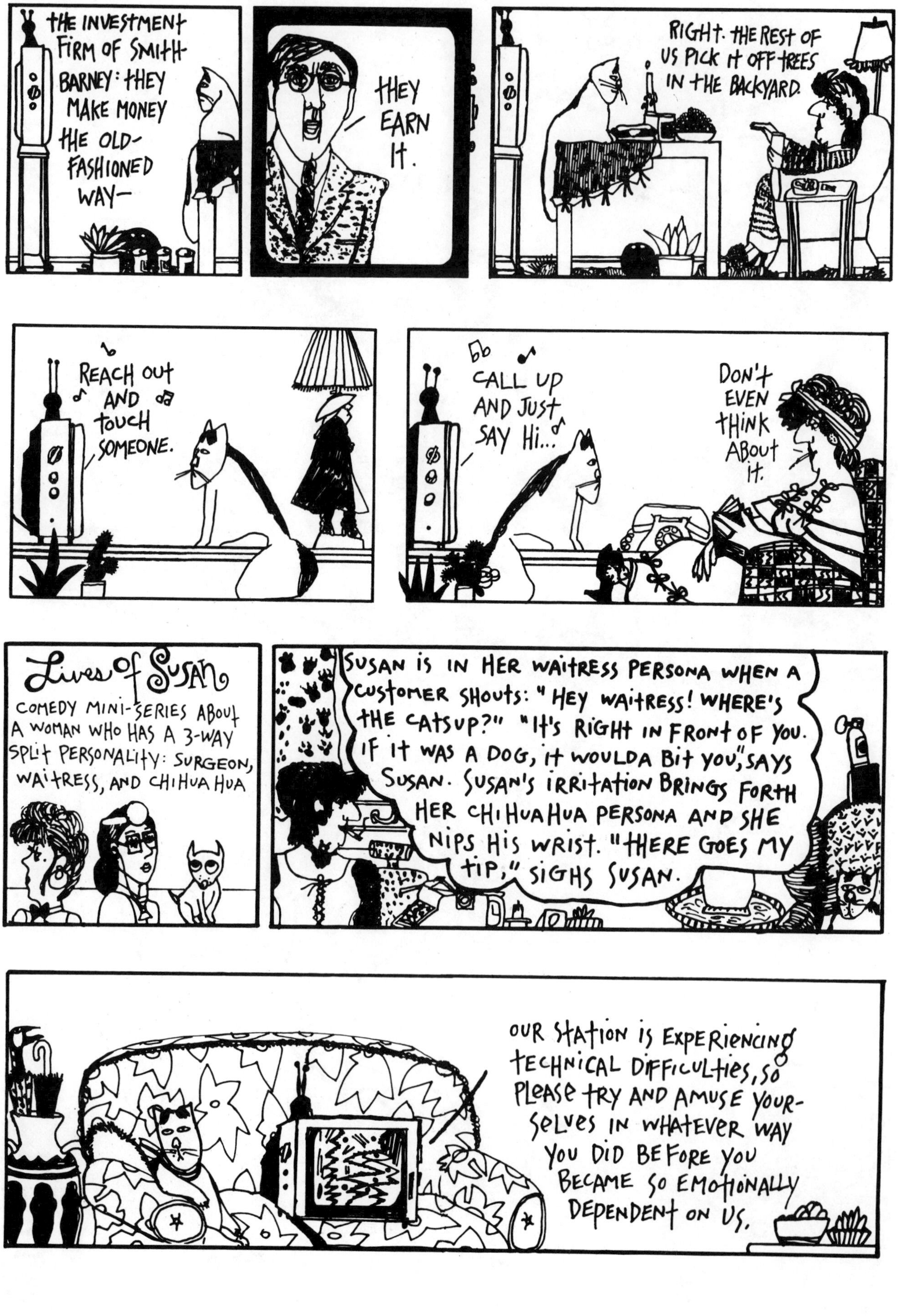
THE INVESTMENT FIRM OF SMITH-BARNEY: THEY MAKE MONEY THE OLD-FASHIONED WAY—
THEY EARN IT.
RIGHT. THE REST OF US PICK IT OFF TREES IN THE BACKYARD.
REACH OUT AND TOUCH SOMEONE.
CALL UP AND JUST SAY HI...
DON'T EVEN THINK ABOUT IT.
Lives of Susan
COMEDY MINI-SERIES ABOUT A WOMAN WHO HAS A 3-WAY SPLIT PERSONALITY: SURGEON, WAITRESS, AND CHIHUAHUA
SUSAN IS IN HER WAITRESS PERSONA WHEN A CUSTOMER SHOUTS: "HEY WAITRESS! WHERE'S THE CATSUP?" "IT'S RIGHT IN FRONT OF YOU. IF IT WAS A DOG, IT WOULDA BIT YOU," SAYS SUSAN. SUSAN'S IRRITATION BRINGS FORTH HER CHIHUAHUA PERSONA AND SHE NIPS HIS WRIST. "THERE GOES MY TIP," SIGHS SUSAN.
OUR STATION IS EXPERIENCING TECHNICAL DIFFICULTIES, SO PLEASE TRY AND AMUSE YOURSELVES IN WHATEVER WAY YOU DID BEFORE YOU BECAME SO EMOTIONALLY DEPENDENT ON US.

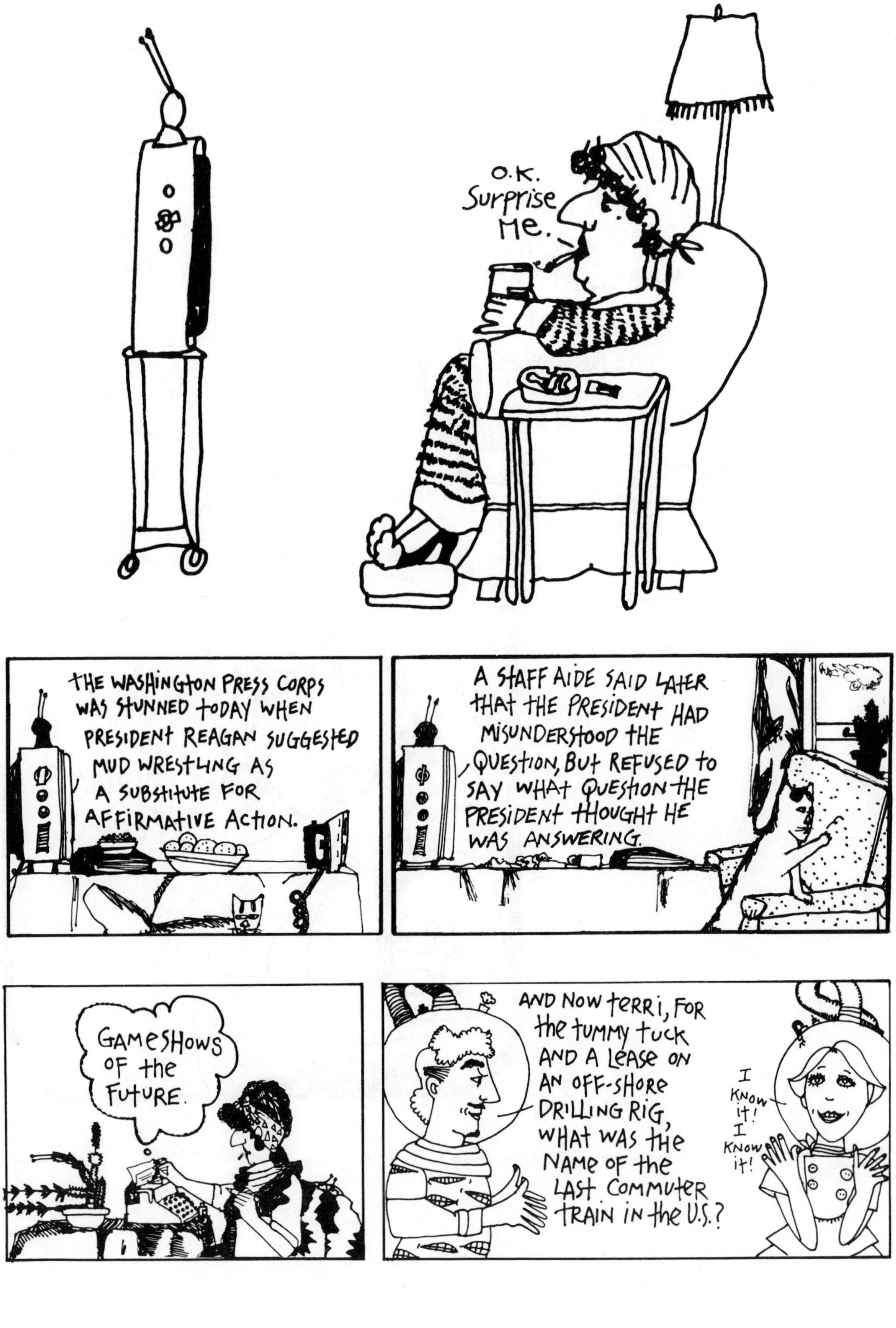

O.K. Surprise Me.
THE WASHINGTON PRESS CORPS WAS STUNNED TODAY WHEN PRESIDENT REAGAN SUGGESTED MUD WRESTLING AS A SUBSTITUTE FOR AFFIRMATIVE ACTION.
A STAFF AIDE SAID LATER THAT THE PRESIDENT HAD MISUNDERSTOOD THE QUESTION, BUT REFUSED TO SAY WHAT QUESTION THE PRESIDENT THOUGHT HE WAS ANSWERING.
GAMESHOWS OF THE FUTURE.
AND NOW TERRI, FOR THE TUMMY TUCK AND A LEASE ON AN OFF-SHORE DRILLING RIG, WHAT WAS THE NAME OF THE LAST COMMUTER TRAIN IN THE U.S.?
I KNOW IT! I KNOW IT!

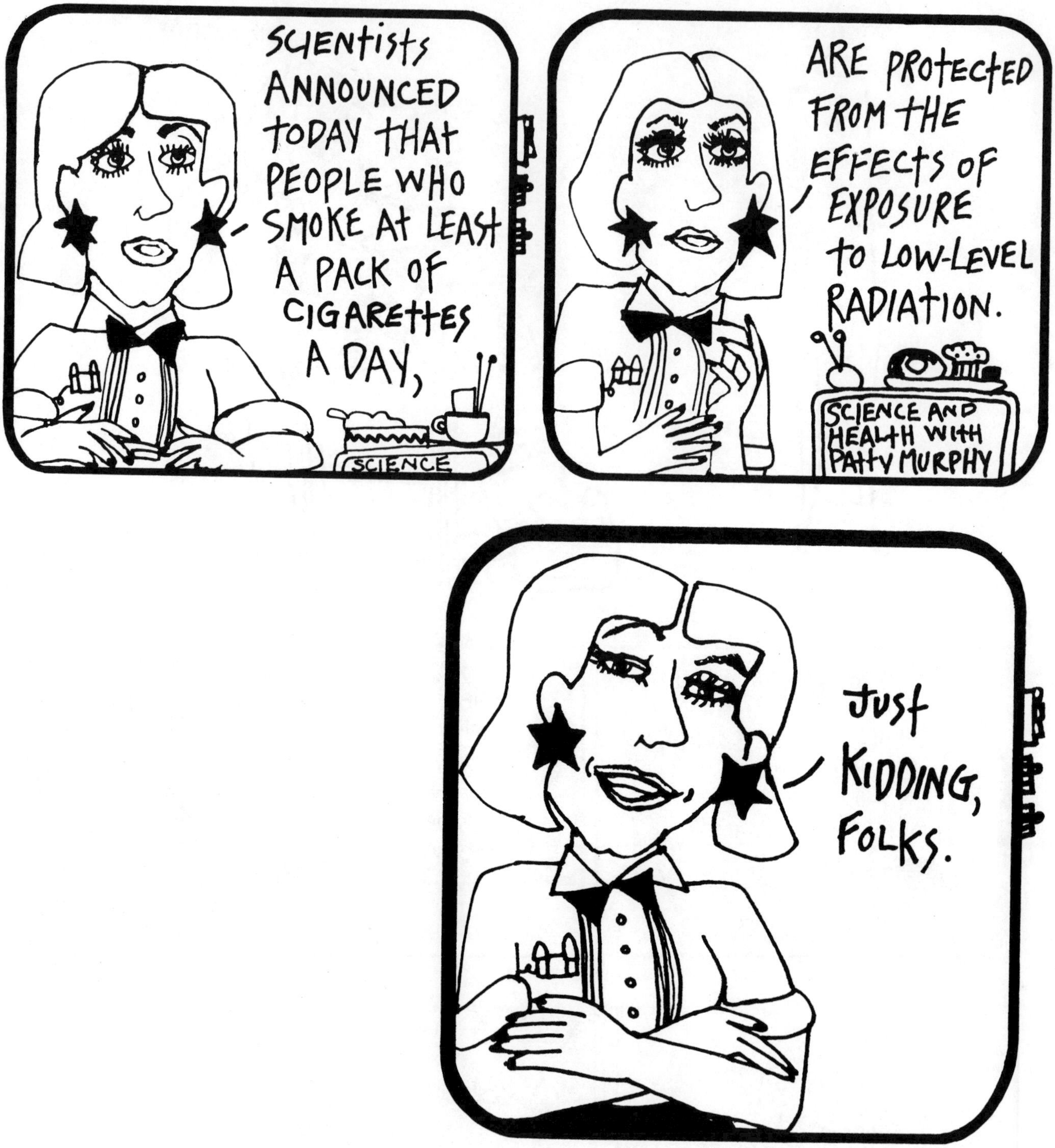
SCIENTISTS ANNOUNCED TODAY THAT PEOPLE WHO SMOKE AT LEAST A PACK OF CIGARETTES A DAY,
SCIENCE
ARE PROTECTED FROM THE EFFECTS OF EXPOSURE TO LOW-LEVEL RADIATION.
SCIENCE AND HEALTH WITH PATTY MURPHY
JUST KIDDING, FOLKS.

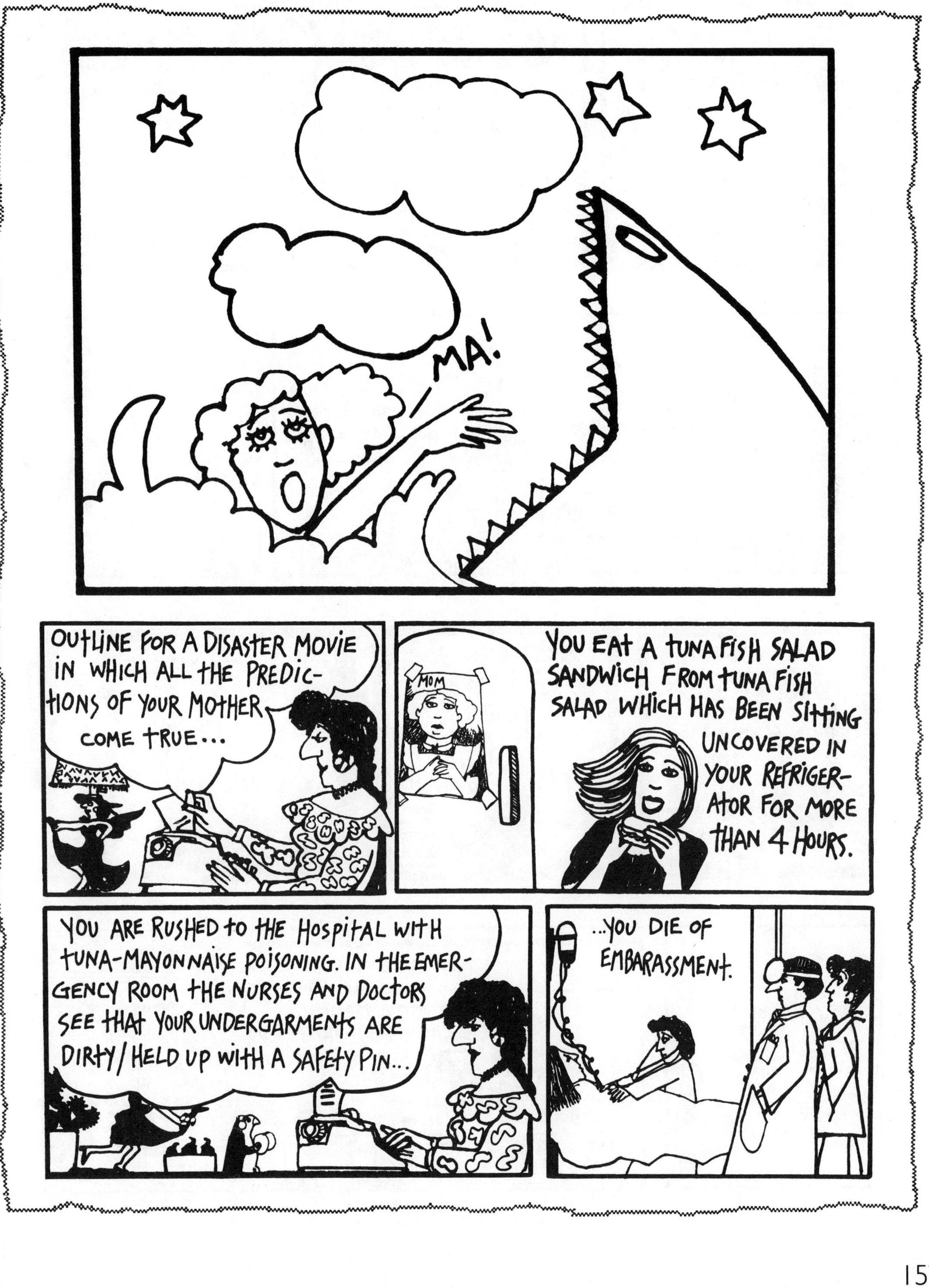
MA!
OUTLINE FOR A DISASTER MOVIE IN WHICH ALL THE PREDICTIONS OF YOUR MOTHER COME TRUE...
MOM
YOU EAT A TUNA FISH SALAD SANDWICH FROM TUNA FISH SALAD WHICH HAS BEEN SITTING UNCOVERED IN YOUR REFRIGERATOR FOR MORE THAN 4 HOURS.
YOU ARE RUSHED TO THE HOSPITAL WITH TUNA-MAYONNAISE POISONING. IN THE EMERGENCY ROOM THE NURSES AND DOCTORS SEE THAT YOUR UNDERGARMENTS ARE DIRTY/HELD UP WITH A SAFETY PIN...
...YOU DIE OF EMBARASSMENT.

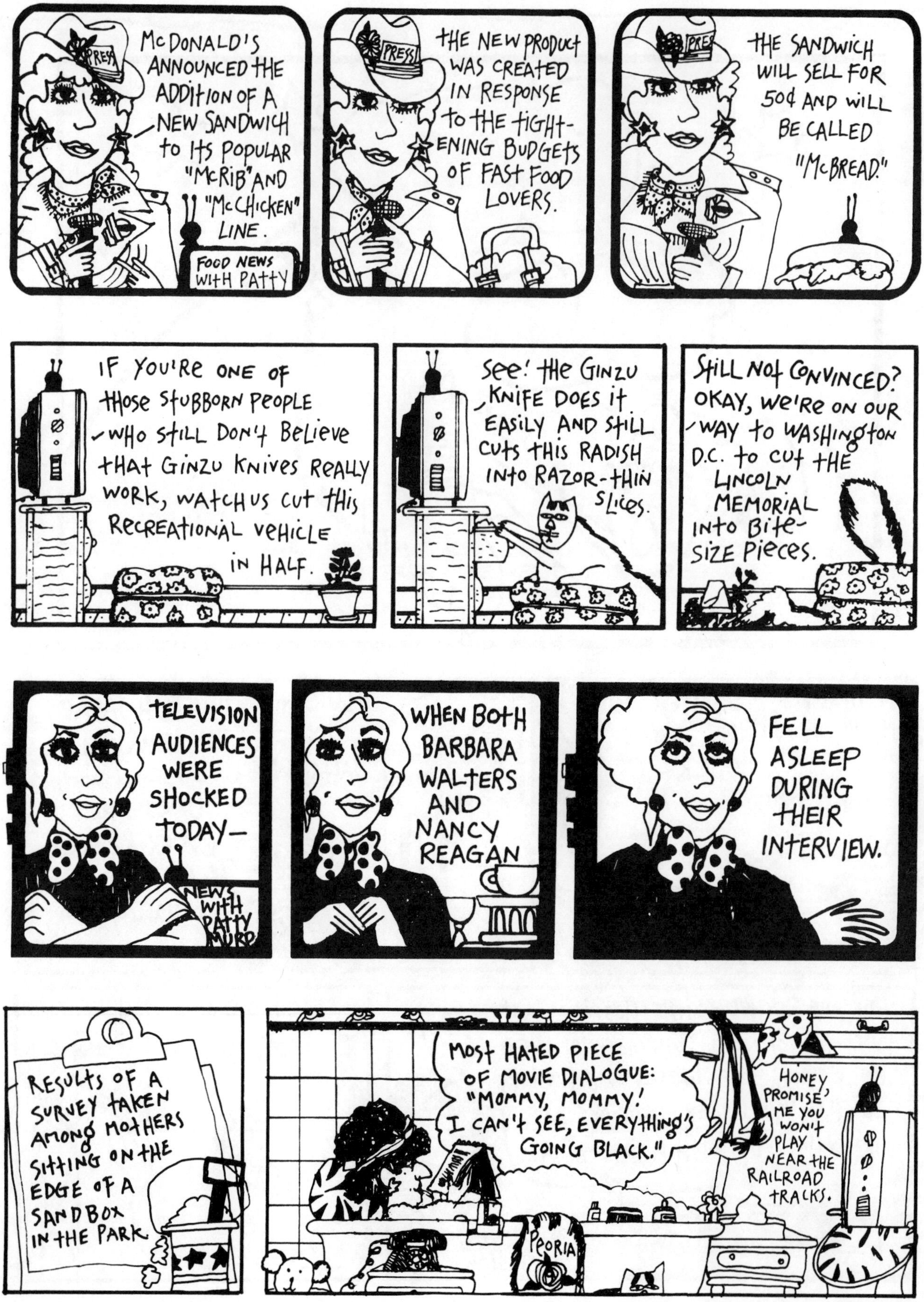

McDONALD'S ANNOUNCED THE ADDITION OF A NEW SANDWICH TO ITS POPULAR "McRIB" AND "McCHICKEN" LINE.
PRESS
FOOD NEWS WITH PATTY
THE NEW PRODUCT WAS CREATED IN RESPONSE TO THE TIGHTENING BUDGETS OF FAST FOOD LOVERS.
PRESS
THE SANDWICH WILL SELL FOR 50¢ AND WILL BE CALLED "McBREAD."
IF YOU'RE ONE OF THOSE STUBBORN PEOPLE WHO STILL DON'T BELIEVE THAT GINZU KNIVES REALLY WORK, WATCH US CUT THIS RECREATIONAL VEHICLE IN HALF.
SEE! THE GINZU KNIFE DOES IT EASILY AND STILL CUTS THIS RADISH INTO RAZOR-THIN SLICES.
STILL NOT CONVINCED? OKAY, WE'RE ON OUR WAY TO WASHINGTON D.C. TO CUT THE LINCOLN MEMORIAL INTO BITE-SIZE PIECES.
TELEVISION AUDIENCES WERE SHOCKED TODAY—
NEWS WITH PATTY
WHEN BOTH BARBARA WALTERS AND NANCY REAGAN
FELL ASLEEP DURING THEIR INTERVIEW.
RESULTS OF A SURVEY TAKEN AMONG MOTHERS SITTING ON THE EDGE OF A SANDBOX IN THE PARK
MOST HATED PIECE OF MOVIE DIALOGUE: "MOMMY, MOMMY! I CAN'T SEE, EVERYTHING'S GOING BLACK."
HONEY, PROMISE ME YOU WON'T PLAY NEAR THE RAILROAD TRACKS.
PEORIA

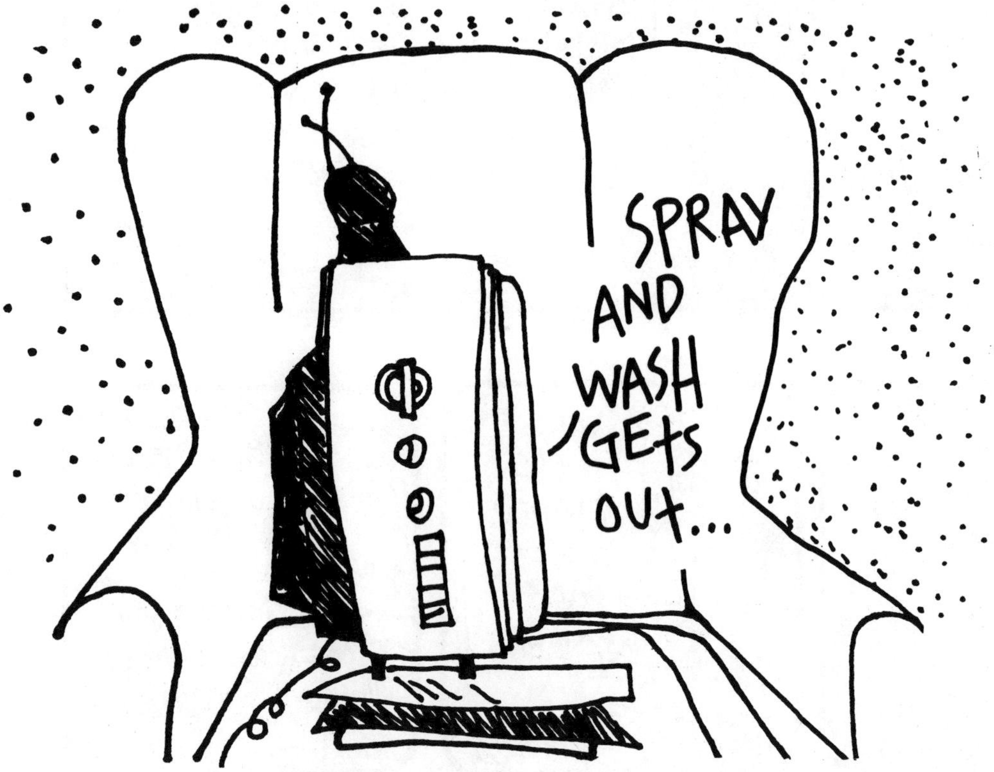
SPRAY AND WASH GETS OUT...

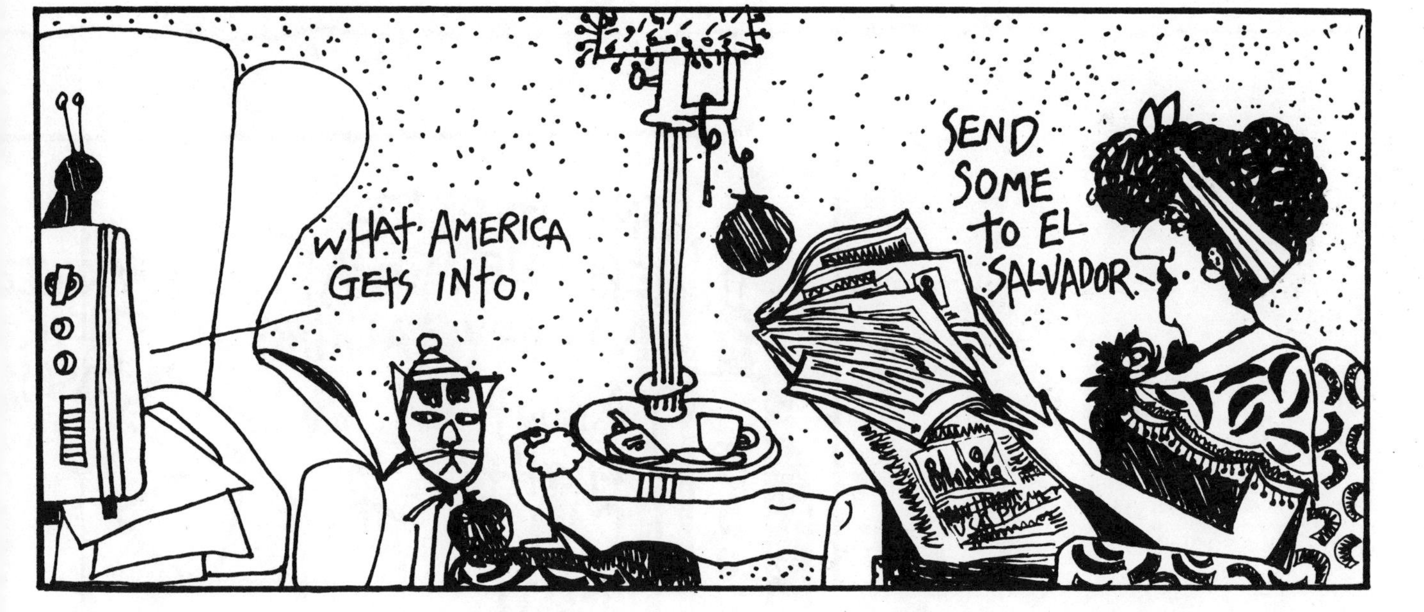
WHAT AMERICA GETS INTO.
SEND SOME TO EL SALVADOR.

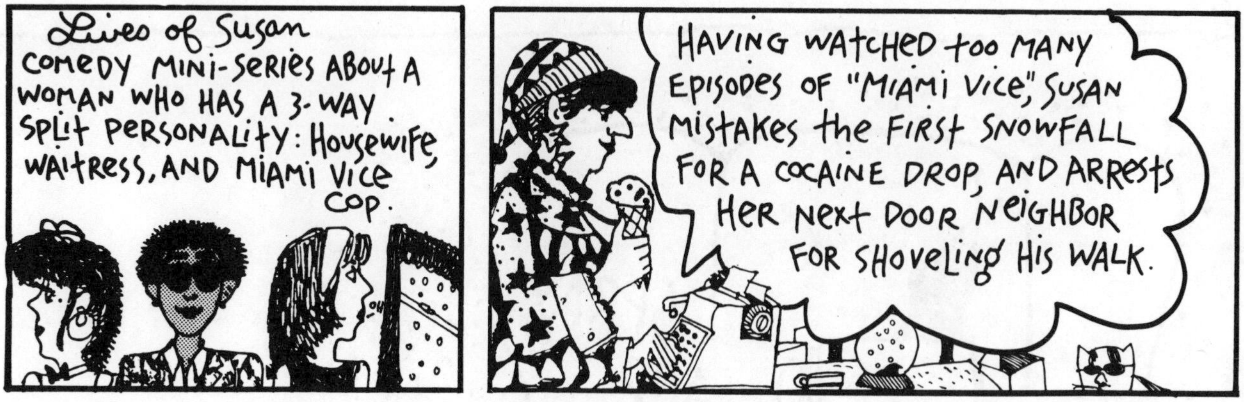
Lives of Susan
COMEDY MINI-SERIES ABOUT A WOMAN WHO HAS A 3-WAY SPLIT PERSONALITY: Housewife, WAITRESS, AND MIAMI VICE COP.
HAVING WATCHED TOO MANY EPISODES OF "MIAMI VICE," SUSAN MISTAKES THE FIRST SNOWFALL FOR A COCAINE DROP, AND ARRESTS HER NEXT DOOR NEIGHBOR FOR SHOVELING HIS WALK.

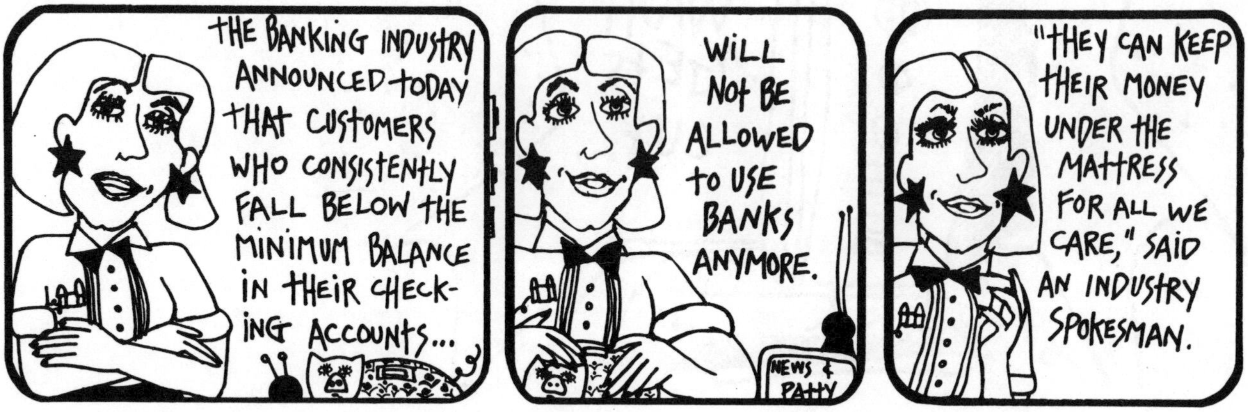
THE BANKING INDUSTRY ANNOUNCED TODAY THAT CUSTOMERS WHO CONSISTENTLY FALL BELOW THE MINIMUM BALANCE IN THEIR CHECKING ACCOUNTS...
WILL NOT BE ALLOWED TO USE BANKS ANYMORE.
NEWS & PATTY
"THEY CAN KEEP THEIR MONEY UNDER THE MATTRESS FOR ALL WE CARE," SAID AN INDUSTRY SPOKESMAN.

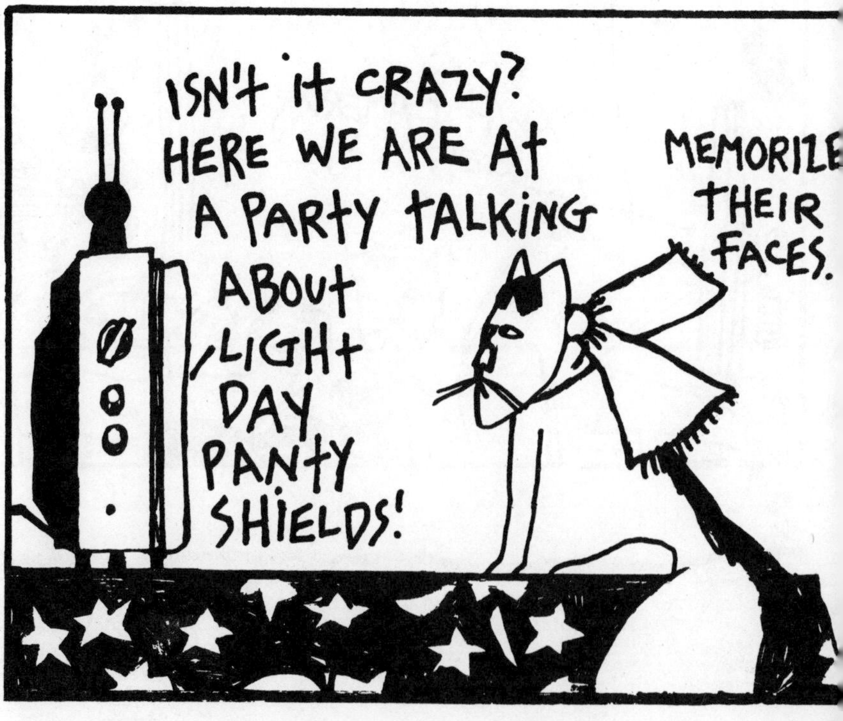
ISN'T IT CRAZY? HERE WE ARE AT A PARTY TALKING ABOUT LIGHT DAY PANTY SHIELDS!
MEMORIZE THEIR FACES.

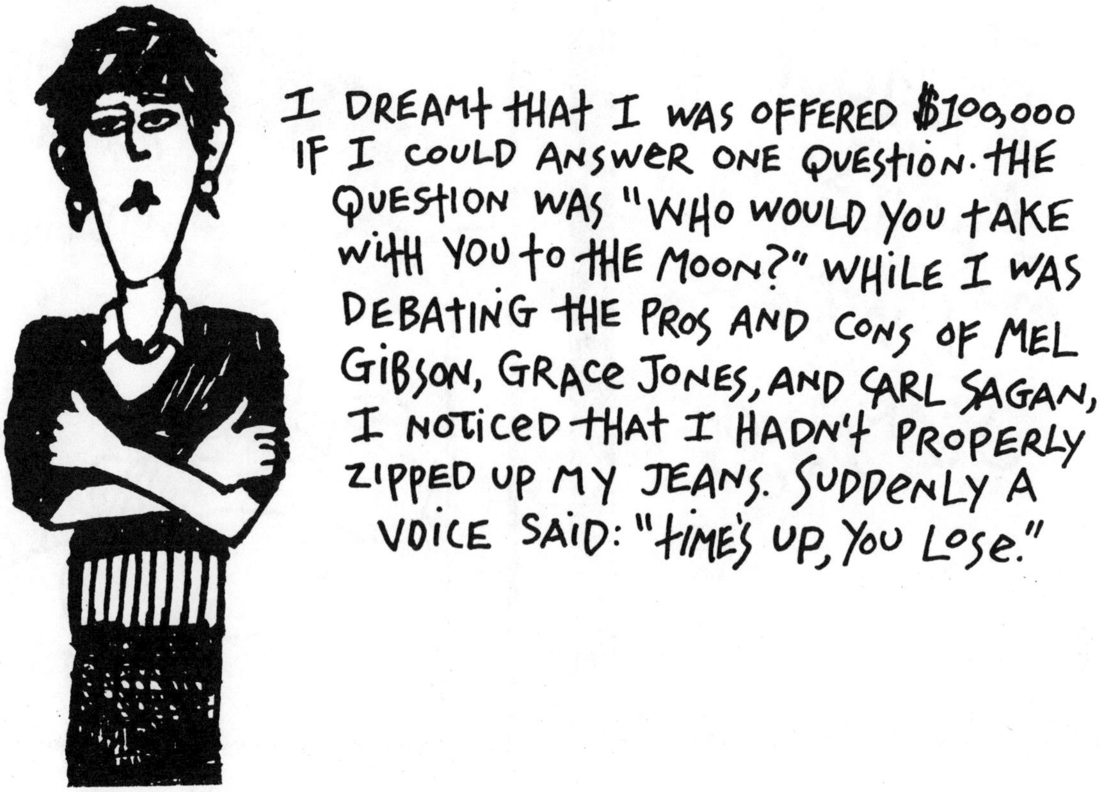
I DREAMT THAT I WAS OFFERED $100,000 IF I COULD ANSWER ONE QUESTION. THE QUESTION WAS "WHO WOULD YOU TAKE WITH YOU TO THE MOON?" WHILE I WAS DEBATING THE PROS AND CONS OF MEL GIBSON, GRACE JONES, AND CARL SAGAN, I NOTICED THAT I HADN'T PROPERLY ZIPPED UP MY JEANS. SUDDENLY A VOICE SAID: "TIME'S UP, YOU LOSE."

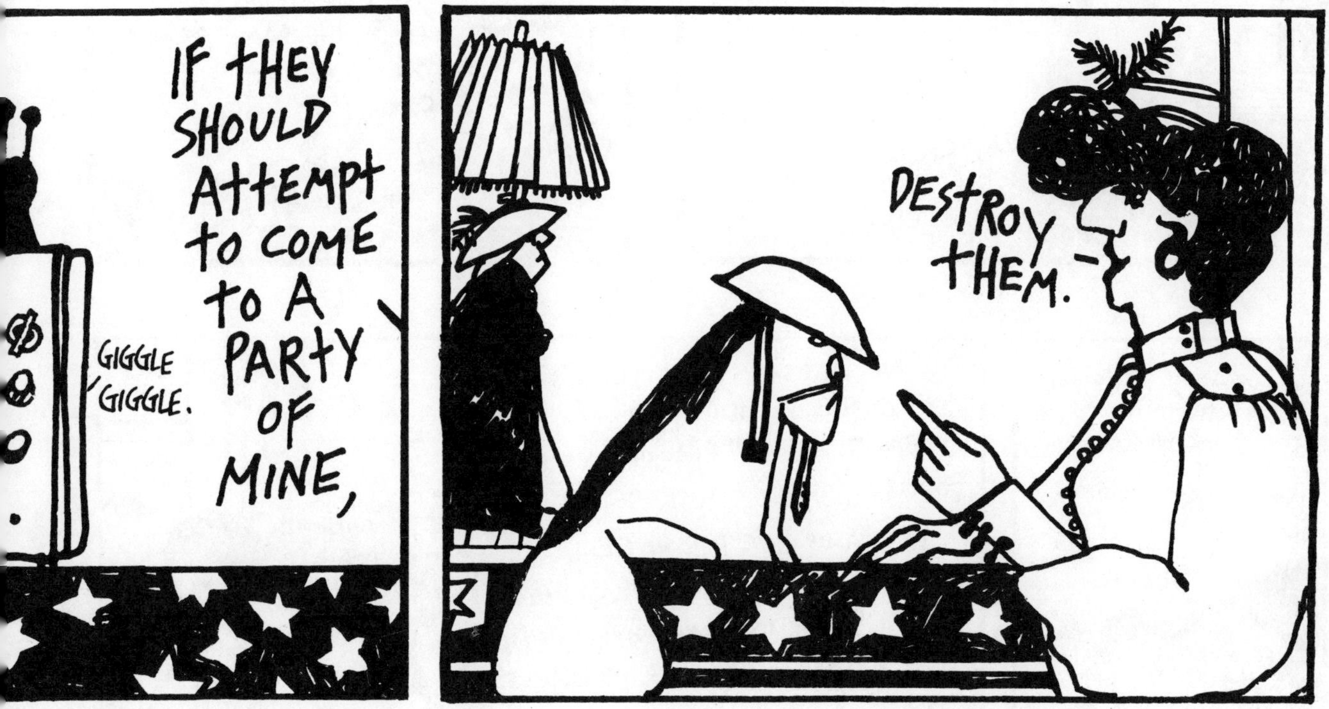
IF THEY SHOULD ATTEMPT TO COME TO A PARTY OF MINE,
GIGGLE GIGGLE.
DESTROY THEM.

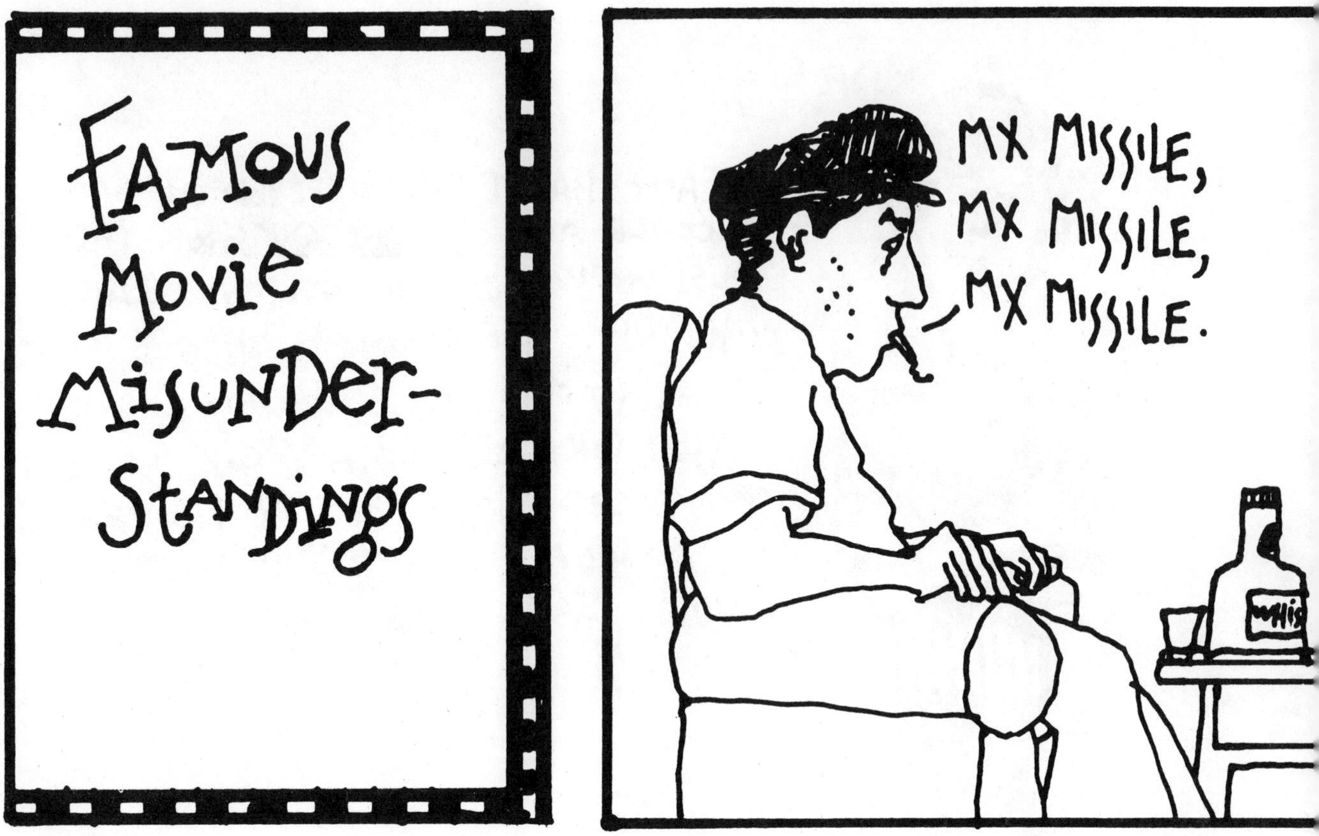
FAMOUS Movie MisunDer-Standings
MX MISSILE,
MX MISSILE,
MX MISSILE.

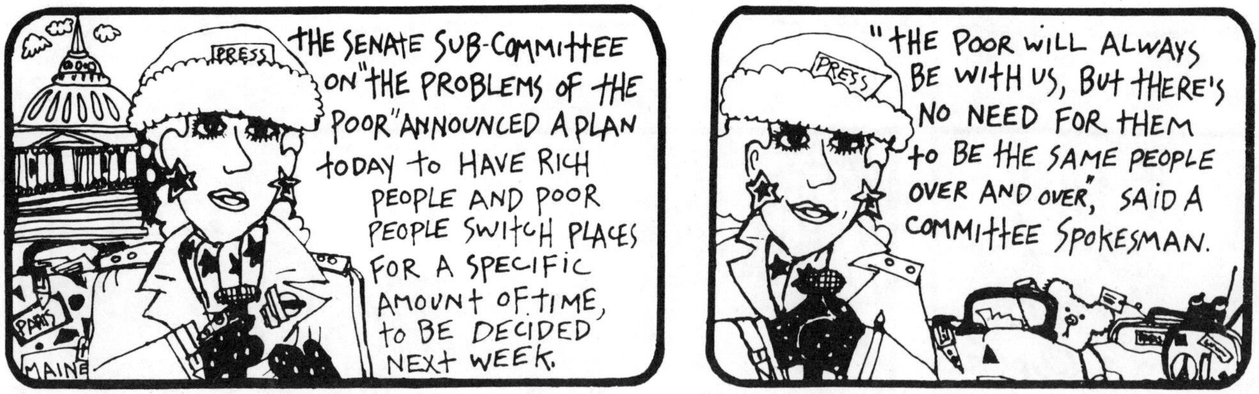
PRESS
THE SENATE SUB-COMMITTEE ON "THE PROBLEMS OF THE POOR" ANNOUNCED A PLAN TODAY TO HAVE RICH PEOPLE AND POOR PEOPLE SWITCH PLACES FOR A SPECIFIC AMOUNT OF TIME, TO BE DECIDED NEXT WEEK.
PARIS
MAINE
PRESS
"THE POOR WILL ALWAYS BE WITH US, BUT THERE'S NO NEED FOR THEM TO BE THE SAME PEOPLE OVER AND OVER", SAID A COMMITTEE SPOKESMAN.

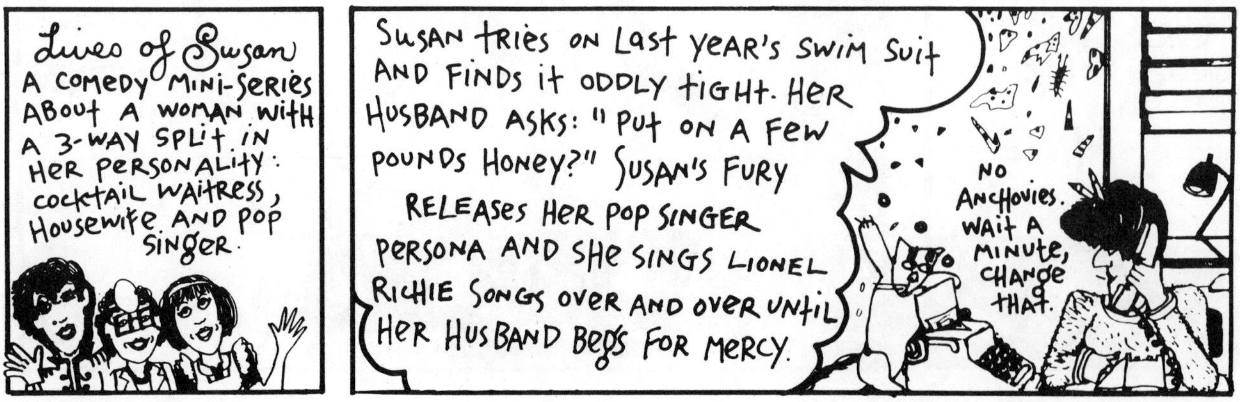
Lives of Susan
A COMEDY MINI-SERIES ABOUT A WOMAN WITH A 3-WAY SPLIT IN HER PERSONALITY: COCKTAIL WAITRESS, HOUSEWIFE AND POP SINGER.
SUSAN TRIES ON LAST YEAR'S SWIM SUIT AND FINDS IT ODDLY TIGHT. HER HUSBAND ASKS: "PUT ON A FEW POUNDS HONEY?" SUSAN'S FURY RELEASES HER POP SINGER PERSONA AND SHE SINGS LIONEL RICHIE SONGS OVER AND OVER UNTIL HER HUSBAND BEGS FOR MERCY.
NO ANCHOVIES. WAIT A MINUTE, CHANGE THAT.

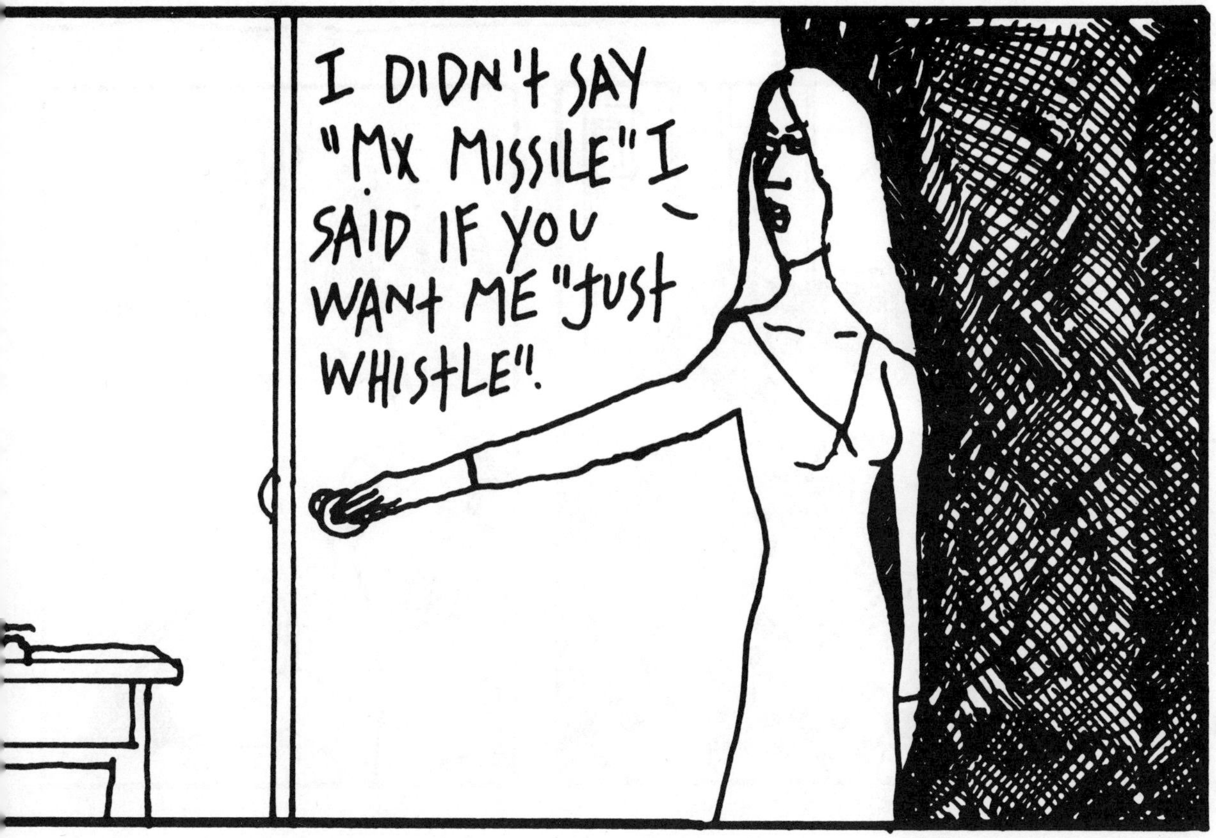
I DIDN'T SAY "MX MISSILE" I SAID IF YOU WANT ME "JUST WHISTLE".

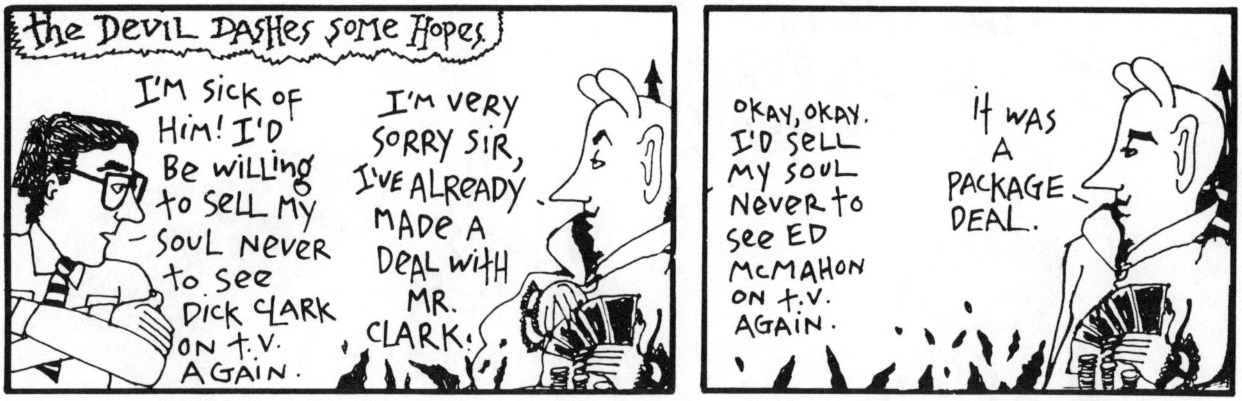
the DEVIL DASHES SOME HOPES.
I'M SICK OF HIM! I'D BE WILLING TO SELL MY SOUL NEVER TO SEE DICK CLARK ON T.V. AGAIN.
I'M VERY SORRY SIR, I'VE ALREADY MADE A DEAL WITH MR. CLARK.
OKAY, OKAY. I'D SELL MY SOUL NEVER TO SEE ED MCMAHON ON T.V. AGAIN.
IT WAS A PACKAGE DEAL.

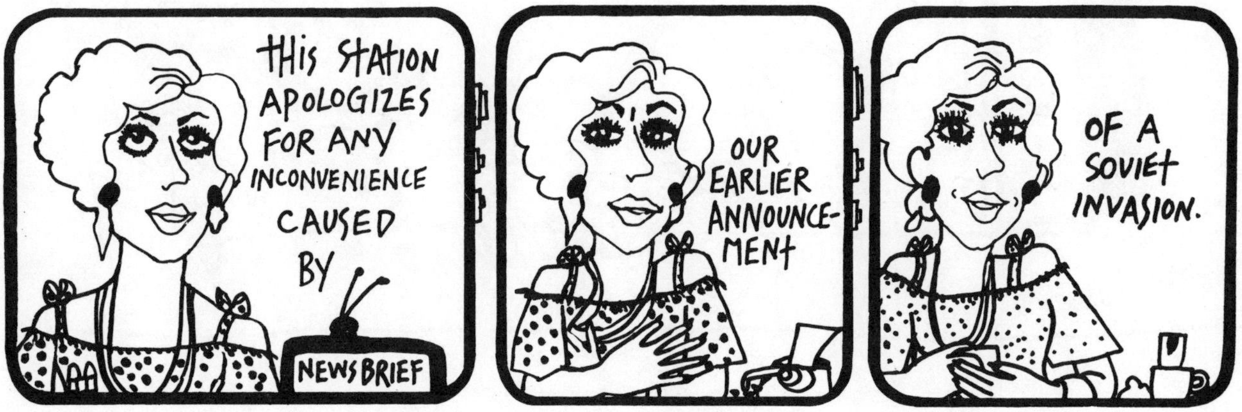
THIS STATION APOLOGIZES FOR ANY INCONVENIENCE CAUSED BY
NEWS BRIEF
OUR EARLIER ANNOUNCE-MENT
OF A SOVIET INVASION.

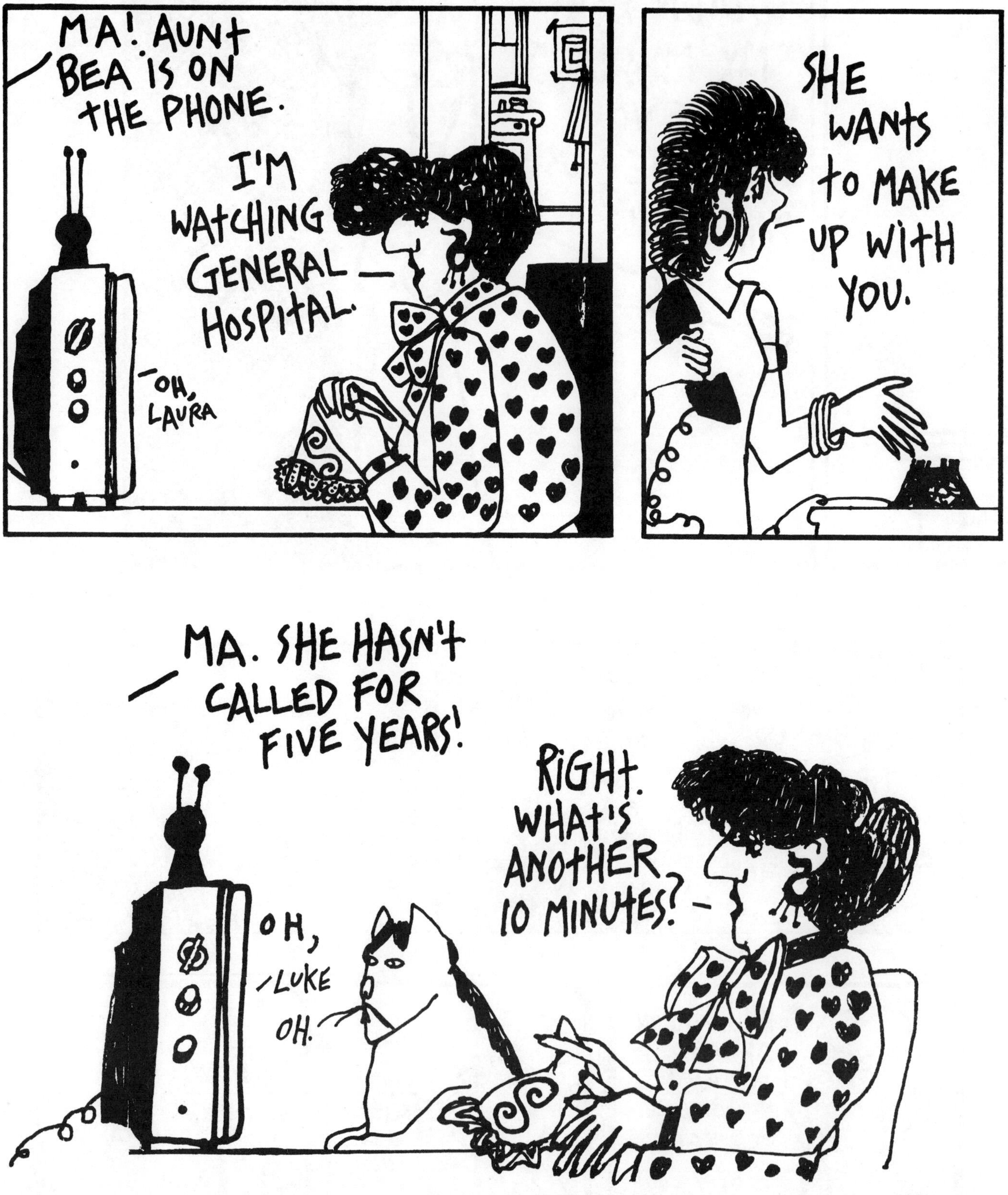
MA! AUNT BEA IS ON THE PHONE.
I'M WATCHING GENERAL HOSPITAL.
OH, LAURA
SHE WANTS TO MAKE UP WITH YOU.
MA. SHE HASN'T CALLED FOR FIVE YEARS!
OH, LUKE
OH.
RIGHT. WHAT'S ANOTHER 10 MINUTES?

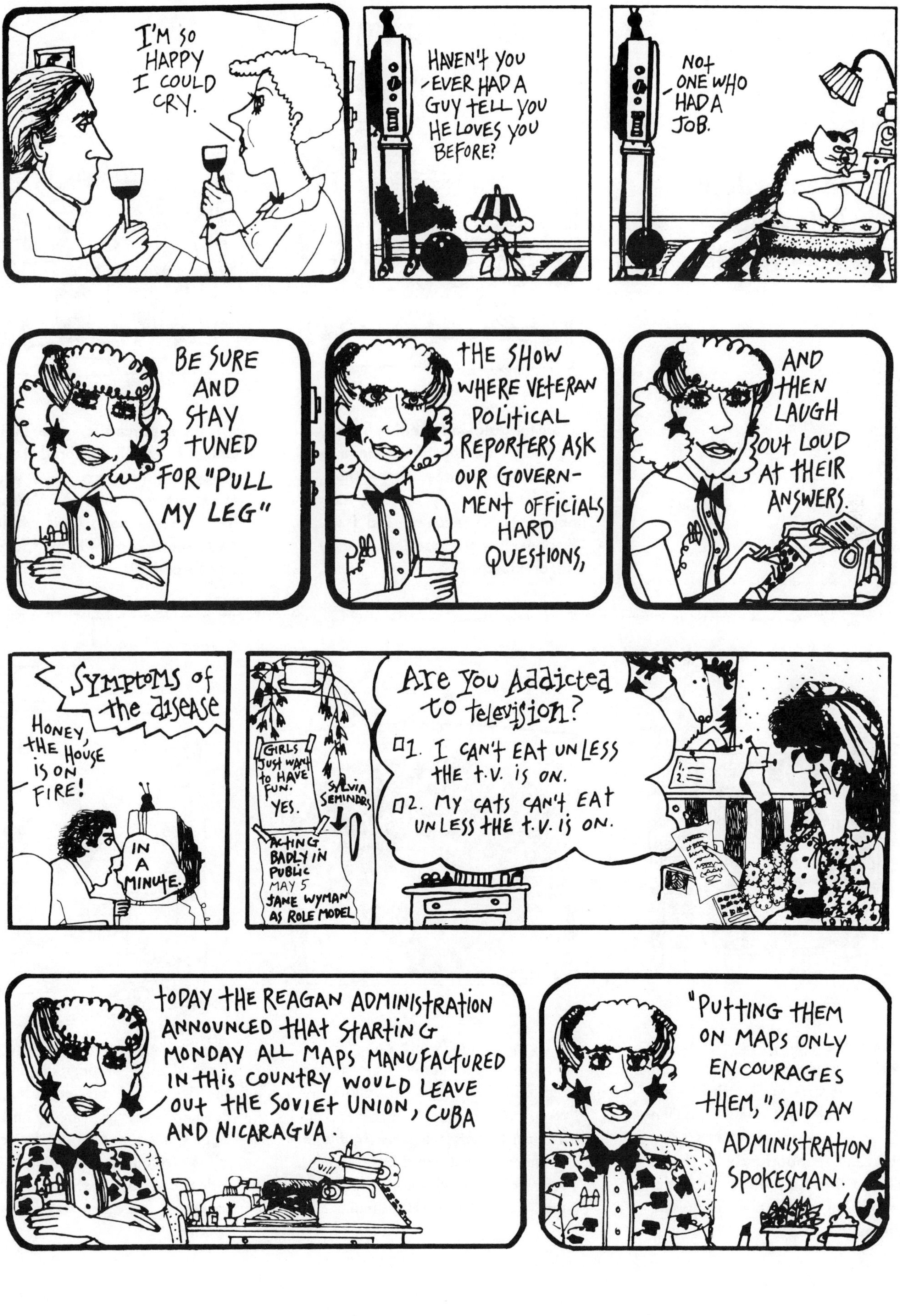
I'M SO HAPPY I COULD CRY.
HAVEN'T YOU EVER HAD A GUY TELL YOU HE LOVES YOU BEFORE?
NOT ONE WHO HAD A JOB.
BE SURE AND STAY TUNED FOR "PULL MY LEG"
THE SHOW WHERE VETERAN POLITICAL REPORTERS ASK OUR GOVERNMENT OFFICIALS HARD QUESTIONS,
AND THEN LAUGH OUT LOUD AT THEIR ANSWERS.
Symptoms of the disease
HONEY, THE HOUSE IS ON FIRE!
IN A MINUTE.
GIRLS JUST WANT TO HAVE FUN. YES.
SYLVIA SEMINARS
ACTING BADLY IN PUBLIC MAY 5
JANE WYMAN AS ROLE MODEL
Are you Addicted to television?
□1. I CAN'T EAT UNLESS THE T.V. IS ON.
□2. MY CATS CAN'T EAT UNLESS THE T.V. IS ON.
TODAY THE REAGAN ADMINISTRATION ANNOUNCED THAT STARTING MONDAY ALL MAPS MANUFACTURED IN THIS COUNTRY WOULD LEAVE OUT THE SOVIET UNION, CUBA AND NICARAGUA.
"PUTTING THEM ON MAPS ONLY ENCOURAGES THEM," SAID AN ADMINISTRATION SPOKESMAN.

Memorable Television Role Models

I am the girlfriend of either Starsky or Hutch. I will die of Leukemia in the last ten minutes of the show, or, alternatively, my past life as a hooker will be revealed and I will disappear for the good of Starsky and/or Hutch.

I am a psychotic/mute/Indian/Chicana who is restored to normalcy and neatness by a young, attractive, white, middle class doctor from the east. (Lots of flashbacks showing me whipped, raped, and force-fed)

I am the sister/daughter of an unjustly imprisoned man or else the witness to a mafia crime. I am also the client of a blind freelance insurance investigator. I scream often and inopportunely. I always fall and twist my ankle when the investigator and I are fleeing the bad guys.

I am a black/white cop. I have a short snappy name. I am tough but feminine. I like to follow my own instincts about a case. This frequently gets me into trouble; I am inevitably rescued by my male, fellow officers, who are devoted to me . . . I never rescue them.

I am the woman behind the man. I spend a lot of time keeping dinner warm for my crusading policeman/coroner, lover/husband. Sometimes I nag about being left alone so much. Sometimes I am kidnapped by mafia thugs. This makes a welcome break in my routine.

166

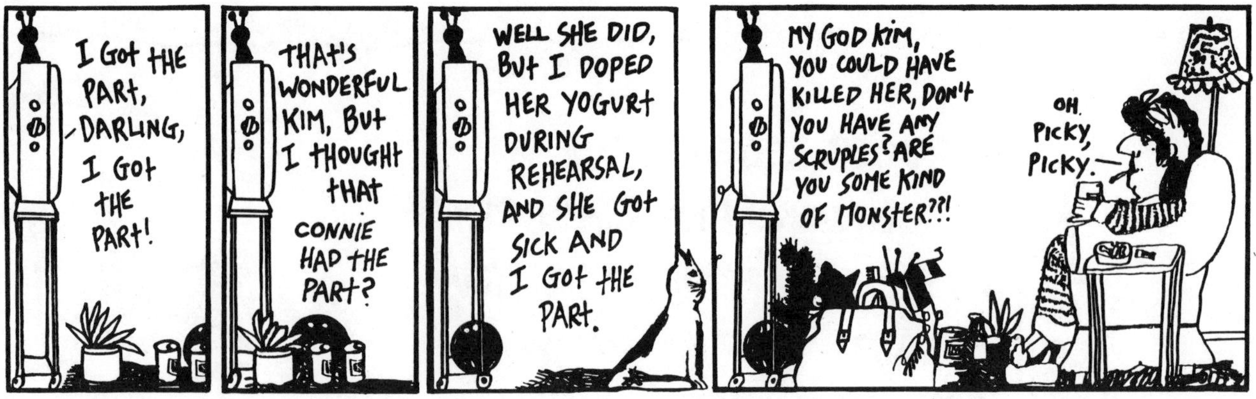
I GOT THE PART, DARLING, I GOT THE PART!
THAT'S WONDERFUL KIM, BUT I THOUGHT THAT CONNIE HAD THE PART?
WELL SHE DID, BUT I DOPED HER YOGURT DURING REHEARSAL, AND SHE GOT SICK AND I GOT THE PART.
MY GOD KIM, YOU COULD HAVE KILLED HER, DON'T YOU HAVE ANY SCRUPLES? ARE YOU SOME KIND OF MONSTER??!
OH. PICKY, PICKY.

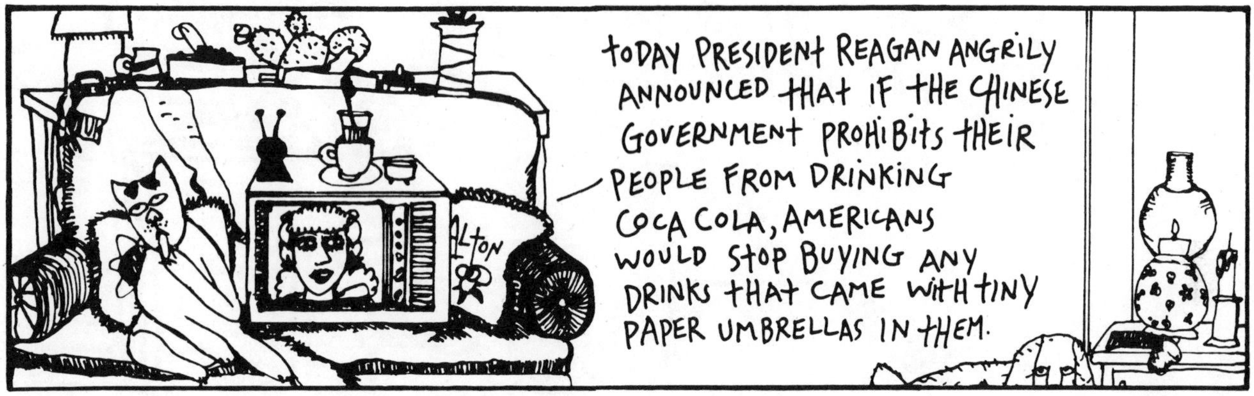
TODAY PRESIDENT REAGAN ANGRILY ANNOUNCED THAT IF THE CHINESE GOVERNMENT PROHIBITS THEIR PEOPLE FROM DRINKING COCA COLA, AMERICANS WOULD STOP BUYING ANY DRINKS THAT CAME WITH TINY PAPER UMBRELLAS IN THEM.
ALTON

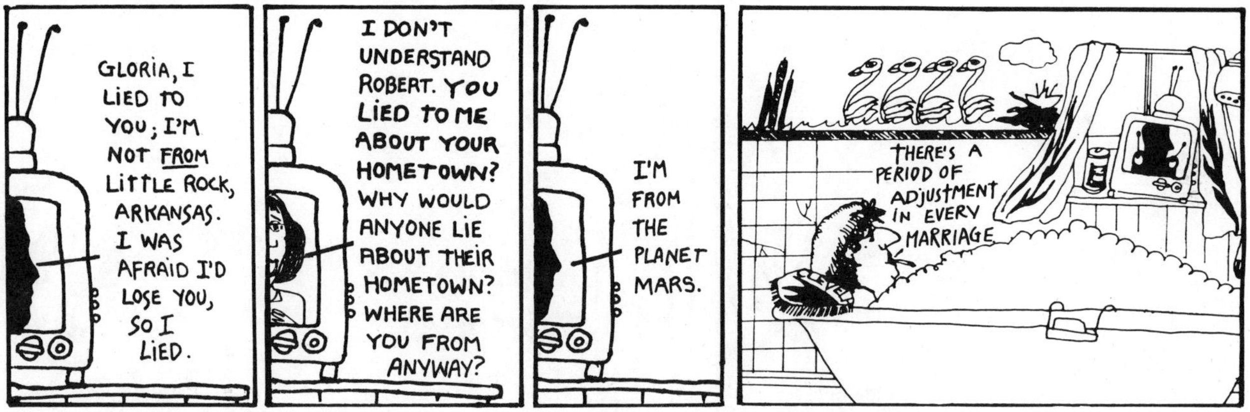
GLORIA, I LIED TO YOU; I'M NOT FROM LITTLE ROCK, ARKANSAS. I WAS AFRAID I'D LOSE YOU, SO I LIED.
I DON'T UNDERSTAND ROBERT. YOU LIED TO ME ABOUT YOUR HOMETOWN? WHY WOULD ANYONE LIE ABOUT THEIR HOMETOWN? WHERE ARE YOU FROM ANYWAY?
I'M FROM THE PLANET MARS.
THERE'S A PERIOD OF ADJUSTMENT IN EVERY MARRIAGE.

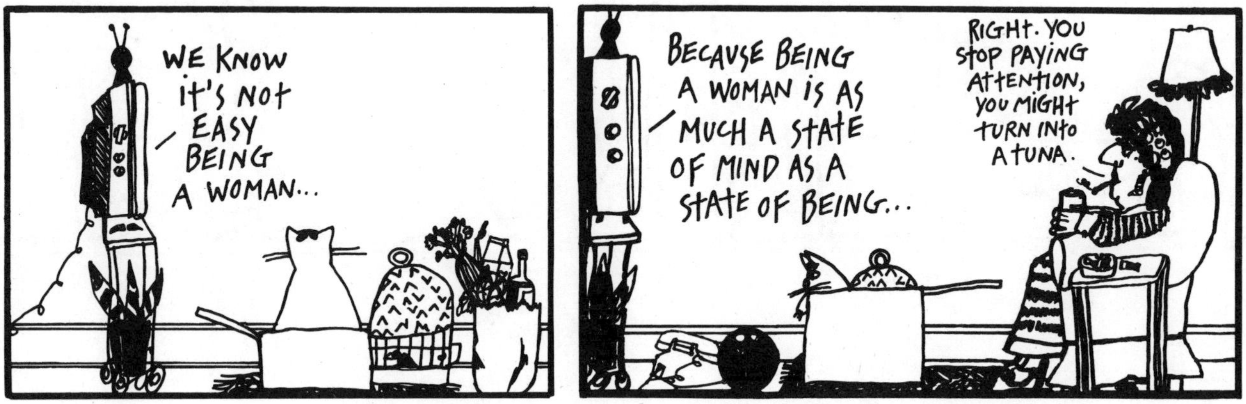
WE KNOW IT'S NOT EASY BEING A WOMAN...
BECAUSE BEING A WOMAN IS AS MUCH A STATE OF MIND AS A STATE OF BEING...
RIGHT. YOU STOP PAYING ATTENTION, YOU MIGHT TURN INTO A TUNA.

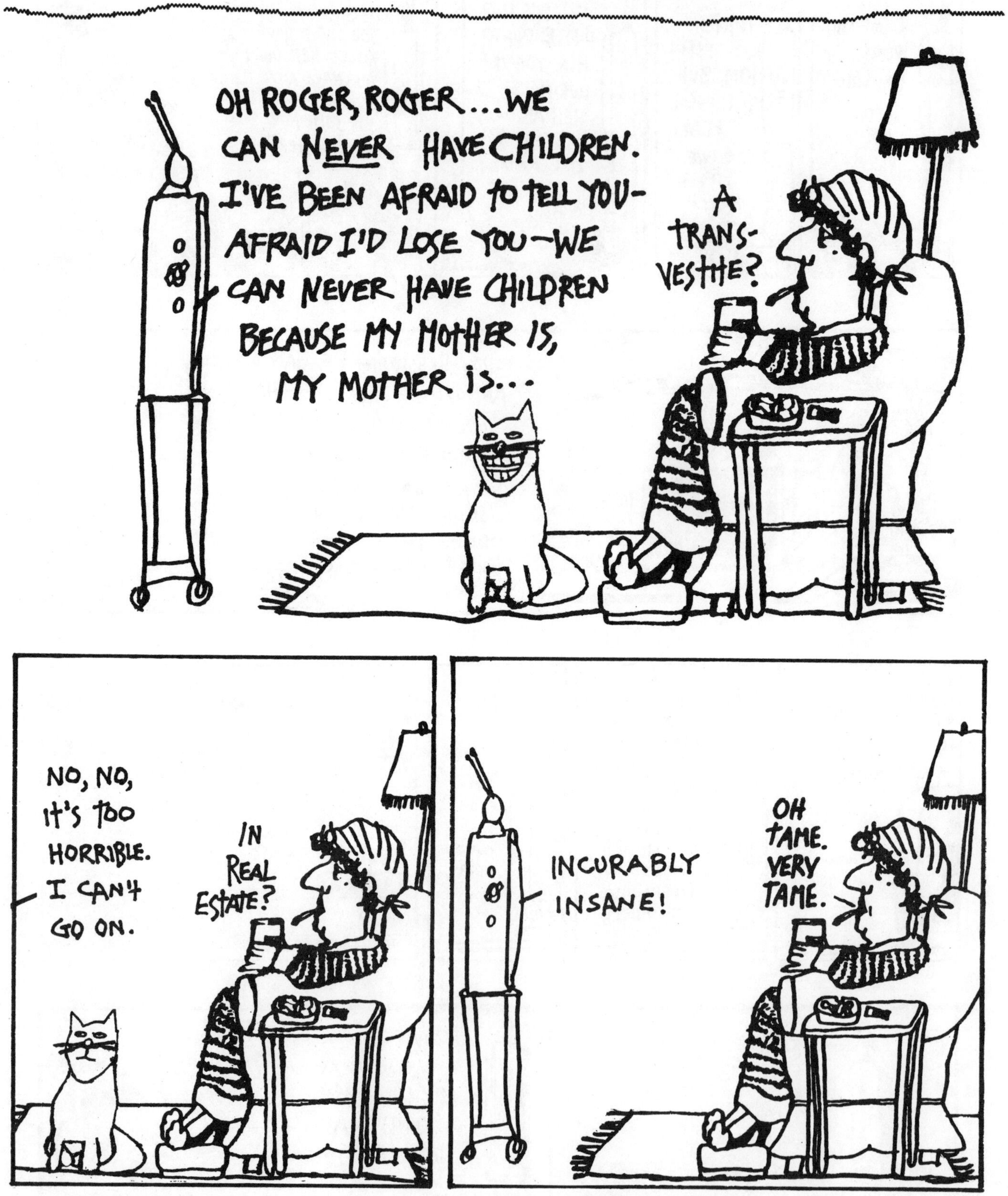
OH ROGER, ROGER... WE CAN NEVER HAVE CHILDREN. I'VE BEEN AFRAID TO TELL YOU- AFRAID I'D LOSE YOU-WE CAN NEVER HAVE CHILDREN BECAUSE MY MOTHER IS, MY MOTHER IS...
A TRANS-VESTITE?
NO, NO, IT'S TOO HORRIBLE. I CAN'T GO ON.
IN REAL ESTATE?
INCURABLY INSANE!
OH TAME. VERY TAME.

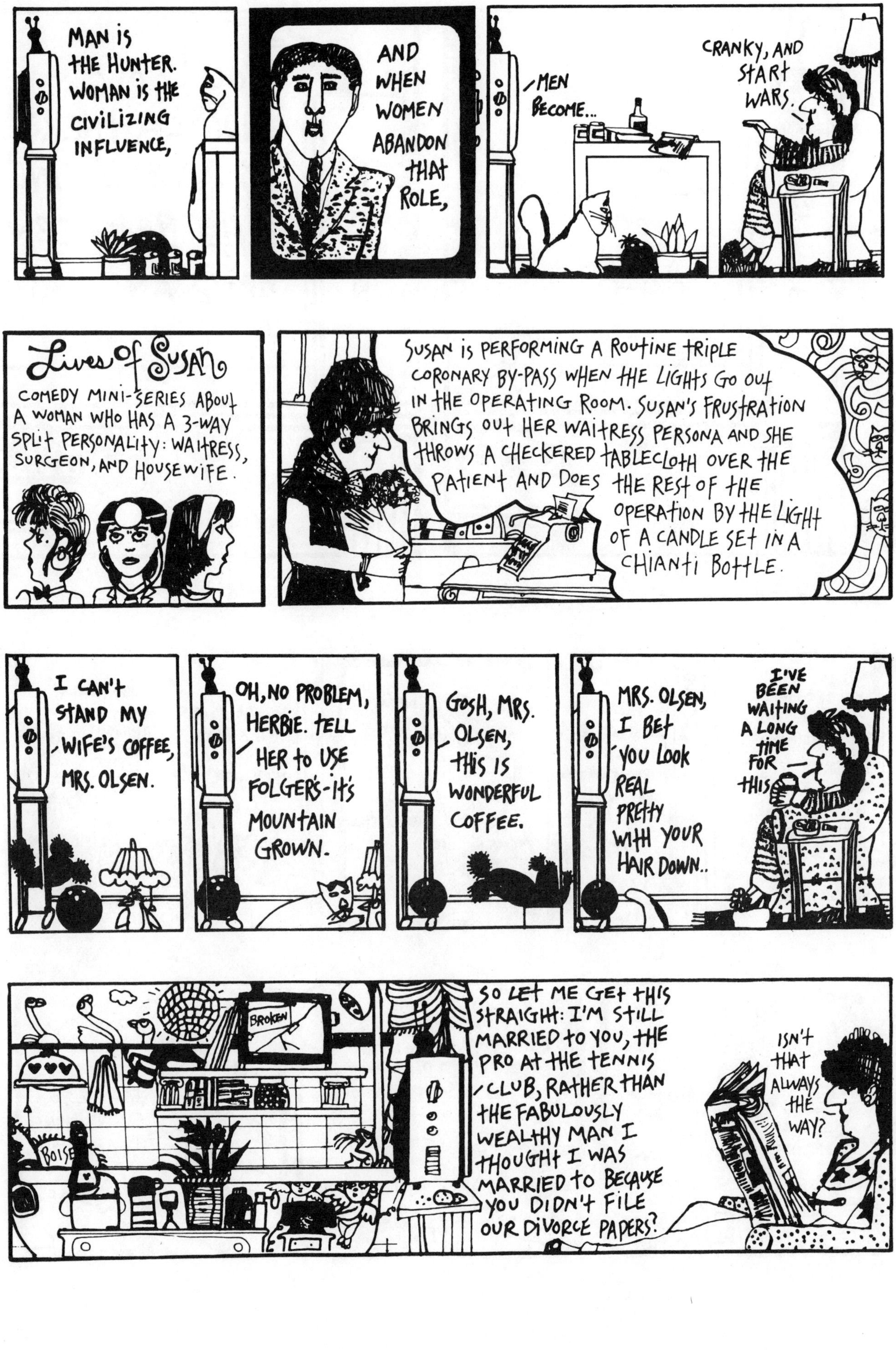

MAN is THE HUNTER. WOMAN is THE CIVILIZING INFLUENCE,
AND WHEN WOMEN ABANDON THAT ROLE,
MEN BECOME...
CRANKY, AND START WARS.
Lives of Susan
COMEDY MINI-SERIES ABOUT A WOMAN WHO HAS A 3-WAY SPLIT PERSONALITY: WAITRESS, SURGEON, AND HOUSEWIFE.
SUSAN IS PERFORMING A ROUTINE TRIPLE CORONARY BY-PASS WHEN THE LIGHTS GO OUT IN THE OPERATING ROOM. SUSAN'S FRUSTRATION BRINGS OUT HER WAITRESS PERSONA AND SHE THROWS A CHECKERED TABLECLOTH OVER THE PATIENT AND DOES THE REST OF THE OPERATION BY THE LIGHT OF A CANDLE SET IN A CHIANTI BOTTLE.
I CAN'T STAND MY WIFE'S COFFEE, MRS. OLSEN.
OH, NO PROBLEM, HERBIE. TELL HER TO USE FOLGER'S-IT'S MOUNTAIN GROWN.
GOSH, MRS. OLSEN, THIS IS WONDERFUL COFFEE.
MRS. OLSEN, I BET YOU LOOK REAL PRETTY WITH YOUR HAIR DOWN..
I'VE BEEN WAITING A LONG TIME FOR THIS
BROKEN
BOISE
SO LET ME GET THIS STRAIGHT: I'M STILL MARRIED TO YOU, THE PRO AT THE TENNIS CLUB, RATHER THAN THE FABULOUSLY WEALTHY MAN I THOUGHT I WAS MARRIED TO BECAUSE YOU DIDN'T FILE OUR DIVORCE PAPERS?
ISN'T THAT ALWAYS THE WAY?

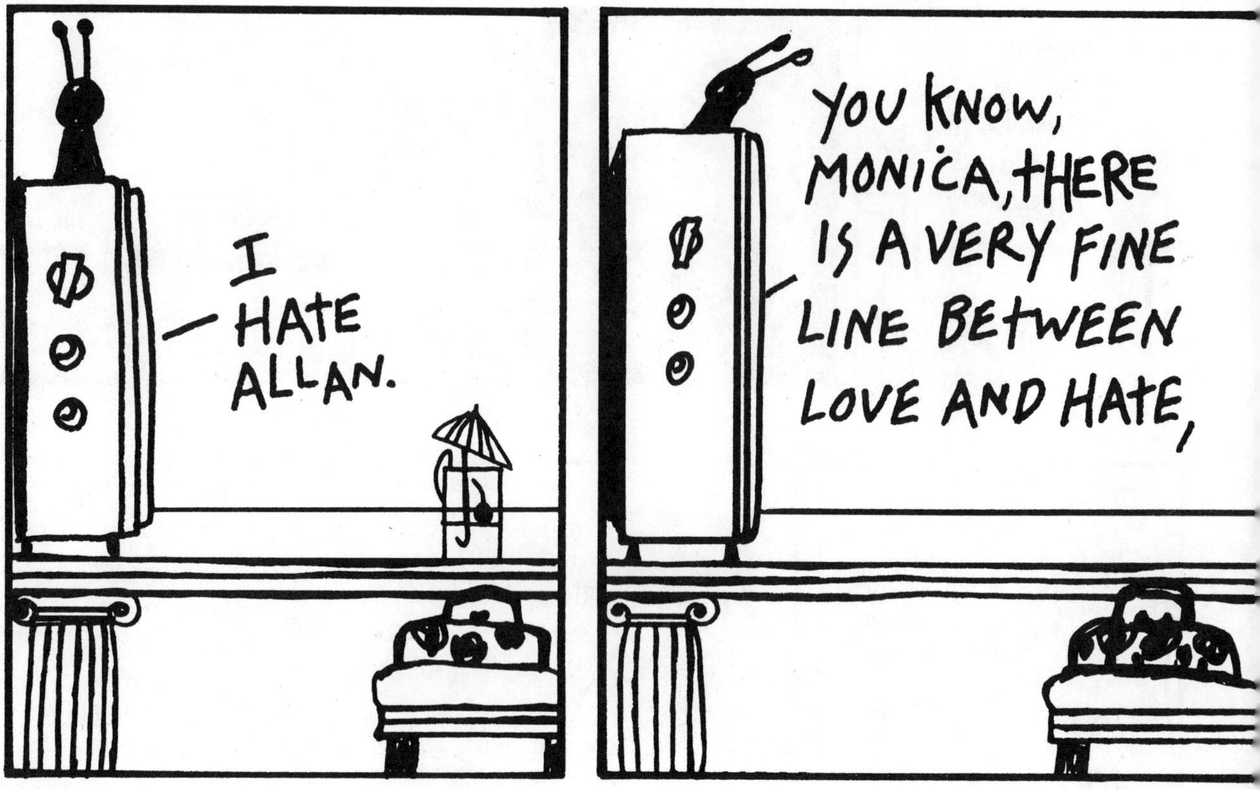
I HATE ALLAN.
YOU KNOW, MONICA, THERE IS A VERY FINE LINE BETWEEN LOVE AND HATE,

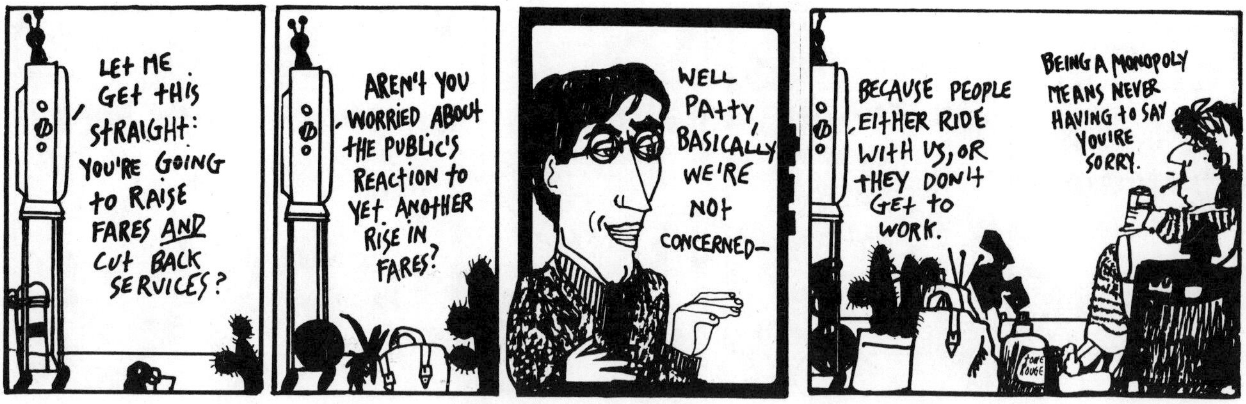
LET ME GET THIS STRAIGHT: YOU'RE GOING TO RAISE FARES AND CUT BACK SERVICES?
AREN'T YOU WORRIED ABOUT THE PUBLIC'S REACTION TO YET ANOTHER RISE IN FARES?
WELL PATTY, BASICALLY WE'RE NOT CONCERNED—
BECAUSE PEOPLE EITHER RIDE WITH US, OR THEY DON'T GET TO WORK.
BEING A MONOPOLY MEANS NEVER HAVING TO SAY YOU'RE SORRY.

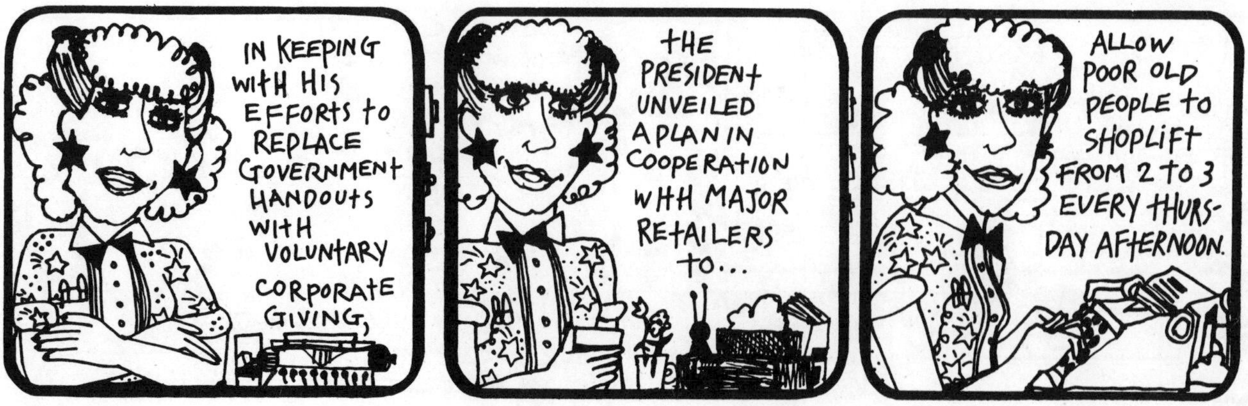
IN KEEPING WITH HIS EFFORTS TO REPLACE GOVERNMENT HANDOUTS WITH VOLUNTARY CORPORATE GIVING,
THE PRESIDENT UNVEILED A PLAN IN COOPERATION WITH MAJOR RETAILERS TO...
ALLOW POOR OLD PEOPLE TO SHOPLIFT FROM 2 TO 3 EVERY THURSDAY AFTERNOON.

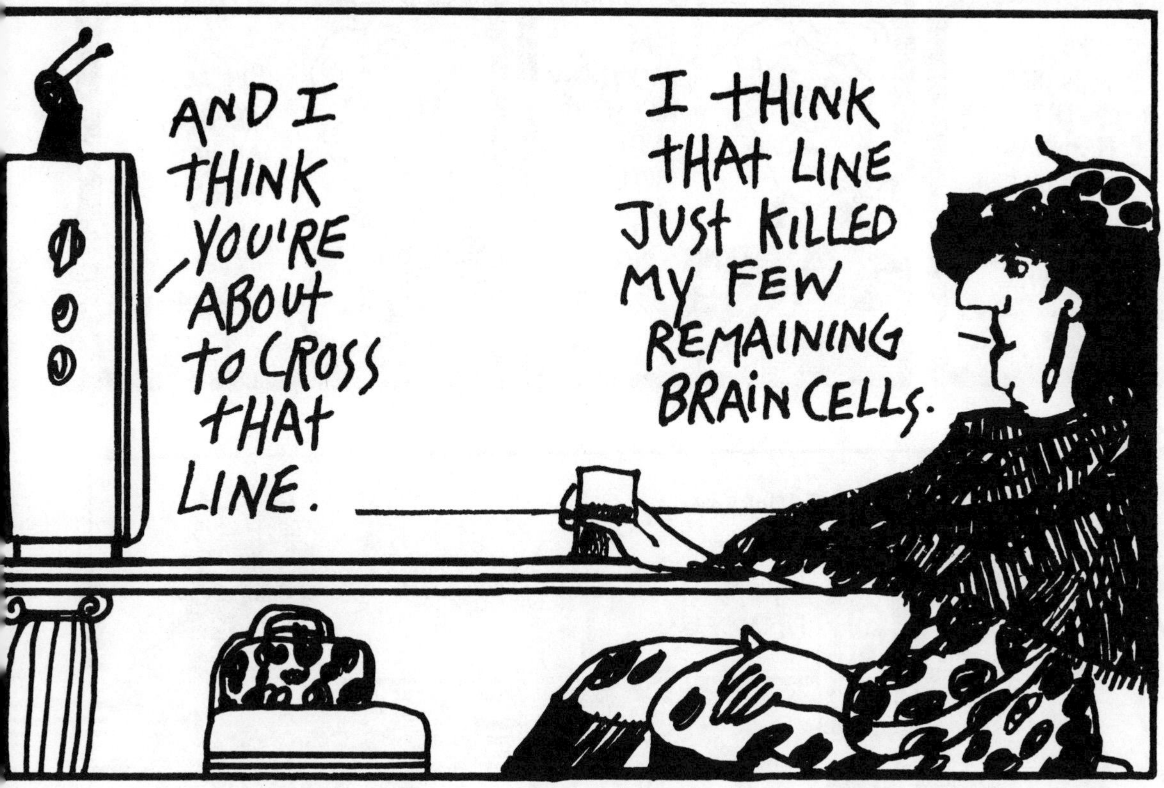
AND I THINK YOU'RE ABOUT TO CROSS THAT LINE.
I THINK THAT LINE JUST KILLED MY FEW REMAINING BRAIN CELLS.

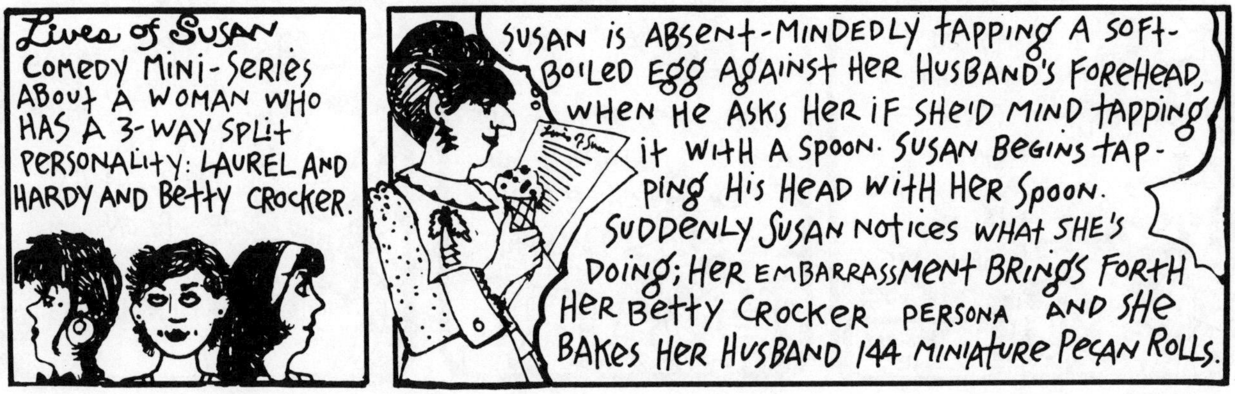
Lives of Susan
COMEDY MINI-SERIES ABOUT A WOMAN WHO HAS A 3-WAY SPLIT PERSONALITY: LAUREL AND HARDY AND BETTY CROCKER.
SUSAN IS ABSENT-MINDEDLY TAPPING A SOFT-BOILED EGG AGAINST HER HUSBAND'S FOREHEAD, WHEN HE ASKS HER IF SHE'D MIND TAPPING IT WITH A SPOON. SUSAN BEGINS TAP-PING HIS HEAD WITH HER SPOON. SUDDENLY SUSAN NOTICES WHAT SHE'S DOING; HER EMBARRASSMENT BRINGS FORTH HER BETTY CROCKER PERSONA AND SHE BAKES HER HUSBAND 144 MINIATURE PECAN ROLLS.

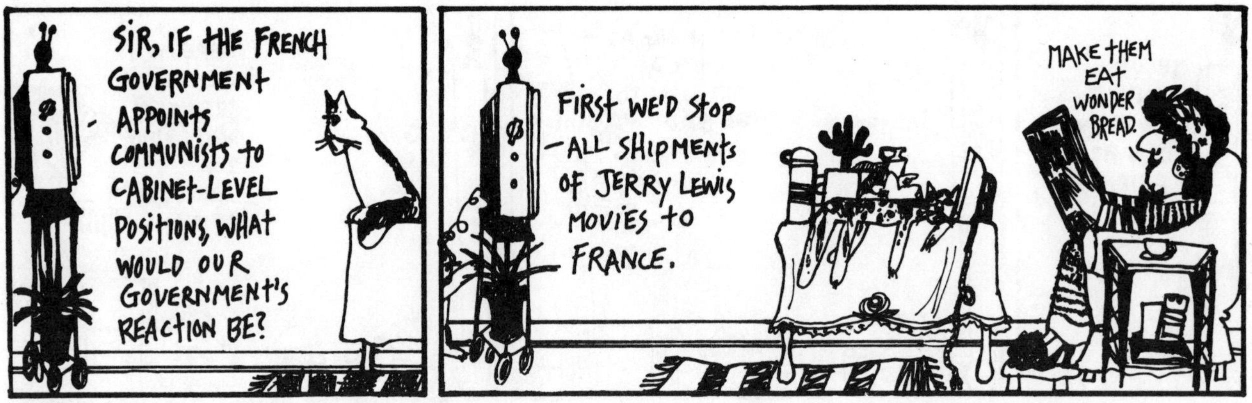
SIR, IF THE FRENCH GOVERNMENT APPOINTS COMMUNISTS TO CABINET-LEVEL POSITIONS, WHAT WOULD OUR GOVERNMENT'S REACTION BE?
FIRST WE'D STOP ALL SHIPMENTS OF JERRY LEWIS MOVIES TO FRANCE.
MAKE THEM EAT WONDER BREAD.

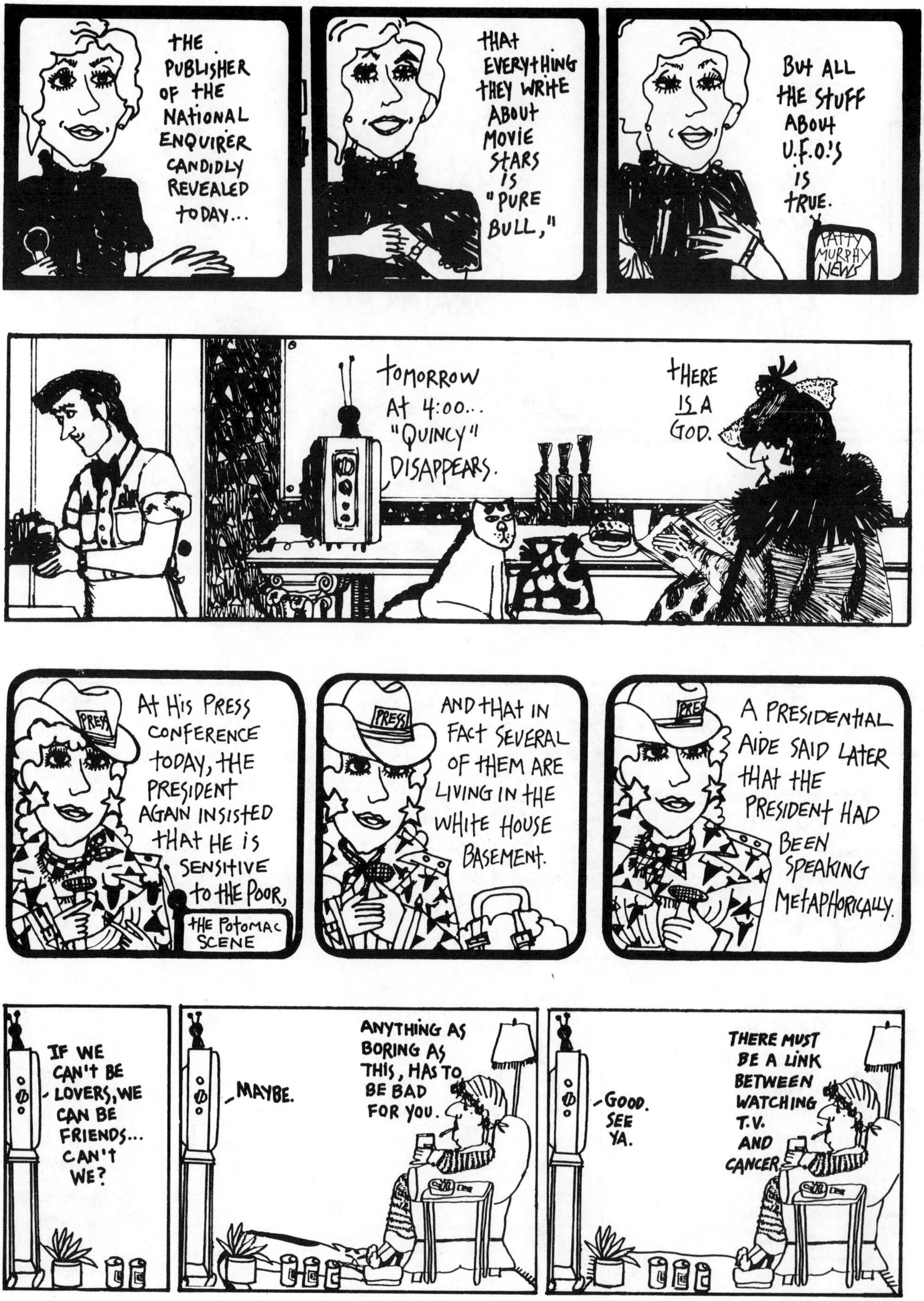
THE PUBLISHER OF THE NATIONAL ENQUIRER CANDIDLY REVEALED TODAY...
THAT EVERYTHING THEY WRITE ABOUT MOVIE STARS IS "PURE BULL,"
BUT ALL THE STUFF ABOUT U.F.O.'S IS TRUE.
PATTY MURPHY NEWS
TOMORROW AT 4:00... "QUINCY" DISAPPEARS.
THERE IS A GOD.
AT HIS PRESS CONFERENCE TODAY, THE PRESIDENT AGAIN INSISTED THAT HE IS SENSITIVE TO THE POOR,
PRESS
THE POTOMAC SCENE
AND THAT IN FACT SEVERAL OF THEM ARE LIVING IN THE WHITE HOUSE BASEMENT.
A PRESIDENTIAL AIDE SAID LATER THAT THE PRESIDENT HAD BEEN SPEAKING METAPHORICALLY.
IF WE CAN'T BE LOVERS, WE CAN BE FRIENDS... CAN'T WE?
- MAYBE.
ANYTHING AS BORING AS THIS, HAS TO BE BAD FOR YOU.
- GOOD. SEE YA.
THERE MUST BE A LINK BETWEEN WATCHING T.V. AND CANCER.

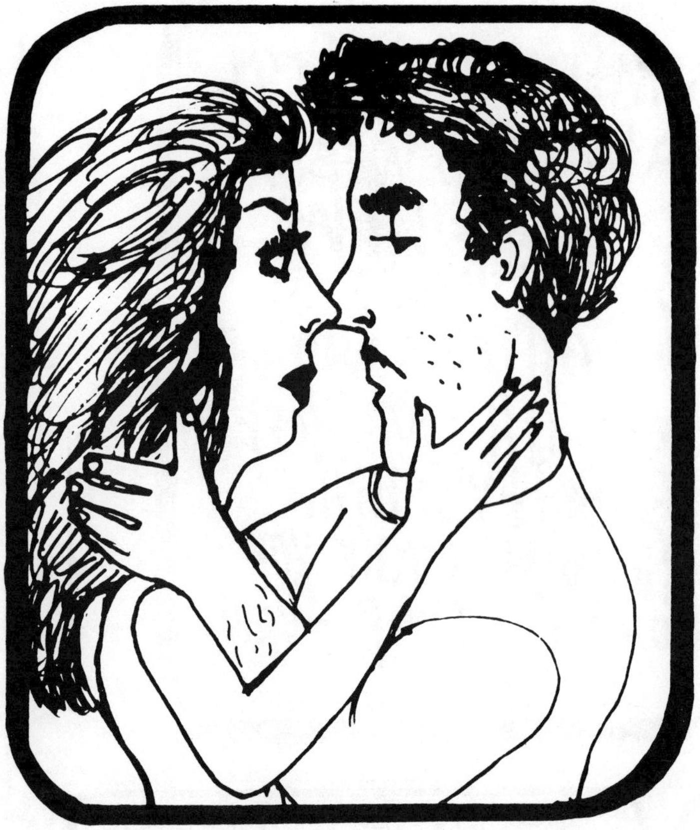

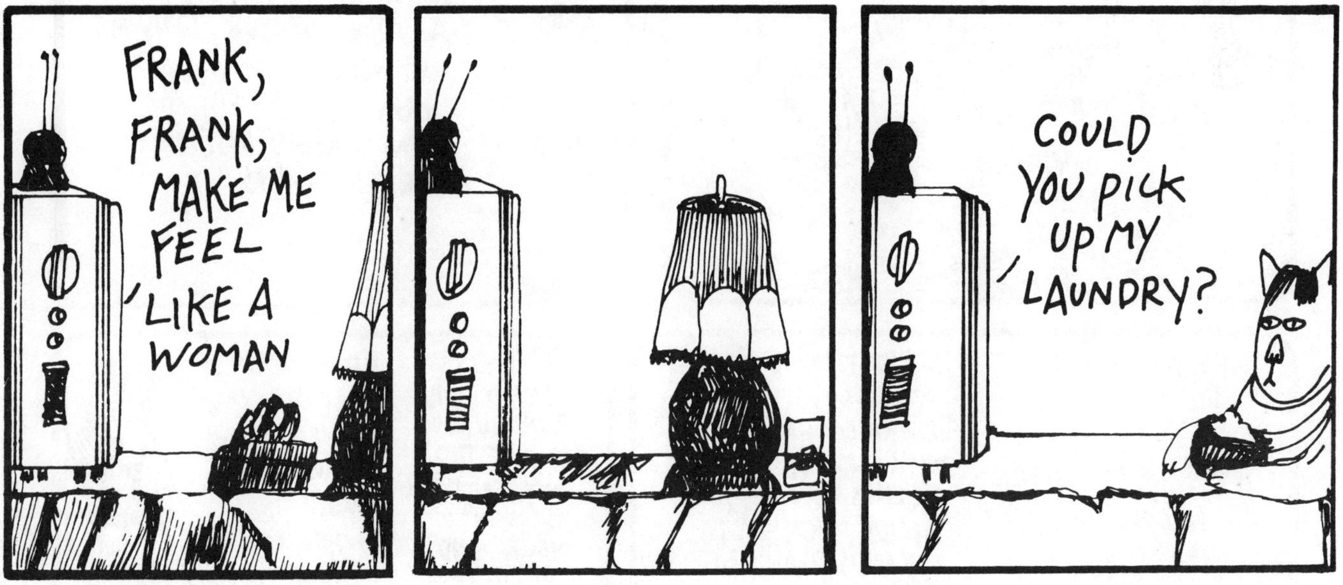
FRANK, FRANK, MAKE ME FEEL LIKE A WOMAN
COULD YOU PICK UP MY LAUNDRY?

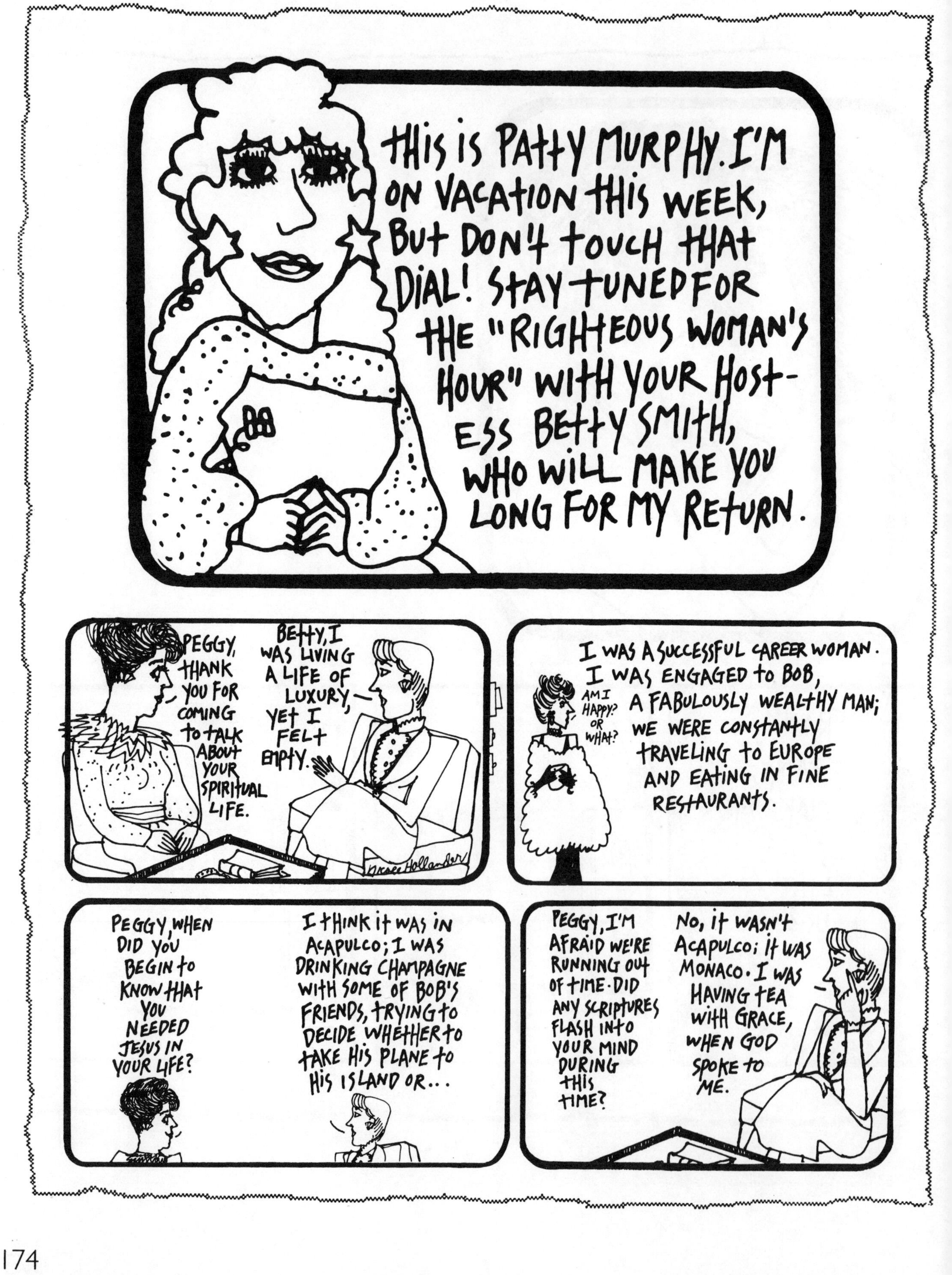
THIS IS PATTY MURPHY. I'M ON VACATION THIS WEEK, BUT DON'T TOUCH THAT DIAL! STAY TUNED FOR THE "RIGHTEOUS WOMAN'S HOUR" WITH YOUR HOST-ESS BETTY SMITH, WHO WILL MAKE YOU LONG FOR MY RETURN.
PEGGY, THANK YOU FOR COMING TO TALK ABOUT YOUR SPIRITUAL LIFE.
BETTY, I WAS LIVING A LIFE OF LUXURY, YET I FELT EMPTY.
I WAS A SUCCESSFUL CAREER WOMAN. I WAS ENGAGED TO BOB, A FABULOUSLY WEALTHY MAN; WE WERE CONSTANTLY TRAVELING TO EUROPE AND EATING IN FINE RESTAURANTS.
AM I HAPPY? OR WHAT?
PEGGY, WHEN DID YOU BEGIN TO KNOW THAT YOU NEEDED JESUS IN YOUR LIFE?
I THINK IT WAS IN ACAPULCO; I WAS DRINKING CHAMPAGNE WITH SOME OF BOB'S FRIENDS, TRYING TO DECIDE WHETHER TO TAKE HIS PLANE TO HIS ISLAND OR...
PEGGY, I'M AFRAID WE'RE RUNNING OUT OF TIME. DID ANY SCRIPTURES FLASH INTO YOUR MIND DURING THIS TIME?
NO, IT WASN'T ACAPULCO; IT WAS MONACO. I WAS HAVING TEA WITH GRACE, WHEN GOD SPOKE TO ME.

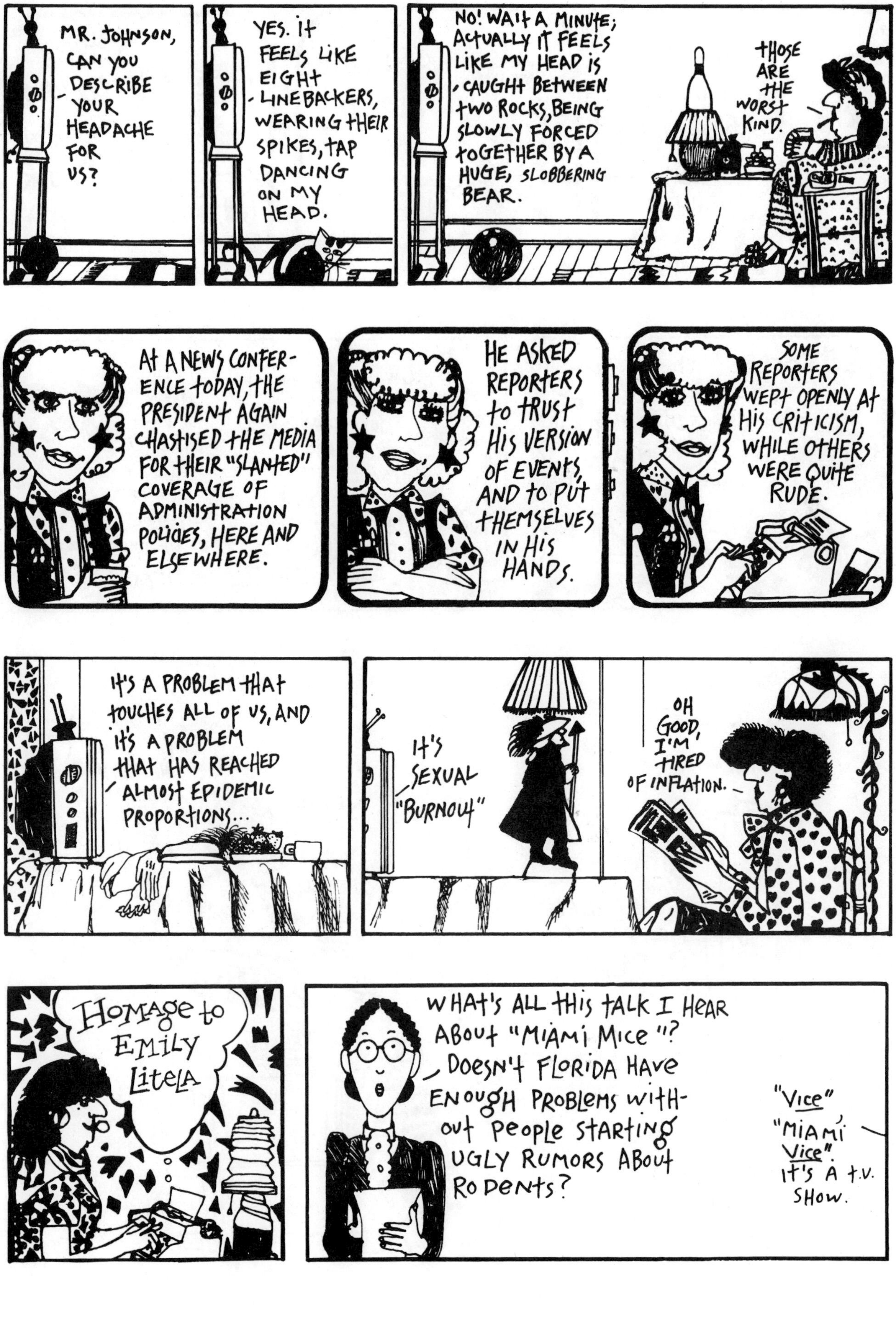
MR. JOHNSON, CAN YOU DESCRIBE YOUR HEADACHE FOR US?
YES. IT FEELS LIKE EIGHT LINEBACKERS, WEARING THEIR SPIKES, TAP DANCING ON MY HEAD.
NO! WAIT A MINUTE; ACTUALLY IT FEELS LIKE MY HEAD IS CAUGHT BETWEEN TWO ROCKS, BEING SLOWLY FORCED TOGETHER BY A HUGE, SLOBBERING BEAR.
THOSE ARE THE WORST KIND.
AT A NEWS CONFERENCE TODAY, THE PRESIDENT AGAIN CHASTISED THE MEDIA FOR THEIR "SLANTED" COVERAGE OF ADMINISTRATION POLICIES, HERE AND ELSEWHERE.
HE ASKED REPORTERS TO TRUST HIS VERSION OF EVENTS, AND TO PUT THEMSELVES IN HIS HANDS.
SOME REPORTERS WEPT OPENLY AT HIS CRITICISM, WHILE OTHERS WERE QUITE RUDE.
IT'S A PROBLEM THAT TOUCHES ALL OF US, AND IT'S A PROBLEM THAT HAS REACHED ALMOST EPIDEMIC PROPORTIONS...
IT'S SEXUAL "BURNOUT"
OH GOOD, I'M TIRED OF INFLATION.
HOMAGE TO EMILY LITELLA
WHAT'S ALL THIS TALK I HEAR ABOUT "MIAMI MICE"? DOESN'T FLORIDA HAVE ENOUGH PROBLEMS WITH-OUT PEOPLE STARTING UGLY RUMORS ABOUT RODENTS?
"VICE", "MIAMI VICE". IT'S A T.V. SHOW.

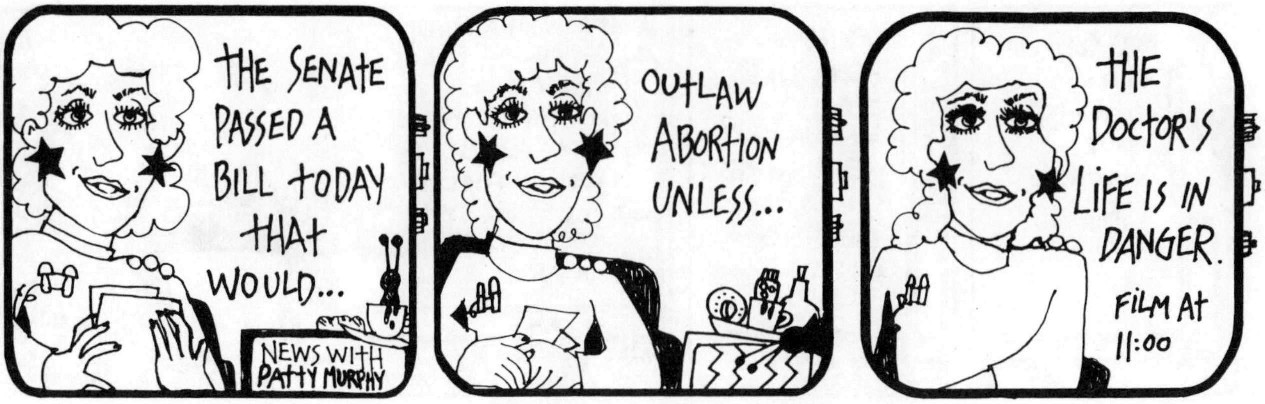
THE SENATE PASSED A BILL TODAY THAT WOULD...
NEWS WITH PATTY MURPHY
OUTLAW ABORTION UNLESS...
THE DOCTOR'S LIFE IS IN DANGER.
FILM AT 11:00

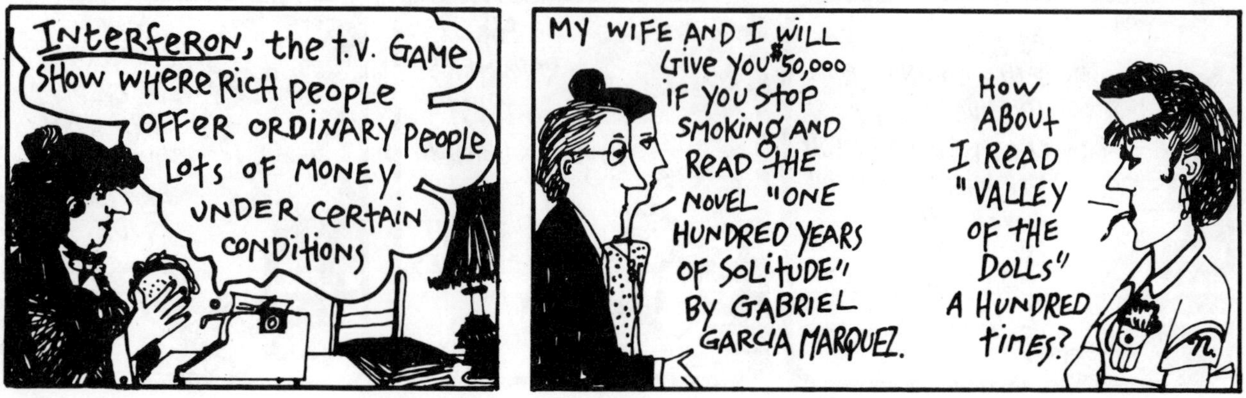
INTERFERON, THE T.V. GAME SHOW WHERE RICH PEOPLE OFFER ORDINARY PEOPLE LOTS OF MONEY UNDER CERTAIN CONDITIONS
MY WIFE AND I WILL GIVE YOU $50,000 IF YOU STOP SMOKING AND READ THE NOVEL "ONE HUNDRED YEARS OF SOLITUDE" BY GABRIEL GARCIA MARQUEZ.
HOW ABOUT I READ "VALLEY OF THE DOLLS" A HUNDRED TIMES?

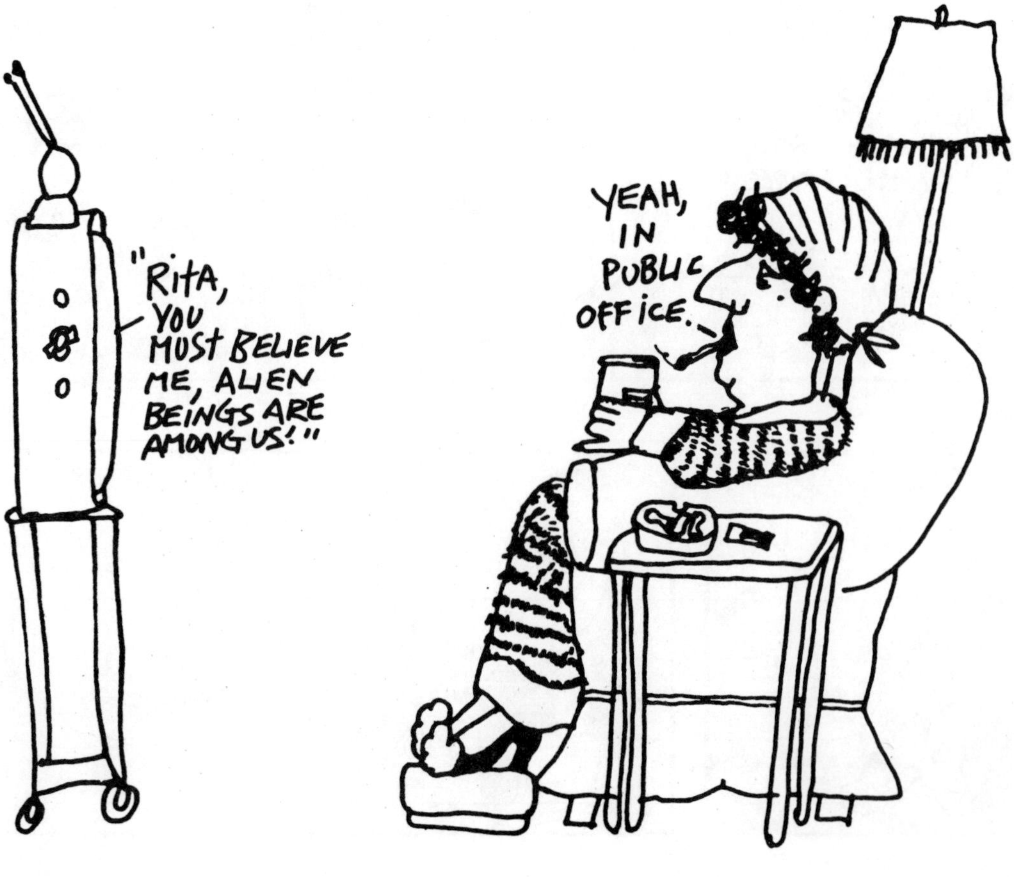
"RITA, YOU MUST BELIEVE ME, ALIEN BEINGS ARE AMONG US!"
YEAH, IN PUBLIC OFFICE.

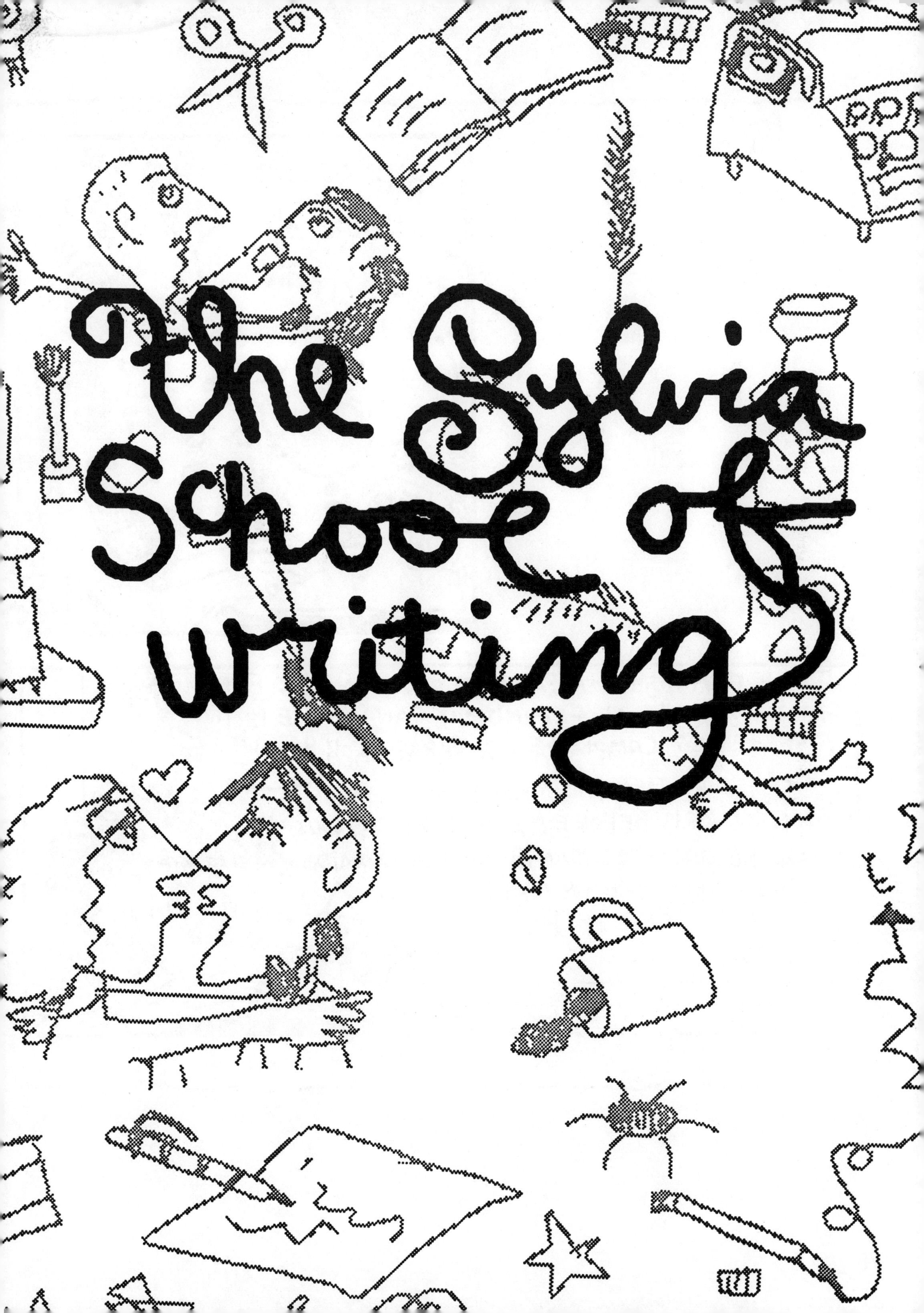
The Sylvia
School of
writing

THE SYLVIA SCHOOL OF MAINSTREAM WRITING. EXERCISE I.

"POST-FEMINISM" IS A POPULAR TOPIC IN THE PRESS. CAN YOU SAY "POST-FEMINISM"? CAN YOU USE IT IN A SENTENCE? COMPLETE THE PARAGRAPH BELOW.
"I HAD TO GET THE MICROFILM TO MAX IN NEW YORK BEFORE MY NEXT RENDEZVOUS WITH THE ONE-EYED MAN, BUT I WAS AFRAID TO TRUST IT TO THE U.S. MAIL. I DECIDED TO SEND IT POST-FEMINISM. HURRIEDLY, I ____."

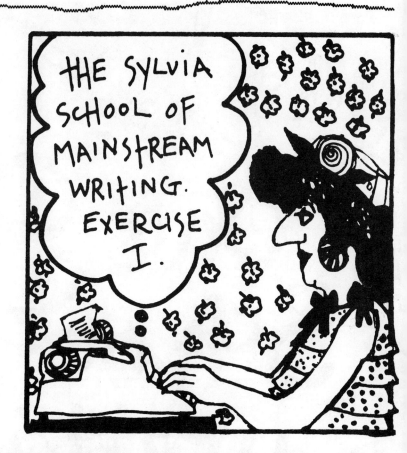

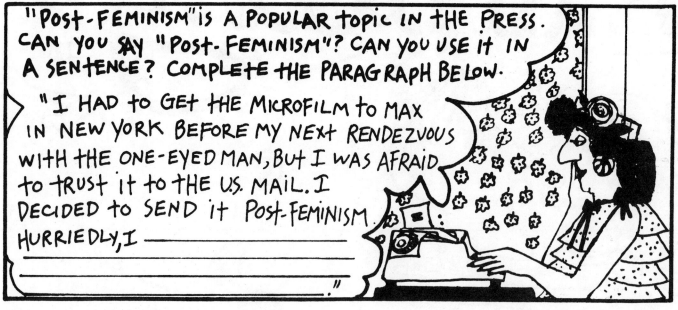

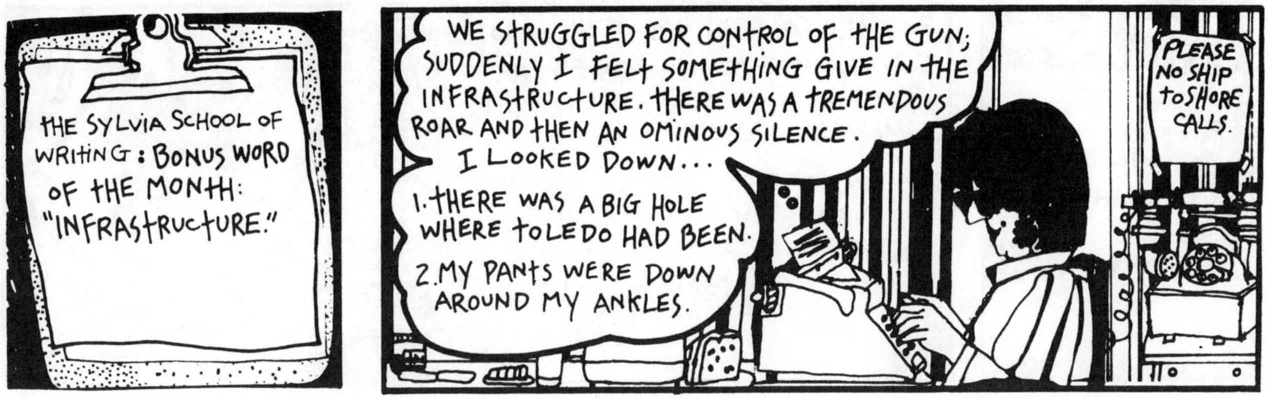
THE SYLVIA SCHOOL OF WRITING: BONUS WORD OF THE MONTH: "INFRASTRUCTURE."
WE STRUGGLED FOR CONTROL OF THE GUN; SUDDENLY I FELT SOMETHING GIVE IN THE INFRASTRUCTURE. THERE WAS A TREMENDOUS ROAR AND THEN AN OMINOUS SILENCE. I LOOKED DOWN...
1. THERE WAS A BIG HOLE WHERE TOLEDO HAD BEEN.
2. MY PANTS WERE DOWN AROUND MY ANKLES.
PLEASE NO SHIP TO SHORE CALLS.

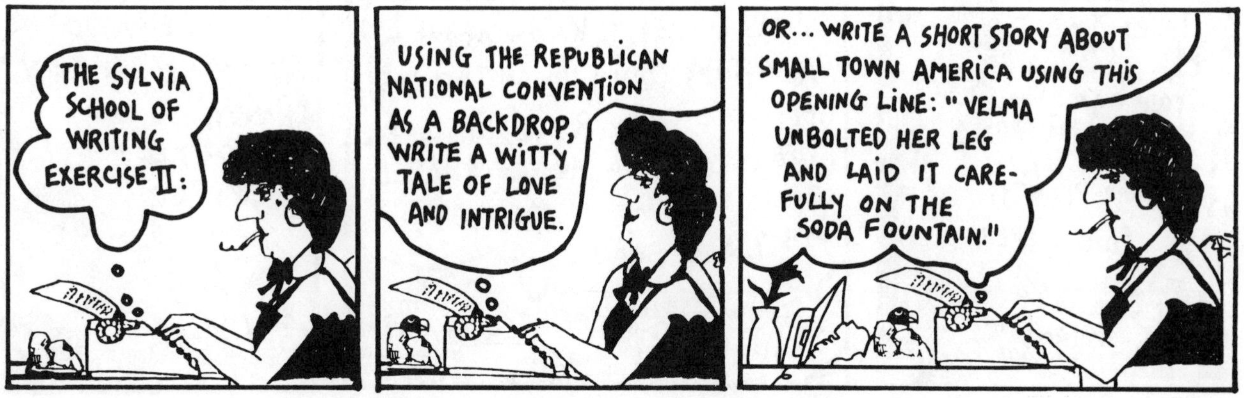
THE SYLVIA SCHOOL OF WRITING EXERCISE II:
USING THE REPUBLICAN NATIONAL CONVENTION AS A BACKDROP, WRITE A WITTY TALE OF LOVE AND INTRIGUE.
OR... WRITE A SHORT STORY ABOUT SMALL TOWN AMERICA USING THIS OPENING LINE: "VELMA UNBOLTED HER LEG AND LAID IT CAREFULLY ON THE SODA FOUNTAIN."

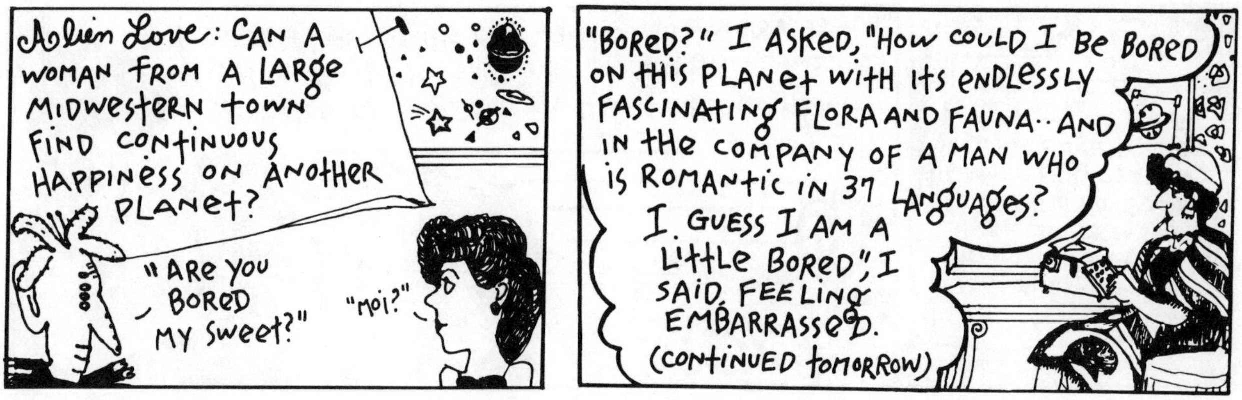
Alien Love: CAN A WOMAN FROM A LARGE MIDWESTERN TOWN FIND CONTINUOUS HAPPINESS ON ANOTHER PLANET?
"ARE YOU BORED MY SWEET?"
"MOI?"
"BORED?" I ASKED, "HOW COULD I BE BORED ON THIS PLANET WITH ITS ENDLESSLY FASCINATING FLORA AND FAUNA.. AND IN THE COMPANY OF A MAN WHO IS ROMANTIC IN 37 LANGUAGES?
I GUESS I AM A LITTLE BORED", I SAID, FEELING EMBARRASSED.
(CONTINUED TOMORROW)

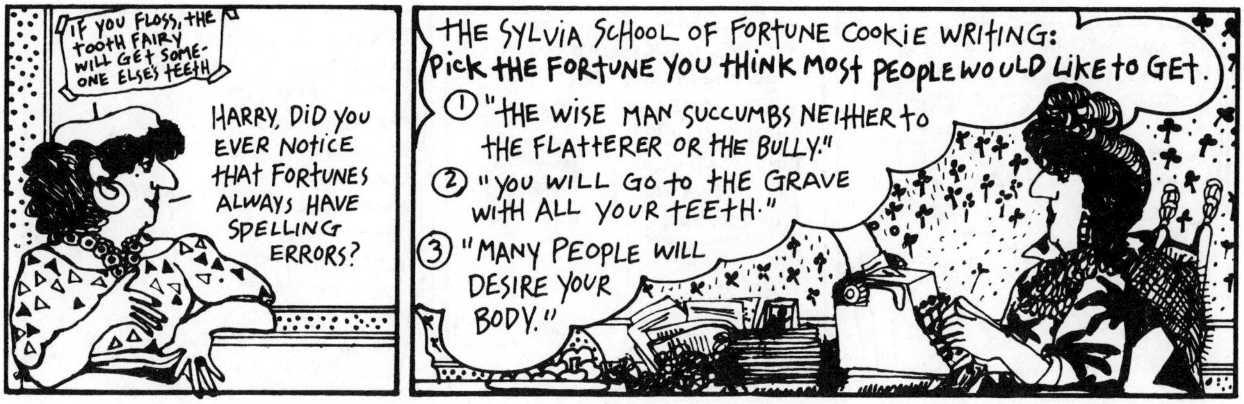
IF YOU FLOSS, THE TOOTH FAIRY WILL GET SOMEONE ELSE'S TEETH
HARRY, DID YOU EVER NOTICE THAT FORTUNES ALWAYS HAVE SPELLING ERRORS?
THE SYLVIA SCHOOL OF FORTUNE COOKIE WRITING: PICK THE FORTUNE YOU THINK MOST PEOPLE WOULD LIKE TO GET.
① "THE WISE MAN SUCCUMBS NEITHER TO THE FLATTERER OR THE BULLY."
② "YOU WILL GO TO THE GRAVE WITH ALL YOUR TEETH."
③ "MANY PEOPLE WILL DESIRE YOUR BODY."

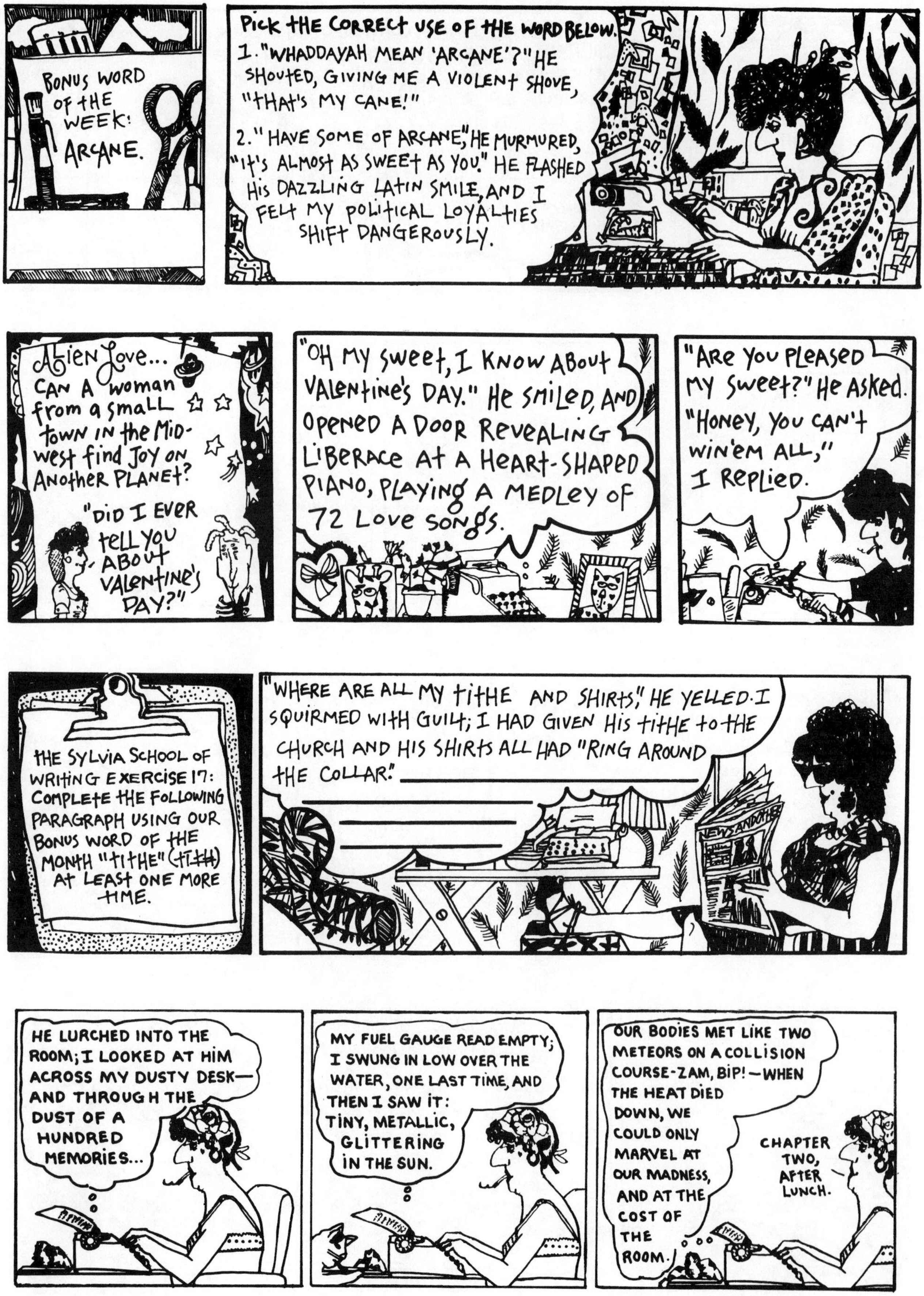
BONUS WORD OF THE WEEK: ARCANE.
PICK THE CORRECT USE OF THE WORD BELOW.
1. "WHADDAYAH MEAN 'ARCANE'?" HE SHOUTED, GIVING ME A VIOLENT SHOVE, "THAT'S MY CANE!"
2. "HAVE SOME OF ARCANE," HE MURMURED, "IT'S ALMOST AS SWEET AS YOU." HE FLASHED HIS DAZZLING LATIN SMILE, AND I FELT MY POLITICAL LOYALTIES SHIFT DANGEROUSLY.
ALIEN LOVE... CAN A WOMAN FROM A SMALL TOWN IN THE MID-WEST FIND JOY ON ANOTHER PLANET?
"DID I EVER TELL YOU ABOUT VALENTINE'S DAY?"
"OH MY SWEET, I KNOW ABOUT VALENTINE'S DAY." HE SMILED, AND OPENED A DOOR REVEALING LIBERACE AT A HEART-SHAPED PIANO, PLAYING A MEDLEY OF 72 LOVE SONGS.
"ARE YOU PLEASED MY SWEET?" HE ASKED. "HONEY, YOU CAN'T WIN 'EM ALL," I REPLIED.
THE SYLVIA SCHOOL OF WRITING EXERCISE 17: COMPLETE THE FOLLOWING PARAGRAPH USING OUR BONUS WORD OF THE MONTH "TITHE" (TĪTH) AT LEAST ONE MORE TIME.
"WHERE ARE ALL MY TITHE AND SHIRTS," HE YELLED. I SQUIRMED WITH GUILT; I HAD GIVEN HIS TITHE TO THE CHURCH AND HIS SHIRTS ALL HAD "RING AROUND THE COLLAR."
NEWS AND OTHER
HE LURCHED INTO THE ROOM; I LOOKED AT HIM ACROSS MY DUSTY DESK— AND THROUGH THE DUST OF A HUNDRED MEMORIES...
MY FUEL GAUGE READ EMPTY; I SWUNG IN LOW OVER THE WATER, ONE LAST TIME, AND THEN I SAW IT: TINY, METALLIC, GLITTERING IN THE SUN.
OUR BODIES MET LIKE TWO METEORS ON A COLLISION COURSE-ZAM, BIP! —WHEN THE HEAT DIED DOWN, WE COULD ONLY MARVEL AT OUR MADNESS, AND AT THE COST OF THE ROOM.
CHAPTER TWO, AFTER LUNCH.

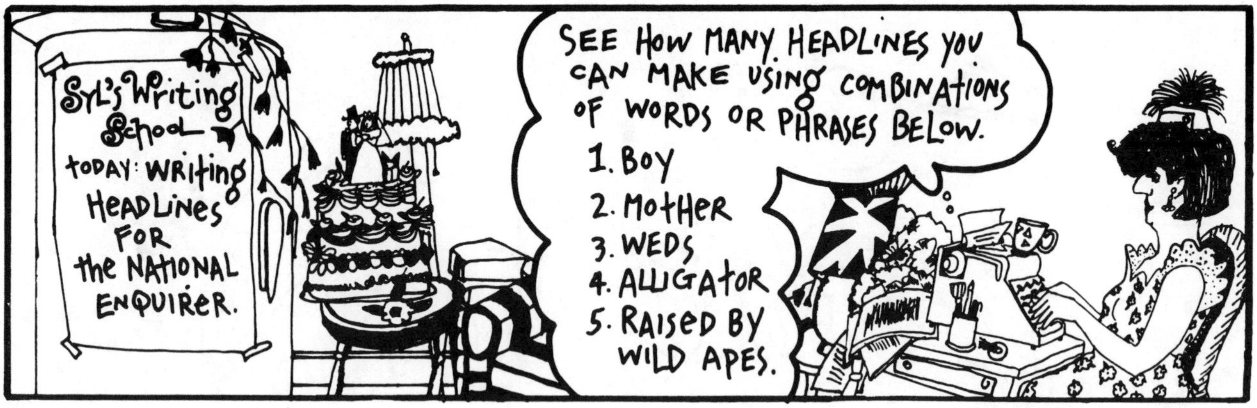
Syl's Writing School
today: writing Headlines for the NATIONAL ENQUIRER.
SEE HOW MANY HEADLINES YOU CAN MAKE USING COMBINATIONS OF WORDS OR PHRASES BELOW.
1. BOY
2. MOTHER
3. WEDS
4. ALLIGATOR
5. RAISED BY WILD APES.

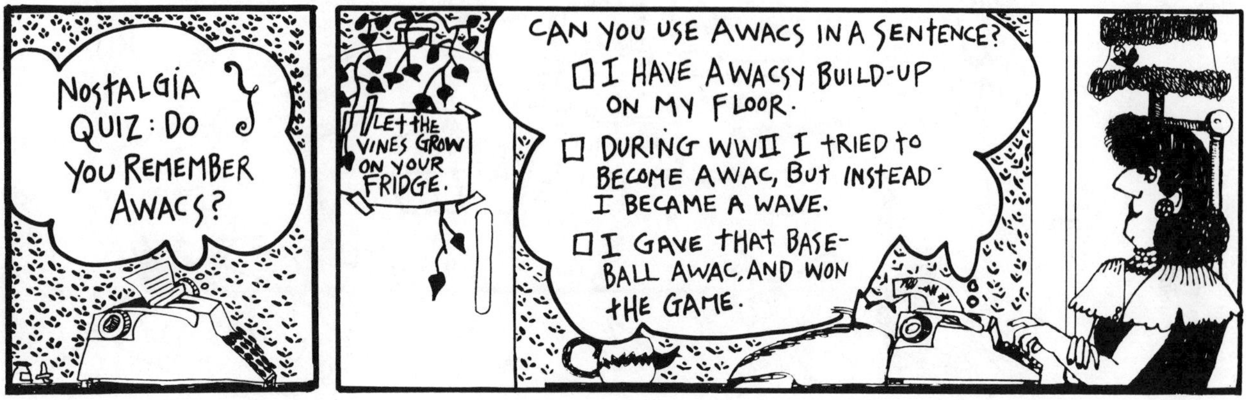
NOSTALGIA QUIZ: DO YOU REMEMBER AWACS?
LET THE VINES GROW ON YOUR FRIDGE.
CAN YOU USE AWACS IN A SENTENCE?
☐ I HAVE AWACSY BUILD-UP ON MY FLOOR.
☐ DURING WWII I TRIED TO BECOME AWAC, BUT INSTEAD I BECAME A WAVE.
☐ I GAVE THAT BASE-BALL AWAC, AND WON THE GAME.

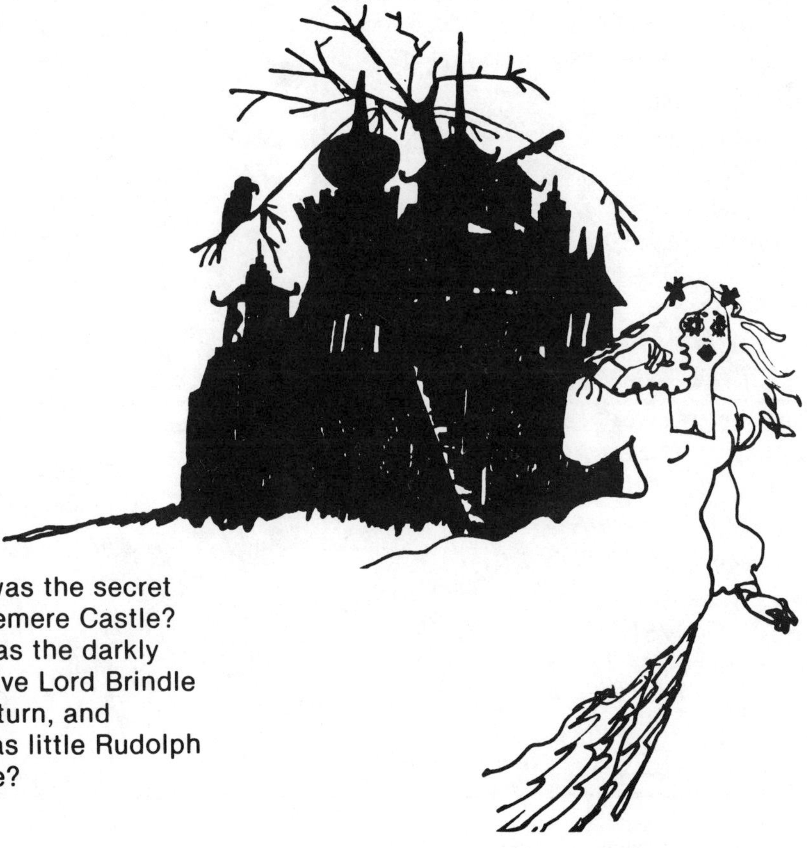

What was the secret
at Edgemere Castle?
Why was the darkly
attractive Lord Brindle
so taciturn, and
why was little Rudolph
so little?

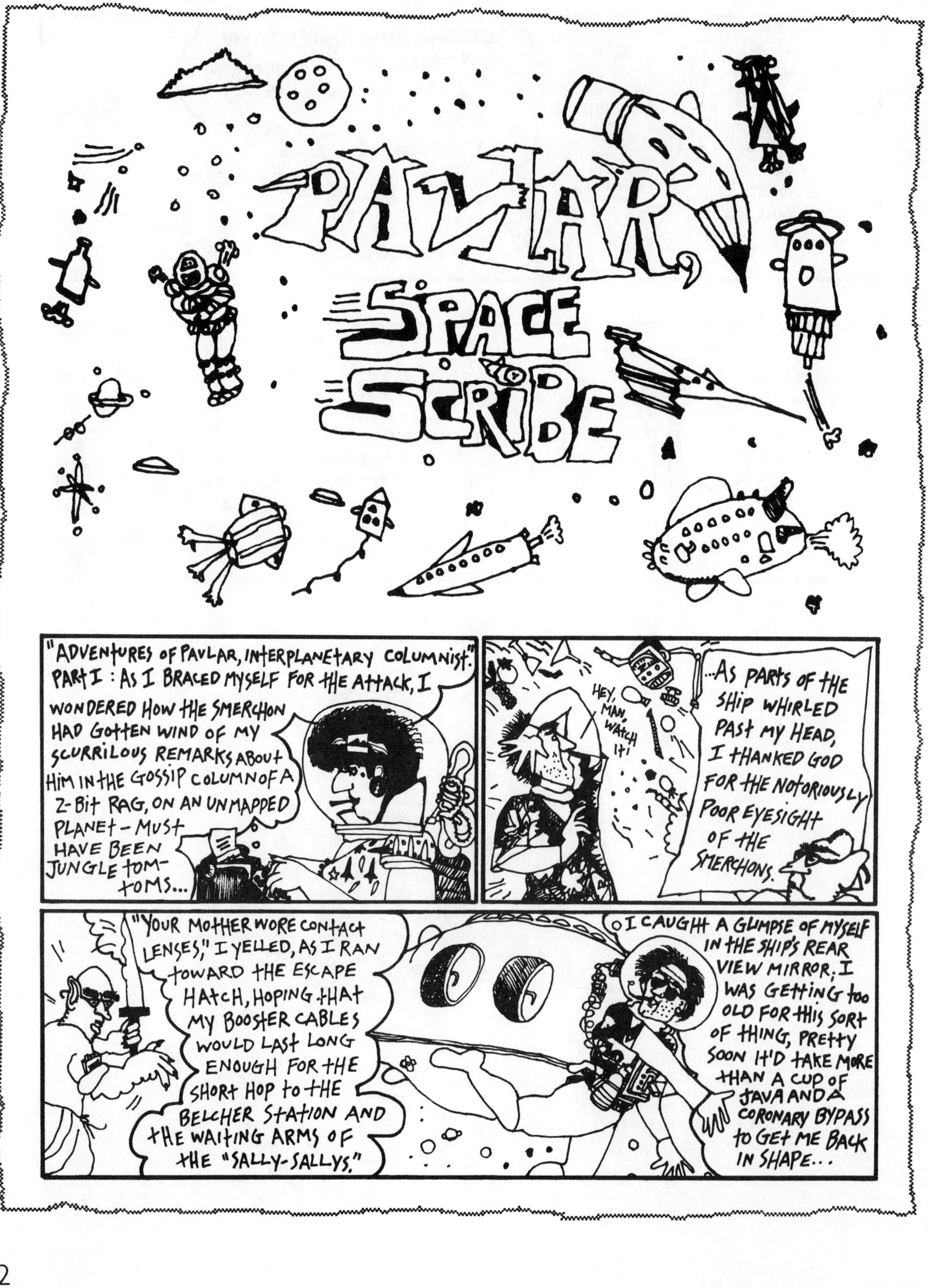
PAVLAR, SPACE SCRIBE
"ADVENTURES OF PAVLAR, INTERPLANETARY COLUMNIST." PART I: AS I BRACED MYSELF FOR THE ATTACK, I WONDERED HOW THE SMERCHON HAD GOTTEN WIND OF MY SCURRILOUS REMARKS ABOUT HIM IN THE GOSSIP COLUMN OF A 2-BIT RAG, ON AN UNMAPPED PLANET - MUST HAVE BEEN JUNGLE TOM-TOMS...
HEY, MAN, WATCH IT!
...AS PARTS OF THE SHIP WHIRLED PAST MY HEAD, I THANKED GOD FOR THE NOTORIOUSLY POOR EYESIGHT OF THE SMERCHONS.
"YOUR MOTHER WORE CONTACT LENSES," I YELLED, AS I RAN TOWARD THE ESCAPE HATCH, HOPING THAT MY BOOSTER CABLES WOULD LAST LONG ENOUGH FOR THE SHORT HOP TO THE BELCHER STATION AND THE WAITING ARMS OF THE "SALLY-SALLYS."
I CAUGHT A GLIMPSE OF MYSELF IN THE SHIP'S REAR VIEW MIRROR; I WAS GETTING TOO OLD FOR THIS SORT OF THING, PRETTY SOON IT'D TAKE MORE THAN A CUP OF JAVA AND A CORONARY BYPASS TO GET ME BACK IN SHAPE...

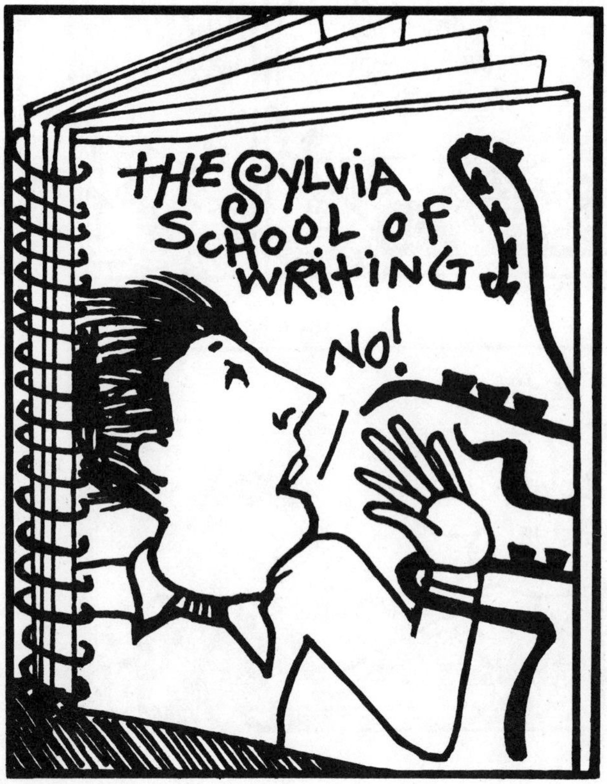
THE SYLVIA SCHOOL OF WRITING
NO!

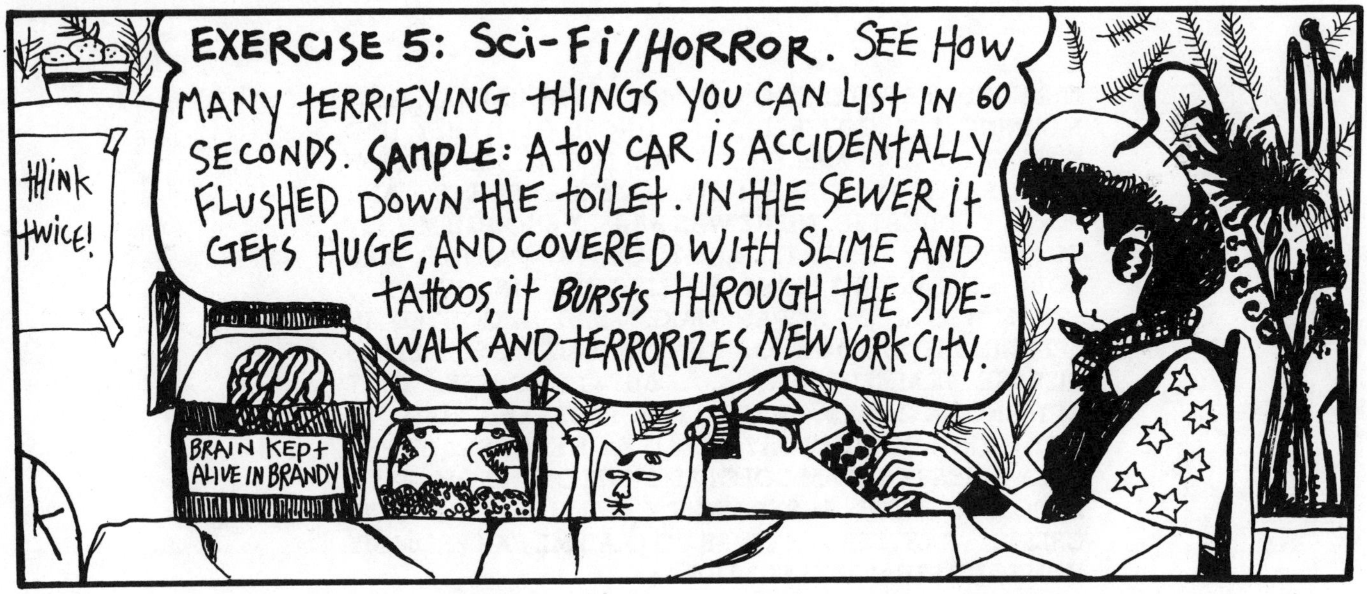
EXERCISE 5: Sci-Fi/HORROR. SEE HOW MANY TERRIFYING THINGS YOU CAN LIST IN 60 SECONDS. SAMPLE: A toy CAR IS ACCIDENTALLY FLUSHED DOWN THE toiLET. IN THE SEWER it GETS HUGE, AND COVERED WITH SLIME AND tattoos, it BURSTS THROUGH THE SIDEWALK AND TERRORIZES NEW YORK CITY.
THINK TWICE!
BRAIN KEPT ALIVE IN BRANDY

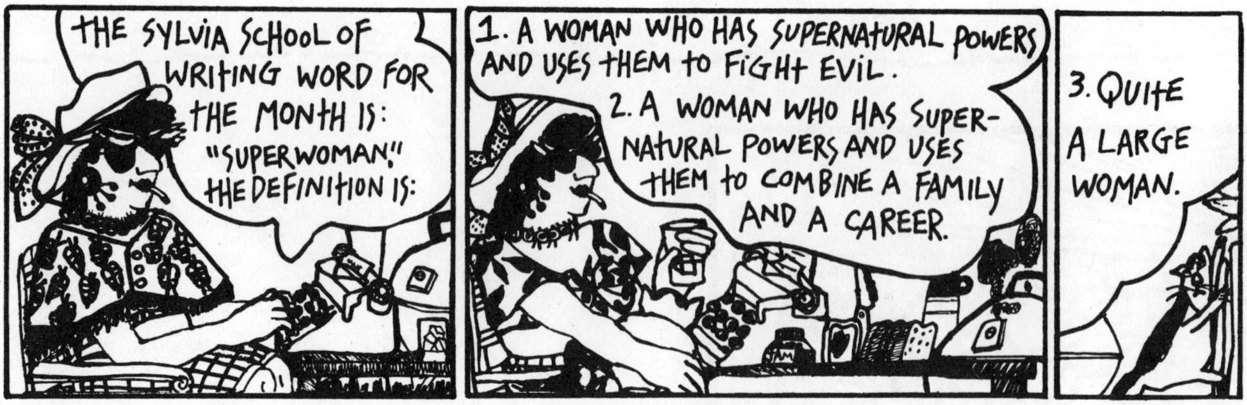
THE SYLVIA SCHOOL OF WRITING WORD FOR THE MONTH IS: "SUPERWOMAN." THE DEFINITION IS:
1. A WOMAN WHO HAS SUPERNATURAL POWERS AND USES THEM TO FIGHT EVIL.
2. A WOMAN WHO HAS SUPERNATURAL POWERS AND USES THEM TO COMBINE A FAMILY AND A CAREER.
3. QUITE A LARGE WOMAN.

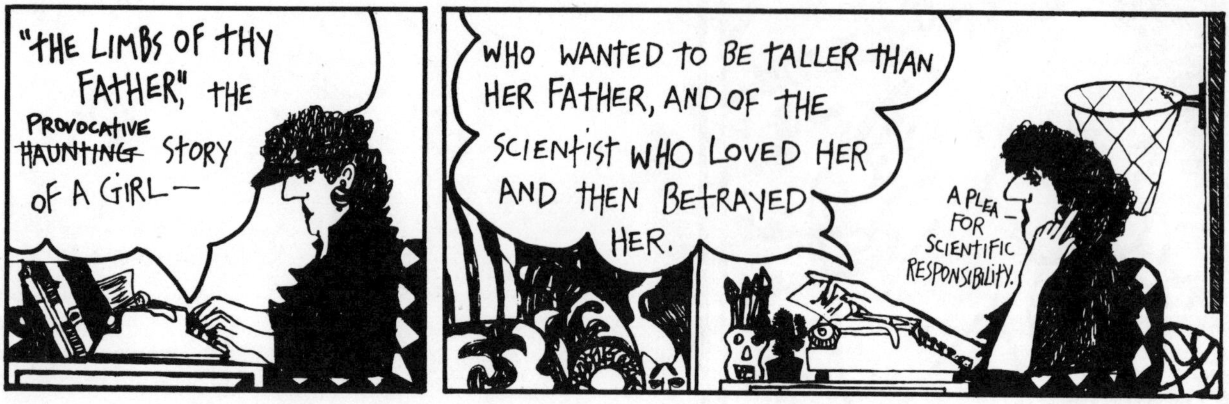
"THE LIMBS OF THY FATHER," THE PROVOCATIVE ~~HAUNTING~~ STORY OF A GIRL—
WHO WANTED TO BE TALLER THAN HER FATHER, AND OF THE SCIENTIST WHO LOVED HER AND THEN BETRAYED HER.
A PLEA—FOR SCIENTIFIC RESPONSIBILITY.

IT RAINED THE AFTERNOON OF MOTHER'S FUNERAL. THAT MORNING I DISCOVERED THAT UNCLE GEOFFREY HAD EMBEZZLED THE FAMILY FORTUNE, LOSING HEAVILY ON THE GREYHOUNDS AND LEAVING ME PENNILESS AND POORLY EDUCATED. THERE WAS BARELY ENOUGH MONEY TO BURY MY DELICATE, ARISTOCRATIC MOTHER. HER BODY SO THIN, SO LIGHT, SO LIKE THE TINY WHIPPED CREAM FILLED MARZIPAN CAKES SHE DELIGHTED IN BEFORE THE SHADOW OF THAT DREAD REMORSELESS DISEASE CLAIMED HER . . . BUT I DIGRESS. THAT AFTERNOON I HAD BURIED THE PAST AND HAD NO INTIMATION OF WHAT LAY AHEAD AS I EAGERLY RIPPED OPEN A HEAVY CREAM COLORED ENVELOPE, FROM ITALY, EMBOSSED WITH A STRANGELY FAMILIAR BARONIAL CREST . . . A LETTER THAT WAS TO LEAD ME FAR FROM MY HOME AND STRAIGHT INTO THE . . .

Arms of Evil

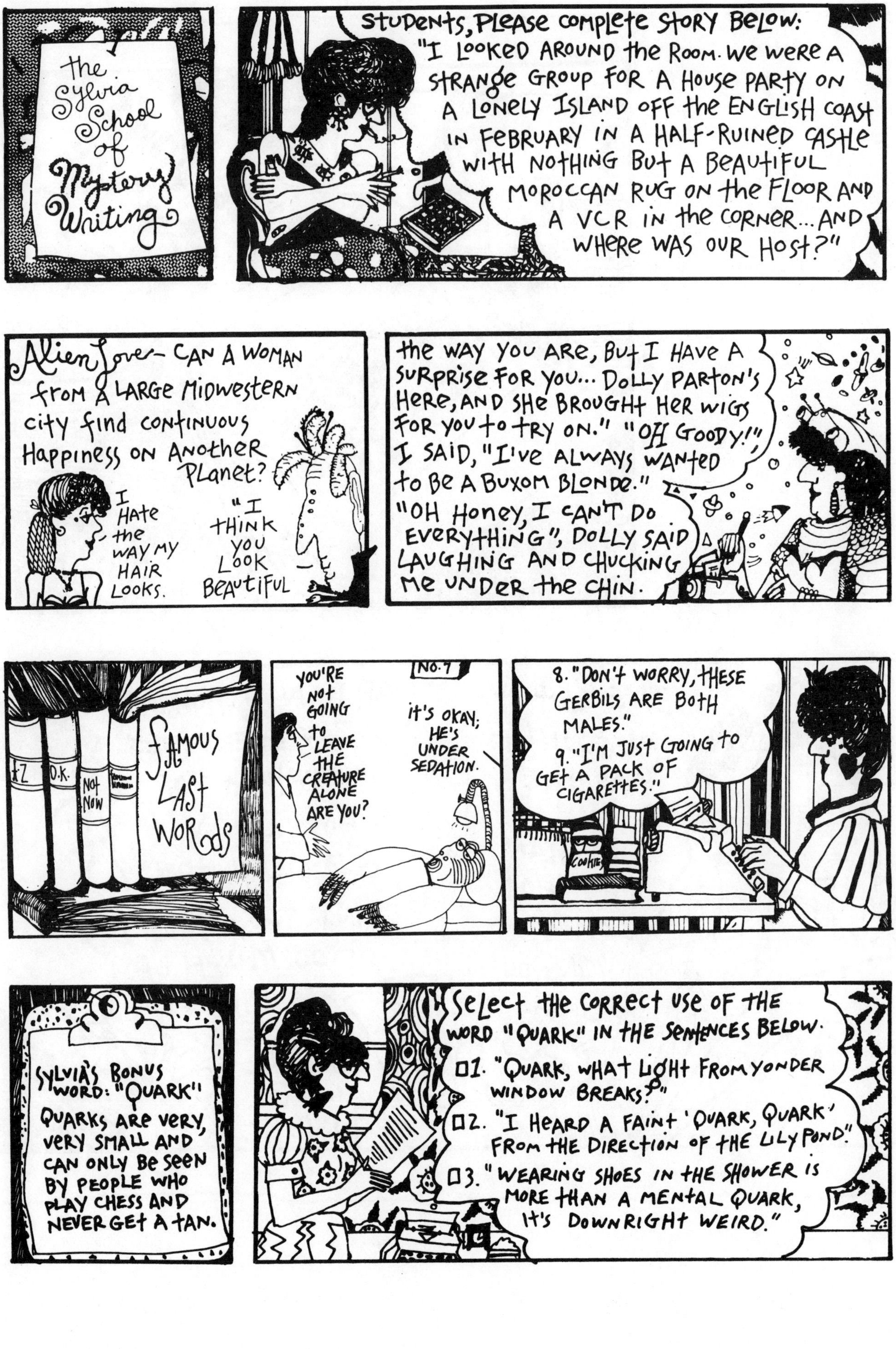
the Sylvia School of Mystery Writing
Students, Please complete story below: "I looked around the room. We were a strange group for a house party on a lonely island off the English coast in February in a half-ruined castle with nothing but a beautiful Moroccan rug on the floor and a VCR in the corner... and where was our host?"
Alien Love— Can a woman from a large Midwestern city find continuous happiness on another planet?
I hate the way my hair looks.
"I think you look beautiful
the way you are, but I have a surprise for you... Dolly Parton's here, and she brought her wigs for you to try on." "Oh goody!," I said, "I've always wanted to be a buxom blonde." "Oh honey, I can't do everything", Dolly said laughing and chucking me under the chin.
Famous Last Words
Z
O.K.
Not Now
No. 7
You're not going to leave the creature alone are you?
it's okay; he's under sedation.
8. "Don't worry, these gerbils are both males."
9. "I'm just going to get a pack of cigarettes."
Cookies
Sylvia's bonus word: "Quark"
Quarks are very, very small and can only be seen by people who play chess and never get a tan.
Select the correct use of the word "quark" in the sentences below.
☐1. "Quark, what light from yonder window breaks?"
☐2. "I heard a faint 'quark, quark' from the direction of the lily pond."
☐3. "Wearing shoes in the shower is more than a mental quark, it's downright weird."

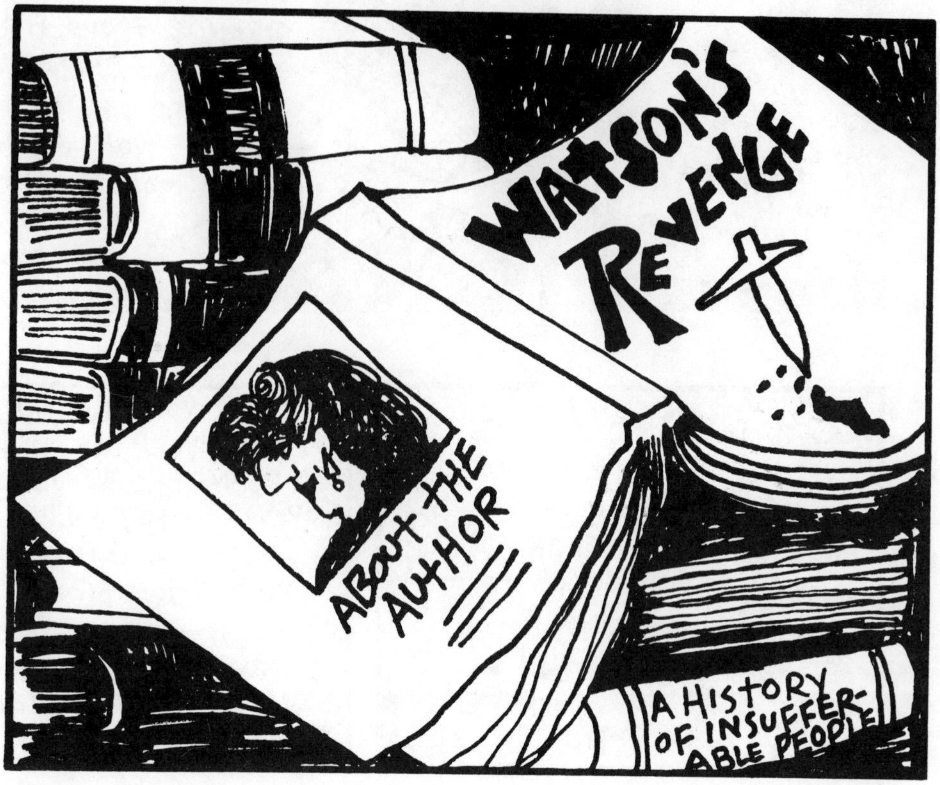
WATSON'S REVENGE
ABOUT THE AUTHOR
A HISTORY OF INSUFFERABLE PEOPLE

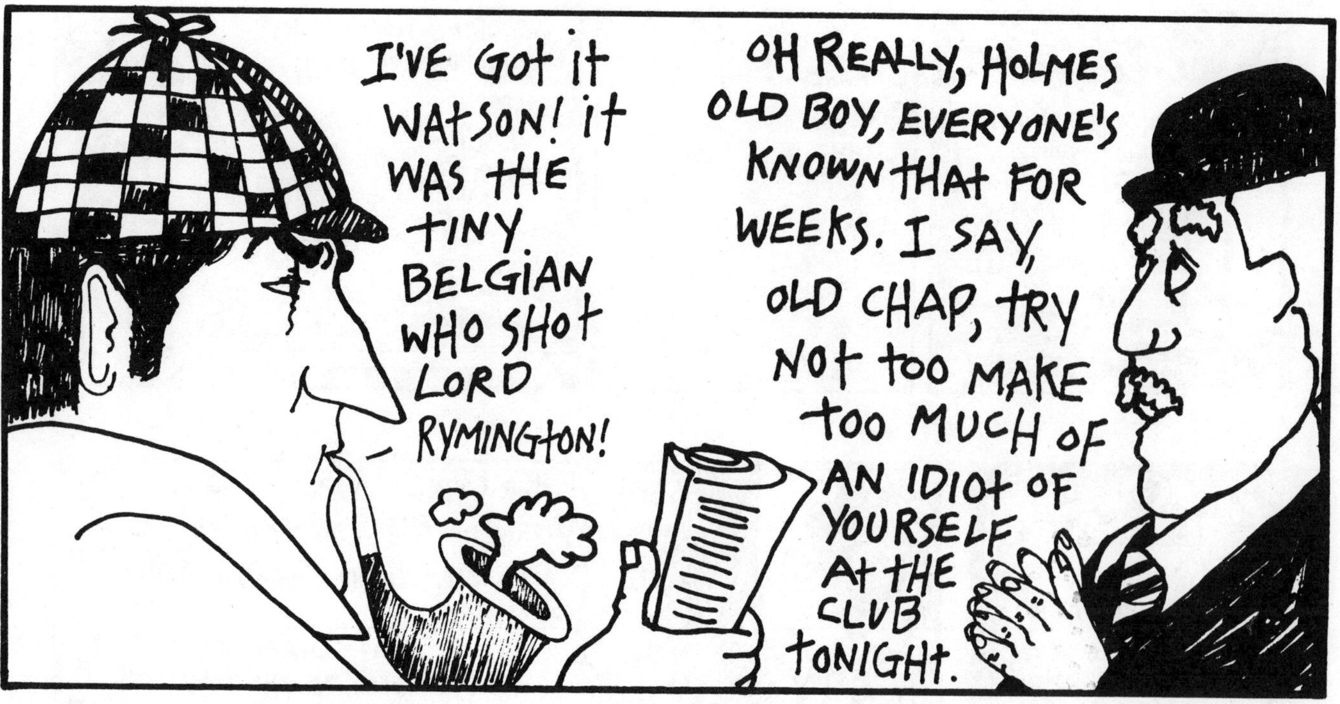
I'VE GOT IT WATSON! IT WAS THE TINY BELGIAN WHO SHOT LORD RYMINGTON!
OH REALLY, HOLMES OLD BOY, EVERYONE'S KNOWN THAT FOR WEEKS. I SAY, OLD CHAP, TRY NOT TOO MAKE TOO MUCH OF AN IDIOT OF YOURSELF AT THE CLUB TONIGHT.

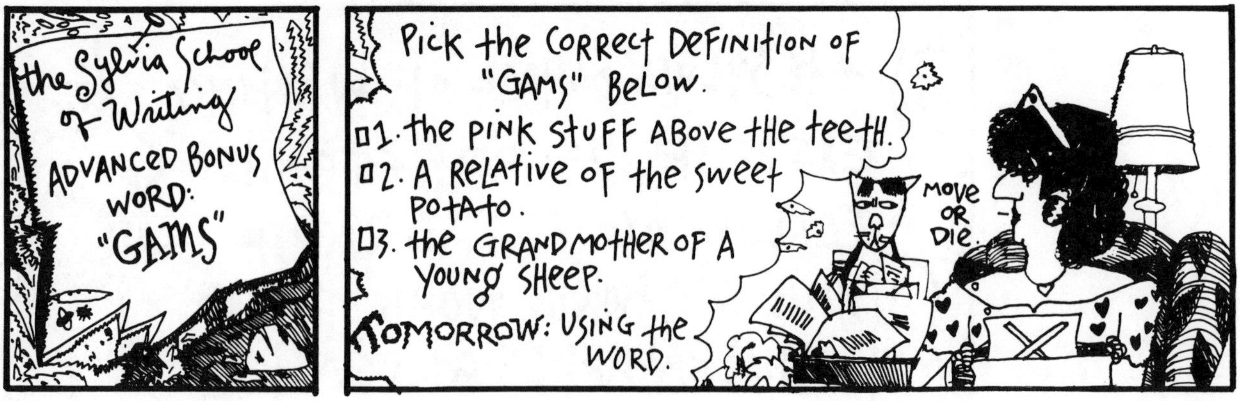
the Sylvia School of Writing
ADVANCED BONUS WORD: "GAMS"
Pick the Correct Definition of "GAMS" Below.
1. the pink stuff above the teeth.
2. A relative of the sweet potato.
3. the grandmother of a young sheep.
TOMORROW: USING the WORD.
MOVE OR DIE.

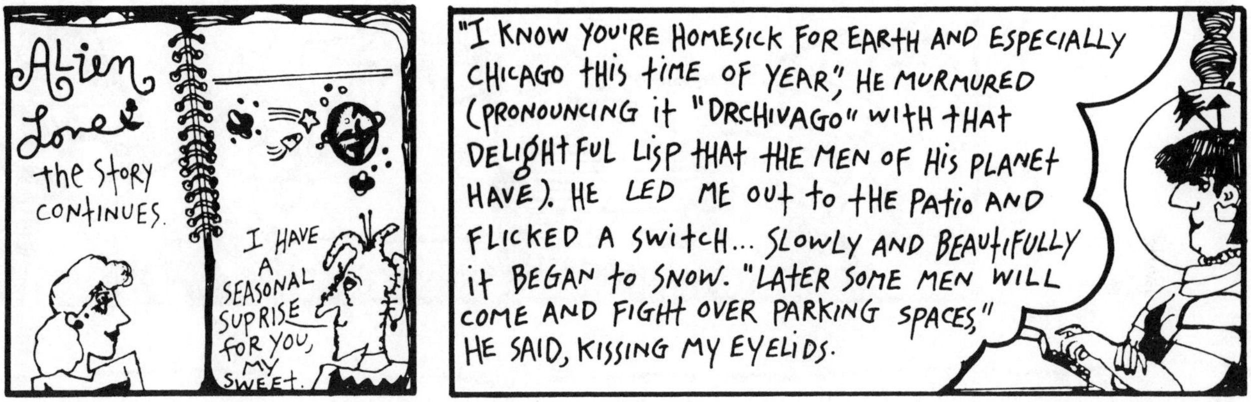
ALIEN LOVE the Story continues.
I HAVE A SEASONAL SUPRISE FOR YOU, MY SWEET.
"I KNOW YOU'RE HOMESICK FOR EARTH AND ESPECIALLY CHICAGO this time of YEAR," HE MURMURED (PRONOUNCING it "DR.CHIVAGO" with that DELIGHTFUL LISP that THE MEN OF HIS PLANET HAVE). HE LED ME out to the PATIO AND FLICKED A SWITCH... SLOWLY AND BEAUTIFULLY it BEGAN to SNOW. "LATER SOME MEN WILL COME AND FIGHT OVER PARKING SPACES," HE SAID, KISSING MY EYELIDS.

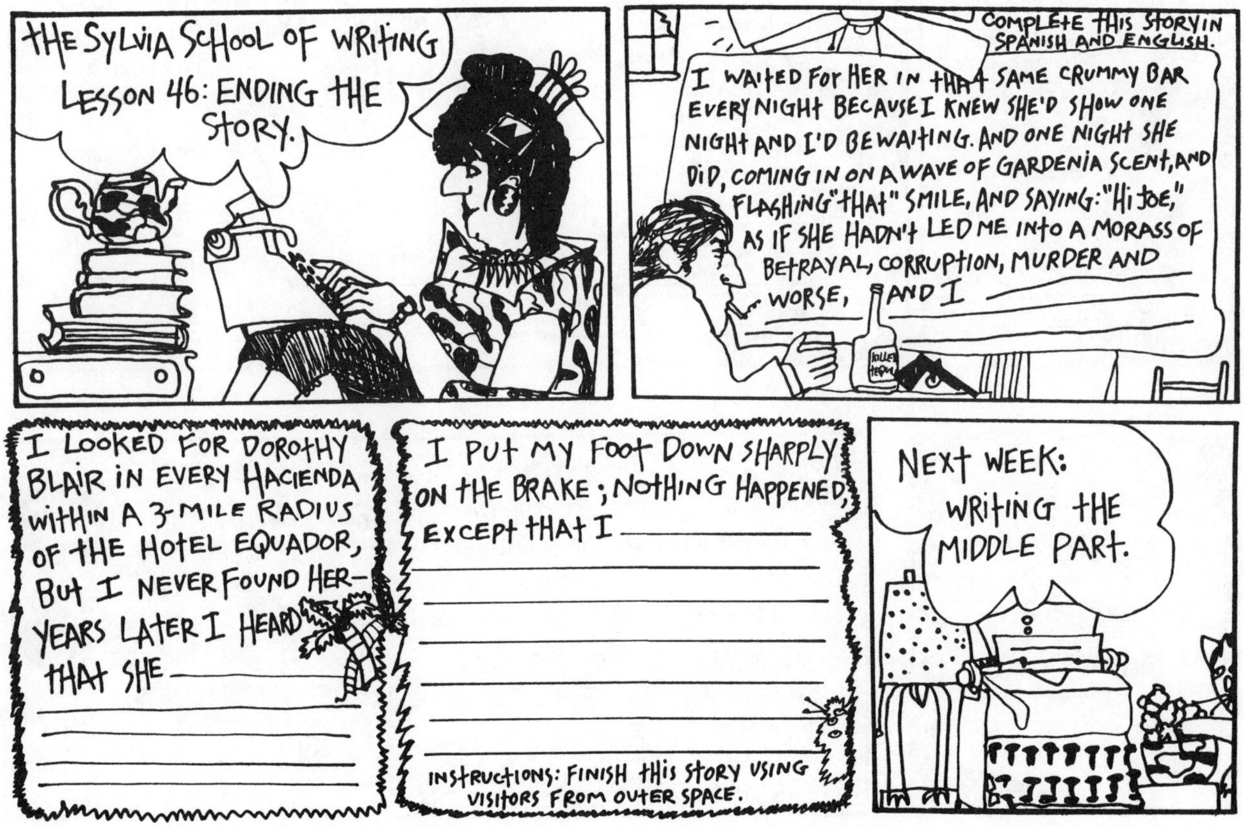
THE SYLVIA SCHOOL OF WRITING
LESSON 46: ENDING THE STORY.
COMPLETE THIS STORY IN SPANISH AND ENGLISH.
I WAITED FOR HER IN THAT SAME CRUMMY BAR EVERY NIGHT BECAUSE I KNEW SHE'D SHOW ONE NIGHT AND I'D BE WAITING. AND ONE NIGHT SHE DID, COMING IN ON A WAVE OF GARDENIA SCENT, AND FLASHING "THAT" SMILE, AND SAYING: "Hi Joe," AS IF SHE HADN'T LED ME INTO A MORASS OF BETRAYAL, CORRUPTION, MURDER AND WORSE, AND I
I LOOKED FOR DOROTHY BLAIR IN EVERY HACIENDA WITHIN A 3-MILE RADIUS OF THE HOTEL EQUADOR, BUT I NEVER FOUND HER—YEARS LATER I HEARD THAT SHE
I PUT MY FOOT DOWN SHARPLY ON THE BRAKE; NOTHING HAPPENED, EXCEPT THAT I
INSTRUCTIONS: FINISH THIS STORY USING VISITORS FROM OUTER SPACE.
NEXT WEEK: WRITING THE MIDDLE PART.

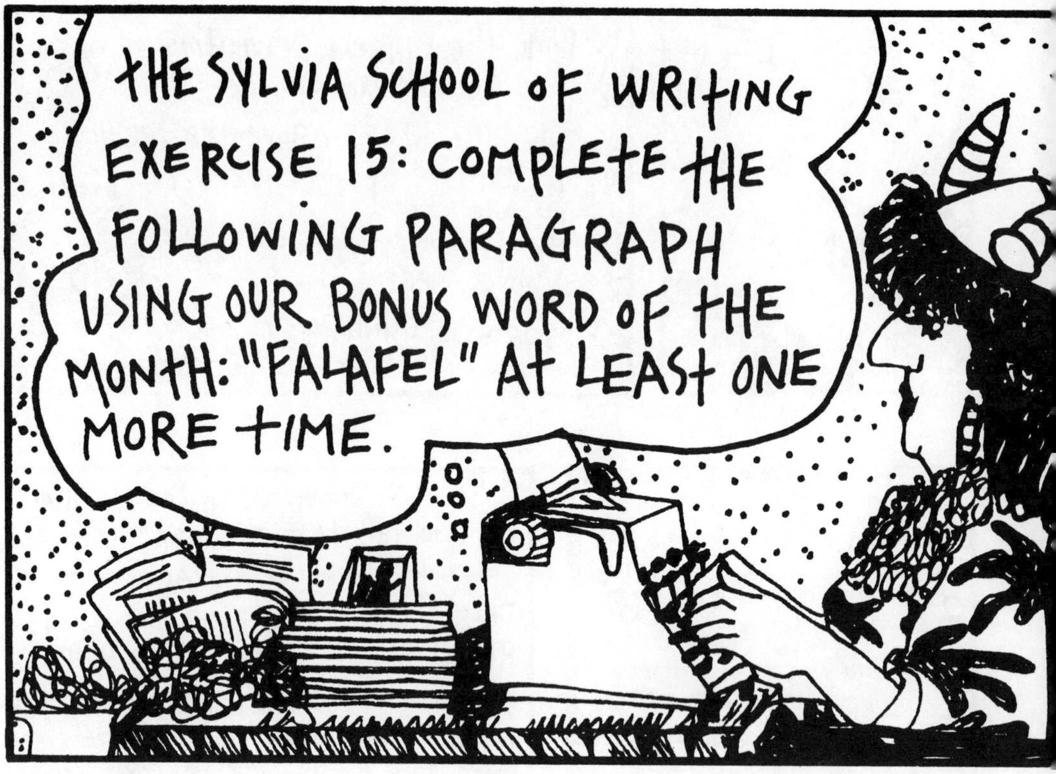
THE SYLVIA SCHOOL OF WRITING EXERCISE 15: COMPLETE THE FOLLOWING PARAGRAPH USING OUR BONUS WORD OF THE MONTH: "FALAFEL" AT LEAST ONE MORE TIME.

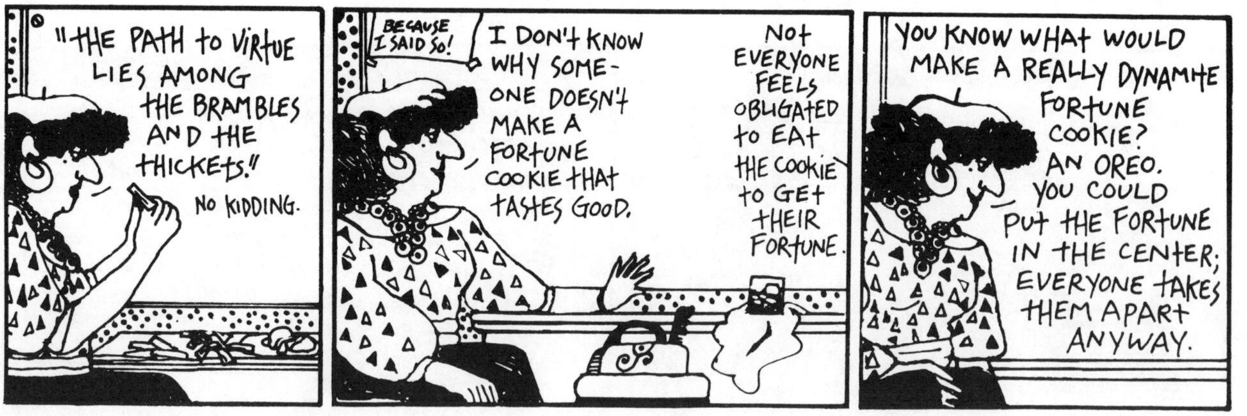
"THE PATH TO VIRTUE LIES AMONG THE BRAMBLES AND THE THICKETS."
NO KIDDING.
BECAUSE I SAID SO!
I DON'T KNOW WHY SOME-ONE DOESN'T MAKE A FORTUNE COOKIE THAT TASTES GOOD.
NOT EVERYONE FEELS OBLIGATED TO EAT THE COOKIE TO GET THEIR FORTUNE.
YOU KNOW WHAT WOULD MAKE A REALLY DYNAMITE FORTUNE COOKIE? AN OREO. YOU COULD PUT THE FORTUNE IN THE CENTER; EVERYONE TAKES THEM APART ANYWAY.

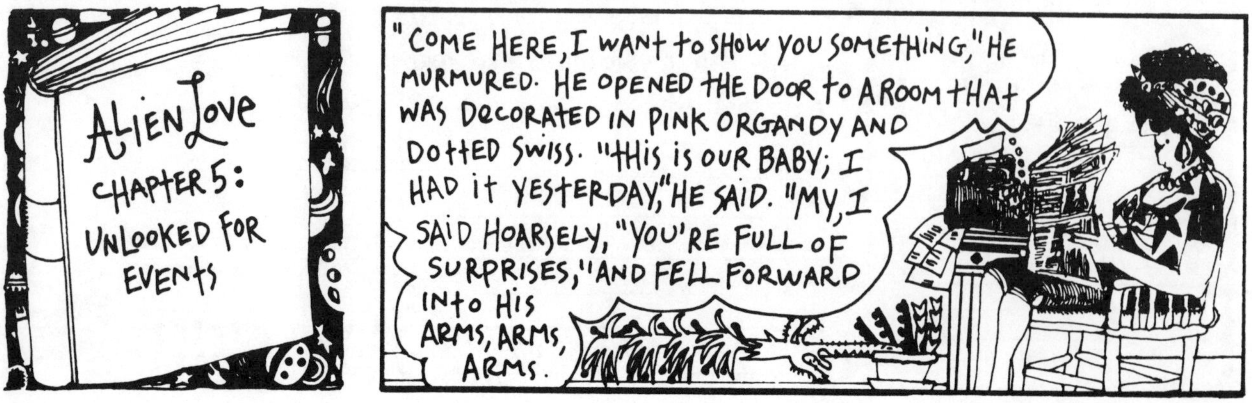
ALIEN LOVE
CHAPTER 5: UNLOOKED FOR EVENTS
"COME HERE, I WANT TO SHOW YOU SOMETHING," HE MURMURED. HE OPENED THE DOOR TO A ROOM THAT WAS DECORATED IN PINK ORGANDY AND DOTTED SWISS. "THIS IS OUR BABY; I HAD IT YESTERDAY," HE SAID. "MY," I SAID HOARSELY, "YOU'RE FULL OF SURPRISES," AND FELL FORWARD INTO HIS ARMS, ARMS, ARMS.

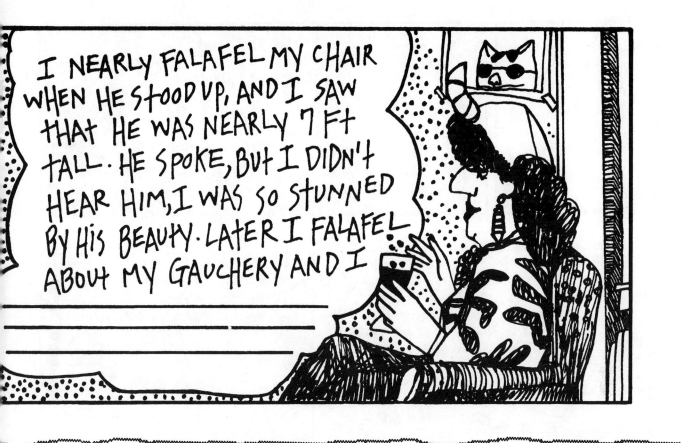

I NEARLY FALAFEL MY CHAIR WHEN HE STOOD UP, AND I SAW THAT HE WAS NEARLY 7 Ft TALL. HE SPOKE, BUT I DIDN't HEAR HIM, I WAS SO STUNNED By His BEAUty. LATER I FALAFEL ABOUT MY GAUCHERY AND I

THE MOTEL WAS A DIRTY PINK, CRAMPED AND FADED, LIKE A DWARF AMONG TALL TREES. I CLIMBED THE SCABROUS IRON STAIRCASE TO THE SECOND FLOOR. I WAS THERE TO MEET A CLIENT; I WAS LATE. I MOVED PAST DARK, DUSTY WINDOWS; WINDOWS LINED WITH FORGOTTEN FRUIT. FRUIT THAT ROTTED BEFORE IT RIPENED; VICTIM OF THE LACK OF LIGHT LIKE THE HUMAN ANTHROPOIDS THAT SHARED THEIR SPACE. *AND THEN I SAW HER. SHE STOOD IN THE SHADOWS, BUT EVEN IN THE SHADOWS SHE WAS SOMEHOW BOTH LIGHTER AND DARKER THAN HER SUR-ROUNDINGS.* THE NEON LIGHTS ON THE BOULEVARD BELOW FLICKERED AND DIED AS I REACHED OUT TO HER.

.......*BEFORE YOU LEAP*

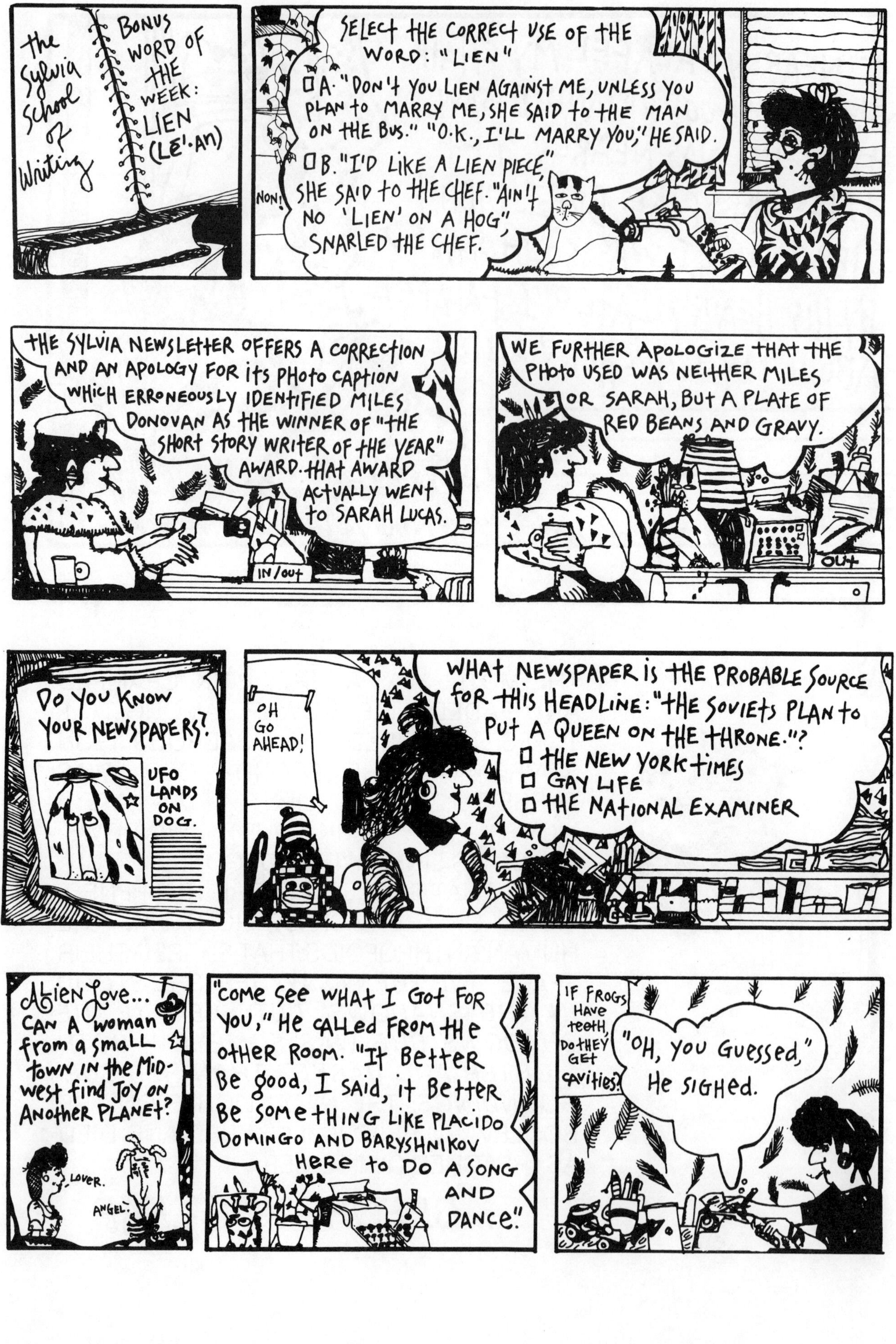

the Sylvia School of Writing
BONUS WORD OF THE WEEK: LIEN (LĒ'·AN)
SELECT THE CORRECT USE OF THE WORD: "LIEN"
☐ A. "DON'T YOU LIEN AGAINST ME, UNLESS YOU PLAN TO MARRY ME, SHE SAID TO THE MAN ON THE BUS." "O.K., I'LL MARRY YOU," HE SAID.
☐ B. "I'D LIKE A LIEN PIECE," SHE SAID TO THE CHEF. "AIN'T NO 'LIEN' ON A HOG," SNARLED THE CHEF.
NON!
THE SYLVIA NEWSLETTER OFFERS A CORRECTION AND AN APOLOGY FOR ITS PHOTO CAPTION WHICH ERRONEOUSLY IDENTIFIED MILES DONOVAN AS THE WINNER OF "THE SHORT STORY WRITER OF THE YEAR" AWARD. THAT AWARD ACTUALLY WENT TO SARAH LUCAS.
IN/OUT
WE FURTHER APOLOGIZE THAT THE PHOTO USED WAS NEITHER MILES OR SARAH, BUT A PLATE OF RED BEANS AND GRAVY.
OUT
DO YOU KNOW YOUR NEWSPAPERS?
UFO LANDS ON DOG.
OH GO AHEAD!
WHAT NEWSPAPER IS THE PROBABLE SOURCE FOR THIS HEADLINE: "THE SOVIETS PLAN TO PUT A QUEEN ON THE THRONE."?
☐ THE NEW YORK TIMES
☐ GAY LIFE
☐ THE NATIONAL EXAMINER
ALIEN LOVE... CAN A WOMAN FROM A SMALL TOWN IN THE MID-WEST FIND JOY ON ANOTHER PLANET?
LOVER.
ANGEL.
"COME SEE WHAT I GOT FOR YOU," HE CALLED FROM THE OTHER ROOM. "IT BETTER BE GOOD, I SAID, IT BETTER BE SOMETHING LIKE PLACIDO DOMINGO AND BARYSHNIKOV HERE TO DO A SONG AND DANCE."
IF FROGS HAVE TEETH, DO THEY GET CAVITIES?
"OH, YOU GUESSED," HE SIGHED.

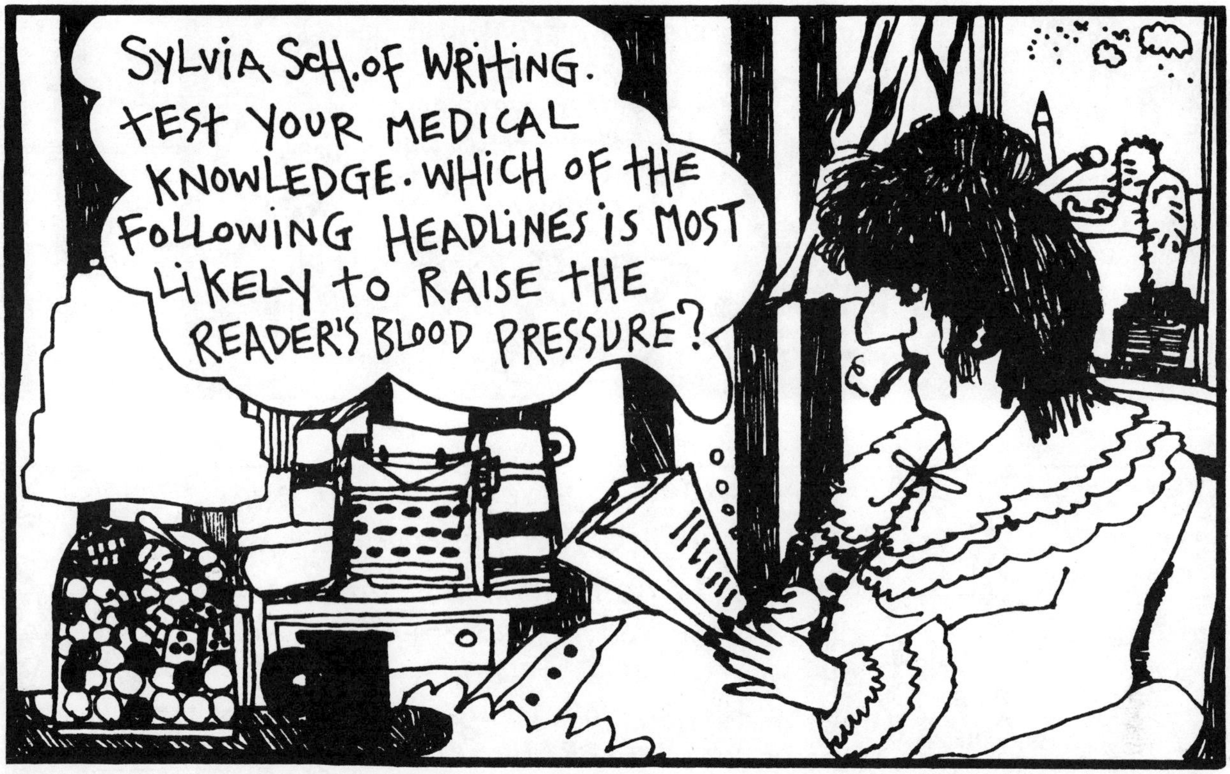
SYLVIA SCH. OF WRITING. TEST YOUR MEDICAL KNOWLEDGE. WHICH OF THE FOLLOWING HEADLINES IS MOST LIKELY TO RAISE THE READER'S BLOOD PRESSURE?

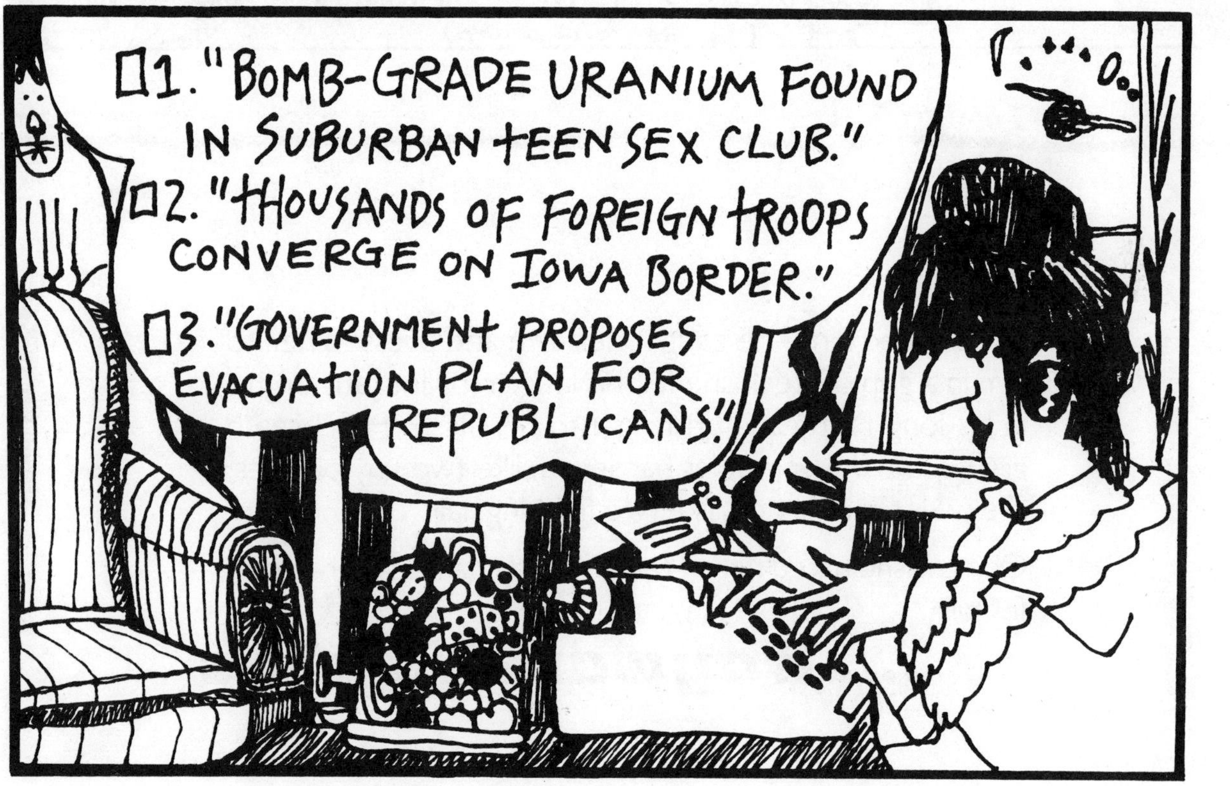
☐1. "BOMB-GRADE URANIUM FOUND IN SUBURBAN TEEN SEX CLUB."
☐2. "THOUSANDS OF FOREIGN TROOPS CONVERGE ON IOWA BORDER."
☐3. "GOVERNMENT PROPOSES EVACUATION PLAN FOR REPUBLICANS!"

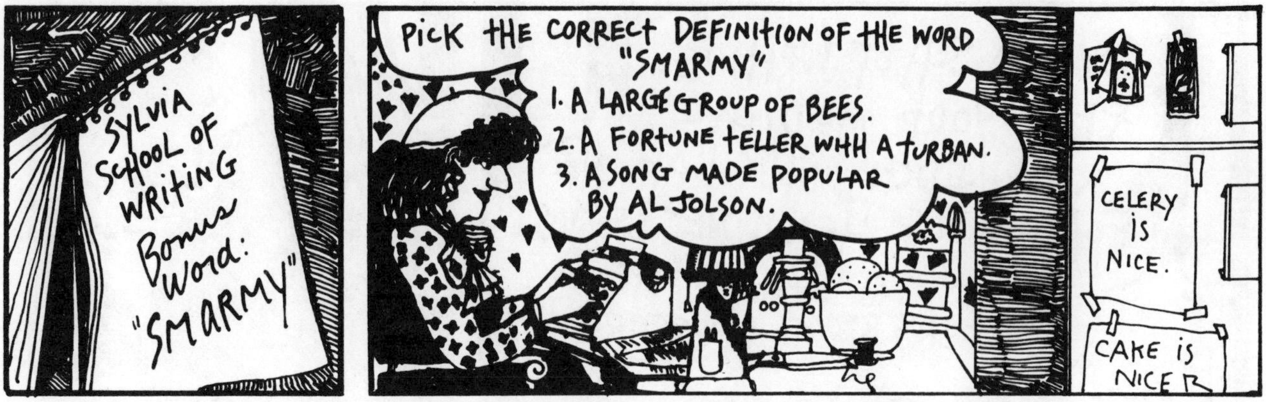
SYLVIA SCHOOL OF WRITING
Bonus Word:
"SMARMY"
PICK THE CORRECT DEFINITION OF THE WORD "SMARMY"
1. A LARGE GROUP OF BEES.
2. A FORTUNE TELLER WITH A TURBAN.
3. A SONG MADE POPULAR BY AL JOLSON.
CELERY IS NICE.
CAKE IS NICER

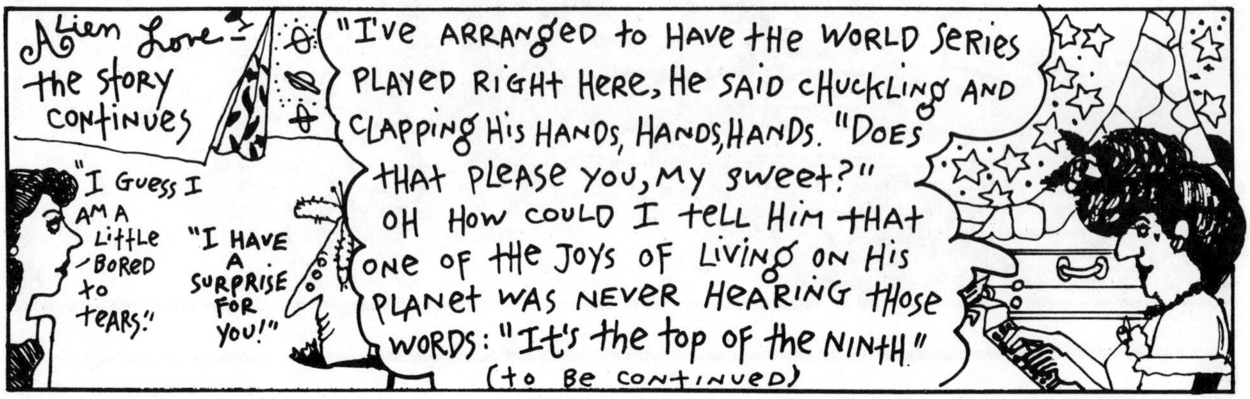
Alien Love— the story continues
"I'VE ARRANGED to HAVE THE WORLD SERIES PLAYED RIGHT HERE, HE SAID CHUCKLING AND CLAPPING HIS HANDS, HANDS, HANDS. "DOES THAT PLEASE YOU, MY SWEET?" OH HOW COULD I TELL HIM THAT ONE OF THE JOYS OF LIVING ON HIS PLANET WAS NEVER HEARING THOSE WORDS: "IT'S THE TOP OF THE NINTH."
(TO BE CONTINUED)
"I GUESS I AM A LITTLE BORED TO TEARS."
"I HAVE A SURPRISE FOR YOU!"

She slapped him—he caught her arm and pressed her to him in a grip of steel; she felt his long arrogant taut thighs in his long taut jeans burning into her flesh. Her breath grew shallow; her nipples hardened, like two tiny pebbles, like sweet hard candy, like two finishing nails.

Oh how she hated him—Yet her body flamed with desire for him.

.... Wayward Nipples

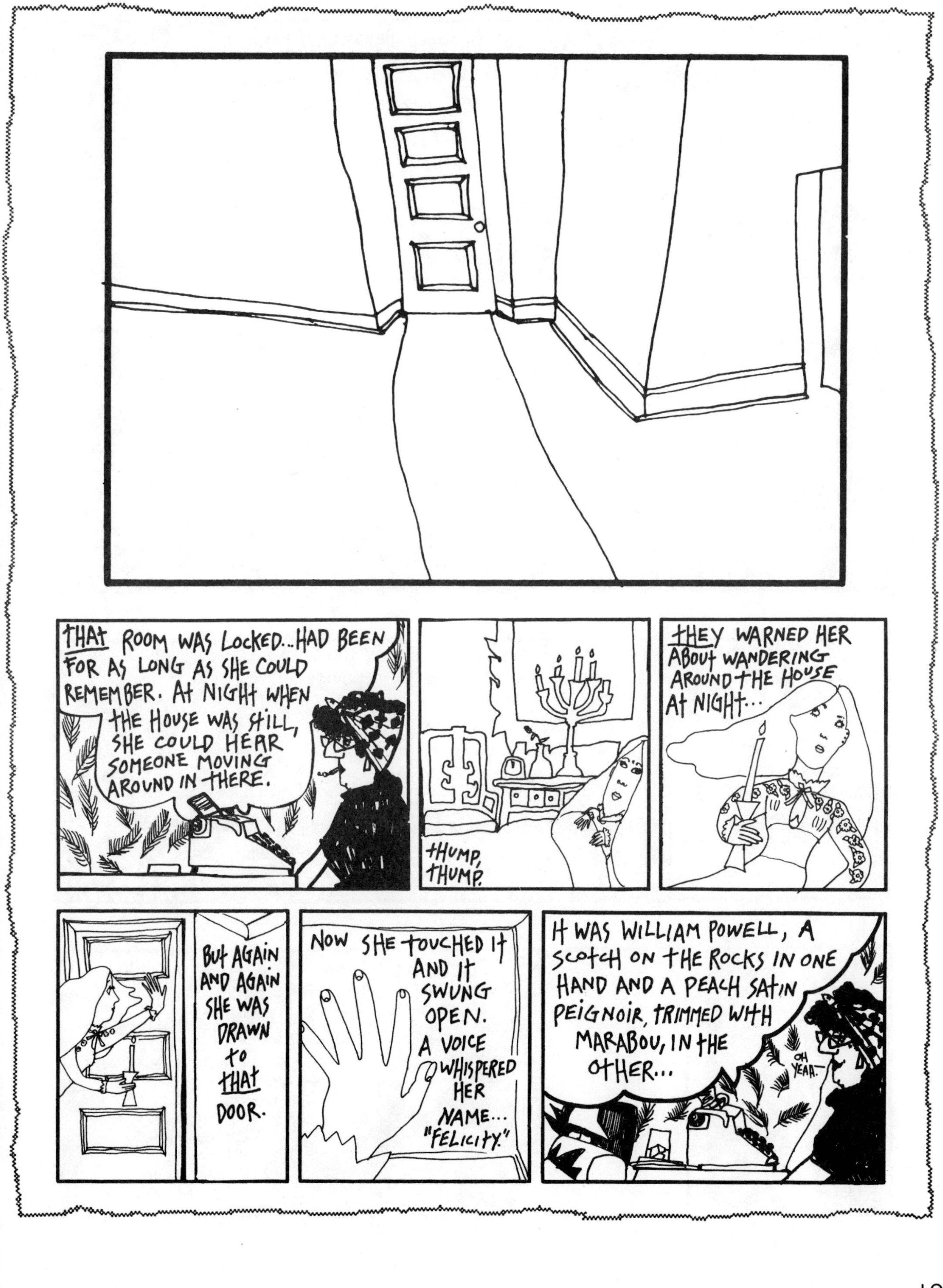
THAT ROOM WAS LOCKED...HAD BEEN FOR AS LONG AS SHE COULD REMEMBER. AT NIGHT WHEN THE HOUSE WAS STILL, SHE COULD HEAR SOMEONE MOVING AROUND IN THERE.
THUMP, THUMP.
THEY WARNED HER ABOUT WANDERING AROUND THE HOUSE AT NIGHT...
BUT AGAIN AND AGAIN SHE WAS DRAWN TO THAT DOOR.
NOW SHE TOUCHED IT AND IT SWUNG OPEN. A VOICE WHISPERED HER NAME... "FELICITY."
IT WAS WILLIAM POWELL, A SCOTCH ON THE ROCKS IN ONE HAND AND A PEACH SATIN PEIGNOIR, TRIMMED WITH MARABOU, IN THE OTHER...
OH YEAH.

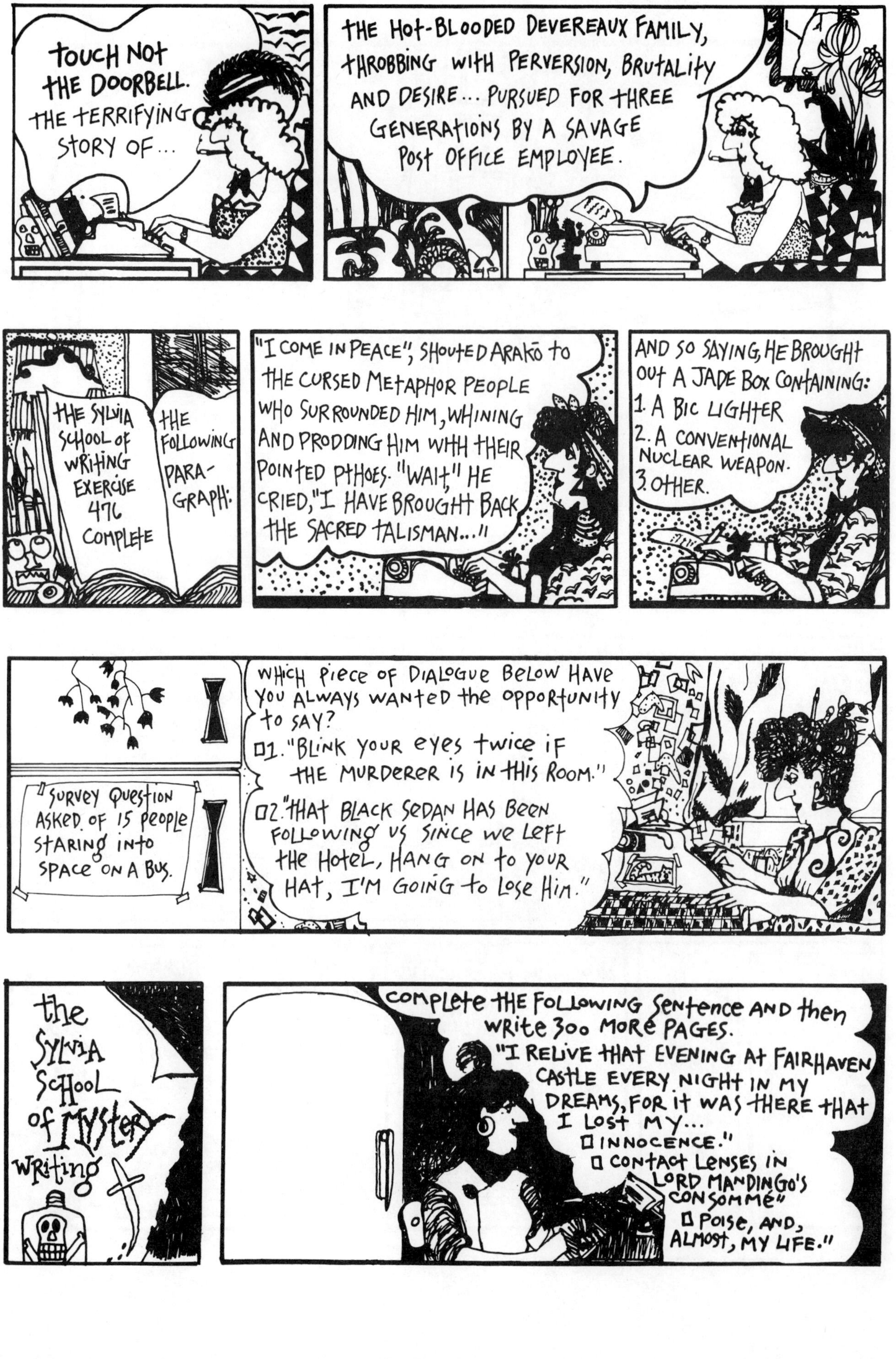
TOUCH NOT THE DOORBELL. THE TERRIFYING STORY OF...
THE HOT-BLOODED DEVEREAUX FAMILY, THROBBING WITH PERVERSION, BRUTALITY AND DESIRE... PURSUED FOR THREE GENERATIONS BY A SAVAGE POST OFFICE EMPLOYEE.
THE SYLVIA SCHOOL OF WRITING EXERCISE 476 COMPLETE
THE FOLLOWING PARA-GRAPH:
"I COME IN PEACE", SHOUTED ARAKŌ TO THE CURSED METAPHOR PEOPLE WHO SURROUNDED HIM, WHINING AND PRODDING HIM WITH THEIR POINTED PTHOES. "WAIT," HE CRIED, "I HAVE BROUGHT BACK THE SACRED TALISMAN..."
AND SO SAYING, HE BROUGHT OUT A JADE BOX CONTAINING:
1. A BIC LIGHTER
2. A CONVENTIONAL NUCLEAR WEAPON.
3. OTHER.
"SURVEY QUESTION ASKED OF 15 PEOPLE STARING INTO SPACE ON A BUS.
WHICH PIECE OF DIALOGUE BELOW HAVE YOU ALWAYS WANTED THE OPPORTUNITY TO SAY?
□1. "BLINK YOUR EYES TWICE IF THE MURDERER IS IN THIS ROOM."
□2. "THAT BLACK SEDAN HAS BEEN FOLLOWING US SINCE WE LEFT THE HOTEL, HANG ON TO YOUR HAT, I'M GOING TO LOSE HIM."
THE SYLVIA SCHOOL OF MYSTERY WRITING
COMPLETE THE FOLLOWING SENTENCE AND THEN WRITE 300 MORE PAGES.
"I RELIVE THAT EVENING AT FAIRHAVEN CASTLE EVERY NIGHT IN MY DREAMS, FOR IT WAS THERE THAT I LOST MY...
□ INNOCENCE."
□ CONTACT LENSES IN LORD MANDINGO'S CONSOMMÉ"
□ POISE, AND, ALMOST, MY LIFE."

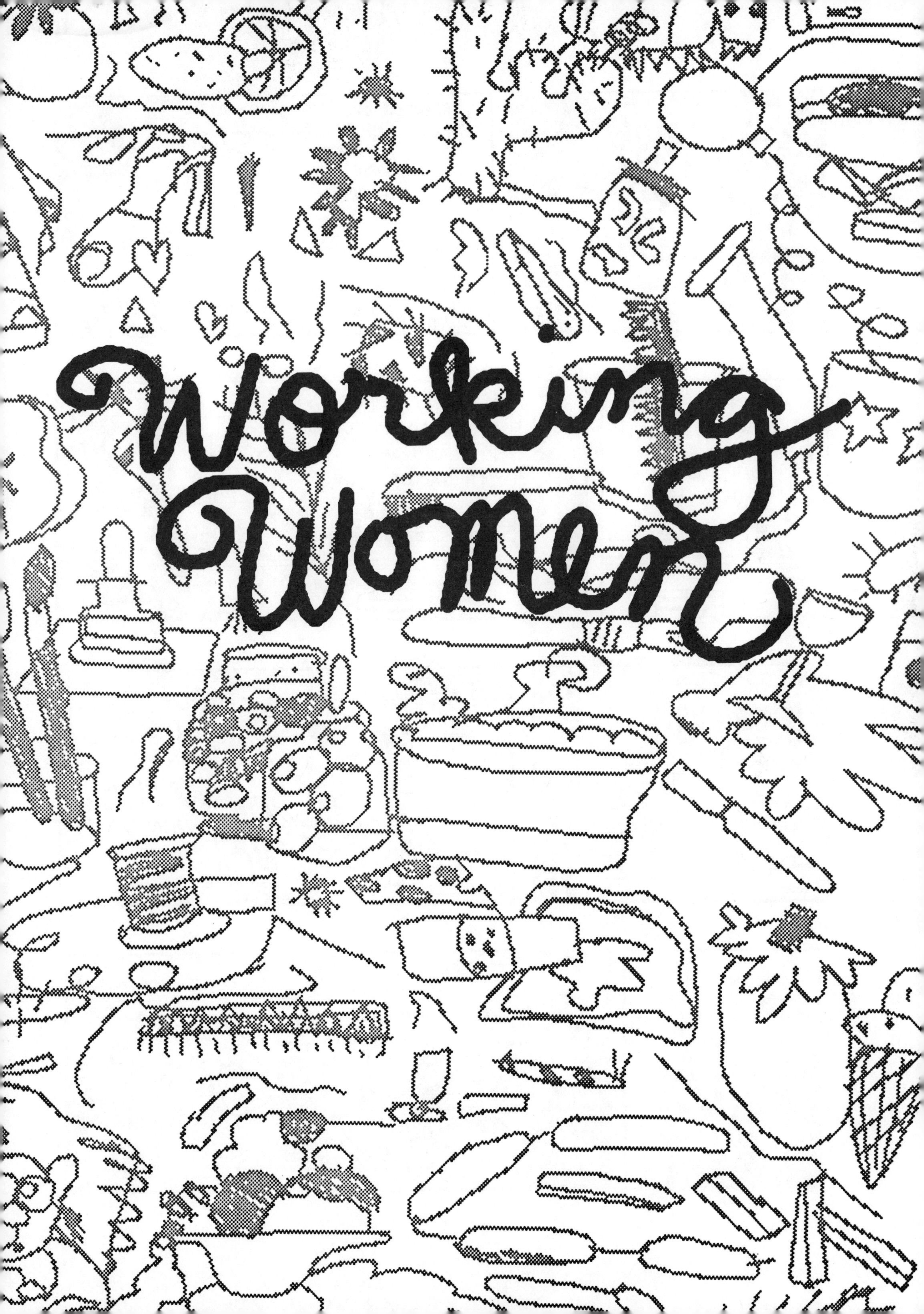
Working Women

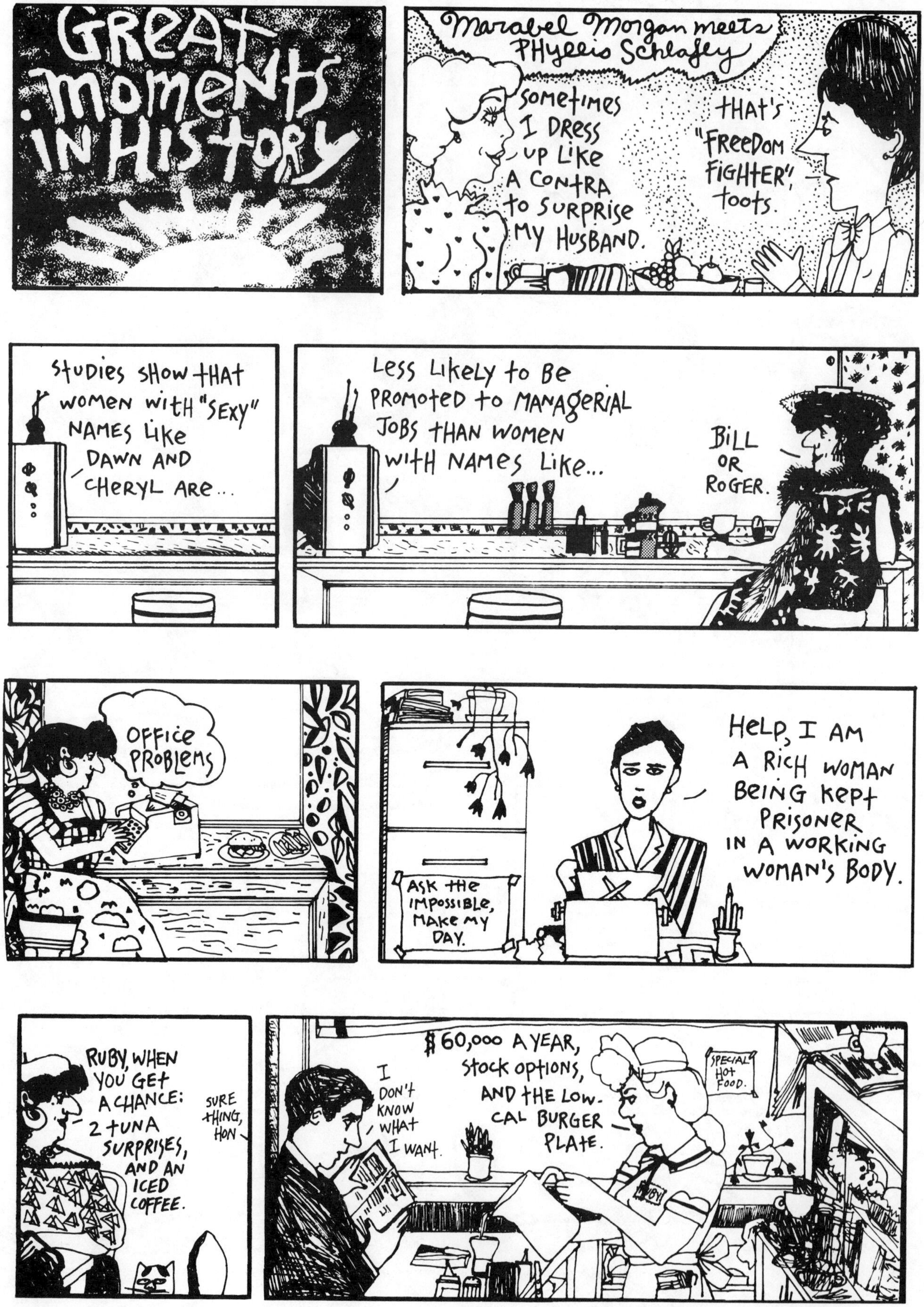
GREAT MOMENTS IN HISTORY
Marabel Morgan meets Phyllis Schlafly
SOMETIMES I DRESS UP LIKE A CONTRA TO SURPRISE MY HUSBAND.
THAT'S "FREEDOM FIGHTER", TOOTS.
STUDIES SHOW THAT WOMEN WITH "SEXY" NAMES LIKE DAWN AND CHERYL ARE...
LESS LIKELY TO BE PROMOTED TO MANAGERIAL JOBS THAN WOMEN WITH NAMES LIKE...
BILL OR ROGER.
OFFICE PROBLEMS
HELP, I AM A RICH WOMAN BEING KEPT PRISONER IN A WORKING WOMAN'S BODY.
ASK THE IMPOSSIBLE, MAKE MY DAY.
RUBY, WHEN YOU GET A CHANCE: 2 TUNA SURPRISES, AND AN ICED COFFEE.
SURE THING, HON
I DON'T KNOW WHAT I WANT.
$60,000 A YEAR, STOCK OPTIONS, AND THE LOW-CAL BURGER PLATE.
SPECIAL HOT FOOD.
RUBY

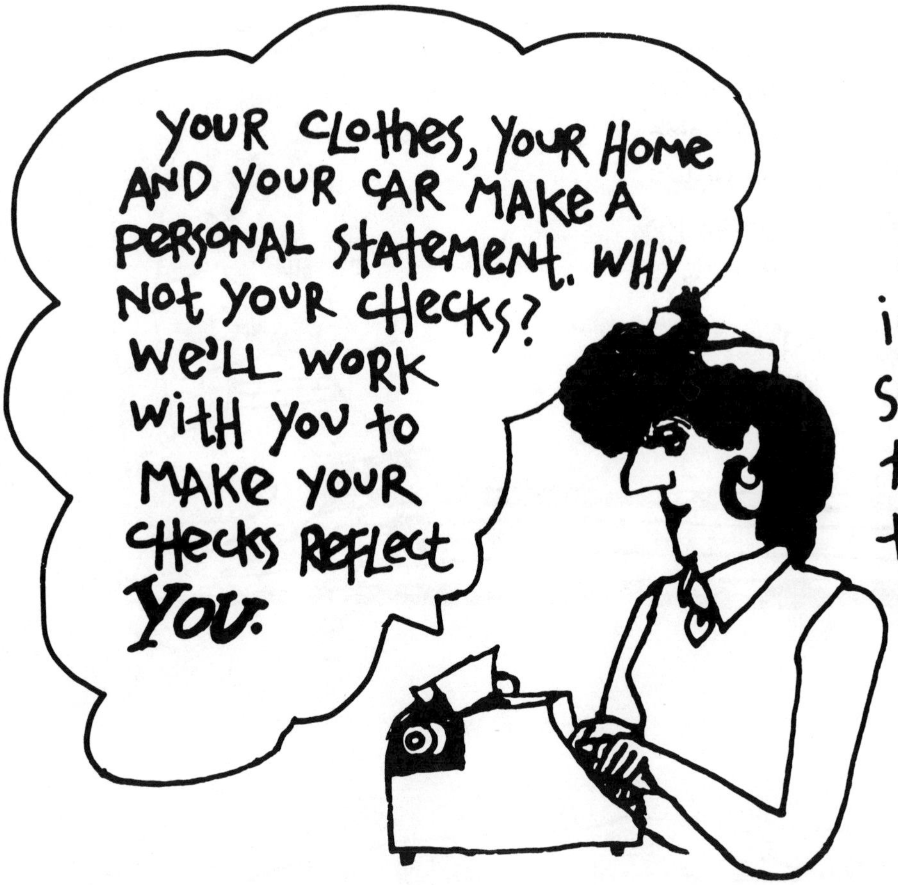
YOUR CLOTHES, YOUR HOME AND YOUR CAR MAKE A PERSONAL STATEMENT. WHY NOT YOUR CHECKS? WE'LL WORK WITH YOU TO MAKE YOUR CHECKS REFLECT **YOU.**

A SAMPLE CHECK FOR PEOPLE WHO FEEL **MONEY** IS TAKEN TOO SERIOUSLY. IT'S FOR THOSE WHO WANT THEIR MORE WHIMSICAL RELATIONSHIP TO MONEY REFLECTED IN THEIR CHECKS.

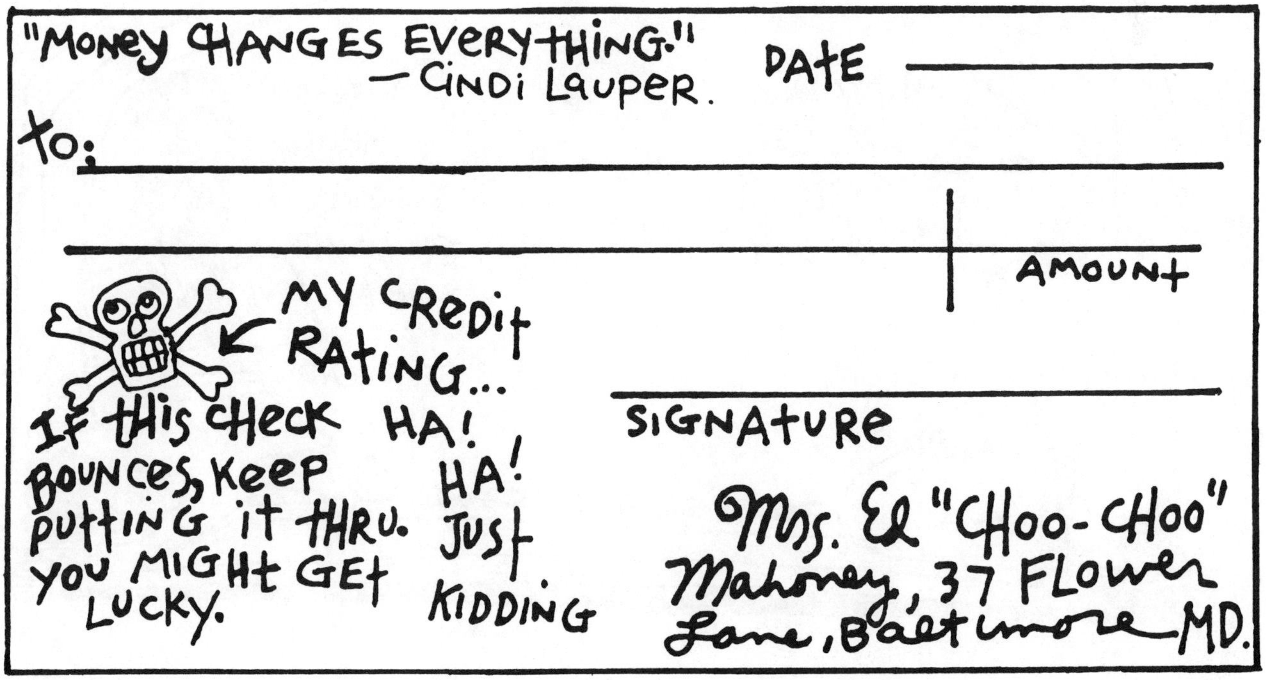
"MONEY CHANGES EVERYTHING."
—CINDI LAUPER.
DATE
TO:
AMOUNT
MY CREDIT RATING...
IF THIS CHECK BOUNCES, KEEP PUTTING IT THRU. YOU MIGHT GET LUCKY.
HA! HA! JUST KIDDING
SIGNATURE
Mrs. Ed "Choo-Choo" Mahoney, 37 Flower Lane, Baltimore MD.

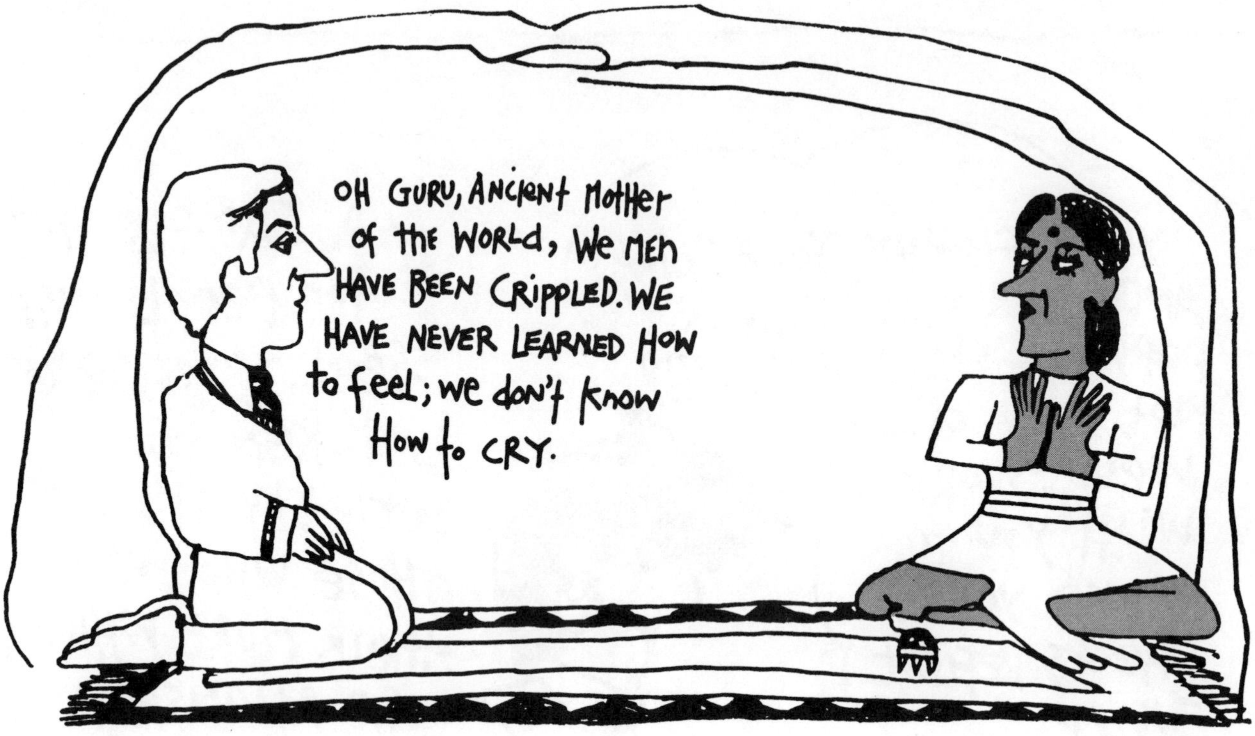
OH GURU, ANCIENT MOTHER OF THE WORLD, WE MEN HAVE BEEN CRIPPLED. WE HAVE NEVER LEARNED HOW TO FEEL; WE DON'T KNOW HOW TO CRY.

1.

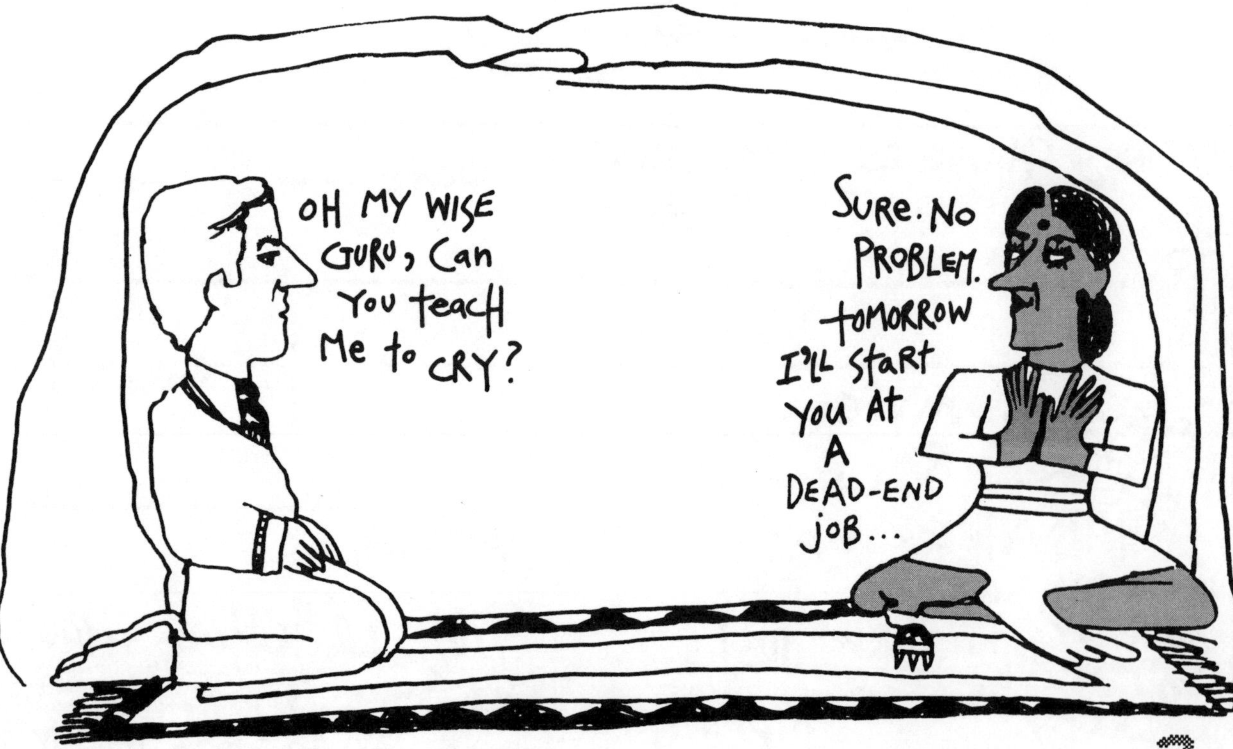
OH MY WISE GURU, CAN YOU TEACH ME TO CRY?
SURE. NO PROBLEM. TOMORROW I'LL START YOU AT A DEAD-END JOB...

2.

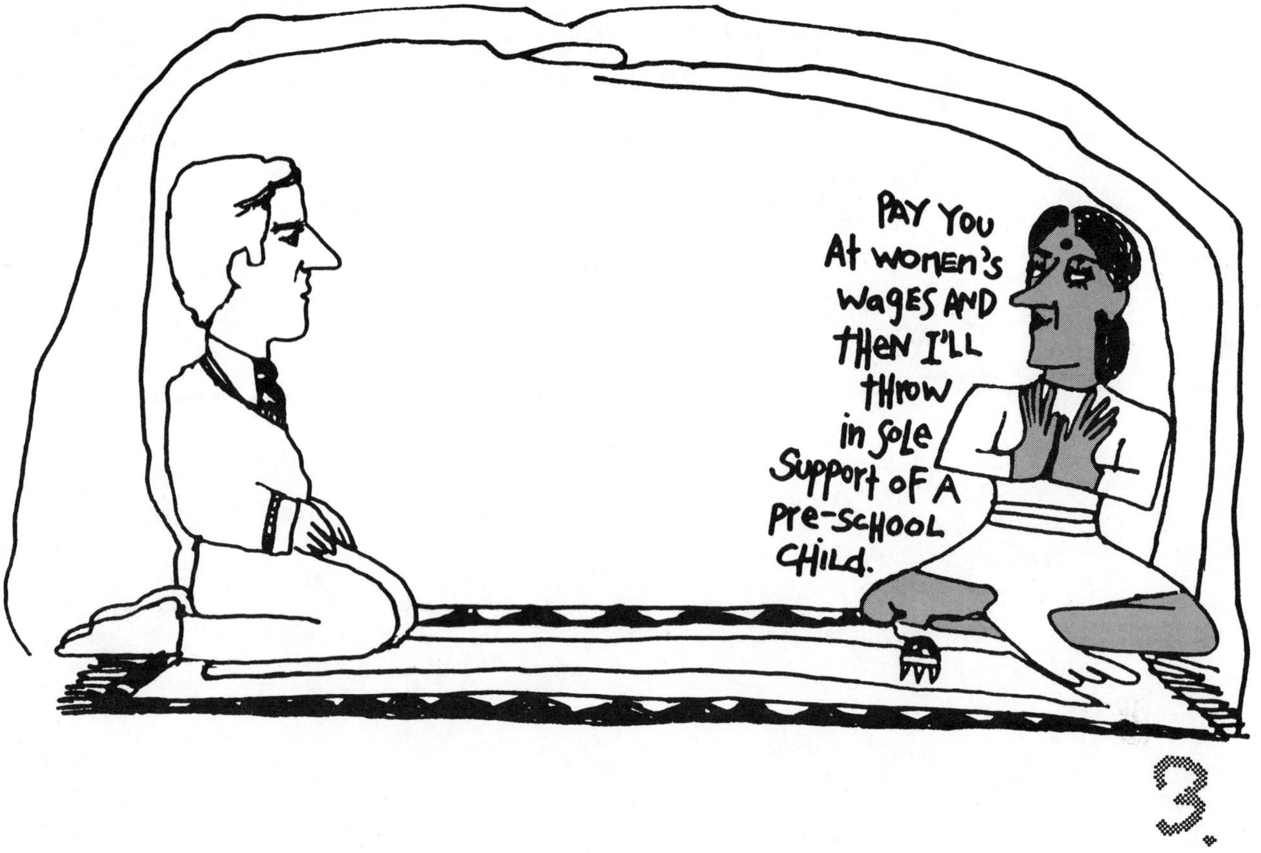
PAY YOU AT WOMEN'S WAGES AND THEN I'LL THROW IN SOLE SUPPORT OF A PRE-SCHOOL CHILD.
3.

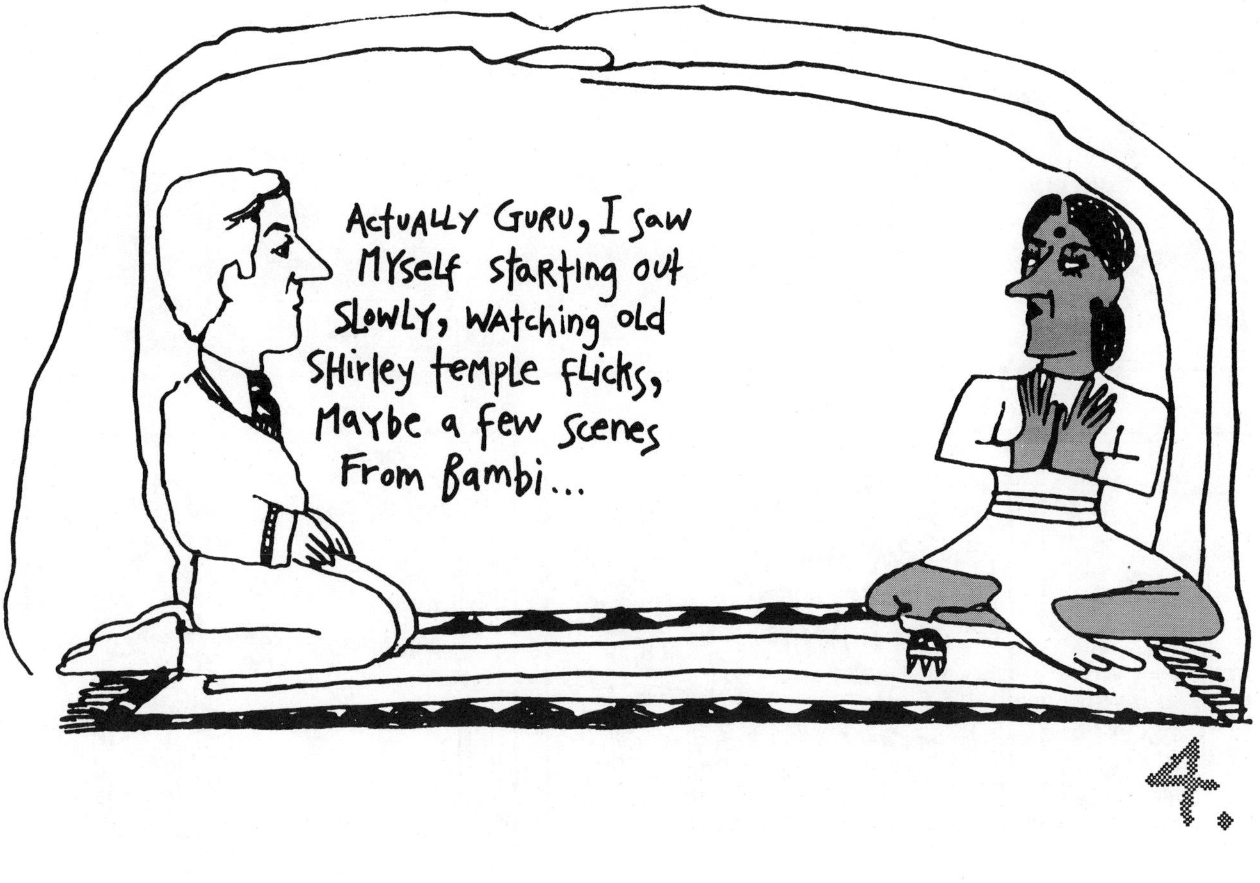
ACTUALLY GURU, I SAW MYSELF STARTING OUT SLOWLY, WATCHING OLD SHIRLEY TEMPLE FLICKS, MAYBE A FEW SCENES FROM BAMBI...
4.

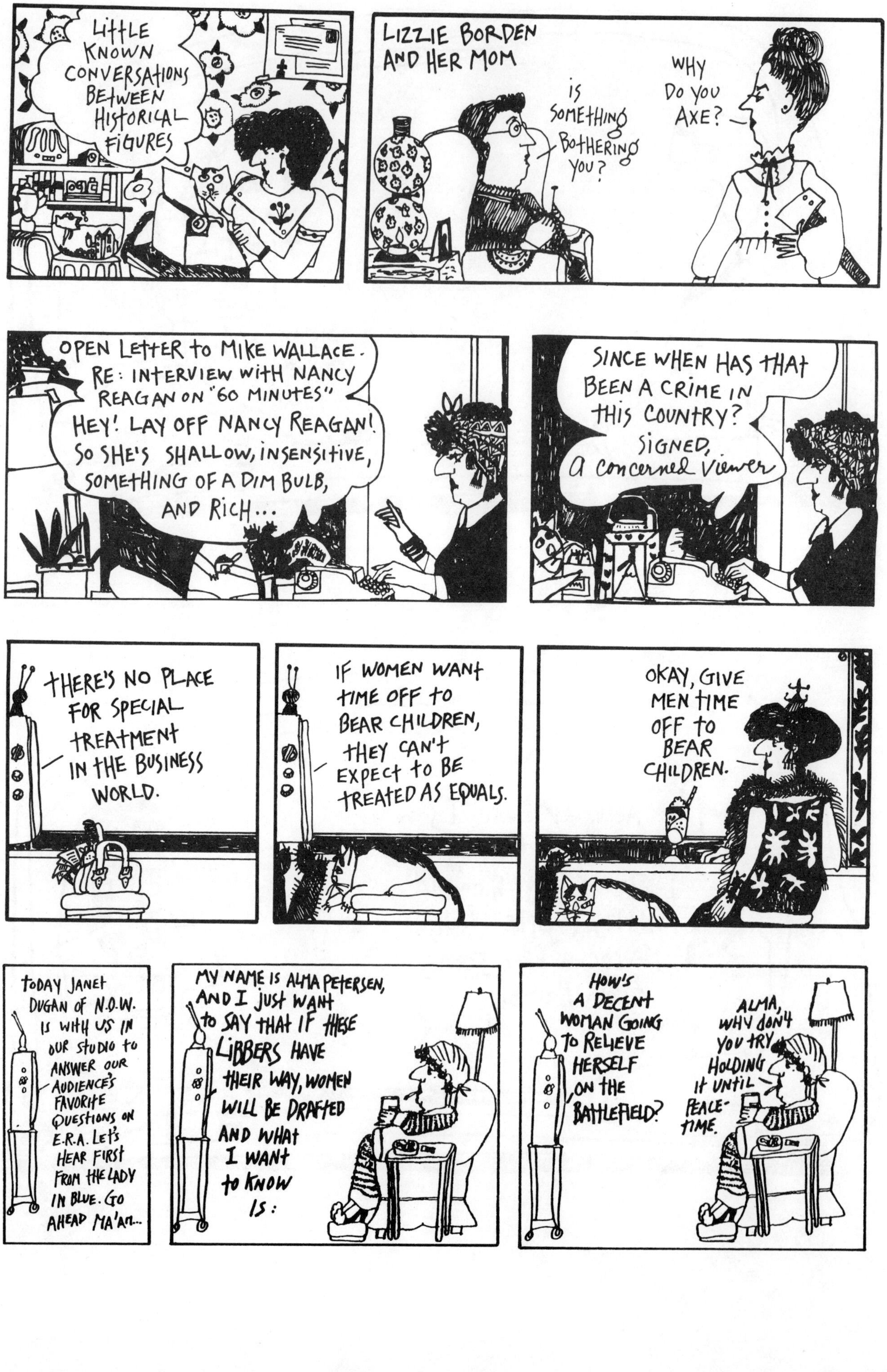
Little Known Conversations Between Historical Figures
LIZZIE BORDEN AND HER MOM
is something bothering you?
WHY DO YOU AXE?
OPEN LETTER to MIKE WALLACE. RE: INTERVIEW WITH NANCY REAGAN ON "60 MINUTES"
HEY! LAY OFF NANCY REAGAN! SO SHE'S SHALLOW, INSENSITIVE, SOMETHING OF A DIM BULB, AND RICH...
SINCE WHEN HAS THAT BEEN A CRIME IN THIS COUNTRY?
SIGNED, a concerned viewer
THERE'S NO PLACE FOR SPECIAL TREATMENT IN THE BUSINESS WORLD.
IF WOMEN WANT TIME OFF TO BEAR CHILDREN, THEY CAN'T EXPECT TO BE TREATED AS EQUALS.
OKAY, GIVE MEN TIME OFF TO BEAR CHILDREN.
TODAY JANET DUGAN OF N.O.W. IS WITH US IN OUR STUDIO TO ANSWER OUR AUDIENCE'S FAVORITE QUESTIONS ON E.R.A. LET'S HEAR FIRST FROM THE LADY IN BLUE. GO AHEAD MA'AM...
MY NAME IS ALMA PETERSEN, AND I JUST WANT TO SAY THAT IF THESE LIBBERS HAVE THEIR WAY, WOMEN WILL BE DRAFTED AND WHAT I WANT TO KNOW IS:
HOW'S A DECENT WOMAN GOING TO RELIEVE HERSELF ON THE BATTLEFIELD?
ALMA, WHY DON'T YOU TRY HOLDING IT UNTIL PEACE-TIME.

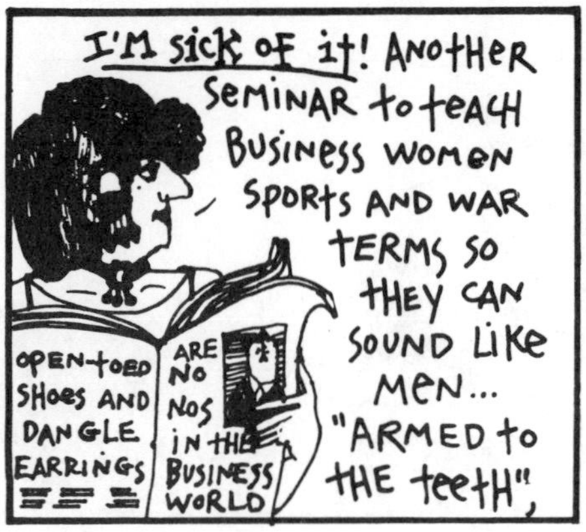
I'M SICK OF IT! ANOTHER SEMINAR TO TEACH BUSINESS WOMEN SPORTS AND WAR TERMS SO THEY CAN SOUND LIKE MEN... "ARMED TO THE TEETH",
OPEN-TOED SHOES AND DANGLE EARRINGS
ARE NO NOS IN THE BUSINESS WORLD

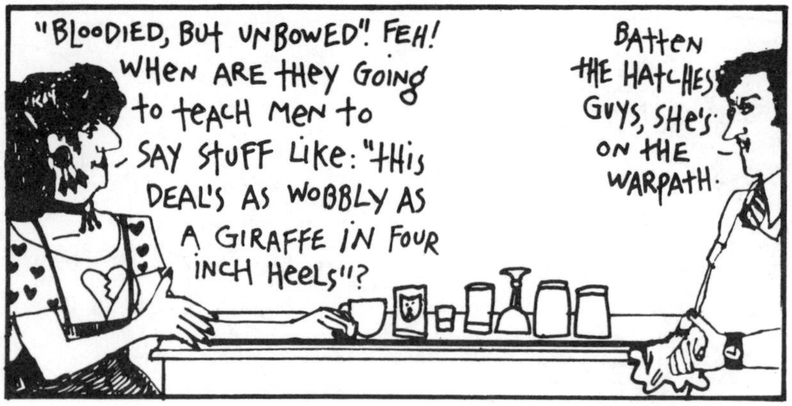
"BLOODIED, BUT UNBOWED". FEH! WHEN ARE THEY GOING TO TEACH MEN TO SAY STUFF LIKE: "THIS DEAL'S AS WOBBLY AS A GIRAFFE IN FOUR INCH HEELS"?
BATTEN THE HATCHES GUYS, SHE'S ON THE WARPATH.

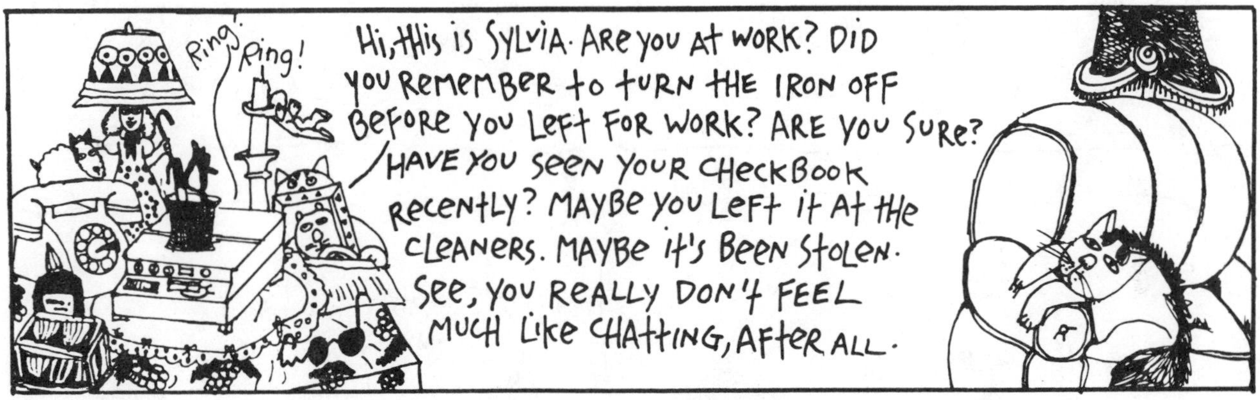
Ring! Ring!
Hi, this is Sylvia. Are you at work? Did you remember to turn the iron off before you left for work? Are you sure? Have you seen your checkbook recently? Maybe you left it at the cleaners. Maybe it's been stolen. See, you really don't feel much like chatting, after all.

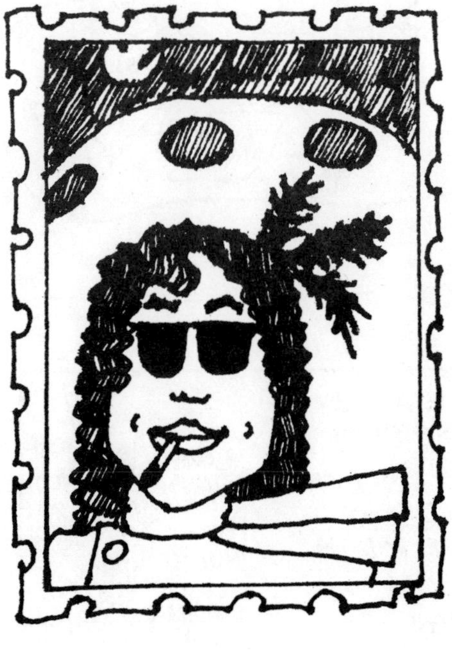

Commemorative Stamp
Ella Sue Whitney
First Woman to Smoke Dope on the Moon.

When asked if she felt the women's movement had anything to do with being honored with a commemorative stamp, Ms. Whitney replied: "Certainly not, I had the qualifications and I worked like hell for the distinction."

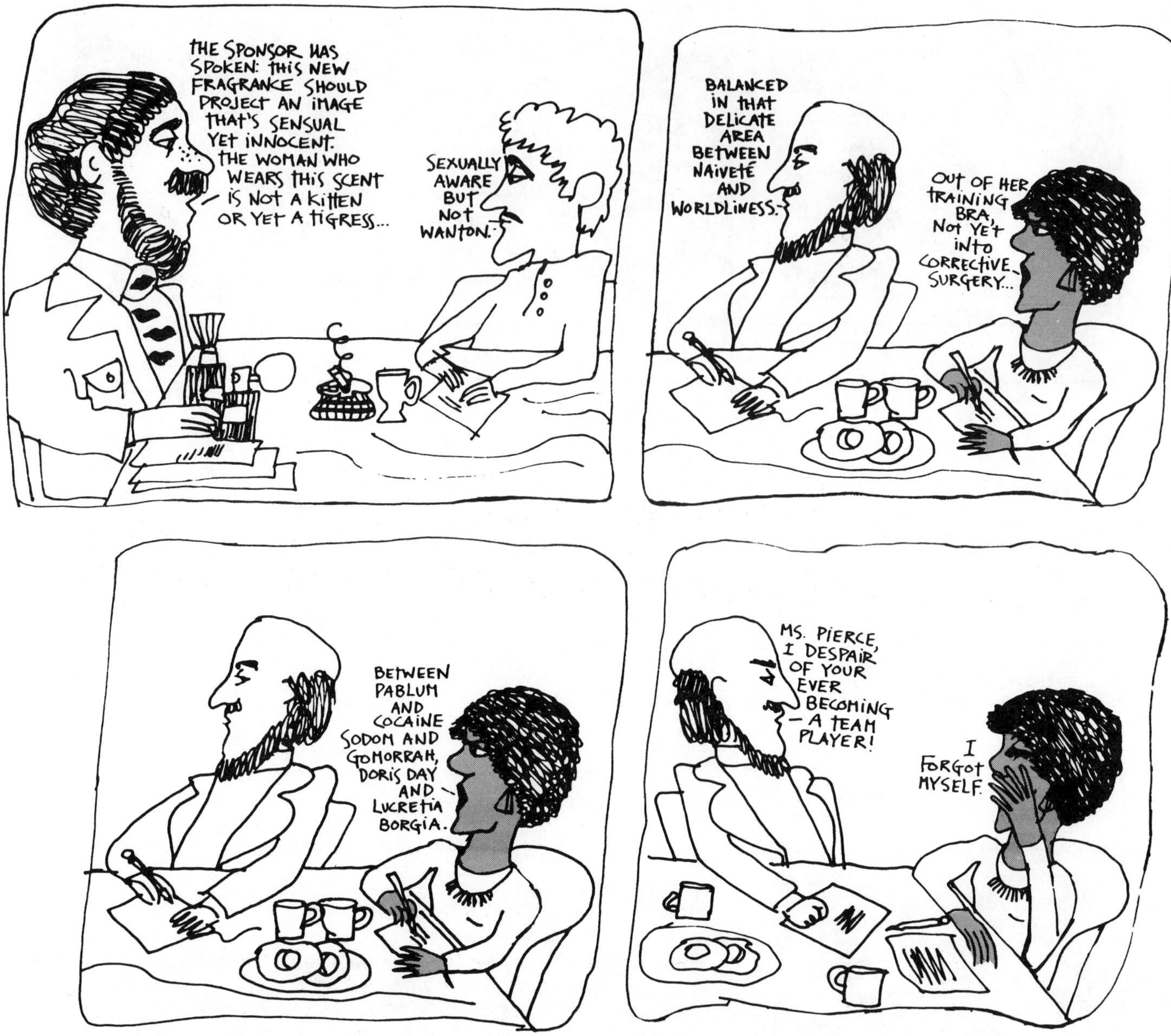
THE SPONSOR HAS SPOKEN: THIS NEW FRAGRANCE SHOULD PROJECT AN IMAGE THAT'S SENSUAL YET INNOCENT. THE WOMAN WHO WEARS THIS SCENT IS NOT A KITTEN OR YET A TIGRESS...
SEXUALLY AWARE BUT NOT WANTON.
BALANCED IN THAT DELICATE AREA BETWEEN NAIVETÉ AND WORLDLINESS.
OUT OF HER TRAINING BRA, NOT YET INTO CORRECTIVE SURGERY...
BETWEEN PABLUM AND COCAINE SODOM AND GOMORRAH, DORIS DAY AND LUCRETIA BORGIA.
MS. PIERCE, I DESPAIR OF YOUR EVER BECOMING A TEAM PLAYER!
I FORGOT MYSELF.

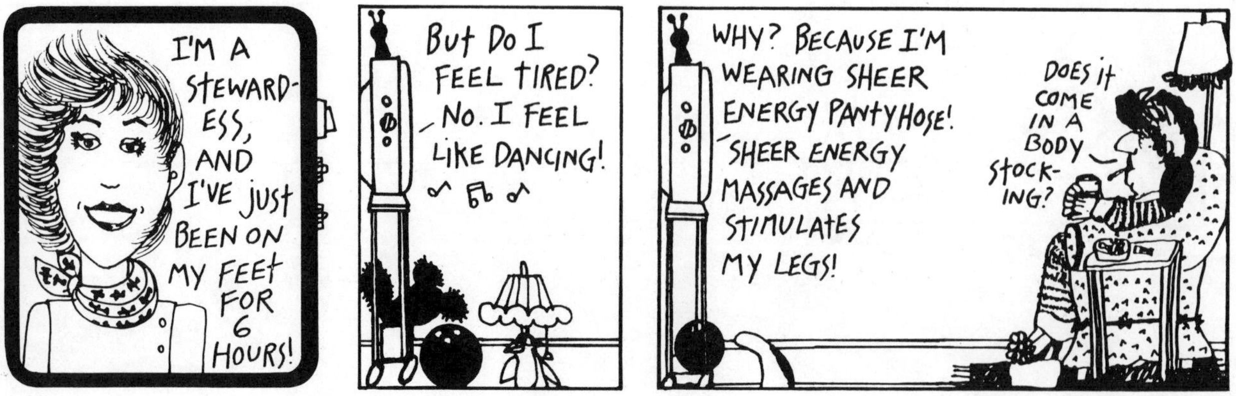
I'M A STEWARDESS, AND I'VE JUST BEEN ON MY FEET FOR 6 HOURS!
BUT DO I FEEL TIRED? NO. I FEEL LIKE DANCING!
WHY? BECAUSE I'M WEARING SHEER ENERGY PANTYHOSE! SHEER ENERGY MASSAGES AND STIMULATES MY LEGS!
DOES IT COME IN A BODY STOCKING?

OKAY. I KNOW YOU'RE GOING to FIND THIS HARD to Believe, But I've Been up FOR HOURS. I WASHED the FLOOR, I wrote 2 CHAPTERS OF MY NOVEL...

RUBY
MENU
WHAT'S GOOD?

PUPPIES, LITTLE CHILDREN LAUGHING, OLD MOVIES, WALKING IN THE RAIN...
CABBAGE À L'ORANGE TODAY.
I'M PROBABLY SAFE WITH THE GRILLED CHEESE.
MENU

SYLVIA SEMINARS
SEPT 22 - RUDENESS
DON'T!
WOMEN! HAVE YOU LOST THE ABILITY TO LOOK TOTALLY ABSORBED IN SOME MAN'S CONVERSATION? DO YOUR EYES WANDER? CONTACT THE SYLVIA SCHOOL FOR TOTAL LISTENING, BEFORE IT'S TOO LATE. THROUGH A COMBINATION OF SELF-HYPNOSIS AND OLD MARILYN MONROE MOVIES, WE'LL HAVE YOU WIDE-EYED AND SLACK-JAWED IN NO TIME.

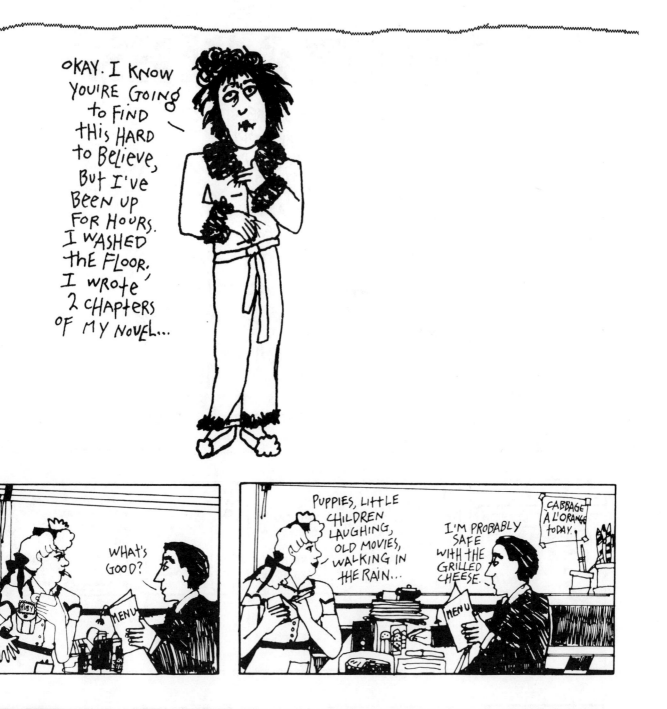

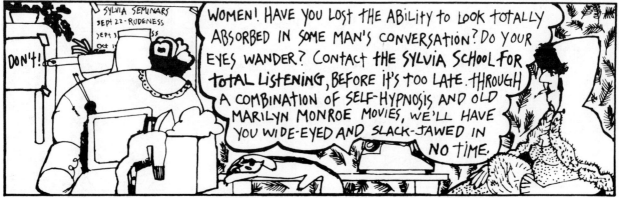

FANTASIES

WOMEN WILL SHAKE OFF THE INFLUENCE OF GODLESS COMMUNISM AND RETURN TO THEIR FIRST DUTY AS WIVES AND MOTHERS EARLY NEXT YEAR.

I'M 28 YEARS OLD... I'M PRETTY INDEPENDENT,

AND A LITTLE UNCONVENTIONAL IN MY DRESS.

I BET YOU CAN'T BELIEVE A WOMAN LIKE ME USES KOTEX.

I BET YOUR MOTHER CAN'T BELIEVE YOU DID THIS COMMERCIAL.

TODAY, THE PRESIDENT ANGRILY REJECTED STATISTICS SHOWING THAT IN 75% OF MIDDLE INCOME FAMILIES BOTH HUSBANDS AND WIVES WORK. HIS VOICE SHAKING WITH EMOTION, HE ASKED: "DOES NANCY WORK? DOES MISS ELLIE WORK? DID THE BEAVER'S MOTHER WORK?"

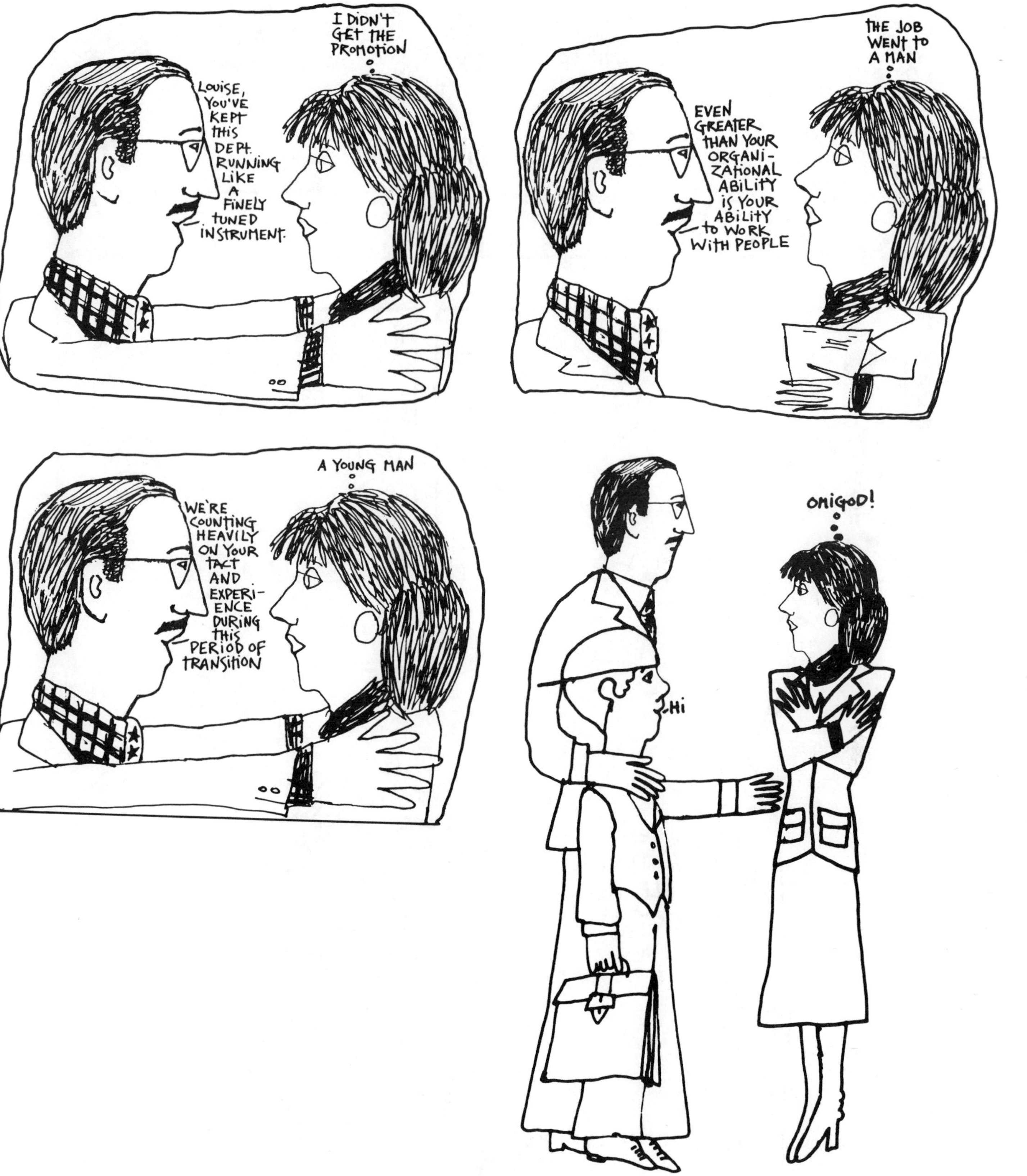
I DIDN'T GET THE PROMOTION
LOUISE, YOU'VE KEPT THIS DEPT. RUNNING LIKE A FINELY TUNED INSTRUMENT.
THE JOB WENT TO A MAN
EVEN GREATER THAN YOUR ORGANI-ZATIONAL ABILITY IS YOUR ABILITY TO WORK WITH PEOPLE
A YOUNG MAN
WE'RE COUNTING HEAVILY ON YOUR TACT AND EXPERI-ENCE DURING THIS PERIOD OF TRANSITION
HI
OMIGOD!

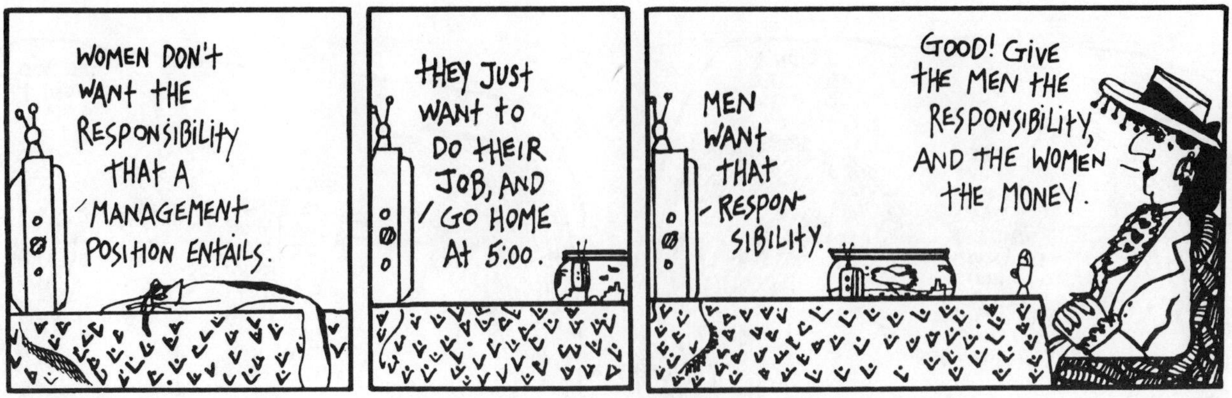
WOMEN DON'T WANT THE RESPONSIBILITY THAT A MANAGEMENT POSITION ENTAILS.
THEY JUST WANT TO DO THEIR JOB, AND GO HOME AT 5:00.
MEN WANT THAT RESPONSIBILITY.
GOOD! GIVE THE MEN THE RESPONSIBILITY, AND THE WOMEN THE MONEY.

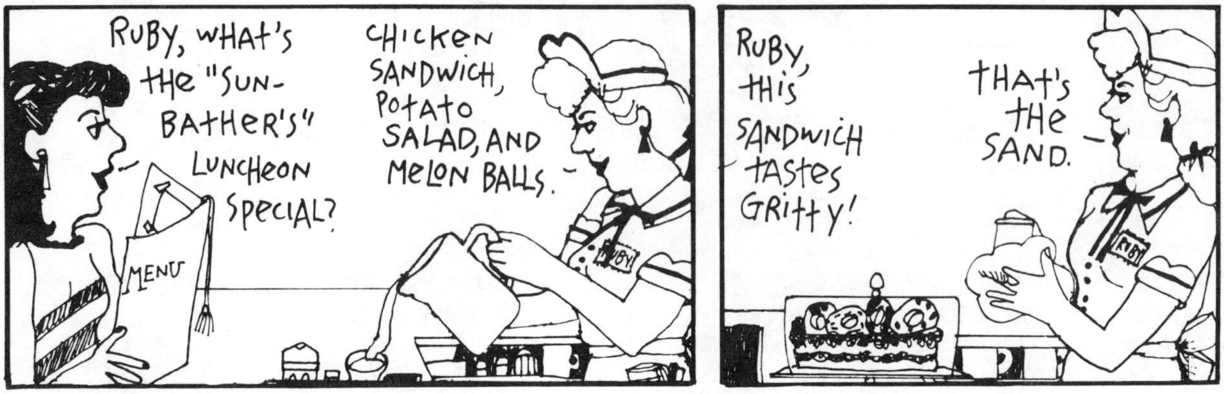
RUBY, WHAT'S THE "SUN-BATHER'S" LUNCHEON SPECIAL?
MENU
CHICKEN SANDWICH, POTATO SALAD, AND MELON BALLS.
RUBY
RUBY, THIS SANDWICH TASTES GRITTY!
THAT'S THE SAND.
RUBY

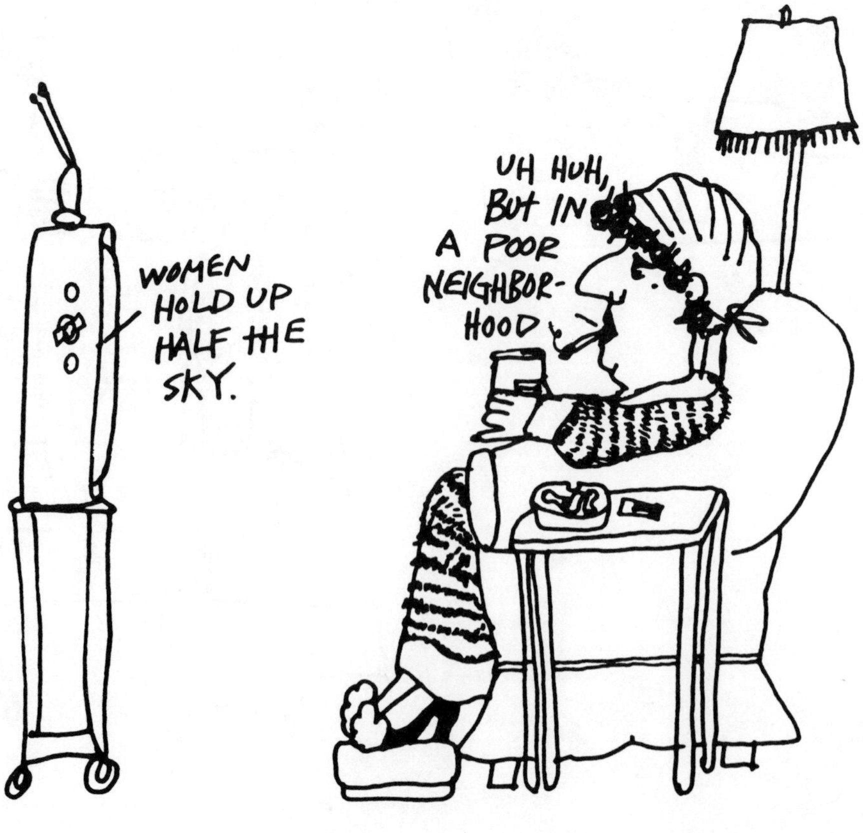
WOMEN HOLD UP HALF THE SKY.
UH HUH, BUT IN A POOR NEIGHBOR-HOOD

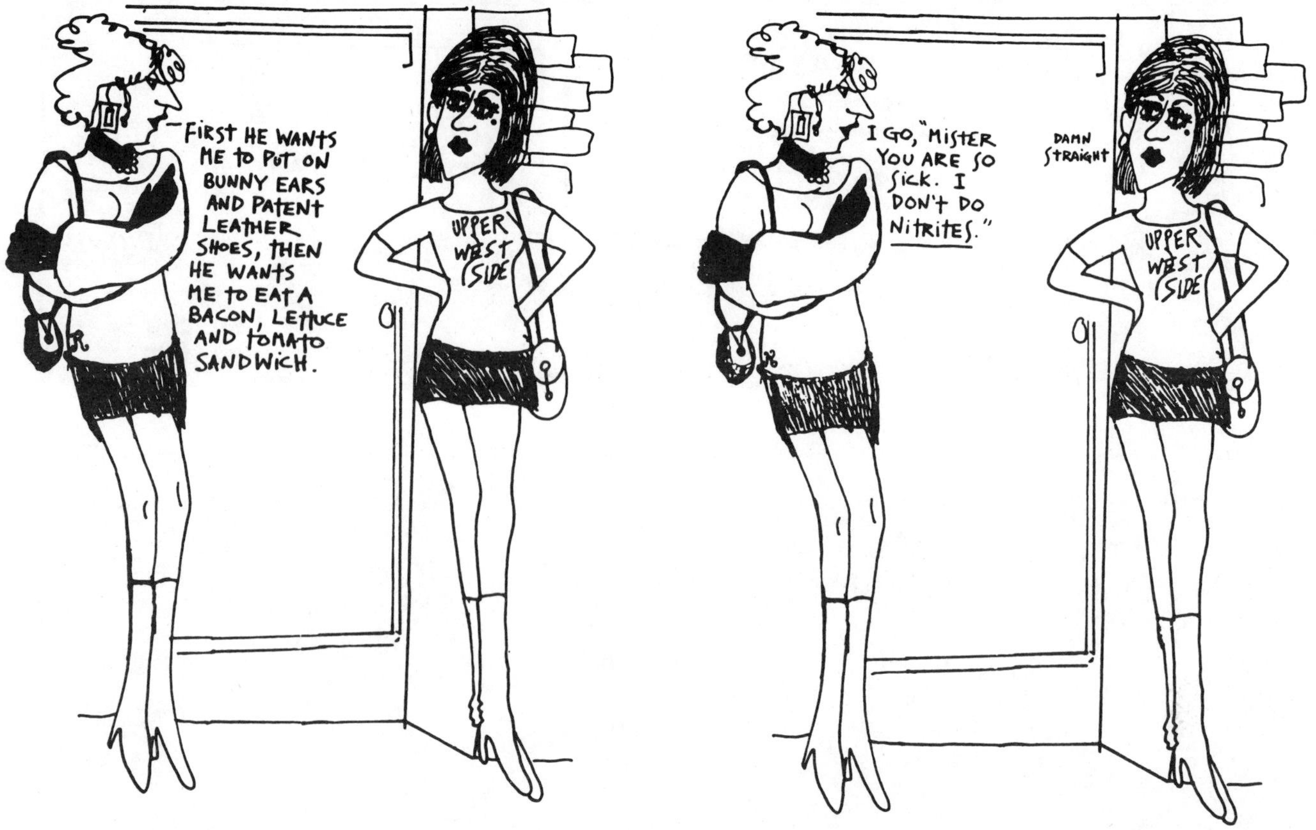
FIRST HE WANTS ME TO PUT ON BUNNY EARS AND PATENT LEATHER SHOES, THEN HE WANTS ME TO EAT A BACON, LETTUCE AND TOMATO SANDWICH.
UPPER WEST SIDE
I GO, "MISTER YOU ARE SO SICK. I DON'T DO NITRITES."
DAMN STRAIGHT
UPPER WEST SIDE

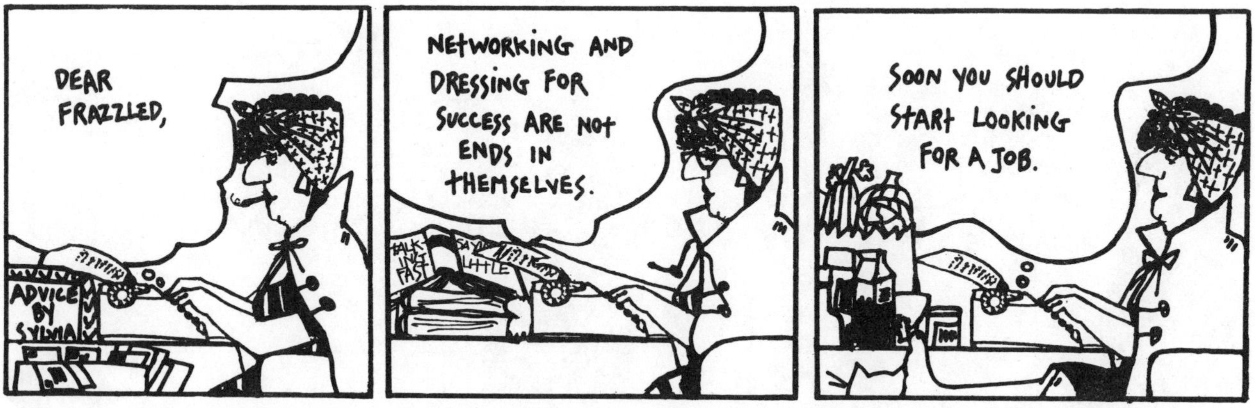
DEAR FRAZZLED,
ADVICE BY SYLVIA
NETWORKING AND DRESSING FOR SUCCESS ARE NOT ENDS IN THEMSELVES.
TALKING FAST
SAY LITTLE
SOON YOU SHOULD START LOOKING FOR A JOB.

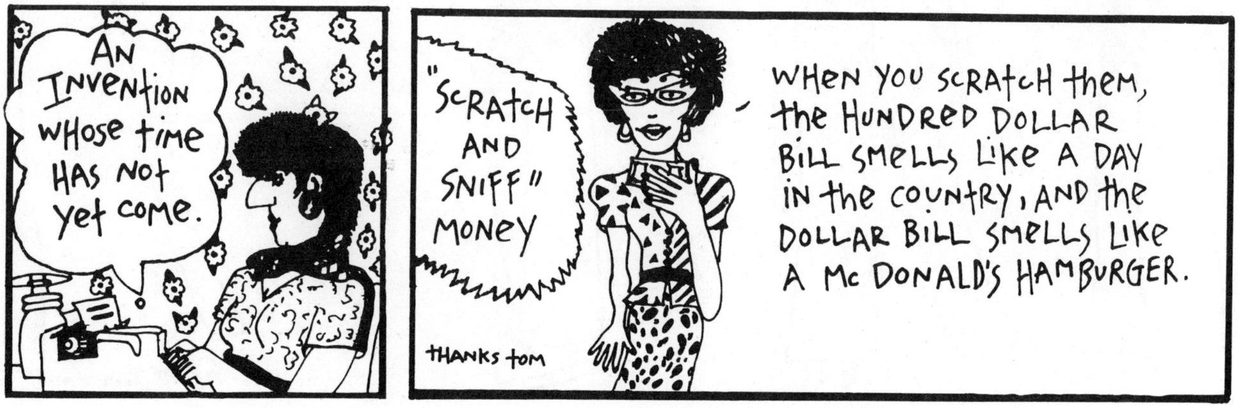
AN INVENTION WHOSE TIME HAS NOT YET COME.
"SCRATCH AND SNIFF" MONEY
WHEN YOU SCRATCH THEM, THE HUNDRED DOLLAR BILL SMELLS LIKE A DAY IN THE COUNTRY, AND THE DOLLAR BILL SMELLS LIKE A MC DONALD'S HAMBURGER.
THANKS TOM

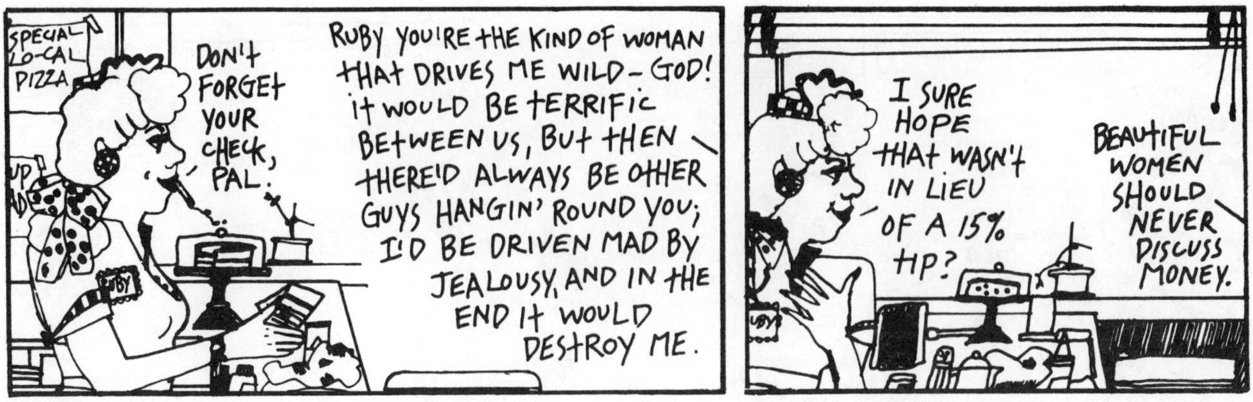
SPECIAL LO-CAL PIZZA
DON'T FORGET YOUR CHECK, PAL.
RUBY YOU'RE THE KIND OF WOMAN THAT DRIVES ME WILD–GOD! IT WOULD BE TERRIFIC BETWEEN US, BUT THEN THERE'D ALWAYS BE OTHER GUYS HANGIN' ROUND YOU; I'D BE DRIVEN MAD BY JEALOUSY, AND IN THE END IT WOULD DESTROY ME.
I SURE HOPE THAT WASN'T IN LIEU OF A 15% TIP?
BEAUTIFUL WOMEN SHOULD NEVER DISCUSS MONEY.

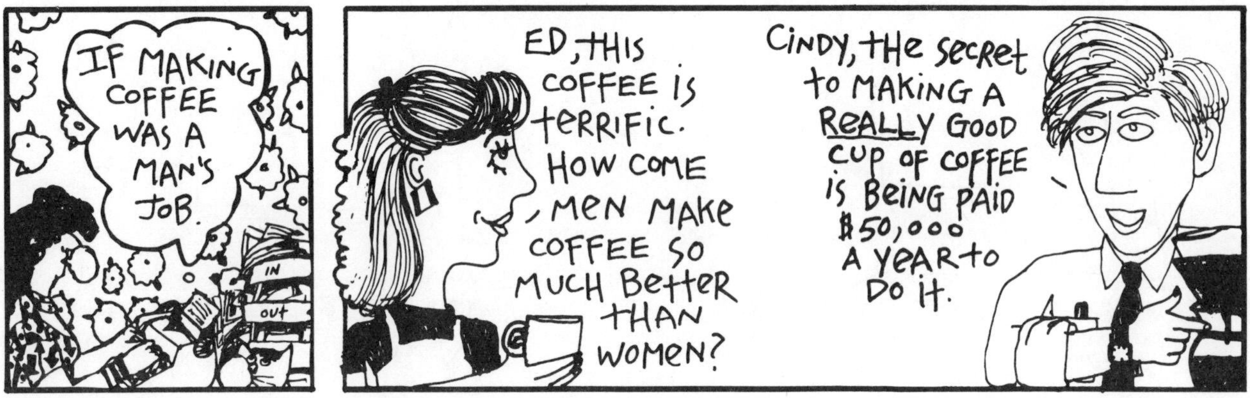
IF MAKING COFFEE WAS A MAN'S JOB.
IN
OUT
ED, THIS COFFEE IS TERRIFIC. HOW COME MEN MAKE COFFEE SO MUCH BETTER THAN WOMEN?
CINDY, THE SECRET TO MAKING A REALLY GOOD CUP OF COFFEE IS BEING PAID $50,000 A YEAR TO DO IT.

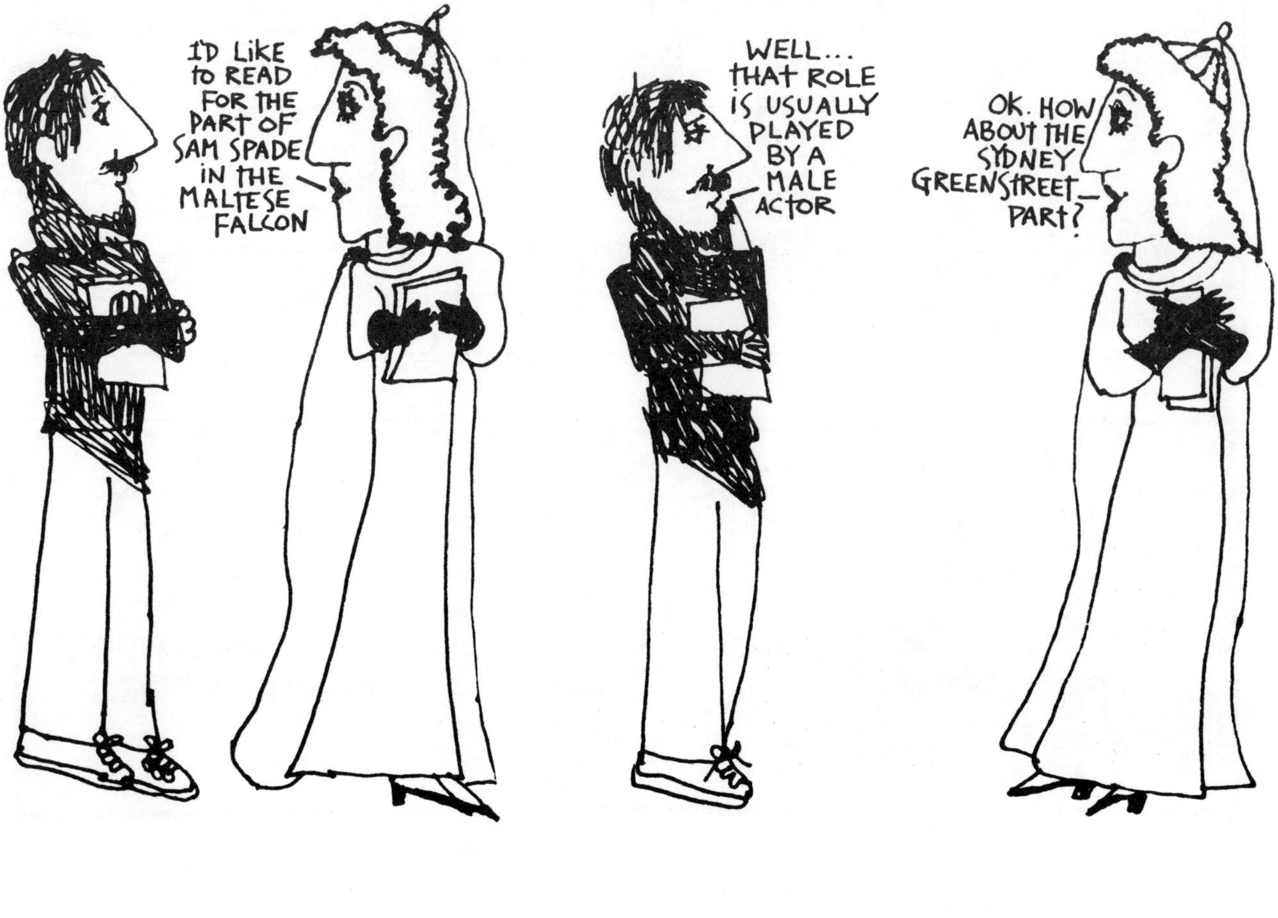
I'D LIKE TO READ FOR THE PART OF SAM SPADE IN THE MALTESE FALCON
WELL... THAT ROLE IS USUALLY PLAYED BY A MALE ACTOR
OK. HOW ABOUT THE SYDNEY GREENSTREET PART?

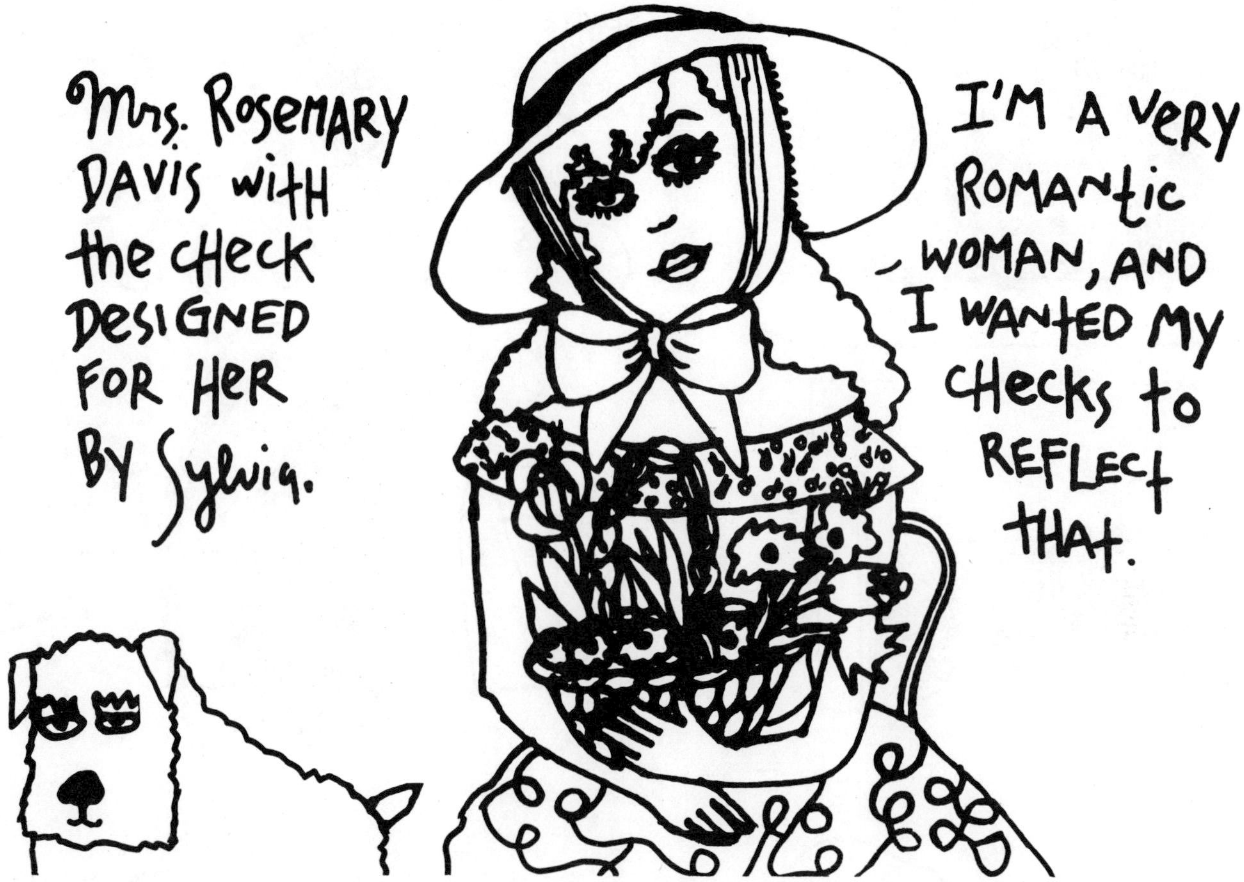
Mrs. Rosemary Davis with the check designed for her by Sylvia.
I'M A VERY ROMANTIC WOMAN, AND I WANTED MY CHECKS TO REFLECT THAT.

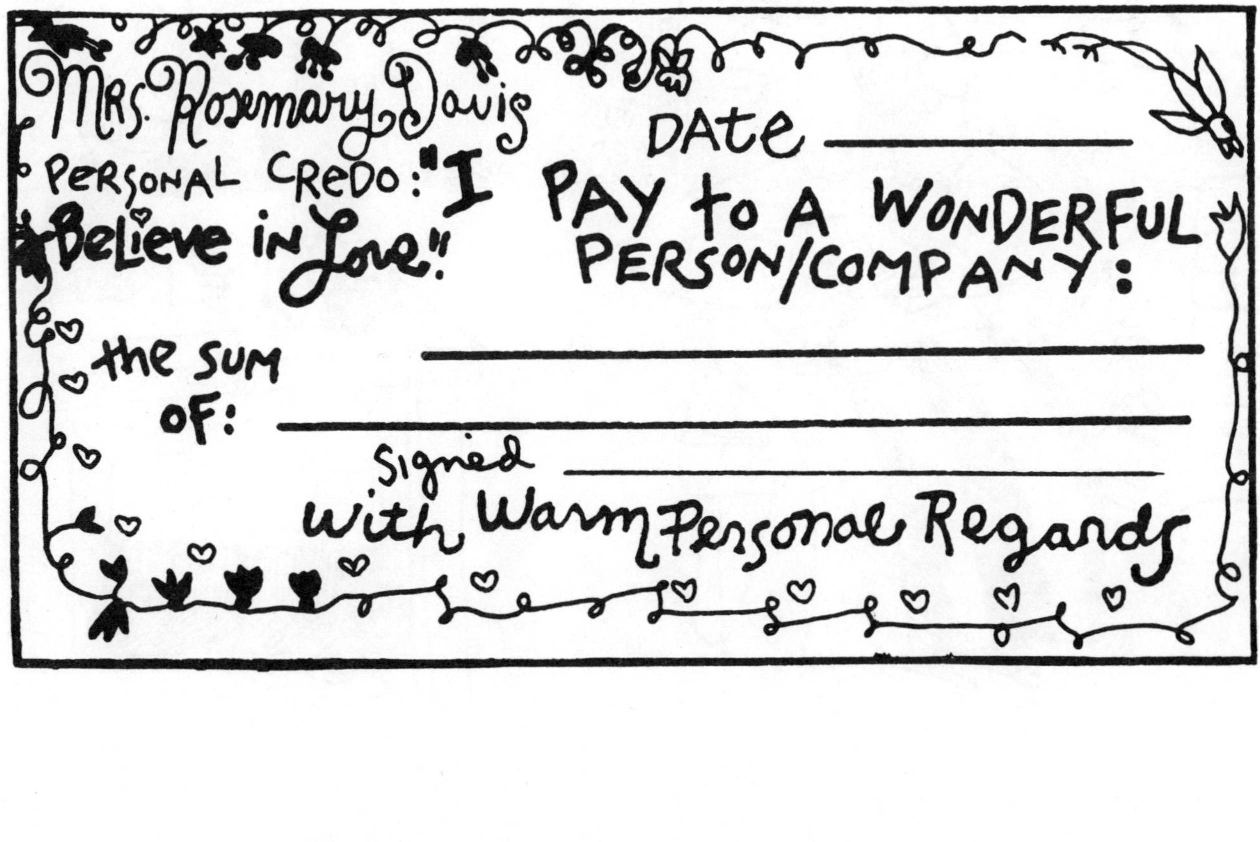
Mrs. Rosemary Davis
PERSONAL CREDO: "I Believe in Love"
DATE
PAY to A WONDERFUL PERSON/COMPANY:
the SUM OF:
Signed
with Warm Personal Regards

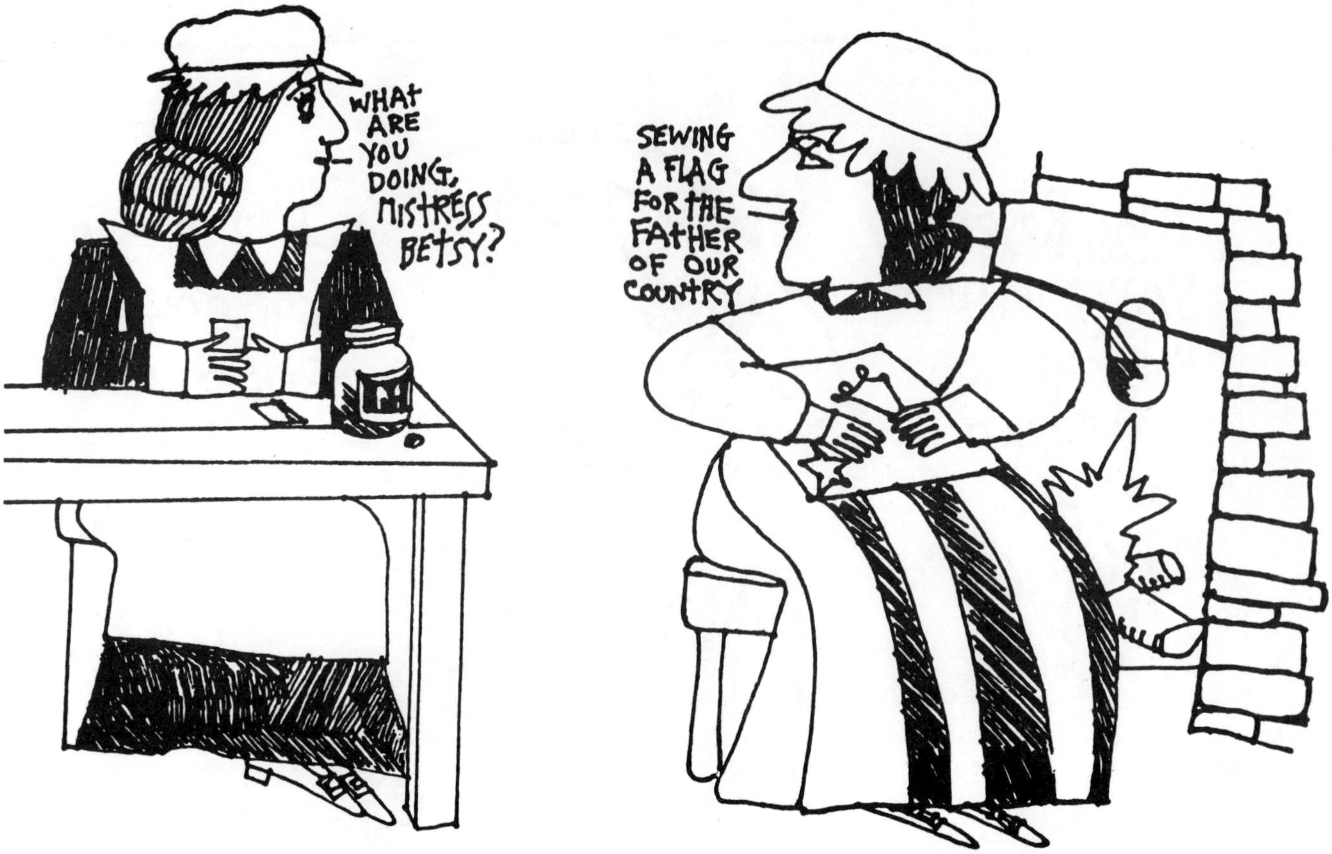
WHAT ARE YOU DOING, MISTRESS BETSY?
SEWING A FLAG FOR THE FATHER OF OUR COUNTRY

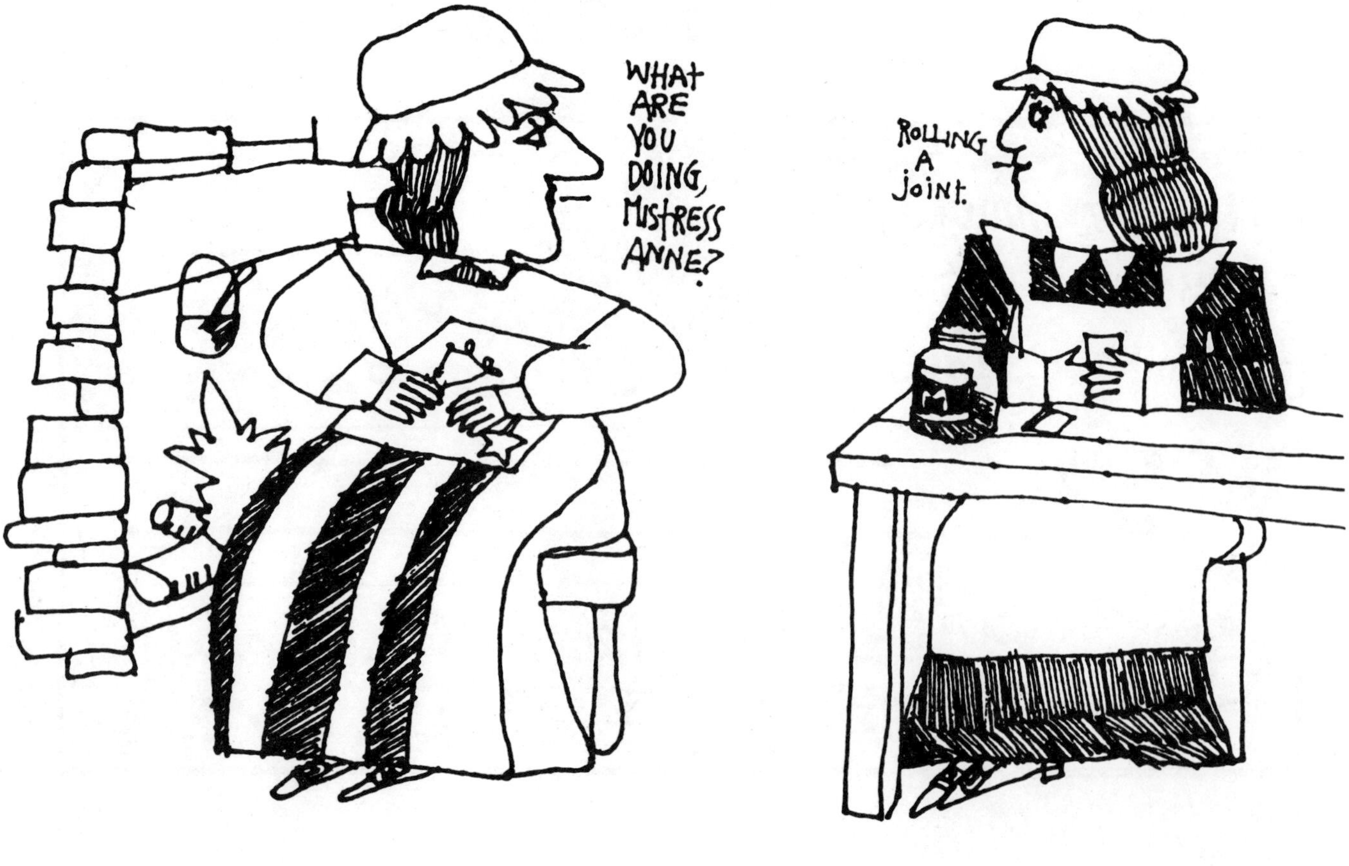
WHAT ARE YOU DOING, MISTRESS ANNE?
ROLLING A joint.

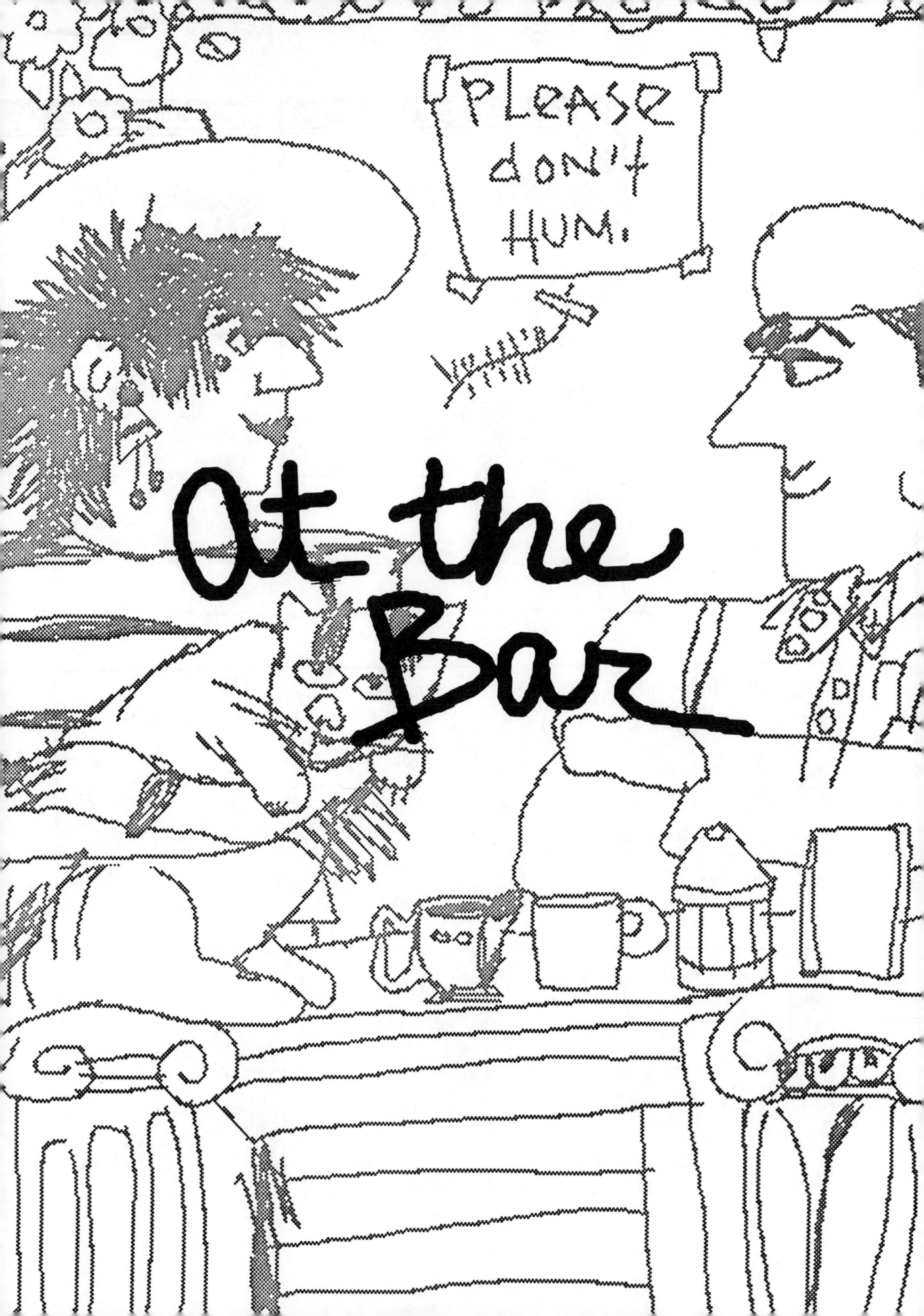
At the Bar
PLEASE don't HUM.

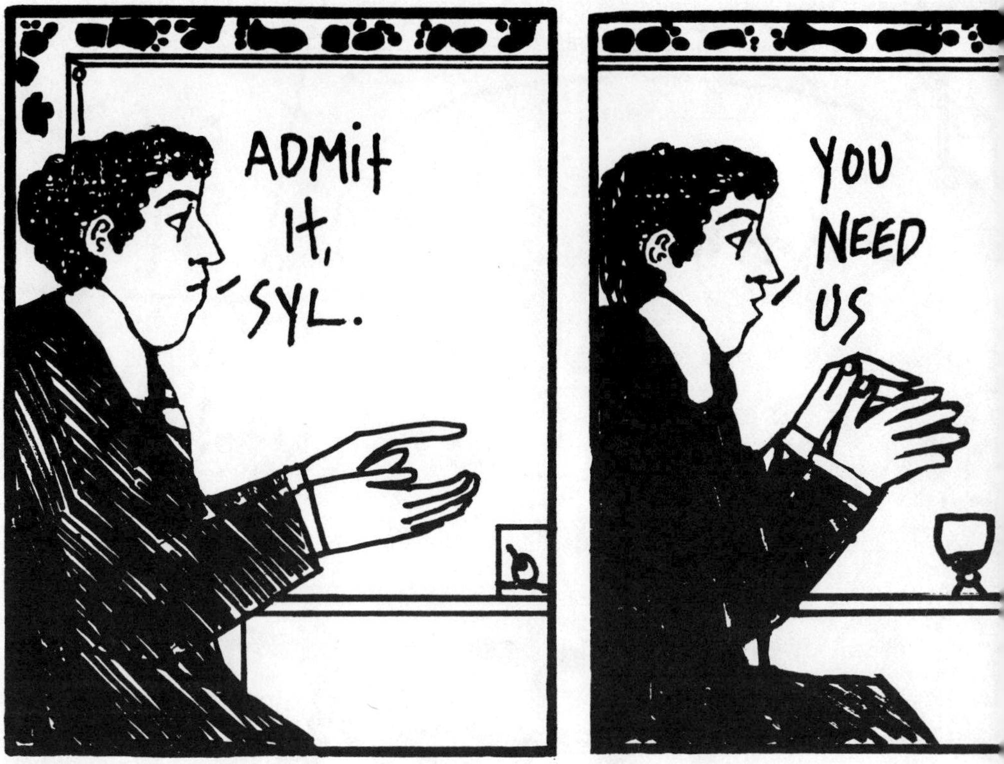
ADMIT IT, SYL.
YOU NEED US

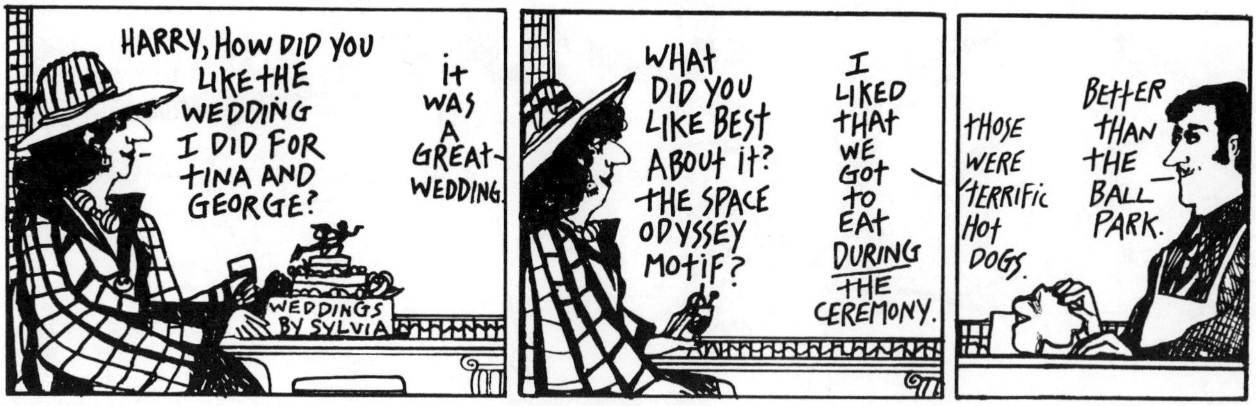
HARRY, HOW DID YOU LIKE THE WEDDING I DID FOR TINA AND GEORGE?
IT WAS A GREAT WEDDING.
WEDDINGS BY SYLVIA
WHAT DID YOU LIKE BEST ABOUT IT? THE SPACE ODYSSEY MOTIF?
I LIKED THAT WE GOT TO EAT DURING THE CEREMONY.
THOSE WERE TERRIFIC HOT DOGS.
BETTER THAN THE BALL PARK.

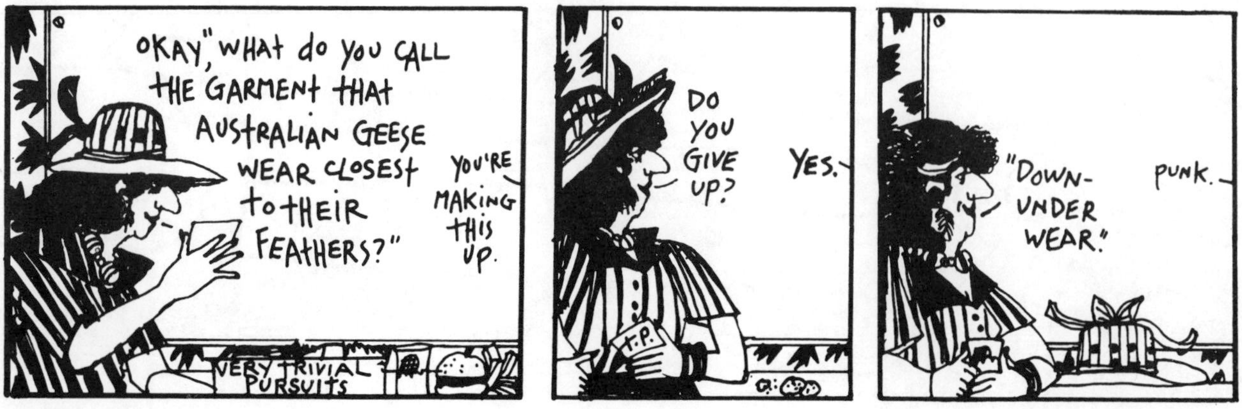
OKAY, "WHAT DO YOU CALL THE GARMENT THAT AUSTRALIAN GEESE WEAR CLOSEST TO THEIR FEATHERS?"
YOU'RE MAKING THIS UP.
VERY TRIVIAL PURSUITS
DO YOU GIVE UP?
YES.
"DOWN-UNDER WEAR."
PUNK.

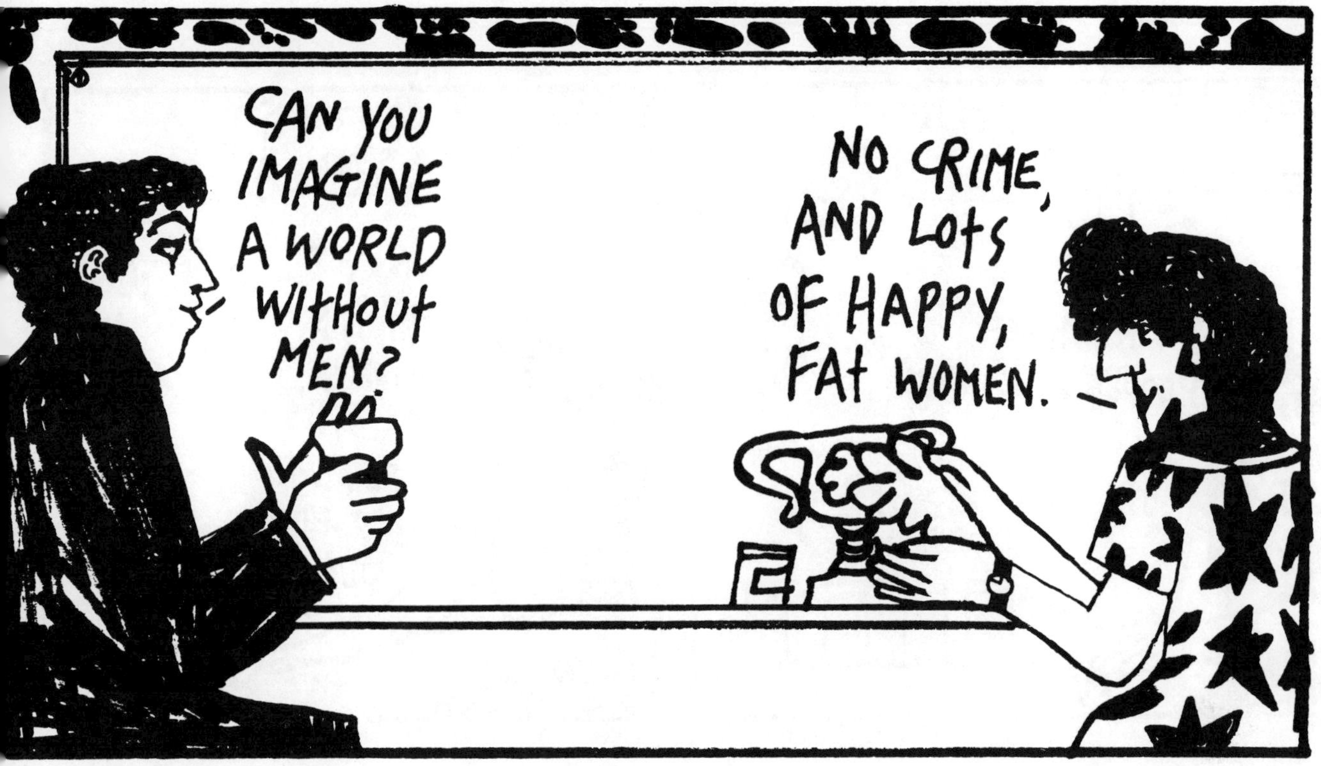
CAN YOU IMAGINE A WORLD WITHOUT MEN?
NO CRIME, AND LOTS OF HAPPY, FAT WOMEN.

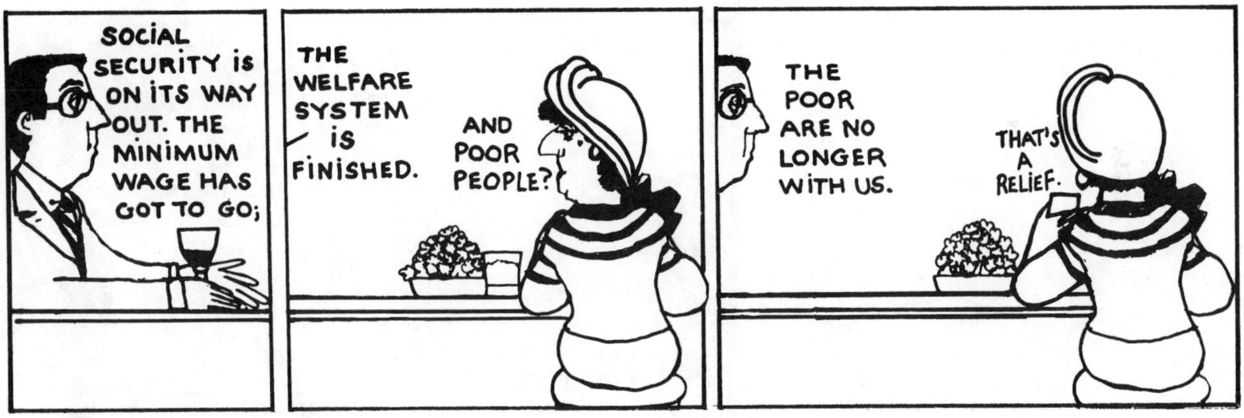
SOCIAL SECURITY IS ON ITS WAY OUT. THE MINIMUM WAGE HAS GOT TO GO;
THE WELFARE SYSTEM IS FINISHED.
AND POOR PEOPLE?
THE POOR ARE NO LONGER WITH US.
THAT'S A RELIEF.

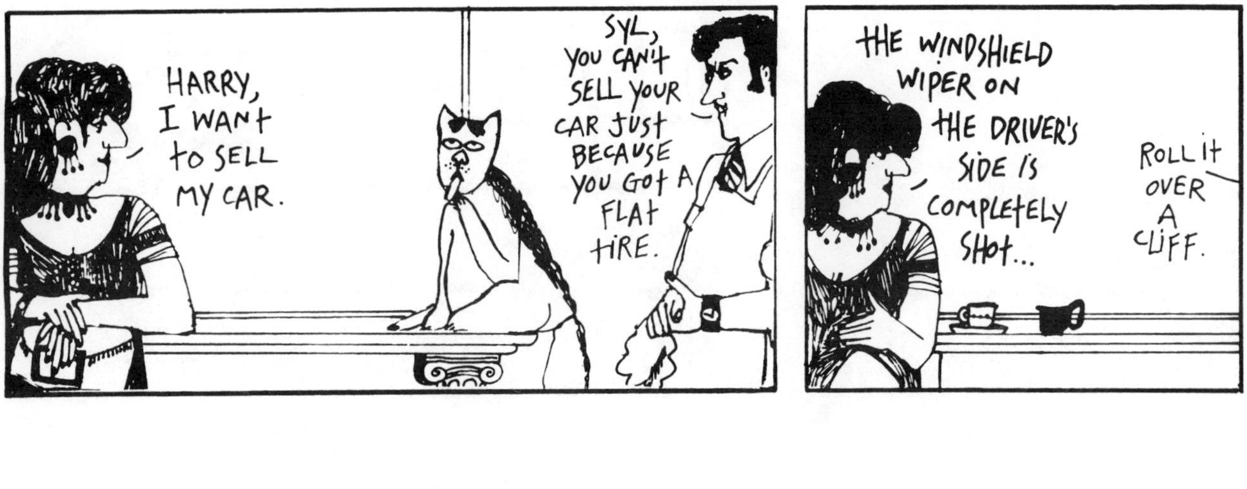
HARRY, I WANT TO SELL MY CAR.
SYL, YOU CAN'T SELL YOUR CAR JUST BECAUSE YOU GOT A FLAT TIRE.
THE WINDSHIELD WIPER ON THE DRIVER'S SIDE IS COMPLETELY SHOT...
ROLL IT OVER A CLIFF.

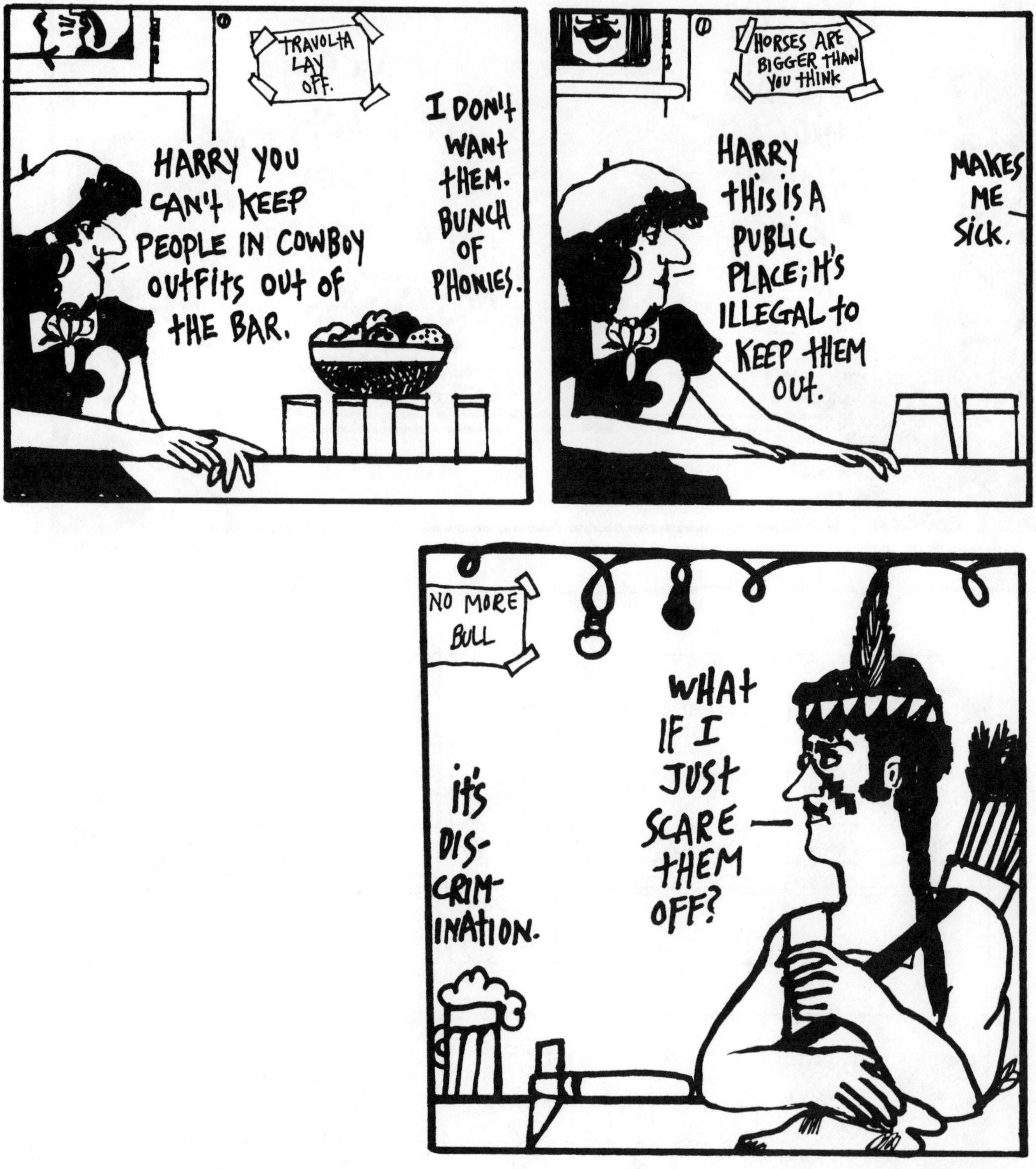
TRAVOLTA LAY OFF.
HARRY YOU CAN'T KEEP PEOPLE IN COWBOY OUTFITS OUT OF THE BAR.
I DON'T WANT THEM. BUNCH OF PHONIES.
HORSES ARE BIGGER THAN YOU THINK
HARRY THIS IS A PUBLIC PLACE; IT'S ILLEGAL TO KEEP THEM OUT.
MAKES ME SICK.
NO MORE BULL
IT'S DIS-CRIM-INATION.
WHAT IF I JUST SCARE THEM OFF?

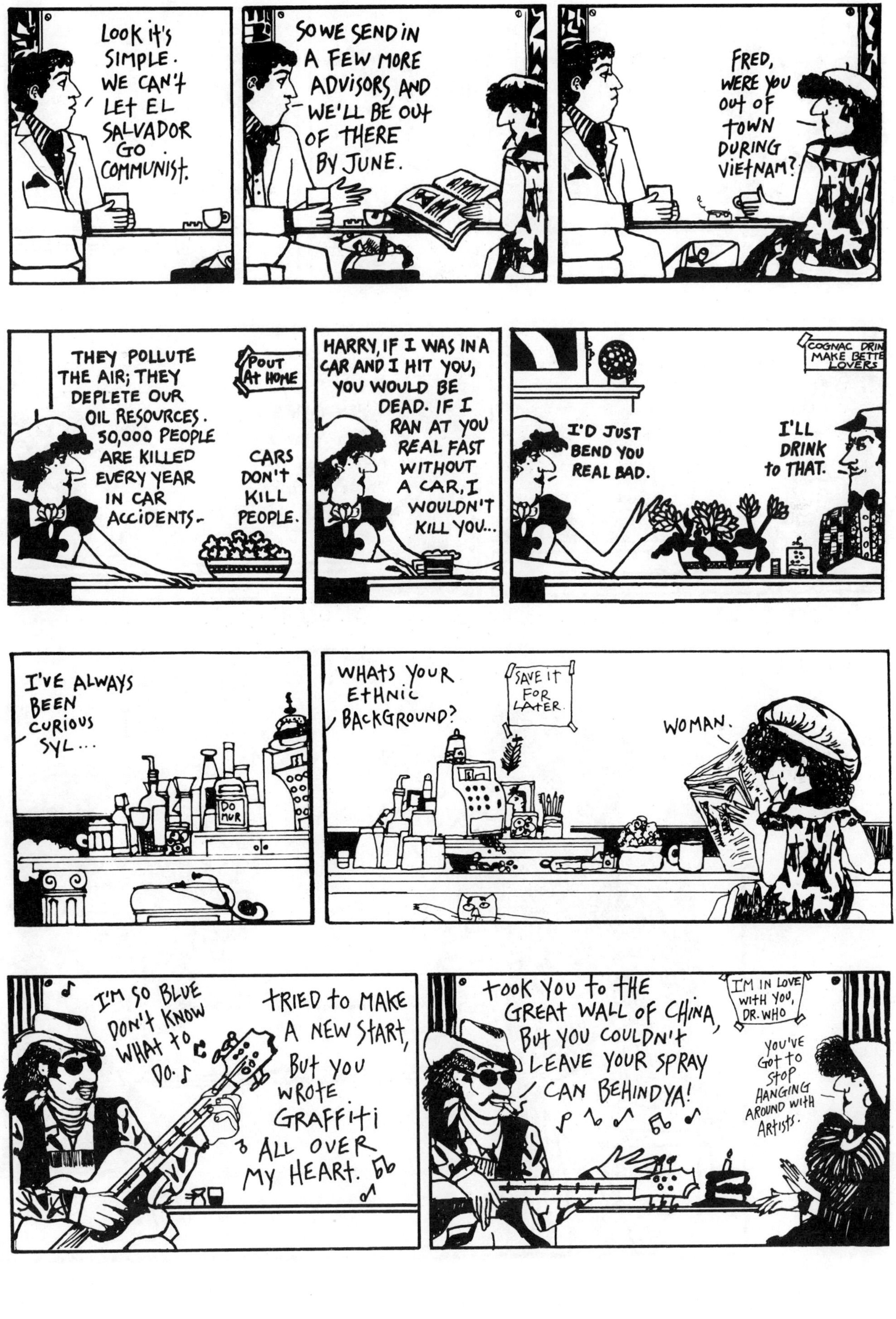
LOOK it's SIMPLE. WE CAN'T LET EL SALVADOR GO COMMUNIST.
SO WE SEND IN A FEW MORE ADVISORS, AND WE'LL BE OUT OF THERE BY JUNE.
FRED, WERE YOU OUT OF TOWN DURING VIETNAM?
THEY POLLUTE THE AIR; THEY DEPLETE OUR OIL RESOURCES. 50,000 PEOPLE ARE KILLED EVERY YEAR IN CAR ACCIDENTS.
POUT AT HOME
CARS DON'T KILL PEOPLE.
HARRY, IF I WAS IN A CAR AND I HIT YOU, YOU WOULD BE DEAD. IF I RAN AT YOU REAL FAST WITHOUT A CAR, I WOULDN'T KILL YOU...
COGNAC DRIN MAKE BETTE LOVERS
I'D JUST BEND YOU REAL BAD.
I'LL DRINK to THAT.
I'VE ALWAYS BEEN CURIOUS SYL...
DO MUR
WHATS YOUR ETHNIC BACKGROUND?
SAVE IT FOR LATER.
WOMAN.
I'M SO BLUE DON'T KNOW WHAT TO DO.
TRIED TO MAKE A NEW START, BUT YOU WROTE GRAFFITI ALL OVER MY HEART.
TOOK YOU TO THE GREAT WALL OF CHINA, BUT YOU COULDN'T LEAVE YOUR SPRAY CAN BEHINDYA!
I'M IN LOVE WITH YOU, DR. WHO
YOU'VE GOT TO STOP HANGING AROUND WITH ARTISTS.

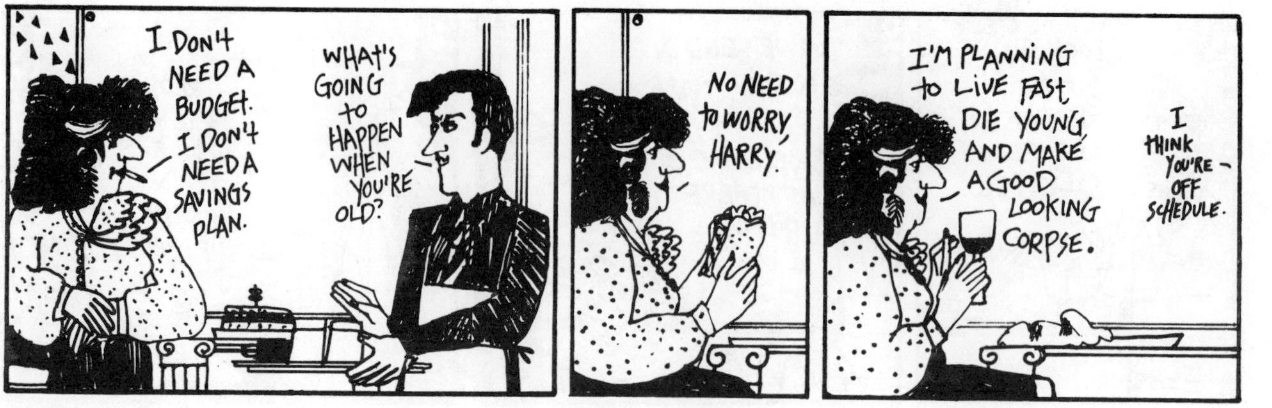
I DON'T NEED A BUDGET. I DON'T NEED A SAVINGS PLAN.
WHAT'S GOING to HAPPEN WHEN YOU'RE OLD?
NO NEED to WORRY HARRY.
I'M PLANNING to LIVE FAST, DIE YOUNG, AND MAKE A GOOD LOOKING CORPSE.
I THINK YOU'RE OFF SCHEDULE.

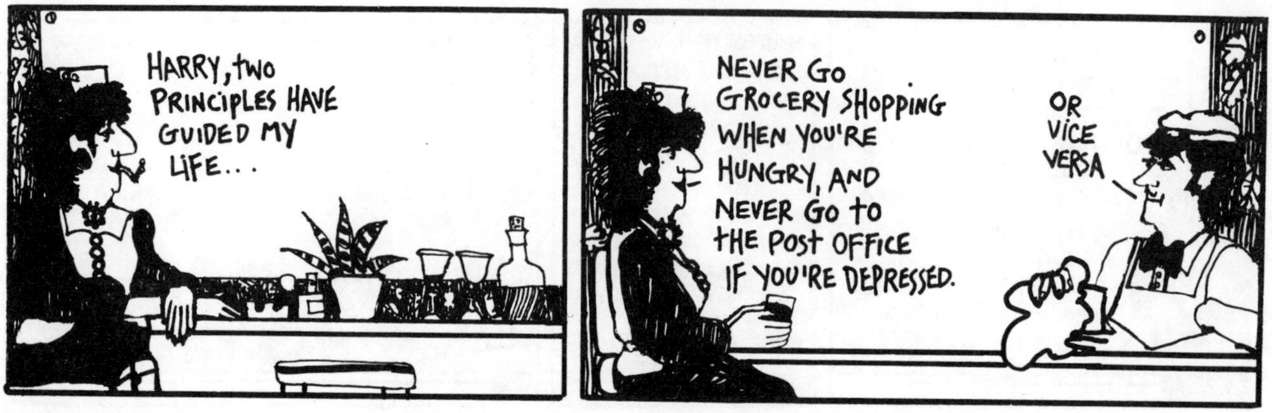
HARRY, two PRINCIPLES HAVE GUIDED MY LIFE...
NEVER GO GROCERY SHOPPING WHEN YOU'RE HUNGRY, AND NEVER GO to the POST OFFICE IF YOU'RE DEPRESSED.
OR VICE VERSA

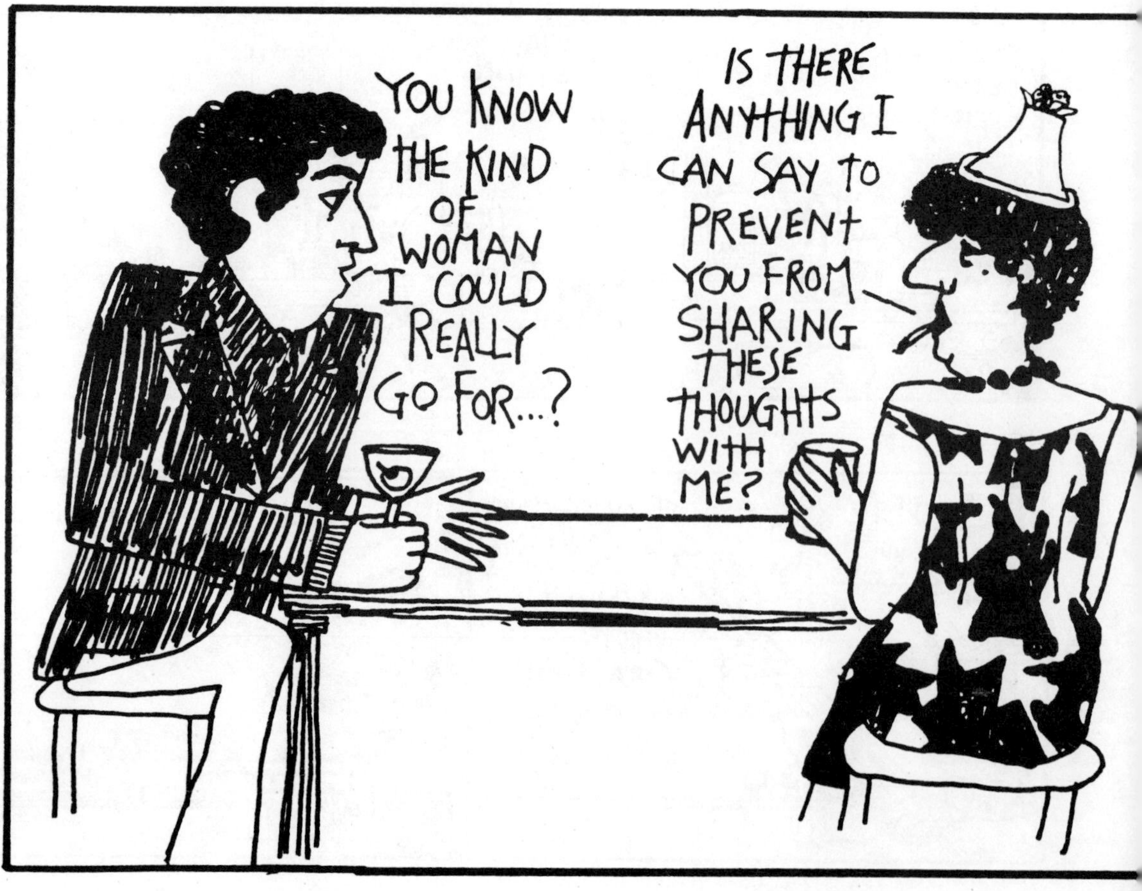
YOU KNOW THE KIND OF WOMAN I COULD REALLY GO FOR...?
IS THERE ANYTHING I CAN SAY TO PREVENT YOU FROM SHARING THESE THOUGHTS WITH ME?

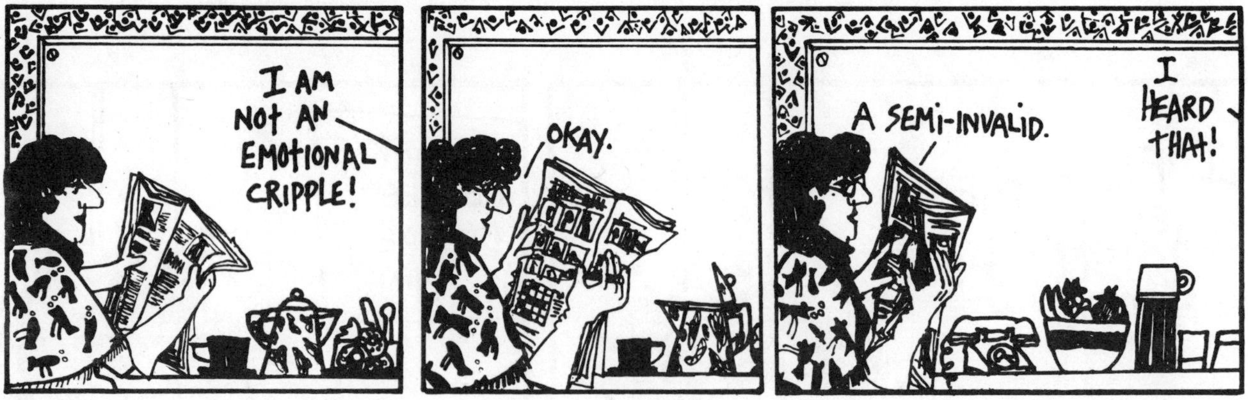
I AM NOT AN EMOTIONAL CRIPPLE!
OKAY.
A SEMI-INVALID.
I HEARD THAT!

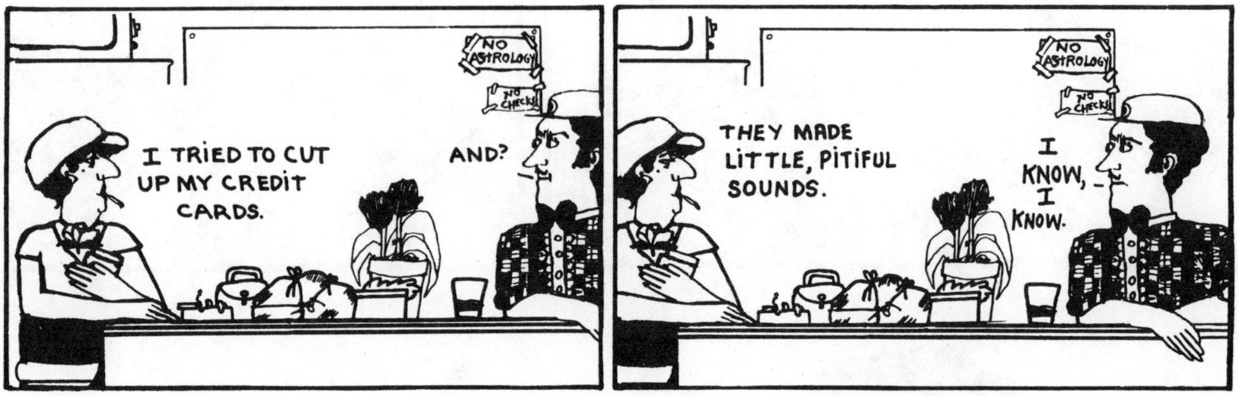
NO ASTROLOGY
NO CHECKS
I TRIED TO CUT UP MY CREDIT CARDS.
AND?
NO ASTROLOGY
NO CHECKS
THEY MADE LITTLE, PITIFUL SOUNDS.
I KNOW, I KNOW.

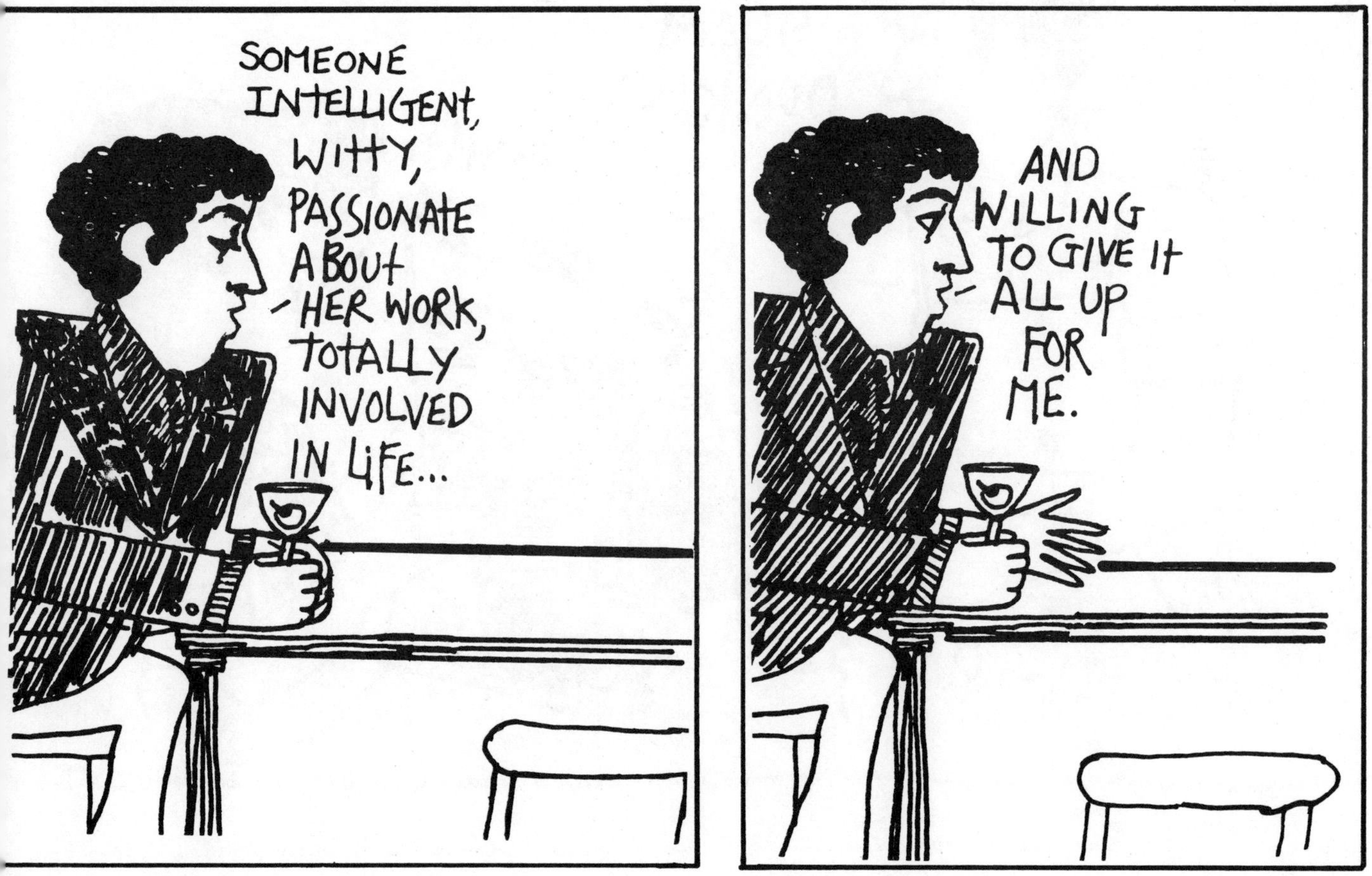
SOMEONE INTELLIGENT, WITTY, PASSIONATE ABOUT HER WORK, TOTALLY INVOLVED IN LIFE...
AND WILLING TO GIVE IT ALL UP FOR ME.

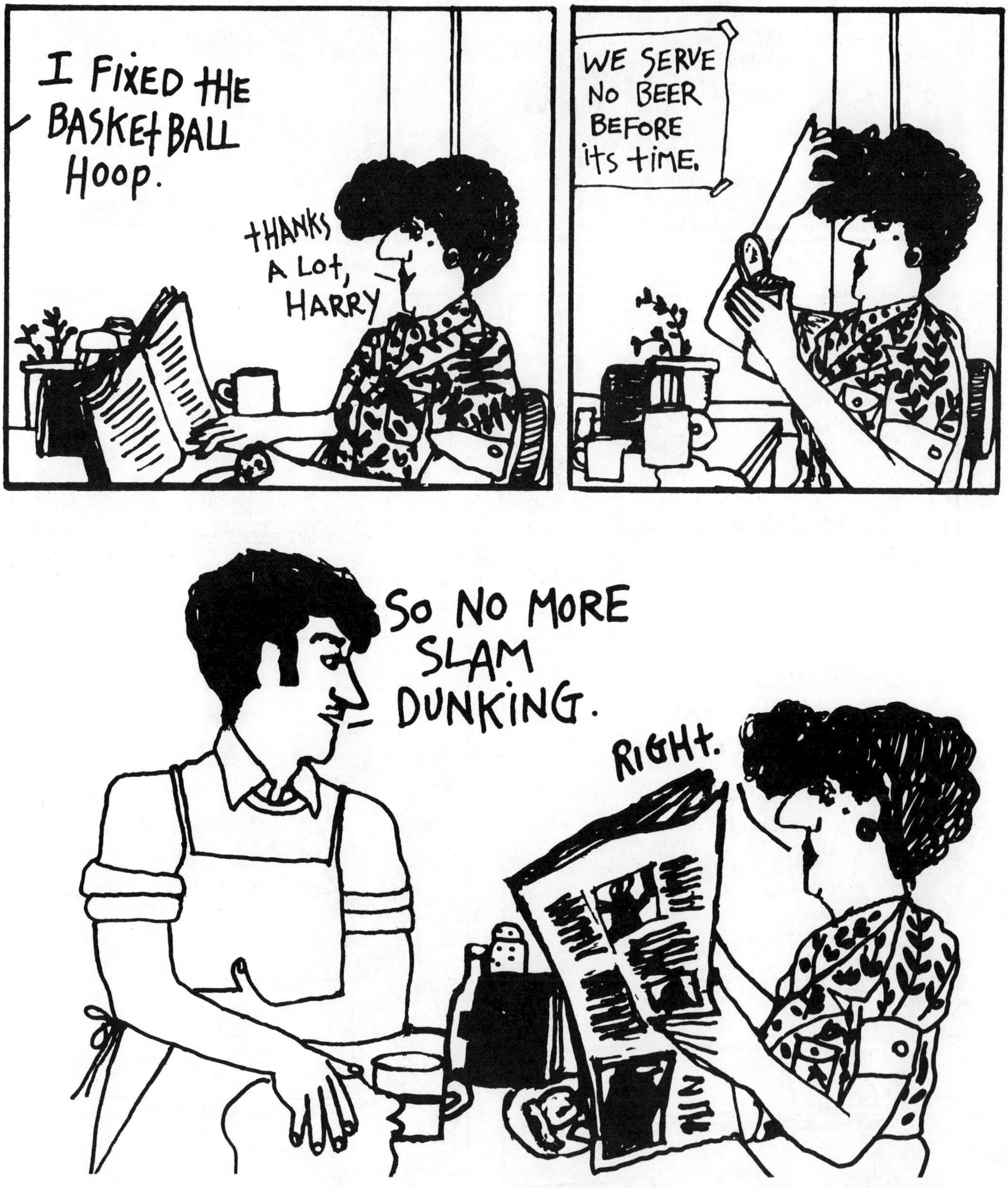
I FIXED THE BASKETBALL HOOP.
THANKS A LOT, HARRY
WE SERVE NO BEER BEFORE ITS TIME.
SO NO MORE SLAM DUNKING.
RIGHT.

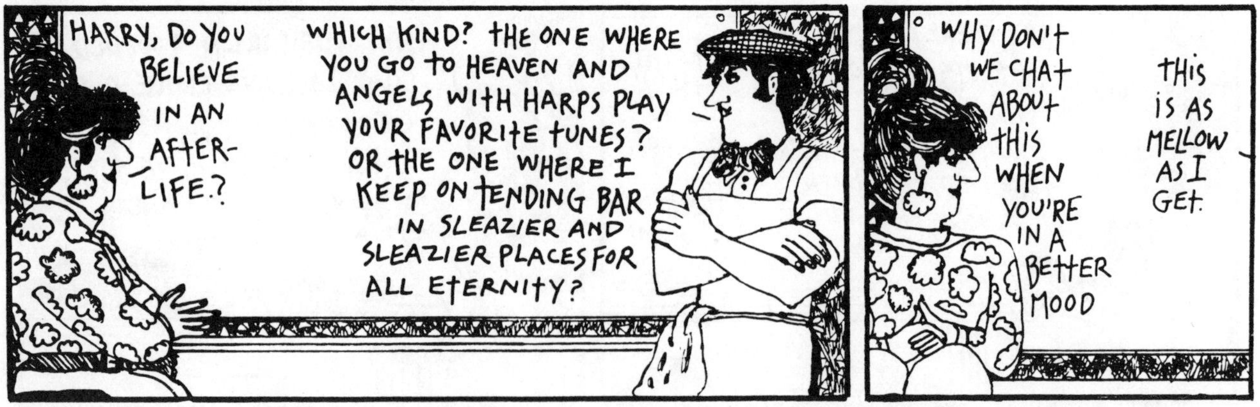
HARRY, DO YOU BELIEVE IN AN AFTER-LIFE?
WHICH KIND? THE ONE WHERE YOU GO TO HEAVEN AND ANGELS WITH HARPS PLAY YOUR FAVORITE TUNES? OR THE ONE WHERE I KEEP ON TENDING BAR IN SLEAZIER AND SLEAZIER PLACES FOR ALL ETERNITY?
WHY DON'T WE CHAT ABOUT THIS WHEN YOU'RE IN A BETTER MOOD
THIS IS AS MELLOW AS I GET.

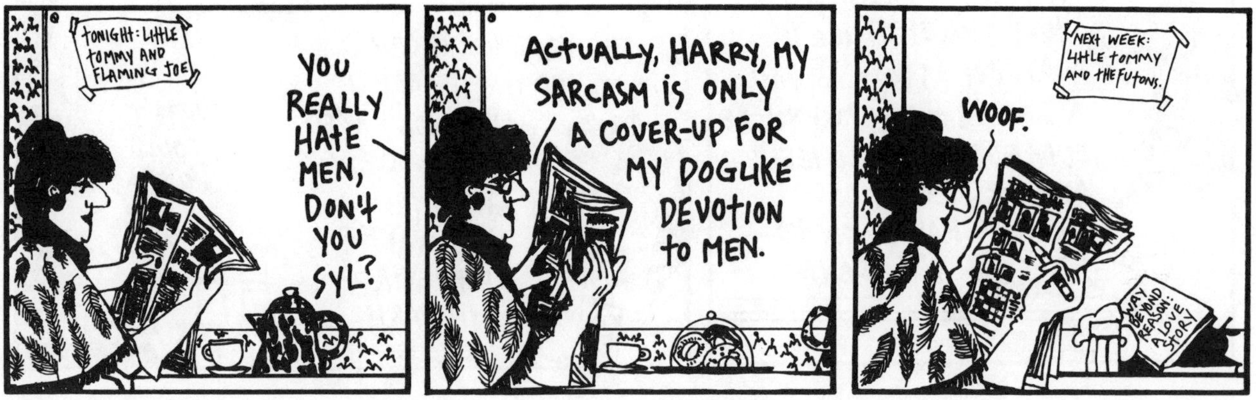
TONIGHT: LITTLE TOMMY AND FLAMING JOE
YOU REALLY HATE MEN, DON'T YOU SYL?
ACTUALLY, HARRY, MY SARCASM IS ONLY A COVER-UP FOR MY DOGLIKE DEVOTION TO MEN.
NEXT WEEK: LITTLE TOMMY AND THE FUTONS.
WOOF.
WAY BEYOND REASON: A LOVE STORY

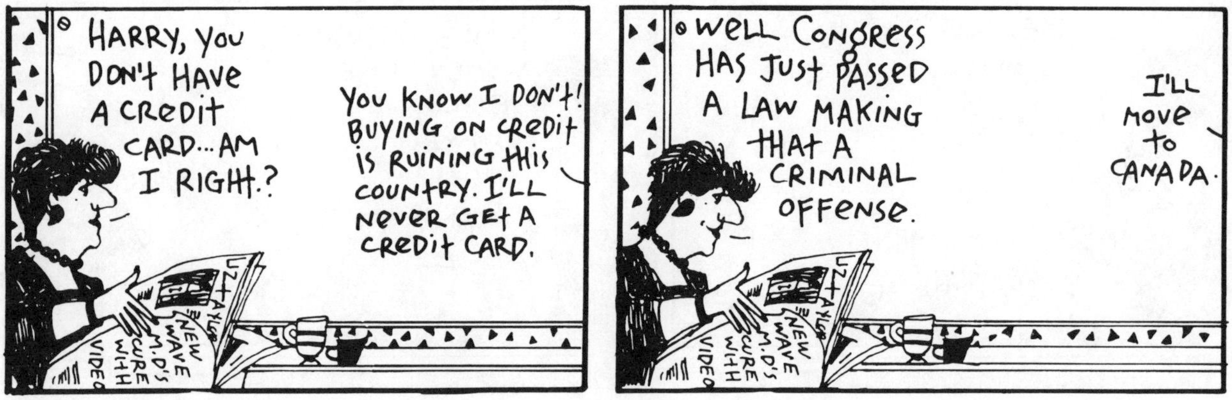
HARRY, YOU DON'T HAVE A CREDIT CARD... AM I RIGHT?
YOU KNOW I DON'T! BUYING ON CREDIT IS RUINING THIS COUNTRY. I'LL NEVER GET A CREDIT CARD.
LIZ TAYLOR
NEW WAVE M.D.'S CURE WITH VIDEO
WELL CONGRESS HAS JUST PASSED A LAW MAKING THAT A CRIMINAL OFFENSE.
I'LL MOVE TO CANADA.

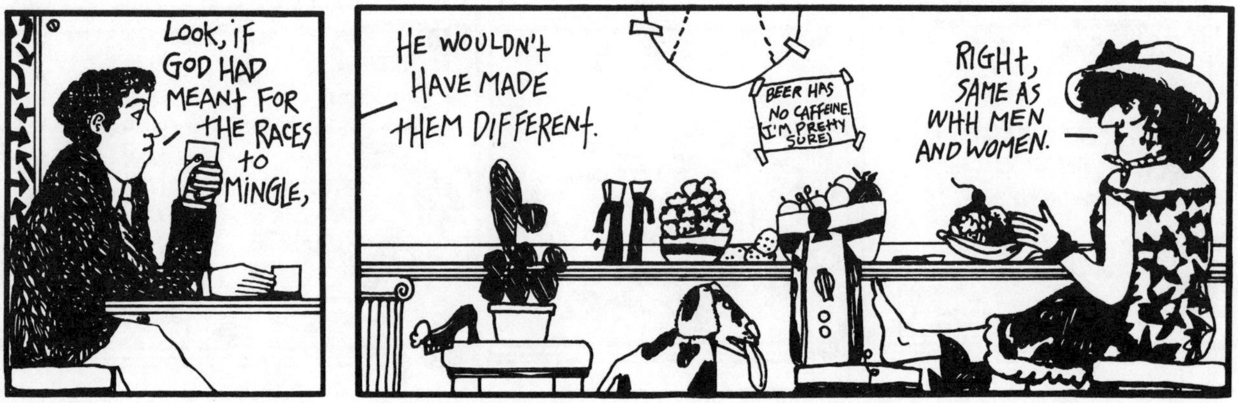
LOOK, IF GOD HAD MEANT FOR THE RACES TO MINGLE,
HE WOULDN'T HAVE MADE THEM DIFFERENT.
BEER HAS NO CAFFEINE. (I'M PRETTY SURE)
RIGHT, SAME AS WITH MEN AND WOMEN.

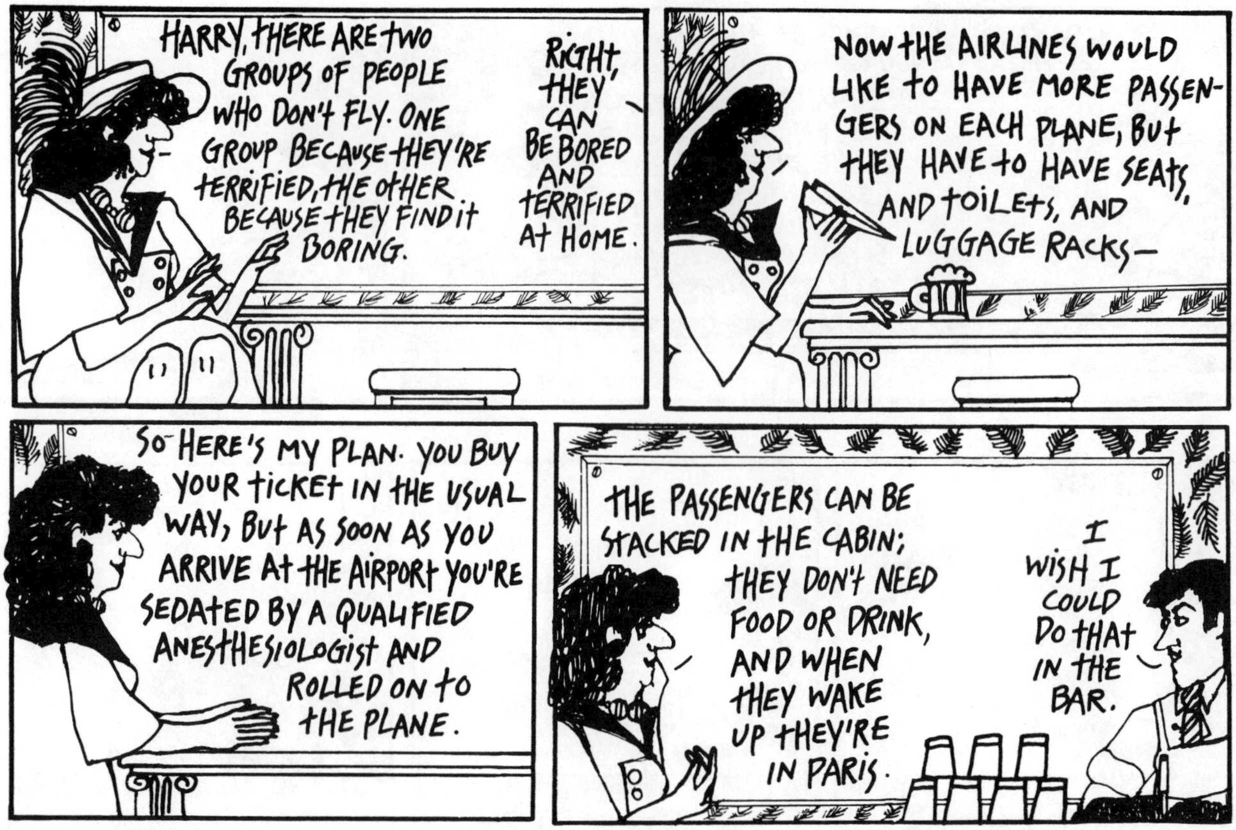
HARRY, THERE ARE TWO GROUPS OF PEOPLE WHO DON'T FLY. ONE GROUP BECAUSE THEY'RE TERRIFIED, THE OTHER BECAUSE THEY FIND IT BORING.
RIGHT, THEY CAN BE BORED AND TERRIFIED AT HOME.
NOW THE AIRLINES WOULD LIKE TO HAVE MORE PASSENGERS ON EACH PLANE, BUT THEY HAVE TO HAVE SEATS, AND TOILETS, AND LUGGAGE RACKS—
SO HERE'S MY PLAN. YOU BUY YOUR TICKET IN THE USUAL WAY, BUT AS SOON AS YOU ARRIVE AT THE AIRPORT YOU'RE SEDATED BY A QUALIFIED ANESTHESIOLOGIST AND ROLLED ON TO THE PLANE.
THE PASSENGERS CAN BE STACKED IN THE CABIN; THEY DON'T NEED FOOD OR DRINK, AND WHEN THEY WAKE UP THEY'RE IN PARIS.
I WISH I COULD DO THAT IN THE BAR.

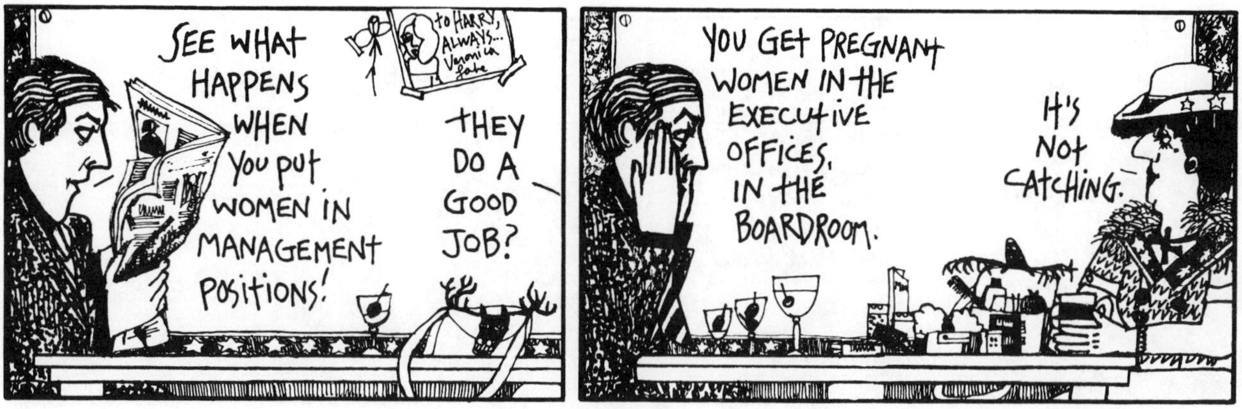
SEE WHAT HAPPENS WHEN YOU PUT WOMEN IN MANAGEMENT POSITIONS!
to HARRY, ALWAYS...
THEY DO A GOOD JOB?
YOU GET PREGNANT WOMEN IN THE EXECUTIVE OFFICES, IN THE BOARDROOM.
IT'S NOT CATCHING.

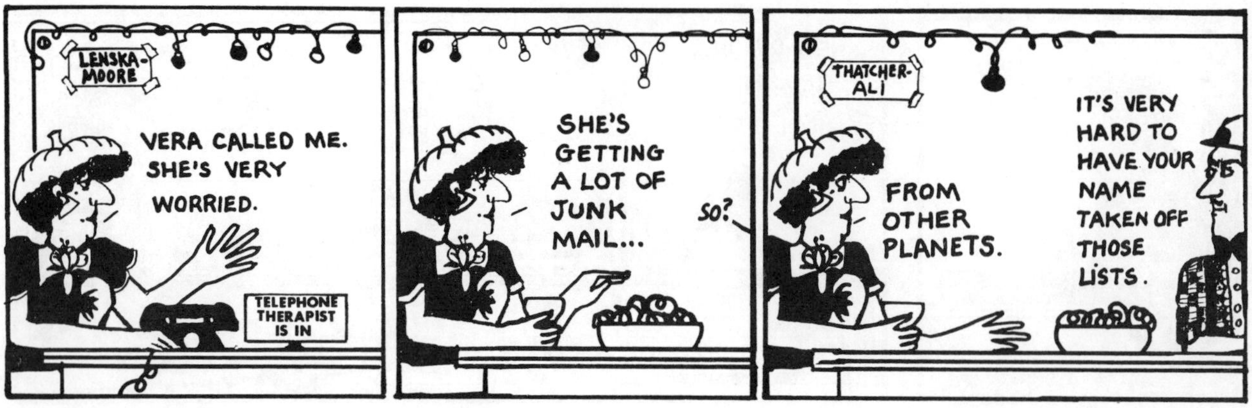
LENSKA-MOORE
VERA CALLED ME. SHE'S VERY WORRIED.
TELEPHONE THERAPIST IS IN
SHE'S GETTING A LOT OF JUNK MAIL...
SO?
THATCHER-ALI
FROM OTHER PLANETS.
IT'S VERY HARD TO HAVE YOUR NAME TAKEN OFF THOSE LISTS.

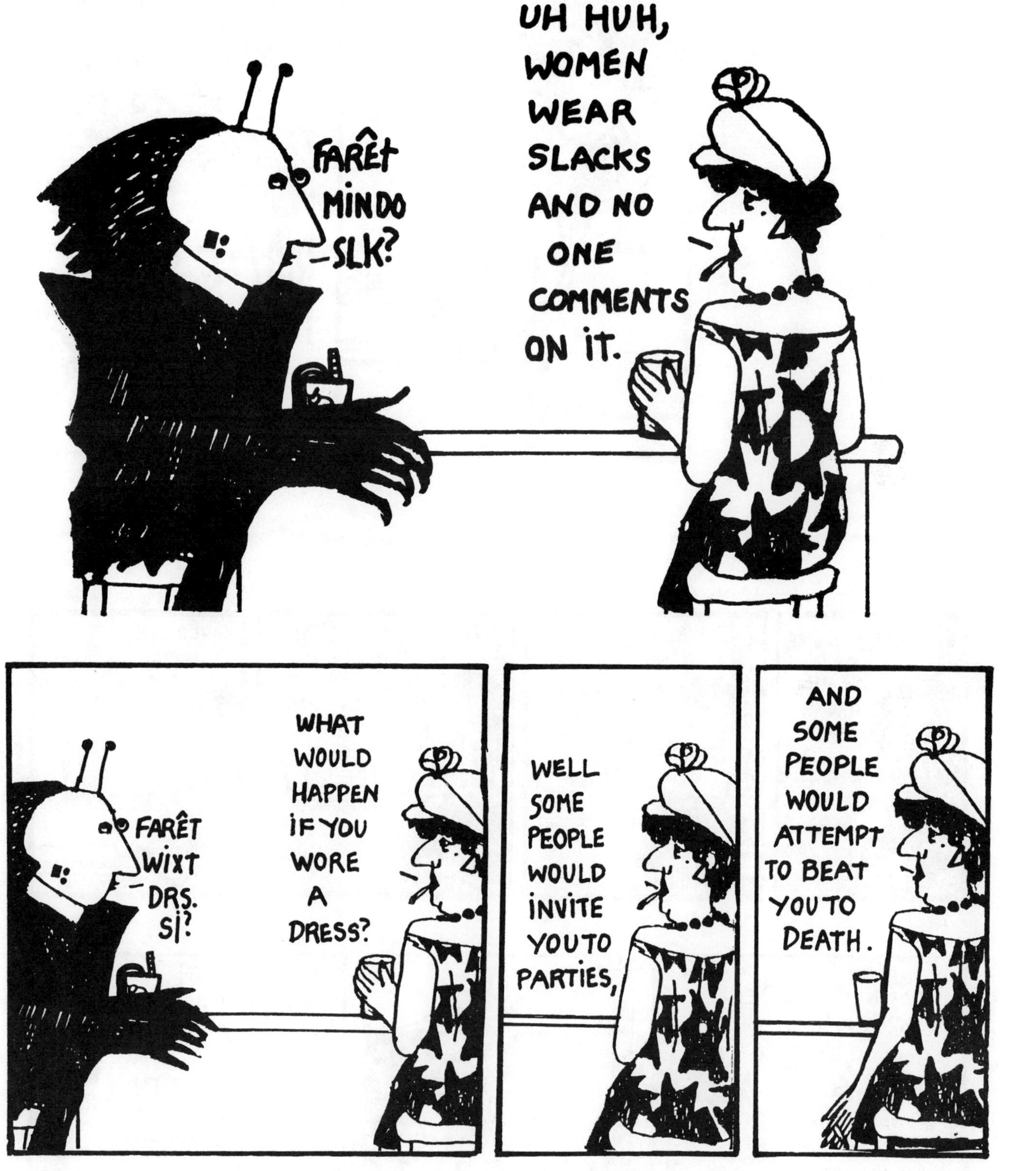

FARÊT MINDO SLK?
UH HUH, WOMEN WEAR SLACKS AND NO ONE COMMENTS ON IT.
FARÊT WIXT DRS. SI?
WHAT WOULD HAPPEN IF YOU WORE A DRESS?
WELL SOME PEOPLE WOULD INVITE YOU TO PARTIES,
AND SOME PEOPLE WOULD ATTEMPT TO BEAT YOU TO DEATH.

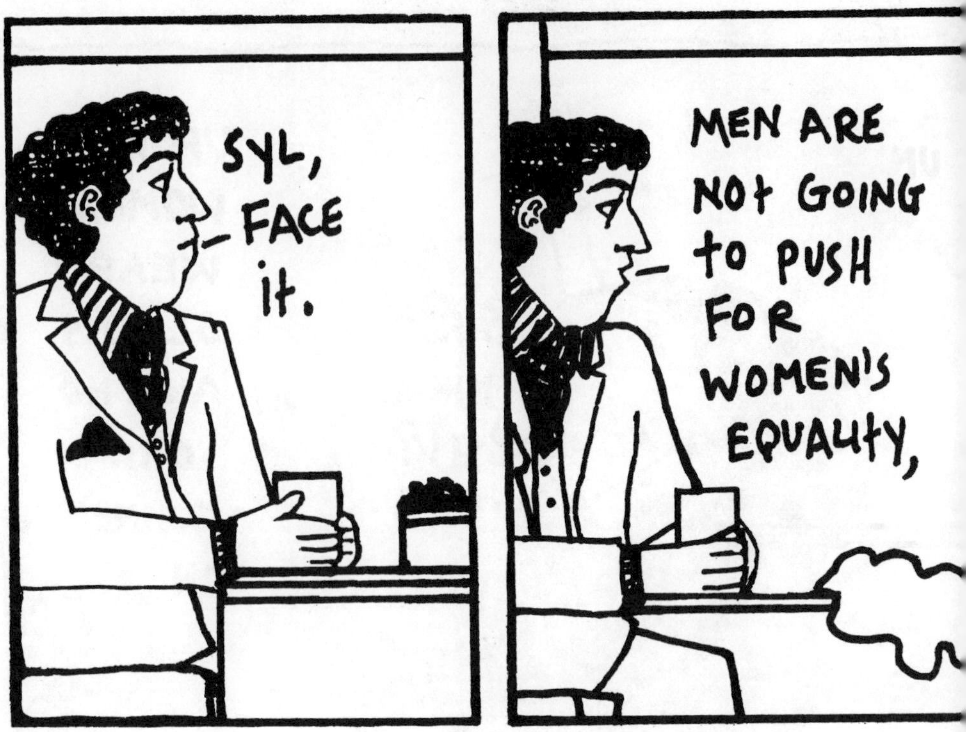
SYL, FACE it.
MEN ARE NOT GOING TO PUSH FOR WOMEN'S EQUALITY,

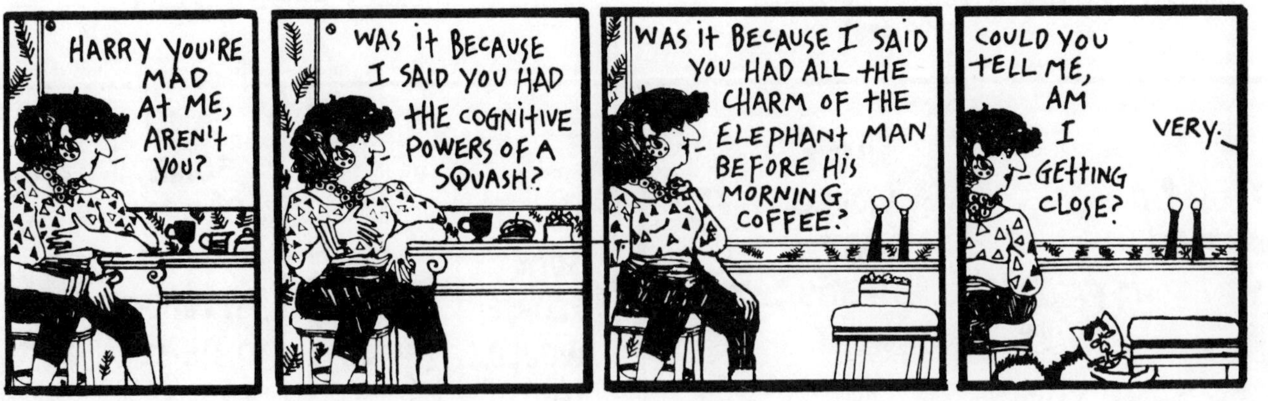
HARRY YOU'RE MAD AT ME, AREN'T YOU?
WAS IT BECAUSE I SAID YOU HAD THE COGNITIVE POWERS OF A SQUASH?
WAS IT BECAUSE I SAID YOU HAD ALL THE CHARM OF THE ELEPHANT MAN BEFORE HIS MORNING COFFEE?
COULD YOU TELL ME, AM I GETTING CLOSE?
VERY.

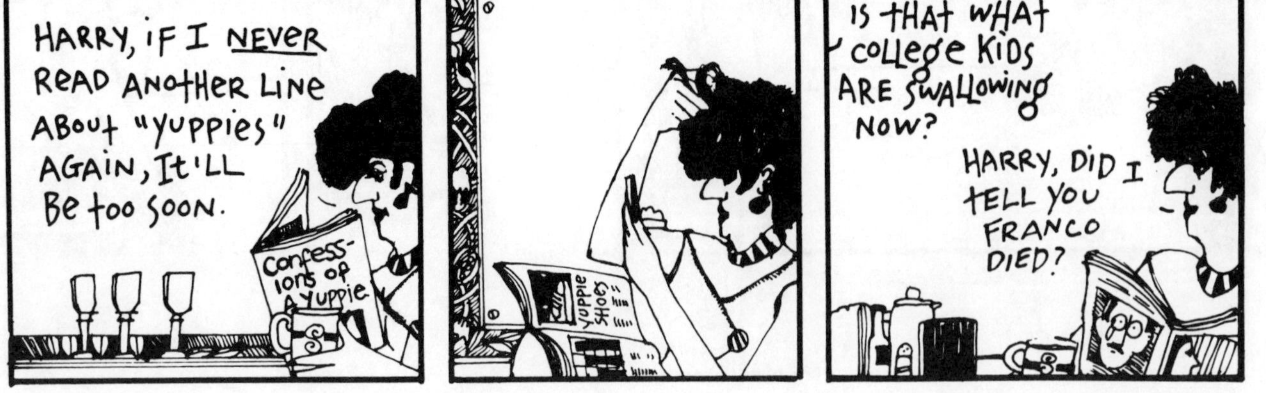
HARRY, IF I NEVER READ ANOTHER LINE ABOUT "YUPPIES" AGAIN, IT'LL BE TOO SOON.
Confess-ions of A Yuppie
Yuppie Shops
IS THAT WHAT COLLEGE KIDS ARE SWALLOWING NOW?
HARRY, DID I TELL YOU FRANCO DIED?

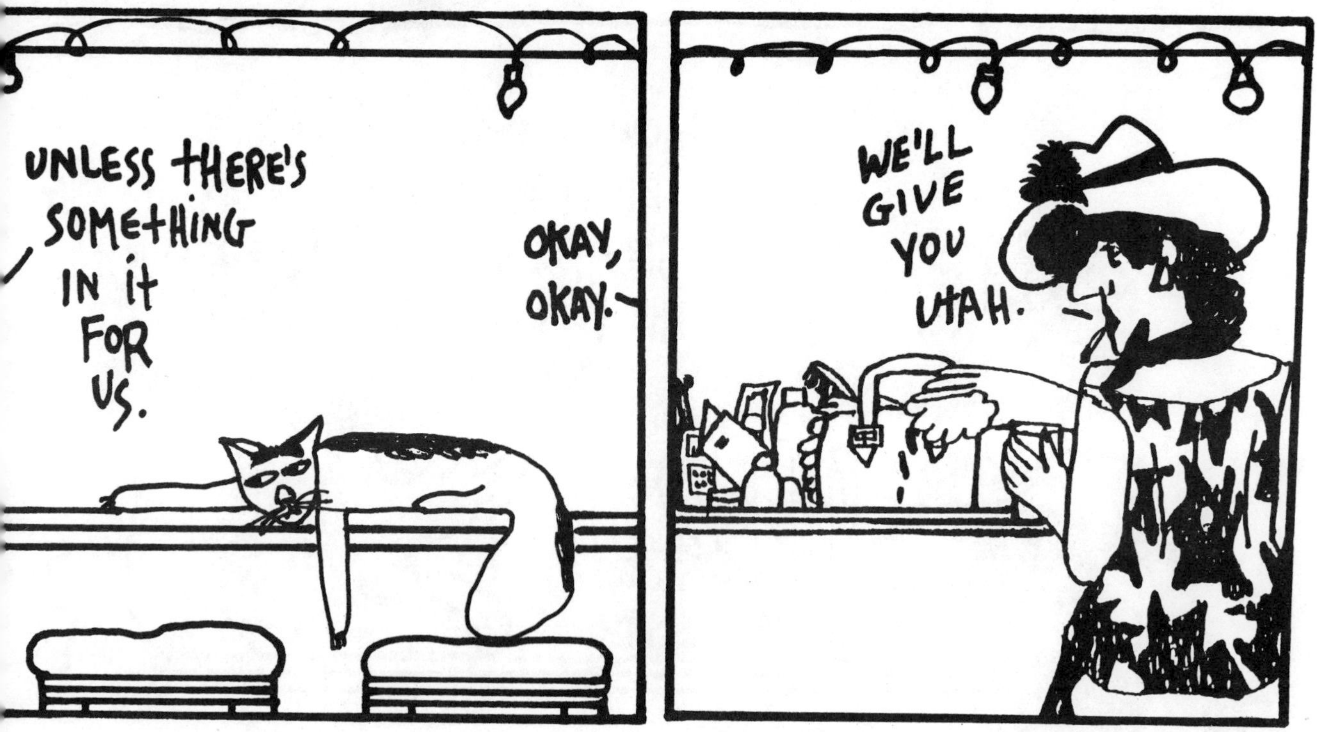
UNLESS THERE'S SOMETHING IN IT FOR US.
OKAY, OKAY.
WE'LL GIVE YOU UTAH.

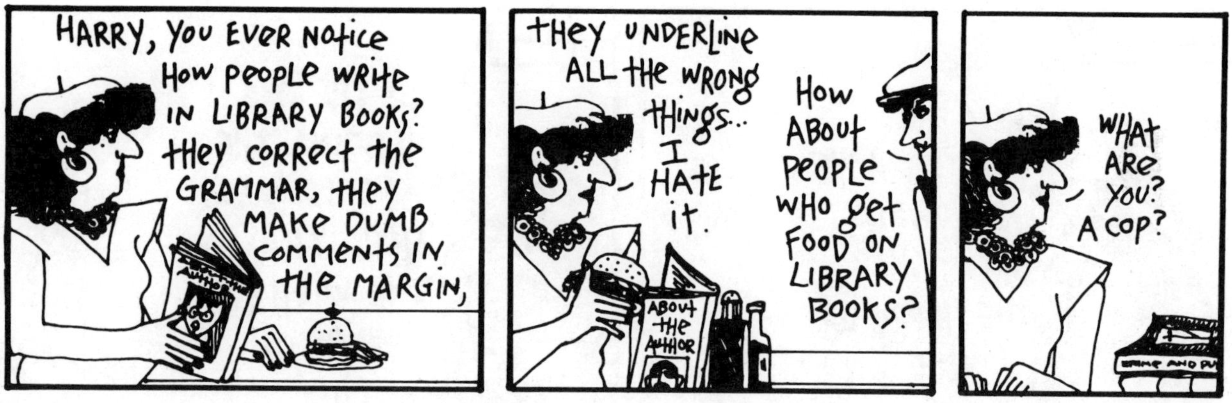
HARRY, YOU EVER NOTICE HOW PEOPLE WRITE IN LIBRARY BOOKS? THEY CORRECT THE GRAMMAR, THEY MAKE DUMB COMMENTS IN THE MARGIN,
THEY UNDERLINE ALL THE WRONG THINGS... I HATE IT.
ABOUT THE AUTHOR
HOW ABOUT PEOPLE WHO GET FOOD ON LIBRARY BOOKS?
WHAT ARE YOU? A COP?

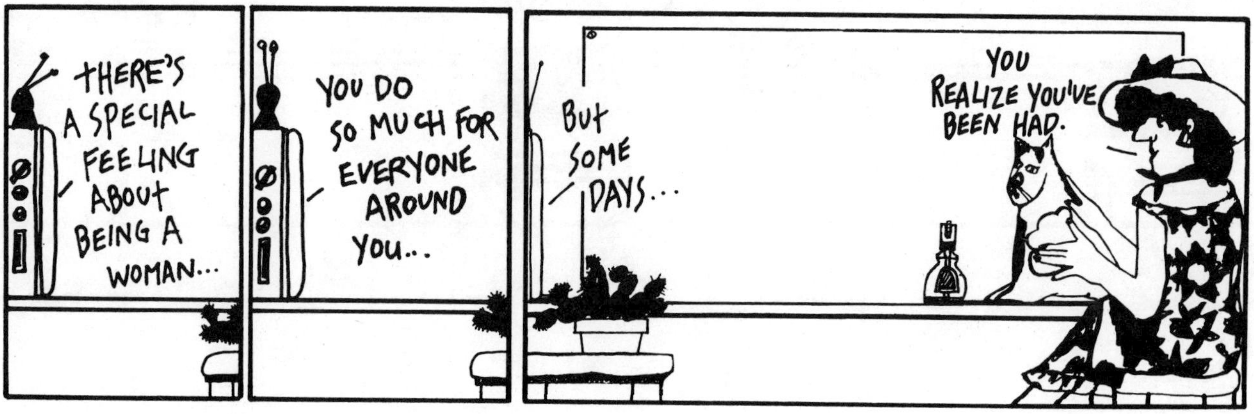
THERE'S A SPECIAL FEELING ABOUT BEING A WOMAN...
YOU DO SO MUCH FOR EVERYONE AROUND YOU...
BUT SOME DAYS...
YOU REALIZE YOU'VE BEEN HAD.

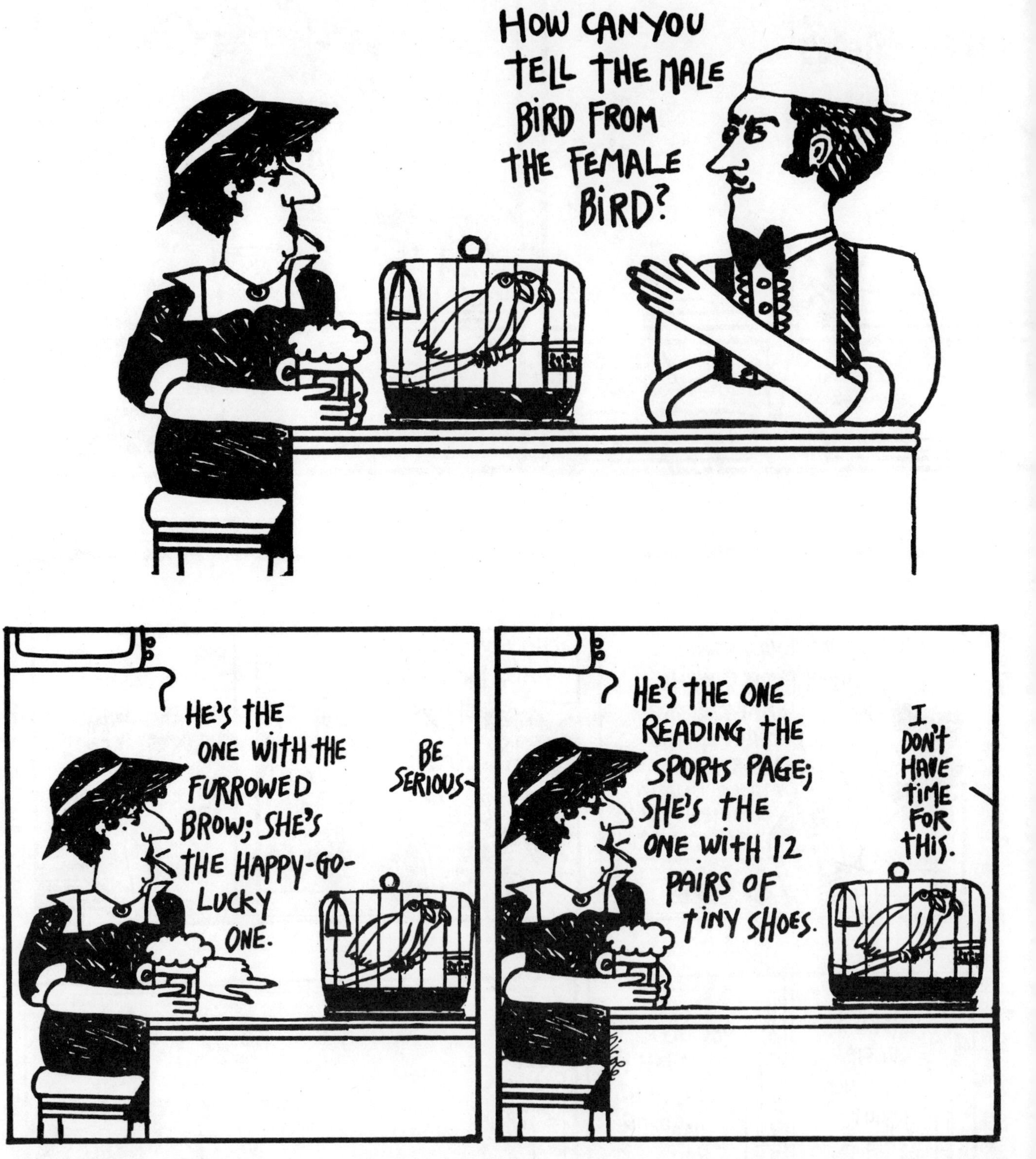
HOW CAN YOU TELL THE MALE BIRD FROM THE FEMALE BIRD?
HE'S THE ONE WITH THE FURROWED BROW; SHE'S THE HAPPY-GO-LUCKY ONE.
BE SERIOUS-
HE'S THE ONE READING THE SPORTS PAGE; SHE'S THE ONE WITH 12 PAIRS OF TINY SHOES.
I DON'T HAVE TIME FOR THIS.